Handbook of Big Data and Analytics in Accounting and Auditing

Tarek Rana · Jan Svanberg · Peter Öhman ·
Alan Lowe
Editors

Handbook of Big Data and Analytics in Accounting and Auditing

Springer

Editors
Tarek Rana
Department of Accounting
RMIT University
Melbourne, VIC, Australia

Peter Öhman
Centre for Research on Economic Relations
Mid Sweden University
Sundsvall, Sweden

Jan Svanberg
University of Gaevle
Gävle, Sweden

Alan Lowe
Department of Accounting
RMIT University
Melbourne, VIC, Australia

ISBN 978-981-19-4459-8 ISBN 978-981-19-4460-4 (eBook)
https://doi.org/10.1007/978-981-19-4460-4

This Springer imprint is published by the registered company Springer Nature Singapore Pte Ltd.
The registered company address is: 152 Beach Road, #21-01/04 Gateway East, Singapore 189721, Singapore

Dedicates this book to his late father-in-law Eng. Siddique Ali Miah, who passed away in April 2022, always encouraged his academic endeavors, and loved him unconditionally. He also acknowledges parents Kabir Ahmed & Ranuara Begum, wife Afsana, and boys Sabir & Jabir for their endless love, support, and patience throughout his academic career.

Tarek Rana

Dedicates this book to his children Esmeralda and Alvar, to his wife Katinka and his father-in-law Jan Svanberg Sr. for their love and support.

Jan Svanberg

Dedicates this book first and foremost to his mother Marianne who has turned 93 and always been supportive, in good times and bad. He also dedicates the book to his research fellows in Sweden end elsewhere.

Peter Öhman

Dedicates this book to all those budding accounting, management, and information systems academics who may find interest and build on this collection of contributions. Research is about sharing ideas and building community. We all need support and encouragement in this activity. It has never been more important to join with others in creating research knowledge.

Alan Lowe

Preface

There is a massive proliferation of data from largely unstructured and non-traditional sources. Not only do they contain very rich information but are updated much more frequently than traditional data sources, thus providing faster access to the latest information and developments. However, relatively little is known as to how accountants' and auditors can deal with the big data and utilize such information by using emerging technologies of analytics to enhance the decision-making capacity of traditional accounting information. Due to the proliferation of big data, a variety of rich and frequently updated information has become available. Accounting academics and practitioners are yet to delve deeply into utilizing this information. While there has been considerable research in exploring the role of big data, data analytics, and textual analytics in accounting and auditing, we still lack evidence on what kinds of best practices academics, practitioners, and organizations can implement and use.

This handbook focuses on both conventional and contemporary issues facing academics, practitioners, and organizations particularly when technology and business environments are changing faster than ever. The book project thus provides various approaches for accounting and auditing academics and practitioners to venture into the age of big data and analytics technologies and their usage. Moreover, the accounting literature lacks empirical evidence on how analytics, machine learning, artificial technologies enhance financial reporting, auditing, management control systems, performance management, and risk management by accessing such big data from multiple sources. Furthermore, accountants and auditors need to learn about the challenges and opportunities of big data and how this will change their professional roles in the digital age.

This book collects the most up-to-date scholarship, knowledge, and new developments of big data and analytics in accounting and auditing by bringing together many strands of contextual and interdisciplinary research. The handbook is interdisciplinary although it is grounded in the disciplines of accounting and auditing but utilizes expertise in management, marketing, information technology, computer science, human resource management, and supply chain disciplines. The chapters provide both retrospective and contemporary views and commentaries by leading and knowledgeable scholars in the field, who offer unique insights on the changing role of accounting and auditing in today's data and analytics driven environment. All chapters address gaps in the literature and provide information about various technologies that are available for analytics, established and emerging models, and applications of practical tools by heavily drawing on conceptual, analytical, literature review, and case-based insights. This enriches future direction for research on accounting and auditing analytics.

Melbourne, Australia — Tarek Rana
Gävle, Sweden — Jan Svanberg
Sundsvall, Sweden — Peter Öhman
Melbourne, Australia — Alan Lowe

Acknowledgments

The authors of the chapters and the editors are equal partners in producing this volume. The editors are extremely grateful to the authors for their contribution whose chapters are published in this volume. We cannot thank enough the authors for their hard work in writing chapters during Covid-19 pandemic and patiently waiting for the compilation of the volume during this difficult time (which has caused many changes and delays by the impact of Covid-19 pandemic). Special thanks to the reviewers for their constructive comments and suggestion for improvement on the chapters included in this book. The editors greatly acknowledge the support from Daniela Argento, Timur Uman, Ling Mei Cong, and Jeanette Ng Po Tin in managing chapters for procuring the book. The editors would also like to thank Lucie Bartonek, Mokshika Gaur, Kavitha Sathish, Jacob Arun Raj, and Parasuraman Aiya Subramani of Springer Nature for their excellent support during this project.

Introduction

In recent years, the demands for accountants, auditors, business analysts, and financial consultants to extend their analysis and interpretation of big data for planning, control, and strategic decision-making are increasing. The academics and practitioners are increasingly interested in helping organizations to rapidly develop and contextualize the analytics means by which to incorporate big data, machine learning, artificial intelligence technologies, and capabilities that will allow them to make sense out of the exponentially growing data captured within and outside organizational domains from structured and unstructured sources. Increased competition for revenues, market share, sustainability, technological advancement, proliferating government regulations, and increased social and community expectations for greater transparency and accountability have introduced more challenges and pressures on business and professional organizations to develop capability to leverage the benefit of big data through appropriate innovation and diffusion of analytics capability.

To this end, the academic and professional community as a whole will greatly benefit as we learn more about data analytics and how organizations successfully innovate and use such systems in the age of big data. The emerging importance and significance of big data and data analytics suggests that organizations need to get a handle on how to use this data earlier rather than later. There are limited documented instances on how organizations could use these large data warehouses to gain competitive advantage but lacks a comprehensive coverage. In a rapidly changing business environment which is increasingly volatile, this handbook can help academics, professionals and organizations to develop capabilities to explore further into the realms of big data with a focus not only on managing threats of declining revenues, but on identifying opportunities to increase revenue and improve customer satisfaction by adding value across the whole supply chain of the business.

The handbook's content will be highly desirable and accessible to accounting and non-accounting audiences across the globe. Aimed at academics, practitioners, students and consultants in the areas of accounting, auditing, management, and other business disciplines, the handbook provides high-level insight into the design, implementation, and working of big data and analytics theories and practices for all types of organizations worldwide. The scholars from interdisciplinary fields provide theoretical perspectives, critical evaluations, and practical guidance on big data and data analytics by illustrating issues related to various sectors such as public, private, not-for-profits, and social enterprises.

Tarek Rana
Jan Svanberg
Peter Öhman
Alan Lowe

Review Process

This book is a collection of peer-reviewed chapters. Springer Nature is one of the leading scientific and commercial publishers in the world for edited books and major reference works. Springer Nature is an interdisciplinary publisher of research books and monographs. This book is a part of Springer Nature's research handbook series that seeks to advance new and scholarly knowledge and debate by providing leading edge and contemporary research outputs. To maintain the high quality of publishing, peer-review is an essential and integral process and fundamental element of Springer Nature's publication process for research books like this one. For each chapter, reviewers and editors have provided anonymous review comments on the content, quality, and contribution. The book has an International Standard Book Number (ISBN), and each chapter has a unique Digital Object Identifier (DOI). The authors and the editors share responsibility for the entire book.

Contents

1 **Introduction: Analytics in Accounting and Auditing** 1
Tarek Rana, Jan Svanberg, Peter Öhman, and Alan Lowe

Part I Emerging Technologies, and Accounting and Auditing Challenges

2 **A Picture Is Worth a Thousand Words: Audit Efficiency and Risk Management Through Data Visualization** 17
Lutfa Tilat Ferdous, Chetanpal Singh, and Tarek Rana

3 **The Challenges Facing Vietnamese Accountants and Auditors with the Adoption of Emerging Technologies** 41
Thuy Thu Nguyen, Lan Anh Nguyen, Michael Kend, and Van Anh Thi Pham

4 **Prediction of Controversies and Estimation of ESG Performance: An Experimental Investigation Using Machine Learning** 65
Jan Svanberg, Tohid Ardeshiri, Isak Samsten, Peter Öhman, and Presha Neidermeyer

5 **Artificial Intelligence and Environmental, Social and Governmental Issues: A Current Perspective** 89
Jonathan Fluharty-Jaidee and Presha Neidermeyer

6 **Sweet Spots or Dark Corners? An Environmental Sustainability View of Big Data and Artificial Intelligence in ESG** 105
Beatrice Crona and Emma Sundström

7 **Digitalization of Bookkeeping in Small Organizations: The Case of Sweden** 133
Anna Alexandersson, Andreas Jansson, and Karin Jonnergård

8 Cloud Accounting: A New Business Model in Challenging Context of China 163
Md. Jahidur Rahman, Gao Yangfan, Md. Moazzem Hossain, and Tarek Rana

9 Exemplifying the Opportunities and Limitations of Blockchain Technology Through Corporate Tax Losses 177
Elizabeth Morton and Michael Curran

Part II Data Analytics and Managerial Accounting

10 Data Sources for Predictive Analytics and Decision Making: A Management Perspective 209
Dennis Fehrenbacher and Alessandro Ghio

11 The Use of Internet of Things, Big Data Analytics and Artificial Intelligence for Attaining UN's SDGs 235
David Teh and Tarek Rana

12 Integrating ESG Risks into Control and Reporting: Evidence from Practice in Sweden 255
Jason Crawford and Fredrik Nilsson

13 Digitalization and Management Control in the Public Sector: What is Next? 279
Laura Broccardo, Elisa Truant, and Daniela Argento

14 Applying Text Mining to Understand Customer Perception of Mobile Banking App 309
Mouri Dey, Md. Zahedul Islam, and Tarek Rana

Part III Digitalization and Accounting Education

15 Integrating Blockchain Technology into Accounting Curricula: A Template for Accounting Educators 337
Manpreet Singh, Mahesh Joshi, and Sharad Sharma

16 Digitized Simulation and Gamified Pedagogy in a First Year Accounting Core Subject 361
Viktor Arity, Gillian Vesty, and Belinda Moloney

17 Roleplay and Interpersonal Skills Self-Efficacy in a Financial Analytics Course 395
Ling Mei Cong

18 Data Analytics in an Undergraduate Accountancy Programme: The Spaced Retrieval Method 415
SzeKee Koh, Hwee Hoon Lee, and Arif Perdana

19 Learning Analytics in Informal, Participatory Collaborative Learning 439
Michelle L. F. Cheong, Aditya V. Singh, Jean Y.-C. Chen, and Bing Tian Dai

20 A Research on Digitalization and Performance in Higher Education Between Hybridity and Algorithms 463
Lino Cinquini and Sara Giovanna Mauro

21 Online Household Waste Management: Measurement, Reporting and Awareness Education 491
Elspeth McKay, Tehmina Khan, and David Teh

22 Does Virtual Reality Enhance Taxation (Capital Allowances) Learning? An International Study 509
Terry Filer and Marc Holmes

23 How Blockchain Is Transforming Accounting, Auditing and Finance: A Systematic Review 535
Manpreet Singh, Mahesh Joshi, Sharad Sharma, and Tarek Rana

Index 561

Editors and Contributors

About the Editors

Tarek Rana is an Associate Professor of Management Accounting and Analytics at RMIT University, Melbourne, Australia. He earned a Ph.D. in Management Accounting at the University of New South Wales (UNSW) Australia. He has considerable professional and industry experience in the areas of business services, taxation, auditing, and financial planning as well as consulting services including performance measurement and risk management. He has formed many industry partnerships and undertaken practice focused research projects to deliver long-term social and organizational impact. His current research focuses on the intersection of accounting and data analytics including the implications of data analytics on management control systems, performance measurement, risk management, and sustainability where he draws on textual analytics, machine learning, and artificial intelligence theories and practices. His research papers appeared in international and interdisciplinary scholarly journals such as *The British Accounting Review, Accounting Auditing and Accountability Journal, Financial Accountability & Management, Intelligent Systems in Accounting, Finance & Management, Business Strategy and the Environment, Public Money & Management, Journal of Accounting & Organisational Change, Journal of Cleaner Production, and Journal of Intellectual Capital.*

Jan Svanberg is an Associate Professor of Business Administration at University of Gävle, and associated with Centre for research on Economic Relations (CER), Sweden. He earned his Ph.D. in Business Administration at Stockholm University, Sweden, and was recently a research fellow at RMIT University, Melbourne, Australia, for a period of two years. In addition to these studies, he has a diverse education with degrees in engineering, mathematics, and physics (M.Sc.) and law (LL.M). His current research focuses on how core problems in accounting, auditing, and finance can be solved by interdisciplinary approaches with tools made available by advances in data science, especially machine learning. His work has been published in scholarly journals such as *The British Accounting Review, Behavioral Research* *in Accounting, Accounting Auditing and Accountability Journal, Journal of Cleaner Production, and Intelligent Systems in Accounting, Finance and Management.*

Peter Öhman is a Professor and Head of Business Administration at Mid Sweden University in Sundsvall, and director of Centre for research on Economic Relations (CER), Sweden. His research focuses on behavioral issues, primarily in accounting and auditing, but also in the banking and property industries. He has published a significant number of scholarly articles, published books, book chapters and reports, and presented papers at international conferences. He has received international awards for excellent research, is a member of Editorial Boards, and a reviewer of several well-known international journals. His work has been published in leading scholarly journals such as *Contemporary Accounting Research, Behavioral Research in Accounting, Accounting Auditing and Accountability Journal, European Accounting Review, and The British Accounting Review.*

Alan Lowe is an Honorary Professor of Management Accounting at RMIT University, Melbourne, Australia. He served as a joint Editor of the *British Accounting Review*. His research interest has included management controls, ERP, technologies, and internet reporting using case studies and interpretive methodology. Recent projects include ethical identity and financial innovation in Islamic financial institutions, ICT service provision in health care sector, and governing climate change.

Contributors

Anna Alexandersson Linnaeus University, Växjö, Sweden

Tohid Ardeshiri University of Gävle and Centre for research on Economic Relations, Sundsvall, Sweden

Daniela Argento Kristianstad University, Kristianstad, Sweden

Viktor Arity RMIT University, Melbourne, VIC, Australia

Laura Broccardo University of Turin, Turin, Italy

Jean Y.-C. Chen Singapore Management University, Singapore, Singapore

Michelle L. F. Cheong Singapore Management University, Singapore, Singapore

Lino Cinquini Institute of Management, Sant'Anna School of Advanced Studies of Pisa, Pisa, Italy

Ling Mei Cong RMIT University, Melbourne, VIC, Australia

Jason Crawford Uppsala University, Uppsala, Sweden

Beatrice Crona Royal Swedish Academy of Sciences, Stockholm, Sweden

Michael Curran Barrister, Victorian Bar, McKinney, TX, USA

Bing Tian Dai Singapore Management University, Singapore, Singapore

Mouri Dey University of Chittagong, Chittagong, Bangladesh

Dennis Fehrenbacher St. Gallen University, St. Gallen, St. Gallen, Switzerland

Lutfa Tilat Ferdous University of Leicester, Leicester, UK

Terry Filer Swansea University, Swansea, Wales, UK

Jonathan Fluharty-Jaidee Washington, DC, USA

Alessandro Ghio University of Laval, Quėbec City, QC, Canada

Marc Holmes Swansea University, Swansea, Wales, UK

Md. Moazzem Hossain Murdoch University, Murdoch, WA, Australia

Md. Zahedul Islam University of Chittagong, Chittagong, Bangladesh

Andreas Jansson Jönköping International Business School, Jönköping, Sweden

Karin Jonnergård Lund University, Lund, Sweden

Mahesh Joshi RMIT University, Melbourne, VIC, Australia

Michael Kend RMIT University, Melbourne, VIC, Australia

Tehmina Khan RMIT University, Melbourne, VIC, Australia

SzeKee Koh Singapore Institute of Technology, Singapore, Singapore

Hwee Hoon Lee Singapore Institute of Technology, Singapore, Singapore

Sara Giovanna Mauro University of Modena and Reggio Emilia, Modena, Italy

Alan Lowe RMIT University, Melbourne, VIC, Australia

Elspeth McKay RMIT University, Melbourne, VIC, Australia

Belinda Moloney Deakin University, Geelong, VIC, Australia

Elizabeth Morton RMIT University, Melbourne, VIC, Australia

Presha Neidermeyer Department of Accounting, West Virginia University, Morgantown, WA, USA

Lan Anh Nguyen RMIT University, Melbourne, VIC, Australia

Thuy Thu Nguyen National Academy of Public Administration, Hanoi, Vietnam

Fredrik Nilsson Uppsala University, Uppsala, Sweden

Peter Öhman Centre for Research on Economic Relations, Mid Sweden University, Sundsvall, Sweden

Arif Perdana Singapore Institute of Technology, Singapore, Singapore

Van Anh Thi Pham Hanoi Academy of Finance, Hanoi, Vietnam

Md. Jahidur Rahman Wenzhou-Kean University, Wenzhou, China

Tarek Rana RMIT University, Melbourne, VIC, Australia

Isak Samsten Stockholm University, Stockholm, Sweden

Sharad Sharma RMIT University, Melbourne, Australia

Aditya V. Singh Singapore Management University, Singapore, Singapore

Chetanpal Singh RMIT University, Melbourne, VIC, Australia

Manpreet Singh RMIT University, Melbourne, VIC, Australia

Emma Sundström Stockholm Resilience Centre, Stockholm University, Stockholm, Sweden

Jan Svanberg University of Gävle and Centre for research on Economic Relations, Sundsvall, Gävle, Sweden

David Teh RMIT University, Melbourne, VIC, Australia

Elisa Truant University of Turin, Turin, Italy

Gillian Vesty RMIT University, Melbourne, VIC, Australia

Gao Yangfan Wenzhou-Kean University, Wenzhou, China

Chapter 1
Introduction: Analytics in Accounting and Auditing

Tarek Rana, Jan Svanberg, Peter Öhman, and Alan Lowe

Abstract Big data and analytics offer new opportunities and challenges for academics and practitioners in all business disciplines including accounting and auditing. In the backdrop of increasing growth of emerging technologies, the organizations in public, private and not-for-profit sectors are embracing digital economy and the fourth industrial revolution journey. This requires knowledge of better practice examples, lessons learned and future directions in addressing the new challenges and seizing new opportunities. In this chapter, we discuss the implications of data analytics, artificial intelligence and machine learning on the accounting and auditing practices. We focus on the technological, social, political, economic, institutional, and behavioral aspects of these technologies in the public, private, non-governmental and hybrid contexts. We present state-of-the-art research directions on philosophical, theoretical, methodological, and practical issues, new developments and innovations of big data, analytics, artificial intelligence, machine learning, blockchain, cryptocurrencies and other emerging technologies related to accounting and auditing.

Keywords Big data · Analytics · Artificial intelligence · Machine learning · Digital economy · Accounting · Auditing

T. Rana · A. Lowe
RMIT University, Melbourne, VIC, Australia
e-mail: tarek.rana@rmit.edu.au

A. Lowe
e-mail: alan.lowe@rmit.edu.au

J. Svanberg (✉)
Gävle University and Centre for Research on Economic Relations, Gävle, Sweden
e-mail: jan.svanberg@hig.se

P. Öhman
Centre for Research on Economic Relations, Mid Sweden University, Sundsvall, Sweden
e-mail: peter.ohman@miun.se

T. Rana et al. (eds.), *Handbook of Big Data and Analytics in Accounting and Auditing*,
https://doi.org/10.1007/978-981-19-4460-4_1

1 Point of Departure

The change to accounting and auditing that is caused by the emerging use of autonomous decision support systems has been described as if this change would concern only the simple repetitive and labor-intensive tasks and not at all the complex judgement-based work accountants and auditors do in the upper end of the value chain. In accounting that would be the work performed by bookkeepers or a stock inventory, and in auditing that would be to perform substantive testing by digging through thousands of items in a ledger. The pervasive arguments are that the effects of artificial intelligence (AI) are likely to be highest on such tasks that have already been computerized because they can be defined in a computer-friendly manner. Typical tasks suitable for computerization are the verification of mathematical accuracy of supporting schedules, tracing the cash receipts journal and cash disbursement journal to general ledger postings and bank statements.

The expected AI revolution of accounting and auditing happens in conjunction with the technological breakthroughs such as robotics, blockchains, mobile applications, and collaboration platforms. The Big 4 audit firms are involved in AI-projects aimed at developing methods to improve efficiency and effectiveness of their services. However, so far the impact of AI in audits is pronounced only in the area of data acquisition. This means that there is AI-enabled methods to locate information for example by extracting it from documents with the purpose of providing information to human auditors. This type of application liberates the accountants' and auditors' time for high level judgment tasks. As long as the use of AI is limited to this non-judgment type of task neither accounting nor auditing needs to feel any threat because such analytics are tools under the user's control. We find, however, that the picture painted in previous literature is based on a layman's perspective on AI and that the real potential is much broader and deeper than automation of hands-on tasks. Analytics using software capable of learning on its own can be used much like statistical methods to make multidimensional decisions concerning the most complex tasks. As any investor or medical practitioner knows, this type of multi-criteria decision-making is the hardest because the human mind does not seem fit to weigh many factors against each other and make accurate predictions on such data.

The many significant contributions to the accounting and auditing analytics literature presented in this volume should be seen in the light of the fact the previous analytics literature has underestimated the capacity of analytics in accounting and auditing. Big audit firms unconstrained by the beliefs and predictions of the academic literature are beginning to make progress towards fully autonomous decision support systems based on AI. For example, KPMG runs a cooperation with IBM about a large AI implementation to experimentally improve the audit process. The precise topics which this system is proposed to address is not yet publicly known but it is obvious that a system like IBM's Watson is capable of doing more than just scraping up pieces of information and presenting them in accessible graphs to auditors. The real potential lies in enhancing the limitations of human judgment when confronted with the most complex and fuzzy problems in accounting and auditing. Information extraction is just a starting point.

2 Part I: Emerging Technologies, and Accounting and Auditing Challenges

The adoption of emerging technologies in accounting and auditing is obviously not without challenges. Challenges relate to the clash between autonomous software and current standards and to how accountants and auditors make sense of the emerging technologies and their properties (Salijeni et al., 2021). Most academic contributions exploring the rise of big data and analytics in accounting and auditing offer a normative perspective on how technologies may better equip accountants and auditors to analyze client data and the practical challenges (Vasarhelyi et al., 2015), while underlying adoption issues are seldom analysed. Adoption issues which are not directly a matter of how to most effectively employ analytics include security, privacy, too much or too little reliance on a system, ownership, and training. For example, auditors may integrate data from multiple sources (Issa & Kogan, 2014) but when doing so auditors need to comprehend the appropriateness of their collected data for the decision they are about to make and that requires knowledge of the inner logic of the analytics tools they are using. Sometimes this is straightforward but there are cases when the manner in which questions are asked through the use of AI-methodology to deal with a measurement problem in business calls for conceptual development. New ways of viewing measures lead to new understandings of the problem and what it means to solve it.

Another adoption issue is obviously who owns the data and the methods with which it is analyzed. As long as the company that pays for the development of a method owns its data all will be fine. When external data is needed, such as the case with ESG ratings, the problem is that the company developing the ratings can only use them within the legal limits of their rights to use the purchased data. A ground-breaking discovery that could change the world would then require costly and time-consuming investments in independent data acquisition before the method can be offered. The organization's use of certain methods may hinge on that data and analytics will be available at a certain cost in the future but ownership and distrust can obstruct a business technology adoption for strategic reasons. Some analytics must become strategic core competencies which may never be delivered from the outside. The book addresses adoption issues in Chap. 3. The chapter illustrates that some adoption issues can be specific for an institutional context while other are generic.

The implementation of new technology in accounting and auditing undoubtedly collides with the current standards at some point because the standards define tasks as performed and fully controlled by a human decision-maker. For example, audit standards require of the signing auditor that he or she is personally responsible for the performance of the audit, including how the statistical sampling of items to control was done. If this procedure is conducted with an autonomous decision support system, which most likely will be the case very soon in many external audits, the auditor will have to be knowledgeable about the inner cognitive processing of the AI-based decision-support tool and currently there is not much discussion in the audit profession how this knot can be untied.

In this context there are some challenges that are easier to solve than others. One of them is the context-dependence of technology adoption. When new decision-support systems are developed, they cannot be used in all countries in the same manner due to country-specific regulation. Some standards relate to, for example, tax issues which are specific to the institutional context (country) and therefore make technology adoption context specific. In accounting this is clearly the case with software for small businesses' bookkeeping which is covered in Chap. 7.

A difficult challenge for accounting and auditing is the understanding and measurement of corporate social performance, or the popular terms ESG (Environment, Social, Governance). The sustainability reporting standards, most notably the GRI (Global Reporting Initiative) has made corporate social performance a new bottom line concept equivalent to what income and balance is for financial reporting. The similarities end about there, however, because while the meaning of financial income is absolutely clear, the bottom line of a sustainability report is unknown both to accountants and auditors.

ESG experts in banks and insurance companies need to deal with this uncertainty. If you ask the leading experts in a large investment banks such as Deutsche Bank or Morgan Stanley they would probably say they know what sustainability is. However, if you ask them to compare the ESG of two car manufacturers or two pharmacy companies they would stutter and eventually they would say that they prefer one because of their strong governance or their lower pollution. If you then ask on what basis they assess the trade-off between a company's governance against their pollutions, water and energy use, the number of work-place accidents and their number of female directors you would not get a straight answer. They might refer to an ESG rating from Sustainalytics or MSCI they have purchased as a state-of-the-art rating. If you press them on causes for believing that these ratings provide legitimacy (you do not ask for evidence that the ratings are valid measures of sustainable performance because you realize that the people you are talking to do not know these concepts) for their investment portfolios, their troubled faces would be painful for you to watch so when they say something about materiality or financial materiality you let them go. The problem is that there is no method to even at some modest level of objectivity measure a company's sustainable performance.

As demonstrated by the research group at Harvard Business School (Christensen et al., 2022), all investigated methods to measure the sustainable performance of companies for investment purposes lack validity, or as Chatterji et al. (2016) state it more bluntly, they are all wrong. Fortunately, a solution to what is the greatest challenge to the finance industry today is presented in the chapter on ESG and machine learning in this handbook. Chapter 4 explains the conceptual difficulty that accountants and auditors face with the undeterminable bottom line and how machine learning can be used to develop ESG predictions, or ratings, that constitute the only ESG ratings with predictive validity and the only ratings for which there is evidence of accuracy known to the literature.

The development of a valid methodology for ESG ratings is important because it suggests a more solid basis for how institutional investors compose socially responsible investment portfolios, and it can be used as decision support in accounting and auditing. For example, the literature describes no validated method that can be used by auditors as they perform their materiality assessments in sustainability audits. On the contrary, recent evidence indicates that auditors are confused about the meaning of the bottom line of sustainable performance, and therefore they cannot assess which company features that constitute the most important sustainability items to report (Canning et al., 2018). The sustainability reporting framework GRI (Global Reporting Initiative) states that auditors should engage broad stakeholder groups in the assessment of which are the material sustainability items to report. In practice this is impossible.

Chapter 4 can be viewed as a proposal to solve the problem with predicting corporate social performance in several different contexts such as reporting (i.e. when companies determine the materiality of sustainability information and therefore whether it should be reported), auditing (i.e. when auditors verify the materiality assessment and thus companies' sustainability reporting focus), and investors (i.e. when composing responsible investment portfolios). When several studies have reported that current ESG ratings lack validity, the development of a valid ESG rating methodology is perhaps the greatest challenge for current research in accounting, auditing and finance.

There are other challenges related to the use of big data and analytics in accounting and auditing to solve problems with sustainable reporting, auditing and socially responsible investment. Chapter 6 describes the current status of the use of AI to collect information that is not found in annual reports but collected from other sources like the Internet by AI applications. The analysis is premised on the assumption that environmental sustainability can only be achieved when societies and economies curb negative impacts on the climate and biosphere. The biosphere refers to the Earth's ecosystems, comprised of all living things and the chapter addresses the issue of dark corners in ESG ratings by its focus on the limits to the anthropogenic pressure the planet can sustain before its ability to support our economies and societies is significantly undermined. This focus differs from the relative approach adopted in current ESG investment practices that compare companies on the basis of within-sector performance.

The growing amount of unstructured available ESG related data provides new possibilities to capture company related information of potential relevance for ESG, that can offer a more unbiased view of companies than simply relying on self-reported sustainability information delivered on an annual basis. AI technologies are invaluable tools in "reading" and analyzing these large datasets. However, until advanced analytical methods are available there are challenges with overreliance on simply collecting more information because important information about biodiversity is not available at all. Current use of AI in ESG will capture issues that are of direct importance for absolute sustainability, while also being financially material. Many environmental issues do not lend themselves to easy capture by news headlines and therefore become dark corners. It is important for all users of ESG to recognize the existence of these dark corners of current AI-ESG approaches, and be cognizant of what this means for the capacity of ESG to measure progress towards sustainability.

Finally, the use of the blockchain technology has been described as a fundamental technology that solves many problems but few if any examples exist to show that this is in fact true. The usefulness of blockchain in key use cases across numerous business sectors is reviewed in Chap. 9, and is then examined regarding its role and function in the context of corporate tax losses, where complex rules apply. The main finding is that while in theory blockchain could enable key efficiencies in tax compliance of corporate tax losses, in practice the complexity and discretion within tax law creates real barriers for this technology's use. The chapter describes blockchain and its many possible uses and then analyses its usefulness for solving problems with tracking and accounting for carry forward tax losses in Australia. Blockchain offers an ability to track and flag resource allocation to broad, high-level elements of the corporate tax compliance and therefore offers potential for the greater digital ecosystem. Blockchain smart contracts may be established to provide the basic checks for changes in ownership, or even facilitate the carry-back refundable tax offset. However, the analysis raises significant concern over relying solely on blockchain technology to execute tax losses without holistic checks and balances. The chapter finds that blockchain does not offer a solution to the investigated corporate tax loss context in Australia but that future simplified rules can enable the use of such digital tools for rapid administration of legal rights.

3 Part II: Data Analytics and Managerial Accounting

Managerial accounting including internal control and internal auditing are the areas that have lent itself more than any other area of accounting to the use of advanced analytics. These areas differ from the environment of external audits because analytics can be tailored to the specific organization in which managerial accounting internal controls or internal auditing is conducted.

Methods such as machine learning require training on data which represents the typical behavior of the system being monitored. This is the case with systems that are tailored for a specific organization but it is not the case for an audit tool that is supposed to work on any organization an auditor is auditing. It is not surprising to find that most of the AI related analytics research has been done in the managerial accounting context. Managerial accounting is an information system, or a company navigation system intended to help managers make rational decisions in the interest of the organization. As such there is little regulation of how managerial accounting may be carried out. Thus, managers have a lot of freedom to design the information systems they would like to have and what type of information the systems should operate on. There are many data sources that organizations could use in their management decision-making process in parallel with the traditional accounting-type of data. The new type of data offer advantages compared to traditional accounting data. For example, search trend data and social media data can be used for predicting sales with higher predictive accuracy than traditional accounting data would enable. The Chartered Institute of Management Accountants (CIMA) encourages organizations to discover how to use analytics related to financial results. In this context, machine learning is adopted to identify business drivers as means to improve financial results.

The data obviously determines the outcome of the analysis, so the choice of data is crucial to the information system managers decide to develop. Despite its importance, little is known about how managers view new data sources and whether new data sources are seen as value adding and whether managers want them in the decision-making process. Management preferences is an important concern for management accounting to improve its role of providing relevant information to managers. Due to the emergence of the machine learning technique, management accountants will increasingly become internal consultants providing business-oriented and strategic information, playing a role in the data evolution. Chapter 10 examines management perceptions of new data sources relative to longer-standing data sources, particularly how the perceptions on data sources differ by management demographics, attitudes and resource constraints. This knowledge is important for management accountants to have because they need to understand managers as users of predictive analytics. The chapter finds that the management demographics and credibility attitudes towards social media influences the preference for data sources for sales prediction. Unsurprisingly, attitudes towards social media is a key to whether such data can be trusted by managers when making decisions about their company.

The issue of trust is not only relevant for such data sources as social media. Even data that emanates from the company's internal sources may be trustworthy and seen as relevant to various extent, such as whether ESG risk data is integrated with control, i.e. incorporated into strategic and operational decision-making. ESG risk should be important because many companies have been hit by the consequences of not complying with their corporate social responsibilities and paid the consequences financially and reputationally, for example BP, Volkswagen and Wells Fargo. It is not clear even in this light that companies pay attention to ESG risks in their management practice. Chapter 12 investigates the extent that ESG risks are used for management control in large companies and finds that while companies have well developed processes and structures for integration ESG risks into reporting there is little formalized use of ESG risk data in the management decision making. The study also finds that cultural controls seem to be more important than well-developed ESG risk management processes and structures, especially in taking meaningful actions. It seems as if ESG data is not viewed as important to the large companies under study as would be expected from the public debate when it comes to organizational structures.

4 Part III: Digitalization and Accounting Education

Analytics can be used to teach and learn accounting and auditing. In the light of a vast transition over accounting and auditing into an AI supported profession with numerous autonomous decision support systems it is obviously imperative to familiarize the coming generations of accountants and auditors with the new applications the previous generations could only imagine. Some IT-based tools for teaching and learning do not in themselves target knowledge of AI decision support systems (but traditional accounting and auditing knowledge).

Chapter 16 provide insights into curriculum designs and student responses to the use of innovative assessment in accounting education. The chapter examines how digitized simulation and serious games can enhance student engagement and help to address cognitive load challenges experienced by students. It investigates how serious games and simulations can effectively reduce the extraneous and intrinsic cognitive load in education. It seems that the cognitive load can be reduced and that learning through games also contribute positively to a student's germane load enabling them to navigate the more complex topics, including debits, credits, and capital budgeting through the simulated activity. Students do not see this activity as burdensome because of the design features within the context of the simulation. Other potential benefits include reducing student attrition, whereby students may previously give up the course, potentially even the degree, based on their perceptions that accounting is difficult and inaccessible from their first encounter.

The transformation of accounting and auditing towards the use of autonomous decision support systems causes a dire need for a certain type of IT-related knowledge among accountants and auditors. The users of autonomous decision support systems that operate as AI-applications must be able to assess the validity, reliability and accuracy of decision support systems that they do not completely control (i.e. they are autonomous systems) and not fully understand the inner logic of. The replacement of mundane tasks and manual work require of accountants and auditors to have knowledge of data science tools. Professional accounting bodies address this need by emphasizing continuing professional education and developing guidelines for data analytics. At the same time, higher education institutions are taking the initiative to integrate data analytics into their accounting curricula.

Given the numerous professional accreditation requirements that higher education institutions must fulfil, a big challenge remains for any institution to insert rigorous data analytics training into their existing curriculum. Following Chap. 20 which reviews the literature on digitalization in higher education, Chap. 18 describes the development of a data analytics roadmap for undergraduate accountancy education, from reviewing our academic and industry data analytics curricula and evaluating existing modules that could be integrated with relevant data analytics topics, to seeking feedback from industry partners regarding the curriculum model that is developed. The chapter also finds that while coming generations of accountants and auditors need to embrace digital transformation and be savvy about using data analytics tools there is a current shortage of data analytics talent. Even though data analytics is increasingly gaining traction in business and industry, the supply of data analytics talent remains inadequate which means that there is a risk that accountants and auditors may not be able to play the advisory role to top management that would be possible in the emerging data driven business models.

AI can be used in the process of accounting education and strong improvements of the process through which students learn can be expected. Education methods that connect students with AI software that keeps track of and engages in the students' learning has been shown to dramatically increase the amount and depth of learning. The approach to use Learning Analytics (LA) was defined as "the measurement, collection, analysis and reporting of data about learners and their contexts, for purposes of understanding and optimizing learning and the environments in which it occurs" during the First International Conference on Learning Analytics and Knowledge (LAK11) in 2011. In the same year LA was said to be "the third wave of large-scale developments in instructional technology", after the first wave where learning management system (LMS) was used in education in the 1990s, and the addition of social networking and cloud-based applications into LMS during the second wave. Developing and using such systems must be a primary goal for higher accounting education as we move towards satisfying the need for more data science aware accounting students because the use of this technology during students' time at university will automatically stimulate reflection on how autonomous learning support and decision support systems operate.

Chapter 19 addresses this potential by developing and testing an integrated telegram mobile application and a web-based portal discussion forum, to enable informal, participatory and collaborative learning beyond the classroom. The chapter analyzes student-initiated question-and-answer discussion posts where a machine learning algorithm predicts the quality of the posts, and prompts the students to improve their posts. With six in-built engagement features, the proposed system generates higher number of high-quality posts, resulting in better learning outcomes among the students. In fact, the proposed methodology provides revolutionary improvements compared to conventional teaching and student support methods such as conventional forums in which students can discuss. Being exposed to this AI-driven method at the same time as students learn data science in relation to accounting and auditing should provide the ideal platform for future generations of accountants and auditors.

A new technology that does not have any obvious practical use in accounting and auditing is virtual reality but for learning accounting and auditing where it instills a sense of reality to the learning environment. Universities provide often alienated environments by students and teachers work completely detached from the actual environment in which students' future work will be conducted. Students are not exposed to the time pressures and conflicting interests that an actual corporate environment entails. They do not learn how to prioritize between accuracy and timely deliveries that they will have to do in the future. Using virtual reality mitigates some of this difference between university and the real world so that students can put their academic learning also in a realistic perspective. Virtual reality also enables the exposure of students to technological advances that are yet not operational of today. For example, AI powered auditing tools which will be used in a couple of years as decision support systems when graduated students are out in the real world working with tools we are only able to write about because they do not yet find practical use.

Chapter 22 offers concrete and detailed insight into how virtual reality can be used in practical teaching of accounting and auditing. The chapter examined the effects of virtual reality on learning about a taxation problem. Because virtual reality moves the students' perception to a fictive environment in which they can use their senses to capture what they are supposed to learn, students are more likely to be able to recall their visual experiences and therefore to learn. Virtual reality has the benefit of participators experiencing "presence" in their learning, putting themselves in the virtual world making it a memorable and often enjoyable experience. The results of the study include improved student understanding, strengthened learning experience, and, not least important, that students enjoyed virtual reality.

5 We Look Forward

Amidst all the problems and difficulties identified in this book (and to which some solutions are provided), there are plenty of reasons to be optimistic when looking at the coming decade. Several of the greatest challenges of our society could be solved with the analytical techniques discussed in this book. However, there is good cause to be skeptical to buzzwords and phenomena which gain momentum in some applications and which are claimed by many to be the solution to a large amount of unspecified and undescribed problems.

We think of blockchain as a concept and method that might have valuable applications where information needs to be transferred and protected in ways that are not possible without packaging it in encrypted boxes. As we see it, there is no evidence in the literature that blockchain would solve any problems relevant to accounting and auditing. In contrast, AI as an umbrella concept for the many techniques to read and understand text and to analyze patterns of numbers, has unlimited capacity to solve fundamental problems in accounting and auditing. Many companies offer fully automated bookkeeping already today and several audit firms claim that they are developing and testing autonomous systems to be used as decision support in external audits. Research groups like the one lead by professor Vasarhelyi at Rutgers Business School in New Jersey have for a long time demonstrated how analytics based on machine learning can be used for the improvement of internal control and internal audits. We therefore find it most likely that internal audits and internal control will be revolutionized in the coming decade through the employment of machine learning and related techniques in AI.

Three suggested areas where big data and analytics will provide revolutionary breakthroughs in the coming few years are: (1) audits of AI-enabled automation of business processes, (2) measurement instruments for the ESG investment industry, and (3) emerging technologies for risk management. They are given space below.

AI-enabled office automation may comprise the majority of the information processing that auditors need to assess the quality of information. Robotics is widely used for assembly of cars. Most series production is suited for automation, and automation of manufacturing is therefore only a matter of time and cost. Office automation is tricky because people in offices do interconnected tasks and the functions to be automated cannot always be defined as a copy of the tasks people say they do. Administration can be partly replaced by computers as far as the jobs can be systematically understood. Inefficient and ineffective administrative processes that fulfils primarily social purposes for the people in an organization must first be rid of its unnecessary parts before they can be described in information comprehensible to machine learning. These formalized descriptions of business processes will eventually take place and much administration will be done with interconnected machine learning algorithms. When this phase of administrative development is reached, auditors will be faced with the task of understanding the inner logic of chains of autonomous decision support systems.

Fortunately, the tools for this are here, and the major breakthrough occurred 2017 with the work of Lundberg and Lee (2017). These American data science researchers have built a generalized framework for explaining machine learning models of any kind on the discovery in economics of the Shapley values for which Shapley was awarded a Nobel prize in 2012. The so called SHAP method (SHapley Additive exPlanations) makes it possible to explain the inner thoughts of machine learning in terms of the contribution from each input feature to the output of the model as contributions of conditional probability. For an auditor who wants to understand why an individual decision was made by an administrative robot it will be possible to connect a SHAP model to the robot and obtain easily comprehensive explanations of each and every decision ever made by the robot. The level of transparency available to the auditor is far beyond what can be achieved in audits of human decision processes that often occur with a logic hidden even for the decision maker. Our estimate is that explainable AI will eventually be the most useful of all aspects of big data and analytics in accounting and auditing.

Regarding measurement instruments for the ESG investment industry, a breakthrough is not only likely but also necessary is the measurement of corporate social performance, or ESG. The need for a more solid foundation for the substantially growing socially responsible investment business in the finance sector is as obvious as sunshine at Miami Beach. Institutional investors are responsible for the allocation of the majority of the global capital, and many institutional investors are honestly motivated to mitigate the climate threat, protect biodiversity and address many social issues affected by or caused by businesses. The problem is that no one knows which direction is the right one. This is certainly the case with the ESG ratings that all aspire to be the most accurate measures of ESG but for which all scientific evidence univocally shows that they all lack validity and accuracy. The main reason for this weakness is that the ESG ratings represent each rater's subjective perceptions of good corporate behavior. The raters' inclination to adopt the 'doing good' perspective on ESG provides no support for the need to develop objective ESG ratings in the sense that they are rater independent and that they represent the preferences of society.

ESG ratings should reflect the fact that the definition of corporate social performance must come from society because it is towards society that companies have their environmental, social and governance responsibilities, not towards a particular stakeholder group. This fact has not had any apparent impact on the design of currently popular ESG ratings. However, we estimate that the finance sector will soon discover the advantage of using the far less subjective ESG ratings that can be developed with the rating methodology described in this handbook.

Risk management is topical for future research in the emerging technologies context. The recent Covid-19 pandemic has necessitated the management of risks around many essential public services, and it has signified the importance of using technologies for financial management, budgeting, supply chain management, indigenous and gender equity. For example, future research may unearth how risk can be identified, predicted and managed in areas of concern. Due to recent geo-political crisis, there has been an increasing demand for national security and safety concerns where technology can play roles in managing supply chains and ensure stability. This has implications for food security, defence, cyber security risk management for public organizations, private businesses and not-for-profits. Recently, digital security has emerged as one of the greatest risks which arises from the use of technology but the solutions also lays with the technology. In addition, climate change risk is another challenge for many governments entrusted with setting climate change agendas and appropriate mitigation strategies. All public and private organizations now need to consider climate change which probably is the greatest existential threats to mankind.

Future research may explore debates, and theory and method developments on these issues of climate change risk and associated transformations of accounting, auditing, management control, performance management and risk management by using data analytics, machine learning, and artificial intelligence. To this end, researchers may pursue critical-interpretive analyses and reflections on risk management patterns and capabilities towards a better understanding of how we can assess and manage these challenges in an integrated way.

References

Canning, M., O'Dwyer, B., & Georgakopoulos, G. (2018). Processes of auditability in sustainability assurance—The case of materiality construction. *Accounting and Business Research, 49*(1), 1–27. https://doi.org/10.1080/00014788.2018.1442208

Chatterji, A. K., Durand, R., Levine, D. I., & Touboul, S. (2016). Do ratings of firms converge? Implications for managers, investors and strategy researchers. *Strategic Management Journal, 37*(8), 1597–1614. https://doi.org/10.1002/smj.2407

Christensen, D., Serafeim, G., & Sikochi, A. (2022). Why is corporate virtue in the eye of the beholder? *The Accounting Review, 97*, 147–175. https://doi.org/10.2308/tar-2019-0506

Issa, H., & Kogan, A. (2014). A predictive ordered logistic regression model as a tool for quality review of control risk assessments. *Journal of Information Systems, 28*(2), 209–229. https://doi.org/10.2308/isys-50808

Lundberg, S. M., & Lee, S. I. (2017, December). A unified approach to interpreting model predictions. *Advances in Neural Information Processing Systems*, 4766–4775.

Salijeni, G., Samsonova-Taddei, A., & Turley, S. (2021). Understanding how big data technologies reconfigure the nature and organization of financial statement audits: A sociomaterial analysis. *European Accounting Review, 30*(3), 531–555. https://doi.org/10.1080/09638180.2021.1882320

Vasarhelyi, M. A., Kogan, A., & Tuttle, B. M. (2015). Big data in accounting: An overview. *Accounting Horizons, 29*(2), 381–396. https://doi.org/10.2308/ACCH-51071

Tarek Rana is an Associate Professor of Management Accounting and Analytics at RMIT University, Melbourne, Australia. He earned a Ph.D. in Management Accounting at the University of New South Wales (UNSW) Australia. He has considerable professional and industry experience in the areas of business services, taxation, auditing, and financial planning as well as consulting services including performance measurement and risk management. He has formed many industry partnerships and undertaken practice focused research projects to deliver long-term social and organizational impact. His current research focuses on the intersection of accounting and data analytics including the implications of data analytics on management control systems, performance measurement, risk management, and sustainability where he draws on textual analytics, machine learning and artificial intelligence theories and practices. His research papers appeared in international and interdisciplinary scholarly journals such as *The British Accounting Review, Accounting Auditing and Accountability Journal, Financial Accountability & Management, Intelligent Systems in Accounting, Finance & Management, Business Strategy and the Environment, Public Money & Management, Journal of Accounting & Organisational Change, Journal of Cleaner Production, and Journal of Intellectual Capital.*

Jan Svanberg is an Associate Professor of Business Administration at University of Gävle, and associated with Centre for research on Economic Relations (CER), Sweden. He earned his Ph.D. in Business Administration at Stockholm University, Sweden, and was recently a research fellow at RMIT University, Melbourne, Australia, for a period of two years. In addition to these studies, he has a diverse education with degrees in engineering, mathematics, and physics (M.Sc.) and law (LL.M). His current research focuses on how core problems in accounting, auditing and finance can be solved by interdisciplinary approaches with tools made available by advances in data science, especially machine learning. His work has been published in scholarly journals such as *The British Accounting Review, Behavioral Research in Accounting, Accounting Auditing and Accountability Journal, Journal of Cleaner Production, and Intelligent Systems in Accounting, Finance and Management.*

Peter Öhman is a Professor and Head of Business Administration at Mid Sweden University in Sundsvall, and director of Centre for research on Economic Relations (CER), Sweden. His research focuses on behavioral issues, primarily in accounting and auditing, but also in the banking and property industries. He has published a significant number of scholarly articles, published books, book chapters and reports, and presented papers at international conferences. He has received international awards for excellent research, is a member of Editorial Boards, and a reviewer of several well-known international journals. His work has been published in leading scholarly journals such as *Contemporary Accounting Research, Behavioral Research in Accounting, Accounting Auditing and Accountability Journal, European Accounting Review, and The British Accounting Review.*

Alan Lowe is an Honorary Professor of Management Accounting at RMIT University, Melbourne, Australia. He served as joint Editor of the *British Accounting Review*. His research interest has included management controls, ERP, technologies, and internet reporting using case studies and interpretive methodology. Recent projects include ethical identity and financial innovation in Islamic financial institutions, ICT service provision in health care sector, and governing climate change.

Part I
Emerging Technologies, and Accounting and Auditing Challenges

Chapter 2
A Picture Is Worth a Thousand Words: Audit Efficiency and Risk Management Through Data Visualization

Lutfa Tilat Ferdous, Chetanpal Singh, and Tarek Rana

Abstract The chapter aims to discuss impact of data visualization on auditors' analytical procedures and propose practical approaches to address audit efficiency through data visualization techniques. To ensure that efficient presentation of data improves audit efficiency and effectiveness, it is essential that auditors are aware of and effectively apply data visualization techniques in auditing. This chapter presents more profound data visualizations applications in audit procedures that can assist auditors in finding data discrepancies for improving audit risk management through insight development capacity. Further, this chapter considers numerous data visualization analysis tools that audit professionals can use in their specific audit procedures. Finally, this chapter provides avenues for future research in audit data analytics and recommends future research that will allow auditors to realize how technology-driven data visualization tools interact with the audit's standard features.

Keywords Data visualization · Audit analytics · Analytical procedures · Audit efficiency

1 Introduction

Data visualization is a process of presenting information in a graphical display for the purpose of sense making and effective communication that considers user's cognitive abilities and visual experiences. This process assists in analyzing unfiltered data and presenting it to users in an organized form through data visualization. Stakeholders

L. T. Ferdous
University of Leicester, Leicester, UK
e-mail: ltf4@leicester.ac.uk

C. Singh
RMIT University, Melbourne, VIC, Australia
e-mail: chetanpal.singh2@rmit.edu.au

T. Rana (✉)
RMIT University, Melbourne, VIC, Australia
e-mail: tarek.rana@rmit.edu.au

T. Rana et al. (eds.), *Handbook of Big Data and Analytics in Accounting and Auditing*,
https://doi.org/10.1007/978-981-19-4460-4_2

often use performance dashboards such as graphs, charts, maps, bubble cloud, and some other visual aids to understand complex and technical financial and analytical information. The data visualization tools and techniques are essential in delivering vast amount of information in a more novel and meaningful way for stakeholders data-driven decision making. Recent technological advancement provides auditors with various data visualization tools and techniques. Automated tools and techniques are available to auditors that can enhance the efficiency and effectiveness of audit procedures as well as help managing risk in audits. This chapter focuses on data visualization as an auditing tool and how data visualization can assist auditors to obtain better information, leading to better audit output, and overall improving the audit procedure.

Given the continuous technological advancement and organizations adoption of emerging technologies in their business operation and management, the audit profession must consider audit analytics for undertaking audits. Data visualizations as an audit analytics tool can maximize efficient management of audit tasks, particularly in conditions of a large and complex business and high-risk clients (Kinkeldey et al., 2014; Padilla et al., 2018). With the introduction of "Big data", corporations are swamped by using big data and analytics to sustain themselves in a new competitive business world. In a modern audit engagement environment, auditor's client information systems are more incorporated with the internet, social media and cloud computing systems. Therefore, in this new competitive and informative audit environment, auditors are evolved with large volumes, different varieties, high velocities, and more veracities data flow in all areas. Therefore, the necessity for "visualizing effects, possibilities, and consequences" increases to deliver adaptable data and concentrate on deep insight to produce intelligence for audit decision making.

This chapter presents a synthesis of the opportunities and difficulties experienced by the auditors with the expanding use of big data and data analytics by their clients and how visualization can enhance their efficiency in this journey. This chapter contributes to the recent literature by investigating the application of different data visualization techniques in auditing. Further, this understanding contributes to the audit professional and accounting community by expanding upon these emergent concerns about audit procedure efficiency through data visualization method and providing opportunities for future research.

2 Relevant Literature

2.1 Data Visualization

Prior literature used a different term to explain visualization, such as "data visualization" (Green, 1998) "information visualization" (Chen, 2010). Iliinsky and Steele (2011) define collection, transformation and presentation data stream in a visual way which allows user investigation and decision making. From a big data perspective, audit professionals need not explore the data instead manufacture more meaningful insight from data (Zhu & Watts, 2010). Data visualization should be constructing visuals that present clarification and thoughtful impact on users' mindset, persuading them to think better, develop judgment, or be curious about raising new questions ultimately. The efficiency of data visualization depends on observation, cognition and users' specific tasks and goals. Thus, visualization creates different meanings to the user's mind based on how a user observes a visualization on visual awareness, lighting settings, color balances, and previous experience (Ware, 2012). The primary objectives of data visualization are to facilitate users improve insights, persuade better outcomes and eventually generate hypotheses (Keim, 2001).

Auditors play a crucial role in verifying the accuracy and integrity of client organization's financial records. They are organized with tools and techniques to do the auditing and data visualization is one essential practice that the auditors use in performing audits (Buchheit et al., 2020). Data visualization helps the user have better insights, come up with better conclusions, and provide hypotheses. This is done by considering the possible ability of the user (Barr-Pulliam et al., 2021). According to Alles and Gray (2016), it has been figured out that data visualization and the presentation format play a crucial role in the judgment development process by considering the analytical procedure. Necessary evidence is provided by analytical procedures required for initial planning, substantive test, and audit review (Buchheit et al., 2020). But the environmental complexity model (Raveh et al., 2020) has highlighted that dealing with various amounts of information may hinder decision making. Backof et al. (2018) used the trend analysis for an experimental task and has found that the presentation format has no impact on the accuracy of dealing with the sales dollar. However, another study carried out by (Dilla & Raschke, 2015) has highlighted that participant have used graphs to perform comparatively better in dealing with correlation and in making predictions at the time of review of the sales account.

2.2 *Visualization Tool Used in Auditing*

In auditing, data visualization assists in dealing with highly diverse and complex data set without a required in-depth understanding of complex mathematical or statistical algorithms and allows users for quicker data investigation and finally valuable for quality control and risk assessment audit procedures (Anderson & Reckers, 1992). Prior auditing research discusses data visualization impact on auditing. Moriarity (1979) reports multi-dimensional graphic presentations are more resourceful in communicating financial information than tabular presentations. Auditors can take advantage of presenting data in a graphical format for their practical financial judgments (Wright, 1995); charts and graphs aid the auditor's decisions in evaluating correlations in analytical procedures (Anderson & Reckers, 1992).

Auditing literature has also documented that data visualization and graphical presentation impact the audit judgment development process concerning analytical procedures (Anderson & Kaplan, 1992; Anderson & Mueller, 2005; Anderson &

Reckers, 1992; Anderson et al., 2020; Schulz & Booth, 1995). During the concept of recent big data, auditors may experience large volume, unfiltered multifaced data, and urge to present the information in an organized visual format that may allow auditor in crucial decision making and analytical procedures (Cao et al., 2015; Joshi & Marthandan, 2020). Auditing research by Anderson and Mueller (2005) suggest that graphical performs pointedly efficient in analyzing correlations and developing estimates during the analytical review of the sales account.

3 Analysis of How Data Visualization Can Enhance Auditing Efficiency

This chapter explains to research community and practices in auditing in the presence of big data visualization tools and should be of interest to audit regulators and practitioners. The importance of visualization discusses different sectors of audit practices of enhanced professional judgments by using data visualizations to evaluate client data (Anderson & Mueller, 2005; Anderson et al., 2020). Prior research explains the importance of data visualization over various tabular formats (Anderson & Mueller, 2005; Kelton et al., 2010). Research has demonstrated the different manner of data presentation format such as tabular, chart, graphical or combination in assessing judgement development process in an analytical or substantive procedure in the auditing practices (Anderson & Kaplan, 1992; Schulz & Booth, 1995).

Alawadhi (2015) report data visualization significance in auditing studies and assesses numerous presentation formats and their effects on audit procedures. The outcome of research indicates that visualization methods empower data exploration in the presence of highly complex and noisy data, which are particularly effective in identifying deviations patterns and potential outliers in the data. Further, this study reveals that data visualization complements analytical procedures to discover and control risks that ultimately improve audit quality. In recent research, Rodríguez-Quintero et al. (2021) reported that the audit approach related to fraud combines visual analytics and process mining techniques. They explained some importance of this analytics such as: (i) a method is included that guides the use of the visual capabilities of process mining to detect fraud data patterns during an audit; (ii) the approach can be generalized to any business domain; (iii) well-known process mining techniques are used (Dotted Chart, Trace Alignment, or Fuzzy Miner) (pg. 1).

Both innovative data visualization tools and audit analytics coexist in audit professions and practice (Susskind & Susskind, 2015). Therefore, as the advancement of visualization tools introduces, it becomes progressively effective to comprehend how visually data stream cooperates with characteristics of both audit methodologies and auditor decision processes to influence auditor judgments (O'Donnell et al., 2017).

3.1 Compare Transactions and Journal Entries

An auditor can compare transaction activity or journal entries history through the data visualization technique. Primarily, when a company attempts a large volume of transactions, complex transactions, visualization can facilitate auditors to understand the unusual trend of transactions or locate risky transactions which can save them a debt, going concern, liquidation or bankruptcy prediction. Along with this, data visualization enables auditors to understand abnormalities, outliers, deviations or take corrective actions. For example, data visualization allows auditors to filter and relate to understanding data patterns—who entered the transaction, timing of transactions, who approved this transaction, and then identify if any revision is required.

Journal entry testing is another advantage of data visualization. Journal entry testing: the user is a chart that gives an example about how visualization helps make an outlet obvious. The total number of transactions processed in each accounting user has been depicted in the chart. The companies that process an enormous volume of transactions and have many accounts find it challenging to figure out unusual patterns or activities (International Auditing and Assurance Standards Board [IAASB], 2018). With the help of data visualization, the engagement team can quickly identify and compare data to figure out the patterns, like the accounts used and who have created the account and approved the journal's entries. Data visualization is also beneficial for the auditors as they can identify outliers that would be rather difficult to figure out (Alles & Gray, 2016). Moreover, the audit engagement team can quickly look at the distribution using basic client information.

3.2 Managing Risk

Risk assessment is one of the basic audit requirements that is done at the beginning as well as throughout the process of the audit. The engagement team plays a crucial role in the process of the audit so that it becomes effective and efficient (Alles, 2015). The engagement team judges the risk associated with material misstatement and figures out high-risk accounts that are prone to errors as well as manipulation.

One of the most popular examples of this case is a forecast which is regarded as a type of visualization that is useful for figuring out such areas (Appelbaum et al., 2017). In the case of forecasting, historical values are taken to provide expectation, as well as other factors, are considered that reflects the previous patterns. The auditors look at the results of the forecast and compare them with the actual result to judge the changes or unexpected scenes (Raveh et al., 2020). The reason why data visualization is beneficial to other forms of auditing is the capability to filter dynamically and sort depending on the underlying accounts or the various classes of transactions. The team gets easy to identify the unusual trends based on the forecasted level.

ASA 330.5 (ISA 330.5) requires that the auditor determine overall responses to assessed risks at the financial report level. The Auditor's assessment of the auditor's identified risks provides a basis for designing and performing further audit procedures (ASA 330.6 /ISA 330.6). In evaluating and managing risk, the auditor must consider: the potential risk, the likelihood of material misstatement, the significance of the risk, the possibility that a misstatement occurs, different classes of transaction and balance accounts, whether IT control or manual control exist in the client internal control system, and further auditor need to gather related audit evidence which is effective in controlling and correcting material misstatement. In this case, the auditor's responses to assessed risks need to reflect in the overall audit strategy and comprehensive audit plan or audit program.

A major obligation of an auditor is overall risk assessment, starting from audit procedures to the end of completion of the audit. In delivering a better-quality audit report and minimizing overall audit risk, the audit team is prone to analyze the risks of material misstatement accounting misreporting and detect high-risk accounts that are more sensitive to error or misreporting. In this case, managing and communicating risk with management have become the crucial task of an engagement auditor. An auditor can reveal unusual balances or transactions that differ from visualization's expected level. Auditors can employ risk visualization through charts, mapping techniques, or conceptual diagrams to realize the potential risk and develop a strategy to control risk. Except for this risk visualization, the auditor presents strategic management techniques such as Strengths Weaknesses Opportunities Threats (SWOT) analysis, Political Economic Social Technological (PEST) risk analysis, value-chain analysis and non-financial performance measurement (Gay & Simnett, 2017). Data visualization can make this information more accessible to understand information about potential risks arising due to the entity's nature and its environment.

3.3 *Inspecting Fraudulent Reporting*

ASA 240.11 (ISA 240.11) defines fraudulent financial reporting as an intentional act by one or more individuals among management, those charged with governance, employees, or third parties, involving the use of deception to obtain an unjust or illegal advantage'. ASA 240.3 (ISA 240.3) indicates that fraud is a comprehensive legal concept; the auditor is focused on fraud that produces a material misstatement in the financial report. During the audit procedure, auditors must discover high-risk accounts that need to be scrutinized more for aggressive accounting practices, fraudulent financial reporting, or intentional errors. Data visualization may assist in better demonstrating the amount, timing and reference person related to discounts and refunds and confirm which staff could connect in each activity which can reveal potential fraud areas that may control through analysis.

There is a lack of research in auditing on how data visualization impacts audit practice. Data visualization dramatically influences the efficacy of data visualization techniques for fraud detection. In this regard, Dilla and Raschke (2015) present a theoretical outline to calculate how auditors or fraud analysts might use data visualization techniques to expose fraudulent transactions and financial reporting. Vona

(2012) suggested that data visualization may use an alternative method of fraud data analytics, where data visualization can be used to analyze data for red flags that correlate with a specific fraud scenario. In effect, the fraud data analytics follows finding audit objectives, risk assessment, fraud data analytics, audit procedures and concluding the findings. Vona (2012) suggested that data visual analysis assists in different stages of fraud analytics.

3.4 Communication with Client

Data visualization techniques can facilitate collating different data concerning the client business that an auditor is observing. The visualization techniques also offer proper means of communicating findings to potential clients. They can assist the clients in learning about what the auditor has figured out at the time of engagement (International Auditing and Assurance Standards Board [IAASB], 2018). Clients can use this information to enhance their risk environment, which can be through a simple chat or a complete dashboard. The auditors can see the company to figure out the problems in the financial report by good communication and proper sharing of data before the year-end (Backof et al., 2018). Visualizations provide a practical idea of the quality of information of the client, which provides a valuable notion of communicating risks and findings to clients and can help clients understand what the auditor result during the audit procedure. Auditors can develop a visual connection with clients through performance dashboards or trend analyses which clients can utilize to recover their risk environment, improve internal controls, and grasp the insight from the auditor's assessment.

This would help the company know about the accounting and control issues that arise in a year.

3.5 Observe Results

Data visualizations provide data insights; some of the insights about data have already been revealed, and other insights might be uncovered. Some new senses might offer a new story, while others could be the result of potential misstatement, this finding can be exposed by visualizing data. Data visualization techniques such as line graphs or bar charts may help auditors compare the previous year to the current year, even monthly, quarterly, semi-annually, or yearly trends of revenue or cash flows or disclosure activity. Auditors can use visualization tools to validate and observe the degree and control of client journal entries or accounts activity to the ending of the financial period.

3.6 Compare Budget and Actual Performance

Budgeting generates a standard to compare actual results to establish how the outcome differs from the expected performance. Based on this difference, corporations forecast financial performance. Performance dashboard and bar chart indicate to validate that companies' performances are on the correct path, which determines how companies should allocate their budgets for a future period. Auditors can uncover substantial deviations through data visualization tools that help auditors analyze the causes of abnormalities from internal such as misappropriation of account or accounting manipulation or external such as business risk or economic reasons. Auditors derived results from this visualization facilitates management to decide the strategic measure and corrective actions.

3.7 Testing Cut-Off

Cut-off testing is one of the significant substantive procedures in auditing. Cut-off testing determines whether transactions and events for the period under audit that transactions and events are recorded in the correct period. For example, the auditor needs to check that last purchases recorded before the balance date and first purchases recorded after the balance date are recorded in the correct period, considering when received by evidence of goods received a note. This testing procedure requires corroborating supporting evidence, which may need scrutinize assessments of related departments like sales, cash management, requisition and delivery. It becomes challenging to figure out whether transactions were recorded at the proper period; instead, it is time-consuming and requires adequate comparison of parameters such as shipping, delivery, and sales date from the documents (Dilla & Raschke, 2015). With the help of data visualization software, the auditors can perform this task quickly based on the corresponding reschedule.

From the cut-off testing chart that visualizes the various transactions that happen daily for the year (Raveh et al., 2020), the auditor can observe from the chart that there was a particular uptick in the sales in December, whereas there was a drop in sales in January. Data visualization through the matrix or line graph presents monthly or daily transactions for a specific year. While transactions for each quarter or period or end-of-year necessitate systematic analysis, though, data visualization software can facilitate auditors to identify irregularities, observe the complete pattern of the data and evaluate related audit.

3.8 Checking Employee Activity

Employees may involve unintentional mistakes or omissions, for example, mathematical or clerical errors in the underlying records and accounting data, misinterpretation of facts, and misapplication of accounting policies (Gay & Simnett, 2017). Data visualization can help auditors to check employee activity in the accounts department. Methods such as pie charts or line graphs provide auditors insight into the volume, amount, timing and accounts reference number of each transaction entered by each employee in the finance and accounts or payroll department. The auditor may identify journal misreporting or reveal payroll discrepancies within different departments from data visualization. Later, management can use this procedure for developing internal control for the transaction, operation or payroll.

3.9 Data Visualization and Analytical Procedure in Auditing

The objective of audit technology is to facilitate auditors to analyze audit risk and respond to these risks more effectively by the better realizing appropriate client and industry data. Due to the rapid growth of audit technology, it becomes evident that, while data analytics and visualization may assist audit professionals in visualizing and examining entire data populations, visualization manages professional judgment and decision-making. Auditors can benefit from effective data visualization through analytical procedures such as either risk assessment or substantive audit procedures. ASA 315.6 (ISA 315.6) explains the auditor to employ analytical procedures at the planning stage as a method of the risk-assessment procedures. Data visualization tools can be used as analytical procedures through the inquiry and assessment of fluctuations and establish a connection whether there are any abnormalities with expected performances.

Visual data shows the auditor to (1) validate previous years' financial report data so that absolute and percentage comparisons can be made, and (2) calculate financial report ratios for current and previous years. Visualization tools such as PowerBI can also perform this type of analysis. Effective data visualization allows the auditor to portray audit evidence classified as substantive analytical procedure as even more credible and drive auditors to less detailed and thorough supplementary proposed procedures relative to evidence (Anderson et al., 2020; Matthews & Chesney, 2015).

4 Data Visualization Techniques

The graphical representation of data and information is known as data visualization. Charts, graphs, maps, and data visualization tools are used to represent the information and data. All these elements offer a straightforward way to look at and understand the patterns trends in the data (Appelbaum et al., 2017). According to big data, data visualization tools and technologies are very important for looking at a large amount of information and making proper decisions accordingly. Below are some of the essential data visualization techniques that one should know Common general type of data visualization.

4.1 Charts

Chat is regarded as the easiest way to present the development of the various data sets. The bar and line charts are the two popular options that depict a relationship between the elements over time concerning pie charts (Alles & Gray, 2016).

4.2 Tables

Similar to mini spreadsheets that show data in the rows and columns. The tables represent the pricing for service and display the comparative features of a product (Gandhi & Pruthi, 2020). The data visualization type is prevalent for visual documents such as reports, proposals, and training manuals.

4.3 Graphs

Line graphs, bar graphs, pie charts, histograms are the popular types of graphs that are a great way to visualize the data and display statistics (Barr-Pulliam et al., 2021). An example of a representation of a bar graph or chart is that it is used for displaying numerical data that is not dependent on one another (Fig. 1).

4.4 Maps

Another popular data visualization technique is the maps used in different industries. With the help of a map, the industry can locate elements on objects and various areas. Popular techniques are geographical maps, building plans, website layout, etc. (Buchheit et al., 2020). Heat maps and dot distribution maps are the most popular visualizations used in different industries.

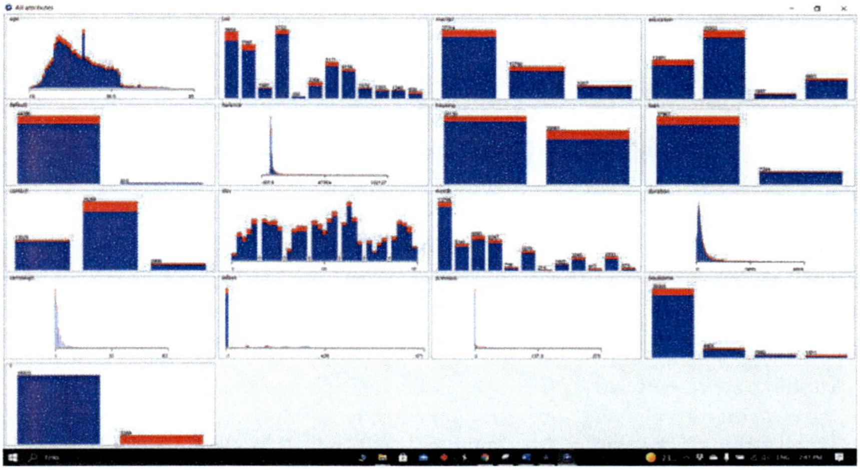

Fig. 1 Bar graph or chart

4.5 *Infographics*

The visual representation of a vast information collection is known as an infographic. The infographics highlight a complete story rather than single data visualization and subjectivity to the topic (Raveh et al., 2020). The infographic comprises one or more data visualization and is often supported by short blurbs or other text pieces that discuss the topic (Fig. 2).

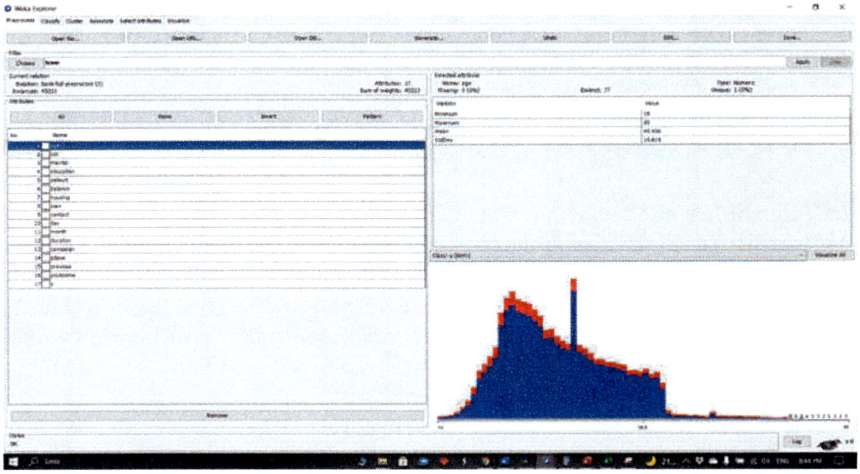

Fig. 2 Infographic

4.6 Dashboard

Data visualization dashboards play a crucial role in displaying visual objects such as charts and graphs and are one of the most popular techniques. The data visualization dashboard is useful for conveniently communicating the message and learning about the pattern. Apart from this, it is also helpful to understand the relationship between the data in a better way. More specific examples of methods to visualize the data.

4.7 Area Chart

Area charts are essential to represent the total value of every data point. It is a variation of the basic line graph where the area on the line is appropriately shaded to highlight the total value of the data point (Dilla & Raschke, 2015). The data visualization method plays a crucial role in showcasing the changes in one or more quantities over time.

4.8 Bar Chart

Another easy-to-use option of data visualization is the classic bar chart. The traditional bar chart or the bar graph is also regarded as a column chart that uses horizontal and vertical bars to compare the various items of different segments (Raveh et al., 2020). One axis depicts the categories being compared in the bar chart, and the other axis shows the measured value. The bar length highlights how the age group measures concerning the value. However, the disadvantage of the bar chart is that labelling, and clarity become problematic if there are many categories included (Fig. 3).

4.9 Box and Whisker Plot

Box and whisker plot is another standard method of data visualization that offers a visual summary of data with the help of its quartiles. At first, a box is drawn in the box and whisker plot. The box is drawn from the first quartile till the target of the data set (Alles & Gray, 2016). This plot is helpful to determine the interquartile range where most of the details of the data are located, and it provides you with a clear concept about the data set outliers. The box and whisker plot is very useful in identifying whether the data is symmetrical or not; it also provides a visual summary of the data set that can be interpreted easily (Fig. 4).

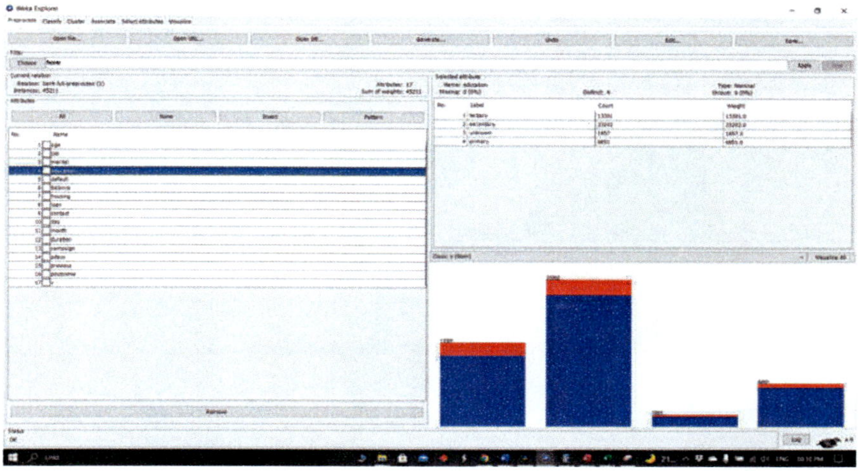

Fig. 3 Classic bar chart

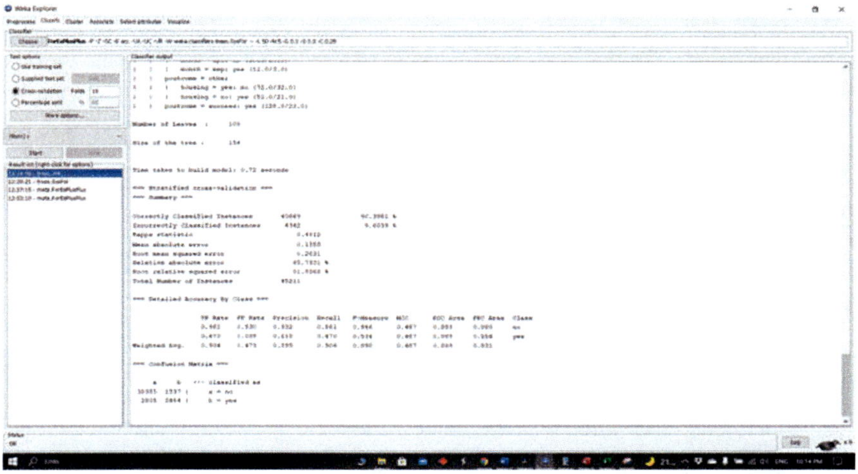

Fig. 4 Whisker Plot

4.10 Bubble Cloud

Bubble cloud is the variation of scattered plots where the makers are replaced using the bubbles. There are three measures required in the bubble cloud plots, where two are for the plot axes, and the third is for the bubble's size to showcase the relationship (Buchheit et al., 2020). A bubble cloud plot is a popular choice where a large data set is present.

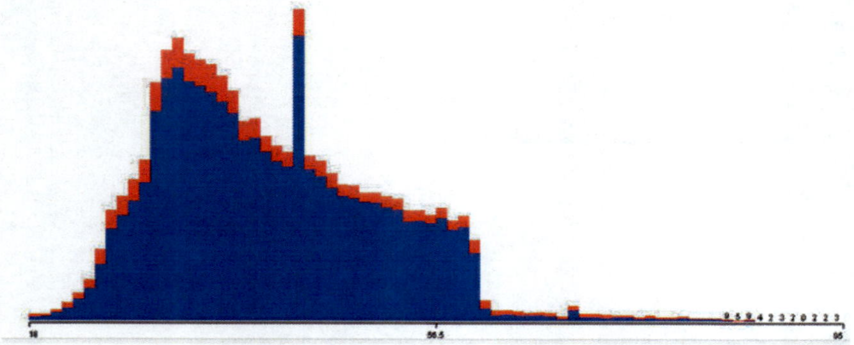

Fig. 5 Bullet graph

4.11 Bullet Graph

Bullet graphs are one of the most popular forms of graphs. It is also known that variation of a bar graph is used in place of dashboard Gauges for representing the performance data. The bullet graphs are useful to provide information to the viewers about the business performance compared to the benchmark of the business metrics (Backof et al., 2018). The actual value is represented by the vertical-horizontal bar that is present in the middle of the bullet graph chart, whereas the particle line talks about the comparative value. However, the target is suppressed if the horizontal bar in the bullet graph passes through the vertical line (Fig. 5).

4.12 Cartogram

This is also known as value by area maps; the geographic regions are modified like the countries in proportion to the interest variable, for example, the population. The cartogram is useful to illustrate the various patterns. Many georeferenced data visualizations have been utilized for over a century (Fig. 6).

4.13 Circle View

Another powerful popular visualization used for competitive analysis is the circle view. A circle view is similar to a scatter plot, but it has a circle marker, and every mark is of the circle shape and is used for operations (Raveh et al., 2020). The technique includes a combination of hierarchical visualization techniques like tree map, circular

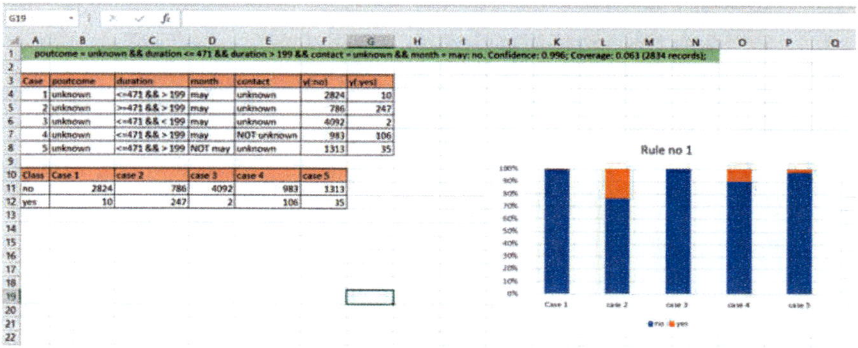

Fig. 6 Cartogram

layout technique etc. The primary objective of the circle view visualization is to compare the continuous data changing the characteristics over some time so that patterns and exceptions can be easily identified.

4.14 Dot Distribution Map

In the case of dot distribution maps in the density of the dot, symbols are used to highlight the presence of the feature, and these maps are widely used to highlight the intensity of the attribute.

4.15 Gantt Chart

In project management, the Gantt chart plays a crucial role in illustrating the timeline of the project as well as the progression of the particular job. The vertical axis of the Gantt chart talks about the task that is to be performed, whereas the horizontal axis represents the time intervals (Gandhi & Pruthi, 2020). Gantt chart is useful to display timelines and is helpful as it provides the team members with a proper track of the various aspects of the project (Fig. 7).

4.16 Heat Map

This is a popular form of visualization used to show the data difference. Heat map uses the help of variation of color. To communicate the values, the heatmap uses color in a way that helps the viewers to identify the trend easily. Moreover, the heat

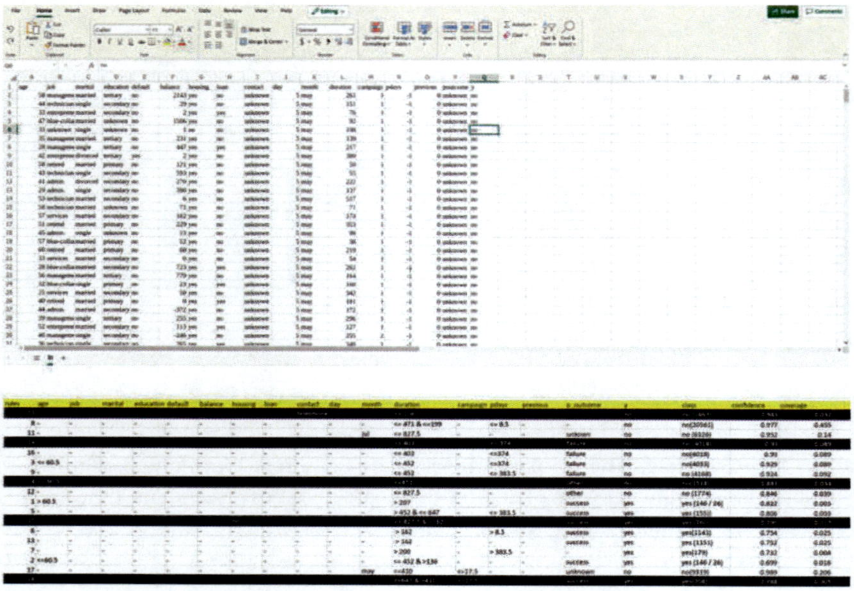

Fig. 7 Gantt chart

map has a clear legend as it allows the user to read and interpret the heatmap correctly (Backof et al., 2018). One of the best examples of the usage of heat maps is that it can be used to highlight the best cases using green color where the average cases are used with yellow color, and worst cases are highlighted in red color. Thus, it offers users to compare the various performance of the task in one go. The heat map has a lot of possible applications; if the user wants to look at which time of the day the retail store experiences the most sales, they can easily look at the heat map to analyze the aspect.

4.17 Highlight Table

Compared to traditional tables, highlight tables are much more beneficial and engaging because they highlight cells inside the table with the help of color. The viewers get it easier to identify the spot quickly and patterns in the given data. The highlight table visualizations are extremely useful to compare the categorical data (Barr-Pulliam et al., 2021). The user can add conditional formatting rules to the highlight table based on the data visualization tool.

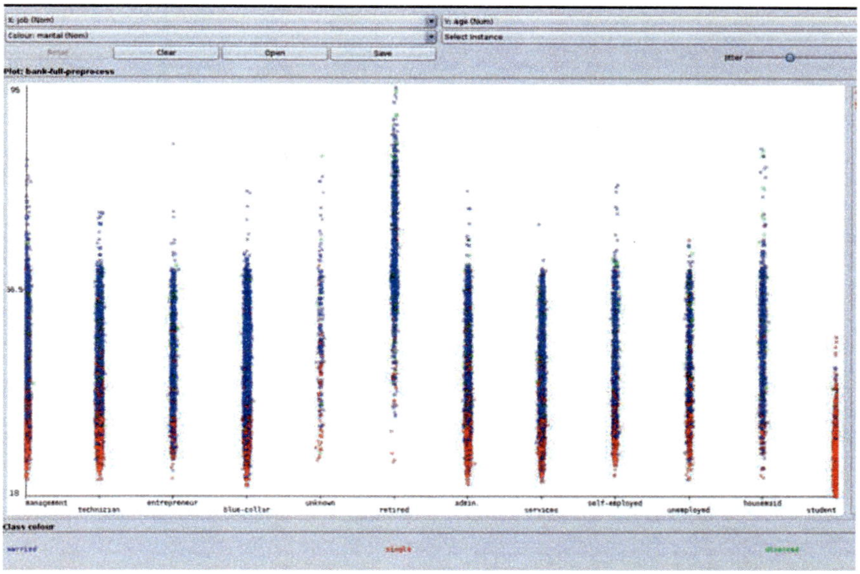

Fig. 8 Histogram

4.18 *Histogram*

The histogram is a popular alternative to bar charts, where the data is distributed over the continuous interval for the period. The reason histogram illustrations are helpful is that it helps in figuring out where the values are concentrated (Raveh et al., 2020). This type of visualization is advantageous to show the frequency of the particular occurrence. For example, suppose the user is looking for how many clicks the website has received each day over the past week. In that case, the histogram is very useful with its visualization. It can quickly help the user determine which day the website has got the most significant clicks (Fig. 8).

4.19 *Matrix*

Another widely used visualization graph is Matrix which compares data groups within a category of information. With the help of the data visualization, the user can get an idea about how the various groups communicate and influence each other. The matrix data visualization can help the viewer to make effective mode decisions.

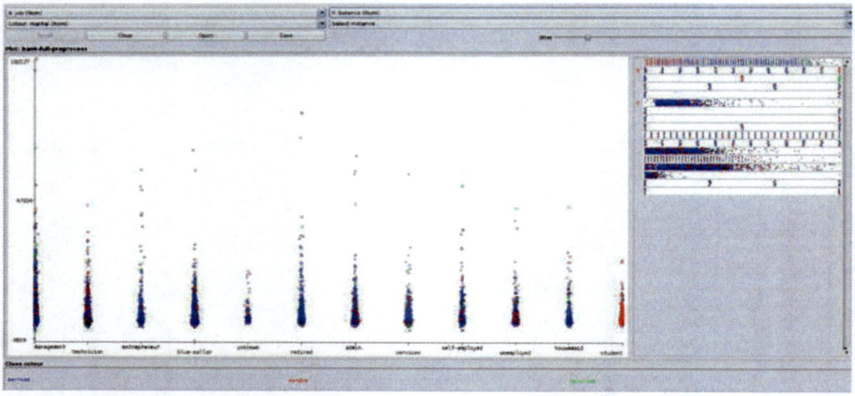

Fig. 9 Network

4.20 *Network*

Another popular form of data visualization is the network diagram that presents the relationship between the qualitative data points. The network diagram visualization comprises nodes and links known as edges (Backof et al., 2018). The singular data points are known as nodes connected to the other nodes with the help of edges that represent the relationship between multiple nodes. The network diagram has many use cases, such as depicting the social network and connection between the workers at our company (Fig. 9).

4.21 *Polar Area*

The polar charts are utilized for data visualization to display multivariate observations using arbitrary variables. This chart form is also called radar charts, web charts, spider charts. This chart is similar to the pie chart in many ways.

4.22 *Radial Tree*

This tree layout algorithm is applicable for any diagram. The radial tree is also a radial map used to display the tree structure. The diagram features are arranged using the layout algorithm to get functions from the root junction with the help of the circle center so that trees can be appropriately arranged starting from the root (Fig. 10).

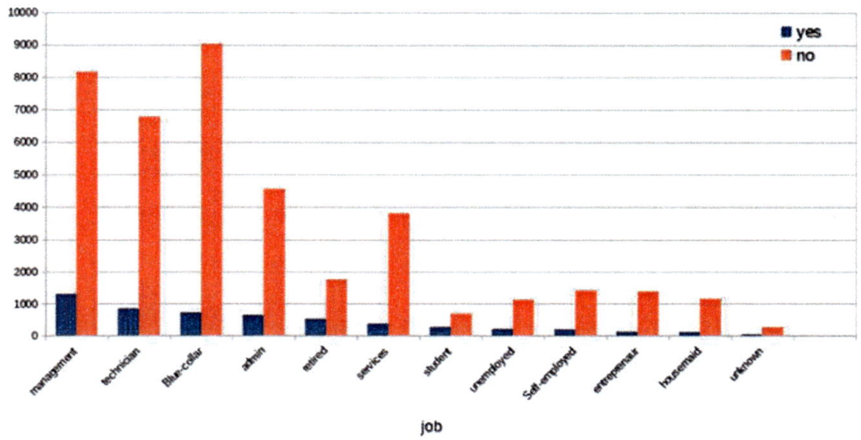

Fig. 10 Radical Tree

4.23 Scatter Plot

The data for two variables are displayed in a scatter plot, and the scatter plot data visualization helps illustrate the relationship between variables. The scatter plot is useful to figure out the trends of correlation in the data (Appelbaum et al., 2017). This form of data is most effective for large data sets as it is easier to figure out the trend where there are many data points (Fig. 11).

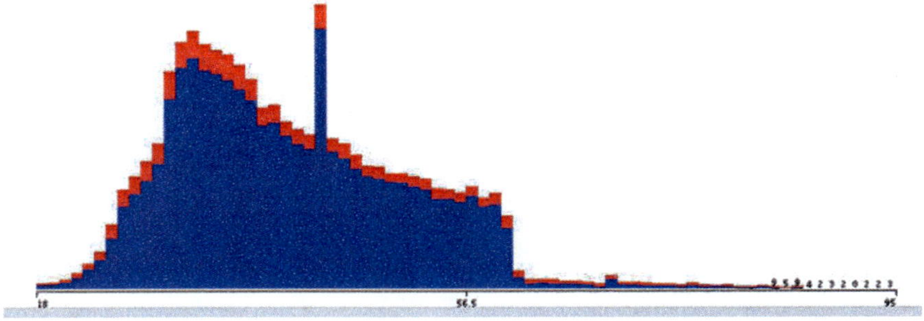

Fig. 11 Scatter Plot

4.24 Stream Graph

The stream graph is a data visualization graph known to be a variety of stacked area charts. The values are not plotted against the customary y-axis; the steam graph balances the baseline of the stack to illustrate to make it even around the x-axis.

4.25 Text Tables

This form of table visualization allows the user to display data from the matrix with the help of a tabular view. This is also known as the data grid or the data table and is the default type of visualization used for selecting the first data (Gandhi & Pruthi, 2020).

4.26 Timeline

To visualize the sequence of tasks in a chronological order timeline plays a crucial role. The timeline is linear that consists of events outlined along the axis. With the help of a timeline, the user can highlight the most vital events.

4.27 Tree Map

This approach is a popular approach that showcases the data in hierarchical form. Here the objects can be divided into divisions as well as subdivisions according to the requirement (Alles & Gray, 2016).

4.28 Wedge Stack Graph

This is another popular data visualization technique that illustrates hierarchical data in a radial system. The graph is extremely useful to show multilevel frequency data.

4.29 Word Cloud

This visualization can be done using word cloud or tag cloud, where the size of the word is directly proportional to the frequency. The word cloud is used on the website as well as blogs to figure out the keywords and differentiate textual data between a couple of sources.

5 Conclusion

Data visualization is all about big data and analytics. Visualisation is an increasingly essential tool that helps the auditor in audit planning, risk assessment and testing procedures. With the help of data visualisation, an auditor can understand the story by removing the noise from the data and presenting useful information for data-driven decision making. This chapter has discussed only a handful of research studies in accounting and auditing literature that have highlighted the recent types and forms of visualisation tools and techniques, and their benefits and challenges. As discussed in this chapter, for the audit, the data visualisation process can help the auditors to filter and compare data to highlight the trends and patterns and present the various complex issues for discussion with the management.

The chapter has not given the importance of data visualisation software that are available for auditors but has highlighted how auditors and audit firms can take advantage of the data visualisation tools and techno agues to improve audit quality, add value to the process of auditing, and manage risk in the audit process. Future research can explore the new innovation, dissemination, and in-depth processes of audit data visualisation by using survey and case study approaches.

References

Alawadhi, A. (2015). *The application of data visualization in auditing* (Doctoral dissertation). Rutgers University.

Alles, M. G. (2015). Drivers of the use and facilitators and obstacles of the evolution of big data by the audit profession. *Accounting Horizons, 29*(2), 439–449.

Alles, M., & Gray, G. L. (2016). Incorporating big data in audits: Identifying inhibitors and a research agenda to address those inhibitors. *International Journal of Accounting Information Systems, 22*, 44–59.

Anderson, J. C., & Kaplan, S. E. (1992). An investigation of the effect of presentation format on auditors' non-investigation region judgments. *Advances in Accounting Information Systems, 1*, 71–88.

Anderson, J. C., & Mueller, J. M. (2005). The effects of experience and data presentation format on an auditing judgment. *Journal of Applied Business Research (JABR), 21*(1).

Anderson, J. C., & Reckers, P. M. J. (1992). An empirical investigation of the effects of presentation format and personality on auditor's judgment in applying analytical procedures. *Advances in Accounting, 10*(1), 19–43.

Anderson, S. B., Hobson, J. L., & Peecher, M. E. (2020). *The joint effects of rich data visualization and audit procedure categorization on auditor judgment*. Available at SSRN 3737234.

Appelbaum, D., Kogan, A., & Vasarhelyi, M. A. (2017). Big Data and analytics in the modern audit engagement: Research needs. *Auditing: A Journal of Practice & Theory, 36*(4), 1–27.

Backof, A. G., Carpenter, T. D., & Thayer, J. (2018). Auditing complex estimates: How do construal level and evidence formatting impact auditors' consideration of inconsistent evidence? *Contemporary Accounting Research, 35*(4), 1798–1815.

Barr-Pulliam, D., Brown-Liburd, H. L., & Sanderson, K. A. (2021). The effects of the internal control opinion and use of audit data analytics on perceptions of audit quality, assurance, and auditor negligence. *Auditing: A Journal of Practice & Theory* (upcoming).

Buchheit, S., Dzuranin, A. C., Hux, C., & Riley, M. E. (2020). Data visualization in local accounting firms: Is slow technology adoption rational? *Current Issues in Auditing, 14*(2), A15–A24.

Cao, M., Chychyla, R., & Stewart, T. (2015). Big data analytics in financial statement audits. *Accounting Horizons, 29*(2), 423–429.

Chen, C. (2010). Information visualization. *Wiley Interdisciplinary Reviews: Computational Statistics, 2*(4), 387–403.

Dilla, W. N., & Raschke, R. L. (2015). Data visualization for fraud detection: Practice implications and a call for future research. *International Journal of Accounting Information Systems, 16*, 1–22.

Gandhi, P., & Pruthi, J. (2020). Data visualization techniques: Traditional data to Big Data. In *Data Visualization* (pp. 53–74). Springer.

Gay, G., & Simnett, R. (2017). *Auditing and assurance services in Australia.* McGraw-Hill Education Australia.

Green, M. (1998). Toward a perceptual science of multidimensional data visualization: Bertin and beyond. *ERGO/GERO Human Factors Science, 8*, 1–30.

Iliinsky, N., & Steele, J. (2011). *Designing data visualizations: Representing informational Relationships.* O'Reilly Media, Inc.

International Auditing and Assurance Standards Board (IAASB). (2018). *Feedback statement: Exploring the growing use of technology in the audit, with a focus on data analytics.* IAASB.

Joshi, P. L., & Marthandan, G. (2020). Continuous internal auditing: Can big data analytics help? *International Journal of Accounting, Auditing and Performance Evaluation, 16*(1), 25–42.

Keim, D. A. (2001). Visual exploration of large data sets. *Communications of the ACM, 44*(8), 38–44.

Kelton, A. S., Pennington, R. R., & Tuttle, B. M. (2010). The effects of information presentation format on judgment and decision making: A review of the information systems research. *Journal of Information Systems, 24*(2), 79–105.

Kinkeldey, C., MacEachren, A. M., & Schiewe, J. (2014). How to assess visual communication of uncertainty? A systematic review of geospatial uncertainty visualisation user studies. *The Cartographic Journal, 51*(4), 372–386.

Matthews, P. G., & Chesney, D. L. (2015). Fractions as percepts? Exploring cross-format distance effects for fractional magnitudes. *Cognitive Psychology, 78*, 28–56.

Moriarity, S. (1979). Communicating financial information through multidimensional graphics. *Journal of Accounting Research*, 205–224.

O'Donnell, R., O'Mara, B., Rast, C., & Sand, H. (2017). *Data and analytics in the audit: Driving up trust in the capital markets.* Publication number 133846-G. KPMG International.

Padilla, L. M., Creem-Regehr, S. H., Hegarty, M., & Stefanucci, J. K. (2018). Decision making with visualizations: A cognitive framework across disciplines. *Cognitive Research: Principles and Implications, 3*(1), 1–25.

Raveh, E., Ofek, Y., Bekkerman, R., & Cohen, H. (2020). Applying Big Data visualization to detect trends in 30 years of performance reports. *Evaluation, 26*(4), 516–540.

Rodríguez-Quintero, J. F., Sánchez-Díaz, A., Iriarte-Navarro, L., Maté, A., Marco-Such, M., & Trujillo, J. (2021). Fraud audit based on visual analysis: A process mining approach. *Applied Sciences, 11*(11), 4751.

Schulz, A., & Booth, P. (1995). The effects of presentation format on the effectiveness and efficiency of auditors' analytical review judgments. *Accounting & Finance, 35*(1), 107–131.

Susskind, R. E., & Susskind, D. (2015). *The future of the professions: How technology will transform the work of human experts.* Oxford University Press.

Vona, L. W. (2012). *Fraud risk assessment: Building a fraud audit program.* Wiley.

Ware, C. (2012). *Information visualization: Perception for design.*
Wright, W. F. (1995). Superior loan collectibility judgments given graphical displays. *Auditing, 14*(2), 144–155.
Zhu, B., & Watts, S. A. (2010). Visualization of network concepts: The impact of working memory capacity differences. *Information Systems Research, 21*(2), 327–344.

Lutfa Tilat Ferdous, Ph.D. is a Lecturer in the Department of Economics, Finance and Accounting at the University of Leicester, UK. Her research interests are financial reporting, auditing, corporate governance, sustainability, data analytics.

Chetanpal Singh, Ph.D. is an ICT and Cyber Security Lecturer in RMIT University, Melbourne, Australia. He has exceptional technical and industry experience of 10 years in leading organizations in Australia including Telstra, KPMG, and Wilson. He has extensive experience in Higher Education course development, compliance and course accreditation, governance oversight. His research specializations are Image Processing, Business Integration, Computer Vision, Software Engineering and Computer Networks.

Tarek Rana is an Associate Professor of Accounting and Data Analytics at RMIT University, Melbourne, Australia. He earned a Ph.D. in Accounting at the University of New South Wales (UNSW) Australia. He has considerable professional and industry experience in the areas of business services, taxation, auditing, and financial planning as well as consulting services including performance measurement and risk management. He has formed many industry partnerships and undertaken practice focused research projects to deliver long-term social and organizational impact. His current research focuses on the intersection of accounting and data analytics including the implications of data analytics on management control systems, performance measurement, risk management, and sustainability where he draws on textual analytics, machine learning and artificial intelligence theories and practices. His research papers appeared in international and interdisciplinary scholarly journals such as *The British Accounting Review, Accounting Auditing and Accountability Journal, Financial Accountability & Management, Intelligent Systems in Accounting, Finance & Management, Business Strategy and the Environment, Public Money & Management, Journal of Accounting & Organisational Change, Journal of Cleaner Production, and Journal of Intellectual Capital.*

Chapter 3
The Challenges Facing Vietnamese Accountants and Auditors with the Adoption of Emerging Technologies

Thuy Thu Nguyen, Lan Anh Nguyen, Michael Kend, and Van Anh Thi Pham

Abstract There are many potential factors that are causing challenges in using emerging technologies in accounting and auditing in developing economies. This study focuses specifically on the transitional emerging economy of Vietnam and just some of the factors are discussed that have been identified as limiting the implementation and usage of emerging technologies in accounting and auditing. To focus on this aim, prior literature was used to collate, summarize, and analyze studies, which broadened the usual goal of directed content analysis, which is to extend theory. The strategy of selecting relevant articles (both academic and from practice) to be reviewed, consisted of a combination of the main concepts of the challenges in using emerging technologies in accounting and auditing. As research relating to emerging technology is still gaining prominence, where necessary, online searching for supplementary information were accessed from the websites of accessible sources such as the 'Big Four' audit firms and professional accounting bodies. We report that in this developing economy, in the Vietnamese context, there are some major challenges we believe are significantly related to emerging technology adoption and usage in the accounting and auditing fields.

Keywords Emerging Technologies · Accounting · Auditing · Document Review · Vietnam

T. T. Nguyen
National Academy of Public Administration, Hanoi, Vietnam

L. A. Nguyen · M. Kend (✉)
RMIT University, Melbourne, VIC, Australia
e-mail: michael.kend@rmit.edu.au

L. A. Nguyen
e-mail: lan.nguyen@rmit.edu.au

V. A. T. Pham
Hanoi Academy of Finance, Hanoi, Vietnam
e-mail: vananhpham@hvtc.edu.vn

T. Rana et al. (eds.), *Handbook of Big Data and Analytics in Accounting and Auditing*,
https://doi.org/10.1007/978-981-19-4460-4_3

1 Introduction

In the recent years, the use of emerging technologies such as audit data and business analytical tools have greatly increased in many business sectors, including in the accounting and auditing sector (Ajana, 2015). In the new technological era, techniques such as pattern recognition, data mining, and natural-language processing (NLP) have improved the predictive power of data analysis routines in both the accounting and auditing fields (Yoon et al., 2015). While the adoption of these emerging technologies brings greater tensions to these sectors (Enget et al., 2017; Marshall et al., 2015; Verma & Bhattacharyya, 2017), at the same time, accounting and auditing firms are facing many challenges as an outcome (Dagilienė & Klovienė, 2019). Despite the importance of using audit, big data, and business analytical tools there is only thus far broad research conducted in this area, especially in accounting and auditing, which remains scant, and especially in developing countries, such as Vietnam.

Major audit firms have all made significant investments in the development and acquisition of artificial intelligence tools which include big data analytics, making claims that these tools are directly relevant to how they conduct their audits (Salijeni et al., 2021). This present study was motivated by the call from Bhandari and Hassanein (2012) to understand the challenges of overcoming the implementation and usage of these emerging technologies, and further motivated by prior studies that indicated there has been only limited attention drawn to how auditors and accountants make sense of the emerging technologies and their properties (Salijeni et al., 2021).

This following chapter is thus motivated due to the following reasons. Firstly, emerging technologies such as audit, big data and business analytics are expected to dramatically change the business environment and the capabilities of business processes. The accounting and auditing functions are changing, the capabilities of accounting firms are being added to at the same time, eliminating the functions that are no longer adding value (Appelbaum et al., 2017). Secondly, most academic contributions exploring the rise of this emerging technology have provided only normative perspectives on how ‘optimal’ application of these technologies may better equip accountants and auditors to analyses client data and the practical challenges ensuing from this new direction (Vasarhelyi et al., 2015; Yoon et al., 2015). Regulators have also added their voices to the debate, for instance, focusing on the extent to which auditors’ claims of using this technology fulfills their commitment for audit quality (Salijeni et al., 2021). So, a lot remains to be explored, and rarely have emerging economies been considered within this debate. While Vietnam had received plenty of focus in recent accounting studies (Nguyen, 2019; Nguyen et al., 2020, 2021) and auditing studies (Nguyen & Kend, 2017, 2019), none of these prior studies considered the emerging technology debate as we presented above, and considered the challenges faced by Vietnam in that respect, as presented below. Thus, this chapter aims to help answer the following research question:

RQ. What key factors are causing challenges in using emerging technologies in accounting and auditing in the developing economy of Vietnam?

The main contributions of this chapter are as follows. Prior literature has examined the challenges of using big data, and audit data analytics from a Westernized setting context. To the best of our knowledge, this study is one of the first to examine the key challenges in using the emerging technologies in a developing economy, such as Vietnam. We explain and analyze how different institutional and company-related challenges are expressed and influence the decision of using emerging technologies in accounting and auditing. Furthermore, this study also to a limited extent, highlights the differences in the emerging technology adoption between the developed and developing countries. These insights will enhance our understanding of the big data and audit data analytics tools available in accounting and auditing context, and how they are used in different settings. The study also makes a theoretical contribution by applying the diffusion of innovation theory (Rogers, 1962, 2003) in the context of the key challenges and issues in the adoption of emerging technologies in Vietnam.

The chapter is organized as follows. The literature review and the theoretical framework pertaining on the general understanding of audit, big data, and business challenges of the adoption of emerging technologies are presented in Sects. 2 and 3 of this chapter. Section 4 presents the methodology used, then Sect. 5 presents the findings and discussion. The conclusion, limitations and further research directions are presented in Sect. 6 of this chapter.

2 Literature Review

2.1 *Prior Literature on Audit, Big Data and Business Analytics in the Accounting and Auditing Fields*

Big data is mainly generated from external sources with different formats such as videos, images, maps, and text. It is also often referred to as vast datasets containing varieties of unstructured, semi-structured, and structured data collected from different sources that can be used for data analytics when needed (Cao et al., 2015). Big data and data science principles enable accountants and auditors to capture data by gaining access to both internal and external parts of their client's financial data sources (Rezaee et al., 2018).

The 5Vs that characterize big data are as follows:

- wide variety (breadth of data generated and captured from multiple sources and in different formats),
- high velocity (generating, capturing, and processing the large amount of data at quite high speed),
- a huge volume of data (amount of data that is very large) (Mayer-Schönberger & Cukier, 2014; Zhang et al., 2015),

- uncertain veracity (data that is messy, inconsistent, incomplete, biased, noisy, and abnormal) (Reimer & Madigan, 2018),
- value (generating and capturing valuable data) (Nepal et al., 2015).

Vasarhelyi et al. (2015) argue that big data has changed the manner that auditors acknowledge information in the same way that it has already influenced business practitioners. The information technology world has defined 'big data' as follows:

> Big data is high-volume, high-velocity and high-variety information assets that demand cost-effective, innovative forms of information processing for enhanced insight and decision making. (Gartner IT glossary, n.d.)

Similarly, TechAmerica Foundation has defined 'big data' as follows:

> Big data is a term that describes large volumes of high velocity, complex and variable data that require advanced techniques and technologies to enable the capture, storage, distribution, management, and analysis of the information. (TechAmerica Foundation's Federal Big Data Commission, 2012)

Tang et al. (2017) defined data analytics as tools that enable the timely analysis and transformation of large, heterogeneous set of data into appropriate structured information used for decision making. Data analytics is a "process by which insights are extracted from operational, financial, and other forms of electronic data internal or external to the organization" (KPMG, 2012, p. 2).

Data analytic tools would add a substantial benefit for auditors, especially in overcome cognitive limitations associated with ambiguity in audit procedures (Tang et al., 2017). For example, in identifying potential abnormal transactions, trends or patterns, the technology provides auditors with the ability to integrate and utilize collected information from both structured and unstructured data sources and recognize unauthorized disbursements or fraudulent transactions from past transaction data (Tang et al., 2017). The auditing profession is being challenged by advances in information technology like never before, allied with real-time approaches to managing of business processes. Rezaee et al. (2018) pointed out that the increasing intricacy of business processes has urged accounting firms to gradually incorporate big data and data analytics into their inherent audit procedures. The same idea also presented by Brynjolfsson et al. (2011) that companies that applied data-orientated decision-making processes could achieve a five to six percent enhancement in their productivity through the usage of this emerging technology. Despite the undeniable importance of data analytics, the remaining challenges center around the possibility for a comprehensive technological integration into current auditing procedures and practices (Vasarhelyi et al., 2015).

The advancement in big data technologies is believed to have leveraged off the existing audit environment to a certain extent. Zhang et al. (2018) stated that development of emerging technologies could drive the establishment of audit informatization, systematic innovation of current working methods, as well as promote audit transformation. Furthermore, the burgeoning rate of novel automation technology application is believed to potentially bring in new opportunities to the current auditing landscape, especially within China (Wen & Yi, 2018). Tian et al. (2019) made a concluding remark that with the background of the Big Data era, the form of the audit work was more enriched and convenient for auditors moving forward.

A more voluminous data landscape implies the need for faster data processing speeds; however this as well has led to the growing concerns over data security (Wen & Yi, 2018). Wen and Yi (2018) emphasized the need for well-clarified property rights and data privacy, and the authors identified the central social challenges for auditing in big data environment revolves around the large volume of data, data sharing and exchange level, data security and privacy and the auditor's ability to effectively make use of data information. Wen and Yi (2018) pointed out improvements in aspects that could boost performance of applications that use big data, namely: in the design, big data audit analysis platforms, integration sources, data security and talented human resources. Strict regulations in inherent audit systems, as indicated by Tian et al. (2019) have unintentionally generated potential threats and difficulties for audit work in the Big Data era.

Regarding the application of emerging technologies (big data, data analytics) for example, Schneider et al. (2015), report can improve the audit cost-effectiveness throughout the information inputting process, which essentially enhances business profitability (Littley, 2012). Other studies also suggest the enhancement of existing audit procedures as better-quality information provided by big data technology will be incorporated into audit procedures (Dai & Vasarhelyi, 2016), future tax liabilities predictions (Schneider et al., 2015), fraud recognition (Cao et al., 2015), prepositions on authentication (Littley, 2012) and risky transactions identification (Alles & Gray, 2014). Another study, Alles and Gray (2016) also shared the same idea that better audit quality will be achieved with the increased competency, reliability, and relevance of audit evidence mainly thanks to emerging big data applications.

Alles (2015) claimed that the underlying reasons for auditors' increasing use of emerging technologies together with existing audit procedures was to improve their already-damaged credibility caused by past audit failures (Enron, WorldCom, Carillion, and WireCard). The adoption of big data technologies allows auditors to enhance the effectiveness of their procedures and ensure the reliability of their work (Alles, 2015). However, Alles and Gray (2016) shared a contrasting approach, that the motivation for rapid big data applications by auditors is a client-side demand orientation. This means the increment in clients' dependency on big data would be the extrinsic factor that urges auditors to embrace big data practice to mitigate the novel risks generated by these advance technologies (Alles, 2015). The same pattern of changes is also observed in the past—clients' widespread integration of Enterprise Resource Planning systems (ERPs) has enabled the corresponding adoption of IT-based auditing as auditors simply follow the lead of their clients (Alles, 2015).

It is certain that big data applications would possess potential risks to some extent, however, according to Yoon et al. (2015), the balance between detailed evidence collection and analytical procedures needs to be maintained. However, this process cannot be so black and white. Transactional performance tests were required in the audit standards; however, the procedures of analytical review are still underdeveloped and contain certain ambiguity (Rezaee et al., 2018). It is up to the auditor's professionalism to determine which techniques to apply, nevertheless, there is always an existing trade-off between those kinds of approaches.

2.2 Technology Adoption in the Emerging Economy of Vietnam—Accounting and Auditing

More research has been called for by prior studies such as Nguyen and Nguyen (2020) and Le and Cao (2020) on investigating factors affecting the quality of accounting information systems and other IT advancements, such as Cloud Computing and Blockchain, used in accounting and auditing, to supplement empirical testimony; especially in Vietnam because this topic has rarely been studied by academics. Currently, the use of accounting software in operation is no stranger to any business in Vietnam, as that type of software has been in use for many years. In Vietnam, the rapid development of the internet has made Vietnam become a potential market to which to exploit and supply products and services via the internet (Ha et al., 2020). Cloud based computing is considered a great advancement in information technology for instance because it provides an open environment for online integration and data sharing among users at long distances (Le & Cao, 2020). However, in Vietnam, cloud computing technology is still very new compared to the rest of the world and has only recently been introduced to key business enterprises.

Knowledge is viewed as the primary determining factor of organizational success and is considered the foundation of competitive advantage for most enterprises. Nguyen and Nguyen (2020) suggest that Vietnamese managers should learn basic knowledge of computer science, software technology, computer engineering, information systems, computer and communications networks, and network information security. Also, Vietnamese managers should participate regularly and continuously in all jobs to build, operate, and develop the systems such as determining the need of developing accounting information systems and controlling the accounting information systems. Finally, Nguyen and Nguyen (2020) conclude that the training needs to be conducted periodically to ensure that all people in the system are proficient in using the systems, updating the system's new points to make the system operate smoothly and bring in higher efficiency. These issues remain concerns for Vietnamese businesses and are not well implemented or resolved currently, thus they impact the quality of the information produced by the information technology used and the accounting systems that auditors and accountants rely upon.

In sum, although Vietnam has been following the general trend of the world, specifically we report, that the application of online accounting software in Vietnamese enterprises is still in its initial stages. Users are still concerned about confidentiality, information privacy, usefulness, ease of use compared to traditional accounting software (Le & Cao, 2020). One potential solution maybe the application of Blockchain technology in Vietnam. The combination of Blockchain technology with accounting software may help accounting work in businesses optimize the security, safety, and transparency of accounting information (Duong, 2020). Most recently, the application of Blockchain technology has started to be deployed on electronic invoicing software. Pioneering in the development of solutions and the application of Blockchain technology on electronic invoice software has been more available recently in Vietnam. In the field of accounting, for example, MISA developed *MeInvoice.vn*—the first e-invoice solution in Vietnam that applied Blockchain technology to increase the security, safety, and transparency of invoices for Vietnamese businesses (Duong, 2020). MISA is one of the top 10 companies in developing new technology in Vietnam for accounting.

2.3 Challenges That Businesses Face in the New Technological Era

2.3.1 Security

Overcoming the challenges that come from data itself is vital to facilitate the integration of emerging technologies into auditing and accounting practices. Unwanted risks, (for example, data breaches) might arise because of companies' overly scrutinized approach toward data processing (Pentland, 2014). Thus Pentland (2014) proposed that unintentional information disclosure would lead to stricter regulations, which subsequently generate greater hindrance to future application of data into auditing and accounting practice (Pentland, 2014). Moreover, given the detailed information stored in big data systems compared to aggregated information, it is likely the loss suffered from big data information leakage would be much more enormous than that of aggregated information (Huerta & Jensen, 2017). Since the mechanism of big data allows the entire community, rather than a single trusted third party, to verify the records (Zheng et al., 2017), the data becomes more exposed to potential privacy and security risks.

Limitations in computational capacity pose great difficulty in tackling voluminous sets of data, for instance the inapplicability of common auditing methods in the big data environment (Cao et al., 2015). The solution is either to use simple analytical techniques that require less computational resources, or to select subsets of data that could be managed by more complex analytical tools (Cao et al., 2015). In the latter case, auditors could use big data technology to determine a more pertinent subset. Based on prior literature (e.g., Settles, 2009), there exists appropriate techniques to detect sub setting data that could result in better-performing analytical models (Cao et al., 2015).

Security measures depend not only on the volume of data, but where the data is hosted on external servers (Huerta & Jensen, 2017). The increasing volume of data processed has driven companies to switch from their regular dedicated hosting servers to cloud-based repositories. This means companies mainly base their data security on measures implemented by a third party, namely, the server or host providers. According to Huerta and Jensen (2017), a significant growth in demand for server or host suppliers was observed in their study.

The unavailability of third-party authorization in current processes could create potential data security and privacy breaches, especially in sensitive sectors such as healthcare (Siyal et al., 2019). In that industry, the lack of verification processes forced patients to provide the right to access private information (such as their medical records) to their representatives in case of an emergency. As a result, the patient's sensitive information was put under constant threat of privacy breaches as the representatives could enable further accessibility on the patient's behalf (Siyal et al., 2019). However, the incorporation of high-security mechanisms into data did subsequently generate difficulty in the data transferal process, in which, lead to limiting data accessed by the receivers (Siyal et al., 2019).

2.3.2 Privacy

The increasing application of information technology into incumbent processes requires auditors to raise the awareness about the legality, as well as threats associated with the usage of inappropriate data. Studies such as one conducted by PWC (2017) pointed out that stakeholders' trust will be negatively impacted by the breaches in data privacy and regarding ethics over the span of the next five years or so. Furthermore, the process of re-building lost client's trust will be a difficult and demanding task, especially when the distrust is caused by a firm's improper application of its processed data (Huerta & Jensen, 2017). Regarding the confidentiality and anonymity, the applicability of anonymity is already in question here. To be specific, a firm' s employees owned the accessibility of customers' personal data, however, the center of the problems lies in how they deal with acquired information—which involves the company's policies (Huerta & Jensen, 2017). For example, Google was also put under intensive examination by the European Union (EU) for a privacy controversy, over its application of big data technology earlier this decade (Mayer-Schönberger & Cukier, 2014).

Fundamentally, big data systems are designed to recognize potential trends from enormous amounts of data and demonstrate the results by using visualization tools (Huerta & Jensen, 2017). The technology possesses the ability to investigate all past transactions and detect possible frauds to the extent that no inherent tools could surpass. Given its dominant technological advances, however, big data could not holistically eliminate cognitive biases (irrationality in individual perceptual judgement) and systematic bias (inherent biases in software systems) (Huerta & Jensen, 2017). Cognitive bias is defined as human's deviation during the process of evaluating information, which results in inferior decisions (Huerta & Jensen, 2017). This is different from system bias, that are not caused by a human's inherent nature, but are programmed bias that were established in the systems as the result of designers' decisions during the system development process (Huerta & Jensen, 2017).

2.3.3 Reliance on the System Itself

Reliance on big data applications is the degree to which people trust and use the information generated by a system (Triki & Weisner, 2014). The effectiveness of big data or data analytic tools relies on their actual use with any tool to support decision making process. The absence of accountants' dependence on system-based outputs—under-reliance, could lead to the loss of significant insights that could be retrieved from the processed data. Similarly, the same oversight could occur in cases of over-reliance, in which auditor irrationally base most of their judgements on the outputs produced by the system (Huerta & Jensen, 2017). Therefore, the act of relying on systematic outputs requires auditors' ability to maintain a balancing degree of trust—both under and over-reliance pose great threats in the use of big data applications.

A constructive guidance on sufficient levels of reliance has yet to be established, however, it is important that accountants and auditors consider the pros and cons of big data applications in the process of decision-making (Huerta & Jensen, 2017). The essence of big data lies in its ability to retrieve empirical evidence and patterns from enormous amount of data to support fact-based decisions, which subsequently reduce the inaccurate possibilities derived from "educated guesses" and unwarranted "gut feelings" (Huerta & Jensen, 2017).

2.3.4 Ownership

Davis (2012), have presented in their study three main questions concerning the issue of ethics and data ownership, namely: (i) who owns the data? (ii) can rights to the data be transferred? and finally, (iii) what are the obligations of companies who use that data? Challenges regarding ownership-related issues have been raised several years ago under the context of rapidly growing dot-com retailers, as well as Facebook (FB), when it was accused of mining FB users' private messages and selling them onto commercial advertisers. McKinsey (2011) emphasized the importance of data ownership in the light of the growing integration of big data in sensitive sectors, such as healthcare. And thus, as conveyed by Kroft (2014), data ownership plays a significant role in the context of the activities of "data broker" companies.

2.3.5 Training

The extraction of enormous quantity of data is enabled by current data analytical tools, however, the underlying problems centered around auditors' ability to analyze and explicate results from the overwhelming amount of collected data continue to exist (Issa & Kogan, 2014). For example, facilitated by sophisticated analytic software, auditors could easily apprehend and integrate vast amount of data from multiple sources (Issa & Kogan, 2014). Meanwhile, the effectiveness of data mining tools depends on the extent that auditors comprehend the appropriateness of their collected data on its quality, and relevance. Furthermore, the assertions of auditing context must be carefully examined for an accurate interpretation and evaluation of data mining outputs (Peecher et al., 2007). All these required training of accountants and auditors. Furthermore, training is important because, considering the nature of big data technologies, information overload could pose potential risks that reduce audit quality despite auditors' familiarization to the integration of non-financial data into their analysis procedures—i.e., strategic systems auditing (Peecher et al., 2007; Zhao & Harding, 2013).

Big data presents auditors with novel and leading challenges regarding their inadequate skills to conduct proper audit data analysis using these tools. Companies had been familiar working with inherent traditional data analysis processes, however, Russom (2011) has pointed out accounting firms' lack the skills development as required with respect to the big data environment. In fact, sufficient training and appropriate skills are perceived to play a significant role in the process of analytical tools adoption. Papagiannis (2012) claimed company's adjustments to their big data management processes is inevitable with the continuous evolution of data in its form, variety, and accessibility. As these sophisticated evolving technologies implied a higher operational cost for the companies: larger quantity of data drives technological costs upward, thereby, increasing firms' demand for data scientists and better-quality accounting software (Golia, 2013).

3 Theoretical Framework

Rogers (1962, 2003) developed a theoretical framework known as 'diffusion of innovation'. This theoretical framework is helpful when determining the adoption of specific innovations related to technology. Rogers defines diffusion as "the process in which an innovation is communicated thorough certain channels over time among the members of a social system" (Rogers, 2003, p. 5). The diffusion of innovations theory has been used extensively in prior literature to examine the process of technology adoption in different areas (Medlin, 2001; Parisot, 1995), for example when investigating IT usage and skills in the university environment (Anderson et al., 1998); or the improvement of technology in the oil and gas industry (Salazar et al., 2020), or when exploring the innovation in electric mobility (Noel et al., 2019), or how technology applies in the healthcare and nursing environment (Pashaeypoor et al., 2016).

In our study, we apply the diffusion of innovation theory when examining the challenges that Vietnamese accountants and auditors are facing through each stage of the diffusion of innovation adoption curve. We believe this theoretical framework will provide a comprehensive explanation on the challenges impacting a developing economy such as Vietnam. Rogers (1962, 2003) diffusion of innovation theory applied in the present research study will help examine how the innovation in technology has been adopted in audit and accounting industries within Vietnam. By investigating the technology adoption at each stage, the study assists to explore the difficulty that these industries are facing during their current journey in the transitioning economy of Vietnam.

The innovation-decision process is described as "an information-seeking and information-processing activity, where an individual is motivated to reduce uncertainty about the advantages and disadvantages of an innovation" (Rogers, 2003, p. 172). There are five stages of the process as follows:

The knowledge stage: during this phase, the individual attempts to determine "what the innovation is and how and why it works" (Rogers, 2003, p. 21). The adoption of emerging technology (BDA, AI, robotics) in accounting and auditing context, is about training or communicating through the emerging technologies to the accountants and the auditor/audit firm so that they are aware of this process. The accountants and auditors may have the knowledge about the emerging technologies; however, it does not guarantee that they will accept the idea of adopting the innovation. At this stage, the individual's attitudes also shape the decision of whether they are willing to adopt or reject the innovation.

The Persuasion Stage: occurs when the individual has a negative or positive attitude toward the innovation, but "the formation of a favorable or unfavorable attitude toward an innovation does not always lead directly or indirectly to an adoption or rejection" (Rogers, 2003, p. 176). At this stage, the accountants and auditors would have more influence on their attitude toward the technology after the collection of more information related to the innovation. While the knowledge stage is more cognitive centered (recognizing), the persuasion stage is more affective centered (feeling). Therefore, at this stage, accountants and auditors will have more involvement to the emerging technologies than in the knowledge stage. The attitude of colleagues and peers would also influence individuals at this stage.

The Decision Stage: at this stage, the individual chooses to adopt or reject the innovation (Rogers, 2003). Colleagues and peers will continually have influence over individual accountants or auditors at this stage.

The Implementation Stage: during this stage, the innovation is put into practice. However, an innovation brings the newness in which "some degree of uncertainty is involved in diffusion" (Rogers, 2003, p. 6). In an accounting and auditing context, an uncertainty about the outcomes of the technology/innovation can be a problem at this stage. Therefore, it is vital to have support and technical assistance or training at this stage. Reinvention may incur during this process to ensure the technology adoption is better than needed.

The Confirmation Stage: the confirmation stage reveals how the individual looks for support to confirm their decision (Rogers, 2003). The attitudes of accountants and auditors become vital at this stage. Subject to the level of support for the adoption of the innovation and the overall attitude of the individual, later on adoption or discontinuance can occur.

4 Methodology

The empirical data collection for this study was gathered from documentary sources through searching and reviews conducted by the authors. Electronic online searches were performed using the following the sources, tools, and databases: Scopus, Google Scholar, Web of Science, Google Search Engine, and the Vietnamese Ministry of Finance (MoF), Big Four and the State Audit Organization websites. This study used directed content analysis to provide greater clarity on emerging technological challenges in Vietnam (Carpenter & McGregor, 2020a). To focus on the research question, prior literature was used to collate, summarize, and analyze studies, which broadened the usual goal of directed content analysis, which is to extend theory (Carpenter & McGregor, 2020b). The strategy of selecting relevant articles (both academic and from practice) to be reviewed, consisted of a combination of the main concepts of the challenges in using emerging technologies in accounting and auditing in Vietnam. The abstracts of these studies were then scrutinized to ascertain whether they contained information relevant to this study. As research relating to emerging technologies is still gaining prominence, where necessary, online searching for supplementary information were accessed from the websites of accessible sources such as the 'Big Four' audit firms, MoF and professional accounting bodies. The selected literature was then reviewed in terms of the research question and aims of this study. Relevant keyword variations of the concepts were used resulting in the following search combinations in both English and Vietnamese: 'data analytics in accounting and auditing Vietnam', 'big data accounting and auditing Vietnam', and '4.0 technology accounting and auditing Vietnam'.

The period for this search was open ended, however, as we are dealing with emerging technologies in the accounting and auditing context, most of the articles that came up were written within the last seven years (2013–2020) and in the Vietnamese context. Around 47 articles were collected by the authors. However, only 17 were relevant to the research question and to this study. These articles were read in detail for the data analysis purposes. These final 17 articles were then reviewed by the authors to identify the challenges that Vietnamese auditors and accountants face. The findings are now identified and reported below in the findings section of this chapter.

5 Findings and Discussion

5.1 The Knowledge and Persuasion Stage

The substantial number of challenges facing accountants and auditors creates issues in attempting to narrow down and focusing on this study's research question. Therefore, we focus only on the key challenges that we identified in Vietnam, which helps provide a more valuable and detailed analysis. Due to practical limitations, only those challenges that recur or a consistent with those identified in the prior literature have been highlighted and analyzed below.

At the Knowledge stage along the diffusion of innovation adoption curve, Vietnamese accountants and auditors acknowledge that the use of emerging technologies (e.g., big data analytics, AI, etc.) in auditing and accounting are considered as very important to the Vietnamese accounting profession (Le, 2020). Vietnamese accountants and auditors recognize that the most important reason to use emerging technologies in the audit process for instance is to improve audit quality, to minimize audit time, audit costs, and at the same time, simplify the auditing process (Pham et al., 2018). Furthermore, these new technologies in auditing help support the minimization of risk in the audit process (Pham et al., 2018). These findings are extending arguments that emerging technologies contribute to identifying fraudulent transactions (Tang et al., 2017) and useful in improving the audit process through higher quality (Tian et al., 2019; Wen & Yi, 2018). Furthermore, Vietnamese accountants and auditors are aware that it has been forecasted that smart software and systems will replace manual work and automate complex and multifaceted processes (such as completing financial agreements), supporting outsourcing trends and internal reuse of some other services in the next three to ten years (ACCA, 2016).

The matter of job security has significant influence on Vietnamese accountants and auditors at the Knowledge and Persuasion Stage based on Rogers (2003) framework. For example, in the interview in November 2018 with the Financial News Magazine, Mr. Vu Duc Chinh—Director of the Accounting and Auditing Supervision Department (Ministry of Finance) expressed his opinion that: "emerging technology can do many tasks in accounting and auditing such as collecting, processing, and calculating data, but with stages such as analysis and case handling, there is always a need for human involvement". Therefore, accountants and auditors understood that while the emerging technologies cannot completely replace humans, it is making significant changes to the work environment, and efficiency of accounting and auditing work activities. This aspect is not consistent with Western culture (see, for example, Brown-Liburd et al., 2015). We reveal that while emerging technologies are new to Vietnam, accountants and auditors are still clearly identifying the human role of the accountants and auditors in this field.

The difference between the Western world and developing economies such as Vietnam in relation to job security is that, in the West, there is more fear of technology (i.e., job security is at risk), however, this is not found to be the case in Vietnam. This is evidenced recently, by the Vietnam Association of Certified Public Accountants

(VACPA) study that investigated the impact of the Industry 4.0 (including big data, audit data analytics, Cloud Technologies) on the accounting and auditing field. Most of the participants in the VACPA study, who are auditors, viewed that the adoption of emerging technology has or will have very little impact on their work activities or job security. Also, some participants expressed the view that they do not understand how these emerging technologies will impact the accounting and auditing field.

Around 98% of financial leaders in Vietnam viewed that soft skills such as communication skills, leadership skills, teamwork skills, critical thinking, problem solving as vital, and that they are at least equivalently important as professional skills (Nguyen, 2020). Vietnamese employees, including accountants and auditors are either lacking in or are weak in these soft skills according to some studies (VACPA, 2014). This issue led them to having difficulty in taking on a more challenging requirements such as emerging technology adoption. Lacking in these skills is a real disadvantage for Vietnamese accountants and auditors compared to their Western peers. Perhaps, this disadvantage was cemented or grounded from their prior education in high school or University studies, whereas in Western society there is much more opportunities to develop soft skills.

Training required for emerging technologies is also another factor that impacts the accountants and auditors' knowledge of this new technology. However, there are no findings or documentation related to Vietnam, that implies the necessary training is provided at the Knowledge and Persuasion Stage for accountants and auditors. Instead, we find the required training is provided at the implementation stage, which is discussed further below.

5.2 *The Decision Stage*

While these emerging technologies (big data and audit data analytics, AI, etc.) have only recently been introduced to Vietnam, we find that they are only being used within several leading organizations. For example, Big Four auditing firms, Telecommunication organizations, banks, and some other enterprises such as DEHA Vietnam, FPT Corporation, MISA Joint Stock Company, Nashtech Vietnam, Sao Bac Dau Technology Joint Stock Company, VNEXT Joint Stock Company, and Vietnam Payment Solution Joint Stock Company (VNPAY) are all using these technologies. For example, in July 2020, VIB International Bank announced the successful application of big data processing technology and artificial intelligence for the credit scoring and the credit card limit approval processes, based on cooperation with a Fintech company providing credit scoring solutions via technology 4.0—Trusting Social. This is the first time a bank in Vietnam has pioneered the application of big data and AI in the card limit review process. The system allows for the card limit review process to take only 5 min for the filling of information, around 15 to 30 min for the approval without any meetings with customers, no need for sales staff, no approver needed, or no proof of income required.

The level of engagement within the profession that leads to any implementation decision for emerging technologies is quite high. A study conducted by VACPA found that 50% of participants who are auditors and accountants are highly interested in these emerging technologies while only 5% of the participants did not or have very little interest in Industry 4.0 (including big data and audit data analytics, AI, Cloud Technologies). Around 33% of participants think that adoption of emerging technologies is part of the normal course of their business.

Most of multinational organizations in Vietnam, especially in banking and telecommunications and the large audit firms have decided to implement either big data or audit data analytics in their organizations. The adoption of these emerging technologies is also being supported greatly by the Vietnamese Government through the MoF and the State Audit Organization. Vietnam has often been one of the leading countries in Asia in these aspects of Government support. Other challenges that face the decision on whether to adopt emerging technologies in audit and accounting is that there is lack of enthusiasm from some of the more senior practitioners. This could delay the process of adopting emerging technologies (Hoang, 2020).

However, there are also some drawbacks in banking and insurance industry in Vietnam. For example, some applications of AI in Banking such as automatic account opening; in insurance such as contract setting, fraud detection in insurance claims, customer valuation, premium pricing, products, and services towards personalization ... have not received adequate attention and deployed sufficient investment. It is acknowledged by IPT Cooperation's expert the sooner businesses with a large customer base such as Banking and Insurance apply AI, the AI application control will increase the competitive advantage by reducing their costs and increasing revenue. This is also a vital condition in the trend of competing with new business models in the financial services sector not only for Vietnam but also for the world.

5.3 The Implementation Stage

While some of the larger organizations in Vietnam have implemented emerging technologies discussed thus far, the current percentage of successful implementation of emerging technologies such as big data analytics and AI in auditing and accounting in Vietnam is somewhat limited (Le, 2018). The fact that many other local audits firms still use Excel in undertaking audits and analytical procedures, and not yet are applying audit specialist software and more advanced data analytical tools is a concern to some (Le, 2018). This limitation in technology usage is also a leading to challenge in applying big data analytics and emerging technology tools in auditing processes across the big and smaller audit's firms in Vietnam. However, to accelerate this, Big Four audit firms and some other smaller firms that have memberships or associations with international audit firms, are using the professional audit procedures to prepare and implement their audit work in this emerging technological environment (Le, 2018). In some instances, the application of high-level technologies has not yet been widely applied in audit firms causing limitations in performing audit tasks (Le, 2018; Pham et al., 2018). This is the challenge for auditing and accounting in general in Vietnam. Big four audit firms that operate in the West, for example, like in Australia, are very focus on the adoption of big data and audit data analytical tools (Kend & Nguyen, 2020). Vietnam is trying to follow suit given the constraints discussed above.

Further challenges that exist for Vietnam is that there is a gap between the usage rate and the implementation rate related to these emerging technologies in accounting and auditing. When evaluating the importance of using the audit software and technology in auditing procedures for instance, Pham et al. (2018) found that 44% of participants viewed that the technology is important for fraud assessment, while only 25% confirmed that technology has been used. Similarly, 65% of participants believed that IT has a significant impact in audit evidence assessment, however only 10% auditors actually used it (Pham et al., 2018). This implies that Vietnamese organizations and the Government need to focus on both the adoption of these emerging technologies and have a further aim of improving their usage rates.

The support in training when adopting emerging technologies is also important as discussed. Auditors and accountants think that the training and application of the technology in real life is critical for them to adapt to the use of emerging technologies (Hoang, 2020). Furthermore, it is viewed that the training work just stops at the transmission of background knowledge stage, and is not in-depth, or multidisciplinary, especially for knowledge of specific technology, data security, and artificial intelligence (Nguyen, 2020). It is suggested that training and structure should also be more of a focus. Training can help to provide within a digital economy, support for high level accounting and auditing, as demanded by the society (Duc, 2019). These findings further extend the Russom (2011) and Golia (2013) findings that training is critically important and needs to be focused on significantly.

5.4 *The Confirmation Stage*

Data security is indicated, through the articles read, as a major challenge in using these emerging technologies in Vietnam (Cao et al., 2015; Chi, 2019). Concern related to information leakage mainly when sending the client information via a digital format (Chi, 2019) is a problem highlighted in Vietnam. Exchanging audit information between external organizations is also a security issue of concern. Unofficial information and audit results can adversely affect the image of the business and cause unpredictable consequences (Chi, 2019). While this security concern has been raised in Vietnam, the extent of it when investigating prior literature (see, for example Cao et al., 2015) is rather limited. Perhaps, this is because of the level of big data or data analytical tools in Vietnam has not yet been developed to the same levels as in Western countries, therefore we only find limited references to these issues.

The local auditing standards is another challenge for auditors in Vietnam when adopting the emerging technologies. There is a significant gap between International Auditing Standards (IAS) and Vietnamese Accounting Standards (VAS) (Nguyen &

Kend, 2019; Nguyen et al., 2020). For example, the concept of fair value is not clearly identified in Vietnam and is quite vague to many Vietnamese accountants (Nguyen, 2016). Based on VAS, businesses are required to prepare financial statements based on historical costs in Vietnam, however, many multinational companies are required to prepare the financial statement using fair value also as per the International Accounting Standards (Nguyen et al., 2020), thus this is an example of the gap in accounting standards that still exists.

Prior literature raised the issue that accountants and auditors are lacking job skills (see, for example, Russom, 2011). However, the lack of high-quality human resources is more serious problem in Vietnam than other Asian countries such as China and Singapore, and this is one of the biggest challenges for Vietnam (Phan et al., 2016). Prior studies indicated that accountants and auditors are ready to integrate with emerging technologies. However, up to 60% of the graduates in accounting and auditing fields are not ready for the workforce or are not job ready to match the employer skill requirements in many aspects related to technology adoption (Phan et al., 2016; VACPA, 2014).

Finally, we found some discussion and comments from, Dr. Nguyen (2020)—of the Accounting Department (Finance academy, National University), predicting that emerging technologies will create competition among audit firms leading to reduced market share among these firms. Together with that trend, these emerging technologies will also increase issues related to data security, and the increasingly sophisticated development of digital technology that leads to security gaps, facilitating high-tech criminals to continue to operate within Vietnam (Duc, 2019).

5.5 *Recommendation for the Development and Adoption of Emerging Technology*

The Government, and the MoF, have provided support in the adoption of emerging technologies. However, amendments should be made to the accounting framework, and the accounting, and auditing regulations. The development of further accounting and auditing standards with the involvement of international accounting bodies is highly recommended for Vietnam (Duc, 2019).

The investment in high-level technologies by the Government in Vietnam should be made in a timelier manner. The Vietnamese Government should also support the development of the higher-level technology to follow the global trend in digital systems, especially helping to facilitate the application of high-level technologies in accounting and auditing fields. This includes building a higher level of security systems required.

According to Dr. Nguyen, of the National Economics University, the other factors that impacted directly into emerging technologies adoption are the management and regulation of practicing surrounding business ethics in accounting and auditing, which need to be strengthened. This is an important factor to improve the status of professional accountants and auditors in Vietnam (Duc, 2019). The role of Vietnamese professional organizations such as the VACPA should also be enhanced, especially in providing ethical training and increasing the number of member guidelines and related publications on the ethical standards. VACPA can also improve the requirements for members to update their professional knowledge on other relevant regulations. Accountants and auditors should also receive extensive training on soft skills such as organization skills, analytical skills, consulting work capacity, network operations, information usage and data security, as discussed above.

6 Conclusions

This chapter examined the challenges in adoption of emerging technologies such as big data, and audit data analytical tools in accounting and auditing in Vietnam. The findings found that at the Knowledge and Persuasion stage, compared to other stages, some concern exists in Vietnam, but not as significant as the challenges as in the other stages. Accountants and auditors were more concern about the knowledge, understanding and skills (both technical and soft skills) required to adapt to the emerging technologies. In the Decision stage, accountants and auditors are ready for the adoption of the emerging technologies in Vietnam. Many businesses have already made the move. However, greater support is required from MoF and regulators to accelerate the process. At the Implementation stage, it was challenging for Vietnam to implement the technologies because historically they have limited usage of technology (i.e., using excel instead of emerging AI and analytical technology) leading to low readiness in the adoption of these emerging technologies. The usage of newly adopted technology is low, and the level of training has not yet met the requirements needed. Data security and regulation/standards issues are raised at the next stage, i.e., the Confirmation stage.

While Western cultures express some fear on their job security as emerging technologies will take over the auditor and accountants work, Vietnamese auditors and accountants have shown no or little concern in this regard. They are confident that emerging technologies will only contribute for improving their own work, but not replacing their roles. These findings show a confident viewpoint of accountants from this developing economy. It is identified that accountants and auditors in Vietnam have limitations in soft skills compared to Western employees. This finding opens or leads to the suggestion that the education system in Vietnam needs some reform to include the soft skills, or training much earlier in the education of accounting students, for them to improve in this respect.

This chapter contributes to the relevant literature by analyzing the challenges facing the auditors and accountants when adopting emerging technologies in Vietnam such as big data, or audit data analytics, AI, etc. The findings contribute to the literature and practice related to the concerns of accountants and auditors during the technology adaption process, especially when applied within a developing economy.

The findings would encourage or inspire ideas for further research that is useful for accounting professionals, regulators, and academic researchers.

While these issues discussed in this chapter should not be ignored by the accountants and auditors, out of the many challenges found in this developing economy, in the Vietnamese context, there are some challenges we believe are significant (for example the lack of resources, the limited support from the government, MoF and other regulators, which was not such an issue in the past).

This chapter contributes to the adoption of emerging technology literature as follows. Firstly, the prior research on the challenges of the adoption of these emerging technologies mostly focused on developed economies, like the U.K. (Salijeni et al., 2021) and Australia (Kend & Nguyen, 2020). Thus, more research is needed on the developing economy context as it remains scant. Secondly, Vietnam was evaluated as one of the pioneers in IT in Asia. Hence it is a good focus, to examine the challenges of technological adoption within this country. Finally, this study has practical contributions in that it provides a good guidance on accountants' experiences from a practical perspective, as it provides relevant lessons from businesses that currently adopt or plan to adopt these emerging technologies. It also provides a background for the regulators, MoF and the Government for the development process during the adoption of these technologies, which can help with the standard setting process.

References

ACCA. (2016). *Professional accountants—The future: Drivers of change and future skills.*

Ajana, B. (2015). Augmented borders: Big Data and the ethics of immigration control. *Journal of Information, Communication and Ethics in Society, 13*(1), 58–78.

Alles, M. G. (2015). Drivers of the use and facilitators and obstacles of the evolution of Big Data by the audit profession. *Accounting Horizons, 29*(2), 439–449.

Alles, M., & Gray, G. L. (2014). *Developing a framework for the role of Big Data in auditing: A synthesis of the literature* (Unpublished Working Paper). Rutgers Business School.

Alles, M., & Gray, G. L. (2016). Incorporating big data in audits: Identifying inhibitors and a research agenda to address those inhibitors. *International Journal of Accounting Information Systems, 22*, 44–59.

Anderson, T., Varnhagen, S., & Campbell, K. (1998). Faculty adoption of teaching and learning technologies: Contrasting earlier adopters and mainstream faculty. *The Canadian Journal of Higher Education, 28*(23), 71–78.

Appelbaum, D., Kogan, A., & Vasarhelyi, M. A. (2017). Big Data and analytics in the modern audit engagement: Research needs. *Auditing: A Journal of Practice & Theory, 36*(4), 1–27.

Bhandari, G., & Hassanein, K. (2012). An agent-based debiasing framework for investment decision-support systems. *Behaviour & Information Technology, 31*(5), 495–507.

Brown-Liburd, H., Issa, H., & Lombardi, D. (2015). Behavioral implications of big data's impact on audit judgment and decision making and future research directions. *Accounting Horizons, 29*(2), 451–468.

Brynjolfsson, E., Hitt, L. M., & Kim, H. H. (2011). *Strength in numbers: How does data-driven decisionmaking affect firm performance?* Available at SSRN 1819486.

Cao, M., Chychyla, R., & Stewart, T. (2015). Big Data analytics in financial statement audits. *Accounting Horizons, 29*(2), 423–429.

Carpenter, R., & Mcgregor, D. (2020a). The implications, applications, and benefits of emerging technologies in audit. *The Business & Management Review, 11*(2), 36–44.

Carpenter, R., & Mcgregor, D. (2020b). Potential threats for the auditing profession, audit firms and audit processes inherent in using emerging technology. *The Business & Management Review, 11*(2), 45–54.

Chi, K. (2019). *Hóa giải thách thức cho dịch vụ kế toán, kiểm toán trước "cơn bão" Cách mạng công nghiệp 4.0* [Online]. http://tapchitaichinh.vn/ke-toan-kiem-toan/hoa-giai-thach-thuc-cho-dich-vu-ke-toan-kiem-toan-truoc-con-bao-cach-mang-cong-nghiep-40-312552.html. Accessed 3 March 2021.

Dagilienė, L., & Klovienė, L. (2019). Motivation to use big data and big data analytics in external auditing. *Managerial Auditing Journal, 34*(7), 750–782.

Dai, J., & Vasarhelyi, M. A. (2016). Imagineering Audit 4.0. *Journal of Emerging Technologies in Accounting, 13*(1), 1–15.

Davis, K. (2012). *Ethics of Big Data: Balancing risk and innovation.* O'Reilly Media, Inc.

Duc, V. (2019). *Cách mạng công nghiệp 4.0: Nhiều thách thức cho nghề kế toán, kiểm toán* [Online]. http://thoibaotaichinhvietnam.vn/pages/kinh-doanh/2019-12-13/cach-mang-cong-nghiep-40-nhieu-thach-thuc-cho-nghe-ke-toan-kiem-toan-80283.aspx. Accessed 2 March 2021.

Duong, T. L. (2020). Impact of blockchain technology to field accounting and auditing. *European Journal of Economics and Management Sciences* (4), 3–6.

Enget, K., Saucedo, G. D., & Wright, N. S. (2017). Mystery, Inc.: A big data case. *Journal of Accounting Education, 38*, 9–22.

Gartner It Glossary. (n.d.). *Gartner IT glossary* [Online]. http://www.gartner.com/it-glossary/big-data/. Accessed 1 March 2021.

Golia, N. (2013, May). What Big Data means for infrastructure costs. *Insurance and Technology*, 30–31.

Ha, G. N., Bui, V. N., & Tran, Q. N. (2020). The influence of website quality on consumer's e-loyalty through the mediating role of e-trust and e-satisfaction: An evidence from online shopping in Vietnam. *Uncertain Supply Chain Management, 8*(2), 351–370.

Hoang, V. L. (2020). Kiểm toán viên sử dụng kỹ thuật kiểm toán hỗ trợ bằng máy tính (CAATs): Thách thức và Cơ hội [Online]. *Financial Magazine.* http://tapchitaichinh.vn/ke-toan-kiem-toan/kiem-toan-vien-su-dung-ky-thuat-kiem-toan-ho-tro-bang-may-tinh-caats-thach-thuc-va-co-hoi-317428.html. Accessed 28 February 2021.

Huerta, E., & Jensen, S. (2017). An accounting information systems perspective on data analytics and Big Data. *Journal of Information Systems, 31*(3), 101–114.

Issa, H., & Kogan, A. (2014). A predictive ordered logistic regression model as a tool for quality review of control risk assessments. *Journal of Information Systems, 28*(2), 209–229.

Kend, M., & Nguyen, L. A. (2020). Big Data analytics and other emerging technologies: The impact on the australian audit and assurance profession. *Australian Accounting Review, 30*(4), 269.

KPMG. (2012). *Leveraging data analytics and continuous auditing within internal audit* [Online]. https://www.kpmg.com/US/en/IssuesAndInsights/ArticlesPublications/Documents/leveraging-data-analytics-auditing-effectiveness.pdf. Accessed 27 February 2021.

Kroft, S. (2014). The data brokers: Selling your personal information. *CBS News.*

Le, T. (2020). *Information technology audit and technology application trends in accounting—Auditing* (Working Paper).

Le, O. T., & Cao, Q. M. (2020). Examining the technology acceptance model using cloud-based accounting software of Vietnamese enterprises. *Management Science Letters, 10*(12), 2781–2788.

Le, T. T. H. (2018). *Ứng dụng công nghệ thông tin trong kiểm toán báo cáo tài chính* [Online]. http://www.hoiketoanhcm.org.vn. Accessed 4 February 2021.

Littley, J. (2012). *Leveraging data analytics and continuous auditing processes for improved audit planning, effectiveness, and efficiency* (KPMG White Paper).

Marshall, A., Mueck, S., & Shockley, R. (2015). How leading organizations use big data and analytics to innovate. *Strategy & Leadership, 43*(5), 72–89.

Mayer-Schönberger, V., & Cukier, K. (2014). Big Data: A revolution that will transform how we live, work, and think. *American Journal of Epidemiology, 179*(9), 1143–2114.

McKinsey. (2011). Big data: The next frontier for innovation, competition, and productivity. *McKinsey Global Institute*, pp. 1–6.

Medlin, B. D. (2001). *The factors that may influence a faculty members' decision to adopt electronic technologies in instruction.* Virginia Polytechnic Institute and State University.

Nepal, S., Ranjan, R., & Choo, K.-K. R. (2015). Trustworthy processing of healthcare Big Data in hybrid clouds. *IEEE Cloud Computing, 2*(2), 78–84.

Nguyen, H. T., & Nguyen, A. H. (2020). Determinants of accounting information systems quality: Empirical evidence from Vietnam. *Accounting, 6*(2), 185–198.

Nguyen, L. A. (2016). *Accountants' perceptions of financial reporting quality in Vietnam and their ethical sensitivity to earnings management* (PhD thesis). RMIT University.

Nguyen, L. A., O'Connell, B., Kend, M., Pham, V., & Vesty, G. (2021). The likelihood of widespread accounting manipulation within an emerging economy. *Journal of Accounting in Emerging Economies, 11*(2), 312–339.

Nguyen, L. A., Vesty, G., Kend, M., Nguyen, Q., & O'Connell, B. (2020). Intertwined institutionalization: Pressures on Vietnam's accounting profession during transition to IFRS. *Pacific Accounting Review*, 1–25.

Nguyen, L. U. (2019). The construction of accountant identity in a transitioning economy: The case of Vietnam. *Accounting & Finance, 59*(3), 1709–1740.

Nguyen, P. T., & Kend, M. (2017). The perceived motivations behind the introduction of the law on external audit in Vietnam. *Managerial Auditing Journal, 32*(1), 90.

Nguyen, P. T., & Kend, M. (2019). An examination of the Vietnamese emerging market economy: Understanding how and why auditors have responded to the audit law reforms. *Accounting & Finance, 59*(3), 1553–1583.

Nguyen, V. B. (2020). *Cơ hội và thách thức đối với kế toán - kiểm toán Việt Nam trong bối cảnh mới* [Online]. Trường Đại học Công nghệ TP. Hồ Chí Minh. http://tapchitaichinh.vn/ke-toan-kiem-toan/co-hoi-va-thach-thuc-doi-voi-ke-toan-kiem-toan-viet-nam-trong-boi-canh-moi-318241.html. Accessed 3 March 2021.

Noel, L., Sovacool, B. K., Kester, J., & De Rubens, G. Z. (2019). Conspicuous diffusion: Theorizing how status drives innovation in electric mobility. *Environmental Innovation and Societal Transitions, 31*, 154–169.

Papagiannis, S. (2012, November). Staying ahead of the data tsunami. *Canadian Underwriter*, 12–15.

Parisot, A. H. (1995). *Technology and teaching: The adoption and diffusion of technological innovations by a community college faculty.* Montana State University-Bozeman, College of Education, Health & Human.

Pashaeypoor, S., Ashktorab, T., Rassouli, M., & Alavi-Majd, H. (2016). Predicting the adoption of evidence-based practice using "Rogers diffusion of innovation model." *Contemporary Nurse, 52*(1), 85–94.

Peecher, M. E., Schwartz, R., & Solomon, I. (2007). It's all about audit quality: Perspectives on strategic-systems auditing. *Accounting, Organizations and Society, 32*(4–5), 463–485.

Pentland, A. S. (2014). Saving big data from itself. *Scientific American, 311*(2), 64–67.

Pham, B. N., Nguyen, T. Q., Tran, M. D., & Nguyen, T. T. P. (2018). Auditor's perception of usage and importance of audit technology in Vietnam. *Asian Business Research, 3*(3), 14.

Phan, D. H. T., Joshi, M., & Mascitelli, B. (2016). Are Vietnamese accounting academics and practitioners ready for International Financial Reporting Standards (IFRS)? In *Economics and political implications of International Financial Reporting Standards.* IGI Global.

PWC. (2017). *Global State of Information Security* [Online]. https://www.pwc.com.au/consulting/global-state-information-security-survey-2017.html. Accessed 4 February 2021.

Reimer, A. P., & Madigan, E. A. (2018). Veracity in Big Data: How good is good enough. *Health Informatics Journal, 25*(4), 1290–1298.

Rezaee, Z., Dorestani, A., & Aliabadi, S. (2018). Application of time series analyses in big data: Practical, research, and education implications. *Journal of Emerging Technologies in Accounting, 15*(1), 183–197.

Rogers, E. M. (1962). *Diffusion of innovations*. Free Press of Glencoe.

Rogers, E. M. (2003). *Diffusion of innovations*. Free Press.

Russom, P. (2011). Big data analytics. *TDWI Best Practices Report, Fourth Quarter, 19*(4), 1–34.

Salazar, R. J., Rauniar, R., Mora-Monge, C., & Shah, S. (2020). Diffusion of innovative technology in US oil and gas industry: An empirical study. *International Journal of Technology, Policy and Management, 20*(1), 1–20.

Salijeni, G., Samsonova-Taddei, A., & Turley, S. (2021). Understanding how Big Data technologies reconfigure the nature and organization of financial statement audits: A sociomaterial analysis. *European Accounting Review, 30*(3), 531–555.

Schneider, G. P., Dai, J., Janvrin, D. J., Ajayi, K., & Raschke, R. L. (2015). Infer, predict, and assure: Accounting opportunities in data analytics. *Accounting Horizons, 29*(3), 719–742.

Settles, B. (2009). *Active learning literature survey* (Computer Sciences Technical Report).

Siyal, A. A., Junejo, A. Z., Zawish, M., Ahmed, K., Khalil, A., & Soursou, G. (2019). Applications of blockchain technology in medicine and healthcare: Challenges and future perspectives. *Cryptography, 3*(1), 3–7.

Tang, F., Norman, C. S., & Vendrzyk, V. P. (2017). Exploring perceptions of data analytics in the internal audit function. *Behaviour & Information Technology, 36*(11), 1125–1136.

TechAmerica Foundation's Federal Big Data Commission. (2012). *Demystifying big data: A practical guide to transforming the business of government* [Online]. http://www.techamerica.org/Docs/fileManager.cfm?f=techamerica-bigdatareport-final.pdf. Accessed 9 February 2021.

Tian, H., Chen, Z., Chang, C.-C., Huang, Y., Wang, T., Huang, Z.-A., Cai, Y., & Chen, Y. (2019). Public audit for operation behavior logs with error locating in cloud storage. *Soft Computing, 23*(11), 3779–3792.

Triki, A., & Weisner, M. M. (2014). Lessons from the literature on the theory of technology dominance: Possibilities for an extended research framework. *Journal of Emerging Technologies in Accounting, 11*(1), 41–69.

VACPA. (2014). *MỘT SỐ VẤN ĐỀ VỀ NHÂN LỰC NGÀNH KẾ TOÁN- KIỂM TOÁN VIỆT NAM TRONG BỐI CẢNH TOÀN CẦU HÓA* [Online]. http://www.vacpa.org.vn/Page/Detail.aspx?newid=4695. Accessed 9 March 2021.

Vasarhelyi, M. A., Kogan, A., & Tuttle, B. M. (2015). Big data in accounting: An overview. *Accounting Horizons, 29*(2), 381–396.

Verma, S., & Bhattacharyya, S. S. (2017). Perceived strategic value-based adoption of big data analytics in emerging economy. *Journal of Enterprise Information Management, 30*(3), 354–382.

Wen, L., & Yi, L. (2018). Government audit in the age of Big Data opportunities and challenges. *Journal of Shandong University of Science and Technology, 6*, 90–96.

Yoon, K., Hoogduin, L., & Zhang, L. (2015). Big data as complementary audit evidence. *Accounting Horizons, 29*(2), 431–438.

Zhang, J., Yang, X., & Appelbaum, D. (2015). Toward effective big data analysis in continuous auditing. *Accounting Horizons, 29*(2), 469–476.

Zhang, Y., Yu, J., Hao, R., Wang, C., & Ren, K. (2018). Enabling efficient user revocation in identity-based cloud storage auditing for shared big data. *IEEE Transactions on Dependable and Secure Computing, 17*(3), 608–619.

Zhao, Y., & Harding, N. (2013). Improving the interpretation of complex audit evidence: The beneficial role of order effects. *Abacus, 49*(4), 476–505.

Zheng, Z., Xie, S., Dai, H., Chen, X., & Wang, H. (2017). An overview of Blockchain technology: Architecture, consensus, and future trends. In *2017 IEEE international congress on big data (BigData congress)* (pp. 557–564). IEEE.

Thuy Thu Nguyen, Ph.D. is the Deputy Director of Planning and Finance at the National Academy of Public Administration, Vietnam. Her research focus is on public sector accountability, especially focusing on public-private partnerships in different areas such as infrastructure and design. She is also undertaking research on education and technological development.

Lan Anh Nguyen, Ph.D., CPA, ACCA is a Lecturer in the School of Accounting, Information Systems and Supply Chain at RMIT University, Melbourne, Australia. During the last 10 years she has worked as an academic, engaging herself in both qualitative and quantitative research projects. Her research interests are in areas such as audit markets, business ethics, and work culture.

Michael Kend, Ph.D., CPA is a lecturer in the School of Accounting, Information Systems and Supply Chain at RMIT University, Melbourne, Australia. He has research experience covering archival, empirical, and interview-based research. Previously he completed work on an ARC Linkage Grant funded by the Australian Government and is best known for his co-authored research book called "The Future of Audit: Keeping Capital Markets Efficient" published in 2010.

Van Anh Thi Pham, Ph.D. is the Deputy Head of the Corporate Finance Department at the Hanoi Academy of Finance, Vietnam. She has been working in the education sector for about 20 years and participated in about 28 major research projects, and published 11 book chapters, and 48 research papers in various scientific journals. Her major research interests are the financial management mechanisms of government, corporate finance, and financial risk management.

Chapter 4
Prediction of Controversies and Estimation of ESG Performance: An Experimental Investigation Using Machine Learning

Jan Svanberg, Tohid Ardeshiri, Isak Samsten, Peter Öhman, and Presha Neidermeyer

Abstract We develop a new methodology for computing environmental, social, and governance (ESG) ratings using a mode of artificial intelligence (AI) called machine learning (ML) to make ESG more transparent. The ML algorithms anchor our rating methodology in controversies related to non-compliance with corporate social responsibility (CSR). This methodology is consistent with the information needs of institutional investors and is the first ESG methodology with predictive validity. Our best model predicts what companies are likely to experience controversies. It has a precision of 70–84 per cent and high predictive performance on several measures. It also provides evidence of what indicators contribute the most to the predicted likelihood of experiencing an ESG controversy. Furthermore, while the common approach of rating companies is to aggregate indicators using the arithmetic average, which is a simple explanatory model designed to describe an average company, the proposed rating methodology uses state-of-the-art AI technology to aggregate ESG indicators into holistic ratings for the predictive modelling of individual company performance.

J. Svanberg · T. Ardeshiri
University of Gävle and Centre for research on Economic Relations, Sundsvall, Sweden
e-mail: jan.svanberg@hig.se

T. Ardeshiri
e-mail: tohid.ardeshiri@ri.se

I. Samsten
Stockholm University, Stockholm, Sweden
e-mail: samsten@dsv.su.se

P. Öhman (✉)
Centre for Research on Economic Relations, Mid Sweden University, Sundsvall, Sweden
e-mail: peter.ohman@miun.se

P. Neidermeyer
West Virginia University, Morgantown, WA, USA
e-mail: presha.neidermeyer@mail.wvu.edu

T. Rana et al. (eds.), *Handbook of Big Data and Analytics in Accounting and Auditing*,
https://doi.org/10.1007/978-981-19-4460-4_4

Predictive modelling using ML enables our models to aggregate the information contained in ESG indicators with far less information loss than with the predominant aggregation method.

Keywords Artificial Intelligence · Controversies · Corporate Social Performance · ESG · Machine Learning · Socially Responsible Investment

1 Introduction

Global capital is by far the strongest force in the world, more powerful than any government or political order. Nothing can be done without capital being allocated, at least not in the commercial world, indicating that capital allocation can help stop unsustainable activities. For a long time, however, there was no clear evidence of whether institutional investors have any impact on their portfolio companies' compliance with corporate social responsibility (CSR) demands. Recent findings indicate that divestment campaigns decrease stock value by 8–10 per cent and may achieve five per cent greenhouse gas (GHG) emission reductions in high-emission companies (Choi et al., 2020).

The portion of institutional investors considering the divestment of CSR-noncompliant companies is growing rapidly. Early estimates held that about a quarter of market capital would have to be allocated according to such preferences to have any real effect on capital costs (Ambec & Lanoie, 2008). We are above that level, with the total amount of socially responsible investment (SRI) in 2018 being one in every four USD (USD 12 trillion) of investment in the USA and one in every two euros (EUR 22 trillion) in Europe (EUROSIF, 2018; USSIF, 2018). Such an important task as directing global capital towards sustainable projects requires a sophisticated navigation system. Unfortunately, there has been no good method to measure or rate the level of sustainable performance of individual companies. The most advanced measures of corporate social performance (CSP) are the environmental, social, and governance (ESG) ratings, which are considered the standard measures of CSP, i.e. the extent to which companies comply with compulsory CSR policies (cf. Drempetic et al., 2020; Oikonomou et al., 2018). A Google Scholar search on 4 October 2020 using the terms' corporate social performance' and KLD (representing Kinder, Lydenberg, Domini) found 10,200 hits for one such rating.

As popular as ESG ratings are, their aggregation methodology has several shortcomings. First, research has found that aggregated ESG ratings are invalid (Chatterji et al., 2016; Delmas et al., 2013; Semenova & Hassel, 2015; Trumpp et al., 2015). These studies unequivocally concluded that the methodology with which information-rich ESG indicators are aggregated to form composite ratings is inappropriate for the broad, heterogenous, and nonlinear construct of CSP. Notably, the critique articulated in the cited studies does not claim that the ESG indicators do not contain a treasure trove of information about CSP, but that the methods with which indicators are aggregated and holistic ratings computed are far from accurate.

Second, the ESG aggregation methodology does not generate ratings that meet the information needs of institutional investors. Nofsinger et al. (2019) found that these investors were indifferent to whether companies had features that were not compulsory environmental, social, or governance requirements, but were underweight stocks in companies that did not meet compulsory requirements. This information preference for compulsory CSR compliance is inconsistent with the lack of discrimination between obligatory and discretionary aspects of CSR produced with conventional ESG aggregation methodology. The aggregated ratings are an arithmetic average of both aspects (Chen & Delmas, 2011), making these ratings more or less irrelevant for informing investment decisions, even though the information underlying ESG indicators likely contains information that would be useful to institutional investors.

This chapter summarizes the findings of a research project using artificial intelligence (AI) to develop a new type of ESG rating methodology with predictive validity and relevance to institutional investors (see e.g. Svanberg et al., 2022). Because of the broad, heterogenous, and nonlinear CSP concept, it is preferable to develop an ESG rating methodology using predictive rather than explanatory modelling. In this regard, we quote Wood (2010, p. 57): "CSP is a complex system and its measurement requires complex tools". Furthermore, a rating describes the state of a single observation (i.e. the performance of an individual company), which is what predictive modelling provides, whereas explanatory modelling generates relationships between variables generalizable to all observations, but no precise prediction of the state of a particular case. Deriving a rating is therefore an inappropriate task for explanatory modelling but an ideal application of predictive modelling with machine learning (ML).

The purpose of this chapter is to describe a rating methodology with which high-precision ESG ratings can be generated within a project including various studies. Because predictive validity and the choice of institutional-investor–relevant proxies for CSP are the keys to a rating that is useful to institutional investors, we discuss the proxies and their predictive performance on several performance measures.

2 The ESG Indicator Aggregation Problem

2.1 Limitations of ESG Indicator Aggregation

Institutional investors need to know if one company is more sustainable than another to compose portfolios that consider ESG risks. The more ESG criteria an investment assessment covers, the more difficult the process becomes for the investment manager, because the investment decision ultimately merges all criteria into one, and ESG contains too many disparate features to be considered separately (Gond & Crane, 2010). For example, how should an investment manager determine the relative financial materiality of two such different ESG features as 'employee turnover' and 'hazardous waste'? If considering disaggregated raw data, such weighing of one feature against another would have to be done with hundreds of ESG features. A central problem with ESG ratings is therefore how to aggregate all features without losing too much information.

In the early ESG literature, ESG was measured using questionnaires (Aupperle, 1984), regulatory compliance (Wokutch & Spencer, 1987), and content analysis (Wolfe, 1991). Another method was indexing, as in the Fortune corporate reputation index (Sharfman, 1996), but the problem of aggregating measures to form composite rating indexes has not been convincingly solved. For example, some studies have used stakeholder questionnaires to assess the relative importance of ESG features, but this method is considered arbitrary and is unpopular (Chatterji & Levine, 2006; Hillman & Keim, 2001). Another method is to use the 'data envelope' technique from operations management to estimate an aggregated ESG measure (Chen & Delmas, 2011). The fact that this method generates identical ratings for most companies makes it useless in practice. In reality, there is no alternative to using the large ESG indicator databases that raters supply. No other information source comes close to compiling hundreds of ESG indicators, most of them company self-reported. The question, then, is how to aggregate these data.

ESG rating methodology is as simple as it is popular. ESG ratings are in effect the arithmetic average of ESG indicators. However, due to scale differences (i.e. binary versus continuous), ranking formulas need to be used, and company performance is computed via within-industry comparison between companies. Previous reviews of ESG methodology confirm our assessment: "Most empirical studies on CSP use simple linear aggregations, weighted or non-weighted, to derive a composite CSP score from a selection of CSP metrics" (Chen & Delmas, 2011, p. 789).

It is surprising that accounting and finance articles in high-ranked journals such as The Accounting Review refer to this aggregation methodology as providing a fairly unproblematic measure of ESG. There are few critical studies of the validity of ESG aggregation methodology (Berg et al., 2019; Chatterji et al., 2016; Drempetic et al., 2020; Semenova & Hassel, 2015; Trumpp et al., 2015), but one indication that something is wrong with the way ESG indicators are aggregated in research is the amount of conflicting evidence regarding the returns of sustainable performance (Margolis et al., 2012; Orlitzky et al., 2003). For example, some find that the financial performances of portfolios with and without SRI screening are indistinguishable (Statman, 2006; Renneboog et al., 2008).

The few studies of the validity of ESG ratings tell the story of the harm that inappropriate aggregation does to a composite rating. Semenova and Hassel (2015) investigated the aggregation of indicators of the environmental part of three ESG ratings and found that the ratings were uncorrelated. Similarly, Trumpp et al. (2015) found that environmental performance is a multidimensional and aggregate construct as opposed to a subordinate construct and claimed that the reduction of this collection of uncorrelated features to one dimension causes information loss. Sharfman (1996) examined the correlation between ESG ratings based on KLD data and the Fortune reputation index, finding that they were not correlated. Among the most thorough studies of aggregated ESG rating validity is that of Chatterji et al. (2016), who examined the convergent validity of six different ratings and found that none of them was correlated with any other rating. Their results indicate that different ratings judge the same company fairly differently, leading to the conclusion that most or all of the ratings must be wrong and that much empirical research relying on ESG ratings must be reassessed.

Two methodological problems with ESG ratings may explain why it is difficult to find evidence that aggregated ESG ratings have validity. The first problem with this rating methodology is its aggregation of indicators using arithmetic averaging. Arithmetic averaging is a linear estimator, but the underlying CSP construct is likely nonlinear due to feature interaction (Chen & Delmas, 2011; Oikonomou et al., 2018). This incapacity is related to arithmetic averaging's low capacity to represent complexity, because averaging treats ESG indicator patterns as if they were expressions of a uniform underlying construct (Semenova & Hassel, 2015) and as if there were no interactions between indicators (Sigrist & Hirnschall, 2019). As a reference point from which to understand the complexity of the rating task, our rating assesses more than 100 indicators per ESG component, among which there may be patterns that exhibit their own distinct behaviors. The arithmetic average is an aggregation method that accounts for none of this.

The second problem is the equal weighting of indicators. The assumption that all aspects of ESG are equally important for overall sustainability performance is clearly wrong (Callan & Thomas, 2009; Chen & Delmas, 2011; Sharfman, 1996). The equal weighting scheme has survived because there has been no viable alternative. From a legitimacy perspective on ESG, a weighting scheme would have to mirror the relative importance of areas of CSP as they appear to society.

These two constraints are due to the manner in which ESG indicators are aggregated and could apply to any complex hypothetical construct. A different constraint arising from the aggregation of ESG indicators is that it does not produce ratings that disclose information relevant to institutional investors. Notably, this problem is not because the ESG indicators lack this information, but because aggregation by means of averaging cannot represent it. As evidenced in several studies, institutional investors view ESG as financially relevant, but they are focused exclusively on ESG weaknesses. The weaknesses refer to features related to the risk of ESG controversies. Nofsinger et al. (2019) claimed that the reason for institutional investors' asymmetric information preference is that any positive effects of delivering ESG performance beyond minimum compliance with CSR demands are so small that they are offset by the costs of achieving those benefits. They argued, in contrast, that non-compliance with binding, compulsory CSR, which we for clarity refer to as corporate social *responsibilities* because we emphasize the obligatory, non-discretionary aspect of this part of CSR, causes irreparable financial damage.

The adverse economic effects associated with CSR controversies include lawsuits, disrupted production, and consumer boycotts (Luo & Balvers, 2017) as well as strikes and government investigations. These effects are relevant only to the extent to which company behaviors are compliant with compulsory CSR, but not at all to the discretionary 'doing good' part of ESG. The cost asymmetry resonates with how institutional investors use ESG information, which is predominantly for managing investment risk rather than out of moral concern with doing good (Amir & Serafeim,

2018). Similar findings were reported in a recent survey study (Krueger et al., 2020): investor reputation protection is the primary motivation to use ESG data when making investments, and a reputation is best protected by avoiding investment in controversy-prone companies. Financial incentives and a desire to protect one's reputation may explain why institutional investors underweight stocks in companies prone to ESG controversies and why their information preferences are one-sided (Nofsinger et al., 2019). Consistent with these observations is the evidence that stock markets show small or no reactions to good news but large negative reactions to bad news (Capelle-Blancard & Petit, 2019; Krüger, 2015).

These findings have consequences for how ESG indicators should be aggregated. An ESG rating needs to be a high-precision estimate of the extent to which individual companies comply with those parts of CSR that could trigger controversy if violated by a company. As an arithmetic average of indicators is highly unlikely to be such an estimate, this aggregation method is inappropriate for ESG ratings.

2.2 *Controversies as Proxies for Non-Compliance with Compulsory CSR*

In contrast to the current ad hoc explanatory approach to aggregating ESG indicators, we claim that ratings should be constructed using predictive modelling because such modelling generates ratings that are far more accurate than those computed using explanatory modelling (cf. Ding et al., 2020; Fiaschi et al., 2020; Shmueli, 2010). Predictive modelling is data driven and therefore not evaluated relative to how consistent it is with theory. The validity of predictive modelling is evaluated using performance measures that indicate the extent to which the model predicts a variable of interest. Our variable of interest is determined by the information preferences of institutional investors. As they are interested in predicting the extent to which potential portfolio companies comply with the compulsory parts of CSR, and because non-compliance with such norms is associated with the risk of controversies, our variable of interest is CSR controversies.

As noted, institutional investors' strongest motivation to integrate ESG assessment in investment is to protect investor reputation. Negative legitimacy caused by social controversies in portfolio companies spills over to the owners (Zavyalova et al., 2012), so avoidance of controversy-prone companies is a priority. An ESG rating predicting the likelihood that a company will become embroiled in a social controversy would serve this purpose. Krueger et al. (2020) found that the second strongest motivation for integrating ESG risk assessment into the investment process is institutional investors' perceived fiduciary obligation towards beneficiaries to invest responsibly. When beneficiaries are dissatisfied with how a fund invests their money, there is a risk that they will withdraw their money from the fund (Grappi et al., 2013). Withdrawing money as an expression of dissatisfaction with the sustainability of investments can be expected when beneficiaries feel that too many portfolio companies are associated with CSR controversies. An ESG rating predicting CSR controversies would therefore not only protect the institutional investor's reputation but also help them perform in line with beneficiaries' expectations.

Another reason for institutional investors to value an ESG rating that predicts CSR controversies is that stocks associated with recent controversies tend to experience high volatility and price declines (Cui & Docherty, 2020; Muller & Kräussl, 2011). This would be viewed as negative by the investors, because investment managers are often evaluated based on their short-term performance (Harmes, 2011). Nofsinger et al. (2019) argued, however, that the avoidance of companies that have ESG weaknesses is more pronounced among institutional investors with a long-term than a short-term investment focus. Taken together, these pieces of evidence and theoretical arguments indicate that CSR controversies should be the proxies for ESG performance when developing an ESG rating using predictive modelling.

The use of CSR controversies as the variable of interest and ESG indicators as input variables produces an ML model conceptually different from conventional ESG ratings. The conventional aggregation of ESG indicators does not assess ESG relative to a performance standard. Describing behaviors is not the same as assessing the extent to which behaviors constitute performance, because a prerequisite for performance is that behaviors should exceed or comply with a standard. We therefore refer to ESG indicators as company behavior indicators and to our estimation of the risk of controversy as our assessment of these behaviors relative to a performance standard of corporate social requirements. As previously indicated, these requirements refer to obligatory CSR norms. Some of those are legally binding, for example, as set forth in labor, environmental, and corporate law; some are 'soft law', such as international standards, for example, for accounting; and some are moral norms, such as the emerging norm to recognize the threat of climate change and reduce GHG emissions. The binding or obligatory nature of these requirements suggests that noncompliance with them is associated with a risk of controversy, which may arise, for example, through litigation initiated by government or international organizations or through boycotts and strikes initiated by stakeholders.

Our definition of ESG performance as formed by behaviors assessed relative to obligatory CSR (referred to below as corporate social *responsibilities*, CS*R*), means that while our ML ratings estimate companies' compliance with norms, conventional aggregation methodology simply summarizes behavioral indicators. For example, having a 'salary gap' and having an 'inappropriate salary gap' are not the same thing, although conventional ratings treat them as if they were. There has been no criticism of the methodological aspects of this conceptual distinction in the ESG rating literature. In contrast, worker performance is assessed by observing achievement relative to a performance standard (Groover, 2007). Judges in all courts of law judge behaviors relative to a standard called law without which their judgments would be arbitrary, questionable, or meaningless. Auditors assess company accounting relative to accounting standards and recommendations (Öhman & Wallerstedt, 2012), and so on.

When aggregating ESG indicators to form a composite rating, it is common practice to define performance as the sum of behaviors, with no reference to any performance standard (cf. Wood, 2010). The lack of performance standard in ESG rating methodology deprives the assessment of such ratings the guidance offered by norms, leaving institutional investors and empirical researchers with an unanswered question: What does the unanchored aggregated ESG indicator actually measure?

Our use of CS*R* controversies as proxies for ESG performance anchors our ML ratings to a system of binding standards and makes the ratings reflect the risk of legitimacy loss described by legitimacy theory (Deegan, 2019). A company non-compliant with CS*R* is one that per definition risks its legitimate right to pursue its business and makes itself a target of controversy. A rating anchored in ESG controversies regarding non-compliance with CS*R* would therefore be a rating that sets out to measure the most fundamental antecedents of legitimacy at the same time as it is consistent with institutional investors' information needs.

Controversies are assessments and reactions to CS*R*-relevant company behaviors (e.g., inappropriate or illegal waste management). As such, they provide different information from that provided by ESG indicators. CS*R* controversies also tell something about whether the transgressor has the structures and processes necessary to ensure CS*R* compliance (Nieri & Giuliani, 2018) regarding, for example, management quality and supply-chain management structures (Chiu & Sharfman, 2018). Identifying the lacking structures is a complex task because they can be related to errors in many areas, each complex in itself, for example, the environment, anti-competitive behavior, patents and intellectual property, lack of respect for human rights, poor labor relations, tax fraud, child labor, and inappropriate management compensation. Predictive modelling accomplishes this through associating indicator patterns with meanings conveyed by controversies. These associated meanings of controversies can be generalized because controversies often arise from intended, systematic breaches of CS*R*. Companies embroiled in controversies often violate moral and legal norms when pursuing financial goals (Fiaschi et al., 2017; Surroca et al., 2013) because performance pressures cause corners to be cut and reward inappropriate behavior, eventually normalizing it (Earle et al., 2010). Predictive modelling extrapolates the likelihood of controversies from known controversies to other companies exhibiting ESG indicators similar to those of the controversial companies.

3 Research Design and Measures

We adopt cross-sectional designs in predictive modelling. The predictive design sacrifices theoretical explanation for substantially higher empirical precision in describing individual companies' performances (Collopy et al., 1994; Gurbaxani & Mendelson, 1990). While explanatory modelling investigates relationships between features in a population, predictive modelling examines the state of specific companies. A rating unable to distinguish between individual companies is as useless to an investor as a poor diagnostic instrument is to a medical practitioner. Differences between explanatory and predictive modelling are described by Shmueli (2010) and Bzdok et al. (2018). Predictive modelling is superior to explanatory modelling for developing diagnostic methods such as image assessment in rheumatology (Hügle et al., 2020), for credit assessment (Kruppa et al., 2013), and for predicting bankruptcy (Heo & Yang, 2014). In such diagnostic applications, it would be inappropriate to use explanatory modelling. Predictive modelling is therefore the most effective ESG rating methodology.

The three studies in our research project use nine ML algorithms and the task is to predict CS*R* controversies in companies by examining ESG indicators. The achievement of this task is evaluated using five measures of predictive performance: precision, recall, Fmeasure, area under receiver operating characteristic (ROC) curve (hereafter AUC), and precision recall curve (PRC).

We obtain data from Refinitiv Eikon and use all available indicators—nearly 400 in the selected ten-year window. An enumeration of the indicators used in each of the three studies is provided in the appendices to the three working papers that this chapter summarizes. In addition, we include the additional indicators 'market capital', 'return on assets', 'industry', 'country of headquarters', 'total assets', and 'net assets'. The three studies are based on a sample of 2517 companies for the 2009–2018 period.

In a first step, the companies are divided into two groups: one of companies having experienced controversies (i.e. environment and governance controversies) or having experienced more than an average number of social controversies, and another of companies having experienced no controversies (i.e. environment and governance controversies) or having experienced fewer than average social controversies. While environmental and governance controversies are rare, social controversies are more common, with an average number of 5.17 during the ten-year window. We therefore use a different approach to define the disjoint classes. For environmental and governance controversies, we use the absence of controversy as indicating high ESG. For social controversies, the definition of high ESG is that a company has experienced fewer than average controversies. The high-ESG class includes negative cases and companies in the low-ESG class are considered positive cases.

The idea behind the cross-sectional research design is not to model the risk of future controversies based on a company's past ESG indicators, but to model the likelihood that an indicator pattern is associated with a company's risk of experiencing a controversy. The longitudinal aspect of the data is reduced to a cross-sectional format, with indicators averaged over the ten years if numerical or encoded with dummy variables if binary.

The models are developed in ML experiments in which one algorithm at a time is extracting information from ESG indicators by associating patterns of indicators with CS*R* controversies. The nine ML algorithms, representing a full range of algorithms for supervised learning, have different functionalities and therefore capture different aspects of this learning task. The algorithms used are nearest neighbors, linear support vector machine (linear SVM), radial basis function support vector machine (RBF

SVM), random forest, logistic regression, artificial neural network, gradient boosting, naïve Bayes, and quadratic discriminant analysis (QDA).

4 Experiments

An overview of the settings with which the nine ML algorithms are executed is presented in Table 1. The hyper-parameter settings ensure that our studies can be reproduced and provide additional background to support their interpretation. For simplicity, we have used the default settings of scikit-learn (Pedregosa et al., 2011), version 0.22.

Predictive modelling evaluates the trained algorithms using an unseen set of test instances. A method to do this that economizes on scarce data is k-fold cross-validation. It partitions the data in k disjoint folds and conducts training iteratively on $k - 1$ folds, with one fold for testing. This repeated training/testing uses the entire dataset for training and testing, with the advantage that predictive performance is evaluated from k different angles. In total, k performance measures are obtained, the mean of which is a better estimate of the generalization performance than if the predictive performance were calculated using only one partition. This study employs stratified tenfold cross-validation. Stratification ensures an equal number of positive and negative cases in each test set.

As mentioned, five measures of performance—precision, recall, F-measure, AUC, and PRC—are used to evaluate predictive performance. The definition of these measures must be understood from initial standard distinctions described in a similar way in all ML literature (see Table 2). Precision (Eq. 1) is the sensitivity of the predictor, i.e. the fraction of positive cases in relation to all predicted positive cases. Recall (Eq. 2) measures the specificity of the classifier, which is its ability to identify as large a fraction as possible of the positive cases. The true positive is the number of times the predictor can correctly label a controversy. The false positive is the number

Table 1 Hyper parameters

Algorithm	Notes
Nearest neighbor	Three nearest neighbors
Linear SVM	Linear kernel with $C = 0.025$
RBF SVM	RBS kernel with $C = 0.025$
Random forest	100 trees
Logistic regression	Ridge regularization with $C = 1$
Artificial neural network	Four hidden layers of size 100 using the RELU activation function
Gradient boosting	Learning rate of 0.1
Naïve Bayes	No hyper-parameters
QDA	No hyper-parameters

Table 2 Basic measures

Measures of performance	Equation
$Precision = \frac{True_{positive}}{True_{positive}+False_{positive}}$	(Eq. 1)
$Recall = \frac{True_{positive}}{True_{positive}+False_{negative}}$	(Eq. 2)
$F-measure = \frac{2\times Precision \times Recall}{Precision+Recall}$	(Eq. 3)
$True_{positive} = \frac{True_{positive}}{True_{positive}+False_{negative}}$	(Eq. 4)
$False_{positive} = \frac{False_{positive}}{False_{positive}+True_{negative}}$	(Eq. 5)

of times the predictor falsely believes a company has experienced a controversy. The true negative is the number of correct observations of a company as not having experienced a controversy. The false negative is the number of contrary-to-fact predictions that a company has not experienced a controversy.

There is a performance trade-off between precision and recall. For example, a predictor that predicts every company as a positive case and having a recall of 100 per cent would often have a very low precision, in our case zero. The F-measure (Eq. 3) captures the trade-off.

Another measure of the relationship between two other measures is the AUC. This is the area under the true positive rate versus false positive rate curve as defined in Eqs. 4 and 5. This measure estimates the probability of a predictor rating a true positive instance ahead of a false positive instance and is therefore a measure of its aggregated rating performance. The PRC shows the mean precision for multiple thresholds of recall and is therefore an average of the trade-off between precision and recall. The PRC is obtained by plotting precision versus recall.

5 Results

5.1 Predictive Performance of Different ML Algorithms

Before examining the prediction results, we investigate whether an ESG rating would provide appropriate data for classifying companies as involved or not involved in ESG controversies. The following is a simple way to illustrate whether a conventional ESG rating contains any information of the type demanded by institutional investors. Figure 1 displays two distributions of companies across overall ESG ratings. The yellow bars show company-years with more than an average number of social controversies on the y-axis and the total ESG rating from Refinitiv on the x-axis. Company-years with fewer than average social controversies are shown by the blue bars. The distributions are similar with no cut-off point defining the two classes. The ESG rating is particularly insensitive to the likelihood of controversies in the ESG range where most companies are situated. We find that the same types

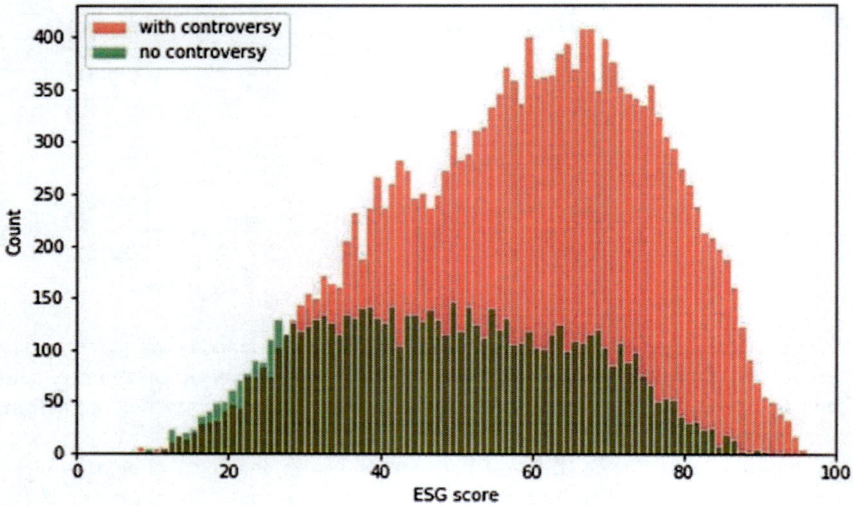

Fig. 1 The distribution of social controversies over company-years and ESG ratings. Company-years with fewer than average social controversies in a ten-year window are classified as 'no controversy' on the *y*-axis and company-years with more than an average number of controversies are classified as 'with controversy'

of overlapping and non-distinguishable distributions are repeated for environmental, social, and governance component ESG ratings and for environmental, social, and governance controversies.

5.2 Prediction Results

We first address the static measures precision, recall, and F-measure, which show the performance of each ML algorithm at a given probability threshold for predicting a positive case. Table 3 shows the performance of two of the ML algorithms for the three types of controversies: environmental, social, and governance. We are contrasting the most capable model, random forest, with one of the less capable but still well-performing ones, logistic regression. We pay special attention to the precision column, because precision should be the priority for institutional investors who are about to allocate large sums of money based on a decision to include a company in their portfolios. Random forest is the most precise of the two models for all three types of controversies (70–84 per cent of the controversies are correctly predicted), but the two models perform more similarly for the dynamic measures and logistic regression has higher recall. Random forest's high precision can be linked to its learning capabilities, because it produces models that have uncalibrated

Table 3 Predictive and learning performance

	Precision	Recall	F-measure	AUC	PRC
Environmental					
Random forest	0.6994	0.1942	0.2990	0.8849	0.5090
Logistic regression	0.3045	0.7253	0.4282	0.8727	0.4814
Social					
Random forest	0.8417	0.5756	0.6823	0.9165	0.8104
Logistic regression	0.6132	0.7788	0.6852	0.8982	0.7898
Governance					
Random forest	0.7506	0.1700	0.2756	0.7787	0.5110
Logistic regression	0.3387	0.6513	0.4444	0.7531	0.4699

probability estimates, requiring that the model have high confidence in predictions. Identical training and testing folds were used for all nine algorithms under study.

In the separate studies we find that random forest, artificial neural networks, and gradient boosting are the best for precision, with the bottom group of naïve Bayes, RBF SVM, and QDA far behind with small variations among them. We also find that the differences between the high- and lower-precision predictors over the five performance measures are similar to those in Table 3. All the lower-precision models (i.e. naïve Bayes, RBF SVM, and QDA) have the same pattern of low precision and relatively higher recall. From the investment manager's point of view, this difference is important because it indicates that the lower-precision algorithms are prepared to guess wrong many more times to get one guess right than the more cautious high-precision models random forest, artificial neural networks, and gradient boosting. This wrong screening of the lower-precision algorithms would limit diversification for institutional investors and encourage investment on false premises. As a reference point, an insurance company may own 2000–5000 equities, which can be compared with the approximately 8000 companies making up 80 per cent of global capital for which Refinitiv provides ESG indicators. A negative screening tool that reduces the investment universe too much due to low precision would not satisfy investment decision support requirements.

Furthermore, we evaluate the ranking and predictive performance of the algorithms using the AUC and PRC in Figs. 2 and 3. Discrimination, equivalent to the probability that a randomly chosen positive instance is ranked higher than a randomly chosen negative instance, is measured by the AUC, i.e. it is equivalent to the two-sample Wilcoxon rank-sum statistic.

The AUC should be as close to the top-left corner as possible. If the curve is below the dashed line, it represents a prediction worse than a random guess. Overall, the plots in Fig. 2, the yellow curve for predicting positive cases and the blue curve for negative cases, confirm our interpretation of Table 3. The differences between the models are more difficult to discern graphically, but we find that random forest has a steeper rise in the true positive rate than does logistic regression, corresponding to

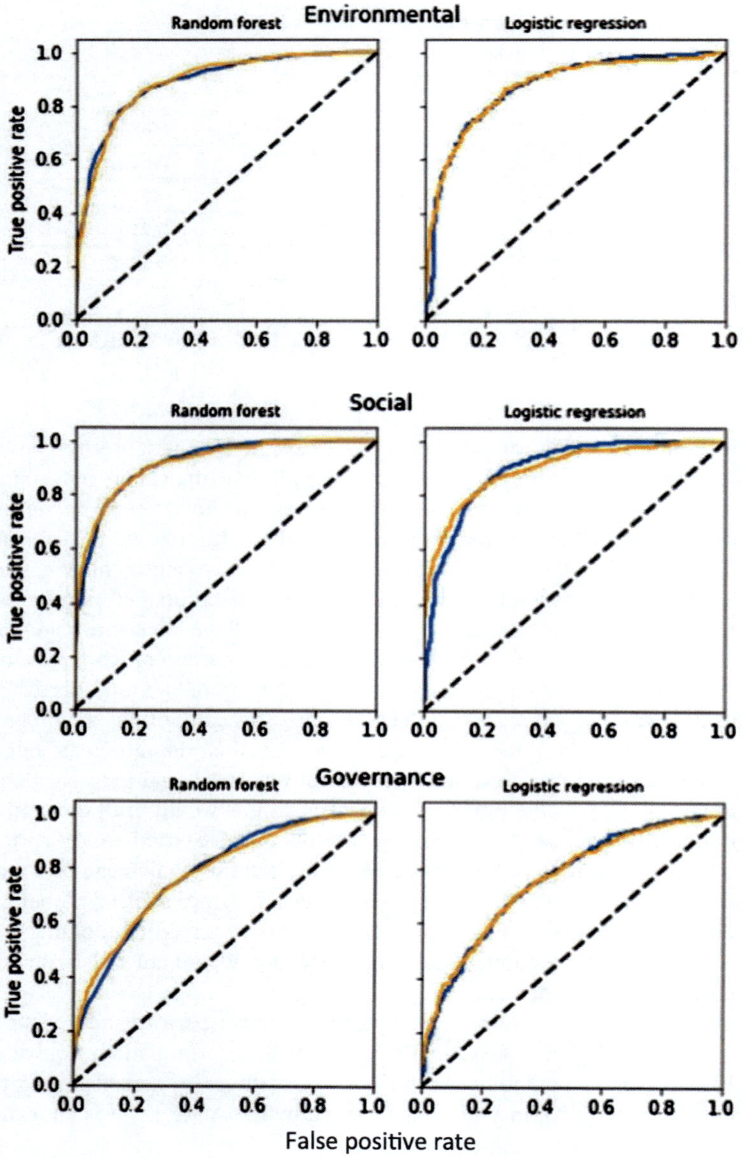

Fig. 2 Area under the ROC curve (AUC) for three different ratings (environmental, social, and governance) and for two algorithms (random forest and logistic regression). The blue line represents the AUC for predicting non-controversy proneness and the yellow line represents the AUC for predicting controversy proneness

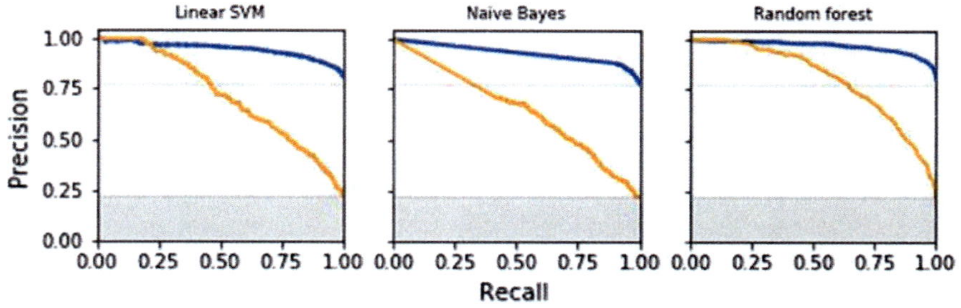

Fig. 3 Precision recall curves (PRC). The blue lines represent the PRC for predicting non-controversyproneness and the yellow lines represent the PRC for predicting controversy-proneness for social controversies. The PRC shows the precision of a classifier as the recall increases. The top region (above the grey area) is where a predictor performs better than random guessing for the non-controversy cases, and the region between the bottom and top region show the region where a predictor performs better than random guessing for the controversy cases

the difference between the high-precision and lower-precision algorithms found in our separate studies, i.e. logistic regression is a linear model with limited complexity representation capacity. Any increase in the false positive rate is costly considering the small fraction of companies defined as controversy prone. It is therefore important that the model have a steep rise in the AUC.

Figure 3 contains PRC and contrasts linear SVM, naïve Bayes, and random forest for predicting positive and negative cases of social controversies. The PRC curve is a dynamic measure of the predictive performance of the algorithms, showing the trade-off between precision and recall. For the investment screening application, it is ideal to have both high precision and high recall, but as Table 3 demonstrates, this is not attainable because none of the models can quite produce the ideal output.

In terms of the graphic presentation in Fig. 3, the ideal is a PRC curve in the topright corner and as far as possible from the bottom-left corner. As long as the algorithms need to predict controversy-prone companies with absolute certainty, they can maintain high precision, but as they are also required to find a large proportion of the total number of such companies, the algorithms sacrifice the certainty of predictions to pursue more positive cases. The PRC curves confirm what we see in Table 3. Both the non-controversy and controversy prediction curves are in the top-right corner for random forest, and our separate studies demonstrate that this applies to the whole group of competent algorithms, i.e. random forest, artificial neural network, and gradient boosting, as well as to logistic regression. They accomplish a more efficient trade-off between precision and recall than do the other algorithms. As seen in Fig. 3, the trade-off drops off significantly more steeply with linear SVM and naïve Bayes than with random forest. The grey area at the bottom of each graph represents the class distribution. Several algorithms offer precision of around 0.8 at a recall well above 0.5 for social controversies, which are high numbers.

5.3 Controversy Prediction as ESG Rating

Having seen that the predictive modelling of environmental, social, and governance controversies is possible and that the results indicate that controversy-prone companies can be detected with our high-precision screening, we now focus on how the corresponding MLbased methodology performs at rating. We expect that any ESG rating and our rating in particular should be negatively correlated with the number of controversies a company experiences. While many company CSR activities can be symbolic and inauthentic, controversies are instances in which companies are accused of not following required practices in the CSR area and ratings measuring this non-compliance are what institutional investors need.

Our best model extrapolates from what it has learnt by studying the association between indicator patterns and controversies. It expects certain patterns to be associated with controversies and should typically give lower ratings to companies experiencing more controversies. However, there may be many deviations from the normal. For example, companies experiencing more controversies than average may have ESG indicator patterns typical of very compliant companies. They 'look good' from the rating model's point of view and are therefore awarded high ratings. Other companies may have experienced no or fewer than average controversies despite exhibiting a pattern of features typical of companies that are controversy prone. They are awarded low ML ratings. On average, however, a negative correlation between an ESG rating and the number of controversies is expected.

The rating distributions are described in Fig. 4. The x-axis in the graph shows the number of controversies per company and the y-axis the ratings. We illustrate the results of our studies by showing the performance of four algorithms for predicting social controversies. (The graphs for environmental and governance controversies are similar.) How closely the rating models are dictated by actual controversies may depend on the complexity of the model. A simplistic rating model would typically have a less tight alignment between the ESG ratings and controversies because it misses relevant interactions between features and controversies, which is called under-fitting to the training data with possible bias as a result. With under-fitting we would anticipate finding some models giving high ratings to companies experiencing many controversies, and this should be expected for linear SVM and logistic regression, but we observe none of that. A complex nonlinear model may instead lead to over-fitting to the data with lower generalizability as a result. There seems to be a mixed pattern in Fig. 4, however, with logistic regression and gradient boosting being unwilling to give any company experiencing many controversies a high rating, whereas random forest (and artificial neural networks) of the complex models and linear SVM (and RBF SVM) of the less complex models appear to use more discretion and sometimes give companies with many controversies a rating around 40–50.

Figure 4 reveals, as expected, a negative correlation between the four ML-based ESG ratings and the number of social controversies experienced by companies. The models with the highest predictive performance have smooth distributions. There is a difference between logistic regression and gradient boosting, on one hand, and

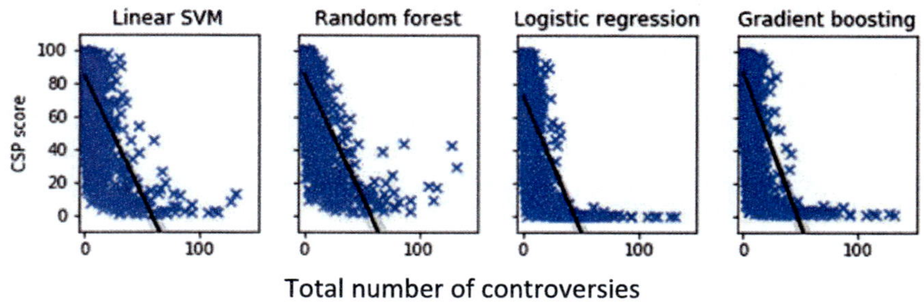

Fig. 4 Correlation between the social component ESG rating produced by four of the machine learning algorithms and the number of years with social controversies. (Total number of controversies)

random forest and linear SVM, on the other, in assigning low ratings to all companies experiencing many controversies. There is a considerably wider distribution in the ratings for companies experiencing many controversies for random forest and linear SVM than for logistic regression and gradient boosting. Because random forest and gradient boosting represent two of the more complex models, whereas logistic regression and linear SVM are linear and therefore less complex, strict adherence to a many controversies–low rating rule can be accomplished using linear and nonlinear models. All the models have a steep downward slope of the correlation, which is evidence that all models operate according to the logic we require of an ESG rating. Except for relatively few companies in which there are good reasons to believe that controversies are not associated with structural weaknesses in governance, many controversies should result in a low ESG rating because CS*R* controversies are the best available proxies for noncompliance with CSR.

6 Conclusions

SRI is endorsed by a large fraction of institutional investors in most parts of the world. Those investors believe that they have the power to make companies more sustainable through the way they exercise ownership power, and recent finance research (Choi et al., 2020) gives them right. However, it is difficult for institutional investors in good faith to try to invest responsibly and influence portfolio companies to become more sustainable if they do not know what a sustainable company looks like.

The problem is that institutional investors need to assess sustainable performance manually by scrutinizing the huge amounts of ESG information companies now tend to disclose. The task is demanding. Assume that an institutional investor was to devote one minute to each of 400 ESG indicators. If so, it would take more than 25 years for one sustainability expert to manually screen the approximately 8000 companies for which there are ESG data today. Consider the difficulty of such manual work competing in this task with the precision (70–84 per cent of controversies correctly predicted) and speed (in seconds once the training is done) of state-of-the-art ML models. There is no lack of information regarding the growing complexity of financial reporting, but the analytical tools with which institutional investors can assess ESG issues have to be hand crafted by each investor because no available tools meet the accuracy and information content demands of institutional investors. The problem is how data are aggregated to form valid and intelligent ratings. Conventional ESG indicator aggregation methodology is more likely to measure the capacity for sustainability rhetoric in large companies than it is to measure sustainable performance (Drempetic et al., 2020).

We find a conceptual weakness that propagates into methodological weaknesses in the aggregation methodology used in ESG ratings. The conceptual weakness is that the ratings do not assess ESG relative to a performance standard. Conventional ratings assume that an average of ESG indicators accurately represents CSP. This is a misperception of the performance concept. This concept has escaped theoretical scrutiny in the CSR and CSP literature despite being established in, for example, the education and work performance literatures. Omitting the idea of performance as behavior relative to a standard causes aggregated ESG ratings to be arbitrary, because an estimator that averages the indicators conveys no information about what is sufficient or good performance on the respective indicators or about the extent to which performance on one indicator could or could not make up for deficient performance on another. The use of equally weighted averages in aggregated ESG ratings is the result of this conceptual error. The methodological problems include raters mainly using equally weighted arithmetic means to aggregate ESG indicators. This aggregation method is, as several studies of ESG rating validity show, unable to produce valid aggregated ESG ratings (e.g. Berg et al., 2019; Chatterji et al., 2016; Semenova & Hassel, 2015; Trumpp et al., 2015).

As a solution to the challenge posed by institutional investors' need for accurate SRI decision support systems, we develop a new type of ESG rating methodology. Our rating methodology uses ML to predictively model ESG. This is a data-driven solution to the problem of assessing company behaviors relative to a performance standard, because we anchor our rating methodology in CSR controversies, which are proxies for companies' compliance with compulsory corporate social *responsibilities* (CS*R*). This data-driven approach studies associations between a broad list of ESG indicators and more than 20,000 controversies with the goal of predicting controversies involving individual companies. Since the prediction of controversies is equivalent to the prediction of compliance with CS*R*, the best ML model (i.e. random forest) assesses companies' behaviors relative to CS*R*. Based on how each indicator is associated with the likelihood of a company experiencing a CS*R* controversy, state-of-the-art ML algorithms learn how to assess the weights on ESG indicators in their models. The best ML model not only produces an unequal weighting scheme that mirrors companies' compliance with CS*R*, it also produces a complex and nonlinear model of ESG that represents the abundant interactions that may occur between ESG indicators. Extrapolating the relationships between ESG indicator patterns and CS*R* controversies to all companies, this ML model can predict compliance with CS*R* for any company for which there is indicator data.

The best ML model has high predictive validity and is consistent with the information needs of institutional investors. These investors need ratings that predict CS*R* controversies so that they can avoid investing in controversy-prone companies. This is the most important feature of any ESG rating, because institutional investors underweight stocks that exhibit traits typical of controversy-prone companies (Nofsinger et al., 2019) and because the strongest motivation for institutional investors to integrate ESG concerns in their investment decisions is the reputation protection they can gain by not investing in controversy-prone companies (Krueger et al., 2020). Our best ML model provides ESG information that meets these needs.

Our various studies have several limitations. First, we use models of the temporal distribution of data. Future modelling could use longitudinal designs with the aim of predicting future controversies. Second, our models do not consider whether controversies in the environmental, social, and governance categories differ from one another, which may introduce bias in the assessment of a company's likelihood of experiencing a controversy because different controversies may have different associations with ESG indicators. Third, we do not adjust the models for unequal media attention paid to companies. Company size and media attention are likely positively correlated, resulting in size-biased ratings. Future work to refine our rating methodology could investigate how to replace CS*R* controversies with a company-level wrongdoing index, which is a scaled and filtered metric of the wrongdoing signaled by controversies (cf. Fiaschi et al., 2020).

Despite these limitations, we argue that our ratings have more merit than the conventional method of simply aggregating ESG indicators. We demonstrate how moving away from explanatory to predictive modelling and how exploiting AI can make ESG a visible target to institutional investors. Future rating research might benefit from investigating how investment managers use additional information to construct supporting arguments for decisions based on ratings. As demonstrated, the importance of individual ESG indicators to the ML ratings can be described using ML models. This is not relevant to conventional ESG rating methodology because the relative importance of indicators does not reflect the relative importance of different features of CSP.

Acknowledgements We gratefully acknowledge the financial and material support from Länsförsäkringars Forskningsfond and the Asset Management Department at Länsförsäkringar. We are particularly indebted to Lars Höglund, Kristofer Dreiman, and Alexander Elfving for their valuable input to this research project.

References

Ambec S, Lanoie P (2008) Does it pay to be green? A systematic overview. *Academy of Management Perspectives, 22*, 45–62. https://doi.org/10.5465/amp.2008.35590353

Amir, A. Z., & Serafeim, G. (2018). Why and how investors use ESG information: Evidence from a global survey. *Financial Analysts Journal, 74*, 87–103. https://doi.org/10.2469/faj.v74.n3.2

Aupperle, K. (1984). An empirical measure of corporate social orientation. *Research in Corporate Social Performance and Policy, 6*, 27–54.

Berg, F., Kölbel, J., & Rigobon, R. (2019). Aggregate confusion: The divergence of ESG ratings. *SSRN Electron Journal*. https://doi.org/10.2139/ssrn.3438533

Bzdok, D., Altman, N., & Krzywinski, M. (2018). Points of significance: Statistics versus machine learning. *Nature Methods, 15*, 233–234. https://doi.org/10.1038/nmeth.4642

Callan, S.J., & Thomas, J. M. (2009). Corporate financial performance and corporate social performance: An update and reinvestigation. *Corporate Social Responsibility and Environmental Management, 16*, 61–78. https://doi.org/10.1002/csr.182

Capelle-Blancard, G., & Petit, A. (2019). Every little helps? ESG news and stock market reaction. *Journal of Business Ethics, 157*, 543–565. https://doi.org/10.1007/s10551-017-3667-3

Chatterji, A., & Levine, D. (2006). Breaking down the wall of codes: Evaluating non-financial performance measurement. *California Management Review, 48*, 29–51. https://doi.org/10.2307/41166337

Chatterji, A. K., Durand, R., Levine, D. I., & Touboul, S. (2016). Do ratings of firms converge? Implications for managers, investors and strategy researchers. *The Strategic Management Journal 37*, 1597–1614. https://doi.org/10.1002/smj.2407

Chen, C.-M., & Delmas, M. (2011). Measuring corporate social performance: An efficiency perspective. *Production and Operations Management, 20*, 789–804. https://doi.org/10.1111/j.1937-5956.2010.01202.x

Chiu, S. C., & Sharfman, M. (2018). Corporate social irresponsibility and executive succession: An empirical examination. *Journal of Business Ethics, 149*, 707–723. https://doi.org/10.1007/s10551-016-

Choi, D., Gao, Z., & Jiang, W. (2020). Global carbon divestment and firms' actions. *SSRN Electronic Journal*. https://doi.org/10.2139/ssrn.3589952

Collopy, F., Adya, M., & Armstrong, J. S. (1994). Principles for examining predictive validity: The case of information systems spending forecasts. *Information Systems Research, 5*, 170–179. https://doi.org/10.1287/isre.5.2.170

Cui, B, & Docherty, P. (2020). Stock price overreaction to ESG controversies. *Monash Centre for Financial Studies*. Retrieved from: https://papers.ssrn.com/sol3/papers.cfm?abstract_id=3559915

Deegan, C. (2019). Legitimacy theory: Despite its enduring popularity and contribution, time is right for a necessary makeover. *Accounting, Audit Account J, 32*, 2307–2329. https://doi.org/10.1108/AAAJ-08-2018-3638

Delmas, M. A., Etzion, D., & Nairn-Birch, N. (2013). Triangulating environmental performance: What do corporate social responsibility ratings really capture? *Academy of Management Perspectives, 27*, 255–267. https://doi.org/10.5465/amp.2012.0123

Ding, K., Lev, B., & Peng, X., Sun, T., & Vasarhelyi, M. A. (2020). Machine learning improves accounting estimates: evidence from insurance payments. *Review of Accounting Studies, 25*, 1098–1134. https://doi.org/10.1007/s11142-020-09546-9

Drempetic, S., Klein, C., & Zwergel, B. (2020). The influence of firm size on the ESG score: Corporate sustainability ratings under review. *Journal of Business Ethics, 167*, 333–360. https://doi.org/10.1007/s10551-019-04164-1

Earle, J. S., Spicer, A., & Peter, K.S. (2010). The normalization of deviant organizational practices: Wage arrears in Russia, 1991–98. *Academy of Management Journal, 53*, 218–237. https://doi.org/10.5465/amj.2010.49387426

EUROSIF. (2018). *European SRI study 2018*. Brussels, EUROSIF. Retrieved from: http://www.eurosif.org/eurosif-2018-sri-study-launch-event/

Fiaschi, D., Giuliani, E., & Nieri, F. (2017). Overcoming the liability of origin by doing no-harm: Emerging country firms' social irresponsibility as they go global. *Journal of World Business, 52*, 546–563. https://doi.org/10.1016/j.jwb.2016.09.001

Fiaschi, D., Giuliani, E., Nieri, F., & Salvati, N. (2020). How bad is your company? Measuring corporate wrongdoing beyond the magic of ESG metrics. *Business Horizons, 63*, 287–299. https://doi.org/10.1016/j.bushor.2019.09.004

Gond, J.-P., & Crane, A. (2010). Corporate social performance disoriented: Saving the lost paradigm? *Business & Society, 49*, 677–703. https://doi.org/10.1177/0007650308315510

Grappi, S., Romani, S., & Bagozzi, R. P. (2013). Consumer response to corporate irresponsible behavior: Moral emotions and virtues. *Journal of Business Research, 66*, 1814–1821. https://doi.org/10.1016/j.jbusres.2013.02.002

Groover, M. P. (2007). *Work systems: The methods, measurement & management of work*. Pearson Education International

Gurbaxani, V., & Mendelson, H. (1990). An integrative model of information systems spending growth. *Information Systems Research, 1*, 23–46. https://doi.org/10.1287/isre.1.1.23

Harmes, A. (2011). The limits of carbon disclosure: Theorizing the business case for investor environmentalism. *Glob Environ Polit, 11*, 98–119. https://doi.org/10.1162/GLEP_a_00057

Heo, J., & Yang, J. Y. (2014). AdaBoost based bankruptcy forecasting of Korean construction companies. *Applied Soft Computing, 24*, 494–499. https://doi.org/10.1016/j.asoc.2014.08.009

Hillman, A. J., Keim, G. D. (2001). Shareholder value, stakeholder management, and social issues: What's the bottom line? *Strategic Management Journal, 22*, 125–139. https://doi.org/10.1002/1097-0266(200101)22:2<125::AID-SMJ150>3.0.CO;2-H

Hügle, M., Omoumi, P., van Laar, J. M., et al. (2020). Applied machine learning and artificial intelligence in rheumatology. *Rheumatology Advances in Practice, 4*. https://doi.org/10.1093/rap/rkaa005

Krueger, P., & Sautner, Z., & Starks, L. (2020). Importance of climate risks for institutional investors. *The Review of Financial Studies, 33*:1067–1111.

Krüger, P. (2015). Corporate goodness and shareholder wealth. *Journal of Financial Economics, 115*, 304–329. https://doi.org/10.1016/j.jfineco.2014.09.008

Kruppa, J., Schwarz, A., Arminger, G., & Ziegler, A. (2013). Consumer credit risk: Individual probability estimates using machine learning. *Expert Systems with Applications, 40*, 5125–5131. https://doi.org/10.1016/j.eswa.2013.03.019

Luo, H.A., & Balvers, R. J. (2017). Social screens and systematic investor boycott risk. *Journal of Financial and Quantitative Analysis, 52*, 365–399. https://doi.org/10.1017/S0022109016000910

Margolis, J. D., Elfenbein, H. A., & Walsh, J. P. (2012). Does it pay to be good...and does it matter? A meta-analysis of the relationship between corporate social and financial performance. *SSRN Electronic Journal*. https://doi.org/10.2139/ssrn.1866371

Muller, A., & Kräussl, R. (2011). Doing good deeds in times of need: A strategic perspective on corporate disaster donations. *Strategic Management Journal, 32*, 911–929. https://doi.org/10.1002/smj.917

Nieri, F., & Giuliani, E. (2018). International business and corporate wrongdoing: A review and research agenda. In D. Castellan, R. Narula, Q. Nguyen et al. (Eds.), *Contemporary issues in international business* (pp. 35–53). Springer International Publishing.

Nofsinger, J. R., Sulaeman, J., & Varma, A. (2019). Institutional investors and corporate social responsibility. *Journal of Corporate Finance, 58*, 700–725. https://doi.org/10.1016/j.jcorpfin.2019.07.012

Öhman, P., & Wallerstedt, E. (2012). Audit regulation and the development of the auditing profession: The case of Sweden. *Accounting History, 17*, 241–257. https://doi.org/10.1177/1032373211434723

Oikonomou, I., Platanakis, E., & Sutcliffe, C. (2018). Socially responsible investment portfolios: Does the optimization process matter? *The British Accounting Review, 50*, 379–401. https://doi.org/10.1016/j.bar.2017.10.003

Orlitzky, M., Schmidt, F. L., & Rynes, S. L. (2003). Corporate social and financial performance: A meta-analysis. *Organization Studies, 24*, 403–441. https://doi.org/10.1177/0170840603024003910

Pedregosa, F et al. (2011). Scikit-learn: Machine learning in python. *Journal of Machine Learning Research, 12*, 2825–2810.

Renneboog, L., Ter Horst, J., & Zhang, C. (2008). The price of ethics and stakeholder governance: The performance of socially responsible mutual funds. *Journal of Corporate Finance, 14*, 302–322. https://doi.org/10.1016/j.jcorpfin.2008.03.009

Semenova, N., & Hassel, L. G. (2015). On the validity of environmental performance metrics. *Journal of Business Ethics, 132*, 249–258. https://doi.org/10.1007/s10551-014-2323-4

Sharfman, M. (1996). The construct validity of the Kinder, Lydenberg & Domini social performance ratings data. *Journal of Business Ethics, 15*, 287–296. https://doi.org/10.1007/BF00382954

Shmueli, G. (2010). To explain or to predict? *Statistical Science, 25*, 289–310. https://doi.org/10.1214/10-STS330

Sigrist, F., & Hirnschall, C. (2019). Grabit: Gradient tree-boosted Tobit models for default prediction. *Journal of Banking & Finance, 102*, 177–192. https://doi.org/10.1016/J.JBANKFIN.2019.03.004

Statman, M. (2006). Socially responsible indexes. *The Journal of Portfolio Management, 32*, 100–109.https://doi.org/10.3905/jpm.2006.628411

Surroca, J., Tribó, J. A., & Zahra, S. A. (2013). Stakeholder pressure on MNEs and the transfer of socially irresponsible practices to subsidiaries. *Academy of Management Journal, 56*, 549–572. https://doi.org/10.5465/amj.2010.0962

Svanberg, J., Ardeshiri, T., Samsten, I., Öhman, P., Rana, T., & Danielson, M. (2022). Prediction of environmental controversies and development of a corporate environmental performance rating methodology. *Journal of Cleaner Production, 342*, 130979. https://doi.org/10.1016/j.jclepro.2022.130979

Trumpp, C., Endrikat, J., Zopf, C., & Guenther, E. (2015). Definition, conceptualization, and measurement of corporate environmental performance: A critical examination of a multidimensional construct. *Journal of Business Ethics, 126*, 185–204. https://doi.org/10.1007/s10551-013-1931-8

USSIF. (2018). *Report on US sustainable, responsible and impact investing trends.* US SIF and US SIF Foundation. Retrieved from: https://www.ussif.org/files/Trends/Trends%202018%20executive%20summary%20FINAL.pdf

Wolfe, R. (1991). The use of content analysis to assess corporate social responsibility. *Res Corp Soc Perform Policy, 12*, 281–307.

Wood, D. J. (2010). Measuring corporate social performance: A review. *International Journal of Management Reviews, 12*, 50–84. https://doi.org/10.1111/j.1468-2370.2009.00274.x

Wokutch, R. E., & Spencer, B. A. (1987). Corporate saints and sinners: The effect of philanthropic and illegal activity on organizational performance. *Calif Manag Rev, 29*, 62–77.

Zavyalova, A., Pfarrer, M. D., Reger, R. K., & Shapiro, D. L. (2012). Managing the message: The effects of firm actions and industry spillovers on media coverage following wrongdoing. *Academy of Management Journal, 55*, 1079–1101. https://doi.org/10.5465/amj.2010.0608

Jan Svanberg, PhD, is an Associate Professor of Business Administration at University of Gävle, and associated with Centre for research on Economic Relations (CER), Sweden. He earned his PhD in Business Administration at Stockholm University, Sweden, and was recently a research fellow at RMIT University, Melbourne, Australia, for a period of two years. In addition to these studies, he has a diverse education with degrees in engineering, mathematics, and physics (M.Sc.) and law (LL.M). His current research focuses on how core problems in accounting, auditing and finance can be solved by interdisciplinary approaches with tools made available by advances in data science, especially machine learning.

Tohid Ardeshiri, PhD, is a Postdoctoral Fellow at the Division of Automatic Control at the Department of Electrical Engineering at Linköping University and Research fellow at the Centre for research on Economic Relations, Sweden. His research interests are in analytical approximations for and various aspects of Bayesian learning, such as variational Bayes, maximum entropy kernels for Gaussian process regression, and mixture reduction.

Isak Samsten, PhD, is a Senior Lecturer in the Department of Computer and Systems Sciences at Stockholm University, Sweden. His main research interest includes machine learning, especially focused on classification and interpretable machine learning, and on complex and temporal data.

Peter Öhman, PhD, is a Professor and Head of Business Administration at Mid Sweden University in Sundsvall, Sweden, and director of Centre for research on Economic Relations (CER). His research focuses on behavioral issues, primarily in accounting and auditing, but also in the banking and property industries. He has published a significant number of scholarly articles in leading academic journals, for example Contemporary Accounting Research, and Behavioural Research in Accounting. He has published books, book chapters and reports, and presented papers at international conferences. He has received international awards for excellent research, is a member of Editorial Boards, and a reviewer of several well-known international journals.

Presha Neidermeyer, PhD, is a Professor of Accounting at the West Virginia University, USA. She is a proud graduate of the West Virginia University College of Business & Economics and the Eberly College of Arts and Sciences. Her research investigates the way culture impacts auditor decision-making. She is serving as an ADVANCE Fellow and is coordinating the Women's Leadership Initiative on campus. Her philanthropic work includes collaborating with various groups both domestically and internationally to assist business growth primarily with micro businesses.

Chapter 5
Artificial Intelligence and Environmental, Social and Governmental Issues: A Current Perspective

Jonathan Fluharty-Jaidee and Presha Neidermeyer

Abstract This chapter analyses the potential impact of Artificial Intelligence on the opportunities to measure ESG, and the climate in which regulations of ESG disclosures are being set. To date, while many ratings agencies provide estimates of overall corporate ESG scores, the scoring systems lack accuracy. Several problems with the current ESG rating approach are identified and the prospect of using Artificial Intelligence to resolve them is discussed. In concluding the chapter, the use of Artificial Intelligence to predict deficient sustainability reporting practices caused by behavioral issues relating to incentives to improper sustainability reporting is identified.

Keywords Sustainability Reporting · ESG Ratings · Artificial Intelligence · Reporting Standards · Fraud Detection · Measurement Error

1 Introduction

2022 will be the year that Environmental, Social, and Governmental (ESG) reporting becomes more mainstream and begins moving markets, according to Aniket Shaw, who leads the Environmental, Social, and Governmental Reporting and Sustainability Research for Jeffries Global.[1] Investors are becoming more interested in these areas, and regulation is continuing to evolve for publicly traded companies. This chapter reports on the potential impact of Artificial Intelligence on ESG, and the current climate in which these regulations are being set. To date, while many ratings agencies provide estimates of overall corporate ESG scores, the scoring systems lack accuracy. Artificial Intelligence may hold a key to unlocking the true potential of ESG metrics

[1] https://news.yahoo.com/humans-most-important-asset-company-144347419.html.

J. Fluharty-Jaidee (✉)
Washington, DC, USA
e-mail: fluharty.jaidee@gmail.com

P. Neidermeyer
Department of Accounting, West Virginia University, Morgantown, WA, USA
e-mail: Presha.Neidermeyer@mail.wvu.edu

T. Rana et al. (eds.), *Handbook of Big Data and Analytics in Accounting and Auditing*,
https://doi.org/10.1007/978-981-19-4460-4_5

in firm valuation; however, ESG suffers from a crisis of poorly reported data—a crisis that could soon be abated.

In April 2021, Chairman of the Securities and Exchange Commission (SEC), Gary Gensler, announced that the commission would begin reviewing the use and disclosure of environmental, social, and governance-related materials in corporate financial statements. The Chairman further stated that the commission would move promptly in examine rulemaking in 2021.[2] In furtherance of these goals, the SEC accepted comments and public input on climate-change disclosures beginning on March 15, 2021.[3]

In the United States, disclosure of ESG-related information is not required; while many companies do provide ESG related information, most do not provide such disclosures within their official financial statements (e.g., 10-K filings).[4] Furthermore, no regulations govern what is—or isn't—an ESG-related disclosure, what is included in those disclosures, or how the disclosures are measured (Kaplan & Ramanna, 2021; Christen, Serafeim, and Sikochi 2022). By committing the SEC to regulating and standardization of ESG disclosure, Gensler's SEC has set the course for a revolution in ESG reporting and provided a strong indication that, within a very short time, these metrics will be required disclosure in annual reports.

As a result, the only questions that remain concern what will be reported and how. To a significant extent, reporting on governance-related issues has been plentiful for many years, as corporates often declare such information openly in their proxy statements (e.g., DEF14As), including information on the makeup of the board of directors (necessary when voting for the slate of directors), the level of board independence, and the existence of a lead independent director or CEO-Chairman duality, as well as through abundant reporting on compensation afforded to directors and executive officers (see, 17 CFR § 240.14a-101—Schedule 14A. Information required in proxy statement).

On the other hand, disclosures regarding environmental and social matters are legally obligated only when a significant risk, or contingency, exists for the corporation (Kaplan & Ramanna, 2021). Firms in certain industries retain accounts on liabilities or obligations against future (or current) environmental expenses. Corporates that face hazards of occupation (OSHA) may disclose and maintain significant accounts related to the likelihood of current (or future) labor settlements. These obligations already require disclosure, and often an explanation in the footnotes, if they are material to the overall financial disclosure (see, e.g., ASC 410–20 and ASC 410–30). Apart from these instances, US publicly traded corporations have no

[2] https://www.banking.senate.gov/imo/media/doc/Gensler%20Resp%20to%20QFRs%203-2-21.pdf.

[3] https://www.sec.gov/news/public-statement/lee-climate-change-disclosures.

[4] https://www.whitecase.com/publications/article/survey-and-depth-review-sustainability-disclosures-small-and-mid-cap-companies; https://www.thompsonhine.com/uploads/1135/doc/An_ESG_Snapshot.pdf.

requirement in reporting ESG disclosures under securities law, FASB standards, or US-GAAP (Katz & McIntosh, 2021).[5]

It is perhaps the lack of reporting requirements, the disparity in the willingness or capacity to report, and the paucity of rules on the measurement of ESG metrics that has created such discrepancies in ESG ratings (Chatterji et al., 2016). Should the requirements for ESG disclosures come to fruition, they would carry with them requirements of assurance and attestation as to the veracity of the figures and statements being reported (see PCAOB's AS 2710, *Other Information Documents Containing Audited Financial Statements*). This increased regulation and monitoring (by auditors) will have two predominant outcomes: (1) corporates will have a standard they must meet in reporting, at a minimum, the metrics and statements required under any new securities regulations, and (2) that those metrics and statements will be the same across corporations in their underlying measurement (Kaplan & Ramanna, 2021).

The first outcome will be of major benefit to nearly all market participants. Currently, any firm may decide whether it wishes to disclose a particular ESG-related issue. This "as you wish" paradigm has led to a sparsity of reporting comparable metrics across firms, even within the same sector or peer groups (Chatterji et al., 2016; Kotsantonis & Serafeim, 2019). This lack of comparable measures means that one-size-fits-all ESG ratings fail to truly capture the underlying sustainability and governance model of the firm (Aouadi & Marsat, 2018). For example, information on smaller companies has been relatively scant in the past,[6] but once all publicly traded firms are required to report specific metrics, there will be an increased ability of market participants to rate and ascertain how smaller firms perform in the sustainability space. Notably, however is that the more ESG data available. In turn, this cohesion across firms will improve the consistency of ESG ratings. Adding this requirement is not without drawbacks, however, as firms are likely to lobby against specific metrics and statements.[7] Some metrics will be chosen over others, which may reduce the variety of metrics reported. Thus, in favoring consistency, we may lose variety. This could lead to a reduction in reporting of potentially important issues for the sake of compliance (WEF, *Measuring Stakeholder Capitalism Report* 2020).

The second outcome will ensure that metrics and statements are rendered upon the same underlying conditions. It will also, naturally in most cases, require the substantiation of the reported ESG disclosure to be reviewed by an audit firm, as is the case with other financial disclosures (CAQ, *ESG Reporting and Attestation*, 2021). The impact upon audit engagements and attestations is outside the scope of this chapter, but the resulting increased monitoring ensures comparability of the

---

[5] While there is no requirement, the SEC has issued guidance on climate change related disclosures. https://www.sec.gov/rules/interp/2010/33-9106.pdf; additionally, IFRS established the International Sustainability Standards Board 'ISSB' in November 2021, to promulgate ESG disclosure requirements with the same governance authority as IASB.

[6] https://www.whitecase.com/publications/article/survey-and-depth-review-sustainability-disclosures-small-and-mid-cap-companies.

[7] https://news.bloomberglaw.com/securities-law/sec-climate-disclosure-push-brings-corporate-lobbying-flood.

specific ESG disclosures across firms (Kaplan & Ramanna, 2021). Previously, firms could report however they desired: there were limited requirements regarding how firms were to measure the figures reported in their disclosures, and such requirements existed only in specific circumstances (see, e.g., mineral sourcing and use disclosures *Sect. 1502, Dodd Frank Act*). As a result, a firm could report a carbon emission of 150,000 M-Tonnes, while another could report 75,000 M-Tonnes; yet there would be no consistency over what emissions were included in either count, and firms would rarely report how they obtained the numbers. As a result, reliance on this "honor system" has hampered the usability and consistency of ESG ratings, which has earned the entire field of ESG disclosures and their ratings agencies the consternation of academics (Berg et al., 2020; Chatterji et al., 2016; Doyle, 2018). Without consistency in the underlying metrics and statements, it is no wonder ESG ratings fail to converge or function as a valuation and pricing metric (Bruno et al., 2021; Li & Polychronopoulos, 2020; Taparia, 2021).

Despite its advantages, the new standardization will have potential drawbacks, chief among them being the costs to implement the new reporting requirements, and to assure, attest, or audit them. Yet, these unintended consequences will provide substantive financial benefit and social good (Freiberg et al., 2020). As Freiberg et al. (2020) points out, if socially responsible corporate activity is a favorable component of the efficient pricing dynamic and corporate investment strategies, corporations that outperform in the ESG field should—when compared to underperforming sustainability firms—experience temporary abnormal gains as the market re-prices in favor of the sustainable corporates (if the information is comparable). This improved information set will lead to a reduction in miss-pricing, and thereby improved market efficiency, as do most increases in required information disclosures, provided, of course, that investors can understand the implications of those disclosures (Chung, Hrazdil, & Suwanyangyuan, 2016; Chung & Suwanyangyuan, 2019). In this way, standardization will allow investors to make more-informed decisions in the allocation of funds, which may provide a supremely capitalistic means to affect social good, and in turn, the requirement of ESG disclosures in financial reports will cyclically improve the social welfare if investors favor sustainable firms over others.[8] Firms that do not "play the game" will suffer reduced access to equity financing, as their valuations decline relative to the more sustainable firms. As a result, there will become a risk to underperforming in environmental, social, and governance areas that may additionally impact firms' access to multiple financing sources such as through banking and bond markets (see, e.g., El Ghoul et al., 2011; Giese et al., 2019; Feng & Wu, 2022). Banks, for their part, routinely report sustainable finance initiatives and where they place their funds. As the ESG ratings improve following the required disclosures, banks may be less willing to provide funding to firms with lower ESG ratings, in much the same way they treat credit ratings.

[8] If investors favor sustainable firms over less-sustainable firms, firms that are perceived to be sustainable will have lower costs of capital and greater access to liquid capital markets. These capital accessibility gains would in-turn lead to increased sustainable investing—improving social welfare and, in theory, further increasing their access to lower cost capital. Furthermore, as the costs of capital decline, these firms become more profitable on a risk-adjusted basis.

While this may appear to have only positive benefits—i.e., net of the costs to implement the increased ESG disclosures—it may unfairly affect smaller firms. Not only is the cost to collect, examine, and report metrics for ESG more intrusive for smaller issuers, they may have fewer metrics to report at all.[9] This in turn could result in lower ESG ratings and impaired valuations or access to capital for these smaller issuers. Furthermore, as larger suppliers and customers seek to retain sustainability and ethical considerations along the entire value-chain, smaller reporters that lack the capacity to produce relevant metrics may be pushed out in favor of larger competitors. In this way, ESG reporting requirements may stifle innovation and cause market concentration, though it is left to be seen to what degree that may occur.[10]

Given that the above required disclosures will provide consistently reported metrics, with consistent measurement, across all firms, market participants will soon have the benefit of applying machine learning models to this forthcoming tsunami of high-quality data. The remainder of this chapter covers the possible improvements to measurements of ESG ratings brought about by the advent of artificial intelligence and the behavioral aspects of market participants in the context of the use of AI in ESG reporting, and concludes with the implications of artificial intelligence in ESG reporting.

The portion of institutional investors considering the divestment of CSR-non-compliant companies is growing rapidly. Early estimates held that about a quarter of market capital would have to be allocated according to such preferences to have any real effect on capital costs (Ambec & Lanoie, 2008). We are above that level, with the total amount of socially responsible investment (SRI) in 2018 being one in every four USD (USD 12 trillion) of investment in the USA and one in every two euros (EUR 22 trillion) in Europe (EUROSIF, 2018; USSIF, 2018). Such an important task as directing global capital towards sustainable projects requires a sophisticated navigation system. Unfortunately, there has been no good method to measure or rate the level of sustainable performance of individual companies. The most advanced measures of corporate social performance (CSP) are the environmental, social, and governance (ESG) ratings, which are considered the standard measures of CSP, i.e. the extent to which companies comply with compulsory CSR policies (cf. Oikonomou et al. 2018; Drempetic et al. 2020). A Google Scholar search on 4 October 2020 using the terms 'corporate social performance' and KLD (representing Kinder, Lydenberg, Domini) found 10,200 hits for one such rating.

As popular as ESG ratings are, their aggregation methodology has several shortcomings. First, research has found that aggregated ESG ratings are invalid (Chatterji et al., 2016; Delmas et al., 2013; Semenova & Hassel, 2015; Trumpp et al., 2015). These studies unequivocally concluded that the methodology with which information-rich ESG indicators are aggregated to form composite ratings is inappropriate for the broad, heterogenous, and nonlinear construct of CSP. Notably, the critique articulated in the cited studies does not claim that the ESG indicators do not contain a treasure trove of information about CSP, but that the methods with

[9] https://www.esgthereport.com/the-barriers-to-esg-reports-for-midsize-small-cap-companies/.

[10] https://www.sec.gov/spotlight/investor-advisory-committee-2012/esg-disclosure.pdf.

which indicators are aggregated and holistic ratings computed are far from accurate. Second, the ESG aggregation methodology does not generate ratings that meet the information needs of institutional investors. Nofsinger et al. (2019) found that these investors were indifferent to whether companies had features that were not compulsory environmental, social, or governance requirements, but were underweight stocks in companies that did not meet compulsory requirements. This information preference for compulsory CSR compliance is inconsistent with the lack of discrimination between obligatory and discretionary aspects of CSR produced with conventional ESG aggregation methodology. The aggregated ratings are an arithmetic average of both aspects (Chen & Delmas, 2011), making these ratings more or less irrelevant for informing investment decisions, even though the information underlying ESG indicators likely contains information that would be useful to institutional investors.

This chapter summarizes the findings of a research project using artificial intelligence (AI) to develop a new type of ESG rating methodology with predictive validity and relevance to institutional investors (see, e.g., Svanberg et al., 2022). Because of the broad, heterogenous, and nonlinear CSP concept, it is preferable to develop an ESG rating methodology using predictive rather than explanatory modelling. In this regard, we quote Wood (2010, p. 57): "CSP is a complex system and its measurement requires complex tools". Furthermore, a rating describes the state of a single observation (i.e. the performance of an individual company), which is what predictive modelling provides, whereas explanatory modelling generates relationships between variables generalizable to all observations, but no precise prediction of the state of a particular case. Deriving a rating is therefore an inappropriate task for explanatory modelling but an ideal application of predictive modelling with machine learning (ML).

The purpose of this chapter is to describe a rating methodology with which high-precision ESG ratings can be generated within a project including various studies. Because predictive validity and the choice of institutional-investor–relevant proxies for CSP are the keys to a rating that is useful to institutional investors, we discuss the proxies and their predictive performance on several performance measures.

2 Measurement

2.1 *Introduction to Measurement Errors*

Corporate Social Responsibility (CSR) is proxied through ESG metrics. Environmental, Social, and Corporate Governance are the three major factors that measure the social investment programs that firms undertake. Components of each of the areas must be weighted to form an aggregate score for each of the factors, and each of these factors is weighted to form the overall ESG score for a company.[11] The weighting

[11] https://www.thomsonreuters.com/content/dam/openweb/documents/pdf/tr-com-financial/methodology/corporate-responsibility-ratings.pdf.

schemes might seem straightforward at first because the relevance of the weighted indicators appear unquestionable but a high weight on one means a low weight on another and vice versa. The weights then actually define the composite construct and thus which companies and portfolios we find socially responsible. Nothing could be more problematic because, as we shall see, there is no objective foundation for the weights and therefore there can be no objective, or conceptually valid, ESG ratings.

The incremental measurement items, the ESG indicators, are meant to improve the overall scope of ESG measurement for a firm by incorporating various ESG features that intuitively point to overall sustainability. While many firms do report ESG metrics that are relevant to their industry type and business operations, the overall scores still suffer from an arbitrary weighting schedule because there is no method to determine objective, or mathematically speaking constrained, weights. Each ratings agency may choose from an unlimited set of weighting schemes between which there is no difference in validity.

In the face of this apparently unsurmountable obstacle many business data-analytics services, such as Reuters, Bloomberg, and MSCI, provide aggregate ESG measurements for firms; They seem to ignore that recent research by such research groups as Chatterji et al. (2016) have shown that these measurements lack convergent validity, making them unsuitable for e.g. finance research. Such lack of performance can be found in how badly ESG measurements predict asset returns. Several papers posit a positive relationship (i.e., increases in ESG ratings correlate to higher returns), while others cast doubt on such connections (Cao et al., 2018).

With arbitrary measures of ESG the relationship between return and ESG should be around zero on average, which is what the literature finds. Chatterji et al. (2016) argue that both firms and academics should address these problems in determining whether it is appropriate to use ESG measurements that are arbitrarily constructed. The arbitrary selection by reporting agencies of ESG score-component weights is where artificial intelligence can reduce inefficiencies in the measurement of ESG. The remainder of this section of the chapter will cover how ESG measurement can be improved through the use of artificial intelligence.

2.2 How AI Can Improve Measurement Problems

Many researchers have noted that artificial intelligence (AI) could improve ESG measurements in many ways: starting by potentially automating the collection of data needed for reporting ESG metrics. Admittedly this is an appropriate use of AI, yet it is perhaps not the most significant use. The more ESG data available about a company the greater the ESG score inconsistence between ratings agencies Christensen et. al., 2022), which suggests that it is not the amount of data that is the essence of ESG scores but the aggregation of data to scores. AI can be used to reduce the errors not only in the collection of data but also in the aggregation of the measurements because of the ability of such methods to perceive information in complex patterns of data. Machine learning can help to relate the abundance of ESG data for a particular company to a benchmark, or objective foundation on which to anchor a weighting scheme and therefore avoid the high degree of arbitrariness in traditional ESG scores.

2.2.1 ESG Measured Against a Benchmark

To fix the weights appropriately, the provider or constructor of the ESG score would need to fit it against an external benchmark that provides a source of validity to the holistic metric. For the finance industry the external benchmark is always returns on the firm or long-run market performance. It might seem awkward that sustainable business could only be counted as company returns or equity price growth because it is highly unlikely that all effects on the environment or the society of a business would impact these metrics. It might also be strange that the long run would have to be as long as 10 to 50 years because it is in that time horizon that technological paradigms shift, e.g. energy sources are phased out. Looking 10 to 50 years back in time, however, is like looking at a different universe and businesses change for so many reasons in this time that it is questionable whether return on equity within a firm or on the stock market can be seen as representing ESG-related effects. Furthermore, as ESG measures have recently shown, such fitted values, when used in investing, tend not to bear out over time. The reason for this problem might be difficulties with the fitting process rather than the lack of relationship between features and long-run returns. If this is so, then AI offers more complex models with which the fitting can become more non-linear and more allowing for interaction effects. In addition to this there are the option, described in the chapter by Svanberg and colleagues in this book, to divert from the common practices in the finance industry and anchor the ESG ratings on a measure of the extent that the rated companies comply with ESG responsibilities. With the latter approach the ESG scores contain information completely 'out of sample' in relation to what is conventionally regarded as financial information.

AI can improve the outcomes also of a more financially traditional ESG score construction if the underlying relationship between CSR activities and long-run financial performance exists. ESG indicators' significance would then be determined by a machine learning model that predicts or regresses a variable of interest that would be return on assets or long-run market-adjusted return. It is even possible to do this analysis with ridge or elastic net regressions, these analyses assume linear relationships where the relationship between ESG and other variables in the corporate world may be highly cointegrated or non-linear.[12]

As a result, supervised machine learning may be the most efficient method for determining ESG scores because some such methods are suited for complex relationships between indicators and predicted outcome variable. An appropriate method for analyzing such a calculation would be to fit a set of features on long-run market performance and select the features that have the highest level of importance based

[12] Econometricians would refer to this as the problems of endogeneity or multicollinearity.

on some threshold. The weights of this prediction or regression model can be understood as representing the explanation of the model's ESG scoring. Only some models have explicit weights in the sense of regression coefficients, so the actual interpretation must be achieved with a local feature importance assessment methodology, preferably the Shapley value-based SHAP method by Lundberg and Lee (2017), for further information see also Lundberg et al. (2019), which outputs the individual contributions from indicators and categories to the ESG score. Because it is benchmarked against long-run market performance, this ESG score should predict long-run market performance. The model's performance can therefore be evaluated regarding its ability to predict the market performance, and evidence is obtained as predictive validity. The approach offers the substantial advantage compared to currently popular ESG ratings because there is no evidence in the literature that traditional ratings from leading ratings agencies would have any type of validity.

2.2.2 A Credit Score Approach

An alternative method of using AI to improve ESG scores would be to train the AI based on human-rated ESG data. This scoring method is, of course, biased towards the individual rater's determination as to what is good ESG and what is bad, as well as the incremental relevance of importance of each component, and it is likely appropriate to use multiple raters to mitigate these effects. This approach has been attempted several times in the past and has been rejected in the literature because it is impractical and because it does not solve the underlying arbitrariness problem (cf. Callan & Thomas, 2009). It benefits, however, from allowing a human to control the direction in which the scoring occurs.

A human-scorer could give a rating to the ESG score similar to how a credit rating agency provides a corporation's credit rating. Based on various corporate metrics—typically related to cash flow, debt levels, and prior history of payments—credit rating agencies provide a score to a corporation of AAA, AA, BBB, BB, etc., based on the risk that the corporation has in repaying their debt. Similarly, a rater could score corporations based on ESG component metrics. Using the scores, an AI algorithm can be trained based on this manually scored ESG set and apply that trained model onto a set of unscored firms. The ML model predicts scores for these firms based on the scores provided by the manual human scorers.

There is a major issue with this methodology: As previously mentioned, the scores mirror the preferences of the rater, which means that the ratings are in effect determined by one person's or a few persons' individual preferences. This fact can lead many investors to wonder what exactly constituted the score and they may default to calling the method a "black box" or an arbitrary rating method with zero legitimacy. Investors tend not to prefer black-box investment criteria or to consider ESG that does not provide their investments legitimacy as a guarantee that they take their responsibilities as responsible investors, and are therefore unlikely to use such scores. Agency-provider scores provide the weights used to construct their ESG ratings but because the reasons for weights are unknown or not comprehensible in terms of how investors think of ESG responsibilities the scores still do not offer any comprehensible interpretation.

Moreover, this method is less preferable than using the market-benchmark model proposed in Sect. 2.2.1, which can be seen as the efficient equilibrium outcome of many raters voting on the ESG rating through market dynamics. If CSR is a major component in investing, then, in the long run, firms that do a lot of CSR will outperform firms that do not do CSR, *ceteris paribus*. Thereby, provided markets are efficient, the overall market performance is an efficient barometer for the economic value of CSR in firms that incorporate all investors' expectations of the value of CSR as it contributes to the self-serving purpose the firms pursue. Hence, in theory, the benchmark method would provide a model with stronger information realization than the scoring based on a few individuals, at least the information about the ability of the firms to convert CSR activities and reporting to money.

In practice, ESG ratings providers will likely incorporate both types of model frameworks, attenuating the market-benchmark based on the scoring of individual "expert" analysts. Leading rating agencies, however, produce their ratings with linear models (Berg et al., 2019) disabling these ratings' effectiveness and there seems to be no evidence that weights are truly the outcome of a market prediction framework. Furthermore, there is no evidence in the literature that the ratings provided by these agencies would predict market performance or that they would in any other conceivable way be valid estimates of the firms' sustainability. The underlying logic of traditional ESG scores is therefore questionable.

Artificial intelligence can provide substantive improvements over ESG scores constructed in the traditional manner by improving the overall relevance and performance of the measures, allowing investors to trust the results to a greater extent. This new disclosure environment presents increasing opportunities for the use of AI, and its use in the CSR arena is not limited to improvements on measurements alone, as it can also be used to determine when firms are fraudulent in their disclosures about the actual amount of CSR that they perform, as discussed below.

3 Behavioral ESG and AI

3.1 Introduction to Behavioral Implications of ESG

Contrary to the logic of ESG metrics, i.e. ESG as a way of making money, managers may view socially responsible investing as being less valuable or producing lower profit for them in the short term. Because managers are subject to pay incentives tied to profitability, managers may be discouraged from investing in socially responsible ways if that reduces short-term profitability.

This disconnect between the incentives that managers face to produce profit for the firm and its shareholders' desire for socially responsible investments is an agency problem specific to CSR. Reducing the agency costs for management is important to consider, but so is the monitoring of management in determining whether their reporting of socially responsible investing (SRI) is accurate.

Managers are incentivized—directly or indirectly—to report SRI. Knowing that investors prefer SRI, but also knowing that SRI produces lower profitability in the short run, managers may report higher levels of SRI while *under*-investing in these activities. This suggests a level of fraudulent behavior on behalf of management. Nevertheless, finding when managers are lying about their SRI is rather difficult. This is where artificial intelligence can be a major benefit to socially responsible investors. While an individual may find it difficult to fetter out whether a manager is lying about their socially responsible investing, a computer can predict the probability that management may be lying and flag to the investor that something is amiss.

3.2 Using AI to Identify Behavioral Issues with CSR Fraud

Identifying whether a manager is lying about their actual investment in socially responsible practices involves either identifying prior issues of fraud and trying to predict whether the current managers fall into these categories, or by comparing the measures of corporate social responsibility of that particular firm against the predicted ESG measures that its characteristics would suggest. In the first method, if a particular firm was identified to have committed fraud with respect to the reporting of their CSR investments, then that firm's attributes could be used in predicting the occurrence of fraud in other companies. Machine learning is adept at discerning patterns humans are unable to perceive. A machine-learning classification system could be used to identify managers who are likely committing fraud at the current time.

Already artificial intelligence is being used in this way to identify fraud in auditing and tax practices.[13] Prior incidences of fraud are being used as a baseline categorical classification for when fraud has occurred. Machine-learning models are trained on the difference between firms that did commit fraud and those that did not, and new firms are then evaluated using these trained models. If a model predicts that a firm is committing fraud, it does not necessarily mean that the firm is committing fraud per se, but it warrants further investigation.

The identification of fraud in accounting has been improved using artificial intelligence, and there is a large stream of literature to support this. Fraud investigators have deployed a wide range of machine-learning programs to varying degrees of success in identifying accounting fraud in the reporting of financial statements and tax fraud on behalf of the IRS. In much the same way, machine learning can be applied to identify cases where managers say they have been investing in CSR practices but are under-investing due to the conflicts in incentives. There are two methods to achieve this goal.

---

[13] https://stahlesq.com/irs-artificial-intelligence-detects-tax-evaders/.

The first method requires distinguishing firms that historically underinvested in CSR practices, but where management disclosed higher levels of investment, from those that invested the actual amount that they stated or disclosed in their reports. Using this bifurcated sample, one can train a machine-learning model based on selected firm features to predict when a manager may lie about their SRI levels.

The second method of classification is to predict the appropriate ESG score based on various features of the firm. Rather than assuming the ESG metrics provided by the firm are correctly constructed, an ESG score based on other features of the firms, such as their profitability, number of employees, employee turnover, etc., can be used to predict what the ESG score *should* be. These predicted ESG scores then could be used to construct dispersions of the ESG score reported based on core ESG metrics and the predicted ESG score. When the two scores do not agree, it points to a misalignment between the reported value and what would otherwise be predicted based on other metrics. Either solution is quite tractable and easy to construct provided a reasonable data set.

3.3 Identifying Bias in CSR Proclamations

Another area where artificial intelligence can significantly improve the analysis of CSR is identifying where managers have a bias in their CSR proclamations. For example, managers may directly lie about the amount of corporate social responsibility that they are undertaking, or they may make announcements that exaggerate their firm's CSR practices. We can try to identify where the managers are lying, but we can also use machine learning to determine whether proclamations about corporate social responsibility are living up to reality.

A facet of CSR is that firms need to publicly identify SR investing or it provides little benefit to the firm. As a result, the press announcements of corporate social responsibility are as important as the activity itself, and the announcements provide a wealth of information as to the legitimate nature of the CSR practice. They can also shed light on how management views the practice of SR investing, and whether it is aligned with the manager's core strategic focus.

AI can be used to analyze the tone, sentiment, diction, and impact of media announcements regarding CSR investment by firms. These features of announcements can be tied to target outcome variables—such as return on the announcement event, or long-term investment return of the firm—to identify profitability in making the CSR announcement and whether one can believe certain aspects of the news releases.

A great deal of research focuses on how managers abuse news releases when lying about their actual actions (see Larcker & Zakolyukina, 2012 for a review). To brush over controversial topics, they will use difficult but general language to get the point across, as a means of obscuring what they are describing. When managers prioritize CSR investment and undertake it sincerely, we expect they will communicate their SRI directly and clearly and indicate their benefits for shareholder value.

AI can benefit investors by making it easier to determine whether or not news announcements are credible. Applying these artificial-intelligence analyses to determine whether CSR news announcements are credible or not can provide investors with easy access to information.

References

Aouadi, A., & Marsat, S. (2018). Do ESG controversies matter for firm value? Evidence from international data. *Journal of Business Ethics., 151*, 1027–1047.

Berg, F., Kolbel, J. F., & Rigobon, R. (2020). *Aggregate confusion: The divergence of ESG ratings*. Corporate Governance & Finance.

Brown, S., Hinson, L. A., & Tucker. J. W. (2021). *Financial statement adequacy and firms' MD&A disclosures* (SSRN Working Paper).

Bruno, G., Esakia, M., & Goltz, F. (2021). Honey, I Shrunk the ESG Alpha: Risk-adjusting ESG portfolio returns. *The Journal of Investing.*

Callan, S., & Thomas, J. (2009). Corporate financial performance and corporate social performance: An update and reinvestigation. *Corporate Social Responsibility and Environmental Management, 16*(2), 61–87.

Cao, J., Titman, S., Zhan, X., & Zhang, W. (2020). *ESG preference, institutional trading, and stock return patterns* (NBER Working Paper Series).

CAQ. (2021). *ESG reporting and attestation: A roadmap for audit practitioners*. Center for Audit Quality.

Chatterji, A. K., Durand, R., Levine, D. I., & Touboul, S. (2016). Do ratings of firms converge? Implications for managers, investors and strategy researchers. *Strategic Management Journal., 37*(8), 1597–1614.

Chen, C. M., & Delmas, M. (2011). Measuring corporate social performance: An efficiency perspective. *Production and Operations Management, 20*(6), 789–804. https://doi.org/10.1111/j.1937-5956.2010.01202.x

Christensen, D. M., Serafeim, G., & Sikochi, A. (2022). Why is corporate virtue in the eye of the beholder? The case of ESG ratings. *The Accounting Review., 97*(1), 147–175.

Chung, D. Y., Hrazdil, K., & Suwanyangyuan, N. (2016). Disclosure quantity and the efficiency of price discovery: Evidence from the Toronto Stock Exchange. *Review of Accounting and Finance, 15*(2), 122–143.

Chung, D. Y., Hrazdil, K., Novak, J., & Suwanyangyuan, N. (2019). *Journal of Contemporary Accounting & Economics, 15*(1), 36–52.

Delmas, M. A., Etzion, D., & Nairn-Birch, N. (2013). Triangulating environmental performance: What do corporate social responsibility ratings really capture? *Academy of Management Perspectives, 27*(3), 255–267. https://doi.org/10.5465/amp.2012.0123

Doyle, T. M. (2018). *Ratings that don't rate: the subjective world of ESG ratings agencies*. American Council for Capital Formation.

Edmans, A. (2011). Does the stock market fully value intangibles? Employee satisfaction and equity prices. *Journal of Financial Economics., 101*(3), 621–640.

El Ghoul, S., Guedhami, O., Kwok, C., & Mishra, D. R. (2011). Does corporate social responsibility affect the cost of capital. *Journal of Banking & Finance., 35*(9), 2388–2406.

EUROSIF. (2018). *European SRI study 2018*. Retrieved November 14, 2022 from https://www.eurosif.org/news/eurosif-2018-sristudy-is-out/

Feng, Z., & Wu, Z. (2022). ESG disclosure, REIT debt financing and firm value. *The Journal of Real Estate Finance and Economics.*

Freiberg, D., Rogers, J., & Serafeim, G. (2020). *How ESG issues become financially material to corporations and their investors* (Harvard Business School Working Paper Series).

Giese, G., Lee, L. E., Melas, D., Nagy, Z., & Nishikawa, L. (2019). Foundations of ESG investing: How ESG affects equity valuation, risk, and performance. *The Journal of Portfolio Management., 45*(5), 65–83.

Kaplan, R. S. & Ramanna, K. (2021). *How to fix ESG reporting* (Harvard Business School Working Paper Series).

Katz, D., & McIntosh, L. A. (2021). Corporate governance update: "Materiality" in America and Abroad. *New York Law Journal.*

Kotsantonis, S., & Serafeim, G. (2019). Four things no one will tell you about ESG data. *Journal of Applied Corporate Finance, 31*(2), 50–58.

Larcker, D., & Zakolyukina, A. (2012). Detecting deceptive discussions in conference calls. *Journal of Accounting Research., 50*(2), 495–540.

Li, F., & Polychronopoulos, A. (2020). What a difference an ESG ratings provider makes! *Research Affiliates*, 24.

Lundberg, S. M., & Lee, S. I. (2017). A unified approach to interpreting model predictions. *Advances in Neural Information Processing Systems (NIPS), 30*, 4768–4777.

Lundberg, S. M., Erion, G., Chen, H., DeGrave, A., Prutkin, J. M., Nair, B., … & Lee, S. I. (2019). *Explainable AI for trees: From local explanations to global understanding*. ArXiv, abs/1905.04610.

Nofsinger, J. R., Sulaeman, J., & Varma, A. (2019). Institutional investors and corporate social responsibility. *Journal of Corporate Finance, 58*, 700–725, S0929119918304395. https://doi.org/10.1016/j.jcorpfin.2019.07.012

Svanberg, J., Ardeshiri, T., Samsten, I., Öhman, P., Neidermeyer, P. E., Rana, T., ... & Danielson, M. (2022). Corporate governance performance ratings with machine learning. *Intelligent Systems in Accounting Finance and Management, 29*(1), 50–68. https://doi.org/10.1002/isaf.1505

Semenova, N., & Hassel, L. G. (2015). On the validity of environmental performance metrics. *Journal of Business Ethics, 132*(2), 249–258. https://doi.org/10.1007/s10551-014-2323-4

Taparia, H. (2021). The world may be better off without ESG investing. *Stanford Social Innovation Review.* https://doi.org/10.48558/PC0C-TV52

Trumpp, C., Endrikat, J., Zopf, C., & Guenther, E. (2015). Definition conceptualization and measurement of corporate environmental performance: A critical examination of a multidimensional construct. *Journal of Business Ethics, 126*(2), 185–204. https://doi.org/10.1007/s10551-013-1931-8

USSIF. (2018). *Report on US sustainable, responsible and impact investing trends*. Retrieved November 14, 2022 from https://www.ussif.org/files/Trends/Trends%202018%20executive%20summary%20FINAL.pdf

Wood, D. J. (2010). Measuring corporate social performance: A review. *International Journal of Management Reviews, 12*(1), 50–84. https://doi.org/10.1111/j.1468-2370.2009.00274.x

World Economic Forum. (2020). *Measuring stakeholder capitalism: Towards common metrics and consistent reporting of sustainable value creation.* https://www.weforum.org/reports/measuring-stakeholder-capitalism-towards-common-metrics-and-consistent-reporting-of-sustainable-value-creation

Jonathan Fluharty-Jaidee, Ph.D., is a staff economist at a financial markets regulator. The views expressed in this chapter are the views of the author and do not necessarily reflect the views of the author's employer or any other entities with which the author may be associated. He has previously served as the Assistant Department Chair of Finance and Clinical Assistant Professor of Finance at West Virginia University, and as a Visiting Assistant Professor of Accounting and Finance at Clarkson University. As a researcher, he studies executive compensation, incentive alignment, agency theory and information games, and audit practices. His current work focuses in Critical Audit Matters (CAMs), a component of audit reports every auditor of a publicly listed company must provi de to explain issues in the audit that required significant judgement. He also focuses on Environmental, Social and Governance (ESG) reporting disclosures and metrics as it relates to auditors.

Presha Neidermeyer, Ph.D, is a Professor of Accounting at the West Virginia University, USA. She is a proud graduate of the West Virginia University College of Business & Economics and the Eberly College of Arts and Sciences. Her research investigates the way culture impacts auditor decision-making. She is serving as an ADVANCE Fellow and is coordinating the Women's Leadership Initiative on campus. Her philanthropic work includes collaborating with various groups both domestically and internationally to assist business growth primarily with micro businesses.

Chapter 6
Sweet Spots or Dark Corners? An Environmental Sustainability View of Big Data and Artificial Intelligence in ESG

Beatrice Crona and Emma Sundström

Abstract This chapter examines environmental aspects of ESG and risks and opportunities for using big data (BD) and artificial intelligence (AI) to capture these in ESG ratings. It starts by outlining the difference between relative and absolute sustainability and what this means for delivering on globally agreed upon targets, such as the Sustainable Development Goals. We then look at what the state-of-the-art climate and Earth System science has to offer investors interested in absolute environmental sustainability. Next, we discuss the risks associated with a blurring of concepts relating to sustainability and materiality, and examine and contrast conventional ESG rating procedures with new approaches informed by BD and AI to understand what this new generation of tools can offer investors interested in sustainability. We note a current misalignment between stated ambitions of investors, and the ability to deliver on stated goals through the use of current ESG metrics and ratings. We therefore finish with suggestions for how to better align these and how those interested in ESG can become more 'sustainability savvy' consumers of such ratings.

Keywords Absolute Sustainability · ESG ratings · Financial Materiality · Biological Diversity · Earth System

1 Introduction

Environmental, social, and governance (ESG) related topics have never been more central to the investment conversation. Friede et al. (2015) found over 2000 studies relating ESG to corporate financial performance since 1970, and mutual funds and exchange-traded funds designated as sustainable by Morningstar attracted $46 billion

B. Crona (✉)
Royal Swedish Academy of Sciences, Stockholm, Sweden
e-mail: beatrice.crona@su.se

E. Sundström
Stockholm Resilience Centre, Stockholm University, Stockholm, Sweden
e-mail: emma.sundstrom@su.se

T. Rana et al. (eds.), *Handbook of Big Data and Analytics in Accounting and Auditing*,
https://doi.org/10.1007/978-981-19-4460-4_6

of inflows in the first quarter of 2020, with a notable increase in the US.[1] It is highly likely that the recent pandemic and increasing frequency of climate change related fires and other natural disasters have further spurred this development.

This chapter examines environmental aspects of ESG, but the insights may also apply to social sustainability as well. Our analysis is premised on the assumption that absolute environmental sustainability can only be achieved when societies and economies curb negative impacts on the climate and biosphere. The biosphere refers to the Earth's ecosystems, comprised of all living things. By 'absolute' we deliberately focus on the limits to the anthropogenic pressure the planet can sustain before its ability to support our economies and societies is significantly undermined (Bjørn et al., 2020; Chandrakumar & McLaren, 2018). This differs from the relative approach adopted in current ESG investment practices that compare companies on the basis of within-sector performance (best-in-class or negative screening) (GSIA, 2018; Rockström et al., 2020). It also contrasts with broadly accepted views of environmental risk and materiality in the investment community, and we return to this important issue in later sections.

We start with a look at what the state-of-the-art climate and Earth System science can offer investors interested in absolute environmental sustainability. Next, we discuss the risks associated with conceptual blurring of sustainability and materiality, then contrast conventional ESG rating procedures with new approaches informed by big data (BD) and artificial intelligence (AI) to understand what this new generation of tools can offer. We conclude that the stated ambitions of investors cannot be delivered by current ESG metrics and ratings, and suggest how investors can become more 'sustainability savvy' consumers of such ratings.

2 Relative or Absolute Environmental Sustainability

The past decade's growing awareness of environmental risk among investors and companies began with a focus on reporting and monitoring of greenhouse gas (GHG) emissions and capture. However, a growing body of scientific evidence suggests that a stable climate, and an environment where humans can continue to thrive, is determined not only by emissions. Complex interactions between large-scale, bio-geo-physical processes such as forest and other vegetation dynamics, global hydrological flows, and radiative forcing (Lenton et al., 2019; Steffen et al., 2018) also play a role. Land use determines vegetation types and storage of carbon in aboveground biomass, but also in the soil where vast amounts lay captured (IPCC, 2019; Scharlemann et al., 2014). Land use also affects moisture recycling at local, regional and global scales (Gleeson et al., 2020; Wang-Erlandsson et al., 2018), affecting the potential for climate change mitigation by affecting productivity and carbon capture capacity of the land (Lal, 2008; Post & Kwon, 2000). These examples represent only a fraction of the dense network of interactions between so called Earth system

[1] https://blogs.cfainstitute.org/investor/2020/07/20/esg-at-a-tipping-point/.

processes for which evidence exists (Lade et al., 2020; Lenton, 2016), but they show that climate stability hinges on the interaction of many planetary processes—beyond carbon emissions.

An additional complexity emerges from the fact that many of these Earth system processes determining climate change and biosphere integrity exhibit threshold dynamics (also referred to as tipping points, see e.g. Lenton et al., 2019). These tipping points are associated with certain regions of the Earth, and include melting of large ice sheets and sea ice in the polar regions, sudden large-scale change of vegetation cover, including loss of tropical forests, and alteration of oceanic currents (Pachauri et al., 2014; Wuebbles et al., 2017). Combining current observations, with past records and climate models, research shows these regions are likely to flip to new states abruptly and with little immediate warning (Lenton et al., 2019; Steffen et al., 2018). When they do, the change in internal dynamics creates feedbacks that perpetuate the new state, which subsequently causes climate or other global environmental change, through various mechanisms (see Box 1).

Corporate and financial communities increasingly acknowledge the importance of multiple environmental risk factors, such as water and biodiversity in addition to carbon emissions (e.g. Global Reporting Initiative (GRI), Sustainability Accounting Standards Board (SASB), Carbon Disclosure Project (CDP), Science-Based Targets Initiative (SBTi). However, the impact of corporate operations on climate, and associated processes like water cycling and biodiversity, is still not well articulated, or accounted for, in dominant risk frameworks [Taskforce on Climate-related Financial Disclosures, TCFD], Buhr, 2017). As such, risk and materiality continues to be conceptualized and measured as risks to the financial sector from some external source. Yet the way in which companies, and their investors, affect absolute sustainability is through their impacts on the environment, via unpriced environmental and social externalities. Measures purported to help address sustainability by reallocating capital to 'sustainable' businesses should therefore (arguably) aim to capture the environmental impacts of these operations.

A simple example links this assertion to the preceding sections on Earth System dynamics. Companies operating in the Brazilian beef and soy industry, directly affecting one of the Earth System tipping points referred to above. Most company assessments by investors focus on, and measure, environmental risk as the reputational, or even litigation, risk if a company is caught with deforestation-associated products in their supply chains (Drost et al., 2019). Another common risk assessed is the future risk to the company of stricter deforestation policies (see James, 2001 for discussion of political risks and Sjåfjell, 2020 for wider discussion of financial risks). Investors would normally also consider effects on production from extreme weather events. Current risk analyses by investors will generally not, however, consider the fact that deforestation associated with company practices directly contributes to bringing the Amazon rainforest closer to a tipping point, in which it turns to savanna with repercussions for rain fed agriculture in the entire region (Lovejoy and Galaz et al., 2018; Nobre, 2018), but also detrimental effects on global warming and spillover-effects on rainfall patterns in other parts of the world where they are also invested (Wang-Erlandsson et al., 2018). The latter might contribute to increasing

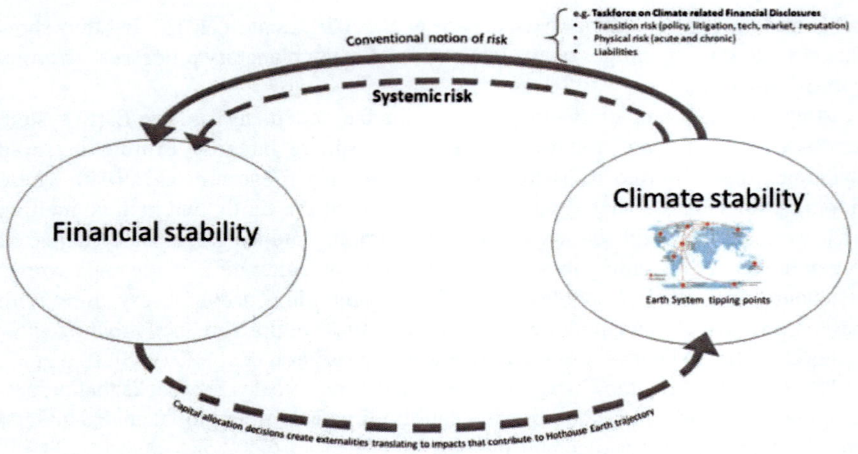

Fig. 1 Closing the cognitive 'risk loop' for sustainable investments (*Solid arrows* = perception of risk by most conventional financial sector risk frameworks. *Dashed arrows* = the 'risk loop' that needs to be acknowledged and incorporated in risk management)

likelihood of systemic failure (Helbing, 2013; Sjåfjell, 2020), as well as acute physical risks. This example illustrates that while risk is affecting companies and investors (Lovejoy and Galaz et al., 2018; Nobre, 2018), it is also directly affected by their actions (Aglietta & Espagne, 2016; Hawley & Lukomnik, 2018). Cognitively closing the 'risk loop' in Fig. 1 means recognizing the direct influence of capital allocation decisions on absolute sustainability and on the risk landscape of the financial sector.

Box 1. Resilience in Reality
Soft commodity trade and the tipping of the Amazon

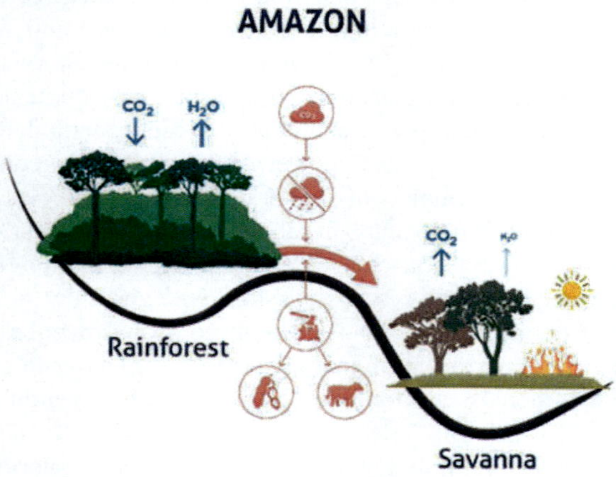

The integrity of the Amazon is threatened by the combined effects of deforestation and climate change. Climate change reduces rainfall, and causes recurrent droughts and floods (Duffy et al., 2015), while deforestation undermines the capacity of remaining forest to generate its own rain, through trees 'breathing' and thus recycling water. There is a threshold beyond which the loss of forest area will very likely cause the Amazon to tip into a Savanna (Steffen et al., 2018; Yang et al., 2018). Savannas are a completely different ecosystem; naturally drier and less diverse, which store less carbon and burn much more easily and frequently. Therefore, if the Amazon tips it will go from being a carbon sink that stores carbon and helps mitigate warming, to a carbon source that contributes to increased temperatures (Steffen et al., 2018; Yang et al., 2018).

The loss of the Amazon is more than the loss of one ecosystem and its biodiversity. It will affect the stability of the climate as a whole, as well as rainfall patterns and agricultural production far beyond Brazilian borders (Koh et al., 2020; Spera et al., 2020; Swann et al., 2015). Most notably it will affect agricultural production in surrounding South American nations, but even as far as the Congo basin (Wang-Erlandsson et al., 2018). The economic activities most important for driving current Amazon deforestation are cattle ranching and soy production, followed by mining and timber extraction (Ometto et al., 2011; Sonter et al., 2017). Since Brazil's Soy Moratorium in 2006, deforestation drastically slowed down, but has been rising since 2015. Soy and meat production are linked in complex ways, as soybean expansion onto previously cleared land is increasing the incentives to clear more, and pushing cattle pastures into pristine rainforest (Barona et al., 2010)

3 What Is Material?

The word 'material' has multiple meanings, but the one of relevance here is defined in most English language dictionaries as "having real importance or great consequences" for a given situation or outcome. Materiality therefore encompasses issues of importance from a particular perspective, and defining this perspective, and hence what materiality specifically refers to, is essential for understanding what ESG is, or should, be.

The concept of ESG grew out of a socially responsible investment movement emerging already in the 1960's, and early versions were motivated by a belief in sustainable development, adopted a systems view, and focused on capturing absolute assessments of corporate externalities (Eccles et al., 2020). As the interest in ESG issues rose in the wake of the 2004 UN Global Compact report (Kell, 2018) the focus of mainstream ESG frameworks shifted away from being impact-oriented, towards financial materiality (see Eccles et al., 2020 for a full historical account). This is reflected in how SASB (Sustainability Accounting Standards Board) now uses ESG to address only that which is seen to be financially material to a business.[2] Put differently, SASB and most financial actors (including the TCFD), consider ESG issues to be those that in some way pose a risk to the businesses in which they invest. Yet, impact materiality has not disappeared from the agenda. It remains a topic of consideration among influential actors like the Global Reporting Initiative (GRI).

Studies which show that investing in financially material sustainability issues leads to financial outperformance, have become very influential and much cited (Khan et al., 2016). Such findings have reinforced a narrative of an emerging win–win situation, where doing good for the environment and reporting on the things that matters to one's company and sector is synonymous with financial logic and economic outperformance. Yet these same analyses simultaneously find that investments in financially immaterial sustainability issues do not lead to better financial outcomes, and may in fact detract from performance. This, in turn, has effectively relegated externalities from the agenda.

Analyses such as Kahn et al. (2016) are based on financial materiality, yet in investment-related fora are often referred to simply as materiality. As a result, over time, the important distinction between financial versus impact materiality (which is the true indication of how environmentally sustainable a company is) has been obscured, as has the fact that reporting on, and accounting for, environmental impact often has a real and tangible cost. A similar blurring has therefore occurred with regards to ESG and what it is and can achieve.[3] While some funds which are labeled as sustainable do in fact include a caveat that they do not address impact, many ESG advisory firms refer to ESG as synonymous to capturing impact caused by corporate activities,[4] and ESG is widely used as a means to communicate the sustainability of investments to retail consumers (see Sect. 1.4.1).

Another factor that arguably adds to the current confusion is that organizations delivering frameworks for measuring impact (e.g. GRI, CDP) and financial (SASB) materiality all use the same (or very similar) linguistic topics/categories to structure their efforts (see next section). Simply looking at these high-level categories can therefore be deceiving. They may indicate alignment while, in fact, two similar categories intend to capture fundamentally different things. One relates to, and captures, financial risk while the other attempts to measure impact (externalities).

In summary, terminology that has become increasingly tangled and confused, and this hampers a transparent discussion about what ESG is, could, or should be. This should not be misconstrued as a critique against the use of materiality as a term—it is certainly important for companies and investors to be able to delineate issues on the basis of how they related to a particular sector, and thereby avoid unrealistic reporting requirements. But attention needs to be paid to which kind of materiality underlies

---

[2] See for example p. 8, Fig. 2, in Statement of Intent to Work Together Towards Comprehensive Corporate Reporting" by SASB, GRI, CDP, IIRC and CDSB: https://29kjwb3armds2g3gi4lq2sx1-wpengine.netdna-ssl.com/wp-content/uploads/Statement-of-Intent-to-Work-Together-Towards-Comprehensive-Corporate-Reporting.pdf.

[3] See e.g. https://business-ethics.com/2019/03/10/1226-what-esg-integration-is-and-what-it-isnt/.

[4] See e.g. https://www.esg-integrate.com/sustainability-integrated-reporting, but many examples exist.

any given analysis. Since today's mainstream corporate and investment community appear to be turning to ESG scores as a means to promote sustainable investments (e.g. World Economic Forum, 2020), neglecting to do so runs the risk of developing sustainability strategies that are widely off the mark (see Fig. 3, C and D). We argue that this is where the sustainable finance community currently finds itself, and as long as strategies aiming to address sustainability do not contain data and measures of impacts they will invariably not capture absolute sustainability, or help societies and economies avoiding transgression of planetary boundaries (Rockström et al., 2009).

4 ESG Metrics and Ranking—Shedding Light on a Complex Process

The growing requirements for non-financial reporting (notably ESG), combined with the difficulties for investors themselves to amass the information and ability to compare companies on these terms, has led to an increasing importance of ESG raters. In the last decade, the ESG rating industry has grown considerably and undergone a phase of consolidation and concentration. Some examples include MSCI, Refinitiv, and Sustainalytics.

Theframeworks used by ESG raters have changed over time, partly as a result of mergers and acquisitions (Escrig-Olmedo et al., 2019), but generally they rate companies' performance on a number of environmental (and social and governance) pillars. Generally, the broad environmental categories used by raters are quite similar and broadly correspond to the categories used in GRI's environmental reporting: materials, energy, water and effluents, biodiversity, emissions, effluents and waste, environmental compliance and supplier environmental assessments. Most raters rely on company self-disclosed data through e.g. sustainability reports; complemented with data from external actors like Carbon Disclosure Project (CDP). However, how the broad environmental topics are practically translated into ratings differs significantly between raters in terms of i) the actual data and metrics used to represent a topic, ii) what metrics are considered relevant for companies in different sectors, and iii) the weight each different metric is given when aggregated together to create a combined environmental score for a given company.

Often metrics are aggregated into one general category of "environmental risk" topics, like emissions and natural resource use, and another capturing "positive opportunities" a company could benefit from if its product or services contribute to a sustainable transition; e.g. if the company gets part of its revenues from green buildings, hybrid vehicles or organic food products. Risk-related categories, like emissions and natural resources, are often divided into a risk component and a preparedness component, where a company that is highly exposed to environmental risk can get a better total score by indicating they are prepared to handle these risks; e.g. by having management plans in place. Furthermore, a reputational risk component is typically included, based on data collected from news media or NGOs, thus being updated on a more frequent basis, and referred to as 'controversies'.

Some ESG topics, such as CO_2 emission are reasonably easy to quantify and not context dependent (see e.g. carbon intensity as defined by the EU Taxonomy (gCO_2/kWh). However, many environmental topics are by definition qualitative, and thus hard to implement and quantify in a standardized way. One example is biodiversity related information, where information is context dependent and no general agreement exists on how, or what, to report. Some examples of metrics used by raters currently are "biodiversity impact reduction", "environmental impact reduction", and "environmental restoration initiatives". Other metrics include "existence of a company-led biodiversity program", assessed by presence/absence, or sometimes ranked on quality; from low to high. A concern with raters relying on these self-reported data for positive environmental initiatives is that data reported may have very tenuous, if any, links to the negative environmental impacts of the company's operations. A review of agrifoods—a sector with documented impacts on land, water and biodiversity—extracted from the Refinitiv Eikon database (2014–2019) shows that over half of the reported environmental restoration and impact reduction initiatives lack concretely stated actions or are not related to the type of impact generally associated with the sector.[5] Tree planting is the most common reported activity but a large majority of reports do not provide any figures to allow meaningful comparison of planting activates to company impacts.

The lack of standardized guidelines or frameworks for what should be included under the 'E' of ESG, or how it should be measured, has resulted in a situation where raters arrive at vastly divergent assessments of what constitutes a sustainable investee (Berg et al., 2019; Chatterji et al., 2016; Dorfleitner et al., 2015). This disagreement prevents comparison of performance of ESG investments across investors relying on different raters (Berg et al., 2019; Chatterji et al., 2016). However, using a diversity of measures should not be critiqued per se. ESG topics are by definition often qualitative, and thus hard to implement and quantify in a coherent way. Also, investors´ different needs may require a diversity of assessments and metrics. A homogenous one-size-fits-all approach may therefore neither be feasible or desirable.

Yet, returning to the overarching objective of ensuring investments are in fact (environmentally) sustainable in the absolute, then transparency must still be strived for. Without it, it is not possible to assess the causal logic on which a sustainability metric is premised, and thus credibility and relevance of the data and metrics includes is undermined. Given the confusion and blurring of terms and purposes noted in the previous section, the current lack of transparency is therefore a concern.

[5] Refinitiv Eikon ESG data for the period 2014–2019 was extracted in May 2020 and included all 7252 publically listed companies with an 'environmental pillar' score in 2019.

4.1 Will Current ESG Ratings Make a Difference to Society's Ability to Meet Sustainability Challenges? A Practical Example of the Use of ESG Scores

Most retail investors or individuals looking to place their pension savings will never be directly exposed to individual company ESG scores, as these are only made available through expensive financial platforms like the Bloomberg Terminal or Refintiv Eikon. Nonetheless, these investors may well be exposed to ESG ratings in the aggregated form, through for example the Morningstar Sustainability Rating for Funds. This tool, sometimes referred to as the Globe ratings, ranks both mutual and exchange traded funds on the basis of their sustainability scores, and uses 1–5 globes to visualize ratings. Beginning in 2016, Morningstar introduced their tool which now ranks over 20,000 funds. The globe ratings are based on the simple logic that the total sustainability of a fund´s portfolio is the assetweighted sum of the sustainability rating of its holdings. Sustainability scores for each individual holding, in turn, is based on the Sustainalytics ESG Risk Rating and are a measure of the degree to which a company's economic value may be at risk by ESG issues.[6]

As noted above, Sustainalytics' ESG Risk Ratings (like most raters) is based on financial materiality, and Morningstar also states that their Sustainability Rating is a measure of financially material ESG risks only.[7] However, the tool was ostensibly developed to help investors compare funds based on sustainability, not just financial performance, and are presented by Morningstar as a means to help investors put their money where their values are and provide a "reliable, objective way to evaluate how investments are meeting environment, social, and governance challenges".[8]

Countless blogs and articles on sustainability geared towards financial audiences reinforce the idea of 'globes' and ESG scores as a mean to shift sustainable investing from a "niche" practice requiring specialized knowledge, to one that is more accessible to a far wider range of prospective investors. Even Investopedia, an influential investing and finance education website with reportedly 17 million unique monthly viewers, state that the globe ratings "make it possible for investors to tilt their portfolios toward a sustainable investment philosophy without having to purchase sustainable, responsible and impact (SRI, formerly Socially Responsible Investing) funds" (our italics).[9] This is achieved by identifying otherwise-desired funds (i.e. funds with high conventional Morningstar star ratings) that also have high sustainability ratings. This invokes the same notion highlighted above (e.g. Kahn et al. 2016); that sustainability can be invested in without any additional costs or financial drawbacks.

---

[6] Morningstar changed its methodology in 2019, as Sustainalytics changed from their previous ESG ratings to ESG Risk Ratings measuring "the degree to which a company's economic value is at risk driven by ESG factors." https://www.sustainalytics.com/esg-risk/.

[7] https://www.morningstar.com/content/dam/marketing/shared/Company/Trends/Sustainability/Detail/Documents/SustainabilityRatingMethodology2019.pdf.

[8] https://www.morningstar.com/articles/745796/introducing-the-morningstar-sustainability-rating-for-funds.

[9] https://www.investopedia.com/terms/m/morningstar-sustainability-rating.asp.

Because of the way the globe rating tool is structured, based on financially material (not impact) ESG scores, it has even resulted in long-established responsible investment funds receiving a lower sustainability score in Morningstar's tool than conventional funds.

4.2 *Why Does This Matter for Sustainability?*

Morningstar is a large, influential actor in the investment domain and their globe rating tool has become highly visible in many locations where investors (large and small) compare and choose funds to invest in. Hartzmark and Sussman (2019) show that in the US alone, the market-wide demand for funds varies as a function of their sustainability ratings, where 5 globe Morningstar funds get a considerable inflow of capital, while 1 globe funds receive less. In the year following the launch of the Morningstar sustainability rating tool, funds scoring high on sustainability (4–5 globes) received a total net inflow of more than $24 billion, while those ranking low lost $12 billion in investments. This shows the power of ESG and rating tools to move markets and is precisely the ambition. Morningstar notes that only a minute part of the fund universe is comprised of SRI funds, and launching the globe ratings was a means to remedy this.

However, once again bringing our focus back to absolute sustainability as defined at the start. The promotion and use of the globe rating tools (and ESG more generally) as a means to address societal challenges does not match what current metrics are able to capture and deliver. As BD and AI now rapidly move into the ESG domain, it is important to understand the following: How will they improve ESG assessments? And to what degree will these improvements further sustainability? The next section examines this in more detail.

5 Will Big Data, Artificial Intelligence and Machine Learning Save the Day?

The last decade has seen an exponential growth in the amount of unstructured textual data, like news posts or social media, available online. In the wake of this development, a number of new actors have entered the ESG arena, with the promise of improving ESG measurements by discerning meaningful, material and potentially predictive information from such unstructured data sources using AI.[10]

Traditional ESG metrics ratings, as described above, are typically based on data that is only updated on an annual basis (like sustainability reports). This is often complemented by a controversies-component to capture some of the reputational

[10] Example of companies include Arabesque, Sensefolio, or TruvalueLabs.

risks companies face from negative ESG related news reporting. With the motivation of getting a more frequently updated analysis of ESG performance, the new generation of raters (from here on referred to as BD/AI raters) put a higher emphasis on information discerned from large, unstructured text datasets; like news sources (financial news or general news media), reports from NGOs or stakeholder groups, and social media. BD/AI raters also argue that using BD allows for data collection that is more independent than that emerging from company reports, thus reducing the bias in sustainability performance assessments.[11] By using technology to automatically scan enormous amounts of texts, the amount of data available in the decision making process greatly increases, and by using AI and machine learning to analyze the data, the human bias in the analysis process is claimed to be reduced.

Efforts at incorporating BD in ESG rating is now driving the growing focus on what some refer to as 'dynamic materiality' (e.g. SASB, True Value Labs, 2020). Dynamic materiality refers to, and is derived from, discernable trends in the forms of BD noted here. It is based on financial materiality, and often BD/AI raters use the ESG factors drawn from the SASB framework. To understand the opportunities and risks of using BD for ESG rating, we now take a closer look at the main data collection tools used.

5.1 Natural Language Processing—A Brief Look Under the Hood

With the growing amount of data available online, techniques for programmatic extraction of value and meaning from unstructured text has grown in importance. These techniques are based on technology called natural language processing (NLP), which is an umbrella term referring to techniques for dealing with language of different complexity and for different purposes.

5.1.1 Language Complexity and the Evolution of Natural Language Processing Approaches

Human language can be represented and analyzed as a hierarchy with increased levels of complexity. This is reflected in NLP methods as well. At the most basic level, language is dealt with as only individual independent words, or collections of words. Using the so called 'Bag of Words' (BoW) approach, word occurrences are counted and texts considered as similar if they use the same words with similar relative frequency. This "shallow" treatment of language leaves out word order, semantic context and ambiguity, and assumes representative words are used in a similar fashion across texts. Capturing the next step in language complexity requires NLP methods

[11] "It´s not about what companies say, it´s what they do" (https://truvaluelabs.com/trends/esg-integration).

based on word embeddings, like the word2vec model, where each word, or collection of words, is mapped to a vector. Mapping is done so that semantically similar words are positioned closer to each other in the vector space, thus providing the ability to capture semantic information about words and their relationship to one another. However, models are still context free, so there is still just a single word embedding representation for each word in the model´s vocabulary (Young et al., 2018). This means there will be no difference to the interpretation of the word "running" in the sentences "He is running a company" and "He is running a marathon".

More advanced NLP models have been developed to represent higher levels of language complexity, and consider the context for each occurrence of a given word (Devlin et al., 2018). These are based on deep neural networks that have been trained for language modeling tasks by scanning through vast amounts of textual data, typically general English corpora. However, the "understanding" that these models have gained is synonymous with a general understanding of language structure. This should not be confused with an understanding of language structure in topic-specific domains, where the model needs to first be trained on large corpora of representative, domain specific texts since the meaning and scope of words are strongly domain-dependent. Even if this representative, domain specific training examples exists, an understanding of domain specific language structure should not be confused with an understanding of the domain itself. Certain types of information, such as common sense knowledge and basic facts about the physical reality, are obvious to humans and thus rarely explicitly stated in text. They are therefore hard for an NLP model to acquire (Lucy & Gauthier, 2017). This also applies to domain specific knowledge and implicit causal connections that are assumed and not explicitly written out. Using a combined approach, where the bottom-up knowledge learned from data is enriched with top-down knowledge inherited from some kind of knowledge base (Zellers et al., 2018) is therefore an approach that might increase (Young et al., 2018). However a single language phrase may be used to inform, mislead about a fact, draw attention, remind, or command, etc. This aspect of language is notoriously difficult for machines to grasp. Thus, regardless of the complexity of NLP approach used, it can only be considered as a proxy to true language understanding.

5.1.2 Natural Language Processing in ESG

The ultimate goal of NLP is (naturally) to extract meaning from, and make sense of, the information collected from the large, unstructured datasets collected. To do this, a common approach used in ESG is the combined use of Named Entity Recognition (NER), Sentiment Analysis (SA), and topic modelling/text classification methods. NER is used to extract "real-world objects", for example a company, brand name, person, country or a product, from texts. This is accomplished using a lexicon with entities, e.g. the CoNLL 2003, which concentrates on four types of named entities: people, locations, organizations and miscellaneous entities and has been a standard English dataset for NER (Young et al., 2018). NER can also be done using statistical approaches, where the model quality strongly depends on training examples. In SA, the goal is to analyze the author's sentiments, attitudes, emotions, and opinions (Beigi et al., 2016). It is used to determine if a text has a positive, neutral or negative tone. Similar to NER, SA could be lexicon-based or based on statistical linguistic analysis on how positive or negative language is expressed in a particular context. To group or classify texts into categories, common approaches include topic modelling, where documents or sentences are grouped together based on some similarity (e.g. similarities of word usage), or text classification, where a classifier is trained on a corpora of labelled documents and each text is assigned to the class most similar. An output of the combined NER, SA and topic modelling approach can be a text having the topic "climate change", including a company name, and the sentiment "negative". A key question, however, is what this piece of data actually represent in a sustainability context.

Several BD/AI raters use text data generated in this fashion to assess whether a topic and sentiment-combination correlates with changes in the value of a company´s stock, and whether it is usable as a tradeable signal. This does not require, nor does it incorporate, any understanding or insight into what the text actually means, or what the causal logic between changes in stock value and environmental indicator is. Therefore, the signal does not necessarily have any connection to absolute sustainability (or impact), and can emerge simply as a result of spurious correlations.

Using BD and AI to create tradeable signals from ESG related sentiments may be a good way to capture proxy variables for trends in consumer preferences or brand perceptions—such as news sources, social media, and blog posts. It is therefore well-suited for assessing rapidly changing risks related to social variables, such as public opinion and reputation. These translate seamlessly into risks to individual companies, and are arguably a good tool for fine-tuning assessments of reputational risk. However, translating these approaches to environmental sustainability risks implies that what is communicated via social media, and how it is perceived, has a real connection to the underlying environmental problem. As shown above, NLP will not, despite a high level of sophistication, be able to detect and distinguish PR activities, or greenwashing, from online reporting of direct relevance to assessing company impact on environmental sustainability; primarily because the technology used to read and evaluate the information has no common sense understanding of the topic itself. To unpack why this can be a concern for investors interested in sustainability we next analyze environmental controversies in more detail and reason around what our findings mean.

5.2 Capturing Environmental Sustainability Using Big Data and Artificial Intelligence

BD sourced from news and social media will most likely only capture environmental issues that make the headline news; so-called environmental controversies alluded to above. Furthermore, to occur in financial news media, the environmental issue would likely need to be considered as financially material in the first place. The explicit focus of BD/AI providers on continuously updated online news data risks creating a strong bias towards this form of tradeable signals. An important question is therefore what this implies from an environmental impact perspective?

Refinitiv provides a dataset on environmental controversies, which is used together with ESG metrics collected from e.g. company sustainability reports, to create the aggregated Eikon ESG scores (a 'conventional', not explicit BD/AI rating service).[12] Controversy data are updated on a continuous basis, as and when such events occur and get picked up by global media. Even though Refinitiv is not a BD/AI ESG rater per se, and the controversy information is gleaned from global media sources and not social media, the logic behind the variable construction by BD/AI ESG providers is similar in that the latter also aim to increase the role of external information to companies in their assessment of ESG scores. Hence we used it to examine and illustrate what environmental controversy data captures, and to test the validity of using it as a measure of absolute environmental sustainability.

Our analysis of the Refinitiv Eikon ESG data on environmental controversies for the 2014–2019 period shows that of the 429 unique environmental controversies captured in the data, 44% related to climate change contribution and 24% to pollution (see Box 2). The former category is dominated by reported associations with fossil fuel extraction and emissions cheating during tests of combustion engines (Fig. 2), while the latter contains a variety of pollutants, followed by pesticide use and toxic leaks from dam failures. This indicates that only a limited set of environmental issues are well captured by environmental controversies, and the issues captured relate primarily to topics already well-established in the media landscape (e.g. carbon emissions since the Paris Agreement in 2016), or those likely to make headline news (such as larger pollution events or blatant fraud).

---

[12] https://www.refinitiv.com/content/dam/marketing/en_us/documents/methodology/esg-scores-methodology.pdf.

Box 2. Environmental controversies—An empirical analysis
Using Refinitiv Eikon ESG data on environmental controversies for the period 2014–2019 we analyzed the types of environmental issues covered by the controversies data. This was done by reading each entry and coding it according to the particular environmental topic it covers. These detailed codes (such as tampering with emissions tests, malpractice in pesticide application, toxic leaks affecting biodiversity, etc.) were subsequently grouped into broader categories, displayed in Fig. 2. Data was extracted in May 2020 and included all 7252 public listed companies with an 'environmental pillar' score in 2019. For these companies, details of their environmental controversies reported since 2015–01-01 where downloaded (equivalent to fiscal years 2014–2019)[13]

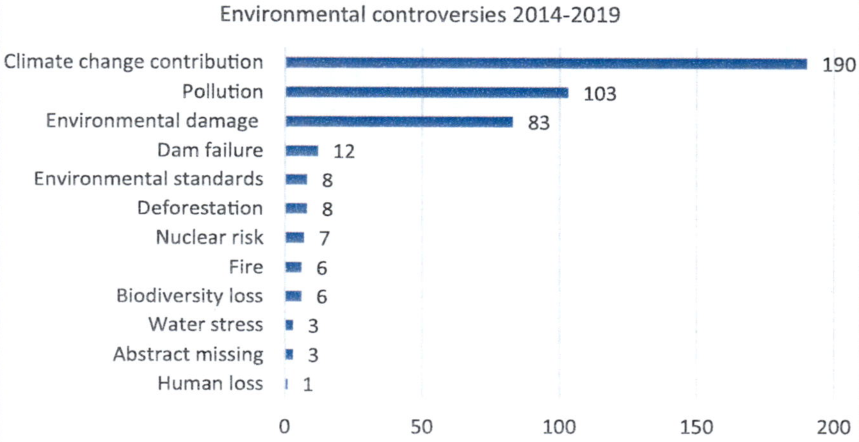

Fig. 2 Frequencies of each category of environmental controversies reported in Refinitiv Eikon during the 2014–2019 period

This analysis therefore highlights that other environmental issues, such as degradation of the environment through diffuse or less apparent pollution over time, or continuous deforestation or land use change leading to gradual (but eventually abrupt, see e.g. Rocha et al., 2018) biodiversity loss, will not be captured. The main reasons for this is that they are (i) unlikely to appear in media (because they are not deemed financially material or otherwise newsworthy), and (ii) particularly problematic in the aggregate and not easily assessed by individually reported events.

The analysis thus underscores the built-in flaw of attempting to rely on media reporting to capture environmental issues from an impact perspective, as this is premised on the idea that such issues are perceived as newsworthy, or for financial

[13] Eikon download details: Equity(active,public,primary); TR.EnvironmentPillarScore(Period = FY0) > = 0;

Fields used: TR.ControvEnv & TR.RecentControvEnv; StartDate': '2015–01-01'; EndDate': '2020–12-31'.

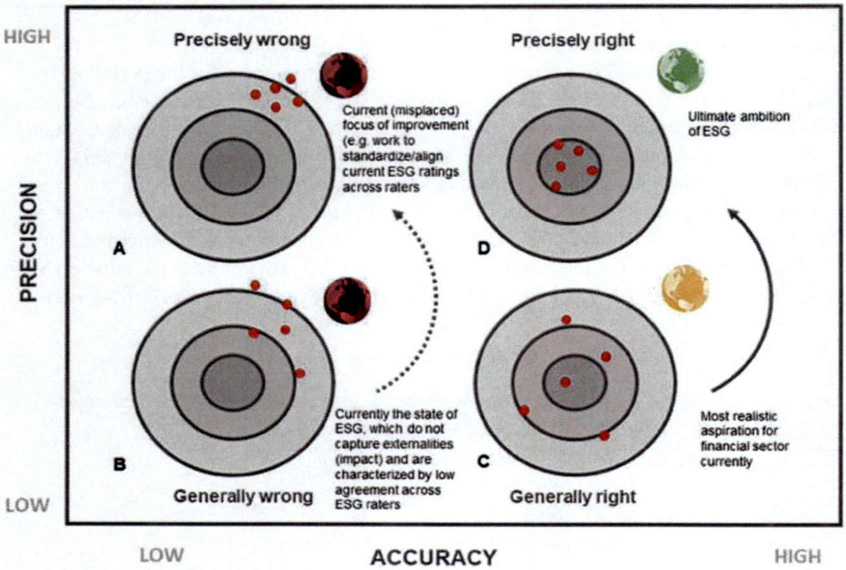

Fig. 3 Environmental sustainability in relation to current achievements and plausible ambitions of ESG frameworks and ratings. The likely environmental sustainability risk incurred by the ESG focus is indicated by colored globes, where; red = high risk of transgressing planetary boundaries, yellow = lower risk, and green = low risk (best possible option)

news media—financially relevant. Environmental issues, like the implications of gradual land use change and agricultural practices for biodiversity and water stress, are sometimes complex and not easily linked to individual companies. Hence they are unlikely to appear in media in relation to companies (or so called 'named entities'). Therefore the environmental ESG data which AI promises to enhance do not currently provide a meaningful assessment of absolute environmental sustainability. Instead, they are largely another measure of reputational risk, detached from causal connections to that which has bearing on sustainability through biosphere integrity and climate stability (Fig. 3).

6 ESG and Impact Investment

Readers of this chapter might argue that those interested in absolute sustainability (or impact) should turn to impact investment and not use ESG as their tool, precisely because it is premised on financially materiality and does not capture causal links between company operations and environmentally sustainable outcomes in a good way. However, the issue is not that simple. As illustrated with the Morningstar example, ESG investments are often used in an impact sustainability context, even though raters providing the underlying metrics may be transparent about their focus on financial materiality. When investors discuss ESG investments in the context of addressing the UN Sustainable Development Goals (SDGs), they are invoking an expectation that investments will somehow contribute to increasing positive, or decreasing negative, impacts on these globally agreed upon goals—not just addressing risks pertaining to the companies in their portfolio. Furthermore, much of the rhetoric in sustainable finance is based on ESG investments as a means to move markets towards sustainability at scale, something which impact investments—with $< 0.5\%$ of total value of SRI (Eurosif, 2018)—currently do not achieve.

Issues get further muddled when the metrics developed from financially material proxy data (such as controversies) are claimed to be directly translatable across to frameworks that explicitly aim to assess impact. An example is Sensefolio (a BD/AI rater), who provide their own ESG/Sustainability framework but state that investors "...can also rely on the frameworks of the Global Reporting Initiative (GRI), the Sustainability Accounting Standards Board (SASB), and the UN Sustainable Development Goals (SDGs) as every (one) of their categories can be classified into the 11 categories of the Sensefolio ESG Framework (SEF)".[14] This once again illustrates how the use of very similar language to structure data categories across frameworks with different ambitions, risks blurring their fundamental differences.[15] In doing so it give investors the impression that a company ESG score from, e.g. Sensefolio, is synonymous with the same company having a measurable impact on one of the SDGs' or GRI impact categories. This mental summersault would equate to believing one is going from B to D, in Fig. 3, when in fact the approach is taking you from B to A.

7 Greenwashing, Accountability, and the Outsourcing of Epistemic Responsibility

Returning to the underlying theory of change for how the financial sector can contribute to sustainability can bring clarity as to the specific hurdles that will need to be overcome to achieve this goal. Broadly speaking investors have two separate but closely linked ways of contributing to absolute sustainability, and both need to be pursued simultaneously. One is by bolstering, through capital allocation decisions, economic activities and businesses that hold a promise of delivering sustainable solutions (and innovation). The other is to use various investment pathways to reduce (and

---

[14] p45 in Sensefolio's technical paper: https://sensefolio.com/Sensefolio_TechnicalPaper.pdf.

[15] Sensefolio scores use three primary sources of information, analyzed via NLP, to assess companies' degree of involvement in ESG topics: Financial News, Sustainability and ESG Reports & Earnings Calls, and Social Media Posts & Company Reviews (all accounting for 1/3 respectively). The source is: https://medium.com/@sensefolio/presentation-of-sensefolio-55699bd144a5, where Sensefolio in a series of articles explains the methodology behind their scores. That the medium account @sensefolio indeed belongs to sensefolio, is stated on the last page of the sensefolio technical paper reference above.

eventually eliminate) the harm currently done to society and planet through unsustainable business practices. Sustainable investments should arguably be synonymous with investments that in various ways ensure that these two ambitions are advanced.

ESG has become the most widespread concept and framework to do this, and is currently used by the financial sector as both a process to guide its engagement with, and thinking around, sustainability issues. Equally important is the fact that it is the primary 'tool' used to classify investments that are promoted vis-à-vis consumers as green or sustainable. In fact, consumers, through their choices and stated preferences, are a cornerstone of the strategy for how the financial industry will achieve change (see Morningstar's globe rating tool as an example); notably by supplying sustainable products to consumers, whether these consumers are institutional or individual retail investors looking for green funds to place their savings.

This logic builds on a much broader trend towards increased consumers liberty to pursue and express individual preferences– well-exemplified by the privatization of pension schemes in several European countries (e.g. Engel & Mccoy, 2002). This trend in beliefs regarding the power of informed and conscious consumers to change market incentives and achieve sustainability is not unique to the financial industry (Haddock-Fraser & Tourelle, 2010; Jones et al., 2008; Maitre-Ekern & Dalhammar, 2019). It mirrors the significant rise in standards and certification schemes to transition production of various soft commodities (such as fish, timber, coffee, palm oil, etc.) onto sustainable trajectories (e.g. Auld, 2014; Schleifer, 2016).

Against this background, this chapter has scrutinized what current ESG frameworks and metrics can deliver, and how the use of BD and AI could affect this capability. Our analysis shows that current approaches to measuring ESG, which are based on financial materiality, cannot address absolute sustainability. And while the BD/AI approaches emerging to enhance ESG will refine the ability of investors to capture real-time trends (becoming more precisely wrong—going from B to A in Fig. 3)—as currently designed and deployed, these approaches capture merely reputational risk and thus will not improve the accuracy with which the capital markets address sustainability (i.e. will not take us from B to D in Fig. 3). This results in a situation where, despite apparently sincere and rising wishes and ambitions of the financial sector to engage with the climate and sustainability challenge, the system is structured in a way that does not allow an assessment of whether we are increasing or decreasing the resilience of the biosphere, approaching Earth System tipping points, or how investments are affecting multiple other social goals (as defined by the UN SDGs) (Gaffney et al., 2018; Galaz et al., 2018; Porter & Kramer, 2006; Rockström et al., 2020). In other words, we are flying blind.

The field of sustainable investments is expanding rapidly, and as noted earlier the marketing discourse abounds with examples of language that suggests ESG can and will help investors contribute to societal transformation towards sustainability. Yet, when penetrating the marketing discourse and reading the fine print, disclaimers by rating tools, such as Morningstar's globe rating tool show that somewhere between the level of stated ambition and the level of execution—i.e. where data is collected and used to deliver company ranking—there is a breakdown of causal logic. It highlights a crucial misalignment between ambition at one level, and the ability to deliver on stated goals.

Just as lack of motivation was overwhelmingly discussed as the moral determinant of the financial crisis of 2008 (Brummer, 2009; Financial Crisis Inquiry Commission, 2011; Larosièrer, 2009; Vickers, 2011), de Bruin (2015) maintains that the currently observed failure to align motivations with actions in a competent way is what continues to undermine the credibility and trustworthiness of the financial sector. Trustworthiness comes from clearly articulating what is required to reach the stated ambitions, and to then perform the duties that these requirements imply, and accounting for how they are executed (O'Neill, 2014). If you are motivated but fail to deliver by suppressing or omitting an intelligible account of what ought to be done (or you account for an illogical or unintelligently constructed metrics as noted here), then O'Neill (2014) refers to it as unintelligent accountability.

Given the responsibility put on consumers to be part of the sustainable transformation through deliberate choice, there has to be transparency regarding the frameworks, processes, analytical tools, and metrics that link actions to ambition. Decision theory would state that the ability to be a responsible consumer rests on knowledge about the diversity and characteristics of products, and about what consequences may result from the decision to buy them, and how likely these consequences are (de Bruin, 2015). Often this is not the case in today's financial markets, and multiple examples exist. One is the erroneous decision made by many UK citizens in switching from State earnings related pension schemes (Serps) to alternative non-government schemes in 1980s (Aldridge, 1998). Another is the failure to grasp the complexities of mortgage pricing and credit scoring among American consumers (Hynes & Posner, 2002). In fact, we often outsource our attempts at acting as responsible consumers to accountants, legal advisers, doctors, consumer organizations, or—in this case—ESG rating providers, simply because we do not have the time, the skills or resources to undertake the research ourselves. De Bruin (2015) refers to this as epistemic outsourcing.

These examples show what can happen when consumers make (or are expected to make) decisions but do not have adequate capabilities to make informed decisions. Financial literacy among the general public has been shown to be generally low, and ecological literacy of financial sector equally so (Jouffray et al., 2019). For ESG to deliver on a promise of sustainability it will have to become a tool that can accurately capture and measure the dimensions relevant for assessing the increasing or decreasing resilience of our biosphere and climate. In doing so, it could provide a means for both consumer and investors to mitigate their low respective literacy and build trust.

Refraining from a move in this direction is associated with real risks. First and foremost, the risk of surpassing planetary boundaries, to the detriment of societies and economies (Rockström et al., 2009; Steffen et al., 2018). Second, is the risk of creating a 'crisis of trust' (O'Neill, 2014). The latter risk stems from the increasing likelihood that, as large-scale environmental change proceeds and result in more frequent droughts, forest fires, crop failures and ice sheets melting (Wuebbles et al., 2017), the public, political actors, and increasingly informed financial regulators, all

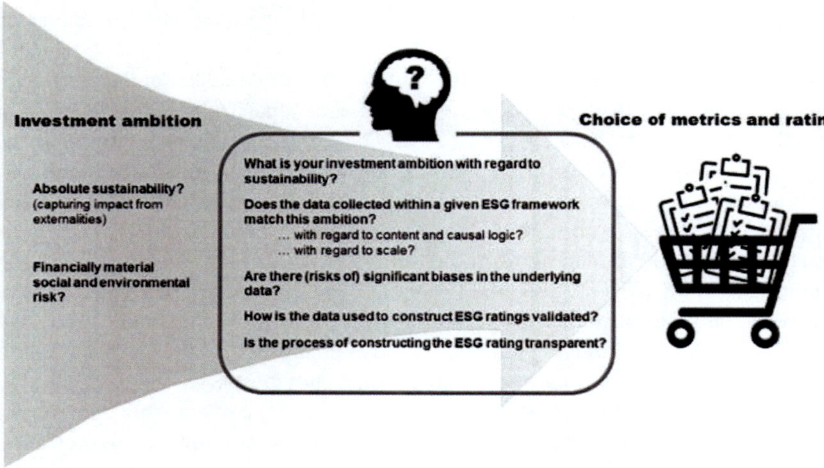

Fig. 4 Becoming a 'sustainability savvy' consumer of ESG ratings. Key questions to pose in order to improve alignment between sustainable investment ambitions and outcomes

realize that the rating systems and metrics used to assess sustainability of investments have not measurably contributed to a sustainable trajectory. Instead valuable time has been squandered in making ESG ever more precisely wrong (Fig. 4), and brought us closer to likely irreversible change (Lenton et al., 2019).

De Bruin (2015: 9) highlights the risk associated with lack of competence and misalignment between purpose and action, by using the example of doctors prescribing drugs. Medical doctors are expected to understand and convey the risks of drugs as well as the reason for taking them. Similarly, promoters of ESG-related investments should arguably be aware of, and accountable for, the risks posed to investors and society if the accuracy with which they can address the sustainability problem (akin to a societal ailment) is overrated/overstated and thus in fact likely to increase the root problem (Fig. 4).

8 How to Become a 'Sustainability Savvy' Consumer of ESG Ratings

Readers of this chapter may argue that current ESG metrics and frameworks are not intended to capture absolute sustainability and therefore should not be unfairly judged against this goal. This is a fair point, and this chapter does not intend to pass judgement on the goal of ESG. Our ambition is simply to tease out and illuminate the misalignment between on the one hand the currently expanding discourse portraying

ESG as a means to help investors address the challenges of climate change, environmental degradation, and labor and human rights (to name a few),[16] and on the other hand the use of tools and metrics that are premised on financially material risk and cannot provide an assessment of how investments contribute to these noted challenges. To aid those interested in understanding the potential of using ESG metrics and ratings to further sustainability through investments the final section is structured around a set of questions we believe every user of these ratings must ask.

8.1 What Is Your Investment Ambition with Regard to Sustainability?

Is your ambition to, in some capacity, contribute to a measurable improvement in absolute sustainability, by allocating your funds to companies with lower environmental (and social) footprints (impact)? Or are you primarily concerned with understanding how environmental and social risks will affect your investments in the short term, and keen to minimize these risks?

If your answer to the former question is yes, then the questions below can guide you as a consumer of ESG metrics and ratings.

8.2 Does the Data Collected Within a Given ESG Framework Match This Ambition?

… with regard to content and causal logic? There are many variables one could imagine or hope to include in a measure of absolute sustainability. While there is growing consensus around the importance of broad impact topics (such as water, biodiversity, etc.), many have no agreed-upon measurement standards. As a consumer of ESG metrics it is therefore paramount to scrutinize the causal logic between your ambition in terms of impact, and the particular data used to capture a specific variable. Is there a clear logic for how the particular data collected for a category—such as school or volunteer projects used as proxies for environmental restoration initiatives—should lead to a sustainable outcome of relevance for that category? An example is the use of company reported data on school or volunteer projects which is used as (an rraneous) proxy for evidence of environmental restoration.

… with regard to scale? The lack of agreed-upon measurement standards for variables to capture the environmental part of ESG measures has resulted in the currently employed metrics capturing vastly different scales of potential impact. As an example, Refinitiv Eikon currently contains data on company initiatives to host rooftop beehives, and conduct beach cleaning events. Yet it is questionable

---

[16] https://www.morningstar.com/articles/745796/introducing-the-morningstar-sustainability-rating-for-funds.

whether these can contribute meaningfully towards a sustainable trajectory, even in the aggregate.

8.3 Are There (Risks of) Significant Biases in the Underlying Data?

Users of ESG ratings should also be aware of the potential bias built into certain types of data. Here we outline two examples:

EXAMPLE 1: : The example of small-scale initiatives like beehives and beach cleaning, noted above should not be critiqued per se. However sustainability minded investors should be aware that there is a real risk that AI approaches will inadvertently misconstrue these as significant and meaningful sustainability contributions, if aggregating individual media occurrences (based on e.g. NER and SA).

EXAMPLE 2: Current approaches using BD and AI for improving the ability of ESG ratings to capture dynamic materiality are biased towards that which can be picked up by the technical tools used (NLP). As such they will be unlikely to capture many of the environmental issues that threaten to undercut social and environmental sustainability (as defined by e.g. the Sustainable Development Goals) (see Box 2).

8.4 How Is the Data Used to Construct ESG Ratings Validated?

Data collected using AI will also be biased by the data used to train the models. Comparing the challenge to the similar task of image classification can be illustrative. An image can be classified as a hierarchy of topics (e.g. animal/dog/Labrador), which is a complicated task. To achieve this requires the machine learning tool to be 'ground-truthed' as to what an image actually shows. Environmental problems, generally display far more ambiguity and nuance than such image recognition tasks, and might also differ depending on context. Current AI ESG approaches do not appear to deal well with the complexity of the environmental topics of relevance (such as biodiversity decline, land-use change), as these do not translate into a simple recognition of a 'named entity' (such as a company name or brand). Human analysts are typically aware of these difficulties and have the kind of implicit understanding of cause and effects and common sense that are difficult to pick up for a machine through NLP.

Inquiring about, and understanding, the data validation procedures is therefore essential to assess the degree to which an ESG rater can provide a reliable metric for absolute sustainability.

8.5 *Is the Process of Constructing the ESG Rating Transparent?*

As noted repeatedly in this chapter, some environmental (and arguably social) concerns are difficult to capture in a simple metric, although this is needed if the goal is to create a quantitative comparable score. This is understandable, yet makes it crucially important to maintain transparency of the chain of causal logic employed in the construction of ESG and impact variables. As a consumer of ESG metrics, it is important to make sure transparency is provided at each level of aggregation to construct a metric—from choice of variable and data collected, to how this data is evaluated and aggregated. Otherwise the causal logic risks being obscured.

9 Conclusion

Is the emergence of BD analytics and use of AI tools to assess ESG misdirected? Certainly not. The growing amount of unstructured ESG related data available provides new possibilities to capture company related information of potential relevance for ESG, with a more unbiased view of companies than simply relying on self-reported company sustainability information delivered on an annual basis. NLP and AI technologies are invaluable tools in "reading" and analyzing these large datasets.

Current use of AI in ESG will capture the sweet spots—that is issues that are of direct importance for absolute sustainability, while also being financially material. However, as we have shown, many environmental issues do not lend themselves to easy capture by news headlines. It is important for all users of ESG to recognize the existence of these dark corners of current AI-ESG approaches, and be cognizant of what this means for the capacity of ESG to measure progress towards sustainability.

In light of this, combining the strength of AI with human analysts could distill the best of both worlds. Human analysts, with the capacity to grasp common sense relations and complex environmental causality, could draw on the capacity of AI to reduce complexity and find patterns in large amounts of data. Human analysts would thus identify and make explicit the causal logic by which a particular proxy variable (dataset) is related to environmental (or social) sustainability, and then leverage the unrivaled data collection and pattern-finding capacity of AI to assess sustainability outcomes in relation to companies or sectors. Herein lies the power of AI and BD.

References

Aglietta, M., & Espagne, E. (2016). *Climate and finance systemic risks, more than an analogy? The climate fragility hypothesis* (CEPII Working Papers), Paris.

Aldridge, A. (1998). "Habitus" and cultural capital in the field of personal finance. *Sociol Rev, 46*, 1–23. https://doi.org/10.1111/1467-954X.00087

Auld, G. (2014). Confronting trade-offs and interactive effects in the choice of policy focus: Specialized versus comprehensive private governance. *Regul ation & Governance, 8*, 126–148. https://doi.org/10.1111/rego.12034

Barona, E., Ramankutty, N., Hyman, G., & Coomes, O. T. (2010). The role of pasture and soybean in deforestation of the Brazilian Amazon. *Environmental Research Letters, 5*, 24002. https://doi.org/10.1088/1748-9326/5/2/024002

Beigi, G., Hu, X., Maciejewski, R., & Liu, H. (2016). An overview of sentiment analysis in social media and its applications in disaster relief. In *Studies in Computational Intelligence* (pp. 313–340). Springer Verlag.

Berg, F., Koelbel, J., & Rigobon, R. (2019). Aggregate confusion: The divergence of ESG ratings. *SSRN Electronic Journal, 0–63*. https://doi.org/10.2139/ssrn.3438533

Bjørn, A., Chandrakumar, C., Boulay, A.-M., et al. (2020). Review of life-cycle based methods for absolute environmental sustainability assessment and their applications. *Environmental Research Letters, 15*, 83001. https://doi.org/10.1088/1748-9326/ab89d7

Brummer, A. (2009). *The Crunch: How Greed and incompetence sparked the credit crisis*. Random House Business Books.

Buhr, B. (2017). Assessing the sources of stranded asset risk: A proposed framework. *Journal of Sustainable Finance & Investment, 7*, 37–53. https://doi.org/10.1080/20430795.2016.1194686

Chandrakumar, C., & McLaren, S. J. (2018). Towards a comprehensive absolute sustainability assessment method for effective Earth system governance: Defining key environmental indicators using an enhanced-DPSIR framework. *Ecological Indicators, 90*, 577–583. https://doi.org/10.1016/j.ecolind.2018.03.063

Chatterji, A. K., Durand, R., Levine, D. I., & Touboul, S. (2016). Do ratings of firms converge? Implications for managers, investors and strategy researchers. *Strategic Management Journal, 37*, 1597–1614. https://doi.org/10.1002/smj.2407

de Bruin, B. (2015). *Ethics and the global financial crisis why incompetence is worse than Greed*. Cambridge University Press.

Devlin, J., Chang, M. W., Lee, K., & Toutanova, K. (2018). Bert: Pre-training of deep bidirectional transformers for language understanding. *arXiv preprint arXiv:1810.04805*.

Dorfleitner, G., Halbritter, G., & Nguyen, M. (2015). Measuring the level and risk of corporate responsibility—An empirical comparison of different ESG rating approaches. *Journal of Asset Management, 16*, 450–466. https://doi.org/10.1057/jam.2015.31

Drost, S., Mishra, K., & Piotrowski, M. (2019). *Cargill's new policies insufficient to fully mitigate deforestation risks in Brazil*. 17

Duffy, P. B., Brando, P., Asner, G. P., & Field, C. B. (2015). Projections of future meteorological drought and wet periods in the Amazon. *Proceedings of the National Academy of Sciences of the United States of America, 112*, 13172–13177. https://doi.org/10.1073/pnas.1421010112

Eccles, R. G., Lee, L.-E., & Stroehle, J. C. (2020). The social origins of ESG: An analysis of innovest and KLD. *Organization & Environment, 33*, 575–596. https://doi.org/10.1177/1086026619888994

Engel, K.C., & Mccoy, P. A. (2002). *A tale of three markets: The law and economics of predatory lending*.

Escrig-Olmedo, E., Fernández-Izquierdo, M., ángeles, Ferrero-Ferrero I, et al. (2019). Rating the raters: Evaluating how ESG rating agencies integrate sustainability principles. *Sustain, 11*,. https://doi.org/10.3390/su11030915

Eurosif. (2018). *European SRI Study 2018*

Financial Crisis Inquiry Commission. (2011). *The Financial Crisis Inquiry Report*. Final Report of the National Commission on the Causes of the Financial and Economic Crisis in the United States. US Government, Washington, DC.

Friede, G., Busch, T., & Bassen, A. (2015). ESG and financial performance: Aggregated evidence from more than 2000 empirical studies. *Journal of Sustainable Finance & Investment, 5*, 210–233. https://doi.org/10.1080/20430795.2015.1118917

Gaffney, O., Crona, B. I., Dauriach, A., & Galaz, V. (2018). *Sleeping financial giants. Opportunities for financial leadership for climate stability.* Stockholm

Galaz, V., Crona, B., Dauriach, A., et al. (2018). Finance and the Earth system—Exploring the links between financial actors and non-linear changes in the climate system. *Global Environmental Change, 53*, 296–302. https://doi.org/10.1016/j.gloenvcha.2018.09.008

Gleeson, T., Wang-Erlandsson, L., Porkka, M., et al. (2020). Illuminating water cycle modifications and Earth system resilience in the Anthropocene. *Water Resources Research, 56*,. https://doi.org/10.1029/2019WR024957

GSIA. (2018). *2018 Global Sustainable Investment Review.*

Haddock-Fraser, J. E., & Tourelle, M. (2010). Corporate motivations for environmental sustainable development: Exploring the role of consumers in stakeholder engagement. *Business Strategy and the Environment, 19*, 527–542. https://doi.org/10.1002/bse.663

Hartzmark, S. M., & Sussman, A. B. (2019). Do investors value sustainability? A natural experiment examining ranking and fund flows. *Journal Finance, 74*, 2789–2837. https://doi.org/10.1111/jofi.12841

Hawley, J. P., Lukomnik, J. (2018). The third, system stage of corporate governance: Why institutional investors need to move beyond modern portfolio theory. *SSRN Electron Journal.* https://doi.org/10.2139/ssrn.3127767

Helbing, D. (2013). Globally networked risks and how to respond. *Nature, 497*, 51–59. https://doi.org/10.1038/nature12047

Hynes, R., & Posner, E. (2002). The law and economics of consumer finance. *Am Law Econ Assoc, 4*, 168–207. https://doi.org/10.1093/aler/4.1.168

IPCC. (2019). *Climate change and land. An IPCC Special Report on climate change, desertification, land degradation, sustainable land management, food security, and greenhouse gas fluxes in terrestrial ecosystems.*

James, D. (2001). *Cooperation, Competition, and the 'science of pricing' in the political risk insurance marketplace.* The World Bank.

Jones, P., Clarke-Hill, C., Comfort, D., & Hillier, D. (2008). *Marketing and sustainability. Mark Intell Plan, 26*, 123–130. https://doi.org/10.1108/02634500810860584

Jouffray, J.B., Crona, B., Wassénius, E., et al. (2019). Leverage points in the financial sector for seafood sustainability. *Science Advances, 5*,eaax3324. https://doi.org/10.1126/sciadv.aax3324

Kell, G. (2018). *The remarkable rise of ESG.* Forbes.

Khan, M., Serafeim, G., & Yoon, A. (2016). Corporate sustainability: First evidence on materiality. *The Accounting Review, 91*, 1697–1724. https://doi.org/10.2308/accr-51383

Koh, I., Garrett, R., Janetos, A., & Mueller, N. D. (2020). Climate risks to Brazilian coffee production. *Environmental Research Letters, 15*, 104015. https://doi.org/10.1088/1748-9326/aba471

Lade, S. J., Steffen, W., de Vries, W., et al. (2020). Human impacts on planetary boundaries amplified by Earth system interactions. *Nat Sustain.* https://doi.org/10.1038/s41893-019-0454-4

Lal, R. (2008). Carbon sequestration. *Philosophical Transactions of the Royal Society B, 363*, 815–830.

de Larosièrer, J. (2009). *Report of the high-level group on financial supervision in the EU.*

Lenton, T. M. (2016). *Earth system science: A very short introduction.* Oxford University Press (OUP).

Lenton, T. M., Rockström, J., & Gaffney, O., et al. (2019). *Climate tipping points—Too risky to bet against.* Nature

Lovejoy, T. E., & Nobre, C. (2018). Amazon tipping point. *Science Advances, 4*, eaat2340.

Lucy, L., & Gauthier, J. (2017). *Are distributional representations ready for the real world? Evaluating word vectors for grounded perceptual meaning.* arXiv

Maitre-Ekern, E., & Dalhammar, C. (2019). Towards a hierarchy of consumption behaviour in the circular economy. *Maastricht Journal of European and Comparative, 26*, 394–420. https://doi.org/10.1177/1023263X19840943

O'Neill, O. (2014). Trust, trustworthiness, and accountability. In N. Morris & D. Vines (Eds.), *Capital failure: Rebuilding trust in financial services*. Oxford University Press, p Part II (8).

Ometto, J. P., Aguiar, A. P. D., & Martinelli, L. A. (2011). Amazon deforestation in Brazil: Effects, drivers and challenges. *Carbon Management*. https://doi.org/10.4155/cmt.11.48

Pachauri, R. K., Allen, M. R., Barros, V. R, et al. (2014). Climate change 2014: Synthesis report. *Working Groups I, II and III to the Fifth Assessment Report of the. Intergovernmental Panel on Climate Change* https://epic.awi.de/id/eprint/37530/. Accessed 28 November 2020.

Porter, M. E., & Kramer, M. R. (2006). Strategy and society: The link between competitive advantage and corporate social responsibility. *Harvard Business Review, 84*, 78–92.

Post, W. M., Kwon, K.C. (2000). *Soil carbon sequestration and land-use change: Processes and potential*

Rocha, J. C., Peterson, G., Bodin, Ö., & Levin, S. A. (2018). Cascading regime shifts within and across scales. *Science, 362*, 1379–1383. https://doi.org/10.1101/364620

Rockström, J., Beringer, A., Crona, B., et al. (2020) Planetary boundaries: A compass for investing for the common good. In H. Bril, G. Kell, A. Rasche (Eds.), *Sustainable investing: A path to a new Horizon* (1st ed., pp 109–128). Routledge.

Rockström, J., Steffen, W., Noone, K., et al. (2009). Planetary boundaries: Exploring the safe operating space for humanity. *Ecology and Society*. https://doi.org/10.5751/ES-03180-140232

Scharlemann, J. P. W., Tanner, E. V. J., Hiederer, R., & Kapos, V. (2014). Global soil carbon: Understanding and managing the largest terrestrial carbon pool. *Carbon Manag., 5*, 81–91.

Schleifer, P. (2016). Private governance undermined: India and the roundtable on sustainable palm oil. *Global Environmental Politics, 16*, 38–58. https://doi.org/10.1162/GLEP_a_00335

Sjåfjell, B. (2020). *The financial risks of unsustainability: A research agenda.*

Sonter, L. J., Herrera, D., Barrett, D. J., et al. (2017). Mining drives extensive deforestation in the Brazilian Amazon. *Nature Communications*. https://doi.org/10.1038/s41467-017-00557-w

Spera, S. A., Winter, J., & Partridge, T. (2020). Brazilian maize yields negatively affected by climate after land clearing. *Nature Sustainability, 3*, 845–852. https://doi.org/10.1038/s41893-020-0560-3

Steffen, W., Rockström, J., Richardson, K., et al. (2018). Trajectories of the Earth system in the anthropocene. *Proceedings of the National Academy of Sciences of the United States of America, 115*, 8252–8259. https://doi.org/10.1073/pnas.1810141115

Swann, A. L. S., Longo, M., Knox, R. G., et al. (2015). Future deforestation in the Amazon and consequences for South American climate. *Agricultural and Forest Meteorology*. https://doi.org/10.1016/j.agrformet.2015.07.006

True Value Labs. (2020). *Dynamic materiality(TM): Measuring what matters.*

Vickers, J. S. (2011). *Independent commission on banking*. Final Report. The Stationary Office, London.

Wang-Erlandsson, L., Fetzer, I., Keys, P. W., et al. (2018). Remote land use impacts on river flows through atmospheric teleconnections. *Hydrology and Earth System Sciences, 22*, 4311–4328. https://doi.org/10.5194/hess-22-4311-2018

World Economic Forum. (2020). *Consultation draft toward common metrics and consistent reporting of sustainable value creation.*

Wuebbles, D., Fahey, D., Hibbard, K, et al. (2017). *Climate science special report: Fourth National Climate Assessment (NCA4), Volume I*. In: Agron. Reports. https://lib.dr.iastate.edu/agron_reports/8. Accessed 28 Nov 2020

Yang, Y., Saatchi, S. S., Xu, L., et al. (2018). Post-drought decline of the Amazon carbon sink. *Nature Communications*. https://doi.org/10.1038/s41467-018-05668-6

Young, T., Hazarika, D., Poria, S., & Cambria, E. (2018). Recent trends in deep learning based natural language processing. *IEEE Computational Intelligence Magazine, 13*(3), 55–75.

Zellers, R., Bisk, Y., Schwartz, R., & Choi, Y. (2018). SWAG: A large-scale adversarial dataset for grounded commonsense inference. In *Proceedings of the 2018 Conference on Empirical Methods in Natural Language Processing, EMNLP 2018* (pp 93–104). Association for Computational Linguistics.

Beatrice Crona, PhD, is a Professor of Sustainability and Deputy Science Director at the Stockholm Resilience Center (Stockholm University) and the Executive Director of the research program Global Economic Dynamics and the Biosphere at the Royal Swedish Academy of Science. Her background is in sustainability science and systems ecology. The last years she has worked on identifying opportunities for financial leadership for climate stability and sustainable development by linking Earth system science to corporate ownership, investment patterns and impact assessment.

Emma Sundström at the time of writing this chapter, she was a research data analyst and systems developer at Stockholm Resilience Centre (Stockholm University), with affiliation to the Global Economic Dynamics and the Biosphere program. She has an MSc in Computer and Systems Sciences. After seven years in the IT industry, she worked to implement technical solutions and methodologies within sustainability science.

Chapter 7
Digitalization of Bookkeeping in Small Organizations: The Case of Sweden

Anna Alexandersson, Andreas Jansson, and Karin Jonnergård

Abstract Bookkeeping and accounting is a prevalent feature of small organizations, which has changed face quite substantially with the advent of personal computers and, later, the Internet. The emergence of digitalized accounting procedures has taken place in a nexus of different types of actors (e.g., software developers, accountancy firms and the businesses themselves), regulatory frameworks (e.g., bookkeeping laws and accounting standards) and technical frameworks (e.g., standards for software interactions with banks and tax authorities). Altogether, this has made the paths taken in this process to be largely national. In general, this process of digitalization is largely undocumented and untheorized in research despite its profound impact on practice. Against this backdrop, this chapter has a descriptive and forward-looking approach, documenting the case of how Swedish bookkeeping practices of small organizations became digitalized, which can work as a reference case for comparisons with other national contexts.

Keywords Accounting · Bookkeeping · Entrepreneurship · Digitalization · Small Business · Regulation

1 Introduction

The bookkeeping that serves as the basis for accounting has been profoundly affected by a number of technological shifts, changing it from an activity performed using

A. Alexandersson (✉)
Linnaeus University, Växjö, Sweden
e-mail: anna.alexandersson@lnu.se

A. Jansson
Jönköping International Business School, Jönköping, Sweden
e-mail: andreas.jansson@ju.se

K. Jonnergård
Lund University, Lund, Sweden
e-mail: karin.jonnergard@fek.lu.se

T. Rana et al. (eds.), *Handbook of Big Data and Analytics in Accounting and Auditing*,
https://doi.org/10.1007/978-981-19-4460-4_7

pens and physical books, via various forms of mechanical machines such as typewriters, calculators and bookkeeping machines using punch cards introduced in the decades around the turn of the twentieth century (Wootton & Kemmerer, 2007), to digital technology. For large organizations, digitalization in the form of computerization started already in the 1950s (Wootton & Kemmerer, 2009) and has morphed into sophisticated information systems of data capture used for control, reporting and compliance, handling massive data quantities (Petkov, 2020). Contemporary research has addressed topics such as how digitalization has made the boundaries of accounting more elusive, allowing for integration of traditional accounting data with non-structured data for use in very compressed decision processes (Knudsen, 2020), among others. Hence, beyond its traditional role in management control, bookkeeping has found its place in contemporary trends of big data analytics and business intelligence.

There is, however, a less told story about digitalization of bookkeeping in smaller organizations, which is addressed in this chapter. Smaller organizations handle less data and often regard bookkeeping as a necessary and sometimes unwanted chore mainly performed to fulfil legal requirements. Digitalization has in this context primarily implied that computers and specialized accounting software have become the main tool for bookkeeping, a set of tools that has undergone substantial development since first introduced as the result of general technological change, but also as a result of entrepreneurial activity among software developers operating in a market. This market is a distinct context for entrepreneurial activities, which is shaped by the fact that the majority of customers (i.e. small business owners) often see the activity the applications are used for as a necessary evil. Bookkeeping is also institutionalized and strictly regulated in ways that some (e.g. Cong et al., 2018) argue hamper development in digitalization.

Research about how digitalization affects bookkeeping is, considering its large practical impact, scarce. If the search is confined to bookkeeping among smaller organizations, the volume of research is even smaller. Rolfe et al. (2003) finds that among remote farmers, digital technology for bookkeeping purposes has become common since it results in cost reductions, which is likely a generalizable result. As an effect of the near wholesale adoption of computerized bookkeeping among smaller organizations (Wyslocka, 2015), professional accountants are expected to have skills in bookkeeping software before entering the profession (Bunn et al., 2005). Gullkvist (2005) suggests that while professional accountants are positive towards technology, formal and informal institution may hinder them from adopting it. More generally, however, digital technology in bookkeeping is argued to increase the timeliness of information that can be extracted from the accounting system (Olivier, 2000). This is a potential that Artificial Intelligence and robotics is believed to contribute towards unleashing (Petkov, 2020), but so far this has mostly become a very partial reality among the largest accountancy firms and major corporations (Baldwin et al., 2006), although some simple robotics technology is built into modern accounting software also for smaller firms (as will be explored later in this chapter). Overall, digitalization and in particular robotic processes requires far-reaching standardization, which indirectly also seems to create a new normativity imposed on areas previously characterized by discretion, including standard setting (Rowbottom et al., 2021; Troshani et al., 2019). Altogether, these kinds of developments are assumed to change the skill set required from a professional accountant serving small firms, which will tend more towards data and technology management (Kruskopf et al., 2020). What effect it may have on other preparers of accounting (e.g., small-business owners) remain largely unexplored.

In sum, digitalization of bookkeeping in small organizations is a nascent research area that paints a very scattered picture of how this process has occurred and is occurring, who the important groups of actors shaping the process are, and how the peculiar context of bookkeeping interacts with the process. Arguably, the field needs both descriptive data and theorization. This chapter represents an attempt to address these issues by describing how digitalization of bookkeeping in small organizations played out in the Swedish context, a relatively technologically advanced society with a Germanic tradition of accounting (Artsberg, 2003), which may serve as a reference case and inspiration for identifying theoretically oriented research questions in future research.

2 Case Context and Methods

Inspired by the case study approach proposed by Flyvbjerg (1998, 2001), the chapter describes the case of the digitalization of bookkeeping in Sweden in detail so that the reader may interpret the case and compare it to other contexts. The bookkeeping practices of Sweden are in line with those of the rest of Europe. Bookkeeping and some form of more or less simplified (depending on legal form and size of the business) yearly financial report is mandatory and forms the foundation for calculating the yearly income tax. Practices are highly structured and regulated. Mandatory bookkeeping for small businesses was introduced by law already in 1855 (Nilsson & Smiciklas, 1993) and most small firms apply the same standardized chart of accounts (the so-called BAS plan), adapted to accounting and tax law, that was first introduced in 1976 together with a new bookkeeping act.

A market for accounting software directed at small firms began to appear in the late 1980s. While not mandatory for sole proprietorships, as opposed to partnerships and business forms with limited liability, more or less all active businesses use accounting software for bookkeeping purposes today. The supply side of the market has ever since been dominated by one, and later two, corporations that have over half of the market share. In general, the market for accounting software is structured according to national borders. This depends both on the fact that accounting regulation is largely issued on national level (although, for example, some EU-level regulation exist), but also because modern accounting software typically is integrated with payment systems, tax reporting systems, various types of industry-specific administrative software, and similar systems, which creates large barriers to entry on a new market.

The chapter places emphasis on the three central aspects of the development: regulation and the discourses surrounding this; the bookkeeping software for use on personal computers and later smartphones; and the entrepreneurial firms which make accounting software into a business model. The starting point is the bookkeeping act of 1976 and the end point is 2020. The chapter describes how technological development is shaped by the entrepreneurial action of a central group of actors—software developers—and how the process is unfolding in the context of the development of regulation of bookkeeping. In Table 1 the development of these aspects over time is described.

The empirical material for the case comes from interviews, document studies and observations. The description of the regulatory development is based on document studies of preparatory work for laws and regulations, and from scanning the accounting professions' magazine *Balans* (issues from 1976 until 2021) for all content relating to digitalization. The sections on digital tools and entrepreneurial processes draw upon twelve semi-structured interviews with entrepreneurs, managers, industry experts, developers, customer support staff and sales representatives from the software developers. The interviews were between one and three hours in length and the interviewees have connections to five different software developers (Visma SPCS, Fortnox, SpeedLedger, PE Accounting and Wint). These represents the major players on the Swedish market, both currently and historically. The description of the digital tools is also built on a study of printed manuals and video tutorials of the bookkeeping programs as these developed over time. Material from observations from industry events, as well as secondary material from annual reports, company websites, and online news articles, is also used to describe entrepreneurial action within the industry.

Following Flyvbjerg (1998, 2001), we have used a narrative approach when constructing the case. When reading the empirical material, we have had the following questions in mind: what happened, where, who acted, and how and why did they act? (O'Connor, 2007). We have aimed to identify the chronology and sequence of events as understood by the participants in the case and how they make sense of the developments in regulation, technology, and industry. By writing the case as narratives we can reconstruct how events, actions and their consequences are connected, and thereby how the development could be understood as a meaningful whole (O'Connor, 2007). The narrative about regulatory development is organized in three phases linked to new bookkeeping acts. The development of digital tools is divided into four phases related to new technology: personal computers, Windows, Internet, and smartphones. The development of the industry for bookkeeping software describes the sequence of entrepreneurial action that has developed the industry and the innovations that these actors have introduced in the field.

Table 1 Overview of the case: the digitalization of bookkeeping in Swedish small organizations 1976–2020

Year	Regulation and introduction of new technology in Sweden	Technological application in bookkeeping	Example of company/software	Comments
1976	Bookkeeping act			Allowing new technical means as punch card, micro cards, and magnetic strips Each second step on paper principle
1980			Hogia Microsoft's first Swedish partner, targeting accounting firms	Bookkeeping software for computers
1981	MS-DOS			
1985	MS Windows			
1986		MS-DOS based software	SPCS introduces SPCS Bokföring Targeting SMEs, less expensive	Bookkeeping, balance sheet and income statement, VAT reports, printing necessary, in MS-DOS Some checking
1994	Internet introduced to general public	Windows-based software	SPCS introduces SPCS Administration	First Window-based system for small firms. As above plus invoicing and simpler ERP system
1999	Bookkeeping act			From (paper-) form to content No demands on each second step on paper
2000	First smartphone introduced			
2001		Software based on Internet platform	SpeedLedger Web-based software in cooperation with bank, targeting micro companies	Bookkeeping based on the information in the bank accounts Machine learning

(continued)

Table 1 (continued)

Year	Regulation and introduction of new technology in Sweden	Technological application in bookkeeping	Example of company/software	Comments
2004	First iPhone		Fortnox, web-based platform Cooperation with Big 4 accounting firms, subscription as business model	Same functions as SPCS Administration above
2010		Smartphone applications		Digitization of supporting vouchers, work-site entries, machine reading
2013			PE Accounting, Hybrid firm	Standardized software to service sector Automation
2015	Archiving issue is debated		Bokio Free of charge, but keep ownership over aggregate information	Automaton, machine learning
2019	New commission for bookkeeping act			Solving the issues of unbroken chains of bookkeeping and the archiving

3 Regulatory Development and Digitalization

3.1 The Bookkeeping Act of 1976

The first regulation in the area of bookkeeping that mentioned computerization was the bookkeeping act from 1976. Since then, the law has changed again in 1999 and currently a governmental commission is assigned to revise the law. The regulatory development of bookkeeping seems to be interwoven with the development of regulation in related areas including EU regulation and standards for bookkeeping and technological devices. Together these four aspects form a pattern that allow for and hinder the use of technology in bookkeeping.

The computerization of bookkeeping in Sweden started in the 1950s. During the 1960s it became more commonplace that registrations of different entries were done through punch cards and magnetic strips. The bookkeeping act at the time originated from 1929 and had, accordingly, not considered modern office technologies. When a governmental investigation for a new bookkeeping act was appointed in 1962, it was based on demands from practice to update the regulation to fit the technology used in the business society. However, it was not an easy task, and an acceptable proposal was not presented until 1973, and a new act of bookkeeping was passed in 1976. The proposal included several "technology-related" changes, amongst others:

- The requirement to use a hardcover book as a journal was repealed, printed lists of entries from the computer could instead pass journal; however, the book containing the annual report still had to be in hardcover.
- Machine-readable material and micro text were allowed. Machine-readable material mentioned at the time was punched card and magnetic strips. However, each second step in the bookkeeping process must be visually readable.
- System documentation and documentation of the treatment of data were mandatory.

The basis was that the bookkeeping and its vouchers had to have *duration,* and this determined which machine-readable material that was accepted. Even though changes to update the regulation to the technology development were implemented, there was a limit on the adaptability to computer development. In the preparatory work to the act (SOU 1973:57: 229; *own translation*) it is stated:

> At the same time there are reasons to be somewhat prudent in the attempts to make the legislation forward looking. The regulatory system should only address those [computerized] system applications that have a clear practical timelessness. Issues about an even more advanced use of computers should, thereby, belong to a more or less distant change of the law in the future.

The act only provided basic rules and principles (a so-called "frame law"), and its more specific application was decided by the Swedish accounting standard board (*Bokföringsnämnden,* BFN). In their statements from the 1970s and 1980s one principle beside duration is salient: the principle of *traceability.* If any change in the bookkeeping process due to technological development was accepted, it followed that the process had to be possible to follow either through information on the voucher or/and a clear description in the system documentation. This is, for example, the basic conditions for presenting more than one transaction on one voucher, the possibility of archiving vouchers in summarized form, the use of electronic invoicing, etc. Over the period the idea of "second-step-visual-form" persisted as well as the demands on the documentation of the bookkeeping system and treatment of different journal entries. Being a frame law the 1976 bookkeeping act as such seems to be flexible enough for the computerization of the Swedish business society's bookkeeping. The one rule that led to several statements from BFN was the hardcover book for annual reports. It was finally agreed that the book could consist of sealed plastic pockets which had been tested and approved by the Swedish institute for standards (SiS). To a certain degree, these early statements reflect not only an application of the law but also a process of learning both from the standard setting board and practice.

In the early 1990s, BFN released a standard for system documentation and documentation of data treatment. It was obvious that the standard board was unsatisfied with the way the companies had fulfilled this part of the regulation. An investigation of practice had shown that the perspective in the system documentation was that of computer professionals, not of accountants. The responsibility as well as the documentation were often in the hand of the company's computer center. The standard board therefore emphasized the aim of the documentation as the importance of traceability. The standard could thereby keep its feature as a part of a frame law. Two officials of the standard board explain (Pyk & Lundqvist, 1992):

> The development within the computer area is, at times, incredibly fast and creates possibilities for new solutions. It had been unfortunate to commit to one model that feels good today but is out-of-date tomorrow.

In the middle of the 1980s the computerization virtually disappeared from the public discourse about accounting. It was still very much "on the move" in practice and the BFN continued to release statements in different areas, but the public discourse rather dealt with issues related to the financial reporting and measurement, and this filled the agenda most of the rest of the 1980s and 1990s. In the 1976 bookkeeping act, a more principle-based accounting based on "best practice" had been introduced. Instead of the intended flexible standards from private standard setters and good compliance from the companies, the result had become flexible compliance from the companies leading to a variety of accounting principles applied for, e.g., goodwill and group accounting. On the top of this, Sweden was in the process of joining the EU. With this as a background a new governmental commission for accounting and bookkeeping was initiated.

3.2 *The Bookkeeping Act of 1999*

The governmental commission consisted of several parts and the one about bookkeeping was first presented in 1996 and decided upon in 1999. To a large degree it is an updated version of the law from 1976. In the report from the commission, it is stated (SOU 1996:157: 20; *own translation*):

> Several of the changes are editorial and linguistic and consist in several cases only of a modernization of the legal rules mostly due to the development in the area of information technology (IT) that occurred since the earlier law. Our point of departure when formulating the legal rules for bookkeeping has been to equalize the demands regarding the function and purposes of the bookkeeping regardless if the bookkeeping is performed manually or computerized. To achieve such general design of the rules of the law it is necessary that the regulation is designed as a frame law to an even larger extent than the act of 1976.

Despite this statement several changes were put into the new legislation, amongst other:

1. A new concept of "voucher" (bookkeeping information) was introduced in order to get rid of the old focus on paper and instead focus on the information regardless of the medium used.
2. A focus on the product of the bookkeeping instead of the process of the bookkeeping. The demand is that the company can always present the bookkeeping regardless of how it has been registered.

3. The principle of "each-second-step-visual-form" was abandoned.
4. If the bookkeeping is computerized, the machine can be located outside of Sweden given that the responsible for the bookkeeping is able to present the bookkeeping in a readable way in Sweden. In addition, supporting vouchers may occasionally leave Sweden.
5. The regulation about a hardcover book containing the annual reports was repealed.

The principles the bookkeeping should rest on were *duration*, *completeness* and *immediate access* and the emphasis should be on the content of the information, not the form it had.

The first years after the new regulation was passed in 1999, it was not widely discussed. Instead, the public discussion evolved around two other laws that likely influenced the development of digitalization of Swedish bookkeeping: EU's directive on secure electronic transformation (EU 1999/93) regarding digital signatures and EU's directive on electronic invoicing (2001/115/EG). The directive on signatures implies that qualified electronic signature is legally applicable. This opened for a practice of electronic signatures in different areas. Regarding electronic invoices this was already a practice within Sweden (see BFN U 89:2) but now it was possible to practice within the whole EU. The practice, however, was not that easily developed, since different business partners often had different computer systems for their bookkeeping. In practice a so-called four corner system was developed in which the invoicing company sends the invoice to its service company (handling issues such as data entry, processing and storage), which sends it on to the customer's service company which sends it on to the customer. Without a clear standard in the area the issues about what was the duration of the supporting vouchers, possibility of information loss during the transformation and where the vouchers should be archived were up in the air.

The bookkeeping act of 1999, on the other hand, seems to be enough of a frame regulation to fit the technological development for at least ten years. Around 2015, however, a discontent with the regulation started to become salient. The discontent addressed two issues: specific rules in the act that were not sufficiently changed between the 1976 and the 1999 acts of bookkeeping, and the issues related to the technological development that had occurred since the act had been put in place.

A rule that was vividly discussed was the principle that any supporting voucher had to be archived in the form it was received. This principle implies that if a receipt for, e.g., a representation dinner was received on paper, it had to be kept and archived in this format for a certain number of years. This took time and money (for an SME, on average SEK 3.7–4.2 per year, according to Trinovo consulting [2021]) and arguments against the principle spanned from its impractical aspects, concern for the forest, to its impact on the Swedish GDP.

Regarding technological development the discussion dealt with the possibility of using cloud-based technology and the development of an unbroken digital chain. The chief officials of BFN describes the development in this way (Pärlhem, 2019; *own translation*):

> A natural development is an increasing use of unbroken digital chains. Invoices and other bookkeeping information are created in a digital way and treated in the bookkeeping system with the support of machine learning and automatic entries. The bookkeeping information is stored in cloud services and cloud distributed databases. The financial reports are compiled from basic data through the support of taxonomies…

The main concern regarding the technological development raised, regards the integrity of the data related to control and potential crime investigations.

3.3 Steps Towards a New Bookkeeping Act

In 2020 a new governmental investigation was formed to overview the bookkeeping act (Dir. 2020:48). This time the investigation was commissioned to address (i) simplification of the rules and administration for the SME, and (ii) modernization of the bookkeeping act. The directives were stated as follows:

> The basic purpose of the assignment is to simplify the bookkeeping process by creating a modern, technologically neutral, and simple frame of rules for the companies. It is important that the regulation can fulfil its purpose over time with consideration that technological development will continue. The simplifications should not open the possibility for abuse of the rules or lead to applications with, e.g., criminal intent. Neither may they imply that the purposes of bookkeeping are being circumvented. (Dir. 2020:48, p.6; *own translation*)

A suggestion for regulatory changes was advanced the summer of 2021 (SOU, 2021: 60). In summary the changes were about modernization of the language in the law, but two more factual changes were also suggested: The concept of machine-read material was exchanged to "electronic documents", allowing for new forms of information, and it was suggested that it would be permittable to dispose documents if they been transformed into a secure electronic document. Much of the demands in the debate above would thereby be met.

4 Technological Development and Digital Tools for Bookkeeping

4.1 The Computerization of Small Business Bookkeeping

Computerized accounting has a history from the 1950s, although then strictly confined to major corporations that could afford and benefit from the substantial initial cost required (Wootton & Kemmerer, 2009). As computer technology became cheaper and more accessible for smaller organizations during the 1980s, computers became increasingly used for bookkeeping purposes. They became more standardized in a format recognizable today, with the gradual dominance of the PC format with the Microsoft-DOS operating system (and the competing proprietary format Macintosh with a different operating system launched in 1984).

There had been bookkeeping software running on other formats than PCs with MS-DOS, but the Swedish market for bookkeeping software took off mainly for this type of computers, which allowed for one standardized set of formatting and writing on floppy discs to work for distribution to all customers. One of the pioneering developers *Hogia* (described below), before the dominance of PCs, had hundreds of computers for writing different disc formats to distribute their software (Hogia PC-museum, n.d.). Such pioneering software, however, generally had a price that was prohibitive for most smaller firms, although it was popular among accountancy firms providing services to small firms. It was the launching of the low-cost bookkeeping software by Scandinavian PC Systems, called *SPCS bokföring*, that popularized computerized bookkeeping among Swedish small firms that practiced bookkeeping themselves.

SPCS Bokföring was an MS-DOS-based, low-cost software for bookkeeping and generation of basic financial accounting reports in the form a balance sheet and income statement, but also some other reports such as a VAT report (for tax reporting purposes) and sales reports for different products (for management control purposes). These early versions of cheap and simple bookkeeping applications for PCs were designed to serve two purposes: to allow bookkeeping in books to be performed in a computerized environment, in which the computer helps with basic checks (i.e. that the sum of debits equal the sum of credits in an entry), summations and compilations into reports, and to adhere to the demands of the bookkeeping act of 1976. Since the act emphasized that every second step must be visually readable, and the durability of machine-readable formats and floppy discs were not considered to be durable enough, this meant that the computer used for bookkeeping had to be supplemented by a printer and that the journal and ledger had to be printed regularly and saved together with vouchers and reports.

Figure 1 shows the interface for a regular entry of an early MS-DOS-based application, which is typical for how this kind of software worked in the mid- to late 1980s. The entries were automatically numbered ("ver. nr") and the user added a date for the transaction ("datum"). By tabbing between fields, the user could then add an explanatory text, and then continue adding rows ("rad") in which a sum ("Belopp") were entered either on the debit or credit side ("D/K") of an account ("konto") that the user had to enter in numeric format. This was picked from a chart of accounts that in the default version was the Swedish standard chart of accounts—the "BAS plan", which in turns were adapted to Swedish reporting requirements—but could be customized within the program. Should the amount of debits and credits not be equal, the application would not register the entry until rectified. The more advanced MS-DOS-based software *Topp* (also released by SPCS), popular during the late 1980s and early 1990s, could (depending on version) perform similar tasks and a few more, such as detailed records of accounts payables and receivables, invoicing, inventory keeping, and simple budgeting and costing, using an interface similar to Fig. 1 but with separate columns for debits and credits and with automatic display of account name once its number was entered. The most advanced applications could also run

```
FIRMA                     860811                    REGISTRERING
=====================================================================
        VER.NR  1                                  DATUM 860811
        TEXT

        RAD KONTO                            KVANT   BELOPP D/K

=====================================================================
         ANGE VER.NR. ELLER ELLER F1
```

Fig. 1 Interface for a regular entry in MS-DOS-based *SPCS Bokföring*. *Source* Scandinavian PC Systems (1986: 4–2)

in a local network. Compared to how bookkeeping on paper worked, this format is very recognizable.

4.2 *The Transfer to Windows*

A major change in the interface of bookkeeping software was prompted by developments in operating systems for PCs: the change from MS-DOS to the graphically oriented Microsoft Windows. While this provided the technology for more graphically appealing and intuitive bookkeeping software, windows-based applications were not quick to be launched on the Swedish market. 1994 saw the release of the first version of what would be the most popular bookkeeping software among Swedish small businesses for around two decades: the Windows-based *SPCS Administration*. This program came in different versions with varying functionality (with corresponding price differential), ranging from a package handling similar tasks as *SPCS Bokföring* combined with invoicing in a Windows-based environment, to simpler ERP systems capable of handling inventory management, orders and offers, packing slips, etc., in a network environment.

While many functions were gradually added, and work in Windows allowed for the use of a mouse when working, many things remained the same. As can be seen in Fig. 2, displaying the interface for a regular entry into the *SPCS Administration 1000* in its 1996 version, the basic prompt was similar to that from MS-DOS-based programs, although more graphical and allowing for more information to be added to each row in the entry, such as cost unit and project number for management accounting purposes (a feature it shared with some versions of *Topp*). The standardized chart of accounts (the BAS plan) was in continuous use providing a structure of accounts that could also be customized by the user. The basic navigation between different tasks was by drop-down menus and buttons with graphical symbols.

The basic problem of storage of the ledger and journal on floppy disks or even a PC hard drive remained as these were not assumed to be durable enough, and users

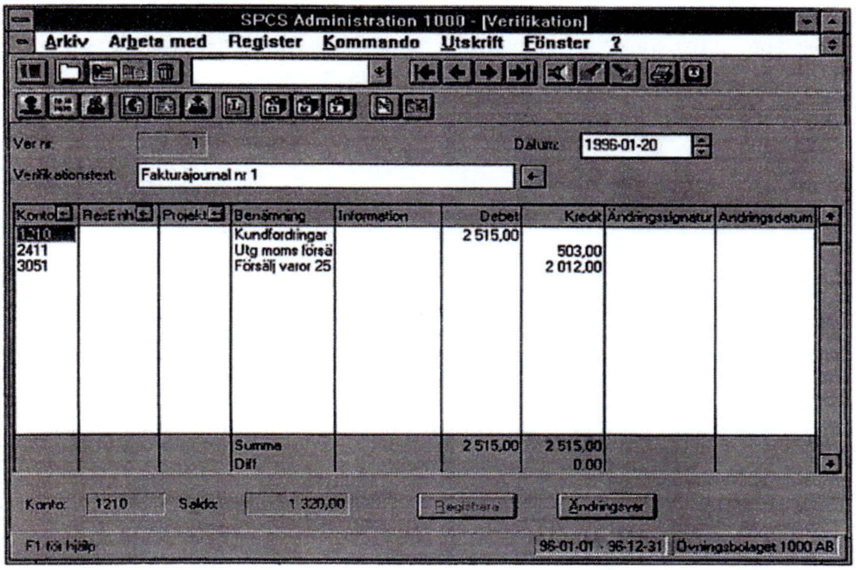

Fig. 2 Interface for a regular entry in MS Windows-based *SPCS Administration*. *Source* Scandinavian PC Systems (1997: 3–9)

kept being expected to print these on a regular basis. This design and technology base of bookkeeping software for small businesses continued until the Internet changed how software was accessed and how data was stored.

4.3 Introduction of Internet-Based Technology

The first applications drawing on Internet-based technology were launched in the first years of the 2000's. There were two main solutions launched: one which was integrated with the retail banks' systems that allowed business owners to do their bookkeeping using the same platform as their online banking, and one which was a standalone system with almost the exact same functionality and interface as the locally installed Windows-based applications. Both solutions allowed the possibility to access the system from any Internet-connected computer and data were being stored by the software company (although it was possible to locally save backup files). The former solution came to be popular among the very smallest businesses, whereas the latter became the norm for slightly larger firms and for accounting firms offering bookkeeping, tax and accounting services.

Some early steps towards machine learning and automation were taken during this era. While it had been possible already in MS-DOS based software for the user to pre-code certain standard transactions (e.g., a certain percentage of VAT to be added when an entry is made on a revenue account), developments in software allowed programs to automatically recognize standard entries to an increasing extent. This introduced the functionality that the program suggested entries based on input information (such as a payment to a certain recipient in online banking systems), allowing the user to simply verify that it is correct.

The main obstacle for Internet-based technology to penetrate the market for bookkeeping software was attitude towards technology: there was a widespread attitude that the technology was not safe enough both in terms of cyber security threats, but also concerns about storage of data by the software companies. While this was a general issue for many online-based activities (e.g., for the emerging e-commerce sector) and was, as discussed above, also up for discussion in the legal process, bookkeeping was considered extra sensitive since organizations by law had to keep records safe since taxes were based on this data.

This obstacle was overcome by the combination of linkage of the new generation of software with well-established players, and interfaces that were very familiar to regular users. The two most successful linkages with established players, were the cooperation with retail banks (which offered the familiar online-banking interface) and with accountancy firms (which offered the familiar interface of locally installed software), of which the latter conferred enough credibility to the technology for it to be increasingly accepted also by firms handling their own bookkeeping. Eventually, Internet-based solutions began to take over the locally installed systems and a new era of more innovation in interfaces and functionality could take place.

4.4 Third Generation of Accounting Software

In the 2010s, the Internet was an integrated part of most computer use and smartphones had become widespread. While it is difficult to determine when online-based bookkeeping software overtook locally installed versions, it is safe to say that by the turn of the decade, the majority of new users opted for online versions, while a lot of old users remained with their familiar software for which they already owned unlimited licenses. The period is characterized by a continued trend of integration of machine learning and automation in bookkeeping software, but also interlinkages through open API's of firms' bookkeeping systems with other systems such as tax reporting systems, online banking systems (for those applications that were not integrated with these platforms already), e-commerce systems and other firms' ERP systems for e-invoicing purposes, and changing user interfaces qualitatively different from the classical user views exemplified by Figs. 1 and 2. An example of a bookkeeping interface of a contemporary system (*Speedledger*) that is integrated with online banking and aimed at micro-businesses is displayed in Fig. 3.

Characteristic of the interface in the Figure is that entries are not done in terms of debits and credits. Rather, by integration with online banking systems, a list of transactions on the banking account is presented to the bookkeeper, who for each payment selects an appropriate revenue or expense account (from the standardized

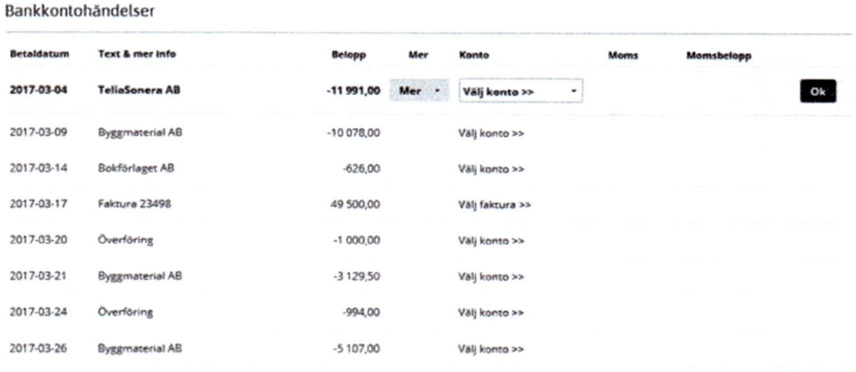

Fig. 3 Interface for a regular entry in online-based *SpeedLedger*. *Source* SpeedLedger (2021)

BAS plan) to which the transaction pertains. The entry into the journal and ledger is then automated. The next time a payment to/from the same recipient arrives, the system will suggest using the same account as the last time, i.e. a simple form of machine learning. Other systems draw on linkages with online banks in other ways; for example, by automatically reconciling transactions on the bank account with the bookkeeping, thus discovering unpaid accounts receivable or transactions that have not been entered into the accounting system. A number of features involving smartphones have also been commonplace, i.e. for digitization of supporting vouchers (however, as described above, a voucher received on paper must still be archived in paper form; this is one of the few areas in which software developers are attempting to pressure the legislator to change regulation), simple entries using an app on work sites, etc. Some degree of automated machine reading of incoming invoices that produce a suggested entry is at hand in some applications but is partly hampered by the lack of a standardized format for invoices.

Despite the macro trends broadly affecting bookkeeping software, the period is also characterized by differentiation in the design of the products. While general bookkeeping software remains the main product, a number of specialized applications aimed at specific segments emerged (e.g., for small service companies, real estate agents, self-employed craftsmen, etc.) handling issues pertaining to that industry. Software was also differentiated in user interface, customer service and payment models, ranging from complete outsourcing of accounting to an accountancy firm working with their self-developed software and highly automated processes for a monthly subscription fee, to simple free-of-charge applications with little support, in which the developers reserve the right to make use of the accounting data for analytical purposes.

5 Entrepreneurship in Small Business Bookkeeping Software

5.1 *Hogia—The OG*

The story of bookkeeping software for small organizations in Sweden started in classic entrepreneurship fashion in the basement of a house in Stenungsund. The founder of Hogia developed software for his wife's accounting firm after work hours and started to sell them on a small scale to other accounting firms. When his wife started her business, he thought she should buy a personal computer and do the bookkeeping digitally, but at the time there was no accounting software for PCs for sale. He learned programming and created a computer program for her. After a year he sold the first program and that was the beginnings of Hogia founded in 1980. He discovered an opportunity to sell the software to other accounting firms and expanded quickly in the Swedish market due to the increasing sales of personal computers during the 1980s.

5.2 *SPCS—A 'Folk' Program Via Mail Order*

In the mid-1980s another main actor in the development of software for bookkeeping entered the market. Scandinavian PC Systems was founded in 1984 in the town of Växjö and started to sell primarily word processing and spreadsheet software, but also video games and other programs to small businesses. The original business idea of SPCS was to supply easy-to-use and low-priced software by mail order. Large resources were spent on developing manuals and sending out catalogues to previous customers several times per year.

SPCS developed its first bookkeeping software for small firms in 1986 (see Fig. 1). The opportunity was discovered when they started to get an increasing number of inquiries about bookkeeping software from their existing customer base. At the time they had a customer directory of 140,000 clients and the majority was small businesses and small accounting firms. A telephone survey of the customers in the register revealed that a bookkeeping application was what they lacked in the offering from SPCS. The main competitor Hogia at this time sold software with support and service which was regarded as expensive by small businesses. The entrepreneurs realized that they had identified a new business area and decided to target firms with less than ten employees, which made up 90% of the market in Sweden at the time. The aim was to create a "folk program" for people less acquainted with computers. The development of the new software was commissioned to an external developer and was developed in dialogue with an expert-group of accounting professionals, since neither of the founders had any background in accounting. The low-priced and basic software filled a niche as it was comparatively cheap relative to existing software used by larger firms. The simple program required the same knowledge about accounting as physical books, but the customers appreciated the possibility of being able to stop hiring accounting firms for bookkeeping. The customers had some concerns regarding the new technology and the company used their mail order catalogue to educate the customers on how it worked. The second software launched by SPCS was a Polish-developed software (TOPP), which was a complete administrative package including bookkeeping, invoicing, and systems for keeping track of accounts receivable and payable. While this software had more functionalities, it was still cheap in comparison to other products mainly aimed at larger firms.

In the beginning of 1990s Windows became the new standard operating system and SPCS developed the first generation of their bestseller and main product SPCS Administration (see Fig. 2; later Visma Administration). Microsoft started to preinstall word processing and spreadsheet software on their personal computers, which killed the market for the other software developed by SPCS. However, bookkeeping software was more difficult to standardize globally, which meant less competition and room for national products such as SPCS Administration.

5.3 Fortnox Among the Clouds

In the late 1990s small businesses were computerized in Sweden and the next technological shift occurred when the Internet emerged. SPCS started early on to plan for developing a platform and program that could be used on the Internet. According to a former employee the company had been late with adopting Windows and did not want to be late again. However, amid the discussions of this new investment SPCS was acquired by a Norwegian company PC Systemer, which then was acquired by Visma, and became Visma SPCS. The original founder of SPCS, and the CEO at the time, pitched the idea of developing a new internet-based platform for the software to the board in 1999. He argued that there were many benefits for the customer and that this was a real opportunity for the company to seize. The product would give the customers constant access to the latest update, to backups and to the system from any computer in the world. However, according to him the board was not interested in a large investment in a product that would compete with their profitable main product. He immediately resigned and started Fortnox in 2001 together with a former employee from SPCS. Both thought the idea of a web-based platform was too good to give up, and that they had come too far in their thinking and preparation for it.

The business idea of Fortnox was the same as SPCS, but with web-based technology. They argued that there were several benefits both for the customers and the company. For the customers there would be less problems with installing new programs with each upgrade and being forced to contact support. For the company it meant a less costly process for upgrades and support. At each upgrade it was expensive to produce the CD-roms and distribute them to all customers and it was difficult and expensive to offer support when the customers had different versions of the software. Distributing new programs to 100,000 customers for each upgrade cost millions of SEK and this had made SPCS postpone upgrades and accept worse quality than necessary. The online upgrade also ensured that all customers always had the same version.

The startup hired a new team of developers for developing software for book-keeping adapted for the Internet. Neither of the entrepreneurs were programmers or had any prior accounting knowledge, both came from marketing and sales, so they found a software-development company that promised that they could build a web-based accounting system for them. However, in late 2003 it was evident that the development company they had been working with did not know web-based technology and they had to start over with another company. Due to this it took 2.5 years until they could offer the first version of the software. The original Fortnox system was very similar to SPCS Administration, although simpler and with less functions, but with the added functions of cloud storage of data and access from any computer that was connected to the Internet.

Sales were slow in the beginning and the new technology presented both a limitation and an opportunity. The potential customers were concerned about the fact that the data was no longer stored on their own computer. The marketing of the product was hindered by the limited number of users of the Internet, but also helped by the increased use of email and search engines. The marketing and sales proved to be a challenge and the entrepreneurs decided to do something drastic. They rented a booth at Arlanda Airport near Stockholm for a week and talked to as many travelers as possible. It turned into a mission of educating the customer about the new technology rather than selling the product. However, the duo managed to catch the attention of key persons from some of the large accounting firms. These representatives recognized the opportunity inherent in Internet-based technology as it allowed them to cooperate with their customers without sending floppy discs or CD-roms with data back and forth. After some time, PwC, one of the big four accountancy firms, integrated the software in their self-branded portal, which led to other firms to follow suit and sales surged. This deal with PwC was deemed as a turning point and crucial by both the founding entrepreneurs.

A major change was the subscription model. Previous iterations of software sold by SPCS and Hogia had been licensed for a lump sum and now the payment model changed to a monthly fee. The co-founder of Fortnox described the new subscription model in the following way:

> It was brilliant commercially that we could get paid every month by the customer. Even if it was little money every month it became a large amount when we had 100 000 customers that paid 100 SEK every month. The only cost we had was for servers and support, but the latter decreased each month when the customer learnt the program.

This model with no initial non-recurring costs, no charges for support, a fixed sum each month and easy to start, switch or cancel subscriptions introduced by Fortnox has since become the norm for the industry.

5.4 Fortnox and the Accounting Firms

Fortnox got their sales going by working with accounting firms and has since been dominant within the segment of larger accounting firms. A manager in charge of the business area accounting firms stated that the accountants were a good entry point because they enjoyed a great deal of trust among their customers. If they managed to make the accountants like the system and recommend it to their clients, it would help when introducing new technology. According to the manager the larger firms understood the benefits of the Internet even before the technology was really established. In the beginning, the web-based software was a complement to locally installed programs when they wanted to cooperate with other offices and their clients. Today, web-based technology is the main software at the accounting firms and no longer a complement.

Fortnox representatives stress how automation gives the opportunity for bookkeeping to be updated in real-time and therefore the accounting firm can provide daily numbers to your client. However, smaller accounting firms are less attracted to such new technologies. There are several reasons for this conservatism: their business model in which they charge per hour, many of them being micro- or solo enterprises, and the high average age among the accountants in this sector. Large accounting firms are pressured to develop their business due to the competition and demands for higher profitability which leads to a higher propensity for change, whereas micro firms with an owner close to retirement are less interested in investing in innovation leading to automation which will decrease billable hours. Automation is projected to change the job of the accountant, putting less time into current recording of transactions, but more on understanding the consequences and making assessment of the numbers. A Fortnox manager explained the company's position as:

> I think the accountant must become much better at being an analyst: observing, analyzing and assessing the data. I would say that one of our goals is that ... recording [of transactions] should be as automated as possible, so you need to do as little as possible manually. However, you need to understand the implications of the data as an accountant.

In the beginning Fortnox spent a lot of time trying to convince both accounting firms and end customers of the benefits and safety of Internet based software. However, the Internet banks changed the perception of the Internet, and thereby, the perception of keeping books in the cloud. The manager described the development as follows: "In 2009 it was so-so, but then came the Internet banks and then it was like, 'Well, this is alright, if they can do it online then I can put the bookkeeping on the web, if I can do bank transactions online, then I can do the bookkeeping online'."

In addition to this, changed perception of safety, the increased speed of the Internet and Google Chrome, according to the manager, changed the situation, since there was no longer a lag when you worked in the program. The close connection with the accounting firms also has led to a particular development of the software at Fortnox. Fortnox engaged accountants from major and smaller accountancy firms as part of an expert panel assisting in the development of the functionality of the product based on their experiences. This involvement from the start meant that they wanted a system that could be used for as many types of companies as possible and that Fortnox today offers a standardized system without any adaptations for different industries.

5.5 *Speedledger and the Internet Banks*

Speedledger was founded in Gothenburg in 2000 and launched their Internet based software a few years ahead of Fortnox in 2001. Fortnox attributed a lot of their success to a change of behavior due to the introduction of Internet banks. Speedledger is the company that took this one step further and established close cooperation with the banks through their platform. The user can buy their software as an add-on in their Internet bank. During the first five years it was not even possible to buy Speedledger as a separate product and in 2019 still most of their customers bought their software through Swedbank E-bokföring. They view themselves as a complement to the banks' services, which both is a strength and weakness for the company since there are some functions they cannot add without competing with the bank.

Their main product is Speedledger e-bokföring (see Fig. 3). The target market is small businesses with 0–10 employees and associations. They offer cloud based and automated bookkeeping through the customer's Internet bank and the software is simple with few options and settings. They describe extensive free customer support as an important part of their offering and a point of pride. The concept is described in these terms on their website (Speedledger, 2019): "Our business concept is to make it easier and more fun to be an entrepreneur by automating routine work and giving the small business owner control over their administration and finances."

The genesis of the company was the cooperation with Swedbank. The founders had an idea, and that was at the same time as the banks launched their Internet bank, they thought that there had to be a way to capitalize on the fact that financial data was now available on the Internet. The first version of Speedledger's software was developed in Swedbank's server halls in Stockholm and had a direct connection to the systems that the Internet banks also used. The API's used by Speedledger are still slightly different from the public PSD2-API's available to the other software developers and they have their own integration with the banks which gives them access to more data than the public ones.

In 2015 the founders sold the company to a British private equity company, HG Capital, that happens to be one of Visma's largest owners. They subsequently sold Speedledger, and its main competitor the Danish company e-economic, to Visma (Visma, 2015). Speedledger is still an independent software developer within Visma and e-economic remains one of their fiercest competitors since the corporate group is run in a very decentralized manner. For many years Visma has had a strategy of growth-through-acquisition and there is head-on competition between the companies within the Norwegian corporate group.

5.6 *PE Accounting—The First Hybrid*

In 2013 a new type of competitor entered the market that in contrast to previous companies also offered bookkeeping services in addition to the software. PE Accounting was the first hybrid of a software developer and an accounting firm, offering to replace the accounting department for their customers. In contrast to the competitors that have entered the market after them such as Wint, Dooer and Bokio, they do not target the smallest firms. Their niche strategy has developed over time and in 2019 they targeted service companies with 5–500 employees and 5–500 Million SEK in net sales. They do not offer any customer specific adaptations and have chosen to decline customers to be able standardize their software. Their payment model is based on a fixed price based on volumes of transactions over one year.

5.7 *WINT—From Accounting Firm to Tech Firm*

If PE Accounting was the first hybrid to start in the industry, then WINT took a longer and more winding road to become a hybrid, transforming from a traditional accounting firm to a tech company. While WINT as a company and trademark was founded in 2011 in Gothenburg, the origin of the firm was a two-person accounting firm from the small town Hagfors.

The founder of WINT resigned as CEO in September 2018, and six months later, the new management announced a new strategic direction to create profit and positive cash flows (Leijonhufvud, 2019). The results had not been satisfactory, and a new niche strategy was launched based on more niched apps, but also downsizing and infusion of new capital from the owners. Instead of creating software for all businesses like Fortnox, the decision was made to focus on microbusinesses and launch specific software for real estate agencies.

In 2020 WINT was a hybrid firm with their own software and 35 accountants employed to service their clients. WINT was at the time known among their competitors for a team-based work process, instead of one consultant per client, which was perceived as more efficient and less dependent on certain employees. The CEO described the work approach as an 'iceberg', where the customer sees very little of the work performed. He stated that these processes below the surface are indeed the major innovation in WINT rather than the technology.

5.8 *Bokio Offers a Bookkeeping App for Free*

In 2015 Bokio entered the market with the same ambition to automate bookkeeping with machine learning and artificial intelligence, but with a new business model. Bokio offered bookkeeping software for free and their business idea was to: "offer free and automated bookkeeping to small and medium sized businesses" (Wallenberg, 2018). Their business model is based on the idea of freemium, which means that one part, in this case the bookkeeping app, is free of charge, but all other services cost money. For example, customer support is not included in the service and, if you need customer support, you are charged a fee much higher than the subscription fee of other companies. Other revenue streams are commission on services that they mediate to the customers such as factoring, credit intermediation, pensions, and other financial services from their business partners (Bokio, 2020; Leijonhufvud, 2017). The stated ambition by the entrepreneurs was to become the Google of bookkeeping and create a new global standard with bookkeeping for free. Bokio has grown organically at a significant rate and had 40,000 clients in 2018.

The development of the company has been supported by venture capital from the start and the company has continuously taken in new capital from investors (Bokio, 2020). The venture capital firm Creandum was one of the investors that invested SEK 30 million and they expressed the following expectations on Bokio: "Bookkeeping should be automated, but it should also be free" (Leijonhufvud, 2017). This statement created questions about how you earn money on a free app. The references to Google, free bookkeeping and a phrasing in their terms and conditions have led to expectations among the competitors that the data will be aggregated and sold to a third party as in the case of Google. Bokio does not openly state that they will sell aggregated data to a third party, but in their general terms and conditions from 2018, they reserve the right to produce statistics based on the customers' data and that these statistics are the property of Bokio (2021).

5.9 The Industry in 2020

In 2020, Visma SPCS and Fortnox are the two main competitors in the market intensely monitoring each other. Figuratively, and quite literally, since Fortnox built their new office building across the road from Visma's headquarter in Växjö. Fortnox got a head start with Internet-based software due to a close cooperation with accounting firms and is the market leader in sales to accounting firms, while Visma SPCS retains the main market share in sales of locally installed products directly to small businesses (and also markets online-based products). The Internet-based systems are the choice of most new customers in a market where few customers change software after the initial purchase. While they dominate, there are several other firms that have emerged contributing to the development of the industry by new forms of strategic alliances, work processes and business models. The firms within the industry either develop and sell software (i.e. Visma SPCS, Fortnox, Bokio, Speedledger), or work as so-called hybrids both developing their own software and providing bookkeeping services (i.e. WINT, PE Accounting). The competition is intensifying, and the number of competitors has increased considerably in the last five years. Notable is the lack of global competitors in the Swedish market, even though global actors such as Zero and Google are mentioned as potential threats.

Even though the corporate group Visma is still growing through acquisitions, there are few signs of consolidations in the market.

A noteworthy trend is the niche strategies adopted by the newer firms. There is a large group of firms targeting the smallest firms, the microbusinesses. Speedledger, Dooer, Bokio, Wrebit and Redflag developed their offer for this group from the start. WINT has recently changed strategy and is now targeting this group, which is approximately 90% of the businesses in Sweden. WINT also stands out with their software developed for a specific industry, real estate agencies. Most software developers seek standardization and offer no, or few, adaptations or complex functionalities suitable for example import/export businesses or wholesalers.

Another trend is that the business model with selling licenses is being replaced with subscription models, freemiums, or payment per transaction. The newest challengers in the industry, such as Bokio and Wrebit, have introduced freemiums.

Lastly, the entrepreneurs within the field advocate a new role for the accounting firms and envision a future in which automated systems are replacing the manual data entry today performed by accountants. The entrepreneurs argue that the accountants should instead focus on business development based on their knowledge about finance and using the bookkeeping data reported in real-time as support for strategic decision-making. However, they identify several factors in the Swedish context that make this transformation slow and recognize that there are few incentives for small accounting firms with owners near retirement to invest in expensive technology when the business model is based on charging the customers by the hour.

6 Conclusion and Implications

Figure 4 summarizes the case in a model which is an adaptation of Orlikowski (1992: 410). There are several external inputs to the process by which bookkeeping software is developed, of which new, more general-purpose technology (personal computers, Microsoft Windows, the Internet, online banking, smartphones, etc.) is among the most important (arrow a). Bookkeeping software manifests as the application of general-purpose technology in the bookkeeping process, although as our case shows, bookkeeping is among the later applications of the technology.

One reason for this late adaptation is the strict and partly formalized institutional environment of the bookkeeping processes, in the form of hard regulation (i.e. the bookkeeping act), highly institutionalized practices (i.e. double-entry bookkeeping) and newer but highly influential soft norms (i.e. the standardized charts of accounts) (cf. Gullkvist, 2005). These institutional properties form a second significant input on the development of bookkeeping software (arrow b). The case shows that software developers are not to any significant extent involved in attempts to change these institutional properties; these properties and general-purpose technology form a largely taken-for-granted framework that is integrated into the bookkeeping software by software developers in an entrepreneurial process (arrow c). Innovation by software developers is rather on the level of finding new ways of applying general-purpose

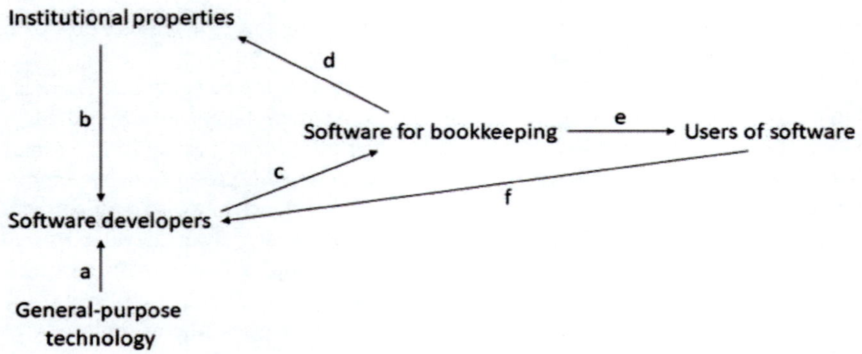

Fig. 4 Model summarizing the case. *Source* Elaboration of Fig. 5 in Orlikowski (1992: 410)

technology to the bookkeeping process within the confines of the existing institutional environment. Some effect of the development of bookkeeping software on the regulation of bookkeeping can, however, be observed (arrow d); especially regarding the issue of electronic record keeping, a development that was clearly driven by the development of software for bookkeeping and accounting purposes.

Finally, bookkeeping software is used by small organizations in their bookkeeping processes and as such influences this (arrow e), an effect that is outside the scope of this chapter. However, what is observable, is how the demand of users of software plays a role in shaping the development of bookkeeping software (arrow f). For example, the early MS-DOS applications were direct responses to demands for simple and cheap bookkeeping software for PCs, and later developments simplifying the bookkeeping process and placing less demands of institutional knowledge about bookkeeping on the user (e.g., through integration with internet banks or automation) can also arguably be interpreted as arising from demand of a segment of customers that may see bookkeeping more as a necessary evil than a value-creating process. However, demand from customers of bookkeeping software should not be overemphasized as a driver for innovation by software developers; as the case illustrates, many important general-purpose technologies required substantial 'selling efforts' before they became more generally accepted by customers (e.g., Internet-based bookkeeping), often involving software developers cooperating with established actors (e.g., retail banks or accountancy firms).

While this chapter is of a descriptive character and the model presented is intended as a summary of empirical findings, we believe it has several implications for the literature and theoretical development in the area of digitalization of accounting in small firms. First, by providing a coherent description of the process by which small-firm bookkeeping became digitalized in Sweden, we demonstrate how this story has multiple aspects that are all interrelated; a finding that is likely to be consisted across contexts and proves important for understanding the development in our case. Digitalization of small-business bookkeeping has been a story of technological development, but also of institutional development and entrepreneurship, and these aspects are clearly interrelated. Our summarizing model represents an attempt to describe the relations among these (and other) aspects, which can serve as a platform for future research and theory development that is discussed more extensively below.

Second the description advances the idea of regulation as not only a restriction for technological development or a mean for hinder misuses of technology which is often emphasized in the Finreg-literature (e.g. Butler & O'Brien, 2019; Lemma, 2020). Instead, it is apparent that the regulation is driven by a desire to protect some fundamental norms, while verbalizing the rules in a way that allow for technological and societal development. This perspective on the legal development opens for studies on the regulative processes as well as on the relationship between norms and technological development.

Third, most of the literature on digitalization of bookkeeping in small firms focus on its positive aspects, such as cost reductions (Rolfe et al., 2003) and more timely information (Olivier, 2000). Our case shows that even in a relatively technologically advanced country as Sweden, innovations in general-purpose technology are not quickly adopted for bookkeeping purposes, which suggests that the literature underemphasize what hinders such adoption. A few such factors are indicated by the case, such as higher set standards for the integrity and security of the data compared to other activities, pricing practices among professional accountants and path dependency (cf. Gullkvist, 2005).

Fourth, the literature emphasizes how digitalization and standardization goes hand in hand (e.g., Rowbottom et al., 2021; Troshani et al., 2019). Our case suggests that this applies also to the digitalization of bookkeeping of small firms. One implication of this, is that less skill may be required to perform the task. While professional accountants may be required to develop IT skills due to digitalization of their clients (Bunn et al., 2005; Kruskopf et al., 2020), small business owners may actually be deskilled as a consequence of simplified and standardized bookkeeping through digital tools.

7 Future Research

From the point of departure that there is a lack of both empirical and theoretical knowledge in the area, this chapter has through a case study established a number of interrelations between different actors and structures in the area (Fig. 4). Our description is, however, only a first step in investing these relations and should serve as an inspiration for future research. Some areas for future research for each relationship in the model are outlined below.

7.1 Arrow A: General-Purpose Technology—Software Developer

This relationship addresses how the inputs from the general-purpose technology are interpreted by reflexive action of the software developer (Orlikowski, 1992). In the Swedish case there seems to be a time-lag between the introduction of a generic new technology for digitalization and its application in this specific field by software developers. In addition, the application often seems to coincide with development in closely related fields instigated by the generic new technology. Often, the design mode seems to be one of combining new opportunities offered by the general-purpose technology, rather than exploring one of them. Further research could thus inquire into the reasons or triggers for when and how a general development gives rise to applications in the bookkeeping field.

7.2 Arrow B: Regulatory (Institutional) Environment—Software Developer

The innovations and entrepreneurial processes in the Swedish case takes place in the field of bookkeeping, a highly institutionalized field. The interrelationship between the regulative environment and the entrepreneurs thereby has a normative feature of acceptable conduct. The case gives very little indication that the entrepreneurs have challenged any regulations, but rather innovated within the limitations of the regulatory framework. An area for future research is to investigate how the societal norms and the software developer co-develop over time. This area is of specific interest as national norms regarding accounting (and therefore bookkeeping) is getting increasingly internationalized, implying that the frame for actions will change.

7.3 Arrow C: Software Developer—Software

This relation relates to what may be called the entrepreneurial mode or the *design* mode (Orlikowski, 1992). None of the firms investigated have developed the technology themselves; the innovations are often combinations of different applications of new technology. They have benefited from a certain maturity in technology use that the customers have developed in other fields. What the entrepreneur appears to add is new business models in the field of bookkeeping both with regards to software developers, hybrids and accounting firms. The business models have so far not been new, but rather translated from other industries. This development has yet to be theorized.

7.4 *Arrow D: Institutional Environment—Software*

The development of the regulation of the bookkeeping area has allowed for technological development due to the conscious decision to apply frame laws (arrow d). However, these "frames" of the law are occasionally stretched by the effects of the application of new technology and experienced opportunities for further efficiency in bookkeeping. Researching this area would add to the growing area of research of the relation between regulation and technology and complement the research about FinTech regulation.

7.5 *Arrow E: Software—User*

This arrow addresses the perspective of small organizations on digitalization and automation of bookkeeping, or what Orlikowski (1992) named *use* mode. The users in our case are both small businesses and accountants. First, our case gives very little indication that the micro and small businesses have been driving the development and to conceptualize their role in the development or their use mode is still an open issue. The expectations in the area are however high of how they will be able to use bookkeeping data for new opportunities and strategic decision-making. Second, the application of the software implies a new role for accountants as business developers and new business models for accounting firms.

7.6 *Arrow F: User—Software Developer*

This chapter has not focused on the way the software developer utilizes user data in the innovative processes, but this is likely to be a large and important area for further research. The aspect of the relation between the user and the software developer that have come to our attention is the secondary use of the users' data. With the new business models bookkeeping data suddenly became "big data", free to use for data analytics while the software became "free" software from the perspective of micro businesses and small businesses. The discussions of ownership of data and new technological possibilities for platform owners to collect data echoes discussions in other fields about 'big data' (e.g. Flyverbom et al., 2017; Zuboff, 2015) (arrow f). The research in the field of entrepreneurship, digitalization and bookkeeping has yet to inquire into this emergent phenomenon and discuss the ethical aspects of handling sensitive data, the exchange of data in return for free software and the possibilities and extent of data aggregation and brokering for commercial purposes.

In sum, by this chapter with our case study as a background, a new agenda for research is opened covering the different relations that reinvent the area of bookkeeping from the slumbers it was put in by Pacioli. There is still a lot to discover in how the technology of bookkeeping influences and is influenced by the surrounding society.

References

Artsberg, K. (2003). *Redovisningsteori*. Liber.

Baldwin, A. A., Brown, C. E., & Trinkle, B. (2006). Opportunities for artificial intelligence development in the accounting domain: The case for auditing. *Intelligent Systems in Accounting, Finance & Management: International Journal, 14*, 77–86. https://doi.org/10.1002/isaf.277

Bokföringsnämnden. (1989). *BFN U 89:2 Överföring av fakturor på elektronisk väg*. BFN.

Bokio. (2020). *Årsredovisning 2019*. Available: Infotorg.

Bokio. (2021). *Allmänna villkor för Bokio Ver 5*, 22 April 2021. https://app.bokio.se/content/legal/swe/eula_v5_20210422.html. Accessed 16 June 2021.

Bunn, P., Barfit, L., Cooper, J., & Sandifer, L. (2005). CPAs in Mississippi: Communication skills and software needed by entry-level accountants. *Delta Pi Epsilon Journal, 47*(3), 154.

Butler, T., & O'Brien, L. (2019). Understanding RegTech for digital regulatory compliance. In T. Lynn, J. G. Mooney, P. Rosati & M. Cummins (Eds.), *Disrupting finance: FinTech and strategy in the 21st century* (pp. 85–102). Springer Nature.

Cong, Y., Du, H., & Vasarhelyi, M. A. (2018). Editorial: Technological disruption in accounting and auditing. *Journal of Emerging Technologies in Accounting, 15*(2), 1–10.

Dir. 2020:48. (2020). *Kommittédirektiv 2020:48: Enklare regelverk för mikroföretagande och en modernare bokföringslag*. Näringsdepartementet.

EU 1999/93. (1999). *EU's directive on secure electronic transformation (EU 1999/93) regarding digital signatures*. https://eur-lex.europa.eu/legal-content/EN/TXT/?uri=celex%3A31999L0093

EU 2001/115/EG. (2001). *EU's directive on electronic invoicing (2001/115/EG)*. https://eur-lex.europa.eu/legal-content/EN/ALL/?uri=CELEX%3A32001L0115

Flyvbjerg, B. (1998). *Rationality & power*. The University of Chicago Press.

Flyvbjerg, B. (2001). *Making social science matter—Why social inquiry fails and how it can succeed again*. Cambridge University Press.

Flyverbom, M., Deibert, R., & Matten, D. (2017). The governance of digital technology, big data, and the internet: New roles and responsibilities for business. *Business & Society*, 1–17

Gullkvist, B. (2005). *Det elektroniska pappret i redovisningen - Studier i förhållningssätt och följder bland redovisningens yrkesmänniskor*. Åbo Akademis Förlag.

Hogia PC-museum. (n.d.). *Persondatorerna*. http://www.pcmuseum.se/datorer75-84/datorer75-84-sida.htm. Accessed 22 June 2021.

Knudsen, D. R. (2020). Elusive boundaries, power relations, and knowledge production: A systematic review of the literature on digitalization in accounting. *International Journal of Accounting Information Systems, 36*, 100441

Kruskopf, S., Lobbas, C., Meinander, H., Söderling, K., Martikainen, M., & Lehner, O. (2020). Digital accounting and the human factor: Theory and practice. *ACRN Journal of Finance and Risk Perspectives, 9*(1), 78–89.

Leijonhufvud, J. (2017, July 12). *Bokio fyller på kassan - vill bli "global standard" för gratis bokföring, DiDigital*. https://digital.di.se/artikel/bokio-fyller-pa-kassan-vill-bli-global-standard-for-gratis-bokforing. Accessed 7 October 2019.

Leijonhufvud, J. (2019, May 10). *Kampen hårdnar - bokföringsappen Wint byter strategi, DiDigital*. https://digital.di.se/artikel/kampen-hardnar-bokforingsappen-wint-byter-strategi. Accessed 26 September 2019.

Lemma, V. (2020). *FinTech regulation: Exploring new challenges of the capital markets union*. Palgrave Macmillan.

Nilsson, S.-A., & Smiciklas, M. (1993). Sweden. *European Accounting Review, 2*(2), 362–365.
O'Connor, E. (2007). Reader beware: Doing business with a store(y) of knowledge. *Journal of Business Venturing, 22*, 637–648.
Olivier, H. (2000). Challenges Facing the Accountancy Profession. *The European Accounting Review, 9*(4), 603–624.
Orlikowski, W. J. (1992). The duality of technology: Rethinking the concept of technology in organizations. *Organization Science, 3*(3), 398–427.
Petkov, R. (2020). Artificial Intelligence (AI) and the accounting function—A revisit and a new perspective for developing framework. *Journal of Emerging Technologies in Accounting, 17*(1), 99–105.
Pärlhem, S. (2019). Bör digitaliseringen påverka utformningen av BFN:s normgivning? Balans, web-version 20191002.
Pyk, P., & Lundqvist, L. (1992). Lagens krav på systemdokumentation och behandlingshistorik: Det handlar mer om bokföring än om ADB! *Balans, 4*, 13–15.
Rolfe, J., Gregor, S., & Menzies, D. (2003). Reasons why farmers in Australia adopt the internet. *Electronic Commerce Research and Applications, 2*(1), 27–41.
Rowbottom, N., Locke, J., & Troshani, I. (2021). *When the tail wags the dog?* Accounting, Organizations and Society. https://doi.org/10.1016/j.aos.2021.101226
Scandinavian PC Systems. (1986). *Bokföringsprogram för IBM PC, XT och AT*. Scandinavian PC Systems.
Scandinavian PC Systems. (1997). *SPCS Administration 1000 - Bokföring & Reskontror*. Scandinavian PC Systems.
SOU 1973:57. (1973). *Förslag till bokföringslag*. Justitiedepartementet.
SOU 1996:157. (1996). *Översyn av redovisningslagstiftningen. Slutbetänkande av redovisningskommittén.* Justitiedepartementet.
SOU 2021:60. (2021). *Förenklingar för mikroföretag och modernisering av bokföringslagen, Betänkande av Utredningen om enklare regelverk för mikroföretagande och en modernare bokföringslag*. Näringsdepartementet.
SpeedLedger. (2019). *Om SpeedLedger e-bokföring*. https://www.speedledger.se/om-speedledger/. Accessed 3 December 2019.
SpeedLedger. (2021). *Autokontering*. https://support.speedledger.se/hc/sv/articles/203240675-Autokontering. Accessed 22 June 2021.
Trinovo consulting. (2021). *Företagens kostnader för att bevara räkenskapsinformation i pappersformat*. Version 1, 26 March 2021. konsekvensutredning_pappersverifikationer.pdf (tidningenkonsulten.se).
Troshani, I., Locke, J., & Rowbottom, N. (2019). *Transformation of accounting through digital standardisation: Tracing the construction of the IFRS taxonomy. Accounting, Auditing & Accountability Journal, 32*(1), 133–162. https://doi.org/10.1108/AAAJ-11-2016-2794
Visma. (2015). *Visma förvärvar e-economic och SpeedLedger*. https://media.visma.se/pressreleases/visma-foervaervar-e-conomic-och-speedledger-1156462. Accessed 3 December 2019.
Wallenberg, B. (2018, August 2). *Gratis bokföring lockar småföretag: "Vi hoppas att växa med 300 procent i år", DiDigital*. https://digital.di.se/artikel/gratis-bokforing-lockar-smaforetag-vi-hoppas-vaxa-med-300-procent-i-ar. Accessed 26 September 2019.
Wootton, C. W., & Kemmerer, B. E. (2007). The emergence of mechanical accounting in the US, 1880–1930. *Accounting Historians Journal, 34*(1), 91–124.
Wootton, C. W., & Kemmerer, B. E. (2009). Mechanisation and computerisation. In J. R. Edwards & S. P. Walker (Eds.), *The Routledge companion to accounting history* (pp. 137–153). Routledge.
Wyslocka, E. (2015). Internet accounting offices. *Procedia Computer Science, 65*, 971–979.
Zuboff, S. (2015). Big other: Surveillance capitalism and the prospects of an information civilization. *Journal of Information Technology, 30*(1), 75–89.

Anna Alexandersson, Ph.D is a senior lecturer at Linnaeus University, School of Business and Economics, Department of Organisation and Entrepreneurship, Sweden. Her research has focused on the topics entrepreneurship, business incubation, digitalization and aesthetics.

Andreas Jansson, Ph.D is an Associate Professor of Business Administration at Jönköping International Business School, Jönköping University, Sweden. His current research centers on issues relating to long-term change of financial accounting regulation and practices, ownership structure, and the mechanisms shaping controlling shareholder behavior.

Karin Jonnergård, Ph.D is a Professor of Accounting and Corporate Finance at Lund University, Sweden. Her research is primarily within the area of corporate governance, and she has studied the development of the Swedish corporate governance system over time. She has also investigated the relation between convergence and development of regulation and practice which delivered a project on the compliance of the Swedish corporate governance code. Recent projects include the digitalization of health care (e-health), and auditing.

Chapter 8
Cloud Accounting: A New Business Model in Challenging Context of China

Md. Jahidur Rahman, Gao Yangfan, Md. Moazzem Hossain, and Tarek Rana

Abstract This chapter presents a descriptive literature review-based research on cloud accounting that published during 2013–2019 to make a comprehensive analysis of the current discourse and impact of cloud accounting in China. This chapter is organized to answer three questions: (a) how cloud accounting a new business model in China, (b) how does cloud accounting influence the business in China and (c) what the accountant's perspective in China is on emerging accounting technology. By comparing the cloud accounting with traditional accounting, we answered the first question. In the second question, this chapter explains from the perspective of opportunity and risks. In the third question, this chapter analyzes perspectives from accountants on accounting discipline and accounting work. All the influence and characters of cloud accounting mentioned in this chapter are all based on Chinese social and institutional background. This chapter promotes the exploration and innovation of the basic theory of accounting informatization and provides a theoretical basis for Chinese enterprises to use cloud accounting.

Keywords Cloud accounting · Cloud computing · Accounting technology · Accounting informatization

Md. J. Rahman (✉) · G. Yangfan
Wenzhou-Kean University, Wenzhou, China
e-mail: mdjahidr@kean.edu

G. Yangfan
e-mail: gaoyan@kean.edu

Md. M. Hossain
Murdoch University, Murdoch, WA, Australia
e-mail: m.hossain@Murdoch.edu.au

T. Rana
RMIT University, Melbourne, VIC, Australia
e-mail: tarek.rana@rmit.edu.au

T. Rana et al. (eds.), *Handbook of Big Data and Analytics in Accounting and Auditing*,
https://doi.org/10.1007/978-981-19-4460-4_8

1 Introduction

In 2013, ACCA and IMA published a report on the technology impact. This report lists top ten technologies that have the capacity to influence the future of business. Cloud technology is in sixth. The following pie chart shows people's expectation of widespread adoption of cloud-based system. Almost 72% expect cloud-based system will be widely used in next 2 years, and only 2% expect in 5–10 years. Accountants and finance departments increasingly adopt cloud computing, the consensus is that cloud computing will be important (Fig. 1).

Cloud accounting is a derivative of cloud computing technology. Wu (2018) defined cloud accounting respectively in the broad sense and in the narrow sense. In broad sense, cloud accounting is a web service that combines delivery and application patterns together, which are available through the network. In narrow sense, cloud accounting is defined as an internet infrastructure that combines delivery and application patterns, and users pay fees through the internet and get the corresponding service. From the perspective of service mode, there are three types of cloud accounting, which are LaaS (Infrastructure as a Service), PaaS (Platform as a Service) and SaaS (Software as a Service) (Marand et al., 2013).

Recent years, the global digital economy is booming, gradually becoming an effective driving force for economic growth. China has entered a new era in which digital economy leads economic development. In China, there is a word to describe the challenging context of China, which is 'Da Zhi Yi Yun'. 'Da' means big, so it represents big data. 'Zhi' represents intelligence. 'Yi' represents mobile internet and 'Yun' represents cloud computing. The proposition of this concept not only reflects

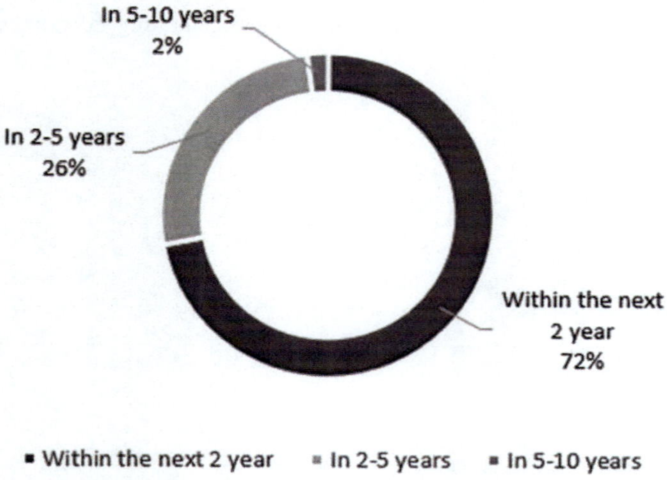

Fig. 1 Expectation of widespread adoption of cloud-based system. *Source* ACCA-IMA, Digital Darwinism (2013)

the closeness of the connection between these four information technologies, but also forecasts the coming of the information age. In the information age, the way people live, and work is changing. Nowadays, people rarely need to bring cash or bank cards. They use We Chat or Alipay. Mobile payments replaced traditional payment methods. Similarly, in such an era, if enterprises want to have a sustainable development in the future, they need to make changes in business management model. Therefore, the requirements for enterprise accounting will inevitably change and challenged.

Another condition is "Internet+". "Internet+" refers that people effectively link various industries to create a certain correlation by using internet technology (Ru, 2019). Ru (2019) points out that "Internet+" brings accounting industry severe challenges, including management mode and control mode. Under the influence of "Internet+", Big Data, Internet of Things and other emerging technology has attracted the attention of many scholars. Ning et al. (2019) analyze cloud accounting from the perspective of Big Data. Big data technology has been applied in the diversified fields of modern enterprise management, greatly impacting the traditional management accounting They found the security of accounting information is the most influential factor for cloud accounting, while network security a system security has little influence. Xu Jinye and Xu Lin consider the application of Internet of Thing. They point out that the development of the Internet of Thing enables enterprises to enter the era of "Big Data" from the era of "Small Data", but it contains huge amount of unstructured data processing which only can be realized by computing technology.

Gradually, traditional accounting can only meet basic financial needs but cannot satisfy the financial needs in the era of big data. Cloud accounting is a new business model with high reliability, high expandability and high-cost performance (Yuan et al., 2019). Wu (2017) points out that cloud accounting is the optimization of traditional accounting principles and business process. Due to various reasons, the accounting informatization developed very slow in China. More than 60% enterprise does not have a network security system and less than 11% of enterprises have complete the construction of all CAD, OA, AND MIS system (Wan, 2019). Compared with other countries, cloud accounting started late in China, and is an emerging technology and service (Geng, 2015).

In the existing literature, there are some research on the comparison between cloud accounting and traditional accounting. Bradshaw et al. (2011) believe that cloud accounting has a greater flexibility than traditional accounting, but people are less certainty for the data location and any contract's legal foundation. Mohammadi and Mohammadi (2014) predict the that cloud accounting software will be widely used. They list advantages and disadvantages of using cloud accounting by comparing with traditional accounting. For example, cloud accounting can accelerate time, follow without physical presence and connect to other computer system, but it requires a constant internet connection and does not work well at low speed.

In addition, Dimitriu and Matei (2015) emphasize the lack of meaningful academic sources regarding the cloud accounting model in their report. They mention that although this technology has been known, few people wrote papers about it. Geng (2015) says although cloud accounting's market share is not high, its prospects are huge, so it is necessary to make some research. Some papers discuss from one specific aspect. Some discuss from a macroscopic perspective. However, there is no outstanding cloud accounting product in China that can make impact on existing accounting information system. And there is a lack of a systematic analysis of cloud accounting which focus on China's current social background. China develops very fast during these years. Recent years, China adjust and optimize the layout of China's strategic scientific and technological forces (Pan, 2019). Therefore, this chapter will focus on China's current social background to analyze the cloud accounting.

Three questions will be answered in this chapter. The first question is how cloud accounting a different business model in China. The second question is how cloud accounting influences the business in China. The last question is what the accountant's perspective is in China. This chapter uses three research method, which are literature research method, comparative analysis method and case analysis method. Though these methods, this chapter collects enough information background for supporting.

2 How Is Cloud Accounting a Different Business Model in China?

Cloud accounting is an accounting information system formed by using cloud computing technology, which can be understood as an organic combination of traditional accounting information and cloud technology (Zhang, 2019). Cloud accounting is considered as a different business model in China, because when companies buy cloud accounting software, what they actually buy is accounting service instead of just a software. The appearance of cloud accounting changes the relationship between enterprises and software provider, providing a different business cooperation model.

The development of accounting software in China has gone through several stages. During 1978–1996, manual accounting software appeared, which was based on Disk Operation System. This accounting software was used to replace manual bookkeeping, so it just needed to have bookkeeping function. After 1996, Windows system was invented. As the Windows operating system matures, the accounting information system began to involve the management content of the enterprise. Some company's systems like invoicing system and physical management system are all included in the company's accounting software (Zhao, 2006). In traditional accounting, two models are used in Chinese companies and enterprises. One is accountants manually write accounting vouchers and edit accounting statements. This model has been eliminated by the times (Xing & Zhang, 2017). Another one is accountants use traditional accounting software to enter data and generate report. This model is most common in China. Recent years, cloud computing-based accounting software appears in China's software market. The most popular cloud accounting products in the Chinese market are Kingdee Jingdou cloud accounting, Yongyou cloud accounting and Inspur cloud accounting.

How the cloud accounting become a different business model in China can be reflected in the cloud accounting software. Following is the comparison of China cloud accounting software and traditional accounting software.

2.1 System Construction and Invested Cost

Traditional accounting is based on Self-built system (Zhao, 2018). In the preliminary stage, company needs to invest a large amount money to purchase financial software, databases and firewalls. The company also needs to introduce the necessary infrastructure. In the later stage, the company should routinize the maintenance of the system, and also update the software in time.

Company that uses cloud accounting software construct its system on external platform. Company leases cloud accounting service platform from website. The Cloud accounting greatly save the cost (Cao, 2018; Chen, 2019; Geng, 2015; Wu, 2018). After the company registers an account on the website, they can enjoy the cloud accounting service. Software service providers will be responsible for the normal operation and update of the software. Many cloud accounting software develop multiple channels that allows companies to enter information from both computer and mobile phone. For example, Kingdee Jiindouyun provides three ways to access the service: APP, Website and applet.

2.2 Data Storage

Traditional accounting software adopt centralized storage technology (Jin, 2019). Centralized storage technology means that all the data and calculation are completed on a host computer. The central computer is connected to multiple terminals. The terminals are used for input and output and does not have data processing capability. All calculations and data storage are performed on the host computer. However, centralized storage technology has an obvious problem. Although host computer has excellent performance and stability, the host computer may break down. Once the host computer fails, the entire system will be unavailable. In addition, with the rapid increase of data and user, computer systems are also growing, which puts forward higher requirements for data storage.

Cloud accounting software adopt distributed storage technology, which means the data is stored on multiple independent devices (Geng, 2015). Under this technology, the data capacity space is very huge. The transition from centralized storage to distributed storage has become a trend, like the 'Take off IOE' program of Alibaba. In 2008, Alibaba put forward 'Take off IOE' program. The biggest purpose of this program is to update the IT architecture. Its mainframes represented by IBM, relational database represented by ORACLE, and high-end storage equipment represented by EMC are all replaced by new cloud computing technologies.

Alibaba's e-commerce system entered the era of distributed systems.

2.3 Update

Traditional accounting software generally has a bookkeeping, report editing and other functions. When the accounting industry has new changes, the traditional software needs to wait for the update or reinstall of the system (Zhao, 2018). For example, if new laws and regulations were issued, enterprises may need to make some change to the accounting treatment method. However, it is difficult to add a new function to the traditional accounting software. The company has to let the system down for update or install new system.

The update of cloud accounting was responsible for the service provider. The service provider has a more professional team for maintenance and update (Geng, 2015; Tian, 2019). When the system needs to update, the accounting service will not be suddenly interrupted, which ensures the progress of accounting work.

2.4 Collaboration Between Different Areas

Traditional accounting software only be used in local area network, so it has a high space limitation. Cloud accounting software is more flexible to use. The system can be accessed anytime and anywhere through the Internet, which can solve the problem of difficult coordination in different places (Table 1).

Table 1 Comparison of cloud accounting and traditional accounting

	Cloud accounting	Traditional accounting
Invested cost	Rental expense of software and little investment in hardware	Heavy investment in hardware and later maintenance
System construction	Lease external platform	Self-built system
Data storage	Distributed storage technology	Centralized storage technology
Update	Service update without interrupted	System down for update
Collaboration between different areas	Terminal equipment and internet	Local area network

3 How Does Cloud Accounting Influence the Business in China?

3.1 Reduce the Cost

Cloud accounting service does not require the company to invest money and human resource on the hardware, office space, the later maintenance and update. The company only has to pay the software lease expense, which can also be paid in monthly installments, without the need for a one-time payment (Chen, 2019). Monthly installments can release enterprise' financial pressure to a certain degree. Table 2 shows the yearly expense of three popular cloud accounting software in Chin. Compared with the traditional accounting information system, the investment of cloud accounting is very low.

When using traditional accounting system, companies need to spend a lot of money on hiring professional teams to train their accountants on the use of software. However, during the application of cloud accounting software, due to the simple operation process of cloud accounting software, accountants can learn how to work with the cloud accounting software by using the accompanying tutorial video. Some software even provides professional training platform for users. For example, Kingdee has a Jindou Cloud practical training teaching-platform. This platform integrates learning, practice, testing and assessment in a unified manner. Kingdee also applies this platform to the course teaching and examination management in colleges and universities.

One final point, in the early stage of establishment, small and micro businesses will reduce their expenses in various aspects in order to survive. Instead of setting up a special financial department, they could find bookkeeping agency to do tax reporting and accounting. The bookkeeping agency is widely favored by small and micro businesses because of its relatively low fees. Cloud accounting software could provide not only the software but also the bookkeeping agency service (Geng, 2015). The small and micro businesses could have a more professional team to deal with company's accounts with little money.

Table 2 The software expense of three cloud accounting software in China

	Kingdee Jindou Cloud	Hao Kuai Ji Cloud accounting	Inspur cloud accounting
Software expense	798 RMB/year	Learning edition: 498 RMB/year Standard edition: 898 RMB/year Professional edition: 1998 RMB/year	Standard edition: 468 RMB/year Personal edition: Free

3.2 Improve Work Efficiency

Traditional accounting software needs to be used under the local area network, while cloud accounting service does not, so cloud accounting allows the accountants to work anywhere at any time, as long as there has network and a terminal. Cloud accounting makes virtual office possible (Shi, 2016). Enterprises do not have to bear the expense of owning or leasing a traditional office.

By using cloud accounting service, the company could achieve the timely sharing of financial data. Accountants can overcome the time and location constraints to communicate directly with customers, suppliers and intermediaries. Within the company, managers can quickly query the financial business data of subsidiaries through the cloud accounting service platform, which will benefit the improvement of corporate management efficiency and financial monitoring efficiency.

Cloud accounting can extend the accounting software's function to improve the work efficiency. For different industries, cloud accounting will provide different service. Companies can choose services according to their own needs. Cloud accounting is based on interest information technology, and its storage space is not limited, so it can acquire new technology in the first time and ensure the rapid adjustment of enterprise financial information. There are many examples of the function extending of accounting software. Take the cooperate of Kindee and Guanyiyun as an example. Guanyiyun C-ERP is a one-stop solution for the stocking-sellingstoring business of e-commerce enterprises. Kindee cloud accounting software provides comprehensive financial accounting system. The combination of Kindee and Guanyiyun provides more complete financial business functions for e-commerce. Cloud accounting software can also combine with payment system, like Alipay, for financial reconciliation.

3.3 Concerns and Risks

Cloud accounting can bring a lot of benefits to enterprises. Especially in the age of Internet, Cloud accounting can be seen as an important resource to improve enterprise competitiveness. However, the cloud accounting still faces many risks and problems in China. We mainly analyze two points. The first point is the security of accounting information. For enterprises, accounting information is high confidential, so security risk has always been the most concerned issue. The second point is the resistance and negative impact that brought by traditional thinking and traditional accounting.

In the context of big data, business accounting information is no longer kept in the archives room in the form of account book and vouchers but is stored in the cloud database. On the one hand, cloud accounting is free from space constraints. On the other hand, cloud database makes the enterprises face some security risks. Cloud database is a virtual storage system. If the cloud database, suffered from malicious code, the password is stolen or virus invaded the system, enterprise accounting information security is seriously threatened (Ning & Liu, 2019). Enterprises will face the risk of information tampering and theft. The security risks also exist in the conversion of accounting information. Accounting information is becoming more diversified than before. In addition to digital information, information of text, pictures, voice and video are increasing, which required the cloud accounting system could accurately transfer the unstructured information to structured information. However, if operator error or other unexpected conditions occur during the conversion process, the authenticity of accounting information will be affected. During the transportation of accounting information, massive access and exchange of data information may cause data delay and network congestion (Ning & Liu, 2019). If the network is severely disabled, accounting information will be lost.

In China, small and medium-sized enterprises have exceeded 40 million by the end of 2016, accounting for more than 90% of the total number of enterprises and contributing more than 60% of China's GDP (Rickards & Ritsert, 2021; Feng, 2019). Therefore, China's small and medium-sized enterprises are playing a decisive role in the national economy. Because big enterprises are difficult to switch to cloud accounting immediately, cloud accounting users are mostly concentrated in small and medium-sized enterprises, but only a few small and medium-sized enterprises are using cloud accounting (Geng, 2015). One of the reasons is that many small and medium enterprise do not fully understand the convenience and value created by cloud accounting and have doubts about whether they need to use such an information platform (Chen, 2019; Wu, 2018). The cloud accounting stored the business accounting information on the cloud database, so the cloud accounting software providers have access to their important information. This increases the concerns of enterprise managers who prefer to hold the data in their own hands. In addition, because of the small scale, small business volume and weak economic strength of the small and medium enterprise in China, few companies want to invest too much money in the construction of accounting information system (Zhang & Wang, 2019). Many companies still use the traditional manual bookkeeping method and believe they can handle daily operations well without using cloud accounting. Recent year, China strengthen the propagation of accounting informationization, but how to break their traditional thinking is still a tough task.

The cloud accounting software that are popular in China have many shortcomings. Software like Yonyou cloud accounting software can meet the needs of most enterprises. However, its strong universality caused it to lose the pertinence, so it cannot effectively combine with the organizational structure of the enterprise and is more difficult to meet the diverse needs of the enterprise in the future (Zhang & Wang, 2019).

4 What Is the Accountant's Perspective in China?

In 2013, ACCA and IMA published a report on the technology impact. This report mentioned that ACCA and IMA members were asked how they expected the cloud accounting affect their career in the future. These members expressed that accountant may no longer be required (2013). In 2019, Shanghai National Accounting Institute launched 'Top Ten Information Technology Affecting Chinese Accounting Industry'. thorough social mobilization, industry recommendation, expert selection, questionnaire survey and other methods, cloud technology stands out as the first place with 72.1% vote rate. This result shows that, in China, cloud technology has a huge impact on accounting industry and has aroused the attention of accounting professionals.

4.1 Accountants

The number of accountants in China has reached nearly 20 million in March 2018. Cloud accounting will provide comprehensive accounting service to enterprises. The demand for accounting professionals will decreased in enterprises, but the demand for accounting professionals will increase in cloud accounting provider. The increasingly intelligent information processing system will allow an accountant to deal with many enterprise tasks at the same time. The employees that engaged in basic accounting operations no longer employed in large numbers and more and more accounting jobs have been replaced. Traditional accountants face the risk of being limited (Shi, 2016).

The cloud accounting also puts forward higher requirements for accounting professional ethics (Shi, 2016). When they deal with the business information, they must guarantee not to disclose the secrets of any company.

4.2 Accounting Discipline

The advent of cloud accounting has made it possible for the financial accounting system to achieve convenient, institutionalized, and standardized. The emphasis of accounting discipline will shift from the accounting and supervision to the forecasting and decision-making of management accounting.

4.3 Accounting Work

Computer technology has developed rapidly in the contemporary accounting industry, and many cutting-edge information technologies will push forward the profound changes in accounting. The management function of accounting will become the primary function of accounting (Zhao, 2006).

5 Conclusion

This chapter presented a comprehensive analysis of the current discourse and impact of cloud accounting in China based on a descriptive literature and document review on cloud accounting published during 2013–2019. It illustrates how Cloud accounting has emerged as an emerging technology and service for accounting, which is very different from traditional accounting. However, in China, the cloud accounting has less service platforms, the market share of cloud accounting software is not high, and the public awareness of cloud accounting is low. The enterprises in China have not fully realized or embraced the potential of cloud accounting is big data and analytics environment. Especially in China the business sector is dominated by SMEs and Cloud accounting can be a powerful technology and competitive tool for this sector's future growth.

The chapter also reveals the challenges and risks of Cloud accounting, especially information security was recognized as one of the biggest concerns for business enterprises. Thousands of years of traditional culture has made Chinese businesses to be more conservative and compliant with local perspectives and values that are consistent and coherence with their social and institutional systems.

The emergence of cloud accounting has implications on the accounting industry. It increases the difficulty of accounting tasks and makes the accounting function focuses more on the management level. Some people think the cloud accounting will replace the accountant in the future. In fact, the emergence of cloud accounting does not mean the end of the accounting profession, but the use of information technology to achieve a leap in accounting work.

In short, with the gradual maturity of big data, mobile Internet, Internet of Things and other technologies in China, Cloud accounting will certainly become a new stage of the development of accounting informatization. The enterprise will establish an accounting information management and analysis platform that does not require pre-capital construction. By paying extremely low fees on time, they can use cloud accounting products on the Internet at any time and get real-time services based on their needs. At the same time, enterprises can purchase information services according to different needs of their business development.

This chapter has two theoretical contributions. Firstly, this chapter promotes the exploration and innovation of the basic theory of accounting informatization and provides a theoretical basis for Chinese enterprises to use cloud accounting. After China enters this rapid developed era, accounting is facing new requirements and challenges. Secondly, this chapter can provide some practical guidance for enterprise in China to apply cloud accounting. This chapter lists some risks and opportunities. The application of cloud accounting in China is still not mature, which means China faces more problems than some other countries. To give more practical theories, this chapter also refers to some locally developed accounting software in China. This chapter does not intend to put forward specific methods and suggestions for the problems existing in cloud accounting and future research can focus on. To this end, despite increasing importance of could accounting the area is a greenfield of research raging from innovation, adoption, evaluation as well as how could accounting is impacted by the proliferation of big data and analytics technologies in accounting and auditing work which is at the forefront of.

References

Association of Chartered Certified Accountants [ACCA] & Institute of Management Accountants [IMA]. (2013). *Digital Darwinism: Thriving in the face of technology change.* Retrieved from http://www.accaglobal.com/content/dam/acca/global/PDFtechnical/other-PDFs/Five-mins-on-Digital-Darwinism.pdf

Bradshaw, S., Millard, C., & Walden, I. (2011). Contracts for clouds: Comparison and analysis of the terms and conditions of cloud computing services. *International Journal of Law and Information Technology, 19*(3), 187–223.

Cao, Y. (2018). Research on the application of "cloud accounting" in SMEs.

Chen, X. (2019). Application of cloud accounting in China's small and medium-sized enterprises accounting informationization. *Intelligent City, 5*(16), 103–104.

Dimitriu, O., & Matei, M. (2015). Cloud accounting: A new business model in a challenging context. *Procedia Economics and Finance, 32*, 665–671.

Geng, Z. (2015). Opportunities and challenges faced by cloud accounting and how to deal with them. *Capital University of Economics and Business.*

Feng, G. (2019). CCPIT has taken many measures to help SMES carry out international economic cooperation. *China's Foreign Trade, 633*(3), 10–13.

Jin, T. (2019). Feasibility analysis of distributed storage replacing centralized storage. *Designing Techniques of Posts and Telecommunications,* (10), 84–87.

Marand, A. A., Marand, E. A., & Dashtebayaz, M. L. (2013). Investigating the effects of cloud computing on accounting and its comparison with traditional models. *Advances in Environmental Biology, 7*(10 S1), 2836–2847.

Mohammadi, S., & Mohammadi, A. (2014). Effect of cloud computing in accounting and comparison with the traditional model. *Research Journal of Finance and Accounting, 5*(23), 104–114.

Ning, Y., Liu, P., & Yi, Z. (2019). Study on security risks and prevention mechanism of cloud accounting under the big data. *Friends of Accounting,* (21), 102–107.

Pan, X. (2019). Thoughts and suggestions on the development strategy of scientific and technological innovation in China. *Zhengce Liaowang* ,(7), 49–52.

Rickards, R. C., & Ritsert, R. (2021). Chinese Enterprises' Use of Management Accounting Tools. In *Management accounting in China and Southeast Asia,* (pp. 7–50). Springer, Cham.

Ru, G. (2019). Innovation and practice of accounting under the environment of "Internet+". *China Market,* (28), 198–194.

Shi, Q. (2016). Discussion on the development of cloud accounting based on the "Internet+" era. *Finance and Accounting Research,* (22), 159–160.

Tian, Z. (2019). Analysis of the application of cloud accounting in enterprise accounting informationization under the background of big data. *Value Engineering, 38*(34), 97–98.

Wan, S. (2019). Research on the reasons and countermeasures restricting the development of China's accounting information system. *Guangxi Quality Supervision Guide Periodical* , (10), 160+139.

Wu, M. (2018). Design and implementation of accounting information system for small and medium sized enterprises in China. *Hubei University of Technology.*

Wu, Q. (2017). A comparative study of cloud accounting and traditional accounting information system. *Economic Research Guide,* (23), 139–140.

Xing, R., & Zhang, J. (2017). Problems and countermeasures of the application of enterprise management accounting informatization. *Agricultural Science & Technology, 18*(8).

Xu, J., & Xu, L. (2013). Big data auditing: Institutional guarantee for the internet of things construction. *Friends of Accounting,* (33), 118–121.

Yuan, Q., Wei, S., & Zhu, Y. (2019). Research on management cloud platform construction of small and medium-sized accounting firms. *Chinese Certified Public Accountant* (1), 28–33.

Zhang, M. (2019). Research on cloud accounting application strategy of small and micro enterprises—Taking L Company as an example. *Beijing Institute of Graphic Communication.*

Zhang Y., & Wang X. (2019). Research on management accounting informatization innovation in manufacturing industry—Based on the background of made in China 2025. *Friends ofAccounting, 2019*(21):96–101.

Zhao, S. (2018). Study on challenges of accounting in the background of big date—Take the accounting of a corporation as an example. *Shenyang University.*

Zhao, Y. (2006). Analysis of the development direction of accounting software. *Friends of Accounting* (6), 63–64.

Md. Jahidur Rahman, Ph.D is an Assistant Professor of Accounting at Wenzhou-Kean University. He received his PhD in Accountancy from the City University of Hong Kong. His research interest includes audit markets, audit quality, Big Data annalistic, and capital markets.

Gao Yangfan graduated from Wenzhou-Kean University in China as an outstanding student. He is especially keen on quantitative research in the accounting field.

Md. Moazzem Hossain, Ph.D is a Senior Lecturer in Accounting at Murdoch University, Perth, Australia. He received his PhD in Accounting from Curtin University, Perth, Australia. His research interests include CSR, Corporate governance, biodiversity, water governance, audit markets, and big data.

Tarek Rana, Ph.D, MBA, CA, ACMA is an Associate Professor of Accounting and Data Analytics at RMIT University, Melbourne, Australia. He has considerable professional and industry experience in the areas of business services, taxation, auditing, and financial planning as well as consulting services including performance measurement and risk management. He has undertaken practice focused research projects to deliver long-term social and organizational impact. His current research focuses on the intersection of accounting and data analytics including the implications of emerging technologies on management control systems, performance measurement, risk management, and sustainability.

Chapter 9
Exemplifying the Opportunities and Limitations of Blockchain Technology Through Corporate Tax Losses

Elizabeth Morton and Michael Curran

Abstract There is an increasing need to recognize the opportunity of blockchain technology beyond cryptocurrencies, such as bitcoin, and instead consider its potential as a technology forming part of the tax regulatory framework. We consider the potential for blockchain technology to play a digital infrastructure role for corporate tax loss compliance in Australia: a "RegTech" solution. In doing so, we identify the key features of blockchain and key use cases across numerous business sectors, then examine the role and function of blockchain in the context of corporate tax losses, where complex carry forward rules (e.g. continuity of ownership, business continuity tests) apply to avoid the erosion of government revenues. We find that in theory, blockchain could enable key efficiencies in tax compliance of corporate tax losses; however, the complexity and discretion within tax law creates real barriers for an effective blockchain solution. We conclude that blockchain offers an ability to track and flag resource allocation to broad, high level elements of the corporate tax compliance. It therefore offers potential for the greater digital ecosystem; however, it does not offer a solution in isolation. As the world progresses towards increased digitalization, this use case highlights the need for continual reflection of complex regulations and high levels of discretion, whilst balancing taxpayer rights, equity and fairness. Through digitalization, we may see increasing simplification for innovations to thrive and digitalization to meet the needs of a digitalized economy.

Keywords Blockchain · Taxation · Australia · Tax compliance · Tax losses · Corporations · RegTech

E. Morton (✉)
RMIT University, Melbourne, VIC, Australia
e-mail: elizabeth.morton@rmit.edu.au

M. Curran
Barrister, Victorian Bar, McKinney, TX, USA

T. Rana et al. (eds.), *Handbook of Big Data and Analytics in Accounting and Auditing*,
https://doi.org/10.1007/978-981-19-4460-4_9

1 Introduction

Blockchain is one of the many emerging technologies we see gracing the news cycles and social media, mostly in relation to cryptocurrencies, such as *bitcoin* and *ether*. The biggest face of blockchain technology has been bitcoin, which was introduced to the world by Satoshi Nakamoto in 2008. Bitcoin allows users to make payments online without a financial institution intermediary (Nakamoto, 2008). However, a growing area of innovation goes beyond digital money. Generally, we are seeing increasing roles for, adoption of, and experimentation with blockchain technology across the economic landscape, as well as other emerging digital technologies (such as AI, big data, cloud) forming the growing digital ecosystem.

As Bentley (2019, pp. 688–689) notes for tax administration, "there are now numerous and increasing instruments, agreements, guidelines, and forums that will support the rapid adoption and use of digital technologies to make tax administration and compliance more domestically and globally effective."

In a recent report, the Australian Government Inspector-General of Taxation (hereafter, "IGT", 2018) highlighted the risk of technology evolution on the tax system, whilst recognizing the important interconnection between the ATO, TPB and tax practitioners, and the need for these parties to 'take collective and well-coordinated action'. COVID-19 has created accelerated disruption that has pushed digital evolution along a much faster continuum of adoption. This chapter focuses on the opportunity for blockchain technology forming part of the tax regulatory framework. We consider blockchain's potential for having a digital infrastructure role for tax compliance: blockchain as a corporate tax loss 'RegTech' solution. We explore this use case and highlight the benefits and limitations of a blockchain solution.

In this chapter we firstly identify the key features of blockchain, and the various use cases espoused. We outline key terms related to blockchain, minus the minute technical aspects of the technology itself. In doing so, we offer a snapshot of the different categories, or types, of blockchains, as well as various digital assets such as tokens, cryptocurrencies, stable coins, and smart contracts. We highlight the benefits of blockchain technology on supply chain provenance, credentialing and identity checks, before reviewing the benefits to the accounting, auditing and taxation space, as well as a number of other use cases. We then turn to the corporate tax loss context in Australia, where complex carry forward rules (e.g. continuity of ownership, business continuity tests) apply to avoid, for example, loss trafficking activities. We also outline the recently enacted temporary carry back mechanism, which was introduced to allow for contemporary tax losses to be used to regain previous income taxes paid as a response to the COVID-19 economic impacts.

This leads to our examination of the potential role and function of blockchain for tax compliance and tax information systems in the context of corporate tax losses. In doing so, we outline the potential RegTech's reach and then the core limitations such a solution would face. We conclude that a use case exists for the provenance of corporate tax losses that combine two key applications of blockchain technology (money and supply chains). In theory, blockchain could enable key efficiencies such as reduced costs, reduced compliance burden, reduce uncertainty and increase responsiveness that is proactive rather than reactive. However, the complexity and discretion within tax law creates a real barrier for an effective blockchain solution. Blockchain smart contracts may be able to incorporate basic checks for changes in corporate ownership, or facilitate the carry back mechanism; however, as we delve deeper into the complexities, blockchain falls short. Blockchain likely offers an ability to track and flag resource allocation to broad, high level elements. It therefore offers potential in the greater digital ecosystem; however, does not offer a solution in isolation.

2 Overview of Blockchain Technology

Blockchain originated with Satoshi Nakamoto's bitcoin dream (Nakamoto, 2008). Although there are numerous definitions, blockchain can be described as a:

> [D]istributed, append-only ledger of provably signed, sequentially linked, and cryptographically secured transactions that's replicated across a network of computer nodes, with ongoing updates determined by a software-driven consensus. (Casey & Vigna, 2018, p. 64)

Blockchain as a distributed ledger technology offers potential across all industries and sectors, including the accounting, auditing and tax functions. In basic terms, we can expect that anything requiring trust or that relates to property, may well be impacted by blockchain technology. With time, for example, it is likely that we will see more and more private monies (such as bitcoin) competing with traditional government money (fiat money, legal tender). This creates complexity with payment systems, business operations and regulation to name a few. Simply put, Blockchain has been described as the economic or digital infrastructure for the next generation.

Without going into the minute technical aspects of blockchain technology, through peer-to-peer networking and cryptography, blockchain is a distributed and decentralized technology connected via the internet. Blockchain is a public ledger of ownership or access of something (almost anything) at any given point, preserving the integrity of ownership (Malekan, 2018). Rather than requiring a central server, blockchain instead shares information directly between participants on the network. The ledger is replicated—distributed—across all participants. Being established via distributed technology, it reduces the risk of central failures causing issues with availability and system security. On a more traditional central system, there is an inherent risk that if something were to happen to that central intermediary, then the entire system crashes.

As information is added to the network, it becomes transparent—every participant on the network has access to the transactions recorded—and due to the decentralized nature, it is incredibly difficult for a 'bad apple' to penetrate, change or corrupt this information (Malekan, 2018). The information is therefore described as immutable. It is essentially impossible to change without substantive collusion. As Malekan (2018, p. 5) summarizes:

In blockchain parlance, a block is a batch of transactions that get entered into the ledger at the same time. Entities that store previous blocks are called nodes; entities that write the newest block in the ledger are called miners.

The blocks interlock to create the chain, which enables participants to view transaction history without being able to modify or tamper with the information (Dai & Vasarhelyi, 2017; Nakamoto, 2008). A consensus mechanism ensures that as new transactions occur, they are verified by the miners before being allowed to proceed to be recorded. There are currently two main forms of consensus: Proof of Work (PoW), which requires significant amounts of energy and computational power for miners to solve cryptographic puzzles, with the first miner solving the problem being rewarded (with coin) and then being able to verify the block and it be added to the blockchain. Miners have financial incentives (e.g. coins, transaction fee), to maintain integrity: 'the highest financial payouts go to the miners that write the truest ledgers. Malekan (2018, p. 5) states:

> Both nodes and miners choose to be involved with the process for their own selfish purposes, either because they run a service that uses data from the ledger, or are being paid to maintain the network.

The alternative, Proof of Stake (PoS), does not rely on energy resources in the same way. Instead, PoS links mining power to the miner's wealth (coins held or the stake they have in blockchain) instead of energy (Frankenfield, 2019). In this case, the process is referred to as 'forging' or 'minting', with the greater the stake making it more likely the participant is to be selected as the validator of the block.

In order to append the records on the blockchain ledger, the creation of a new block is required. This requires a new process of verification by the miners (Nakamoto, 2008). Critically, appending a record may amend theoretically. However, if it is digital money being transferred accidentally, or a wallet lost, the lack of a centralized authority and a lack of regulation means a lack of remedy to resolve the error. If for example there is a transfer in error, the inadvertent recipient may simply accept the transaction with no substantive recourse available to the transferrer. If the private key is lost, unless found, a private key cannot be replaced. In essence crypto-assets are irreplaceable, whether lost, stolen, hacked, or transferred in error (Malekan, 2018).

A key revolution that blockchain technology offers is its ability to shift trust from an intermediary (whether agent or institution, such as a bank) to the technology itself. Rather than requiring an intermediary to verify transactions (centralized system), cryptography and consensus mechanisms replace these in a decentralized system (Deloitte, 2016). The implication is that those wishing to transact, can do so without the need to trust: the trust moves from trusting people to trusting mathematics (Antonopoulus, 2017). They can trust that they will receive fair and honest treatment (Malekan, 2018). This does not remove the need for trust in totality. Those observing or not part of those activities directly, such as an accountant preparing compliance and reporting obligations or an auditor auditing an entity, are still in a position of trust.

All blockchains are not identical. There are generally three categories, or types, of blockchains. The most notable is the public blockchain, such as the Bitcoin and

Ethereum blockchains. These blockchains are open to anyone to check, verify and participate in the consensus process (Lin & Liao, 2017). In contrast, the private blockchain is restricted, it is not open to everyone to participate and incorporates strict authority management (Lin & Liao, 2017). As such, private blockchain's retain central authority and structure and its transparency is limited to participants who have the authority to access (Lin & Liao, 2017). A notable example of private blockchains is the ASX distributed ledger technology system replacing the Clearing House Electronic Subregister System (CHESS) (Barbaschow, 2017), which is anticipated to go live in 2021 (Department of Industry Science Energy and Resources (DISER), 2020), discussed below. Lastly, the consortium blockchain, in which a group of entities control the blockchain in a collaborative manner to form solutions to shared problems. Therefore, this type is a hybrid between public and private blockchains. An example of a consortium blockchain is Hyperledger, which "is focused on ledgers designed to support global business transactions, including major technological, financial, and supply chain companies, with the goal of improving many aspects of performance and reliability" (Lin & Liao, 2017, p. 655).

2.1 *Tokens, Cryptocurrencies and Stable Coins*

One of the most well-known and publicized forms of crypto-assets is bitcoin (BTC), a form of cryptocurrency, introduced in 2009 by Satoshi Nakamoto (2008). Bitcoin makes use of blockchain's consensus mechanisms, cryptographic-algorithms and, therefore, immutability to enable it to serve as a form of digital money without the need of a central bank. Unlike a fiat currency issued by a government, cryptocurrencies such as bitcoin tend not to hold legal tender status. For example, in Australia, the Australian dollar has legal tender status as the official unit of currency: Subsection 8(1) of the Currency Act 1965 (Cth).

Bitcoin is far from the only kind of cryptocurrency available on blockchain, with many altcoins available. Following Nakamoto (2008), in 2013 a white paper espousing features beyond bitcoin (Buterin, 2013), saw the introduction of the Ethereum blockchain platform in 2015. Ethereum introduced another key crypto-asset ether (ETH), comparable to bitcoin (Malekan, 2018). Such coins are stored in digital 'wallets'.

Since 2014, stable coins have also emerged to overcome volatility issues in cryptocurrencies such as bitcoin and ether (Berentsen & Schär, 2019). Stable coins resolve volatility issues by embedding a stability mechanism, such as pegging the stable coin to another asset (e.g. off chain assets such as the US dollar or other on chain crypto-assets such as ether) or through adjusting the supply by creating or selling additional coins ('algorithmic' stability mechanism) (Berentsen & Schär, 2019). Stable coins currently capture a relatively minor share in the market capitalization of all cryptocurrencies (less than three per cent) (Berentsen & Schär, 2019), with fiat-backed stable coins having the highest market share.

Unlike privately issued cryptocurrencies and stable coins, central bank digital currency (CBDCs) are digital forms of fiat currency issued by a central bank (see for example discussions in Andolfatto, 2019; Barrdear & Kumhof, 2016). Many countries are exploring and experimenting with CBDCs, with one survey finding that:

> Central banks are continuing to research CBDCs… a few central banks with sufficient motivation are proceeding to pilot various designs… Although motivations are fairly stable, central banks with firmer plans to issue CBDC are now imminently close to doing so. Some 10% of the central banks surveyed are likely to issue a CBDC for the general public in the short term, representing 20% of the world's population. (Boar et al., 2020, p. 9)

Importantly, Ethereum opened the doorway to tokens beyond a form of digital money, as its introduction enables the execution of programming instructions on blockchain (Buterin, 2013; Malekan, 2018). Tokens on Ethereum can be created for an innumerable number of purposes, representing any asset where ownership tracking is relevant (e.g. bonds, media, gift cards, real estate, collectables etc.) (Chevet, 2018; Malekan, 2018). Smart contracts are programmed agreements established in the form of computer code, between participants that can be executed in real time, in compliance with agreed upon terms (Malekan, 2018). For example, a smart contract can specify an amount to pay a party at an agreed time if set requirements are complied with. Smart contracts utilize blockchain oracles, which are a form of blockchain middleware that provide the bridge to connect on-chain data with off-chain data: i.e. transmitting data such as price feeds from real-world sources to the blockchain (Mammadzada, 2019).

Tokens can be classified as utility tokens, security/asset tokens or commodity/payment tokens (see for example, Chevet, 2018; Nakavachara et al., 2019; Powell & Hope, 2019); however, tokens will often have features across one or more of the three main categories (Nakavachara et al., 2019). Utility tokens offer access to an application or service, a security/asset token will derive value from a pre-existing asset and generally fall under the scope of security laws; whilst, commodity/payment tokens are those used as a means of payment and therefore include cryptocurrencies such as bitcoin and ether (see for example, Chevet, 2018; Nakavachara et al., 2019; Powell & Hope, 2019).

Another key distinction across tokens are their fungibility. Digital tokens that are unique to one another are non-fungible tokens (NFTs). Their uniqueness, scarcity and demand drive their value (Evans, 2019). Blockchain technology confirm ownership rights in anything from digital collectables such as 'CryptoKitties', to digital artwork, gaming accessories, physical assets and even identity. In general, blockchain stored only the proof of ownership, whilst the asset itself may be on a private server or in the real world (Chevet, 2018). This can be compared with cryptocurrencies such as bitcoin and ether, which are fungible. In these instances, each token represents the same value, they carry uniformity and interchangeability, in a similar manner to fiat currency. For digital goods and collectables, blockchain technology enables the necessary scarcity and protection to be achieved: preventing unauthorized copying, distribution and other undesirable uses of materials (Evans, 2019).

2.2 Blockchain Use Cases

There are key use cases across numerous industries, particularly around supply chain provenance, registries and trading (Department of Industry Science Energy and Resources [DISER], 2020). DISER (2020) highlight, or 'showcase', a number of blockchain use cases in particular. Firstly, they explore agricultural supply chains such as wine exports, where safety, quality, taste and regulated production attracts counterfeiting risks (DISER, 2020). Blockchain offers the technology to allow for secure and reliable provenance tracking, in combination with other technologies such as the Internet of Things (IoT) (DISER, 2020). The wine export supply chain includes different participants, such as growers, wineries, bottlers, domestic distributers, international distributors, consumers and regulators. Blockchain can offer real time data tracking, whether for temperature monitoring, tracing data between participants, auto-checking labelling compliance and so on (DISER, 2020, p. 35). As well as this, blockchain can offer the ability for efficient payments by way of smart contracts (DISER, 2020).

Moreover, credentialing is the second use case DISER (2020) used to explore blockchain's potential. Here blockchain can facilitate trust regarding the skills and capabilities of employees by employers as well as consumers in the professional and trade services they seek. Blockchain offers trusted credentialing infrastructure, which is fast becoming a driving force within a digital economy (DISER, 2020). With relevant concern over credential fraud and the time consuming and costly nature of the verification process:

> Blockchain innovation can benefit a major export industry, increasing administrative efficiency and facilitating adoption of digital technology in tertiary education—as well as improve the functioning of Australia's labor markets; increasing the quality of job matching; and lowering the cost of employment process. (DISER, 2020, p. 38)

COVID-19 has no doubt accelerated the importance of the digital technology adoption and therefore the importance of such use cases.

This can extend to identity checks, the third use case that DISER (2020) showcases. DISER (2020) proposes a use case for identity checks within the financial sector in particular. They argue that blockchain technology offers the ability to reduce costs, increase efficiencies, enhance competitiveness and so on. DISER (2020) explores the potential for blockchain to aid in the verification process of financial institutions to 'Know Your Customer' ('KYC' p. 43). They highlight the duplication occurring in the real world: customers often have multiple bank accounts, where KYC has already occurred. If KYC has already occurred in one institution, blockchain offers the ability to share that information across institutions (DISER, 2020). Blockchain technology allows "the results of KYC checks to be transmitted securely, at speed and with the highest level of confidence" (DISER, 2020, p. 44).

2.2.1 Accounting, Auditing and Taxation

Deloitte (2016) has argued that blockchain is highly promising for the accounting profession, as previously indicated. They note:

> From simplifying the compliance with regulatory requirements to enhancing the prevalent double entry bookkeeping, anything is imaginable... Instead of keeping separate records based on transaction receipts, companies can write their transactions directly into a joint register, creating an interlocking system of enduring accounting records. Since all entries are distributed and cryptographically sealed, falsifying or destroying them to conceal activity is practically impossible. It is similar to the transaction being verified by a notary – only in an electronic way. (pp. 2–3)

Blockchain has the ability to improve the transparency of the accounting process (Aste et al., 2017; Bonsón & Bednárová, 2019; Schmitz & Leoni, 2019) and the quality of reported information (Yu et al., 2018), including the reduction of human error in accounting practice (Deloitte, 2016). Similarly, we have seen promising outlooks for auditing (CPA Canada, AICPA, & UWCISA, 2017; Deloitte, 2016; Schmitz & Leoni, 2019). Blockchain technology for example allows auditors to verify large data sets underpinning financial statements, thereby reallocating resources to more complex transactions and internal control mechanisms as well as blockchain's controls, consensus protocols, smart contracts and related policies (CPA Canada et al., 2017; Deloitte, 2016).

From the tax perspective, blockchain offers benefits in improving tax collection efficiencies by maximizing revenue collection, whilst minimizing the cost of that collection:

> It is widely reported that digital collection methods are cheaper for tax authorities to operate than analogue methods. For example, an Australian government survey concluded that the same service could be provided for $1 digitally as against $16 by phone, $32 by post, or $42 in person. (Tech London Advocates & The Law Society, 2020, p. 128)

Technologies such as blockchain open the door to real-time tax collection, real-time tax data, and improved reliability through verification (Bentley, 2019; Tech London Advocates & The Law Society, 2020), although a number of proof of concepts on blockchain technology by the ATO have either failed or had not being progressed (IGT, 2018). The IGT (2018) described, unknowingly how close to that paradigm shift we were, arising from COVID-19:

> Many of the anticipated or touted changes are not unique to the tax profession... the relevant developments have far wider impact. Indeed, at the extreme boundaries, it is the entire social and economic fabric of society that is evolving. We are on the cusp of a total 'paradigm shift' in how we live our lives. (p. 2)

The IGT (2018) was interested in anticipating what professional services consumers or taxpayers would want and what they would be willing to pay for it; however, COVID-19 resulted in an immediate shift in consumer demands along with a decentralization in the production and innovation process (Allen et al., 2020). We are now operating in a new economic environment, requiring new public policy, and these will challenge the traditional approaches to tax regulation and the compliance function.

2.2.2 Other Notable Use Cases

There are numerous use cases outside of the above outlined examples. Further examples include solutions for land titles, which are subject to loss, fraud and mismanagement (Consensys, 2020). Real estate asset tokenization in the United Kingdom, aim to increase the transparency and reduce costs in real estate (Codefi, 2020).

The Australian Stock Exchange (ASX) has addressed inefficiencies using blockchain technology. Within this context, blockchain technology has been adopted for stock exchanges, enabling the efficient and automated processing of trading activities. The ASX distributed ledger technology solution replaces the equity clearing and settlement functions undertaken by the CHESS (ASX, 2020; Barbaschow, 2017). The ASX describes the move as having benefits in "reduced risk, cost and complexity through improved record keeping; reduced need for reconciliation between multiple databases; more timely transactions and better-quality source of truth data" (Nott, 2018, paragraph 12). There is clear potential for the application of blockchain technology to the share market, with other stock market 'powerhouses' such as the Nasdaq investing heavily in blockchain technology (Elliott, 2018). Lee (2016) explores the implications of peer-to-peer solutions for share markets, including the legal implications. Lee (2016) concludes that a blockchain market solution offers the ability to choose between peer-to-peer trading or trading through an intermediary. Such a solution would remove the need for brokers and transfer agencies, but reinforced that the traditional share market would not disappear:

> It is likely there will always be a need for both systems, just as with the advent of email there is still a need for the post office to manage traditional letters. (p. 128)

The technology is a private solution, where only authorized participants can access the database. As such, the ASX maintains central control over the system. We now turn to consider the corporate tax loss context in Australia, in setting the scene to consider further blockchain use cases.

3 Corporate Tax Losses in Australia

The corporate tax loss context in Australia is made up of complex carry forward rules, which seek to protect the Government's revenue base and prevent loss trafficking. In 2020, a temporary "carry-back" mechanism was introduced to allow for contemporary tax losses to be used to regain previous income taxes paid. We briefly summaries the key regulatory framework surrounding tax losses for corporate tax entities.

3.1 *Tax Rules for Corporate Tax Losses*

Division 36 of the Income Tax Assessment Act 1997 (Cth) ('ITAA97') outlines the rules around tax losses, which occur when allowable deductions exceed assessable income and net exempt income: section 36-10 ITAA97. Often tax losses are simply carried forward to future income years to offset against future profits. For individual taxpayers, this can occur indefinitely. Division 35 outlines non-commercial loss rules that individual taxpayers may be subject to; however, different rules apply for corporate tax entities. Companies may choose the extent to which they apply carried-forward tax losses against income (according to section 36-17 ITAA97, for example); however, they can only do so if they meet specific tests. In order to deduct a tax loss, companies must pass either the Continuity of Ownership (CoT) or the Business Continuity (BCT) tests: section 165-10 ITAA97. Only one test needs to be met in order for the tax losses to be applied and each test incorporates anti-avoidance measures (see for example section 165-180 and subsections 165-210(3) and 165-211(3) ITAA97).

The CoT was first introduced in 1964, largely due to problematic loss-trafficking activities as well as to prevent fraud and multiplication of losses, which threatened the government's tax revenue stream (Kent, 2011; Morton & Hinchliffe, 2020; Thomas & Johnson, 2009). As discussed in Kent (2011), there is no justification to allow losses to be claimed by a different set of shareholders, relating to a different, earlier, income year. The SBT was then introduced in 1965 as a way to offer a concession to the strict nature of the CoT (Morton & Hinchliffe, 2020). These tests generally attempt to protect the integrity of the tax system, albeit bringing with them contention around discouraging innovation and criticisms of the asymmetric treatment between profits and losses (Freebairn, 2012; Kent, 2011; King, 2019; Thomas & Johnson, 2009). In particular, Morton and Hinchliffe (2020) summarize that:

> Despite protecting government revenues and integrity, the restrictive nature of some of the tax loss rules (for example, the Same Business Test or SBT) can lead to market concentration which can reduce competition, impede small businesses, start-ups and innovation, as well as add substantial complexity to the tax system. (p. 210, citations omitted)

The rules surrounding tax losses for companies have been described as complex, experiencing frequent scrutiny within the judiciary and experiencing frequent amendments (Kent, 2011). The SiBT was introduced in 2019 pursuant to *Treasury Laws Amendment (2017 Enterprise Incentives No. 1) Bill 2019* (Cth), with retrospective applicability from 1 July 2015, to offer a relaxation to the strict nature of SBT thereby enabling innovation and growth (discussed in Morton & Hinchliffe, 2020; The Parliament of the Commonwealth of Australia, 2019).

3.1.1 The Continuity of Ownership Test

In short, the CoT requires that the same persons collectively own the same exact 'shares that gave them more than 50% of the voting power, rights to dividends, and

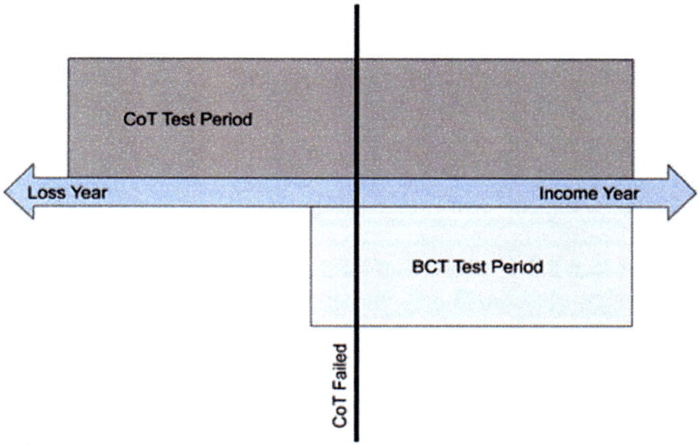

Fig. 1 Relevant test times for CoT and BCT. *Source* Adapted from Morton and Hinchliffe (2020, p. 213)

rights to capital distributions at all times during the 'ownership test period time' (Bevacqua et al., 2021, p. 196). The ownership test period extends from the beginning of the year of loss to the end of the income year: section 165-12(1) ITAA97: Fig. 1. This test looks to beneficial ownership, thereby tracing ultimate individual shareholders who may be indirect shareholders.

However, division 166 ITAA97 provides concessions for entities such as widely held companies (e.g. public companies). As Bevacqua et al. (2021) outlines, these concessions make the CoT less onerous to apply and include:

- maintenance of the same owners between certain points of time is required, rather than proof of maintenance of the same owners throughout the periods in between
- direct shareholdings of less than 10% in the company are treated as if they were held by a single notional entity, so that it is unnecessary to trace through to the persons who beneficially own those shareholdings
- direct and indirect shareholdings of between 10 and 50% in the company held by a widely held company are treated as having been held by that widely held company, so that it is not necessary to trace beyond those companies (p. 196).

If this test is failed—where there is a substantial change in ownership or control—the company is then required to pass the BCT: section 165-13 ITAA97.

3.1.2 The Business Continuity Test

The BCT looks to whether income is derived from new business activity or transactions and is made up of two sub-tests: the same business test (SBT) and the similar business test (SiBT) (Morton & Hinchliffe, 2020). These tests focus on the time immediately before CoT was failed (test time) and the income year (business continuity period). Table 1 outlines the three key tests and integrity measure that form part of the SBT.

The interpretation of what constitutes the 'same' is extremely narrow and the courts have interpreted 'the same' as being almost identical. Following the continued concern over the SBT inhibiting business innovation and growth (see King, 2019), effective from July 2015, the SiBT increases the ability for companies to access prior period losses. The SiBT provides an alternative to the narrow approach under SBT, where companies can access losses if their business is 'similar': Table 2.

The Explanatory Memorandum outlines the importance of the identity of the business:

> [F]our factors allow for differences between the current and former businesses that result from attempts to grow or rehabilitate the business. However, they also mean that there should be a clear similarity in the business identity of the operations of the former business and the current business. If a business changes its essential character or identity, or if there is a sudden or dramatic change in the business brought about by either the commencement, the

Table 1 Components of the Same Business Test (SBT)

Test	Section of ITAA97	Description
The Same Business Test	Subsection 165-210(1)	The primary test that examines whether the same business has been maintained through the business continuity test period as carried on immediately before the test time
The New Business Test	Paragraphs 165-210(2)(a) and 165-210(4)(a)	The SBT is failed if at any time during the business continuity period, the entity derives assessable income or incurs expenditure from a new kind of business it did not undertake before the test time
The New Transaction Test	Paragraphs 165-210(2)(b) and 165-210(4)(b)	The SBT is failed if at any time during the business continuity period, the entity derives assessable income or incurs expenditure from a new kind of transaction it did not previously enter into
The Anti-Avoidance Test	Subsection 165-210(3)	Where an entity starts to carry on a new business or new transaction before the test time for the purpose of satisfying the SBT during the business continuity period, the entity is taken to have failed the SBT

Table 2 Components of the Similar Business Test (SiBT)

Test	Section of ITAA97	Description
The Similar Business Test	Subsection 165-211(1) Subsection 165-211(2)	The primary test that examines whether a similar business has been maintained through the business continuity test period as carried on immediately before the test time In examining what constitutes 'similar,' the following four factors are considered but not limited to: • Firstly, examining what has been maintained: (a) Whether the same assets are generating the same assessable income; (b) Whether the same activities and operations are generating the same assessable income; (c) Whether the same identity of the business is maintained; and, • Then, reflecting on what has changed: (a) Examines the extent of changes resulting from developments or commercialization of assets, products, processes, services, marketing, or organizational methods
The Anti-Avoidance Test	Subsection 165-211(3)	Where an entity starts to carry on a new business or new transaction before the test time for the purpose of satisfying the SiBT during the business continuity period, the entity is taken to have failed the SiBT

> acquisition or the cessation of activities, then the business would fail the similar business test. (The Parliament of the Commonwealth of Australia, 2019, [1.23])

As explored in Morton and Hinchliffe (2020), a key factor that cause a company to fail the SiBT is a sudden or dramatic change or cessation in activities, when exploring SiBT in a COVID-19 environment. A business can change the way in operates, such as expanding activities and operations; however, where a business changes or ceases it core activities, it is more likely to significantly impact its identity and income-producing activities (The Parliament of the Commonwealth of Australia, 2019). King (2019) argued that SiBT is unlikely to meet the needs of start-up companies, who are likely to experience major pivots in business activity as their businesses emerge.

These tests highlight the importance of recording keeping ensuring developments in business are adequately documented to ensure sufficient detail is available to support any claims of prior year tax losses (Kent, 2011; Morton & Hinchliffe, 2020). Sudden changes, such as those imposed by COVID-19 can also blur the difference between normal and abnormal activities, which could lead to problematic applications of the anti-avoidance measures (Morton & Hinchliffe, 2020).

3.2 *Temporary "Carry-Back" Mechanism*

In the 2020–2021 Commonwealth Budget, the Government outlined the introduction of an optional and temporary carry-back mechanism for tax losses, which gained substantial attention within the profession and follows comparable allowances in New Zealand, America and the United Kingdom (for example, see Lian, 2020a). The Government's introduction of the carry-back mechanism (known as the carry back refundable tax offset) has been spurred on by its desire to support businesses and economic recovery, incentivizing investment (such as via the temporary full expensing of eligible assets) to enable increased business cash flow as well as promoting longer term capacity and wage growth (The Parliament of the Commonwealth of Australia, 2020). In its pre-budget submission, the Chartered Accountants of Australia and New Zealand (CAANZ) described the measure as having "the potential to provide Australian businesses with a soft landing during what are tumultuous economic times and would help many businesses survive until they become profitable again" (CAANZ senior tax advocate Susan Franks cited in Lian, 2020a, paragraph 5).

The temporary mechanism received Royal Assent in October 2020 after its introduction into parliament via the Treasury Laws Amendment (A Tax Plan for the COVID-19 Economic Recovery) Bill 2020 (Cth), resulting in the insertion of division 160—Corporate loss carry back tax offset for 2020–2021 or 2021–2022 for businesses with turnover under $5 billion—into ITAA97.

The mechanism allows eligible companies to recover income tax paid in prior years as a result of a contemporary tax loss. In particular, according to section 160-1 ITAA97:

> A corporate tax entity can choose to "carry back" a tax loss it had for 2019-20, 2020-21 or 2021-22 against the income tax liability it had for 2018-19, 2019-20 or 2020-21. The entity gets a refundable tax offset for 2020-21 or 2021-22 that is a proxy for the tax the entity would save if it deducted the loss in the income year to which the loss is "carried back".

Importantly, this mechanism is limited to 'corporate tax entities', which are defined as entities that are either a company, corporate limited partnership or public trading trust: section 960-115 ITAA97. This has raised some concern over businesses operating outside of the corporate structure (see for example, Lian, 2020b).

Furthermore, eligible corporate tax entities must be carrying on a business (not merely engaged in passive investment activities) and meet a threshold criterion. They must have been either:

- A small business entity (SBE) for the income year, which is defined in section 328-110 ITAA97 as:

General rule: based on aggregated turnover worked out as at the beginning of the current income year

(1) You are a small business entity for an income year (the current year) if:
  (a) you carry on a business in the current year; and
  (b) one or both of the following applies:
    (i) you carried on a business in the income year (the previous year) before the current year and your aggregated turnover for the previous year was less than $10 million;
    (ii) your aggregated turnover for the current year is likely to be less than $10 million.

Or,

- Would have been an SBE if instead of $10 million, as stated above, the threshold was $5 billion for the income year: section 160-20 ITAA97.

Moreover, the corporate tax entity is required to have lodged an income tax return for the current year and each of the five immediately preceding years: section 160-5(e) ITAA97. This latter requirement is aimed at providing assurance as to the accuracy and verifiability of the tax liabilities, tax losses and franking account entries (Treasury, 2020). This rule is not applicable to particular years, if the entity was not required to lodge a return for that year: paragraph 160-5(e)(ii) ITAA97.

Eligible loss years include the 2019–2020, 2020–2021, and 2021–2022 years, whilst tax losses can be carried back to relevant previous year (as far back as 2018–2019), where income tax liabilities were incurred: section 160-5 ITAA97. As well as certain categories of losses (see s160-30 ITAA97), capital losses are ineligible to be carried back, these remain applicable to capital gains. Eligible tax losses are generally those arising from when allowable deductions exceed assessable income: see section 36-10 ITAA97, for example.

Entities are not subject to the CoT and BCT for the purposes of this mechanism; however, where an entity enters into a scheme for the purpose of receiving a financial benefit from the carry back mechanism, an integrity rule will prevent entitlement: section 160-35 ITAA97.

The tax offset is based on the corporate tax entity's tax rate in the eligible loss year, and cannot exceed (i) the amount of tax paid previously by the entity, and (ii) the franking account balance at the end of the year in which the refundable tax offset is claimed. Moreover, receipt of the carry back tax offset results in a debit to the corporate tax entity's franking account.

A franking account is summarized by Bevacqua et al. (2021, p. 210) as an account maintained by a corporate tax entity to keep track of 'franking credits' it can pass onto its shareholders. Franking accounts are governed division 205 ITAA97. In terms of franking credits, section 205-5 ITAA97 outlines:

(1) The payment of a PAYG instalment or income tax will generate a franking credit in that account. The amount of the credit is equal to the amount of tax paid. The receipt of a franked distribution by an entity from another corporate tax entity

Table 3 Method of determining loss carry back tax offset

Step	Process
1	Start with the amount of the tax loss the corporate tax entity is deciding to carry back to the relevant income year (as far back as 2018–2019)
2	Reduce the amount in step 1 by any unapplied net exempt income for the year
3	Multiply the resulting amount from step 2 by the corporate tax rate applicable to the corporate tax entity for the loss year

Source Subsection 160-10(2)

will also generate a franking credit. There are other circumstances in which a franking credit arises.

(2) The receipt of a refund of income tax or the payment of a franked distribution by a corporate tax entity will generate a franking debit. There are, however, other cases where a franking debit arises. For example, a franking debit might arise under a determination by the Commissioner because distributions have been streamed.

As such, the newly enacted carry-back provisions will have a direct impact on and are impacted by franking credit balances. The approach to determine the amount of the refundable tax offset is not simple. Table 3 outlines the general process. Note that a refundable tax offset may be made up of a component relating to multiple prior years, outlined in Table 4.

The amount of $268,500 is less than the corporate tax entity's franking account balance of $280,000 for the 2020–2021 year, therefore the full amount is eligible to be claimed as the carry back tax offset: subsection 160-10(2) ITAA97. If the sum had exceeded the franking account balance, the tax offset would be limited to that franking accounting balance: subsection 160-10(2) ITAA97.

Similarly, for the 2021–2022 year, the corporate entity will need to disregard previously amounts claimed pursuant to the carry back tax offset in the prior years: subsection 160-10(4) ITAA97. Moreover, eligible corporate tax entities can choose whether to make use of the carry back mechanism or continue to carry forward losses to future years and deduct against income derived in those later years. We now specifically consider the use case for blockchain in the governance of tax losses.

4 Blockchain for Tax Loss Compliance

Blockchain has been identified as a technology that will particularly impact processes containing verification activities and technology used by the ATO is already having a positive impact regarding income tax return and BAS lodgment and processing (IGT, 2018). Moreover, corporate taxation is a factor applicable and permeating across all industries (IGT, 2018). The value of corporate tax losses makes them a target for undesirable activities (fraud and loss trafficking), impacting the integrity of the tax

Table 4 Example of determining loss carry back tax offset

	Scenario
	A corporate tax entity with a current tax rate of 30% has: • A tax loss of $900,000 in the 2020–2021 year as well as a franking account balance of $280,000 • Paid an income tax liability of $120,000 relating to the 2018–2019 year as well as deriving net exempt income of $5,000 • Paid an income tax liability of $210,000 relating to the 2019–2020 income year The corporate tax entity chooses to carry back the tax loss airing in the 2020–2021 year as follows: • $405,000 to the 2018–2019 income year • $495,000 to the 2019–2020 income year The carry back tax offset for the 2020–2021 year is:
2018–2019 component	*Start with the amount of the tax loss the corporate tax entity is deciding to carry back to the relevant income year (as far back as 2018–2019)* *Reduce the amount in step 1 by any unapplied net exempt income for the year* *Multiply the resulting amount from step 2 by the corporate tax rate applicable to the corporate tax entity for the loss year* Step 1: Tax loss of $405,000 Step 2: Tax loss of $405,000 minus net exempt income $5,000 = $400,000 Step 3: $400,000 multiplied by the tax rate of 30% = $120,000 Carry back tax offset component: $120,000
2019–2020 component	*Start with the amount of the tax loss the corporate tax entity is deciding to carry back to the relevant income year (as far back as 2018–2019)* *Reduce the amount in step 1 by any unapplied net exempt income for the year* *Multiply the resulting amount from step 2 by the corporate tax rate applicable to the corporate tax entity for the loss year* Step 1: Tax loss of $495,000 Step 2: Tax loss of $495,000 minus net exempt income of nil = $495,000 Step 3: $495,000 multiplied by the tax rate of 30% = $148,500 Carry back tax offset component: $148,500
	Sum of components: $120,000 + $148,500 = $268,500 offset amount Given this forms part of the current year income tax return, this offset will form a direct component of the current year income tax payable (refundable) amount

Source Subsection 160-10(2) ITAA97

system. In general tax aggressive activities are not necessarily directly observable, with the ATO making use of a broad range of information to undertake risk analysis to gather intelligence in identifying key flags to establish high risk companies. We consider blockchain technology as offering key benefits to the tax loss management function; however, considerable limitations specific to this context impede it from being fit for purpose in isolation.

4.1 'RegTech' for Corporate Tax Losses

There is a clear use case for blockchain technology relating to supply chain provenance and money. Bitcoin and other similar cryptocurrencies are growing in popularity, whilst a broad range of supply chains are experimenting or implementing blockchain solutions. Records—ledgers—verify ownership of goods being transformed along a supply chain, strengthening trust between participants. When we consider corporate tax losses, we see a uniting of the concepts of money or value on blockchain as well as provenance of ownership—or entitlement to tax losses. Instead of physical goods, we look to the provenance and management of information pertaining to corporate tax losses.

The regulatory context for corporate tax losses is an area impacted by the dynamic business environment and local decision making, which results in key obligations and critical trust between participants: Fig. 2. A company and its advisors hold core knowledge of its activities: ownership, trading activities, transactions etc. Business decisions can impact the availability of losses from current and prior years. The ATO, whilst having access to key information, it is an outsider to the business. Blockchain technology offers the ability to connect the dots between local decision making and the regulatory framework. This technology offers the ability for aiding in the shift towards real-time reporting, pro-active responses: being a key shift for detection.

In essence, blockchain could theoretically enable the reliable—verified—tracking of tax loss "provenance", bringing together core information such as ownership movement and claims of carry-back tax offsets. In this way, the use case would treat losses as comparable to a good on a supply chain, allowing for provenance to be maintained based on a set of smart contracts to monitor activity against core regulatory requirements. The evolution of smart contracts mean that we can provide the governance infrastructure for managing the relationship of companies, shareholders, and the ATO. Moreover, such a coordination mechanism could, in theory, function as the eligibility check for economic stimuli, such as the carry-back tax offset.

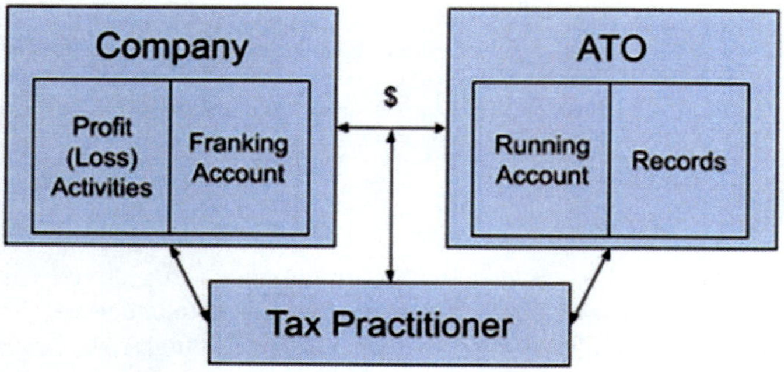

Fig. 2 Core relationships

Trusted information is extremely important for both companies and regulators. Moving away from centralized approaches avoids "silos" of information, which are critical to assessment and compliance, leading to inefficiencies and lags. Similarly, in environments, such as the COVID-19 pandemic, the ability for the government to react with economic stimuli and offer businesses aid is critical. It can be timely but rife with potential of abuse. For example, following the JobKeeper scheme, the ATO is investigating numerous cases of fraudulent claims relating to false or misleading statements, and had already recovered $120 million in JobKeeper payments due to ineligibility of applicants (see for example, McGrath, 2020). Operating proactively with real-time data offers the ability to protect taxpayer rights, avoid unnecessary burdens (compliance, financial, legal), protect government funds, reduce administrative costs and better target resource allocations. Although, as Bentley (2019) highlights, technology and taxpayer rights need careful consideration.

In particular, we summarize two key interrelated aspects to blockchain technology as a form of 'RegTech' for corporate tax loss: (i) Business-orientated benefit, and (ii) Government-orientated benefit. We perceive the benefits of blockchain will aid in the reduction of the compliance burden for companies and tax practitioners in ensuring appropriate records are kept and distributed, enabling accurate claims of prior year losses against income and promoting trust, including justified trust[1] (see for example IGT, 2018, p. 9).

For the Government, we perceive the benefits of blockchain technology espoused will aid real-time automated audit trails facilitating accurate audit resource allocation. The Government has already indicated the technology enabled insights that allow refinement to the ATO's risk assessment models, to direct resources in a more targeted and effective way (IGT, 2018). The Inspector General has already indicated improvements to the risk assessment processes will reduce compliant taxpayers being unnecessarily targeted (IGT, 2018).

Moreover, technology developments have already been posited to enable the detection of vulnerable taxpayers, such as small businesses (Bentley, 2019; IGT, 2018). As the Inspector General notes:

> The ATO could more accurately detect signs of financial distress and ability to pay their tax debt. Earlier identification and intervention would enable the ATO to take more proportional 'lighter touch' actions which would assist the taxpayer to better manage their tax debts. This has clear benefits for the taxpayer, the ATO as well as the broader economy. (IGT, 2018, p. 44, citations omitted)

We see blockchain as having the ability to contribute to this function in terms of the management of corporate tax loss obligations.

Overall, we see the potential for a "loss token", representing the value embedded in corporate tax losses and governable through the use of smart contracts, in order to manage core information needs as well as flag resource allocation. Self-executing

[1] Justified trust stems from the OECD and adopted by the ATO. According to the ATO "Justified trust builds and maintains community confidence that taxpayers are paying the right amount of tax. It also allows us to focus our resources in the right areas" (ATO, 2019).

Table 5 Exemplifying benefits and limitations

Area	Benefits	Limitation
Distributed, decentralized Nature	Offer a registry, with transparency of ownership in real time, create clarity and records. Reduces risk of centralized failures, removes intermediary. Facilitate efficient processes	Accessibility is subject to network connectivity. Instead of a central failure, if a 'hack' or flaw occurs, spreads through network
Transparency and immutability	Reliable provenance tracking. Difficult to reverse engineer tax activities. Facilitates trust between participants	Balance with confidentiality requirements, difficulty in retrospective regulatory change
Suitability of blockchain category	Private blockchain to restrict access and authority to maintain accountability and confidentiality	Private blockchains do not offer the same level of distribution and decentralization as public blockchains
Interoperability	Information can be integrated with other tax related activities (such as franking accounts) and enable real-time compliance and tax functionality. Incorporated into other big data sources, incorporate into existing accounting information systems	Needs broad adoption and investment in a fast-evolving technology
Smart Contracts	Enables real-time automated flagging of key changes (e.g. ownership for CoT), eligibility/non-eligibility, higher risk activities, expiration of losses due to failure of CoT/BCT	Complex nature of regulatory context and discretion goes beyond smart contract capabilities. Cannot be relied upon in isolation nor cater for discretionary issues (BCT)

smart contracts could aid in verifying the authenticity of "loss tokens" that meet requisite conditions (e.g. COT, balance of previous taxes paid available for the carry-back tax offset), thereby offering proactive rather than reactive compliance opportunities: Table 5. In that way, aggressive behavior (including loss trafficking) may be prevented before it can potentially occur, or at minimum resources could be allocated in a more targeted way, therefore reducing disputes.

4.2 Core Limitations

Despite the inherent benefits espoused for blockchain technology, core limitations with respect to managing corporate tax loss data are highlighted, which exemplify more broadly barriers for blockchain technology to swiftly take hold within the accounting, auditing and taxation sphere. We break this down into four key areas of concern: (i) blockchain's ability to capture discretion/interpretation, (ii) tax information requiring protection via confidentiality provisions, (iii) the dynamic tax law at odds with immutability, and (iv) the cost-benefit between existing technology adoption.

4.2.1 Blockchain's Ability to Capture Discretion/Interpretation

Deloitte (2016) suggests that the high regulatory requirements surrounding accounting is partly the cause of digitalization in accounting systems being in their infancy. Smart contracts offer the ability to automate actions when certain conditions are met. However, the technology does not yet have the ability to go beyond basic "if this then that" executions. This creates a major limitation regarding the complexity of the tax regulatory environment and the inherent discretion it allows: Table 6.

For example, blockchain technology could execute actions based on a change of ownership, identified through share sales on the stock exchange (e.g. CHESS), and track majority threshold against the conditions of the CoT. However, CoT is more complex than this. The majority threshold looks to voting power, dividend and capital distribution rights; it provides concessions for certain entities; as well as integrity measures. Moreover, not all changes of ownership occur on the stock exchange (e.g. private companies). Even more problematic is the BCT. The SBT has faced substantial levels of debate within the courts, and the SiBT is yet to be tested by the judiciary. Interpretation of the concepts of similar and same go beyond exact figures within a tax return. It goes to the real-world activities and can be impacted by external factors not directly captured by any records. Records themselves may not be easily interpretable by code.

On this basis, we do not believe that blockchain technology offers a complete solution for corporate loss management. However, it could still offer the ability to reduce administrative costs and create targeted resource allocations as part of the greater digital ecosystem: form part of the technology toolkit. Moreover, with respect to economic stimuli temporarily in place such as the carry-back tax offset, there is greater opportunity to utilize blockchain technology as a means to check eligibility in real-time, to avoid fraudulent and incorrect claims being recovered at a later date. Again, however, we do not see this as an isolated tool. We see any development requiring a holistic appreciation of the digital eco-system including a human element to ensure taxpayer rights are protected (for example, the government's 'robo-debt'[2] offers a case in point where human elements were removed in totality in recovering Centrelink welfare payments, which resulted in horrific outcomes, including suicide:

---

[2] The robo-debt scheme used information collected across government agencies (e.g. ATO) to attempt to determine overpayments, with the system automatically sending letters and raising debts to past and present social security recipients. The Australian Government ultimately conceded that the method of income averaging to raise debts was unlawful: Victoria Legal Aid (2020).

Table 6 Consideration of the level of discretion

Panel	Test	Section of ITAA97	Consideration of discretion elements
Panel A: CoT	The Continuity of Ownership Test	Section 165-12	• Listed company buy/sell activities accessible via CHESS • Non-listed companies, off market transfers less accessible; however, requisite documentation required • Ownership threshold by way of voting power, rights to dividends, rights to capital distributions • Tracing beneficial ownership to ultimate individual shareholder • Application of concessions: single notional entities (<10% holdings grouped), reduced tracing for shareholdings between 10 and 50%, reduced time points
Panel B: BCT	The Same Business Test	Section 165-210	• Broad range of factors from business name, branding, location(s), staffing, assets and equipment, goods, product range, suppliers, client base, head office • Balance between factors to assess what constitutes 'the same', 'new kind of business', 'new kind of transaction' • Extent of documentation available, format of documentation • Assessment of purpose for integrity measure
	The Similar Business Test	Section 165-211	• Broad range of factors from business name, branding, location(s), staffing, assets and equipment, goods, product range, suppliers, client base, head office • An assessment of assets generating income • An assessment of activities and operations generating income • An assessment of identity • An assessment of changes in the business (developments or commercialization of assets, products, processes, services, marketing, or organizational methods) • Balance between factors to assess what constitutes 'similar, 'new kind of business', 'new kind of transaction' • Extent of documentation available, format of documentation • Assessment of purpose for integrity measure

(continued)

Table 6 (continued)

Panel	Test	Section of ITAA97	Consideration of discretion elements
Panel C: Carry-Back Mechanism	Temporary Carry-Back Refundable Offset	Subsection 160-10(2)	• Availability data (across multiple years) of taxable income, prior taxes paid, franking account balances, applicable tax rates, net exempt income • Elective nature of application, amount of tax losses to carry back and be applied against which year, unapplied net exempt income, prior claims • Eligibility criteria, including what constitutes "carrying on of a business", corporate structuring in order to aggregate data, assessment of turnover threshold, lodgment history, impact on and by franking account balance and/or other activities impacting franking account • Assessment of purpose for integrity measure

see for example, Victoria Legal Aid, 2020). Interestingly, blockchain technology shifts trust to the ATO and thereby instead of the taxpayer being incentivized to act in less desirable ways, this may shift to the ATO.

4.2.2 Tax Information Is Protected Via Confidentiality Provisions

A core issue with blockchain is the need for sensitivity over tax information. Division 355 of Schedule 1 of the Taxation Administration Act 1953 (Cth) ('TAA53') outlines the protection of taxpayer information, as well as other obligations that arise through the Privacy Act 1988 (Cth). DISER (2020) for example have highlighted already the uncertainty around increased transparency and "unease" of data usage, storage and control. The IGT (2018) has already cautioned the need to consider the risks of new technologies, including cyber risks. Although blockchain offers immutability and permanence to protect against problematic behavior, there is a clear concern over sensitivity of information. There is a balance needed between auditability and tamper proof data with the Government's obligation to meet privacy concerns and protect taxpayers' rights. Bentley (2019) describes the taxation system as not being well positioned for either cross-jurisdictional activities without central authority. A public blockchain will unlikely be able to achieve the necessary privacy and confidentiality. The question arises as to whether a private blockchain can overcome this, whilst retaining the overall benefits of decentralized ledger technology.

4.2.3 Dynamic Tax Law

DISER (2020) highlight a particularly relevant limitation for tax law: retrospective changes in regulation:

> Regulatory challenges exist for centralized standards and oversight. It is particularly difficult to edit or alter an existing blockchain, meaning that retrospective regulation on blockchains will be difficult to enforce. (DISER, 2020, p. 41)

Taxation is frequently facing regular and dynamic changes, as exemplified by the temporary carry-back provisions as well as the introduction of the SiBT outlined above. Frequently regulations are seen as controversial. For example, Mills (2020) highlights that the corporate tax loss rules are unnecessarily complex and difficult to apply. Mills (2020) posits that there is an arguable basis to remove loss rules in their entirety or simplify them via offering a limited period of recoupment or offering recoupment on a straight-line basis. If the Government were to adopt blockchain for corporate tax losses and the system was overhauled, this would create challenges in the underpinning technology where retrospective impacts would occur. However, at the same time, simplification of the tax regulations around tax losses may be beneficial for innovation and creating certainty. Increasingly innovative technology adoption may push the tax system towards increasingly simplified and automatic tax compliance solutions.

4.2.4 Cost-Benefit Between Existing Technology Adoption

The Government and ATO have invested heavily in existing technologies:

> The ATO has, in recent years, developed and released several significant platforms and services which make it easier for individuals and businesses to engage with the ATO and comply with their tax obligations. These include myTax, the ATO's virtual assistant Alex, the mobile app, voice biometrics as well as cloud authentication and authorization. (IGT, 2018, p. 60)

A clear barrier to entry for any blockchain solution is the risk of obsolescence, the risk of swift evolution in the technology space. As Bentley (2019) rightly considers, the government must balance technology adoption and technology obsolescence. The problem is, blockchain technology is moving fast and governments are inherently slow. Moreover, any system revolutions will need to offer interoperability with existing systems within the digital ecosystem. The ATO has already invested heavily into a suite of technology solutions for tax compliance. Not only will costs of implementation be a barrier to entry, but where multiple participants are required to achieve the espoused benefits of blockchain, this can be difficult to gain collective alignment (DISER, 2020).

5 Conclusion

We outline and exemplify the benefits and limitations of blockchain technology as it currently stands for the management of corporate tax losses. We posit that a use case theoretically exists for the provenance of corporate tax losses, combining two key applications of blockchain technology: money and supply chains. Tax loss money flows become trusted through verification. Blockchain could in theory enable reduced costs, reduced compliance burden, and could reduce uncertainty and increase responsiveness that is proactive rather than reactive. However, the complexity and discretion within tax law creates a real barrier for an effective blockchain solution and creates substantial concern over whether a blockchain solution in this context would be fit for purpose.

Blockchain smart contracts may be established in order to provide the basic checks for changes in ownership, or even facilitate the carry-back refundable tax offset with blockchain's ability to identify and execute contract terms when elections are made. The carry-back refundable offset relies on identifiable elements such as taxable income (loss), prior tax paid and tax rates for relevant tax periods. However, as we delve deeper into the complexities, blockchain falls short. Even with well documented records in clear and consistent formats regarding exact activities being undertaken by corporations, the BCT, for example, is highly problematic from a self-executing point of view and we raise significant concern over relying solely on blockchain technology to execute tax losses without holistic checks and balances. Blockchain offers an ability to track and flag resource allocation to broad, high level elements, as part of a greater, holistic, digital ecosystem. It could offer mechanisms to act swiftly in response to economic conditions (i.e. carry back loss mechanism) by having verified criteria creating a control mechanism for reducing opportunities of abuse.

As the world progresses towards increased digitalization, this use case highlights the need for continual reflection of complex regulations and high levels of discretion, whilst balancing taxpayer rights, equity and fairness. Through digitalization, we may see increasing simplification in order for innovations to thrive and digitalization to meet the needs of a digitalized economy.

Index of terms

Term	Definition
Block	Malekan (2018, p. 5) summarizes, that "*...a **block** is a batch of transactions that get entered into the ledger at the same time*"
Blockchain	"*[D]istributed, append-only ledger of provably signed, sequentially linked, and cryptographically secured transactions that's replicated across a network of computer nodes, with ongoing updates determined by a software-driven consensus*" (Casey & Vigna, 2018, p. 64)
Central bank digital currency	Digital forms of fiat currency issued by a central bank (see for example discussions in Andolfatto, 2019; Barrdear & Kumhof, 2016)
Franking account	An account maintained by a corporate tax entity to keep track of 'franking credits' it can pass onto its shareholders, governed by division 205 ITAA97
Miners	Malekan (2018, p. 5) summarizes, that "*entities that write the newest block in the ledger are called **miners***"
Nodes	Malekan (2018, p. 5) summarizes, that "*entities that store previous blocks are called **nodes***"
Non-fungible tokens	Digital tokens that are unique to one another, with their uniqueness, scarcity and demand driving their value (Evans, 2019)
Smart contracts	Programmed agreements established in the form of computer code, between participants that can be executed in real time, in compliance with agreed upon terms (Malekan, 2018)
Stable coins	Stable coins resolve volatility issues by embedding a stability mechanism, such as pegging the stable coin to another asset (e.g. off chain assets such as the US dollar or other on chain crypto-assets such as ether), or through adjusting the supply by creating or selling additional coins ('algorithmic' stability mechanism) (Berentsen & Schär, 2019)

References

Allen, D. W., Berg, C., Davidson, S., Lane, A. M., & Potts, J. (2020). *Unfreeze: How to create a high growth economy after the pandemic*: American Institute for Economic Research.

Andolfatto, D. (2019). Central bank digital currencies and private banks. In A. Fatas (Ed.), *The economics of Fintech and digital currencies* (pp. 57–64). CEPR Press.

Antonopoulus, A. M. (2017). *Mastering Bitcoin: Programming the open blockchain.* O'Reilly Media, Inc.

Aste, T., Tasca, P., & Di Matteo, T. (2017). Blockchain technologies: The foreseeable impact on society and industry. *Computer, 50*(9), 18–28.

ASX. (2020). CHESS replacement. *ASX.* Retrieved from https://www2.asx.com.au/markets/clearing-and-settlement-services/chess-replacement. Accessed 4 December 2020.

Australian Government Inspector-General of Taxation. (2018). The future of the tax profession: The Australian Government.

Australian Taxation Office (ATO). (2019). *Justified trust.* Retrieved from https://www.ato.gov.au/business/large-business/justified-trust/. Accessed 4 December 2020.

Barbaschow, A. (2017). ASX chooses blockchain for CHESS replacement system. Retrieved from https://www.zdnet.com/article/asx-chooses-blockchain-for-chess-replacement-system/. Accessed 4 December 2020.

Barrdear, J., & Kumhof, M. (2016). *The macroeconomics of central bank issued digital currencies* (Working Paper). Retrieved from SSRN: https://ssrn.com/abstract=2811208 or https://doi.org/10.2139/ssrn.2811208. Accessed 4 December 2020.

Bentley, D. (2019). Timeliness principles of taxpayer protection. *Ejournal of Tax Research, 16*(3), 679–713.

Berentsen, A., & Schär, F. (2019). Stablecoins: The quest for a low-volatility cryptocurrency. In A. Fatas (Ed.), *The economics of Fintech and digital currencies* (pp. 65–74). CEPR Press.

Bevacqua, J., Marsden, S., Morton, E., Xu, L., Devos, K., & Whait, R. (2021). *Australian taxation.* Wiley.

Boar, C., Holden, H., & Wadsworth, A. (2020). *Impending arrival—A sequel to the survey on central bank digital currency* (BIS Papers No. 17: Bank for International Settlements).

Bonsón, E., & Bednárová, M. (2019). Blockchain and its implications for accounting and auditing. *Meditari Accountancy Research, 27*(5), 725–740.

Buterin, V. (2013). *A next-generation smart contract and decentralized application platform* (Ethereum White Paper). Retrived from https://blockchainlab.com/pdf/Ethereum_white_paper-a_next_generation_smart_contract_and_decentralized_application_platform-vitalik-buterin.pdf. Accessed 4 December 2020.

Casey, M. J., & Vigna, P. (2018). *The truth machine.* St Martin's Press.

Chevet, S. (2018). *Blockchain technology and non-fungible tokens: Reshaping value chains in creative industries* (Masters). HEC Paris, SSRN. Retrieved from https://ssrn.com/abstract=3212662. Accessed 12 February 2020.

Codefi. (2020). *HMLR case study real estate asset tokenization in the UK.* Retrieved from https://codefi.consensys.net/hmlr. Accessed 4 December 2020.

Consensys. (2020). *Blockchain solutions for real estate.* Retrieved from https://consensys.net/solutions/real-estate. Accessed 4 December 2020.

CPA Canada, AICPA, & UWCISA. (2017). *Blockchain technology and its potential impact on the audit and assurance profession.* Retrieved from https://www.aicpa.org/content/dam/aicpa/interestareas/frc/assuranceadvisoryservices/downloadabledocuments/blockchain-technology-and-its-potential-impact-on-the-audit-and-assurance-profession.pdf. Accessed 2 June 2020.

Dai, J., & Vasarhelyi, M. (2017). Toward blockchain-based accounting and assurance. *Journal of Information Systems, 31*(3), 5–21.

Deloitte. (2016). *Blockchain technology a game-changer in accounting?* Retrieved from https://www2.deloitte.com/content/dam/Deloitte/de/Documents/Innovation/Blockchain_A%20game-changer%20in%20accounting.pdf. Accessed 2 June 2020.

Department of Industry Science Energy and Resources (DISER). (2020). *The national blockchain roadmap: Progressing towards a blockchain-empowered future*. Retrieved from https://www.industry.gov.au/sites/default/files/2020-02/national-blockchain-roadmap.pdf. Accessed 2 December 2020.

Elliott, A. (2018). *The blockchain technology revolution is about to remake the stock market*. Retrieved from https://www.investors.com/news/technology/blockchain-technology-blockchain-stock-market-revolution/. Accessed 4 December 2020.

Evans, T. M. (2019). Cryptokitties, cryptography, and copyright. *AIPLA Quarterly Journal, 47*(2), 219–266. Retrieved from https://copyrightsymposium.copyright.byu.edu/papers/CryptoKitties_Cryptography_and_Copyright.pdf. Accessed 7 February 2020.

Frankenfield, J. (2019). *Proof of Stake (PoS)*. Retrieved from https://www.investopedia.com/terms/p/proof-stake-pos.asp. Accessed 10 February 2021.

Freebairn, J. (2012). Asymmetric treatment of tax losses. *Australian Tax Forum, 27*(2), 273–286.

Kent, B. (2011). Complexities of the loss carry-forward provisions. *The Tax Specialist, 15*(2), 106–111.

King, A. (2019). Increasing access to company losses: The SiBT. *Taxation in Australia, 53*(10), 534–537.

Lee, L. (2016). New kids on the blockchain: How bitcoin's technology could reinvent the stock market. *Hastings Business Law Journal, 12*(2), 2016.

Lian, J. (2020a, 2 October 2020). Loss carry-back tax offset gains accounting stamp of approval. *Accountants Daily*. Retrieved from https://www.accountantsdaily.com.au/tax-compliance/14900-loss-carry-back-tax-offset-gains-accounting-stamp-of-approval?utm_source=Accountants%20Daily&utm_campaign=05_10_20&utm_medium=email&utm_content=1&utm_emailID=9968c2e857ba1094968c49b803f4d49946bfd356077f48450708791bf05822d0. Accessed 9 December 2020a.

Lian, J. (2020b, 15 October 2020). 'Unnecessary and unfair': Small business shut out from loss carry back. *Accountants Daily*. Retrieved from https://www.accountantsdaily.com.au/tax-compliance/14943-unnecessary-and-unfair-small-business-shut-out-from-loss-carry-back?utm_source=Bookkeeper&utm_campaign=16_10_20&utm_medium=email&utm_content=1&utm_emailID=9968c2e857ba1094968c49b803f4d49946bfd356077f48450708791bf05822d0. Accessed 9 December 2020b.

Lin, I., & Liao, T. (2017). A survey of blockchain security issues and challenges. *International Journal of Network Security, 19*(5), 653–659. Retrieved from http://ijns.jalaxy.com.tw/contents/ijns-v19-n5/ijns-2017-v19-n5-p653-659.pdf. Accessed 11 December 2020.

Malekan, O. (2018). *The story of the blockchain*. Triple Smoke Stack.

Mammadzada, K. (2019). *Blockchain oracles*. Retrieved from https://core.ac.uk/reader/237085000. Accessed 10 February 2021.

McGrath, P. (2020, 9 December 2020). Criminal investigations into JobKeeper rorts ramp up as scheme winds down. *ABC News*. Retrieved from https://www.abc.net.au/news/2020-12-09/tax-office-pursues-jobkeeper-fraudsters/12964266. Accessed 17 December 2020.

Mills, A. (2020). Tax reform: Selected issues. *Taxation in Australia, 55*(2), 71–77.

Morton, E., & Hinchliffe, S. (2020). The potential for the unintentional loss of tax losses in the COVID-19 environment. *The Tax Specialist, 23*(5), 210–223.

Nakamoto, S. (2008, 31 October 2008). *Bitcoin: A peer-to-peer electronic cash system* (Whitepaper). Retrieved from https://bitcoin.org/bitcoin.pdf. Accessed 2 December 2020.

Nakavachara, V., Potipiti, T., & Lertmongkolnam, T. (2019, August 18). *Should all blockchain-based digital assets be classified under the same asset class?* Retrieved from https://ssrn.com/abstract=3437279. Accessed 18 February 2020.

Nott, G. (2018, 4 September 2018). ASX pushes back roll-out of blockchain-based CHESS replacement. *Business Intelligence*. Retrieved from https://www.cio.com/article/3492032/asx-pushes-back-roll-out-of-blockchain-based-chess-replacement.html

Powell, K., & Hope, M. (2019). Shifting digital currency definitions: Current considerations in Australian and US tax law. *EJournal of Tax Research, 16*(3), 594–619.

Schmitz, J., & Leoni, G. (2019). Accounting and auditing at the time of blockchain technology: A research agenda. *Australian Accounting Review, 29*(2), 331–342.

Tech London Advocates, & The Law Society. (2020). *Blockchain legal and regulatory guidance*. Retrieved from https://www.lawsociety.org.uk/en/topics/research/blockchain-legal-and-regulatory-guidance-report. Accessed 4 December 2020.

Thomas, A., & Johnson, S. (2009). Revisiting tax losses. *Australian Tax Forum, 24*(1), 59–76.

The Parliament of the Commonwealth of Australia. (2019). *Explanatory Memorandum, Treasury Laws Amendment (2017 Enterprise Incentives No. 1) Bill 2019 (Cth).*

The Parliament of the Commonwealth of Australia. (2020). *Treasury Laws Amendment (A Tax Plan for the COVID-19 Economic Recovery) Bill 2020 Explanatory Memorandum.*

Victoria Legal Aid. (2020). *Robo-debts*. Retrieved from https://www.legalaid.vic.gov.au/find-legal-answers/centrelink/robo-debts. Accessed 4 December 2020.

Yu, T., Lin, Z., & Tang, Q. (2018). Blockchain: The introduction and its application in financial accounting. *Journal of Corporate Accounting & Finance, 29*(4), 37–47.

Dr. Elizabeth Morton is a Research Fellow at the RMIT Blockchain Innovation Hub as well as coordinator and lecturer of taxation in RMIT's College of Business and Law's, School of Accounting, Information Systems and Supply Chain. Elizabeth's research traverse's both the accounting and taxation systems, with particular concern directed towards blockchain and related technologies, information disclosure and tax compliance. Her research is currently underpinned by three core themes: tax compliance, crypto-related activities, and practitioner competencies. Along with peer-reviewed and industry journals, Elizabeth engages with industry through channels such as discussion groups, policy submissions, articles, blogs, seminars, podcasts and radio. Prior to academia, Elizabeth was an accountant in a small taxation business in regional Victoria, working for all entity types on various aspects of accounting and taxation including capital gains tax and investments, GST and FBT compliance and superannuation. As well as other associations, Elizabeth is a Fellow of the Tax Institute, a Chartered Accountant, member of the Institute of Public Accountants, and member of the Accounting and Finance Association of Australia and New Zealand (AFAANZ).

Michael Curran is a barrister and has been a member of the Victorian Bar for more than 25 years. He is also a Public Accountant, an Australian Registered Tax Agent and a Chartered Tax Advisor with the Taxation Institute of Australia. He has most recently held positions as Senior Lecturer and Program Director at RMIT University. Michael specializes in Taxation Law, representing and advising both Australian and international clients and has undertaken consulting work for the Australian Taxation Office. Michael has also lectured in Law at Melbourne University, Monash University, Deakin University, Swinburne University, the Australian Catholic University, Metropolitan College in Malaysia, the Hong Kong Management Association, the Leo Cussen Centre for Law and the Singapore Institute of Management.

Part II
Data Analytics and Managerial Accounting

Chapter 10
Data Sources for Predictive Analytics and Decision Making: A Management Perspective

Dennis Fehrenbacher and Alessandro Ghio

Abstract This chapter discusses aspects of data sources for budgeting and forecasting. It provides empirical evidence on the preference for data sources for a sample of experienced managers in the context of sales predictions. The authors show that managers still have strong preferences for traditional accounting data sources relative to non-traditional data sources. These preferences change between levels of education. Furthermore, the credibility (and not their use) of social media positively influences the preference for non-traditional data sources. These findings indicate that non-traditional data sources appear to coexist and become complementary to traditional accounting sources and do not substitute them.

Keywords Big Data · Sales predictions · Forecasts · Budgeting · Data sources · Social media

1 Introduction

Organizations possess an increasing amount of data sources that could be included in the management decision-making process (Brown-Liburd et al., 2015; Davenport et al., 2012). New and evolving data sources have been labelled 'Big Data' or from an accounting perspective 'non-traditional' accounting data (Moffitt & Vasarhelyi, 2013; Vasarhelyi et al., 2015). Emerging literature examines the usefulness of some of the new data sources for making predictions into the future. For instance, Geva et al. (2017) find that for predicting sales, adding search trend data to social media data leads to higher predictive accuracy than when predictions are only based on social media data. Indeed, the ultimate goal of using 'Big Data' is to make better decisions and not (only) to automate processes (Nielsen, 2018). In this regard, the professional

D. Fehrenbacher (✉)
St. Gallen University, St. Gallen, St. Gallen, Switzerland
e-mail: dennis.fehrenbacher@unisg.ch

A. Ghio
University of Laval, Québec City, QC, Canada
e-mail: alessandro.ghio@fsa.ulaval.ca

T. Rana et al. (eds.), *Handbook of Big Data and Analytics in Accounting and Auditing*,
https://doi.org/10.1007/978-981-19-4460-4_10

body Chartered Institute of Management Accountants (CIMA) contends that organizations should 'discover how to use analytics to transform finance. Data analytics are becoming the most important means of identifying the business drivers of the organization and therefore can have a major influence on its financial outcome.'[1]

However, little is known about how managers react to some of the new data sources and whether new data sources are seen as value adding by managers and are eventually adopted in the management decision-making process. Knowledge on management preferences is an important concern for management accounting to improve its role of providing decision-making oriented information to managers. Indeed, past research shows that management accountants are increasingly acting as consultants providing business-oriented and strategic information (Quattrone & Hopper, 2001). Moreover, management accountants can play a key role in this data evolution beyond complementing financial accounting (Brands & Holtzblatt, 2015).

Hence, we examine management perceptions of new data sources relative to longer-standing data sources. These perceptions are likely context-dependent and influenced by specific use-cases. Our approach is to investigate how perceptions on data sources differ by *management demographics*, *attitudes* and *resource constraints*. As such, we aim at providing a status-quo perspective of management perceptions to help designers of decision-support systems (e.g. predictive analytics systems) and management accountants to understand managers as users of predictive analytics tools better. This is important because organizations invest increasing amounts in data analytics systems with potential long-term impact on organizational decisions.

The remainder of this chapter proceeds as follows. Section 2 critically reviews the literature on data sources in accounting, and it examines the different types of 'Big Data' used for sales prediction. Section 3 provides empirical evidence on the managers' attitudes towards traditional and non-traditional data sources for sales prediction and how these vary in relationship to managers' demographics, use and credibility of social media. To conclude, Sect. 4 discusses the main take-aways of this chapter, and it provides avenues for future research in the domain of management accounting and Big Data.

2 Background

2.1 Data Sources in Accounting

In accounting, grouping data into financial and non-financial data (or measures) is a widely used practice. A major concern in accounting is to aggregate financial data to prepare balance sheets, income statements and cash flow statements. Protocols such as XBRL are used to tag the data in the financial statement accordingly and to transmit data to stakeholders (Di Fabio et al., 2019). Other groupings include data for

[1] See https://www.cimaglobal.com/Events/Events/Mastercourses/Technical-skills/Management-reporting-and-analysis/Business-analytics/. Last accessed September 10th, 2020.

internal decision-making purposes (e.g. cost data in management accounting) and external purposes (e.g. expense data). The aim of accounting as the processor of data and preparer of information has been to handle such structured data and aggregate it.

With the rise of 'Big data', more unstructured data sources become available to organizations and organizations try to find ways of making use of these sources (Günther et al., 2017). Specifically, new data sources have been termed non-traditional accounting data or more generally 'Big Data'. Accounting as the gatekeeper can play a central role in unearthing the value of new data sources (Deshmukh, 2006). Rikhardsson and Yigitbasioglu (2018) argue that "big data has the potential to radically alter the organization of the management accounting function" (p. 45). Nielsen (2018) indicates that non-traditional data sources such as big data will have a decisive impact on management accountants, in particular in descriptive analytics, i.e., insights into the past, predictive and prescriptive analytics, i.e., understanding the future. Schläfke et al. (2013) indicate that a multilayer performance management framework would help managers to identify the type of data analytics to use in their decision making.

Big data can be characterized according to volume, velocity, veracity, and variety (Davenport et al., 2012). Volume described the pure amount of data that requires data repositories that increase in size. Variety describes the differentiation of data into distinctly different types. Many newer data types cannot be put into simple tabular format anymore (e.g. pictures, videos, social media posts). Veracity captures increased uncertainty about the quality of Big Data. Velocity describes the speed of new data sources in terms of data creation or transfer.

This chapter is particularly concerned with the variety of new data sources and how varying non-traditional data sources are perceived by management. Such an understanding helps management accountants as processors of data and preparer of information to provide targeted reports to management.

2.2 *Variety of 'Big Data' for Sales Predictions*

The variety of data sources that can be relevant for management decision making has evolved. Making accurate sales predictions is at the start of successful sales and operations planning (SOP) and can facilitate the budgeting process. Data sources based on new technologies can facilitate both the collection and the analysis of information for decision making (Rikhardsson & Yigitbasioglu, 2018). From an organizational perspective, such data sources have been broadly categorized to be internal or external to an organization (see e.g. Vasarhelyi et al., 2015; Voleti, 2019). Voleti (2019) provides a summary description of data sources (Table 1). They distinguish between *internal* data, i.e., transaction data, customer preference data, experimental data, customer relationship data, and *external* data, i.e., survey data, biometric data, third party data, government and quasi-government agencies, and social media platforms. These data sources can include numbers, text, image, audio, video, biometric

Table 1 Data sources

Category	Type	Example
Internal	Transaction data	Prior sales
	Customer preference data	Website click
	Experimental data	Clinical trials
	Customer relationship	Loyalty rewards data
External	Survey data	Census
	Biometric data	Immigration data
	Third party data	Google trends
	Government and quasi-government agencies	World Bank
	Social media platforms	Twitter

Source Authors' elaboration based on Voleti

information. An open question is how qualitative and quantitative data visualizations are used in the budgeting and forecasting process considered the larger types of data available. This is important as new data sources provide multiple types of structures beyond traditional graphs and tables.

Lee et al. (2008) document that users' level of expertise affects the perception and use of data sources, highlighting the importance to consider users' characteristics. The visualization of data also plays a role in shaping bias and decision outcomes (Rikhardsson & Yigitbasioglu, 2018). Cardinaels and van Veen-Dirks (2010) document that managers discount non-financial information when they evaluate data in scorecards and encourage the use of performance markers to address potential bias. Chen et al. (2016) highlight that the type of information's users, specifically managers' attitude, rather than data format influence the decision making.

Non-traditional data is increasingly used in multiple management accounting practices, including forecast, budgeting and customer segment profitability (Hee Lee & Park, 2005). Bronzo et al. (2013) show that the use of non-traditional data sources has positive implications for organizational performance. Marx et al. (2012) develop a five-stage maturity model mapping the degree of maturity for technologies across planning, reporting and consolidating task. In this context, Vasarhelyi et al. (2015) show the evolution and expansion of Big Data in accounting as well as their interactions with traditional data sources. Figure 1 provides a representation of the increasing integration between traditional and non-traditional data sources in data collection, data analysis and visualization. The expansion in the data sources is also associated with a growing automatization of data collection, leading also to an increase in data analysis. The advent of the Big Data through web data and mobility data generated an entire ecosystem of new types of data, namely text, video and audio. Importantly, the link between non-traditional data sources can enrich ERPs to analyses economic activities, for instance consumer behaviors. As such, big data have the potential to influence both financial and managerial accounting. They can also be used in the audit domains, for instance by real time tracking of inventory

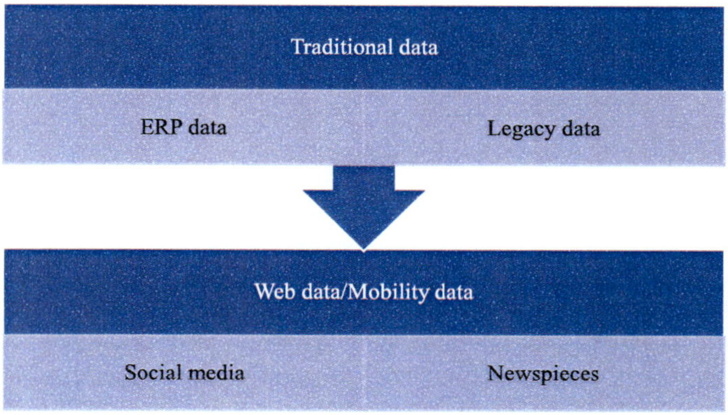

Fig. 1 Changes in Big Data. *Source* Authors elaboration based on Moffitt and Vasarhelyi (2013) and Vasarhelyi et al. (2015)

movements. The use of Big data would allow auditors to complement their traditional audit evidence The main behavioral implications currently concern information overload, information relevance, pattern recognition and ambiguity (Brown-Liburd et al., 2015).

In regards to a management control system, Warren et al. (2015) argue that big data can play a key role, especially to identify behaviors related to specific targets. For instance, the analysis of the tone of emails and phone conversations may provide indications on employees' morale. They also suggest that big data could assist beyond budgeting practices as alternative sources of information for operational planning, performance evaluation, communication of goals and strategy definition. Rikhardsson and Yigitbasioglu (2018) argue that perceptions of big data in terms of timeliness and accuracy in budgeting and forecasting are still unexplored. In a similar fashion, Nielsen (2018) calls for more research on the integration of non-traditional data sources with traditional ones, such as present sales, in the forecasting process.

3 Factors that Influence Management Perception

3.1 Method

To limit the scope of our research, we identified data sources that have been associated with sales predictions in the extant literature, some of which are seen as traditional accounting data, i.e. sales data, market trend data and survey and focus group data, and other data sources have evolved relatively recently and are associated with data mainly becoming available through web and mobile technologies. They include product mentions and likes, textual product data, product search trend data, web traffic data and physical traffic data (Geva et al., 2017; Vasarhelyi et al., 2015; Voleti, 2019). Some of these data sources, such as physical traffic data, may be captured using mobile technologies, but also more traditionally using a simple customer count enabled by staff manually counting.

3.2 *Sample*

Given the explorative nature of our research and our objective to gather insights into managers' current views on data sources for sales predictions, we employed a questionnaire. We electronically surveyed 169 experienced managers from Anglo-Saxon countries in May 2020. We use an online labour market platform to recruit participants. The questionnaire included questions about the use of different data sources, perception of social media and demographic questions. We used a seven-point Likert scale, rating, yes-no questions, and single or multiple-choice questions, to gather richer insights into managers' decisions.

The majority of the respondents are from the United Kingdom (157 respondents; 92.90% of the total sample), followed by Australia (4 respondents, 2.37% of the total sample). 99 (58.58%) of the participants were female and 70 (41.42%) of the participants were male. The majority of the managers were between 25 and 34 years (76 respondents, 44.97% of the total sample), with more than 10 years of work experience (114 respondents, 67.46% of the total sample) and between 1 and 3 years of managerial experience (52 respondents, 30.77% of the total sample). With regards to the education, the majority of the managers surveyed completed an undergraduate degree (84 respondents, 49.70% of the total sample) and attended at least an accounting or finance course (88 respondents, 52.07% of the respondents).

3.3 *Results*

This section reports three main sets of results ($N = 169$). First, we report on the managers' perception of traditional and non-traditional data sources. We then examine how managers perceive multiple social platforms and their credibility. In the last set of results, we analyze the preference for data sources conditional to the use and credibility of social media.

3.3.1 What Are Management Preference for Data Sources in Sales Predictions?

We first investigate managers' preferences on different data sources in their sales predictions. Specifically, we ask the extent they would rely on ten different data sources on a scale ranging between 1 (low extent) to 7 (high extent).

Table 2 Preference for data sources in sales predictions

	p25	median	p75	Mean	sd
Sales data gathered from internal sales records	5	6	6	5.57	1.12
Number of product mentions gathered from external social media platforms	3	4	5	4.02	1.39
Product 'Likes' gathered from external social media platforms	3	4	5	3.70	1.51
Survey and focus group data gathered from internal marketing department	4	5	5	4.73	1.17
Survey and focus group data gathered from external marketing agencies	4	5	6	4.83	1.21
Web product search trend data gathered from external search engines	4	5	6	4.72	1.31
Web traffic data representing visits to your firm's online stores	5	5	6	5.18	1.18
Traffic data representing visits to physical stores	4	5	6	5.13	1.27
Market trend data gathered from external sources	4	5	6	4.90	1.24
Textual data and sentiment about products gathered from external social media platforms	3	4	5	4.24	1.43

If you were able to choose data sources to make sales predictions, how much would you rely on the following data sources? (7-point scale ranging from 1 = Low Extent to 7 = High Extent)

The results of the survey (Table 2) show that managers mostly rely on 'traditional' accounting information, such as prior sales (mean 'Sales data gathered from internal sales records' = 5.57, median = 6), when they have a choice among potential data sources for sales predictions. "Web traffic data representing visits to a firm's online stores" is also highly regarded by managers (mean = 5.18; median 5) as well as traffic representing visits to the physical stores (mean = 5.13; median = 5). Conversely, managers tend to rely less on data from social media. In particular, "Product 'Likes' gathered from external social media platforms" and "Textual data and sentiment about products gathered from external social media platforms" receive the lowest scores (mean = 3.70, median = 4; mean = 4.24, median = 4, respectively). These results suggest that managers still primarily rely on traditional sources of information, while they remain relatively skeptical about social media when making their forecasts. Note, that reliance on social media - type data is nevertheless not at the low end (a rating of 1 would indicate a low extent).

3.3.2 How Do Resource Limitations Influence Management Preferences for Data Sources in Sales Predictions?

In this set of analysis, we investigate managers' preferences for data sources mix. We asked managers to assign weights to ten data sources out of a score of 100. This analysis aims to understand the preference assigned to different data sources in a portfolio of potential choices. Larger weights would indicate more prominence for a certain data source in a managers' data analytics tool for sales predictions.

Table 3 shows that "Sales data gathered from internal sales records" plays a major role in the portfolio of 'ideal' data sources. It accounts, on average, for more than a quarter of the total weights (mean = 26.94; median = 20). Traffic data, both to online stores and physical stores, follow in terms of relevance ("Traffic data representing visits to physical stores" mean = 10.39, median = 10; "Web traffic data representing visits to your firm's online stores" mean = 10.13, median = 10). Again, managers assign lower weight to data sources related to social media. The two sources with the lowest weights are "Textual data and sentiment about products gathered from external social media platforms" (mean = 5.10; median = 5) and "Product 'Likes' gathered from external social media platforms" (mean = 5.41; median = 5).

Taken together, this first set of results shows that, on average, managers continue to mostly rely on traditional data sources for their sales predictions. They also include new data sources, such as social media. Nonetheless, they tend to assign relatively low weights to non-traditional data sources in the overall portfolio for decision-making.

Table 3 Preferences for data sources in a sales prediction portfolio

	p25	median	p75	mean	sd
Sales data gathered from internal sales records	10	20	40	26.94	18.79
Number of product mentions gathered from external social media platforms	4	5	10	6.94	5.95
Product 'Likes' gathered from external social media platforms	2	5	7	5.41	5.25
Survey and focus group data gathered from internal marketing department	5	8	10	8.68	6.44
Survey and focus group data gathered from external marketing agencies	5	8	10	8.82	6.35
Web product search trend data gathered from external search engines	5	5	10	7.52	5.51
Web traffic data representing visits to your firm's online stores	5	10	13	10.13	6.75
Traffic data representing visits to physical stores	5	10	15	10.39	6.93
Market trend data gathered from external sources	5	5	10	8.17	8.09
Textual data and sentiment about products gathered from external social media platforms	0	5	10	5.10	4.53
Other	0	0	0	1.82	6.15

If you were able to choose data sources to make sales predictions, which weights would you assign to the following data sources? (100 points in total)

3.3.3 How Do Managers' Demographics Influence Management Preferences for Data Sources?

We now turn our attention to the association between managers' demographic characteristics and preference for data sources in their sales predictions. Specifically, we aim to capture the different attitudes towards data sources conditional to seniority, education and experience in organizational decision-making. We operationalize these different dimensions with the variables age[2] (as a proxy for seniority), degree accomplished[3] and level of accounting and finance education[4] (as proxies for education), years of work experience,[5] and years of management experience[6] (as proxies for experience in organizational decision-making).

We first examine the extent to which managers rely on different data sources (Panel A of Table 4). In terms of seniority, we observe that more senior people rely slightly less on sales from prior sales while they generally tend to rely more on other data sources. Interestingly, more senior managers would rely more on the data source "Product 'Likes' gathered from external social media platforms" relative to less senior managers (difference = 0.41; statistically significant at less than 10% level). In terms of education, managers with higher levels of education tend to rely less on "Product 'Likes' gathered from external social media platforms". Moreover, managers who took more accounting and finance courses would rely more on "Survey and focus group data gathered from external marketing agencies", "Web traffic data representing visits to your firm's online stores" and "Market trend data gathered from external sources" compared to managers who have less accounting and finance education. Thus, in particular accounting and finance education brings out differences.

Panel B of Table 4 reports no statistical difference among data sources when looking at work experience. Conversely, managers with more managerial experience tend to rely more on "Survey and focus group data gathered from external marketing agencies" and on "Web product search trend data gathered from external search engines" and on "Product 'Likes' gathered from external social media platforms" relative to managers with less experience.

When we look at the different weights managers assign to a hypothetical portfolio of data sources for sales predictions (Table 5), we do not observe significant differences across seniority. Managers with a higher level of education assign a higher weight to "Survey and focus group data gathered from internal marketing department" and less to "Web traffic data representing visits to your firm's online

---

[2] More senior if the manager is above 35 years old, less senior otherwise (i.e., millennial).

[3] Higher education level if the manager has completed at least an undergraduate degree, lower education level otherwise.

[4] High accounting education if the manager has completed at least one accounting or finance course, lower accounting education otherwise.

[5] High work experience if the manager has at least 4 years of work experience, low work experience otherwise.

[6] High managerial experience if the manager has at least 4 years of managerial experience, low managerial experience otherwise.

Table 4 Preference for data sources in sales predictions conditional to managers' characteristics

Panel A: Seniority and Education[a, b]

	More senior	Less senior	Diff	Higher education level	Lower education level	Diff	High accounting education	Low accounting education	Diff
Sales data gathered from internal sales records	5.55	5.58	−0.03	5.85	5.5	0.35*	5.33	5.65	0.32
Number of product mentions gathered from external social media platforms	4.18	3.88	0.30	3.68	4.1	−0.42	4.04	4	0.04
Product 'Likes' gathered from external social media platforms	3.93	3.52	0.41*	3.22	3.82	−0.60**	3.88	3.64	0.24
Survey and focus group data gathered from internal marketing department	4.82	4.67	0.15	4.77	4.73	0.04	4.83	4.7	0.13
Survey and focus group data gathered from external marketing agencies	4.94	4.74	0.20	4.68	4.87	−0.19	5.16	4.72	0.44**

(continued)

Table 4 (continued)

Panel A: Seniority and Education[a, b]

	More senior	Less senior	Diff	Higher education level	Lower education level	Diff	High accounting education	Low accounting education	Diff
Web product search trend data gathered from external search engines	4.89	4.6	0.29	4.42	4.8	−0.38	5.21	4.56	0.65***
Web traffic data representing visits to your firm's online stores	5.29	5.09	0.20	5.28	5.15	0.13	5.52	5.07	0.45**
Traffic data representing visits to physical stores	5.2	5.07	0.13	5.37	5.06	0.31	5.33	5.06	0.27
Market trend data gathered from external sources	5.06	4.77	0.29	4.85	4.91	−0.06	5.21	4.8	0.41*
Textual data and sentiment about products gathered from external social media platforms	4.43	4.1	0.33	3.97	3.32	0.65	4.54	4.14	0.40

Panel B: Decision-making experience[c, d]

	High work experience	Low work experience	Diff	High managerial experience	Low managerial experience	Diff
Sales data gathered from internal sales records	5.57	5.58	−0.01	5.56	5.57	−0.01

(continued)

Table 4 (continued)

Panel B: Decision-making experience[c, d]

	High work experience	Low work experience	Diff	High managerial experience	Low managerial experience	Diff
Number of product mentions gathered from external social media platforms	4.1	3.83	0.27	4.28	3.97	0.31
Product 'Likes' gathered from external social media platforms	3.76	3.58	0.18	4.2	3.61	0.59*
Survey and focus group data gathered from internal marketing department	4.74	4.72	0.02	4.88	4.71	0.17
Survey and focus group data gathered from external marketing agencies	4.78	4.92	−0.14	5.28	4.75	0.53**
Web product search trend data gathered from external search engines	4.71	4.74	−0.03	5.16	4.65	0.51*
Web traffic data representing visits to your firm's online stores	5.09	5.36	−0.27	5.52	5.12	0.40
Traffic data representing visits to physical stores	5.06	5.27	−0.21	5.52	5.06	0.46*
Market trend data gathered from external sources	4.88	4.94	−0.06	5.12	4.86	0.26

(continued)

Table 4 (continued)

Panel B: Decision-making experience[c, d]

	High work experience	Low work experience	Diff	High managerial experience	Low managerial experience	Diff
Textual data and sentiment about products gathered from external social media platforms	4.23	4.27	−0.04	4.56	4.2	0.36

Note * significant at the .1 level, ** significant at the .05 level, *** significant at the .01 level

[a]If you were able to choose data sources to make sales predictions, how much would you rely on the following data sources? (7-point scale ranging from 1 = Low Extent to 7 = High Extent)

[b]*More senior* if the manager is above 35 years old, *less senior* otherwise (i.e., millennial); *Higher education* level if the manager has completed at least an undergraduate degree, *lower education* level otherwise; *High accounting education* if the manager has completed at least one accounting or finance course, *low accounting education* otherwise

[c]If you were able to choose data sources to make sales predictions, how much would you rely on the following data sources? (7-point scale ranging from 1 = Low Extent to 7 = High Extent)

[d]*High work experience* if the manager has at least 4 years of work experience, *low work experience* otherwise; *High managerial experience* if the manager has at least 4 years of managerial experience, *low managerial* experience otherwise

stores" relative to managers with lower levels of education. Lastly, managers with high work experience assign more weight to "Sales data gathered from internal sales records" relative to less experienced managers, suggesting thus a stickiness for more traditional data sources.

3.3.4 How Do Attitudes Towards Technologies Influence Management Preferences for Data Sources in Sales Predictions?

In this section, we focus on the managers' attitude towards social media. Indeed, the preference for social data information as data sources in sales prediction may depend on managers' use and perception of social media.

Table 6 reports managers' use of five different social media, i.e., Twitter, Facebook, YouTube, Instagram and WeChat. These social media have the largest number of users in the world, with Facebook having over 1.785 billion users (Source: Statista.com).[7] In our survey, lower scores indicate a higher frequency in their use. Our data show that Facebook and YouTube are the most used social media, with more than 50% of the managers affirming to use Facebook on a daily base. WeChat appears the least used social media. We explain the apparent low frequency use of WeChat for its large dissemination in China, while our managers are mostly based in Anglo-Saxon countries, i.e., U.K, USA and Australia.

We then asked managers to rate between 0 and 100 the credibility of the different social media platforms. Higher (lower) scores indicate that managers find a certain platform highly (poorly) credible. Table 7 shows that YouTube (mean = 43.40, median = 44) and Twitter (mean = 42.93; median = 42) are the most credible platforms. WeChat (mean = 12.07; median = 3) and Facebook (mean = 33.77; median = 44) are the two least credible social media platforms. Interestingly, none of the platforms reaches the average critical point of 50, suggesting a certain degree of skepticism towards social media platforms among managers.

Next, we investigate the potential variance in the use of social media among managers due to their seniority, education and experience in organizational decision-making. Table 8 shows that managers with more experience use more YouTube and Instagram compared to managers with less experience. Managers with a higher level of education use more Facebook and less Instagram compared to managers with a lower level of education. Looking at the level of organizational decision-making experience, managers with high work experience use more Twitter, YouTube and Instagram relative to managers with low work experience; managers with more managerial experience tend to use more Instagram than those with less managerial experience.

In terms of credibility, we observe differences for Facebook, Instagram and WeChat. Specifically, Table 9 shows that more senior managers find Facebook and WeChat more credible than managers with less seniority. Managers with higher

[7] Further information at https://www.statista.com/statistics/346167/facebook-global-dau/. Accessed on August 23, 2020.

Table 5 Preferences for data sources in a sales prediction portfolio conditional to managers' characteristics

Panel A: Seniority and Education[a, b]

	More senior	Less senior	Diff	Higher education level	Lower education level	Diff	High accounting education	Low accounting education	Diff
Sales data gathered from internal sales records	27.59	26.43	1.16	27.11	26.52	0.59	26.11	27.21	−1.10
Number of product mentions gathered from external social media platforms	6.7	7.12	−0.42	6.9	7.03	−0.13	6.78	6.99	−0.21
Product 'Likes' gathered from external social media platforms	5.25	5.62	−0.37	5.21	6.06	−0.85	4.92	5.63	−0.71
Survey and focus group data gathered from internal marketing department	8.33	8.94	−0.61	9.31	7.18	2.13**	8.07	8.88	−0.81
Survey and focus group data gathered from external marketing agencies	8.39	9.15	−0.76	9	8.4	0.60	9.33	8.65	0.68

(continued)

Table 5 (continued)

Panel A: Seniority and Education[a, b]

	More senior	Less senior	Diff	Higher education level	Lower education level	Diff	High accounting education	Low accounting education	Diff
Web product search trend data gathered from external search engines	7.47	7.55	−0.08	7.46	7.66	−0.20	7.59	7.49	0.10
Web traffic data representing visits to your firm's online stores	10.43	9.9	0.53	9.48	11.68	−2.20*	10.14	10.13	0.01
Traffic data representing visits to physical stores	27.59	26.43	1.16	27.11	26.52	0.59	26.11	27.21	−1.10
Market trend data gathered from external sources	6.7	7.12	−0.42	6.9	7.03	−0.13	6.78	6.99	−0.21
Textual data and sentiment about products gathered from external social media platforms	5.25	5.62	−0.37	5.21	6.06	−0.85	4.92	5.63	−0.71

(continued)

Table 5 (continued)

Panel B: Decision-making experience[c, d]						
	High work experience	Low work experience	Diff	High managerial experience	Low managerial experience	Diff
Sales data gathered from internal sales records	28.73	23.21	5.52*	27.32	26.87	0.45
Number of product mentions gathered from external social media platforms	6.82	7.18	−0.32	6.2	7.07	−0.87
Product 'Likes' gathered from external social media platforms	5.63	5.1	0.53	5.52	5.45	0.07
Survey and focus group data gathered from internal marketing department	8.6	8.83	−0.23	7.96	8.8	−0.84
Survey and focus group data gathered from external marketing agencies	8.63	9.21	−0.58	7.88	8.98	−1.1
Web product search trend data gathered from external search engines	7.07	8.43	−1.36	8	7.43	0.57
Web traffic data representing visits to your firm's online stores	9.65	11.12	1.47	11.44	9.9	1.54
Traffic data representing visits to physical stores	9.82	11.58	−0.176	11.92	10.12	1.8

(continued)

Table 5 (continued)

Panel B: Decision-making experience[c, d]

	High work experience	Low work experience	Diff	High managerial experience	Low managerial experience	Diff
Market trend data gathered from external sources	7.48	9.58	−2.1	6.36	8.48	−2.12
Textual data and sentiment about products gathered from external social media platforms	5.1	5.09	0.01	4.88	5.13	−0.25

Note * significant at the .1 level, ** significant at the .05 level, *** significant at the .01 level

[a]If you were able to choose data sources to make sales predictions, which weights would you assign to the following data sources? (100 points in total)

[b]*More senior* if the manager is above 35 years old, *less senior* otherwise (i.e., millennial); *Higher education* level if the manager has completed at least an undergraduate degree, *lower education* level otherwise; *High accounting education* if the manager has completed at least one accounting or finance course, *low accounting education* otherwise

[c]If you were able to choose data sources to make sales predictions, which weights would you assign to the following data sources? (100 points in total)

[d]*High work experience* if the manager has at least 4 years of work experience, *low work experience* otherwise; *High managerial experience* if the manager has at least 4 years of managerial experience, *low managerial* experience otherwise

Table 6 Social media use

	p25	median	p75	mean	sd
Twitter	1	3	5	2.92	1.67
Facebook	1	1	3	1.89	1.42
YouTube	1	2	3	1.98	1.07
Instagram	1	1	4	2.29	1.67
WeChat	5	5	5	4.88	0.55

How often do you use the following social media? (5-point scale ranging from 1 = Daily to 5 = Never).

Table 7 Credibility of social media platforms

	p25	median	p75	mean	sd
Twitter	20	42	61	42.93	24.84
Facebook	18	30	50	33.77	22.45
YouTube	25	44	60	43.40	22.76
Instagram	17	35	52	36.71	24.59
WeChat	1	3	19	12.07	17.16

To what extent do you perceive the following sources of information as credible (101-point scale ranging from 0 = Low Credibility to 100 = High Credibility)

education levels find Instagram more credible than those with a lower education level. Managers with high work experience find WeChat more credible than managers with low work experience. Finally, more managerial experience is positively associated with Facebook and Instagram credibility.

In the last set of analyses, we examine the preference for data sources conditional to managers' use and credibility towards social media. Specifically, we identify managers with high (low) use of social media depending on whether their use of the five social media platforms previously discussed (Twitter, Facebook, YouTube, Instagram and WeChat) is above (below) the average. Similarly, we define managers having high (low) credibility of social media if the credibility of the five identified social media platforms is above (below) the average.

Table 10 shows that there is no significant difference among managers in the preference for data sources when we focus on the use of social media. Interestingly, the preference for data sources changes quite substantially when we turn our attention to managers' credibility towards social media. Managers exhibiting higher credibility in social media would prefer more social media items, namely 'Number of product mentions gathered from external social media platforms", "Product 'Likes' gathered from external social media platforms", "Web product search trend data gathered from external search engines" and "Textual data and sentiment about products gathered from external social media platforms" as a data source for sales predictions. This set

Table 8 Use of social media conditional to managers' demographic

	Twitter	Facebook	YouTube	Instagram	WeChat
More senior	3.16	1.91	2.22	2.95	4.86
Less senior	2.74	1.88	1.8	1.77	4.89
Difference	*0.42*	*0.03*	*0.42****	*1.18****	*−0.03*
Higher education level	3	2.03	1.97	2.09	4.84
Lower education level	2.74	1.58	2.02	2.78	4.96
Difference	*0.26*	*0.45***	*−0.05*	*−0.69****	*−0.12*
High accounting education	3.09	1.95	2.11	2.59	4.8
Low accounting education	2.87	1.88	1.94	2.19	4.9
Difference	*0.22*	*0.07*	*0.17*	*0.4*	*−0.1*
High work experience	3.11	1.85	2.09	2.6	4.91
Low work experience	2.54	1.98	1.76	1.65	4.81
Difference	*0.57***	*−0.13*	*0.33***	*0.95****	*0.1*
High managerial experience	2.88	1.76	2.08	3.08	4.88
Low managerial experience	2.93	1.92	1.97	2.15	4.89
Difference	*−0.05*	*−0.16*	*0.11*	*0.93****	*−0.01*

Note * significant at the .1 level, ** significant at the .05 level, *** significant at the .01 level
How often do you use the following social media? (5-point scale ranging from 1 = Daily to 5 = Never)
More senior if the manager is above 35 years old, *less senior* otherwise (i.e., millennial); *Higher education* level if the manager has completed at least an undergraduate degree, *lower education* level otherwise; *High accounting education* if the manager has completed at least one accounting or finance course, *low accounting education* otherwise; *High work experience* if the manager has at least 4 years of work experience, *low work experience* otherwise; *High managerial experience* if the manager has at least 4 years of managerial experience, *low managerial* experience otherwise

of data sources appears complementary to traditional accounting sources as we do not observe significant differences with regards to the other data sources.

We next examine managers' preferences with regards to sales prediction portfolio. Table 11 shows no significant difference among managers with different social media use in their sales prediction portfolio. Conversely, managers having a higher degree of credibility towards social media assign a greater weight to data sources related to social media, such as "Number of product mentions gathered from external social media platforms", "Product 'Likes' gathered from external social media platforms" and "Textual data and sentiment about products gathered from external social media platforms". However, this change in the portfolio composition does not come with a decrease in the weight of traditional accounting measures.

Taken together, these results provide evidence that managers' credibility towards social media leads to an increase in the role of social media as a data source for sales prediction. This is not the case when we look at the managers' use of social media. Moreover, managers still assign traditional accounting data sources a key role in sales predictions, with social media playing an increasingly complementary

Table 9 Credibility of social media conditional to managers' demographic

	Twitter	Facebook	YouTube	Instagram	WeChat
High accounting education	38.88	34.54	45.64	37	10.66
Low accounting education	44.27	33.51	42.66	36.62	12.53
Difference	*−5.39*	*1.03*	*2.98*	*0.38*	*−1.87*
More senior	42.28	37.6	43.97	3	16.18
Less senior	43.44	30.78	42.95	2.43	8.86
Difference	*−1.16*	*6.82***	*1.02*	*0.57*	*7.32****
Higher education level	42.26	32.36	43.99	38.89	12.1
Lower education level	44.52	37.12	42	31.52	12
Difference	*−2.26*	*−4.76*	*1.99*	*7.37**	*0.1*
High work experience	42.11	35.11	42.97	37.46	13.86
Low work experience	44.63	31	44.29	35.16	8.34
Difference	*−2.52*	*4.11*	*−1.32*	*2.3*	*5.52***
High managerial experience	43.4	40.48	46.28	44.32	16
Low managerial experience	42.85	32.61	42.9	35.39	11.38
Difference	*0.55*	*7.87**	*3.38*	*8.93**	*4.62*

Note * significant at the .1 level, ** significant at the .05 level, *** significant at the .01 level
To what extent do you perceive the following sources of information as credible (101-point scale ranging from 0 = low Credibility to 100 = High Credibility)
More senior if the manager is above 35 years old, *less senior* otherwise (i.e., millennial); *Higher education* level if the manager has completed at least an undergraduate degree, *lower education* level otherwise; *High accounting education* if the manager has completed at least one accounting or finance course, *low accounting education* otherwise; *High work experience* if the manager has at least 4 years of work experience, *low work experience* otherwise; *High managerial experience* if the manager has at least 4 years of managerial experience, *low managerial* experience otherwise

role. Managers are increasingly turning their attention at non-traditional data sources to triangulate evidence gathered from traditional sources. Interestingly, we do not observe a substitution between traditional and non-data sources. Future research could further investigate whether managers prefer traditional data sources as an anchor because they are considered more reliable while non-traditional data sources provide more timely information. The use of both traditional and non-traditional data sources may also generate unintended consequences, such as information overload. It could also be interesting to further examine the extent to which managers would resolve potentially conflicting predictions between traditional and non-traditional data sources about organizational trends, such as sales forecasts.

Table 10 Preference for data sources in sales predictions conditional to managers' attitude towards social media according to the use of social media

	High use	Low use	Diff	High credibility	Low credibility	Diff
Sales data gathered from internal sales records	5.54	5.6	−0.06	5.61	5.53	0.08
Number of product mentions gathered from external social media platforms	4.03	4	0.03	4.41	3.61	0.8***
Product 'Likes' gathered from external social media platforms	3.7	3.7	0	4	3.4	0.6***
Survey and focus group data gathered from internal marketing department	4.6	4.86	−0.26	4.85	4.61	0.24
Survey and focus group data gathered from external marketing agencies	4.87	4.79	0.08	4.78	4.88	−0.1
Web product search trend data gathered from external search engines	4.74	4.71	0.03	4.96	4.48	0.48***
Web traffic data representing visits to your firm's online stores	5.2	5.15	0.05	5.32	5.03	0.29*
Traffic data representing visits to physical stores	5.14	5.11	0.03	5.07	5.19	−0.12
Market trend data gathered from external sources	4.92	4.88	0.04	4.91	4.9	0.01

(continued)

Table 10 (continued)

	High use	Low use	Diff	High credibility	Low credibility	Diff
Textual data and sentiment about products gathered from external social media platforms	4.3	4.19	0.11	4.51	3.97	0.54***

Note * significant at the .1 level, ** significant at the .05 level, *** significant at the .01 level
If you were able to choose data sources to make sales predictions, how much would you rely on the following data sources? (7-point scale ranging from 1 = Low Extent to 7 = High Extent)

4 Conclusion

Big data are revolutionizing the budgeting and forecasting processes and management accountants are increasingly providing information from data sources beyond traditional accounting measures. Specifically, social media data as a form of non-traditional data can provide a wide new range of information about customers' choices and preferences. We investigate managers' preferences for traditional and non-traditional data sources. Our results suggest that managers still prefer traditional accounting data sources compared to non-traditional data sources. Further, we show that the preference for non-traditional data sources for sales predictions varies with the level of education. In particular accounting and finance education leads to a higher preference for social media data. We also find that the use of social media does not affect the preference for data sources in sales predictions. Conversely, managers that exhibit higher credibility towards social media tend to have a higher preference for non-traditional data sources for sales predictions. However, the higher preference for non-traditional data sources appears to be complementary with traditional accounting sources and does not substitute them.

Our study contributes to an emerging stream of literature on managerial behavior and decision making in relation to new data sources (Fehrenbacher et al. forthcoming). We find that the *management demographics* and *credibility attitudes* towards social media influences the preference for data sources in the context of sales prediction. These are important considerations for management accounting when conceptualizing management accountants as key organizational actors in budgeting and forecasting activities (Granlund & Lukka, 1998). We call for more research on the use of different types of social media information, such as video, images and text. Managers may differently react to the type of data available with regards to their reliability, relevance and timeliness. Our findings have also practical implications for professional bodies. When preparing courses to update management accountants' skills, professional bodies will have to consider managers' pre-conceptions about the use and credibility of non-traditional data sources. Another key aspect concerns the role that demographics play in using new data sources. Management accountants

Table 11 Preference for data sources in a sales prediction portfolio conditional to managers' attitude towards social media

	High use	Low use	Diff	High credibility	Low credibility	Diff
Sales data gathered from internal sales records	25.06	28.67	−3.61	25.34	28.55	−3.21
Number of product mentions gathered from external social media platforms	6.78	7.09	−0.31	7.98	5.89	2.09**
Product 'Likes' gathered from external social media platforms	5.61	5.31	0.3	6.2	4.71	1.49*
Survey and focus group data gathered from internal marketing department	8.38	8.95	−0.57	8.84	8.51	0.33
Survey and focus group data gathered from external marketing agencies	9.58	8.12	1.46	8.32	9.32	−1
Web product search trend data gathered from external search engines	7.54	7.5	0.04	7.98	7.04	0.94
Web traffic data representing visits to your firm's online stores	10.54	9.76	0.78	10.08	10.19	−0.11
Traffic data representing visits to physical stores	10.87	9.95	0.92	10.15	10.63	−0.48
Market trend data gathered from external sources	8.3	8.04	0.26	7.71	8.63	−0.92

(continued)

Table 11 (continued)

	High use	Low use	Diff	High credibility	Low credibility	Diff
Textual data and sentiment about products gathered from external social media platforms	5.32	4.89	0.43	5.89	4.29	1.6**

Note * significant at the .1 level, ** significant at the .05 level, *** significant at the .01 level
If you were able to choose data sources to make sales predictions, which weights would you assign to the following data sources? (100 points in total)

will need to take different routes to embrace holistic models that include multiple data sources to further support organizational decision-makers.

References

Brands, K., & Holtzblatt, M. (2015). Business analytics: Transforming the role of management accountants. *Management Accounting Quarterly, 16*(3), 1–12.

Bronzo, M., de Resende, P. T. V., de Oliveira, M. P. V., McCormack, K. P., de Sousa, P. R., & Ferreira, R. L. (2013). Improving performance aligning business analytics with process orientation. *International Journal of Information Management, 33*(2), 300–307.

Brown-Liburd, H., Issa, H., & Lombardi, D. (2015). Behavioral implications of Big Data's impact on audit judgment and decision making and future research directions. *Accounting Horizons, 29*(2), 451–468.

Cardinaels, E., & van Veen-Dirks, P. M. (2010). Financial versus non-financial information: The impact of information organization and presentation in a balanced scorecard. *Accounting, Organizations and Society, 35*(6), 565–578.

Chen, Y., Jermias, J., & Panggabean, T. (2016). The role of visual attention in the managerial judgment of balanced-scorecard performance evaluation: Insights from using an eye-tracking device. *Journal of Accounting Research, 54*(1), 113–146.

Davenport, T. H., Barth, P., & Bean, R. (2012). How 'Big Data' is different. *MIT Sloan Management Review, 54*(1), 22–24.

Deshmukh, A. (2006). *Digital accounting: The effects of the internet and ERP on accounting.* IGI Global.

Di Fabio, C., Roncagliolo, E., Avallone, F., & Ramassa, P. (2019). XBRL implementation in the European Union: Exploring preparers' points of view. *Organizing for the Digital World* (pp. 33–47). Springer.

Fehrenbacher, D., Ghio, A., & Weisner, M. (forthcoming). Advice utilization from predictive analytics tools: The trend is your friend. *Forthcoming, The European Accounting Review.*

Geva, T., Oestreicher-Singer, G., Efron, N., & Shimshoni, Y. (2017). Using forum and search data for sales prediction of high-involvement products. *MIS Quarterly, 41*(1), 65–82.

Granlund, M., & Lukka, K. (1998). It's a small world of management accounting practices. *Journal of Management Accounting Research, 10*, 153–179.

Günther, W. A., Mehrizi, M. H. R., Huysman, M., & Feldberg, F. (2017). Debating big data: A literature review on realizing value from big data. *The Journal of Strategic Information Systems, 26*(3), 191–209.

Lee, J. H., & Park, S. C. (2005). Intelligent profitable customers segmentation system based on business intelligence tools. *Expert Systems with Applications, 29*(1), 145–152.

Lee, Z., Wagner, C., & Shin, H. K. (2008). The effect of decision support system expertise on system use behavior and performance. *Information & Management, 45*(6), 349–358.

Marx, F., Wortmann, F., & Mayer, J. H. (2012). A maturity model for management control systems. *Business & Information Systems Engineering, 4*(4), 193–207.

Moffitt, K. C., & Vasarhelyi, M. A. (2013). AIS in an age of Big Data. *Journal of Information System, 27*, 1–19.

Nielsen, S. (2018). Reflections on the applicability of business analytics for management accounting—And future perspectives for the accountant. *Journal of Accounting & Organizational Change, 14*(2), 167–187.

Quattrone, P., & Hopper, T. (2001). What does organizational change mean? Speculations on a taken for granted category. *Management Accounting Research, 12*(4), 403–435.

Rikhardsson, P., & Yigitbasioglu, O. (2018). Business intelligence & analytics in management accounting research: Status and future focus. *International Journal of Accounting Information Systems, 29*, 37–58.

Schläfke, M., Silvi, R., & Möller, K. (2013). A framework for business analytics in performance management. *International Journal of Productivity and Performance Management, 62*(2), 110–122.

Vasarhelyi, M. A., Kogan, A., & Tuttle, B. M. (2015). Big Data in accounting: An overview. *Accounting Horizons, 29*(2), 381–396.

Voleti, S. (2019). Data collection. In essentials of business analytics: An introduction to the methodology and its applications In B. Pochiraju & S. Seshadri (Eds.), *Essentials of business analytics: An introduction to the methodology and its applications*. Springer.

Warren, D., Moffitt, K., & Byrnes, P. (2015). How accounting records will change with Big Data. *Accounting Horizons, 29*(2), 397–407.

Dennis Fehrenbacher is an Associate Professor at the Institute of Accounting, Control and Auditing at St. Gallen University, Switzerland. He also holds an Adjunct position at Monash Business School, Monash University, Australia. He is a researcher and educator at the intersection of information systems and management accounting. A focus of his research is to examine digital technologies and their impact on addressing organizational challenges. To understand the potential of digital technologies, he also employs some emerging technologies in his research projects. To better understand the role of information processing in performance evaluation, he and his colleagues have used eye tracking and big data analytics techniques to gain more insights into the nature of a biases related to subjective performance evaluation.

Alessandro Ghio is an Assistant Professor of Accounting at School of Accounting, University of Laval, Canada. As an educator motivated by human connection, they position accounting within its social context. Their research focuses on issues surrounding financial reporting (e.g., corporate social media) and the sociology of the accounting profession (e.g., diversity).

Chapter 11
The Use of Internet of Things, Big Data Analytics and Artificial Intelligence for Attaining UN's SDGs

David Teh and Tarek Rana

Abstract With world's population projected to grow to 9.7 billion in 2050, the demand for food and water will increase drastically. When population increases it also raises consumption and waste, managing waste can be more challenging. If urgent actions not taken, global waste is expected to increase by 70%; to an estimated 4 billion tons by 2050, projected by the World Bank. Further, the link between humanity's impacts on ecosystems and biodiversity, and the rise of emerging and certain diseases, such as the novel coronavirus (COVID-19) shows the severity. This chapter seeks to further understand and explore how the use of emerging technologies such as the Internet of Things, Big Data Analytics and Artificial Intelligence can accelerate the progress on the 17 UN Sustainable Development Goals (SDGs). Brief case studies based one documentary evidence are presented to capture how technologies can create solutions in the areas of smart waste management, water management, and agriculture and farming. Since IoT has offered the opportunity to digitize many operations that can bring many benefits, it can help combat climate change and protect the environment. For instance, IoT can be used to develop smarter and more effective ways of managing and reducing waste. IoT could also impact the sustainability of the planet in different areas, such as water use, water efficiency and harvest productivity. The technologies discussed provide the opportunity to drive success and accelerate the progress of attaining many of the SDGs such as SDG 2, 3, 6, 9, 11, 12, 13, 14, 15.

Keywords Internet of Things · Big Data Analytics · Artificial Intelligence · Sustainable Development Goals · Accounting for sustainability · Smart waste management · Smart Water Utilities Management · Smart agriculture

---

D. Teh · T. Rana (✉)
RMIT University, Melbourne, VIC, Australia
e-mail: tarek.rana@rmit.edu.au

D. Teh
e-mail: david.teh@rmit.edu.au

T. Rana et al. (eds.), *Handbook of Big Data and Analytics in Accounting and Auditing*,
https://doi.org/10.1007/978-981-19-4460-4_11

1 Introduction

In the latest 2019 revision of the *World Population Prospects* (WPP), the United Nations (UN) projected that the world's population would increase by 2 billion people in the next 30 years, from 7.7 billion to 9.7 billion in 2050, and 10.9 billion in 2100. In addition, by 2050, two-thirds of the world population—an estimated 6.3 billion people will be living in urban areas. With close to 90% of this population growth will be taking place in less developed regions of Asia and Africa. Asia, despite its relatively lower level of urbanization, is home to 54% of the world's urban population, followed by Europe and Africa with 13% each (United Nations, 2018a). A sharp increase of urbanization will also place a significant burden on the sustainability of food security and water system. Further, three in five cities worldwide with a population of at least half a million people are at high risk of natural disaster (UN, 2018b). For that reason, critical infrastructures, such as transport, housing, energy supply, health care and waste management will be at the brink of collapse. Global collaborative efforts including implementation of resilience measures is urgently needed to address natural disasters and the related threats in a timely and efficient manner, resulting in least negative economic and social impacts (Teh & Khan, 2021).

In addition, the recent report by Worldwide Fund for Nature (WWF) illustrates the link between humanity's impacts on ecosystems and biodiversity, and the rise of emerging and certain diseases, one example, is the novel coronavirus (COVID-19) which is the pandemic the world encounters (WWF, 2020). This has not only caused serious damage to the local society and world economy, but also the natural environment. The pandemic reignited demand for single-use plastic bags, plastic packaging and many other single-use items like masks, gloves and test kits in which plastic is a key component. According to the nation's Ministry of Ecology and Environment, during the peak of the crisis in Wuhan China, the center of the COVID-19 outbreaks, generated around 240 tons a day of medical waste, producing up to six times more medical waste than usual. Manila produced an additional 280 tons a day of medical trash, while Jakarta generated 212 tons and Bangkok generated 210 tons, based on the estimates of Asian Development Bank (2020).

With many parts of the world in lockdowns or with restriction and movement control, many businesses struggle to survive. For those businesses in the food and beverages industry have opted for only takeaway or delivery service which have used a lot more plastics than usual, such as food container, utensils and single-use plastics bag. This further contributes to the rise in plastic and paper waste. Many other retail businesses have shifted and sold through online platform or e-commerce which results in surge in packaging demand, especially the corrugated board for delivery (McKinsey, 2020).

The risk of pandemics, as highlighted by the current coronavirus crisis, underlines the urgent need for decisive global action to safeguard people's lives and health. The loss of habitats, the modification of natural environments, and more generally the decline in biodiversity are all factors in the spread of emerging infectious diseases (Di Marco et al., 2020). One should also note that, the real environmental impact would be determined by the actions we undertake now to emerge from the crisis—*how we respond and manage the pandemic, how and what we find as longer term and more sustainable solutions.* This chapter explores the role of technologies in addressing the society's most pressing issues—current existential risks and sustainability problems human civilization ever encountered. Based on the analysis of advancement of technologies, this chapter seeks to build on the previous research of Teh (2022), Teh et al. (2020), and Teh and Khan (2019, 2020) to further understand and explore how the use of emerging technologies such as the Internet of Things (IoT), Big Data Analytics (BDA) and Artificial Intelligence (AI) can accelerate the progress on the 17 UN Sustainable Development Goals (SDGs).

2 Research Background

2.1 Sustainable Development and the UN's Sustainable Development Goals

The 2030 Agenda for Sustainable Development and the related 17 Sustainable Development Goals (SDGs) was launched and adopted at the UN General assembly in September 2015. The Agenda of the 17 SDGs are the new agreed blueprint aim to achieve a better and more sustainable future for all in both developed and developing countries (UN, 2015). The SDGs aim to tackle the world's various challenges, specifically, those related to poverty, inequality, climate, environmental degradation, prosperity, and peace and justice (see Fig. 1). The SDGs are interconnected with an aim to leave no one behind. Hence, all 193 UN Member States have agreed to deliver these 17 SDGs and meet 169 targets by 2030 (UN, 2015). In fact, actions are urgently required, as the progress to achieve the SDGs has been slow and challenging (UN DESA, 2019). As a consequence, the window of opportunity to address climate change is getting smaller by each day. Research has suggested that we are in a state of planetary emergency—both the risk and urgency of the situation are acute (Lenton et al., 2019).

Current global consumption patterns supported by consumerism culture are unsustainable from the climate and environmental standpoint of SDGs. Consumerism encourages the acquisition of goods and services in ever-increasing amounts. This has not only increased the production quantity and purchasing amount, but waste has also become a hallmark of consumerism. Developed countries or more advanced economy can lead the way by reinventing many of its industries, to decrease carbon emissions and negative environmental impacts, and reduce material waste costs associated with many facets now considered normal in modern life (UNDP, 2020). The UNDP's report (2020) has shown that achieving economic growth and SDgs requires that urgent actions to reduce our ecological footprint by changing the way we produce and consume goods and resources. We must aggressively support its transitions towards greener energy and increasingly closed-circle product lifecycles.

Fig. 1 United Nations 17 Sustainable Development Goals (UN, 2015)

Why take urgent action now can combat global climate change crisis and achieve its impacts can be the tipping point? First, climate action (SDG13) is fundamentally linked to all other 16 SDGs of the 2030 Agenda for Sustainable Development (see Fuso Nerini, Sovacool et al., 2019). Research shows the issues of climate change and biodiversity are deeply intertwined (Scholes & Scholes, 2020; UNDP, 2019). Healthy ecosystems and rich biodiversity are fundamental to life on the planet; even small changes in average temperatures can have a significant effect on the ecosystems. Changes in temperature and rainfall conditions may trigger extreme weather conditions which may occur with increased frequency and influence transmission patterns for many diseases, including water-related diseases, such as diarrhea, and vector-borne infections, including malaria (WHO, 2020). Climate change may affect patterns of food production and food security (SDG2), which in turn can have health impacts in terms of rates of malnutrition and the overall wellbeing of all (SDG3). In UN, 2019 special report, public investment in agriculture globally is declining, investment in infrastructure and technology for sustainable agriculture is urgently needed. It is also important to note, agriculture is cited as the biggest user of water (SDG6) worldwide, and irrigation now claims close to 70% of all freshwaters for human use (UNESCO, 2019). In the similar vein, actions on climate change (SDG13), including actions to reduce food system emissions via transformative food system is crucial as it can have a synergistic effect on several other SDGs (Campbell et al., 2018). For instance, SDG 13 actions that reduce emissions can have positive impacts on other SDGs, namely SDG3, 6, 12, 14, 15, but such actions should not undermine the adaptation goals of SDG13 and SDGs 1, 2, 5 and 10 (Campbell et al., 2018).

If so, climate change is arguably the root cause of many problems that the human civilization is facing, and it is the major source of many risks including physical hazards and socioeconomic impacts. If solving a single root cause could solve several problems at once, this would help to slow down of climate change, if not, to delay the irreversible change in the climate system and accelerate the progress of attaining the SDGs. The UN's Intergovernmental Panel on Climate Change (IPCC) has also began considering the critically important key scientific findings of its Special Report on Global Warming of 1.5 °C (IPCC, 2020). To address climate change, countries adopted the Paris Agreement and Glasgow Summit to undertake ambitious efforts to combat climate change by limiting the global temperature rise to well below 2 °C—it is reported that greenhouse gas emissions have to be cut by 7.5% for a decade in order to meet the 1.5 °C Paris Agreement goals (UNFCCC, 2019).

2.2 Sustainable Development—A Multi-Dimensional Goal

Sustainable development is a multi-dimensional goal, which can be approached from different perspectives, subsequently, active stakeholder engagement and collaboration of individuals, governments, public and private sector organizations and civil society organizations alike is critical to the success of the mission. The large-scale collaboration is required in order to achieve these ambitious UN SDGs. Governments around the world having their own set of priorities, requiring businesses to implement actions to achieve the SDGs. Further long-term perspectives and pragmatic actions are needed than ever before, by businesses. Organizations' efforts are vital since international business and trade has a significant impact on sustainable development from economic, environmental and social perspectives (Xiao et al., 2017). It is evidenced that economic growth is not the only goal which an organization should focus on to achieve the SDGs; strategic direction needs to incorporate and consider multiple perspectives of stakeholders including environmental and social impacts of the organization (Teh & Corbitt, 2015; Xiao et al., 2017).

In the recent report by McKinsey, managers and investors alike are criticized—too often being fixate on short-term financial performance metrics, particularly earnings per share, rather than focusing on long-term value creation and social impact which considers the interests of all stakeholders, instead of just the shareholders (Goedhart & Koller, 2020). The business needs to be more accountable for their decisions and actions rather than focusing on financial bottom lines. McKinsey's Corporate Horizon Index from 1999 to 2017 shows the tendency toward short-termism has been on the rise. Companies that conflate short-termism with value creation often put both shareholder value and stakeholder interests at risk in the long term because such action is the *anti-thesis of value creation.* In fact, the roots of short-termism are deep and intertwined, a collective commitment of business leaders to change and cultivate future value is therefore highly required immediately (Goedhart & Koller, 2020), especially during a time like this—*first*, what the world will be like after the COVID-19 crisis depends on *how and what business organizations* do to reshape it;

second, with so much uncertainty ahead, businesses need to *think more strategically* in order to survive and thrive after the storms.

SDGs have been redefining how businesses conduct their operations and focus on the environmental impact. Every business has a role to play—different types of companies in different industries may be able to contribute to the SDGs in different ways. It is a matter of what specific SDG(s) mean to the company, and how are the SDG(s) aligned with the overall business, its business model and process, and its business strategy (Teh & Corbitt, 2015). This encourages companies to rethink about the business—how they can integrate sustainability into the business so that they do not become competing interests (Teh & Corbitt, 2015). For instance, companies in the manufacturing can contribute to the SDGs, by rethinking the materials used and product design, better understanding of their product/service life cycle so that they can be more sustainable in their production, consumption (SDG12), and overall business activities, contributing of direct investments to invest in research and development (R&D) and more sustainable and greener operations (SDG9).

In the same way, the United Nations and other development agencies see a pivotal role for institutional investors and private sector to play to solve some of the most urgent problems the world is facing—helping direct more capital, through their public equity holdings to contribute their business investment to the SDGs (Douma et al., 2017; Gestrin, 2019); this can be supported by the principles for Responsible Investment (for more information, e.g. see the PRI). This supports the process of creating and developing a more sustainable global financial system, hence, a more sustainable economy and toward the achievement of the SDGs objectives. For example, the primary focus of SDG17 is strengthening the means of implementation and revitalize the global partnership to get the investors on board for sustainable development finance (Douma et al., 2017). Therefore, achieving SDG17 could address the financing challenges, hence, open more doors to fund other initiatives and achieve other SDGs.

To achieve these ambitious UN SDGs, it has its own set of challenges. The latest UN report (2019) further highlights areas that can drive progress across all 17 SDGs. Some of the areas are financing (this could be solved through SDG17 discussed above); resilience; sustainable and inclusive economies; better use of data; and harnessing science, technology and innovation with a greater focus on digital transformation. For example, lack of quality data for reporting, and reporting on key SDG performance indicators is still relatively new or inconsistent to rely on for investment decision-making (Schramade, 2017). Due to the lack of financial services and inadequate financing, small-scale industries in the poorest countries will not be able to build resilient infrastructure; and to grow and innovate to create a sustainable industrialization. Hence, SDG9 will not be achieved. The UN report further stresses the importance of investing in data for the full implementation of the 2030 Agenda (2019). This indicates the importance of data and technology, the role of analytics-enabled accounting in the process will add values to different stakeholders. Data analytics tools can translate the raw data into valuable decision-making knowledge (Hesse et al., 2015). One point to note, emerging technology is crucial to developing projects on sustainability on a large scale, but the awareness of the importance of sustainability in society must be emphasized.

BDA and AI enhance the processes of data collection, identification of cause-and-effect relations, integration of data, translation of raw data into meaningful information, and the representation of the data through visualization on a manageable and accessible scale more efficiently (Wu et al., 2017). On that note, and with the advancement of technologies, this chapter seeks to further explore and understand how the use of emerging technologies, such as the Internet of Things (IoT), Big Data Analytics (BDA) and Artificial Intelligence (AI) can play a role to help accelerating the progress on achieving some of the 17 UN SDGs, if not all (UN, 2020). These technologies will be considered and discussed in turn.

2.3 *Emerging Technologies*

Technological advancements have fundamentally changed many aspects of life and environment for individual, society and businesses. With new technologies continuously being developed, they revolutionize the way human beings live and how they relate to others; how society interacts and engages; and how businesses operate. For instance, digital technologies such as data pooling and AI are used to track and diagnose issues in agriculture, health, and the environment, or to perform daily tasks such as navigating traffic or paying a bill (Castro & New, 2016; Chui et al., 2018). Similarly, technologies can be considered and leveraged to generate new, innovative and sustainable solutions to address some of the environmental and social issues and to support and accelerate the achievement of each of the 17 SDGs (Teh et al., 2020).

2.3.1 Internet of Things (IoT)

IoT is the network of physical objects—"things" that are embedded with sensors, software, and other technologies for the purpose of connecting, communicating, collecting and sharing real-time data, as well as sensing or interacting with their internal states or the external environment (Gartner, 2020). There are more than 7 billion connected IoT devices in 2018; the number of IoT devices that are active is expected to grow to 10 billion by 2020 and 22 billion by 2025 (IoT Analytics, 2020). The growth will further be fueled by the introduction and evolution of IPv6 along with 5G enabled high-speed connectivity. Consequently, this will also drive organizations' and smart cities nations' demand for more connected technologies.

The World Economic Forum (WEF) (2018) report on IoT, "The Internet of things (IoT) is undoubtedly one of the largest enablers for responsible digital transformation. It is estimated that industrial IoT alone can add $14 trillion of economic value to the global economy by 2030." The WEF report (2018) also found that 84% of IoT technology applications were addressing or could potentially address many of the UN's SDGs. Due to its technical capabilities, IoT can measure and control previously unconnected "things", connect the people and reach objects that technology could not have reached, previously. IoT, hitherto, has supported many SDGs in the process with 75% of these projects (small and medium sized) concentrate on five SDGs:

- SDG9, Industry, innovation, and infrastructure (25%)
- SDG11, Smart cities and communities (19%)
- SDG7, Affordable and clean energy (19%)
- SDG3, Good health and well-being (7%)
- SDG12, Responsible production and consumption (5%)

Extensive usage of sensors and actuators that turn "things" into smart connected devices; co-exist in both the digital and physical universes, with minimal human intervention, paves way for the advent of many smart solutions, especially smart cities applications that makes the fabric of the world smarter and more responsive. This is due to large amount of data that constantly being generated, collected and used by IoT applications to aggregate, analyze, and deliver insights, which helps driving more informed decisions and real-time actions (IBM, 2019). As a result, the IoT has been widely considered as the smart solutions and future fundamental platform to achieve many objectives set in the smart sustainable cities.

2.3.2 Big Data Analytics (BDA)

Although, the massive amount of generated data referred to as "big data" has been the buzzword in business context; and has been intensively researched on, the concept is not entirely new. The way of how the concept of big data is defined is constantly changing. So, what is big data? Put it simply, it is known as big dataset—immense quantities of data that is being generated constantly due to many developed technological trends, including the IoT (discussed in previous section), emergence of cloud computing as well as explosion of use of other various smart devices and applications. Due to the intensification of datafication that constantly generates data—enormous amount of data, IBM data scientists break big data into five main dimensions: *volume*, *variety*, *velocity*, *veracity*, and *value*. They are described in the following:

- Volume: data collected from a variety of sources, including business transactions, social media and information from sensor or machine-to-machine data.
- Velocity: data collected at an unprecedented speed and must be processed within a timely manner. For instance, radio-frequency identification (RFID) tags, sensors and smart metering are driving the need to deal with near-real time data.
- Variety: data collected in all various formats—from structured, numeric data in traditional databases to unstructured texts, email, video, audio.
- Veracity: Inherent discrepancies in all the data collected which affect unpredictability of some data. This might require analysis of big data to gain reliable prediction.
- Value: The extent to which big data generates economically worthy insights and/or benefits is through extraction and transformation, and superior analytics.

There are many applications of IoT and BDA in numerous industries, for instance, agriculture, retail, healthcare, supply chain management, transportation. BDA is also known as one of valuable technologies that help creating a suitable cities and communities, through smart cities' applications and solutions in waste management, water and utilities management. This is because when more data being able to be collected through sensors (as discussed in IoT section) in real time, these data can be fed into big data pools; and become available for some powerful analytics—processed through artificial intelligence on the cloud to enhance data-enabled decision making. However, the key question is how. BDA is a great way to sift through and process large amount of data so that they become valuable information. Accountants who use analytics-enabled accounting in the processes will help businesses and organizations to uncover valuable insights and make better data-informed decisions that can help them optimize their business processes for efficiency and compliance. Auditors have always undertaken large scale of data analysis but the sheer volume of data and the data analytics now possible provide new insights about their client and its risk environment, including a detailed knowledge of the transactions that make up their financial statement balances. Similarly, the information can be used for tracking the progress of SDGs and supporting more critical decision-making around sustainability. Big data can supplement traditional data sources to better keep track of SDGs development and various SDGs performance indicators.

One of the challenges is, although, SDGs offer particular, time-based, and quantifiable targets in sync with national development plans and priorities. With as many as 231 SDG indicators, data being collected require some forms of disaggregation—it is necessary to collect more granular data to monitor, process and track all SDGs and targets simultaneously. It is not an easy task for any national statistical systems, especially those in the developing countries who might lack the infrastructures and other critical resources (Martinez & Albert, 2018). Many national statistical organizations (NSOs) of 16 ADB developing member countries acknowledge that the only way that they will be able to meet SDGs' disaggregated data requirements is to utilize innovative methods and data sourcessmall area estimation (SAE) methods that strengthen direct survey estimates for small areas (or small sub-populations) with auxiliary information such as census records; a small proportion utilizes aerial photos/satellite imagery, mobile data, web-scraped online price data, and social media data (Martinez & Albert, 2018).

Research shows many views that big data as a promising technology to address data gaps for SDGsit improves accuracy, granularity of stats on poverty, welfare. However, only a limited number of these respondents have current Big Data projects. This might be due to some of the major challenges—technological infrastructure, hardware and software, expertise of data scientists who are strong in both data and computational focus (Martinez & Albert, 2018). Since then, through SDG9 and 17, UN launched a number of initiatives such as online courses on big data; UN Statistics Division partners with GIS software company Esri to set up data hub enabling countries to use mapping software to monitor progress of the SDGs; and 12-point plan on privacy and governance issues to unleash big data-driven innovation and strengthen countries' use of big data for sustainable development (IISD, 2018).

2.3.3 Artificial Intelligence (AI)

The volume of data in the world is increasing exponentially because data that is constantly being generated by inexpensive and multiple smart connected devices or sensor-enabled objects. This leads to explosion in the availability of big data; and together with the emergence of artificial intelligence which require these data as the input. This offers another powerful combination of technologies. Other than being used by IoT applications and big data analytics to drive more informed and real-time decisions, new applications to analyze the collected data to make meaningful correlations and possible decisions, has also emerged, this leads to AI. The term AI was first coined by John McCarthy in 1956 when he described while computer programs performing tasks, they seemingly exhibit some intelligence as humans (Rajaraman, 2014). AI is believed to have the technological capabilities and computing power to solve more complex cognitive problems associated with human intelligence. The core concept of AI is on machines that were capable of thinking like humans. It has shown promising opportunities in enhancing human decision-making.

AI technologies have continued to advance, and their transformative impact is increasingly evident across industries. AI can exploit the current BDA capabilities to allow machines to do more of the heavy liftings in the audit, so that auditors can focus on more impactful activities within the audit function (Alles & Gray, 2020). AI has changed the way to generate, process and use information for decision-making; revolutionized the ways of conducting business; stimulate sectors moving towards sustainability by offering competitive and sustainable products or services (Garbuio & Lin, 2019). AI can recognize patterns, problems and create solutions for the benefit of people, society, and business. It offers a wide range of applications that can be game changers for the pursuit of sustainable development (Goralski & Tan, 2020). It is about how to integrate AI into decision-making processes for the achievement of the SDGs.

AI-based technologies are an enabler for SDG1, 4, 6, 7 and 11 by supporting the provision of food, health, water, and energy services to the population. It can also support low-carbon systems, for instance, by supporting the creation of circular economies and smart cities that efficiently utilize their resources (Fuso Nerini, Slob et al., 2019). AI-assisted monitoring platforms use machine learning (a branch of AI where it processes data, finds insights hidden in data without explicitly being told where to look or what to conclude, and learn on their own, with or without constant supervision) algorithm on big data feeds to enable smarter analysis of weather and traffic commuter information to help predict areas of poor air quality. The information can be used by local authorities to reduce pollution by reducing traffic and output from factories. Poor air quality is a major adverse issue in urban areas but is much worse in emerging economies' urban areas; it is therefore a key target under SDG11 (Teh & Khan, 2019). AI can also offer alternative computational approaches to solve solid waste management problems (Abdallah et al., 2020).

3 Methodology: Case Studies

This chapter presents the following brief case studies of how different countries, both developed and emerging countries, or organizations use a combination of various technologies in creating solutions for accounting for sustainability and potentially attaining some of the UN's SDGs, such as SDG2, 3, 6, 9, 11, 12, 13, 14, 15. The brief case studies capture the leveraging of technologies in creating solutions in the areas of smart waste management, smart water management, and smart agriculture and farming (Wolfert et al., 2017) is presented and summarized in Table 1.

4 Discussion, Implications and Conclusion

With the world's population projected to increase to 9.7 billion in 2050; and around two-thirds of the world's people will be urban, this will cause serious environmental, social and economic sustainability implications, and create significant burdens on the on the sustainability of food security and food system, and critical infrastructures, including housing, water utilities management, waste management (UN, 2018a). The Food and Agriculture Organization of the United Nations (FAO) and the International Food Policy Research Institute (IFPRI) have published projections of an increase in global food demand by 70% by 2050. With population growth, the demand for water will also increase. In addition, as consumer-oriented urban populations grow, global waste is expected to increase by 70%; to double from nearly 2 billion tons in 2016 to an estimated 4 billion tons by 2050, if without urgent actions, projected by the World Bank (Kaza et al., 2018). When population growth, it increases consumption and waste, managing waste can be more challenging.

The IoT can be used to develop smarter and more effective ways of managing and reducing waste. As an accurate tracking and monitoring technology, IoT enables automation, through cyber-physical systems to change the way waste management takes place (e.g. see Bin-e, 2020). It helps with problems such as timing of waste collection, waste treatment and disposal (reduce and avoid landfill) and accountability issues associated with the service providers. Some cities are already using a combination of IoT and sensors to operate smart waste management systems. For example, Songdo in South Korea is a purpose-built smart city that uses a combination of IoT and sensors to operate its waste management system. Songdo aims to recycle 76% of its waste by 2020, through its highly efficient and convenient waste management system (Teh & Khan, 2019). This could be particularly beneficial to many states in Australia, such as Victoria, New South Wales, and Queensland; it struggled with a waste crisis after China's ban on trash imports (Teh & Khan, 2020).

It is also suggested that the IoT can help by providing integrated and sustainable solutions to support a circular economy. For example, in waste management, instead of accepting a cradle-to-grave approach, cradle-to-cradle approach should be

Table 1 Emerging technologies for smart solutions and the SDGs

	Smart Waste Management	Smart Water Utilities Management	Smart Agriculture/Farming
Country/ Organization	Poland/ Bin-e	Sub-Saharan Africa countries such as Ghana, Niger, Rwanda and South Africa/CityTaps	USA/Harvest CROO Robotics, Blue River Technology, SkySquirrel Technologies, aWhere
Technology	IoT, sensors, BDA, AI	IoT, sensors and actuators	AI, robotics, aerial technology (drones), IoT, BDA
Solution	Recognize and categorize recycling waster into four categories	Detect anything from changes in temperature and chemical composition to water quantity and soil humidity	Leverage AI-robotics and computer vision to handle essential agricultural tasks, e.g. plant seed, monitor soil and crops health, control pest, monitor and precisely spray weeds on plants, harvest crops
	Waste is compressed, hence, occupies less space; optimize fleet logistics operations	Report a faulty water hand pump	Drones powered by AI can be used to monitor crop health
		Install smart meters to provide access to running water at home by prepaying for the service	Manage livestock and monitor for health issues
Impacts	Detect waste fill level; reducing traffic and automobile CO_2 emissions (part of smart transportation) and fuel consumption	Provide access to safe and clean water to certain areas	Controlled weeds on crops to reduce food wastage, hence, prevent loss of income for farmers
	Save money, time and labor	Improve the accuracy and efficiency in reporting water consumption	Precise cultivation for higher crop yield and better quality while using less resources

(continued)

Table 1 (continued)

	Smart Waste Management	Smart Water Utilities Management	Smart Agriculture/Farming
	Create a resource-efficient and environmentally friendly facility that can reduce waste going to the landfill	Improve productivity when the communities do not need to spend more time in finding clean water away from their homes (e.g. from standpipes)	Increase efficiency, reduce production costs of vegetables and fruits, minimizing environmental impacts
		Water utility companies can provide safe and clean water and run the business more sustainably	Fill the current manpower shortage
SDGs	SDG11, 12	SDG2, 3, 6	SDG1, 2,3, 6, 9, 12, 13,15

considered, which is to rethink and relook at how we can reuse, recycle and repurpose products, components and materials to reduce the use of virgin resources or any other natural resources, with the help of technology. Technology can help where humans struggle.

Since IoT has offered the opportunity to digitize many operations that can bring many benefits, it has the ability to help combat climate change and protect the environment. This could also impact the sustainability of the planet in different areas, such as water use, water efficiency and harvests productivity. Between 70 and 90% of freshwater is abstracted from rivers, lakes and aquifers is used in irrigation for crops; whereas 40% of the global population is affected by water scarcity, and this is projected to increase; an estimated of 1.7 billion people are currently living in river basins where water usage exceeds recharge (UN, 2020; UNESCO, 2019).

The United Nations World Water Development Report reported that 6 billion people around the world will suffer from scarcity of clean water, by 2050 (WWAP, 2019). This was countered by Boretti and Rosa (2019) who suggested that the number may be underestimated, and scarcity of clean water by 2050 may be worse. Regardless, stress levels will continue to increase, as global demand for (clean) water is expected to continue increasing and the effects of climate change exacerbate. Unsustainable rapid urbanizations have also put pressure on water supply and usage. With a rising world population that extracts too much water and pollutes the water sources, the world is heading towards a global water security crisis unless immediate actions are taken. Severe water crisis can further impact the sustainability of agriculture and food systems; this can further affect the progress of SDG2 where it is reported that the world is not on track to achieve Zero Hunger by 2030. If recent trends continue, the number of people affected by hunger would exceed 840 million by 2030. To address this challenge, one of the SDGs—SDG6 is about ensuring access to water and sanitation for all; improving water-use efficiency in irrigation or reducing its use; and increasing water harvesting, wastewater treatment with the help of recycling and reuse technologies (UN, 2020). To protect the water resources, innovative technology should be considered and utilized whenever possible.

UN Africa Renewal reports that start-ups and organizations in sub-Saharan Africa countries are embarking on missions to conserve water, provide clean water, irrigate farms and monitor water usage, among other objectives, with the use of IoT technology (Atanga, 2017). It has also reported that approximately one million hand pumps supply water to over 200 million rural water users across Africa, yet as many as one-third of all hand pumps are alleged to be broken at any given time. A broken water pump that is unfixed can be expensive, dangerous to the community that depends on the water, and exacerbate water security of the community.

Another challenging issue is the water meters which are inaccurate and inefficient in water consumption reporting where consumers are billed for water that they do not use which then result in default in payment or payment dispute. Due to poor infrastructure set up that lead to non-payment for services or unsustainable revenue streams, water utility companies cannot sustainably provide safe and clean water to certain areas; customers could possibly be consuming unsafe water which affect their well-being (SDG3), or spending more time in finding clean water elsewhere. A more serious issue will be, due to the lack of proper water accounting process, the communication of water resources related information and the services generated from consumptive use cannot be efficiently shared with users such as policy makers, water authorities, and water companies (Water Accounting, 2021). CityTaps offers a solution that addresses this issue by creating a win-win relationship to both water utility companies and residents in the underserved. First, utility companies are guaranteed with payment for their water services via a prepaid meter system that uses mobile money. They install the smart pay-as-you-go water meters that help monitor the exact amount of water used so they can charge the customers accordingly. The residents use CityTaps smart meters to gain access to running water at home by prepaying for the service (Atanga, 2017).

In Barcelona, Spain has also used its extensive fiber-optic communication network to extend its individual IoT systems to support various urban services. Barcelona has implemented IoT technologies to remotely sense and control park irrigation and water levels used in public fountains—using sensors to monitor rain and humidity, park workers can work out how much irrigation is needed in each area (Adler, 2016). A system of electrovalves is then remotely controlled to transport necessary water across the city. The program, implemented in 68% of public parks, helped the city achieve a 25% increase in water conservation with a savings of approximately $555,000 per year. In addition to water management, the city also installed 19,500 smart meters to improve energy efficiency, by monitoring and optimizing energy consumption in targeted areas of the city. In waste management, households can deposit waste in municipal smart bins that monitor waste levels and optimize collection routes. These sensors can be further enhanced, and plans have been developed to integrate sensing for hazardous or offensive waste material (Adler, 2016).

Research shows that AI may act as an enabler on 134 targets (79%) across all SDGs, generally through technological improvements, which may address some present limitations (Vinuesa et al., 2020). For instance, AI-based technologies are an enabler for SDG1, 4, 6, 7 and 11 by supporting the provision of food, health, water, and energy services to the population. Climate change, population growth and food security concerns, and water security have driven the industry, e.g. agriculture into seeking more innovative approaches in managing and sustaining farming—crop monitoring and soil management in order to protect and improve crop yield (Liu et al., 2016; Patil & Sakkaravarthi, 2017). Since severe water crisis can further impact the sustainability of agriculture and food systems, AI-enabled technologies can help improving land use efficiency that allow farmers to get more from the land while using resources more sustainably. The emphasis is on preventing defective crops and optimizing the potential for healthy crop production. In addition, machine learning can be deployed to diagnose soil defect (Vincent et al., 2019).

Another example, AI-powered drones fitted with sensors can be used for land scouting and crops, checking for weeds and spot treating plants, monitoring overall crop health as well as managing livestock and monitoring for health issues (Jensen, 2019). Sensors provide real-time and multi-faceted views, but the data has limited use if they are not being converted to useful information. However, data is much more valuable if they can be converted by artificial intelligence into information to support more holistic farm operation, planning and monitoring, to manage crops, livestock and land, to determining management decisions for individual plants, crops and animals. It can provide better guidance to farmers about optimum planting, water and irrigation management, crop rotation, timely harvesting, nutrient management and pest control management (Boursianis et al., 2020; Talaviya et al., 2020). Some of the companies such as SkySquirrel Technologies uses drone-based imaging technology to help users monitor crop health, improve their crop yield and to reduce costs, whereas a Where uses machine learning algorithms in connection with satellites to deliver weather-based agricultural intelligence. Data-driven agriculture, with the support of machine learning algorithms and agricultural robotic solutions incorporate AI are deemed to be one of the important driving forces that will set the grounds for sustainable agriculture of the future (Saiz-Rubio & Rovira-Más, 2020).

Technology is the new frontier for infrastructure and its importance as a driver for real change and transformation has accelerated since Covid-19. The technologies discussed above give us an opportunity to drive success and accelerate the progress of attaining many of the SDGs such as SDG2, 3, 6, 9, 11, 12, 13, 14, 15, demonstrating the significant impact that technologies can have on the achievement of the 2030 Agenda for Sustainable Development. On the other hand, advanced technologies are being used to create smart solutions and transform cities into smart cities, but the process and implementation is not without its risks such as implementation risk, cybersecurity risk, and the risks of overly dependent on the technology. Further, challenges of adoption of such technologies such as availability of quality data, financial commitments, return of investment requirements, and regulatory and ethical challenges should also be taken into consideration. Hence, future research should consider and understand the associated challenges and risks posed by technology implementation in the respective areas such as waste management, utilities management (water and energy), urban planning (smart city), agriculture and farming. Future research can involve more in-depth case study of how the technologies discussed in this chapter are used in each of the respective cases. Future work can also consider how other technology such as blockchain can be integrated with IoT to support IoT-based food traceability for smart agriculture (Wolfert et al., 2017) to turn traditional agriculture into modern sustainable agriculture.

To this end, it is also important to note that no one technology can solve all the world's problems and achieving the SDGs; this will require bold government policies, corporate commitments and individual actions in addition to the use of new technologies. We need to use every tool at our disposal; and with technology becoming more advanced and powerful, we need to utilize them to focus on new ways to address the greatest social and environmental challenges facing the world through attaining the UN SDGs.

References

Abdallah, M., Talib, M. A., Feroz, S., Nasir, Q., Abdalla, H., & Mahfood, B. (2020). Artificial intelligence applications in solid waste management: A systematic research review. *Waste Management, 109*, 231–246.

Adler, L. (2016). *How smart city Barcelona brought the Internet of Things to life*. Viewed 28 September 2020. https://datasmart.ash.harvard.edu/news/article/how-smart-city-barcelona-brought-the-internet-of-things-to-life-789

Alles, M. G., & Gray, G. L. (2020). Will the medium become the message? A framework for understanding the coming automation of the audit process. *Journal of Information Systems, 34*(2), 109–130.

Asian Development Bank. (2020). *Managing infectious medical waste during the COVID-19 pandemic*. Viewed 20 June 2020. https://www.adb.org/sites/default/files/publication/578771/managing-medical-waste-covid19.pdf.

Atanga, I. (2017). *The Internet of everything water—Local communities boosting water monitoring systems using the Internet*. Viewed 28 September 2020. https://www.un.org/africarenewal/magazine/may-july-2017/internet-everything-water

Bin-e. (2020). *The new Bin-e*. Viewed 30 May 2020. http://www.bine.world/

Boretti, A., & Rosa, L. (2019). Reassessing the projections of the world water development report. *NPJ Clean Water, 2*(1), 1–6.

Boursianis, A. D., Papadopoulou, M. S., Diamantoulakis, P., Liopa-Tsakalidi, A., Barouchas, P., Salahas, G., Karagiannidis, G., Wan, S., & Goudos, S. K. (2020). Internet of Things (IoT) and Agricultural Unmanned Aerial Vehicles (UAVs) in smart farming: A comprehensive review. *Internet of Things, 18*, 100187.

Campbell, B. M., Hansen, J., Rioux, J., Stirling, C. M., & Twomlow, S. (2018). Urgent action to combat climate change and its impacts (SDG 13): Transforming agriculture and food systems. *Current Opinion in Environmental Sustainability, 34*, 13–20.

Castro, D., & New, J. (2016). The promise of artificial intelligence. *Center for Data Innovation, 115*(10), 32–35.

Chui, M., Manyika, J., Miremadi, M., Henke, N., Chung, R., Nel, P., & Malhotra, S. (2018). *Notes from the AI frontier: Insights from hundreds of use cases*. McKinsey Global Institute.

Di Marco, M., Baker, M. L., Daszak, P., De Barro, P., Eskew, E. A., Godde, C. M., Harwood, T. D., Herrero, M., Hoskins, A. J., Johnson, E., & Karesh, W. B. (2020). Opinion: Sustainable development must account for pandemic risk. *Proceedings of the National Academy of Sciences, 117*(8), 3888–3892.

Douma, K., Scott, L., & Bulzomi, A. (2017). *The SDG investment case*. https://www.unpri.org/download?ac=5909

Fuso Nerini, F., Slob, A., Ericsdotter Engström, R., & Trutnevyte, E. (2019). A research and innovation agenda for zero-emission European cities. *Sustainability, 11*(6), 1692.

Fuso Nerini, F., Sovacool, B., Hughes, N., Cozzi, L., Cosgrave, E., Howells, M., Tavoni, M., Tomei, J., Zerriffi, H., & Milligan, B. (2019). Connecting climate action with other Sustainable Development Goals. *Nature Sustainability, 2*(8), 674–680.

Garbuio, M., & Lin, N. (2019). Artificial intelligence as a growth engine for health care startups: Emerging business models. *California Management Review, 61*(2), 59–83.

Gartner. (2020). *Internet of Things*. Viewed 1 June 2020. https://www.gartner.com/en/information-technology/glossary/internet-of-things

Gestrin, M. V. (2019). *The contribution of international business investment to the Sustainable Development Goals: Key actors and recent trends*. OECD.

Goedhart, M., & Koller, T. (2020). *The value of value creation*. Viewed 25 June 2020. https://www.mckinsey.com/business-functions/strategy-and-corporate-finance/our-insights/the-value-of-value-creation

Goralski, M. A., & Tan, T. K. (2020). Artificial intelligence and sustainable development. *The International Journal of Management Education, 18*(1), 100330.

Hesse, B. W., Moser, R. P., & Riley, W. T. (2015). From big data to knowledge in the social sciences. *The Annals of the American Academy Political and Social Science, 659*, 16–32.

IBM. (2019). *What is IoT*. Viewed 30 May 2020. https://www.ibm.com/internet-of-things/learn/what-is-iot/

IISD. (2018). *UN launches initiatives to unleash Big Data for Sustainable Development*. Viewed 29 September 2020. http://sdg.iisd.org/news/un-launches-initiatives-to-unleash-big-data-for-sustainable-development

Intergovernmental Panel on Climate Change (IPCC). (2020). *Special report—Global warming of 1.5 °C*. Viewed 28 June 2020. https://www.ipcc.ch/sr15/

IoT Analytics. (2020). *State of the IoT 2018: Number of IoT devices now at 7B—Market accelerating*. Viewed 1 June 2020. https://iot-analytics.com/state-of-the-iot-update-q1-q2-2018-number-of-iot-devices-now-7b/

Jensen, J. (2019). *Agricultural drones: How drones are revolutionizing agriculture and how to break into this booming market*. Viewed 3 October 2020. https://uavcoach.com/agricultural-drones/

Kaza, S., Yao, L. C., Bhada-Tata, P., & van Woerden, F. (2018). *What a waste 2.0: A global snapshot of solid waste management to 2050*. The World Bank Group.

Lenton, T. M., Rockström, J., Gaffney, O., Rahmstorf, S., Richardson, K., Steffen, W., & Schellnhuber, H. J. (2019). Climate tipping points—Too risky to bet against. *Nature, 575*, 592–595.

Liu, N., Cao, W., Zhu, Y., Zhang, J., Pang, F., & Ni, J. (2016). Node deployment with k-connectivity in sensor networks for crop information full coverage monitoring. *Sensors, 16*(12), 2096.

Martinez, A., & Albert, J. R. (2018). *Big Data can transform SDG performance. Here's how*. Viewed 29 September 2020. https://blogs.adb.org/blog/big-data-can-transform-sdg-performance-heres-how

McKinsey. (2020). *How the packaging industry can navigate the coronavirus pandemic*. Viewed 30 June 2020. https://www.mckinsey.com/industries/paper-forest-products-and-packaging/our-insights/how-the-packaging-industry-can-navigate-the-coronavirus-pandemic

Patil, S. M., & Sakkaravarthi, R. (2017). Internet of things based smart agriculture system using predictive analytics. *Asian Journal of Pharmaceutical and Clinical Research, 10*(13), 148–152.

Rajaraman, V. (2014). John McCarthy—Father of artificial intelligence. *Resonance, 19*(3), 198–207.

Saiz-Rubio, V., & Rovira-Más, F. (2020). From smart farming towards agriculture 5.0: A review on crop data management. *Agronomy, 10*(2), 207.

Scholes, M., & Scholes, R. (2020). Climate change, biodiversity loss and other global ills share root causes. Viewed 21 June 2020. https://theconversation.com/climate-change-biodiversity-loss-and-other-global-ills-share-root-causes-140183

Schramade, W. (2017). Investing in the UN sustainable development goals: Opportunities for companies and investors. *Journal of Applied Corporate Finance, 29*(2), 87–99.

Talaviya, T., Shah, D., Patel, N., Yagnik, H., & Shah, M. (2020). Implementation of artificial intelligence in agriculture for optimisation of irrigation and application of pesticides and herbicides. *Artificial Intelligence in Agriculture, 4*, 58–73.

Teh, D. (2022). Sustainable competitive advantage: A leap forward in sustainable strategy with blockchain-enabled LCA. In H. H. Khoo & R. B. H. Tan (Eds.), *Life cycle assessment: New developments and multi-disciplinary applications* (pp. 177–193). World Scientific Publishing. https://doi.org/10.1142/12515.

Teh, D., & Corbitt, B. (2015). Building sustainability strategy in business. *Journal of Business Strategy, 36*(6), 39.

Teh, D., & Khan, T. (2019). Technological innovation for creating sustainable cities and communities. In W. Leal Filho, A. Azul, L. Brandli, P. Özuyar, & T. Wall (Eds.), *Sustainable cities and communities: Encyclopedia of the UN Sustainable Development Goals*. Springer.

Teh, D., & Khan, T. (2020). *As cities grow, the Internet of Things can help us get on top of the waste crisis*. Viewed 21 June 2020. https://theconversation.com/as-cities-grow-the-internet-of-things-can-help-us-get-on-top-of-the-waste-crisis-127917

Teh, D., & Khan, T. (2021). Types, definition and classification of natural disasters and threat level. In S. Eslamian & F. Eslamian (Eds.), *Handbook of disaster risk reduction for resilience* (pp. 27–56). Springer. https://doi.org/10.1007/978-3-030-61278-8_2

Teh, D., Khan, T., Corbitt, B., & Ong, C. E. (2020). Sustainability strategy and blockchain-enabled life cycle assessment: A focus on materials industry. *Environment Systems and Decisions, 40*(4), 605–622.

UN. (2015). *UN adopts new global goals, charting sustainable development for people and planet by 2030*. Viewed 4 June 2020. https://news.un.org/en/story/2015/09/509732-un-adopts-new-global-goals-charting-sustainable-development-people-and-planet

UN. (2018a). *68% of the world population projected to live in urban areas by 2050*, says UN. Viewed 31 May 2020. https://www.un.org/development/desa/en/news/population/2018a-revision-of-world-urbanization-prospects.html

UN. (2018b). *Majority of the world's cities highly exposed to disasters, UN DESA warns on World Cities Day*. Viewed 31 May 2020, https://www.un.org/development/desa/en/news/population/world-cities-day-2018b.html.

UN. (2019). *The Sustainable Development Goals Report 2019*. https://unstats.un.org/sdgs/report/2019/The-Sustainable-Development-Goals-Report-2019.pdf.

UN. (2020). *Sustainable Development Goals*. https://sdgs.un.org/goals#goals

United Nations DESA. (2019). *SDG progress reports 2019: Are we on track to achieve the global goals?* Viewed 10 June 2020. https://www.un.org/development/desa/en/news/sustainable/sdg-progress-reports-2019.html

UNDP. (2019). *2020: A crunch year for the biodiversity and climate emergencies*. Viewed 10 June 2020. https://www.unenvironment.org/news-and-stories/story/2020-crunch-year-biodiversity-and-climate-emergencies

United Nations Educational Scientific and Cultural Organization (UNESCO). (2019). *The United Nations world water development report: Leaving no one behind, facts and figures*. https://unesdoc.unesco.org/ark:/48223/pf0000367276

United Nations Environment Programme (UNDP). (2020). *Goal 12: Responsible consumption and production*. Viewed 10 June 2020. https://www.undp.org/content/undp/en/home/sustainable-development-goals/goal-12-responsible-consumption-and-production.html

UNFCCC. (2019). *Cut global emissions by 7.6 percent every year for next decade to meet 1.5°C Paris target—UN report*. Viewed 30 September 2020. https://unfccc.int/news/cut-global-emissions-by-76-percent-every-year-for-next-decade-to-meet-15degc-paris-target-un-report

Vincent, D. R., Deepa, N., Elavarasan, D., Srinivasan, K., Chauhdary, S. H., & Iwendi, C. (2019). Sensors driven AI-based agriculture recommendation model for assessing land suitability. *Sensors, 19*(17), 3667.

Vinuesa, R., Azizpour, H., Leite, I., Balaam, M., Dignum, V., Domisch, S., Felländer, A., Langhans, S. D., Tegmark, M., & Nerini, F. F. (2020). The role of artificial intelligence in achieving the Sustainable Development Goals. *Nature Communications, 11*(1), 1–10.

Water Accounting. (2021). *Water accounting*. Viewed 10 January 2021. https://www.wateraccounting.org/

Wolfert, S., Ge, L., Verdouw, C., & Bogaardt, M. J. (2017). Big data in smart farming—A review. *Agricultural Systems, 153*, 69–80.

World Economic Forum (WEF). (2018). *Future of digital economy and society system initiative—Internet of Things guidelines for sustainability.* Viewed 30 May 2020. http://www3.weforum.org/docs/IoTGuidelinesforSustainability.pdf

World Health Organization (WHO). (2020). *Climate change.* Viewed 10 June 2020. https://www.who.int/heli/risks/climate/climatechange/en/

World Wide Fund For Nature (WWF). (2020). *The loss of nature and the rise of pandemics: Protecting human and planetary health.* Viewed 31 March 2020. https://d3bzkjkd62gi12.cloudfront.net/downloads/the_loss_of_nature_and_rise_of_pandemics_protecting_human_and_planetary_health.pdf

Wu, K. J., Liao, C. J., Tseng, M. L., Lim, M. K., Hu, J., & Tan, K. (2017). Toward sustainability: Using Big Data to explore the decisive attributes of supply chain risks and uncertainties. *Journal of Cleaner Production, 142*, 663–676.

WWAP (UNESCO World Water Assessment Programme). (2019). *The United Nations World Water Development Report 2019: Leaving no one behind.* UNESCO.

Xiao, Y., Norris, C. B., Lenzen, M., Norris, G., & Murray, J. (2017). How social footprints of nations can assist in achieving the sustainable development goals. *Ecological Economics, 135*, 55–65.

David Teh works in the School of Accounting, Information Systems and Supply Chain at the RMIT University, Melbourne, Australia. He focuses on understanding business's challenges and needs, and creating practical solutions, to make visible outcomes and real impact. He has a strong passion for and/or expertise in sustainability, strategy, process improvement, risk management, and technology (data analytics).

Tarek Rana is an Associate Professor of Accounting and Data Analytics in the School of Accounting, Information Systems and Supply Chain at RMIT University, Melbourne, Australia. He earned a PhD in Accounting at the University of New South Wales (UNSW) Australia. His current research focuses on the intersection of accounting and data analytics including the implications of data analytics on management control systems, performance measurement, risk management, and sustainability where he draws on textual analytics, machine learning and artificial intelligence theories and practices. His research papers appeared in international and interdisciplinary scholarly journals such as *The British Accounting Review, Accounting Auditing and Accountability Journal, Financial Accountability & Management, Intelligent Systems in Accounting Finance & Management, Qualitative Research in Accounting and Management, Meditari Accountancy Research, Business Strategy and the Environment, Public Money & Management, Journal of Accounting & Organisational Change, Journal of Cleaner Production, and Journal of Intellectual Capital.*

Chapter 12
Integrating ESG Risks into Control and Reporting: Evidence from Practice in Sweden

Jason Crawford and Fredrik Nilsson

Abstract As transparency and accountability demands around Environmental, Social, and Governance (ESG) risk control and reporting increase, pressure is mounting on organizations to act as good corporate citizens. One avenue to meet these challenges is to integrate ESG risks into Enterprise Risk Management (ERM) in order to improve control and reporting. The aim of this chapter is to examine ESG risk integration by focusing on: (1) How ESG risk is integrated with control, i.e. incorporated into strategic and operational decision-making; and (2) How ESG is integrated into reporting, i.e. incorporated into financial and sustainability reports. Our analytical framework conceptualizes integration as a technical-social process, which has three integrating dimensions and five integrating components. We use a qualitative approach and conduct short case studies in four ESG leading Swedish organizations. The study finds that social processes are important in ESG integration and lead to increased integration on the cognitive dimension. Findings also show how technical processes support social processes, however the use of Artificial Intelligence (AI) in ESG risk management in the organizations is low, as is internal audits role in promoting ESG risk control effectiveness and reporting quality. As this is a nascent area that connects risk management, management control, and financial accounting concepts, future research should engage with leading organizations to better understand the relationships between these concepts to advance theoretical development and create practical insights useful for practitioners.

Keywords COSO · ERM · ESG · Integrated reporting · Integrated control · Sustainability

J. Crawford (✉) · F. Nilsson
Uppsala University, Uppsala, Sweden
e-mail: jason.crawford@fek.uu.se

F. Nilsson
e-mail: fredrik.nilsson@fek.uu.se

T. Rana et al. (eds.), *Handbook of Big Data and Analytics in Accounting and Auditing*,
https://doi.org/10.1007/978-981-19-4460-4_12

1 Introduction

Organizations face growing transparency and accountability demands from stakeholders to act as good corporate citizens. This requires improvements in Environmental, Social and Governance (ESG) risk identification, mitigation, and reporting. A central facet of that work is integrating ESG risks into Enterprise Risk Management (ERM) to improve control and reporting practices. ERM can improve the identification and management of risks by revealing risks that can have a material impact on financial and sustainability reporting (see Cohen et al., 2017).

This chapter examines ESG risk integration, focusing on: (1) How ESG risk is integrated with control, i.e. incorporated into strategic and operational decision-making; and (2) How ESG is integrated into reporting, i.e. incorporated into financial and sustainability reports. We do so by investigating the integration of ESG into control and reporting in four leading Swedish organizations. This is an interesting context to study ESG risk integration, as Sweden has been active in sustainability issues since the 1990s, and adopted its first national sustainable development strategy in 2002 (United Nations, 2021). In 2016, the government appointed a committee to implement the 2030 Agenda. Sweden is also recognized for its inclusive partnership approach to governance issues (Crawford & Nilsson, 2021).

ESG risks can significantly affect organizations financially and reputationally. The list of organizations experiencing negative ESG implications is rising. In contrast to traditional risk types, ESG risks are more difficult to identify, quantify and mitigate, yet stakeholders demand greater transparency to evaluate organizations' risk exposures and their management. This demand has resulted in work on sustainable finance, Science-Based Targets (SBT) and a taxonomy for sustainable activities (European Commission, 2021). Efforts continue to develop and refine ESG scoring and ratings models to enhance transparency and create mechanisms to increase accountability. However, their theoretical and methodological weaknesses have been criticized (Svanberg et al., 2021 in this volume).

Together, these developments pose challenges for organizations to improve their control and reporting practices, but also opportunities. ESG work is no longer viewed as something done to the detriment of organizational performance. Institutional investors are increasingly interested in ESG, viewing it as key to long-term value creation (Asante-Appiah, 2020), and external actors, such as the Committee of Sponsoring Organizations of the Treadway Commission (COSO), are encouraging organizations to apply their ERM-Integrated Framework to ESG risks. While many organizations actively work with risk management, not all have an ERM framework in place. The components and level of maturity of the frameworks implemented vary substantially (Lundqvist, 2014).

The remainder of the chapter is structured as follows. Section 2 reviews the literature and presents the analytical framework. The method is presented in Sect. 3. Section 4 describes four Swedish organizations' efforts to integrate ESG risk into their control and reporting practices. Section 5 presents the analysis, and Sect. 6 ends the chapter with conclusions and avenues for future research.

2 Literature Review and Analytical Framework

2.1 General Background

The global risk landscape has transformed. The World Economic Forum ranked asset price collapse 1st in the top five global risks in 2010. Extreme weather and climate action failure ranked 1st in 2020. In fact, financial risks disappeared from the top 5 global risks in 2020, to be replaced by climate, biodiversity, weather, and human-made environmental disasters (World Economic Forum, 2021). Because of the changing risk landscape, it is necessary to adapt and implement new risk management practices. This existential crisis is accelerating the pace of sustainability innovation at European, national, and organizational levels.

Several definitions of ESG risk exist which affect the control and reporting of such risks, i.e. those provided by the Sustainability Accounting Standards Board (SASB), the Global Reporting Initiative (GRI), and the International Integrated Reporting Council (IIRC). Flexibility in how to define and report ESG risks has been provided so that organizations can disclose ESG risk information that best suits their unique circumstances. However, the scope and quality of the information reported makes it difficult to conduct individual, cross-company and industry comparisons, as reporting alone does not equate to meaningful action (Henriksson & Weidman Grunewald, 2020).

Efforts are underway to resolve these issues and include the introduction of the EU Non-Financial Reporting Directive (2014/95/EU), the EU Taxonomy with supporting IT tools, voluntary stock exchange guidance (e.g. NASDAQ), the development of ESG scoring models (e.g. Dow Jones Sustainability World Index), and efforts to improve corporate governance. Together, these should enable organizations to continue to discharge their duty of accountability by increasing control and reporting integration (e.g. King IV Report, 2016). In addition, COSO has provided guidance on applying their ERM-Integrated Framework to ESG risks (COSO, 2018). Early ERM adopters may have a distinct advantage over late adopters if they already have good governance, internal control, and reporting practices in place.

To understand, control and report ESG risks effectively, data gathering and analysis needs to improve. The right metrics and Key Performance Indicators (KPIs) should be developed, not for ranking or reporting awards, but to support decision-making and assess progress towards strategic goals and performance targets (Henriksson & Weidman Grunewald, 2020, p. 129). A considerable gap between ERM and digitalization is acknowledged by both practitioner bodies (COSO, 2017) and researchers (Crawford & Lindvall, 2021), which can lead to data gathering and analysis challenges. While COSO actively promotes the use of advanced analytics and data visualization tools in ERM, which could be extended to include ESG risks, evidence reveals that such use is limited at the company level.

Given investors' heightened interest in ESG risk, achieving investment-grade ESG data quality is critical. It means actively working with systems (consolidated IT systems), processes (internal controls), and people (data management responsibilities) to improve information used for control and reporting. Accounting bodies, COSO, and the World Business Council for Sustainable Development (WBCSD) are collaborating to offer guidance (FSR/WBCSD, 2019). While Socially Responsible Investing (SRI) has benefitted from the increased application of AI as part of a general trend towards using advanced analytics within portfolio management, there is limited evidence of individual organizations using AI in their control and reporting activities (Verheyden et al., 2016).

Demands for greater transparency and accountability in the ESG space are changing the relationship between individual companies and external actors, such as investors, banks, competitors, and suppliers, as they are judged on their commitment to improving their understanding, control, and reporting of ESG risks. Currently, evaluation practices are primarily carried out through self-reporting activities and scoring models. However, innovations such as impact-weighted accounting,[1] will transform this space by developing principles and methodologies for calculating the financial value of ESG risk impacts.

ESG risk management requires changes in governance, strategy, risk management, and performance management. This change is apparent in banks, which are increasingly signing up to the Principles for Responsible Banking (PRB) and projects such as the Task Force on Climate-related Financial Disclosures (TCFD) (UNEP FI, 2021). This change requires organizations to work closely together to influence and educate each other to transition to sustainable business models. Best practice organizations have an important role by encouraging others who are lagging behind to catch up.

2.2 *ESG Integrating Dimensions*

ESG integration is important for reducing risk exposures, improving performance, and gaining competitive advantage. ERM, as part of management control, may theoretically drive companies into ESG risk management. How ERM drives better risk control and reporting practices has been based on two interrelated processes: a technical process centered on the use of calculative techniques, models, and tools (Mikes, 2009, 2011; Wahlström, 2009); and a social process centered on risk culture, cross-functional or group interactions, and dialogue (Hall et al., 2015). While technical processes have received the most attention in the ERM literature, new research highlights the importance of, and lack of attention to, social processes (Jean-Jules & Vicente, 2021). Social processes are important in ESG risk management, because high uncertainty makes the quantification of ESG risks difficult, information is limited, and biases against the perceived importance of ESG work may exist. Ideally, technical and social approaches should be mutually supporting (ibid.).

[1] For further information on the Impact-Weighted Accounts Project use the following link: https://www.hbs.edu/impact-weighted-accounts/Pages/default.aspx.

We conceptualize integration as a technical-social process in line with existing ERM literature (Jean-Jules & Vicente, 2021) and Gond et al.'s (2012) theorization of integration in their study of sustainability integration. According to Gond et al., integration has technical, organizational, and cognitive dimensions. The technical dimension focuses on developing ESG accounting systems used for controlling and reporting ESG risk. These systems are important for producing ESG risk information and linking it to other accounting systems, such as performance management. The organizational dimension focuses on developing formal structures and roles, and how they support the transfer and interpretation of ESG risk information across the organization. The cognitive dimension focuses on how ESG risk information is used in interactions between ESG specialists and decision-makers to create shared understandings and redefine or overcome cognitive boundaries.

2.3 ESG Integrating Components

COSO (2018) states that ESG integration occurs through the five components of their ERM framework and provides guidance and examples. Our analytical framework incorporates ESG integration, COSO's five components, and insights from extant ERM literature. The five COSO components are: Governance and culture; Strategy and objective setting; Performance; Review and revision; Information, communication and reporting.

Poor corporate governance and culture (Lundqvist, 2015) were blamed for ineffective risk management during the latest financial crisis. The literature emphasizes corporate governance's role in developing formal structures and mechanisms to support and control ERM. Culture is important in raising risk awareness (Mikes, 2009; Power et al., 2013). The board, executive management, and the risk function have a special responsibility to promote a culture of risk awareness. However, efforts to improve risk culture are primarily focused on technical processes. These include administrative controls, such as policy documents and rules. Technical processes also include the extensive use of risk artefacts, e.g. risk appetite statements, registers, models, and risk maps, as communication and behavioral directing mechanisms. Social processes, e.g. the establishment of risk committees, and other social spaces for actors from different knowledge domains to discuss risks, are also gaining attention in the literature.

ESG risks must be considered in strategy and objective setting. The literature shows that risk functions have attempted to influence strategic decision-making in two ways. Their focus is either on performing complex risk calculations and modelling, sometimes linking risk metrics to other performance metrics, or they focus on risk envisionment, which relies on experience, intuition, and imagination, to provide risk insights to senior management (Mikes & Kaplan, 2015). What organizations consider the most appropriate approach is often a tension filled compromise between institutional regimes and internal dynamics.

The literature shows that organizations rely on various accounting and other tools to identify, control, and report risks. They attempt to transform uncertainty into risk by categorizing and calculating individual risks that, when aggregated, may be linked to performance measurement. This requires consistent definitions and measurement approaches to make comparability possible (Mikes, 2011). The assumption that ERM is like accounting, producing stable and combinable information units, is disputed in the literature (Tekathen & Dechow, 2013). As ESG risks are long-term, slow to materialize and difficult to detect, they are difficult to integrate on the technical dimension. ERM requires a portfolio approach, where the risk function interacts with the wider organization.

Reviewing and revising ESG risks requires ongoing evaluation of the external and internal environments, as well as ESG risk management capabilities. This necessitates effective internal controls and heightened awareness of external and internal risks. According to COSO (2018), changes in the external and internal environment may require changes to risk governance, strategy, and performance measurement. A significant part of this activity involves recognizing and measuring change, which is closely related to information and knowledge acquisition and management. It also involves prompt action in unpredictable conditions. These new conditions necessitate dynamic and flexible ERM, that combines the dual role of compliance champion and business partner (Mikes, 2008).

One of the biggest challenges is minimizing the possibility of misstatements and ensuring timely and accurate reporting practices (Cohen et al., 2017). Appropriate information and communication channels need to be developed for internal and external reporting, so that relevant, concrete and verifiable ESG information is reported. Improving ESG related information quality should also be a top priority.

Providing useful and high-quality information will help raise risk awareness and be used to inform strategic and operational decisions. The format of information affects the user's perception of its usefulness and quality. As ESG reporting requirements increase, the ERM system's role in risk assessment and improving the internal control environment must be considered (Cohen et al., 2017). Internal audit is important in monitoring ERM. However, little is known about the role of internal audit in encouraging the inclusion of ESG risks into ERM, or the relationship between ERM and the financial reporting process (ibid.). One would expect this to change as compliance issues arise and the existing control environment adapts to ESG risk management as external demands for improved control and reporting increase.

3 Method

To provide an overview of ESG risk management practices, we conducted a series of short case studies. By studying organizations that are considered to be in the forefront of ESG risk management development, it is possible to gain valuable insights into how far the area has come (Kaplan, 1986).

The selection process began with two informal interviews with experts (one in internal auditing and one in sustainability management and reporting). Those interviews, together with our knowledge of the field, helped us identify five Swedish organizations in different industries that are considered to be at the forefront of ESG risk management. One organization declined to be included in the study due to time and resource limitations. Four organizations accepted and include: Länsförsäkringar (a large insurance and bank company); Scania (a global truck manufacturer); Svenska Handelsbanken (a large bank); and The Church of Sweden (the largest organization in Sweden).

Following the initial presentation of the project and its objectives, an on-line interview was scheduled for each organization (one interview per organization). The interviewees were working with ESG risk management and/or had in-depth knowledge of the organization's structures and processes. Three interviews were recorded and transcribed, and detailed notes were taken in the fourth. The semi-structured interviews covered the following areas: (a) ESG identification; (b) ESG scoring; (c) The role of AI; (d) ESG as part of ERM; (e) Governance and culture (COSO theme 1); (f) Strategy and objective setting (COSO theme 2); (g) Performance (COSO theme 3); (h) Review and revision (COSO theme 4); (i) Information, communication and reporting (COSO theme 5); and (j) The role of internal auditing.

The transcribed interviews were supplemented by the organization's official descriptions and reports. The data was analyzed to build an account of each organization's unique ESG structures and processes. Using the literature, each case's unique ESG risk management characteristics could be distilled iteratively and abductively (Gehman et al., 2018). In the next phase, a cross-case analysis was conducted.

To enhance the findings' validity, interviewees read and commented on the case descriptions and the conclusions drawn. While every effort was taken to ensure the descriptions and analysis are of high quality, each case is based on interviews with one person in each organization. Thus, the case studies are exploratory, with preliminary findings.

4 Evidence from Practice

4.1 Länsförsäkringar

The Länsförsäkringar group (LF) is an insurance, bank, and realtor company. It is a federation consisting of 23 independent companies, each covering a specific geographic market in Sweden. We have studied one company in LF: Länsförsäkringar Göteborg och Bohuslän (LFGB). In 2019, LFGB had a premium income of 1.77 billion SEK and total assets of 10.76 billion SEK (Länsförsäkringar Göteborg och Bohuslän, 2019a). Both LF and LFGB state that sustainability[2] is an important aspect

[2] Neither LF nor LFGB uses the term "ESG" explicitly. Instead they use the term "Sustainability". We will therefore use this term.

of their businesses and have ambitious objectives in this area. LF has won awards for its achievements. For example, it received the “Sweden’s most sustainable insurance company” award from Sustainable Brand Index in 2019.

The governance structure of LF is unique. Länsförsäkringar AB (LFAB) is a service company owned by 23 companies. These companies are owned by their customers. This unusual governance model affects sustainability risk management at an overall level. A group-level sustainability policy has been developed by the Communication and Sustainability function. The policy defines how sustainability “is to be conducted in terms of governance, approach and monitoring” (Länsförsäkringar AB, 2020, p. 2). There is, for example, a list of United Nations (UN) initiatives (e.g. UN Sustainable Development Goals) that LF is supporting and that the companies are encouraged to follow. The policy is not detailed and the companies have full freedom in choosing a sustainability strategy and how it is going to be implemented. The design of controls is the responsibility of the companies. The results of their actions are reported in the company’s annual sustainability report.

The governance structure of LF and especially the high level of decentralized decision-making is reflected in the culture at the group and company level. This creates an awareness of how sustainability matters and how it relates to risk management. At company-level, LFGB started to emphasize the importance of sustainability and integrate it into their business in 2015. The first step was to establish a culture focused on sustainability by experimenting with activities and by showing tangible results. The CEO explains how he talked to managers and employees.

> We need to change, find new examples on how to be more sustainable. Do not care if we can prove empirically that we are doing something useful in every example. Follow your gut feeling and do a lot of activities that we can communicate in the company and use to create energy so that we can generate even more ideas and involve as many as possible.

When LFGB started to integrate sustainability into the objectives, strategies, and controls, there was some initial skepticism. Today, this is an area that according to the CEO, managers and employees are proud of. There is a realization that the business risks of not being a sustainable company are huge, or in the words of the CEO there is a risk that “you will be out of the market.” The relationship between business risk and sustainability is further developed in the LFGB annual sustainability report (Länsförsäkringar Göteborg och Bohuslän, 2019b, p. 11):

> Sustainability has gone from only managing risks to being a business opportunity. There is an increase in expectations that companies take responsibility – locally and globally. Values can be created and new customers attracted to companies that succeed in producing innovative solutions that combine profitability and sustainability. (our translation)

In the sustainability report, four areas are identified as important for the strategy and operations of LFGB: (1) sustainable products (e.g. sustainable insurance offerings); (2) a sustainable work-place (e.g. better mental health); (3) a sustainable society (e.g. reduction of socio-economic polarization); and (4) a sustainable planet (e.g. reduction of carbon footprint). Each area has targets related to them (e.g. reduce carbon foot-print with 30% in 2023 compared to 2018). Risks attached to the four areas are categorized into: (1) environmental risks; (2) personnel and social relation risks; (3) human rights risks; and (4) risks of corruption. Risks identified and mapped are discussed with the risk management function and with the board and the executive management.

The identification, assessment and prioritization of sustainability risks seem to be rather traditional. Advanced scoring methods (e.g. customer scoring, investment product scoring), including AI solutions, are not used. Instead, the company uses several IT tools to analyze their asset management and especially its risk exposure. According to the CEO, it is important to ensure that investments being made are in line with the sustainability strategy. Therefore, companies in certain industries (e.g. defense and tobacco) are excluded. In addition, investment decisions should be in line with the objective to reduce the carbon footprint of the investment portfolio. However, the formal controls for review and revision are not really focusing on sustainability risk. The CEO explains why:

> It focuses on legal issues, compliance, risk management in general, internal audit etcetera – that is – actuarial knowledge. It is very theoretical in character. These type of issues (sustainability issues, our remark) are not captured that well in the formal control system. You have to find other ways of following it up. We have therefore extended the tasks of the risk management function and the type of risks that are mapped.

According to the CEO, this could be explained by the rapid development of sustainability risk management in the last five years. Earlier a business model built on sustainability could be expected to contribute to creating competitive advantage. Today it is considered a must in many industries. Five years ago, there were few laws and regulations compared to today. In line with these developments internal audit has started to show a lot of interest for sustainability risk management. The opinion of the CEO is that the combined result of these changes will lead to new and better formal controls for sustainability risk management. The level of integration will also be affected, as discussed by the CEO:

> The sustainability issues have a tendency to end up detached, instead of being integrated with other processes and risks; that is to be a natural part of the business [...] All that is added, has a tendency to be kept to the side before it becomes a natural part of the business.

At LFGB, the formal controls for sustainability risk management are in a period of transition and development. The annual sustainability report, even though it is primarily intended for stakeholders outside LFGB, is an important vehicle for information, communication, and reporting. Cultural controls are also important. They have created a sense of importance for the sustainability area and how to manage sustainability risks. The CEO explains.

> Culture is important and in our core focus. It is crucial for success and employee satisfaction to create a commitment in the organization that makes you truly engaged in the company's strategies and goals. That creates an organization focused on performance. Simultaneously, the employees must feel that it is fun to perform and that their performance is sustainable during a long period of time. This is a marathon race and not a short distance race. So, we worked towards establishing our ideas about sustainability. I often experience that showing examples is very effective rather than trying to show that what we do is built 100 % of a solid analysis.

4.2 Scania

Scania is a global transport solution company which produces trucks and buses and has a large product related service offering. It is part of the Traton group, which also includes brands such as MAN and Volkswagen. In 2019, Scania had an operating income of 17.49 billion SEK and net sales of 152.42 billion SEK. Scania's production operations are mainly in Europe, Latin America, and Asia. Scania views sustainability as an integral part of their culture and business model. This is evident in their longstanding commitment to the United Nations Global Compact Principles, their steady climb in global sustainability rankings (e.g. The Corporate Knights List) (Scania, 2012), and more recently, their commitment to science-based targets as part of the Science Based Targets initiative (SBTi) (Scania, 2019).

The corporate governance model is based on legislation, the companies act and the annual accounts act. It is also based on internal governing documents. These include the code of conduct, group policies, processes, standards, and other governing regulations. Together they describe the organizational structure, decision-making procedures, power and responsibilities which form the basis for the internal control environment together with groupwide accounting and reporting instructions (Scania, 2019, pp. 37–39). Scania also adheres to the GRI voluntary framework when reporting on ESG risks. As Scania is a decentralized organization, the ultimate responsibility for the management of ESG risks is that of each of Scania's subsidiaries. In 2016, the executive board decided to create a Governance, Risk and Compliance (GRC) function to ensure that the company complied with legal requirements and international GRC standards. They also created a group risk management function at that time, which is part of the GRC.

Scania's culture is based on six core values (i.e. customer first, respect for the individual, elimination of waste, determination, team spirit, and integrity). Their "sustainable risk culture" promotes organization-wide risk awareness through openness, transparency and accountability. Activities such as Climate Day are arranged, where employees attend workshops to learn about ESG risks and to come up with ideas for carbon-saving actions for example, which can be incorporated into the groups short and long-term plans (Scania, 2019).

According to the Head of Group Risk Management (HGRM), the decentralized structure coupled with a culture that has its foundations in continuous improvement, innovation, and the promotion of ongoing organizational-wide dialogue, supports the development of a shared understanding of the importance of ESG risks. Scania also has a Central Sustainability Advisory Board to help in this work. This awareness is further enhanced by the work of the GRM Team in supporting decision-makers throughout the organization, both in an advisory capacity, but also through the provision of materials, risk tools, and learning and training opportunities. Scania places a strong emphasis on integrating sustainability into its processes, rather than having a large centralized sustainability team. The reason for this, according to the HGRM, is:

> The strength of Scania is that we always try and bring things into the normal processes and then we work with it throughout the whole organization. A centralized team in the sustainability department needs to support that work and everything needs to be integrated. And if it needs to be integrated it really needs to be understood and usable.

The evaluation of Scania's sustainability work is based on their signing of the United Nations Business Ambition for 1.5 degree climate pledge, for which science-based climate targets have been set. While external ESG scoring models are on the rise, the HGRM points out that these models make cross-industry comparisons difficult as ESG scoring is still at an early stage and standardized approaches have not evolved yet. Therefore, Scania does not currently place so much emphasis on external scoring models. However, through their commitment to science-based climate targets, development of sustainability KPIs, and ongoing work to implement TCFD recommendations, Scania places a strong emphasis on risk measurement and aggregation. Internal scoring models are used for suppliers using self-assessment questionnaires. Scania's reporting transparency on sustainability work is high, particularly for a non-listed company. Scania does not use AI in its identification, assessment and mitigation of ESG risks, but according to the HGRM, they are discussing it internally as they are aware of the possibilities that the application of AI in this area could present. Currently, the identification and analysis of ESG risks is carried out manually.

Scania's strategy "2025 and beyond: driving the shift", extends their existing growth strategy and is a response to increasing uncertainty driven by environmental and technological factors. For Scania, integrating sustainability into their strategy is a top strategic priority, and they have been working for several years to transition to sustainable transport solutions. This is evident in their three-pillar approach, which focuses on energy efficiency (vehicle optimization and driving), renewable fuels and electrification (energy optimization), and smart and safe transport (optimizing the transport system). In their efforts to lead the way in decarbonizing the transport system and creating sustainable transport solutions, Scania works in close collaboration with a wide range of stakeholders in society, including academics as their commitment to sustainability requires a range of new competencies. An example of broad stakeholder engagement is perhaps most visible in several electric road projects throughout Europe. And, the extension of competencies is perhaps most visible in their work on autonomous and connected vehicles (Scania, 2019), as well as their founding of the Integrated Transport and Research Laboratory (ITRL) together with the Royal Institute of Technology (KTH) in Stockholm (Scania, 2014).

The identification of ESG risks and the evaluation of Scania's sustainability work is based on ongoing interactions between organizations, customers, suppliers and partners. In addition, Scania carries out a yearly materiality analysis, gathering data from capital providers, political decision-makers, NGOs, students, media and labor unions. Data is gathered using an online survey and the results are used to prioritize issues within the categories of sustainable transport, responsible business, and long-term business value. Scania also uses workshops to identify risks (including ESG risks). They measure ESG risk management performance in 18 KPIs, which are linked to sustainable transport and responsible business.

While Scania has integrated sustainability into its strategy and developed performance metrics which include ESG risks; control and reporting practices for these risks are not as advanced as they are for financial control and reporting. However, by committing to science-based targets and developing KPIs with explicit targets, which are related to their three-pillar approach to sustainable transport, Scania intends to close the gap by further developing its control and reporting systems.

Internal audits role in promoting ESG risk control effectiveness and reporting quality is currently limited. Internal audit does not look specifically at ESG risks, but it is included in their scope. However, there is ongoing dialogue between internal audit and Group Risk Management. They focus this dialogue on sharing knowledge as well as developing a joint understanding of which ESG issues should trigger an audit.

4.3 Svenska Handelsbanken

Handelsbanken (HB) is a bank which has a presence in Sweden, Norway, Finland, Denmark, the Netherlands, and the UK. In 2019, the bank had an income of 44.56 billion SEK, an operating profit of 21.80 billion SEK and a return on equity of 11.9%. Sustainability is an important issue for the bank and its customers and HB is committed working on 6 of the 17 sustainable development goals[3]. Sustainability is integrated into the banks' corporate culture, the business model, and activities at an operational level in all 6 markets (Handelsbanken, 2019a). Sustainability work is reported in adherence to the GRI reporting standards. Commitment to sustainability manifests itself through the promotion of long-term relationships with financially stable clients, a move away from low demand, high risk, and poor earnings products and services, and a zero tolerance for credit losses. More recently, HB has extended its commitment to sustainability by endorsing PRB in 2019 and supporting the Principles for Responsible Investment (PRI) (Handelsbanken, 2019b). HB was ranked as the most sustainable listed company in 2020 in Sweden for the second year in a row in the category of bank and finance (Handelsbanken, 2020).

The governance structure is built on two fundamental pillars. The first is the issuance of policy documents and instructions by the board, e.g. the corporate sustainability policy, the sustainability assessment policy and the risk control policy. The second is corporate culture, goals, working methods and renumeration (Handelsbanken, 2019a). The board also exercises its governance by discussing and setting the overall risk appetite of the bank and sustainability related issues are discussed regularly at board level. HB is a decentralized organization where responsibility for sustainability work is embedded at branch level. It is coordinated by a group-wide specialist function, and the Head of Sustainability reports directly to the CEO. The bank also has a sustainability committee, formed in 2010.

[3] Gender equality; decent work and economic growth; industry, innovation and infrastructure; sustainable cities and communities; climate action; peace, justice and strong institutions.

Evaluation of the bank's sustainability work is based on external and internal analysis, e.g. analysis performed by research teams in investment banks and HB's own materiality analysis (Handelsbanken, 2019a, pp. 46–47). HB's commitment to the PRB and its publication of climate reports for HB Liv and HB Asset Management since 2018, have further driven corporate governance toward sustainability, raising board member awareness, which is also supported by training initiatives. HB has a strong risk culture, which is embedded in formal governance and control mechanisms but also in the mindsets of those working in the bank. Influencing the risk culture to include sustainability issues at the branch level, is achieved through issuing sustainable products, i.e. green financing products and internal training, both acting as a medium for knowledge development and sharing and the evolvement of distributed rather than centralized expertise in this area. Developing knowledge and expertise at the branch level has enabled HB to include sustainability issues as part of their advisory services to clients who have assets under management.

HB strategy is characterized by a low-risk tolerance. Recently, the bank is orientating itself more towards focusing on long-term relationships with core customers, i.e. private customers and SMEs, and on core segments, i.e. private banking, real estate, mortgages. The strategy is linked to the 6 sustainability goals via their product and service offerings. For example, in line with a commitment to sustainable cities and communities, HB offers green loans for multi-family dwellings. In line with a commitment to climate action, they provide green loan products to companies producing renewable energy. Commitment to the sustainability goals also means that HB uses inclusion and exclusion criteria to screen portfolio companies for ESG risk contravening activities, e.g. the exclusion of fossil fuels from actively managed funds (Handelsbanken, 2019b). In integrating sustainability into their strategy, they intend to help their existing corporate and private clients transition towards sustainability. HB is currently working on adding sustainability targets at the strategic level. These targets will be related to the PRB.

The identification, assessment, and prioritization of sustainability risks is based on activities focused on the bank and its customers. External rankings and materiality assessments offer inputs into the identification, assessment, and prioritization of sustainability risks that HB may be exposed to. The materiality analysis is based on a dialogue with stakeholders and provides important input into ESG risk identification, assessment, and prioritization (Handelsbanken, 2019b). In identifying, assessing, and prioritizing customer ESG risks on the financing side of the bank's business; credit scoring models now include ESG risk assessment as part of the credit scoring process. The banks' ability to effectively score customers on ESG risks, is based on a closer client–bank relationship, where client relationship managers collect data in a risk report via dialogue with the client, and quantify that data to improve the credit risk assessment process. While input from external scoring models is used, internal ESG scoring models are considered more sensitive and future orientated, as they include non-publically disclosed information, and information at a greater level of granularity than external models can, in many cases, provide.

In identifying, assessing and prioritizing ESG risks on the asset management side of the bank's business, scoring models are used to select and invest in portfolios. Stress testing towards climate scenarios is currently used, and the use of stress testing towards ESG risks will expand into other areas. While they consider external scoring models useful, different models provide different evaluations of the same industry partly because of the different datasets used, showing a lack of consistency and commensurability. It is also questionable to what extent external models push companies towards sustainable transformation. The Head of Sustainability explains:

> ESG ratings provide valuable guidance but are not the full picture for our assessment purposes. Significantly improving an ESG score is possible if the company implements a lot of ESG related policies that, albeit an important step, do not necessarily reflect improvements in operations nor does the score necessarily reflect the company's level of contribution to global development goals, enabling activities etc.

As HB does not service industries or clients with high exposures to ESG risks, risk related performance has been managed through culture rather than developing a range of KPIs for ESG risks. The Head of Sustainability explains when asked about ESG performance indicator development:

> The low tolerance for risk, including sustainability risk, is a cultural matter. They [employees] are not encouraged to take on certain risks, even if they could be priced favorably. The bank has an originate to hold rather than an originate to transfer model. Credit deals are typically held on the balance sheet to maturity.

HB continues to work on the development of sustainability targets, the first of which were made public in 2021. These will help steer ESG work together with the strong risk culture of the bank. Reporting sustainability targets will be a further step in the banks' work on communicating internally and externally what the bank is doing in the ESG space. The Head of Sustainability explains:

> Sustainability targets help in presenting a clear view of what a sustainable bank means and, making it more concrete what are we striving to do going forward. However, there is a distinction between reporting according to GRI standards and communicating in the form of storytelling. Storytelling is an important aspect in making the sustainability strategy widely known, understood and executable.

The role of internal audit in promoting ESG risk control effectiveness and reporting quality is currently limited, as control and reporting obligations in relation to ESG risks are based on soft law. As this situation develops and ESG risks become increasingly visible in governing policies and activities, it is expected that internal audit will become more involved to ensure that external obligations and internal governance and policy expectations are being fulfilled.

While AI is not currently used for risk identification on the financing side of the business, AI is used in asset management to evaluate funds against the global development goals by screening sustainability reports using textual analysis tools. According to the Head of Sustainability, the extended use of AI in ESG risk management depends on the development of, and adherence to, consistent definitions, common reporting standards and the availability of ESG datasets. Implementing the EU taxonomy and common reporting standards will advance the possibilities for AI to be applied to ESG scoring, controlling and reporting practices in the future.

4.4 The Church of Sweden

The Church of Sweden (CS) is without comparison the largest organization in Sweden. It has 5.8 million members and employs 22 400 people. We have studied the Church of Sweden at the national level (CSN), focusing on its asset management. In 2019, CSN had total revenues of 4.57 billion SEK (of which 1.58 billion comes from asset management) and total assets of 16.58 billion SEK (of which 9.62 billion are assets managed) (Church of Sweden, 2019). However, a long-term trend is that the number of members is decreasing and revenues are decreasing as a result. At the same time, CS has a cost-structure that is difficult to change. For example, there are over 3 400 church buildings that need maintenance. CS and CSN therefore depend on successful asset management.

Asset management has a transparent governance structure. The board of CSN approves the finance policy. The asset management council has overall responsibility for all asset management activities. The present policy is from 2010 (has been updated several times) and states that asset management should be sustainable and build on the following principles: (1) the principle of human dignity (i.e. that all humans are created equal); and (2) the concept of stewardship (i.e. that all assets are gifts from God and that they should be used in the service of mankind) (Church of Sweden, 2020, p. 7). According to the Chief Investment Officer (CIO) this is a manifestation of "Christian thoughts that man should be a good steward and should not leave earth in a worse state to the next generation."

The report "Sustainable investments – Annual report 2018" shows that the practical meaning of this manifestation is that the asset management of CSN should contribute to society by "making a difference with its own capital" and "to drive developments in the financial sector towards increased sustainability and long-termism industry" (Church of Sweden, 2018, p. 17). This ethical orientation is the foundation of the finance policy and an expression of strong cultural controls that affect ESG risk management. The sustainability report shows that both asset management objectives and strategies are strongly orientated towards avoiding ESG risks. The CIO maintains that the use of ESG scores could be one way of avoiding these risks. However, one must be aware of their short-comings; scorings focus on policies, not necessarily what is done. To illustrate his point, he takes an example of a large company that had a good ESG-score partly because its policy focused on areas that were very easy to measure. However, these areas were not necessarily related to the core business and their inherent ESG-risks.

> They had a policy that focused on the wrong things. They got a good score because of their company car policy, etc. But these risks were not important.... There had to be a relation to the identified risk areas.

Alone, a good ESG score is not enough to show that CSN can invest in the company. Company management must be able to show that their operations are sustainable, for example, that the company has an environmentally driven business development. Businesses that are controversial, such as extracting fossil fuel or manufacturing weapons, are excluded from the portfolio of assets. They have developed a detailed instruction to help facilitate these types of decisions. It should be noted however, that companies that are affecting the environment in a negative way, but are "best in their class" (e.g. certain energy intensive companies), could be included in the portfolio (Svenska Kyrkan, 2020). The strategy is expected to lead to lower ESG risks while achieving a 3% yearly real return (average yearly return since 2000 is 4.8%). In 2019, the asset management of CSN was included among the top 10% of the world's leading sustainable asset managers (PRI, 2019).

To achieve this level of performance, the risks and opportunities must be identified, assessed and responded to. CSN only works with external asset managers, as they should "have a good ability to integrate factors that affect environmental, social and governance aspects" (our translation) of their business (Svenska Kyrkan, 2018, p. 10). Hence, ESG risk management is, to a large extent, conducted through the choice of asset managers. They are expected to work in accordance with the values and risk-culture of CSN and make investment decisions in line with the Paris Agreement and Agenda 2030 (Svenska Kyrkan, 2018; www.svenskakyrkan.se). The CIO underlines it is not sufficient for the external asset managers to apply an "ESG-filter" to create a "feel good factor".

> We want our asset managers to have *it* (*ESG*, our remark) in their DNA. We have to see that sustainability is fully integrated in asset management.

Besides choosing funds from the asset managers, CSN has also developed new products together with them. One example is that CSN has been an investor in new solutions for microfinancing (www.svenskakyrkan.se).

Review and revision of which asset managers to use, is important in CSNs ESG risk management. Over time, asset managers must deliver according to the return objectives of CSN but also meet the sustainability demands. To make sure that the asset managers do not breach those demands, different methods are used, such as ESG scoring. Using AI in this process is not something that CSN pays attention to. However, CSN scrutinizes the asset managers' portfolios with the help of external evaluators. There is also a normative screening to identify events that can change the assessment of company ESG risks. The CIO explains:

> An event that does not seem to have an impact on financial return in the short term can nevertheless have long-term consequences. And not only a financial risk but also a reputational risk.

A long-term consequence of such an event could be a deterioration of the company trade-mark leading to a loss of businesses, eventually affecting shareholder return. Reputational risks can have severe consequences for CSN as expressed by the CIO

> The risk for us is to be connected to an asset manager that has invested in a company that do not operate according to the values of the Church. That could absolutely destroy… it can damage the trademark. That is a fact and the reason why we use screening-companies.

Management of companies in the portfolio that do not fulfill the sustainability requirements can be contacted by CSN to start a dialogue. CSN always tries to affect and change the companies and by doing that contribute to a positive development.

Information, communication and reporting of ESG risks is to a large extent directed towards the asset management council. All suggestions for investments are discussed there. There are also ethical reports to the council in which the ESG scores for the portfolios are presented, as well as if there are any dialogues with companies that have breached the CSN requirements. Reports are also sent to the board of CSN. Internal audit does not seem to be particularly involved in ESG risk management, but the external auditors are. The annual sustainability report is used to communicate ESG risks both to internal and external stakeholders. Finally, it should be pointed out that the trade-mark of CSN is strong. If CSN invests in a company, it indicates that their sustainability work is at the forefront and that ESG risks are low. This situation creates a strong sense of responsibility for the decisions that CSN makes and how they are communicated and reported. The CIO explains:

> We have a responsibility related to asset managers and the companies they invest in. So, there are some asset managers that are willing to stretch themselves a lot for being able to include us in their portfolio of clients

5 Analysis

5.1 Analysis of Integrating Dimensions

ESG risks are well-integrated into control and reporting in all four organizations. Not surprisingly, we find that technical processes are important because of increased transparency and accountability demands. These demands are the result of changes in accounting standards, the EU taxonomy, scoring models and ERM frameworks that include ESG risks. We also find that social processes play an important role in ESG integration (Jean-Jules & Vicente, 2021).

All four organizations received early recognition for their ESG best practice approaches where: (1) a variety of ESG definitions, standards, and principles existed; (2) the use of formal controls was limited (but high use of social controls) (see Malmi & Brown, 2008); and (3) there were limited or no use of sophisticated risk measurement techniques or risk managers involved in risk aggregation. Hence, integration was achieved mainly through social processes. This finding is surprising, as it is at odds with normative notions of how ESG risks should be integrated according to ERM frameworks with their emphasis on the technical and organizational dimensions of integration (Gond et al., 2012). The finding draws attention to the informal, social mechanisms of integration discussed in the management control literature (see Chenhall, 2003), and materiality issues associated with ESG risks, i.e. measuring and pricing emissions. Technical processes used to identify financial risks can fail to identify ESG risks which are incubating, only for them to emerge later, causing devastating consequences.

5.2 Analysis of Integrating Components

All four organizations have transparent and well-developed corporate governance models (Lundqvist, 2015). Best practice approaches have emerged because of an early commitment to ESG work supported by the organizational culture, which filtered down into strategic and operational processes. Länsförsäkringar, Scania and Handelsbanken all emphasize that a critical factor in their early success in ESG work was not focusing on technical details. Instead they were starting minor projects, integrating sustainability into processes and developing customer advisory services. The aim was to change mindsets, create awareness and transfer knowledge.

These organizations have been able to integrate ESG risks into strategies and manage uncertainties by having a risk envisionment culture, which combines risk measurement with intuition, expert judgment, and softer instruments, e.g. materiality analysis (Mikes, 2011). Handelsbanken already had a risk-adverse culture, which they extended to include ESG risks. Yet they are only developing and reporting sustainability targets. Scania's current leadership in decarbonizing the transport sector upholds their longstanding commitment to sustainability. Still they have a small and only recently established risk management function. A decade ago, Länsförsäkringar's president described their commitment to sustainability as "an expression of who we are and a natural part of our operations" (Länsförsäkringar, 2011, p. 9). Today, their sustainability work is visible in local communities. However, their structure for measuring and following up ESG risks is, by their own admission, not that mature. The Church of Sweden's inclusion of existentialism as a fourth dimension in their sustainability work shows the extent of their commitment on a human level. Perhaps that is why they are skeptical to using scoring models to evaluate companies in their investment portfolios. Instead they rely on the capacity of investment management firms to capture relevant information based on a dialogue with actors in their network.

As demands for better ESG risk control and reporting practices have emerged, committing to standards and reporting guidelines have been a natural progression for these organizations, necessitating the development of technical processes alongside the social processes already in existence (Jean-Jules & Vicente, 2021). While standards and guidelines are important, as they encourage improved reporting practices (e.g. increased transparency about sustainability work), they guide rather than drive sustainability engagement.

The relationship between corporate governance and culture in ESG risk management is strong. Corporate governance mechanisms can solidify and formalize the organizations' commitment to sustainability work by supporting the development of controls that produce ESG risk information (technical dimension) as well as the establishment of risk control functions and roles (organizational dimension). What is clear from the cases is that the production and transfer of ESG risk information further adds to the organizations' ability to control their risks and report them with increased transparency, accuracy and quality—both internally and externally. Setting sustainability targets also shows a clear methodological link (technical dimension) between risk, strategy and performance. This is a central aspect in achieving a shared awareness of ESG risks, a core ambition of the COSO ERM-Integrated Framework. It promotes integration on the cognitive dimension, by providing information that enables managers and employees to perceive how their individual and collective behavior is contributing to the achievement of those targets.

Using a combination of first order measurements and risk envisionment instead of risk aggregation has proven to be a powerful mechanism for constructing and conveying a sustainable vision of an uncertain future that cannot be expressed in a quantitative format alone. Combining the dual roles of sustainability, champion and partner, plays a decisive role in creating that vision through toolmaking and tool dissemination, as well as interpersonal relations (Hall et al., 2015; Mikes, 2008). This is a crucial social factor in decentralized organizations.

Financial organizations are in a unique situation, as external demands to enhance ESG control and reporting practices are more intrusive. They are also more likely to use ESG scoring models, IT-based risk measurement tools and AI to identify ESG risks and commercial client deviations from incoming ESG standards. Nonetheless, as we see from Handelsbanken and Länsförsäkringar, risk envisionment is still important in controlling and reporting ESG risks. In line with that approach, the use of materiality analysis is an important risk envisionment tool currently used to identify and prioritize ESG risks. It makes it possible to check their alignment with the vision and strategy of the organization.

Finally, we were surprised by internal audit's lack of involvement in promoting ESG risk control effectiveness and reporting quality. We attribute this to ESG risks being new, although the organizations in this study have worked with sustainability issues for many years. We also attribute it to the soft law approach applied by external actors to organizational level ESG requirements. However, when they are eventually embedded into governing policies and formal controls, we expect internal audit to have a more prominent role.

6 Conclusions and Future Research

The analysis shows the importance of integrating ESG risks with control. It also shows the importance of organizational-wide dialogue about ESG issues. It facilitates the identification and analysis of ESG risks, providing board members, managers, and employees with strategic, tactical and operational information. However, the flow of information between organizational levels and decision-makers requires suitable structures and processes. Therefore, it is necessary to achieve a basic level of technical and organizational integration to support ESG strategy formulation and implementation. That means that the information used should relate to the strategies pursued as well as to operations (Nilsson et al., 2020). The analysis shows that the technical processes facilitate the social processes that are necessary for a meaningful strategic dialogue (Gond et al., 2012). What is striking is that cultural controls seem to be more important than well-developed ESG risk management structures and processes, especially in taking meaningful actions (Henriksson & Weidman Grunewald, 2020). One explanation could be that definitions and standards allow for maximum flexibility in formal control. In this context, it is natural that advanced information technologies like AI are not fully utilized, even though some of the organizations' asset managers use them.

The analysis also reveals that organizations have well-developed processes and structures where ESG risk are integrated into reporting. External reporting appears to be critical in how organizations communicate their ESG strategies, performance and risks. This is visible in the formal governance structures, with roles and responsibilities supporting the transfer of ESG risk information in the organization. Like financial reporting, sustainability reporting focuses on developing accounting systems to produce reliable information. Thus, technical processes and organizational integration are emphasized. To some extent, that is due to laws and regulations. Internal sustainability reporting, and especially the reporting of ESG risks, is not as regulated and formalized. That could explain why ESG risks are not as visible as in the external reports. Other explanations are the prevalence of strong cultural controls and the use of external reporting for internal communication to managers and employees.

The study reported in this chapter is limited to four short case studies and it has an explorative character. Hence, the conclusions are preliminary. What we found striking is the strong emphasis on social processes, which is at odds with how ESG risk management best practice is generally described. One explanation for that tendency could be that ESG risk management has not reached the same level of maturity as ERM practices. As a result, organizations are experimenting much more and also relying on cultural controls to create an awareness of the importance of sustainable businesses. This reasoning is however, more of speculation than an empirical fact and future research, especially in-depth case studies, could provide more insight into the actual practices of ESG risk management. By co-operating with organizations in the fore-front of ESG risk management, scholars could also contribute more directly to the development of best practices in the area of sustainable business.

Acknowledgements We would like to thank the interviewees for generously sharing their experience, insights and knowledge with us. The insightful comments by the editors are also acknowledged. Financial support has been received from the Jan Wallander and Tom Hedelius Foundation, as well as the Tore Browaldh Foundation.

References

Asante-Appiah, B. (2020). Does the severity of a client's negative environmental, social and governance reputation affect audit effort and audit quality? *Journal of Accounting and Public Policy, 39*(3), 1–22.

Chenhall, R. H. (2003). Management control system design within its organizational context: Findings from contingency-based research and directions for the future. *Accounting, Organizations and Society, 28*(2–3), 127–168.

Church of Sweden. (2018). *Sustainable investments—Annual report 2018*. Church of Sweden.

Church of Sweden. (2019). *Review and financial summary—The national level of the Church of Sweden 2019*. Church of Sweden.

Church of Sweden. (2020). *Financial policy for the national level of the Church of Sweden*. Church of Sweden.

Cohen, J., Krishnamoorthy, G., & Wright, A. (2017). Enterprise risk management and the financial reporting process: The experiences of audit committee members, CFOs, and external auditors. *Contemporary Accounting Research, 34*(2), 1178–1209.

Crawford, J., & Lindvall, J. (2021). Leveraging digital technologies in enterprise risk management. In P. Ekman, P. Dahlin, & C. Keller (Eds.), *Management and information technology after digital transformation* (pp. 157–171). Routledge.

Crawford, J., & Nilsson, F. (2021). Enterprise risk management in Sweden. In M. Maffei (Ed.), *Enterprise risk management in Europe* (pp. 211–226). Emerald Publishing.

Gehman, J., Glaser, V. L., Eisenhardt, K. M., Gioia, D., Langley, A., & Corley, K. G. (2018). Finding theory–method fit: A comparison of three qualitative approaches to theory building. *Journal of Management Inquiry, 27*(3), 284–300.

Gond, J. P., Grubnic, S., Herzig, C., & Moon, J. (2012). Configuring management control systems: Theorizing the integration of strategy and sustainability. *Management Accounting Research, 23*(3), 205–223.

Hall, M., Mikes, A., & Millo, Y. (2015). How do risk managers become influential? A field study of toolmaking in two financial institutions. *Management Accounting Research, 26*(1), 3–22.

Handelsbanken. (2019a). *Annual report*. https://vp292.alertir.com/afw/files/press/handelsbanken/202002135859-1.pdf

Handelsbanken. (2019b). *Sustainability report*. https://vp292.alertir.com/afw/files/press/handelsbanken/202002135907-1.pdf

Henriksson, H., & Weidman Grunewald, E. (2020). *Sustainability leadership: A Swedish approach to transforming your company, your industry and the world*. Palgrave Macmillan.

Jean-Jules, J., & Vicente, R. (2021). Rethinking the implementation of enterprise risk management (ERM) as a socio-technical challenge. *Journal of Risk Research, 24*(2), 247–266.

Kaplan, R. S. (1986). The role for empirical research in management accounting. *Accounting, Organizations and Society, 11*(4/5), 429–452.

Länsförsäkringar AB. (2011). *Annual report*. https://mb.cision.com/Main/152/9255754/10084.pdf

Länsförsäkringar AB. (2019). *Annual report*. https://mb.cision.com/Main/152/3058516/1210478.pdf

Länsförsäkringar AB. (2020). *Sustainability policy for Länsförsäkringar AB*. https://mb.cision.com/Main/152/3309414/1389097.pdf

Länsförsäkringar Göteborg och Bohuslän. (2019a). *Årsredovising 2019* (eng: Annual Report 2019). https://www.info@gbg.lansforsakringar.se

Länsförsäkringar Göteborg och Bohuslän. (2019b). *Hållbarhetsrapport 2019* (eng: Sustainability Report 2019). https://www.info@gbg.lansforsakringar.se

Lundqvist, S. A. (2014). An exploratory study of enterprise risk management: Pillars of ERM. *Journal of Accounting, Auditing & Finance, 29*(3), 393–429.

Lundqvist, S. A. (2015). Why firms implement risk governance—Stepping beyond traditional risk management to enterprise risk management. *Journal of Accounting and Public Policy, 34*(5), 441–466.

Malmi, T., & Brown, D. A. (2008). Management control systems as a package: Opportunities, challenges and research directions. *Management Accounting Research, 19*, 287–300.

Mikes, A. (2008). Chief risk officers at crunch time: Compliance champions or business partners? *Journal of Risk Management in Financial Institutions, 2*(1), 7–25.

Mikes, A. (2009). Risk management and calculative cultures. *Management Accounting Research, 20*(1), 18–40.

Mikes, A. (2011). From counting risk to making risk count: Boundary-work in risk management. *Accounting, Organizations and Society, 36*(4–5), 226–245.

Mikes, A., & Kaplan, R. (2015). When one size doesn't fit all: Evolving directions in the research and practice of enterprise risk management. *Journal of Applied Corporate Finance, 27*(1), 37–40.

Nilsson, F., Petri, C.-J., & Westelius, A. (Eds.). (2020). *Strategic management control: Successful strategies based on dialogue and collaboration.* Springer Nature Switzerland.

Power, M., Ashby, S., & Palermo, T. (2013). *Risk culture in financial organisations: A research report*. CARR-Analysis of Risk and Regulation.

PRI. (2019). *The PRI leaders' group 2019—Asset owners: Selecting, appointing and monitoring external managers in listed and private equities.* PRI.

Scania. (2012). *Annual report*. https://www.scania.com/content/dam/group/investor-relations/financial-reports/annualreports/2012-en-scania-annual-report.pdf

Scania. (2014). *Annual report*. https://www.scania.com/content/dam/group/investor-relations/financial-reports/annualreports/2014-en-scania-annual-report.pdf

Scania. (2019). *Annual and sustainability report*. https://www.scania.com/content/dam/group/investor-relations/financialreports/annual-reports/Scania_AnnualReport_2019-English.pdf

Svanberg, J., Ardeshiri, T., Samsten, I., Öhman, P., Rana, T., & Danielson, M. (2023). Prediction of environmental controversies and estimation of environmental corporate social performance: An experimental investigation using machine learning. In T. Rana, A. Lowe, & J. Svanberg (Eds.), *Handbook of big data and analytics in accounting and auditing*. Springer Nature.

Svenska Kyrkan. (2018). *Hållbara investeringar—Årsrapport 2018* (eng: Sustainable investments—Annual report 2018). https://www.svenskakyrkan.se/filer/2018%20Svenska_Kyrkan_Hallbara_Investeringar.pdf

Svenska Kyrkan. (2020). *Placeringsanvisningar för etik och hållbarhet för Svenska kyrkans kapitalförvaltning på den nationella nivån* (eng: Investment instructions for the asset management of the Church of Sweden in the area of ethics and sustainability). https://www.svenskakyrkan.se/filer/1709193/Placeringsanvisningar%20etik%20och%20h%c3%a5llbarhet%20uppd%202022-02-15.pdf

Tekathen, M., & Dechow, N. (2013). Enterprise risk management and continuous realignment in the pursuit of accountability: A German case. *Management Accounting Research, 24*(2), 100–121.

Verheyden, T., Eccles, R. G., & Feiner, A. (2016). ESG for all? The impact of ESG screening on return, risk, and diversification. *Journal of Applied Corporate Finance, 28*(2), 47–55.

Wahlström, G. (2009). Risk management versus operational action: Basel II in a Swedish context. *Management Accounting Research, 20*(1), 53–68.

Web Sources

COSO. (2017). *Enterprise Risk Management integrating with strategy and performance executive summary.* https://www.coso.org/Documents/2017-COSO-ERM-Integratingwith-Strategy-and-Performance-Executive-Summary.pdf

COSO. (2018). *Enterprise Risk Management: Applying enterprise risk management to environmental, social and governance-related risks.* https://www.coso.org/Documents/COSO-WBCSD-ESGERM-Guidance-Full.pdf

EU Non-Financial Reporting Directive. (2014/95/EU). https://ec.europa.eu/info/business-economy-euro/company-reporting-and-auditing/companyreporting/corporate-sustainability-reporting_en

European Commission. (2021). *EU taxonomy for sustainable activities.* https://ec.europa.eu/info/business-economy-euro/banking-and-finance/sustainable-finance/eutaxonomy-sustainable-activities_en

FSR/WBCSD. (2019). *Guidance on improving the quality of ESG information for decision making: Developing a roadmap for companies.* https://www.sustainability-reports.com/guidance-on-improving-the-quality-of-esginformation-for-decision-making/

Handelsbanken. (2020). https://www.handelsbanken.com/en/sustainability/news/sustainable-bank-of-the-year

King IV. (2016). https://cdn.ymaws.com/www.iodsa.co.za/resource/collection/684B68A7-B768-465C-8214E3A007F15A5A/IoDSA_King_IV_Report_-_WebVersion.pdf

Svenska Kyrkan. www.svenskakyrkan.se

UNEP FI. (2021). *TCFD for banks*. United Nations Environment Programme Finance Initiative (UNEP FI). https://www.unepfi.org/climate-change/tcfd/tcfd-for-banks/

United Nations. (2021). *Member States, Sweden*. https://sustainabledevelopment.un.org/memberstates/sweden

World Economic Forum. (2021). *The global risks report 2020*. http://www3.weforum.org/docs/WEF_Global_Risk_Report_2020.pdf

Jason Crawford is an Assistant Professor at the Department of Business Studies, Uppsala University, specializing in accounting. His research focuses on regulation, strategy, enterprise risk management, and management control systems in financial and other industries. He has presented his work at European Accounting conferences and has published book chapters. In 2018, Jason was awarded the Wallander Scholarship for his research, and he is presently involved in several research projects that are generously financed by Swedish research foundations.

Fredrik Nilsson is a Professor of Business Studies, specializing in Accounting, at Uppsala University. His research focuses on how different information systems (e.g. related to financial accounting, management control and enterprise risk management) are designed and used in formulating and implementing strategies. He has published his research in books (e.g., Routledge and Springer) and in scientific journals such as Accounting & Finance, The British Accounting Review, British Journal of Management, European Management Journal, Management Accounting Research and Scandinavian Journal of Management. He is the Chairman of the Swedish Academy of Auditing and Chairman of the Swedish Research School of Management and Information Technology.

Chapter 13
Digitalization and Management Control in the Public Sector: What is Next?

Laura Broccardo, Elisa Truant, and Daniela Argento

Abstract Digitalization has become increasingly important over the years because of the potential opportunities and advantages it offers, both in terms of organizations' management and performances and various stakeholder relationships. If integrated with management accounting systems, these benefits—derived from the implementation and use of digital tools—can increase. However, it is argued that there is still a long way to go, especially in the public sector. There is no clarity about the degree of digitalization and whether public sector organizations are prepared to implement digital tools in their management control systems (MCS). Therefore, this chapter, through a systematic literature review, aims to clarify how the implementation of digital tools influences the MCS of public sector organizations. The literature review reveals few studies on such topics for the public sector, which has a greater need of quantitative and qualitative studies. Furthermore, although the internal and external benefits associated with the use of digital tools in MCS are recognized, such tools seem to have an unexpressed potential in the public context. This chapter also adds to the knowledge of both practitioners and academics as it unveils a lack of innovative technical solutions that can support MCS and its integration with digitalization, which should be strengthened to improve decision-making processes.

Keywords Digitalization · Big Data · Management control · Management accounting · Public sector

L. Broccardo (✉) · E. Truant
University of Turin, Turin, Italy
e-mail: laura.broccardo@unito.it

E. Truant
e-mail: elisa.truant@unito.it

D. Argento
Kristianstad University, Kristianstad, Sweden
e-mail: daniela.argento@hkr.se

T. Rana et al. (eds.), *Handbook of Big Data and Analytics in Accounting and Auditing*,
https://doi.org/10.1007/978-981-19-4460-4_13

1 Introduction

Digitalization is the term commonly used to describe 'how social life is organized through and around digital technologies' (Leonardi & Treem, 2020, p 1602). It entails the transformation of organizational processes through the use of digital technologies to increase efficiency and value creation opportunities. Data, documents, and reports are collected and stored via digital solutions, allowing organizations to analyze them and make decisions efficiently and more comprehensively. In turn, the implementation of digital technologies can support the delivery of improved services.

There is a debate on the effects and changes that digitalization may have on and cause in management control systems (MCS; Gärtner and Hiebl, 2017; Manyika et al., 2011). MCS include 'all the devices or systems that managers use to ensure the behaviors and decisions of their employees are consistent with the organization's objective and strategy' (Merchant and Van der Stede, 2007, p 8). Some authors believe that digitalization can lead to positive changes in various areas of MCS such as operational and strategic planning (Davenport, 2014; Wang et al., 2016), decision-making processes (Côrte-Real et al., 2017; Gandomi & Haider, 2015; McAfee and Brynjolfsson, 2012) and data value and management (Bhimani & Willcocks, 2014). It can also lead to more effective relationships with external stakeholders. Meanwhile, other scholars claim that digitalization can lead to challenges in cost structures (Bhimani & Willcocks, 2014), information overload, and faster and erroneous decision-making (Quattrone, 2016). In addition, the claimed improved relationship opportunities with external stakeholders are not always confirmed, leading to discussions about the increased exclusion or segregation caused by the use of digital tools.

It is argued that digitalization has been successfully implemented in the private sector, while the public sector seems to have been falling behind (Mullich, 2013). However, the relevance of digitalization in public sector MCS is currently being recognized, as it can help governments increase their effectiveness, productivity, and accountability (Milakovich, 2012). Digitalization can support the MCS of public sector organizations and offer many advantages because digital applications and features may provide a wide range of opportunities. First, digitalization enables governments to shift from paperwork to e-government services, for example, by improving integration and data flow across various governmental entities. Second, digitalization can play an essential role in establishing partnerships among government and citizens (Bertot et al., 2010). Third, digitalization offers the possibility for public sector organizations to create precise and reliable citizen databases, which can be used to adapt public services to meet citizens' needs, thereby enhancing both internal and external managerial practices. By compiling comprehensive and reliable citizen profiles, public sector organizations can meet citizens' demands more effectively (Bonsón et al., 2015; Heikkila & Isett, 2007). Lastly, digital tools can be a new source of information about public organizations' quality and effectiveness.

It follows that digitalization has the potential of producing positive effects both in terms of how public sector organizations work and in the relationships with various stakeholders. One important aspect of the impact of digitalization on MCS is presented by its capacity to support public managers to make more logical and informed decisions, based on future-oriented and real-time data (Manyika et al., 2011).

When discussing digitalization, big data is often argued to make a relevant contribution to MCS, because it promotes data volumes, velocity, and availability, making the storage and management of data easier and cheaper and providing the ability to mix digital forms and supporting analytics (Bhimani & Willcocks, , 2014). Big data is an information asset that requires unique technologies and analytical methods, generating value through high volume, velocity, and variety (DeMauro et al., 2016; Wamba et al., 2015). It has tremendous impact on innovative and information processing methods, leading to cost savings and improved decision-making (Arnaboldi et al., 2017). Furthermore, effective or almost real-time information in MCS enables organizations to become more agile (McAfee and Brynjolfsson, 2012).

The increasing awareness of the potential advantages of digitalization in MCS has given rise to plans and roadmaps to promote the growth of big data worldwide, including the public sector (European Commission, 2010; Kim et al., 2014). In the public sector, the extent to which digitalization is implemented can also be influenced by political decisions and legislation. Government leaders are increasingly aware of the opportunities generated by digitalization (Chen & Zhang, 2014; Jin et al., 2015; McAfee and Brynjolfsson, 2012; Shaw, 2014). However, digitalization is simultaneously a challenge that can affect the performance of public sector organizations (McConnell, 2015). Governments recognize digitalization opportunities, but it seems unclear whether they are ready for its introduction and prepared to implement digital tools. As argued by Fredriksson et al. (2017), digitalization provides possibilities and challenges, and there are many complex issues to consider when big data is studied in the public sector context. In particular, the main challenges concern the need to ensure transparency and greater closeness to citizen's actual needs.

This chapter aims to clarify how the implementation of digital tools influences the MCS of public sector organizations. Through a systematic literature review, knowledge is provided to both practitioners and researchers interested in digitalization and MCS in the public sector. This chapter addresses the research question: What main evidence does the current literature provide regarding the effects of digitalization on MCS in the public sector?

The remainder of this chapter is structured as follows. After this introduction, the following section explains the review design adopted to conduct the systematic literature review, including the search criteria and queries used to retrieve existing literature on the selected topic. Section 3 presents the descriptive statistics of the studies included in the literature review and the results of the data mining analysis. Section 4 illustrates the findings of the systematic literature review, while Sect. 5 discusses the findings. Finally, Sect. 6 provides the conclusions, limitations, and future research avenues.

2 Review Design

A systematic literature review was carried out through a well-documented process that guarantees the search's replicability, following Tranfield et al.'s (2003) three-stage process: (i) planning, (ii) execution, and (iii) analysis and reporting. The three stages are described below.

2.1 Planning Stage

The first stage, namely, the planning stage, was devoted to identifying the research's objective and the key data sources. We chose to limit our sources to published articles, conference proceedings, books, and book chapters with a focus on the public sector because, as observed by Podsakoff et al. (2003), these types of contributions can be considered validated knowledge. In addition, these contributions have better chances of meeting the basic requirements of theoretical and methodological rigor (Anessi-Pessina et al., 2016). Hence, unpublished conference proceedings and practitioners' sources were excluded. Both theoretical and empirical studies were considered suitable.

2.2 Execution Stage

Following Mauro et al. (2017), the second stage of the systematic review process, that is, the execution stage, consisted of three steps: (a) definition of the search criteria, (b) finding studies through search queries, and (c) elimination of duplicates and loosely focused studies.

2.2.1 Definition of the Search Criteria

The systematic search began with the identification of a set of keywords that could reflect the variety of labels coined and used by practitioners and scholars to refer to digitalization and big data in the public sector, particularly focusing on MCS and their impact and influence. Therefore, in the search process, the following terms were used: big data, digitalization, public sector, management control, management accounting, state-owned, and some related acronyms combined with Boolean logic. The databases powered by EBSCOHost (Business Source Complete), Thomson Reuters (Web of Science) and Elsevier (Scopus) were selected to conduct the search. Furthermore, to confirm the results of the search and find additional contributions, Google Scholar was used as well. Yet, no additional records were found through Google Scholar.

The following parameters were applied when searching for the literature:

- Language: Only contributions written in English were selected to avoid translation problems.
- Time horizon: Contributions published from 2010 to 2020 were included given the growing importance of digital technologies within public sector organizations in this timeframe.
- Source: The search was limited to published articles, conference proceedings, books, and book chapters as decided in the planning stage.

2.2.2 Finding Studies Through Search Queries

A representative dataset of the literature was created by conducting nine search queries in each selected search engine using Boolean logic (combining search terms such as AND, OR, NOT) and the identified keywords for each search round. As explained above, the search was limited by language and time horizon. A total of 123 contributions were retrieved. Table 1 shows the number of contributions retrieved through the nine search strings (SS).

The search strings are based on very similar keywords to avoid missing relevant contributions. For example, 'management control system' and 'management accounting system' were used to identify the features and tools to support operative decision-making processes. In addition, 'impact' was used synonymously as

Table 1 Search strings and number of contributions

Database creation		No
SS1:	'Big data' and 'management control system' and 'public sector'	20
SS2:	'Digitalization' and 'management control system' and 'public sector'	12
SS3:	'Big data' and 'management accounting system' and 'public sector'	27
SS4:	'Digitalization' and 'management accounting system' and 'public sector'	3
SS5:	'Big data' and 'management control system' and 'public sector' and 'impact or influence'	41
SS6:	'Digitalization' and 'management control system' and 'public sector' and 'impact' or 'influence'	4
SS7:	'Big data' and 'management accounting system' and 'public sector' and 'impact' or 'influence'	13
SS8:	'Digitalization' and 'management accounting system' and 'public sector' and 'impact' or 'influence'	1
SS9:	'Digitalization' and 'management control system' and 'state-owned' and 'impact' or 'influence'	2
Total number of retrieved contributions		123

'influence' to search for contributions that focus on the effects of digitalization on management control in the public sector. The term 'state-owned' was used to retrieve contributions that focus on public sector organizations where the government or state has significant control. Further attempts were made by using other terms such as higher education and public utilities, but the search did not lead to additional contributions.

2.2.3 Elimination of Duplicates and Loosely Focused Studies

The 123 records were manually analyzed to eliminate duplicates and loosely focused studies. Specifically, a manual search was conducted by inspecting the list of contributions. After removing four duplicates, the dataset included 119 contributions.

Afterwards, the importance of the remaining contributions was assessed in line with Petticrew and Roberts (2006). The 119 contributions were analyzed by screening their abstract, introduction, literature review and findings. A deep analysis and comparison led to the exclusion of contributions that were not pertinent with the aim of this literature review. Hence, 92 contributions were removed because they did not focus on the intersections among the public sector, digitalization or big data, and management control. In this process, the impact, in terms of citation statistics, of the contributions was not considered.

The entire second stage was executed by two authors who worked separately to increase the trustworthiness of the process. After working separately, the two authors compared the list of studies that were included in their respective sample. The two samples corresponded to a high degree, and after a discussion, the selection process led to a database of 27 contributions: 24 scientific articles, 1 conference proceeding published in the *Series Advances in Economics, Business, and Management Research—Volume 131*, 1 chapter published in the book *Digitalization and Industry 4.0: Economic and Societal Development*, and 1 article published by the *Social Science Research Network (SSRN)*. Table 2 shows the number of the scientific articles per journal.

2.3 Analysis and Reporting Stage

The last stage of the process, named analysis and reporting, involved descriptive and conceptual analyses of the 27 contributions included in the final dataset. Inspired by Manes-Rossi et al. (2020), the contents of each contribution were codified into the six categories explained below.

The first category is named *public sector entity* (A) and refers to the public entity that each contribution is focused on. This literature review focuses on the public sector in a broad sense, meaning that it includes contributions that relate to governments, their agencies, such as defense, police, judicial and legislative structures, and other government institutions that produce public goods and services. Therefore, this

Table 2 Number of Scientific Articles *per* Journal (nr.)

Code	Journal name	No
IJAIS	International Journal of Accounting Information Systems	1
GIQ	Government Information Quarterly	2
IJDST	International Journal of Distributed Systems and Technologies	1
IJPPM	International Journal of Productivity and Performance Management	1
IJSSMET	International Journal of Service Science, Management, Engineering, and Technology	1
IPMJ	International Public Management Journal	1
IRAS	International Review of Administrative Sciences	1
JCG	Journal of Chinese Governance	1
PAR	Public Administration Review	1
PMR	Public Management Review	1
PPMR	Public Performance & Management Review	1
QAE	Quality Assurance in Education	1
PJPA	Asia Pacific Journal of Public Administration	1
ARPA	The American Review of Public Administration	1
ICS	Information, Communication & Society	1
PMM	Public Money & Management	1
IP	Impresa e Progetto—Electronic Journal of Management	1
IJARBSS	International Journal of Academic Research in Business and Social Sciences	1
TGPPP	Transforming Government: People, Process and Policy	1
ESI	Entrepreneurship and Sustainability Issues	1
VPIA	Public policy and administration	1
AOS	Accounting, Organizations and Society	1
JUCPA	Journal of US-China Public Administration	1
	Total	24

category includes the central government (A1), state or regional governments (A2), local governments (A3), state-owned enterprises (A4), healthcare organizations (A5), education institutions (A6), public utilities (A7), others (a residual subcategory used to categorize contributions not specifically traced to previous subcategories or not focused on any specific organization; A8) and mixed (for contributions that cover more than one subcategory; A9).

The second category considers the *country of research* (B) for each contribution. Thus, and similar to Manes-Rossi et al. (2020), we included the following categories: Africa (B1), Asia (B2), Europe and UK (B3), North America (B4), South America (B5), Oceania (B6), not specified (B7) and mixed (for contributions that cover more than one subcategory; B8).

The third category relates to the investigated *MCS* (C). To classify the MCS, four types were identified, in line with the Chartered Institute of Management Accountants (CIMA, 2008), namely, strategic planning (C1), operating system (C2), business performance (C3), and general management accounting systems (C4). Strategic planning refers to long-term tools and documents, including both financial and non-financial information. Operating systems refer to short-term reports and documents such as those relating to the budgeting process, while business performance specifically focuses on key performance indicators. Finally, general management accounting systems refer to management accounting systems in general and do not explicitly focus on a single tool.

The fourth category identifies the *type of digital tools* (D) treated for each contribution. By carefully reading the selected contributions, the following were identified: information technology (IT; D1), e-government (D2), mobile technologies (D3), big data (D4), open data technology (D5), business analytics (D6) and multiple tools (D7) for contributions that focus on more than one digital tool.

IT refers to the use of computers for data or information storage, recovery, transmission, and manipulation (Isaacs, 1996). Digital transformation is considered in this category as the adoption of digital technology, through the replacement of non-digital or manual processes by digital processes or replacement of ageing digital technology with modern digital technologies, to transform services or companies (Lankshear & Knobel, 2008).

E-government is the use of technological communication devices for public services. E-government creates new ways to make public access easier and more directly available to public services through the government (Caves, 2005). Smart Government is also included in this category and understood as managing government and administration business processes through intelligently networked information and communication technologies (Lucke, 2016).

Mobile technology is defined as 'handheld information technology (IT) artifacts that encompass hardware (devices), software (interface and applications) and communication (network services; Jarvenpaa & Lang, 2005).

Big data 'is the Information asset characterized by such a High Volume, Velocity and Variety to require specific Technology and Analytical Methods for its transformation into Value' (De Mauro et al., 2016, p 123).

Open data technology means that the source code can be used, modified and redistributed openly. Data is open when it is published publicly (over the Internet), and when it is distributed freely (Tammisto & Lindman, 2012).

Business analytics (BA) refers to the expertise, technology, and methods used to continuously analyze and explore past business performance to develop a clear understanding, also with the use of statistical techniques (Shah et al., 2014).

The fifth category centers on the research methods (E) used in the reviewed contributions, which are classified into case or field study or interviews (E1); content analysis or historical analysis (E2); survey, questionnaires, or other empirical work (E3); commentary, normative work, or policy (E4); literature review (E5); and mixed (for contributions based on more than one research method; E6).

The sixth category refers to the theories and models (F) used in the studies. Three subcategories were used: No theory or model (F1), in case the contributions did not refer to any theory nor models; reference to previous models (F2), when contributions referred to theories or models already existing in the literature; and proposition of a new model (F3), in case the study developed a new theoretical framework or model related to digitalization.

An excel file was created to codify the 27 contributions. In addition to the six categories discussed above, the following information was coded: authors' names, year of publication, journal name, research questions and hypothesis, main findings, and future developments. The outcomes of this coding activity are described in the next sections.

3 Descriptive Statistics

Figure 1 presents the number of contributions published per year in the period 2010–2020. The figure clearly shows that there has been an increasing interest in conducting research on these topics over the past four years (2017–2020), with a considerable peak in 2020.

Apart from the increased popularity of the focal topic, some reflections on the impact of the selected contributions can be made. Table 3 shows the number of citations of each contribution as of 11 April 2021. The most cited article is authored by Brivot and Gendron (2011), with 175 cites, followed by the article by Taipaleenmäki

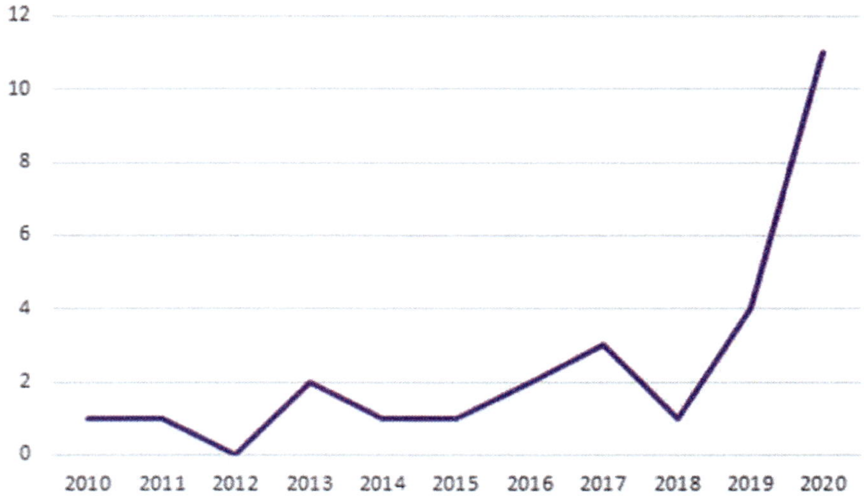

Fig. 1 Number of contributions per year (2010–2020)

and Ikäheimo (2013), with 167 cites. The remaining contributions have a number of citations ranging from 0 to 77.

A second ranking of the 27 contributions, based on the average number of citations per year (CPY), was made to compare more equally the old and new publications (Dumay et al., 2016; Manes-Rossi et al., 2020). A high CPY index indicates that a contribution is interesting and informative to readers and able to generate new knowledge. A high CPY means that a contribution is influential, that is, it has impact because it receives an increasingly considerable amount of citations over a specified period of time. Table 4 provides a list of contributions ranked by CPY (highest to lowest). The CPY was calculated using the Publish or Perish software that retrieves and analyses academic citations.

Table 4 shows that the two articles with the highest CPY are Gao and Yu (2020), with 43 CPY, followed by Wirtz et al. (2019), with 21.5 CPY.

A comparison of Tables 3 and 4 reveals that 10 articles rank high in both categories, namely, Brivot and Gendron (2011), focusing on control in public digital environment; Taipaleenmäki and Ikäheimo (2013), management accounting and IT; Alcaide Muñoz et al. (2017), budgeting in public administration; Maciejewski (2017), big data and public management; Chatfield and Reddick (2018), open government data and management performance; Wirtz et al. (2019), smart government and business model; Safarov (2019), institutional dimension and open government data; Gao and Yu (2020), decision-making support in public governance during emergencies; Clarke (2020), design of MCS and benefit risks and future trajectories of digital governmental units; and Glotko et al. (2020), digital business models for government regulation efficiency.

Furthermore, these top-cited articles are published in Accounting, Organizations and Society (Brivot & Gendron, 2011), International Journal of Accounting Information Systems (Taipaleenmäki & Ikäheimo, 2013), The American Review of Public Administration (Alcaide Muñoz et al., 2017), International Review of Administrative Sciences (Maciejewski, 2017), Government Information Quarterly (Chatfield & Reddick, 2018; Wirtz et al., 2019), Public Performance & Management Review (Safarov, 2019), Journal of Chinese Governance (Gao & Yu, 2020), International Public Management Journal (Clarke, 2020), and Entrepreneurship and Sustainability Issues (Glotko et al., 2020).

3.1 Data Mining Analysis

Data mining is a technique for extracting patterns and combinations from large amounts of data (Provalis Research, 2010). It enables the discovery of structures and patterns in large and complex datasets. The software WordStat was used to execute a frequent pattern extraction.

The following model examines the relationships between the main keywords used to select the contributions included in the systematic literature review and how strong the ties among the keywords are. Stronger ties indicate that the selected contributions

Table 3 Citations by google scholar (as of 11 April 2021)

Ranking	Reference	Contribution	Cites
1	Brivot and Gendron (2011)	Beyond panopticism: On the ramifications of surveillance in a contemporary professional setting	175
2	Taipaleenmäki and Ikäheimo (2013)	On the convergence of management accounting and financial accounting—the role of information technology in accounting change	167
3	Maciejewski (2017)	To do more, better, faster and more cheaply: using big data in public administration	77
4	Alcaide Muñoz et al. (2017)	Transparency in governments: a meta-analytic review of incentives for digital versus hard-copy public financial disclosures	76
5	Gao and Yu (2020)	Public governance mechanism in the prevention and control of the COVID-19: information, decision-making and execution	43
5	Wirtz et al. (2019)	An integrative public IoT framework for smart government	43
6	Kagaari et al. (2010)	Performance management practices, information and communication technology (ICT) adoption and managed performance	40
7	Chatfield and Reddick (2018)	The role of policy entrepreneurs in open government data policy innovation diffusion: An analysis of Australian federal and state governments	35
8	Padovani et al. (2014)	Implementing change in a hospital management accounting system	21
8	Safarov (2019)	Institutional dimensions of open government data implementation: evidence from the Netherlands, Sweden, and the UK	21
9	Glotko et al. (2020)	Main trends of government regulation of sectoral digitalization	15
9	Clarke (2020)	Digital government units: what are they, and what do they mean for digital era public management renewal?	15

(continued)

Table 3 (continued)

Ranking	Reference	Contribution	Cites
10	Clarke (2017)	Digital government Units: origins, orthodoxy and critical considerations for public management theory and practice	11
11	Nielsen et al. (2016)	The power reinforcement framework revisited: mobile technology and management control in home care	8
12	Janjua et al. (2019)	Effective performance management of local governments in Khyber Pakhtunkhwa, Pakistan	5
13	Cosimato et al. (2015)	How to innovate management accounting for public sector: an Italian case study	4
14	Munteanu and Newcomer (2020)	Leading and learning through dynamic performance management in government	3
15	Schmid (2017)	Big data public controlling fundamental changes in public management	2
15	Mahama et al. (2020)	New development: enabling enterprise risk management maturity in public sector organisations	2
15	Silva et al. (2013)	A collaborative model of information technology strategic plan for the government sector	2
15	Alkaabi et al. (2019)	Assets digitalization: exploration of prospects with better control implementation	2
16	Ertl et al. (2020)	Ensuring the success of management accounting change in IT departments of public organisations	1
17	Bray et al. (2020)	Performance management and evaluation meets culture and politics: Australia's experience	0
18	Cristofaro et al. (2020)	Measuring healthcare performance in digitalization era: The Pharmacy Unit of Academic Hospital	0
19	Magnusson et al. (2021)	Closeness and distance: configurational practices for digital ambidexterity in the public sector	0
20	Zvereva et al. (2020)	Improving client-oriented approach in the provision of public services in the context of digitalization	0

(continued)

Table 3 (continued)

Ranking	Reference	Contribution	Cites
21	Kurchenkov et al. (2020)	Features of the development of organizational structures of large Russian state-owned companies (based on the example of SC «Roskosmos», SC «Rostekhnologii», SC «Rosatom»)	0

Table 4 Citation per year (as of 11 April 2021)

Ranking	Reference	Contribution	CPY
1	Gao and Yu (2020)	Public governance mechanism in the prevention and control of the COVID-19: information, decision-making and execution	43
2	Wirtz et al. (2019)	An integrative public IoT framework for smart government	21.5
3	Taipaleenmäki and Ikäheimo (2013)	On the convergence of management accounting and financial accounting – the role of information technology in accounting change	20.88
4	Maciejewski (2017)	To do more, better, faster and more cheaply: using big data in public administration	19.25
5	Alcaide Muñoz et al. (2017)	Transparency in governments: a meta-analytic review of incentives for digital versus hard-copy public financial disclosures	19
6	Brivot and Gendron (2011)	Beyond panopticism: on the ramifications of surveillance in a contemporary professional setting	17.5
7	Clarke (2020)	Digital government units: what are they, and what do they mean for digital era public management renewal?	15
7	Glotko et al. (2020)	Main trends of government regulation of sectoral digitalization	15
8	Chatfield and Reddick (2018)	The role of policy entrepreneurs in open government data policy innovation diffusion: An analysis of Australian federal and state governments	11.67
9	Safarov (2019)	Institutional dimensions of open government data implementation: evidence from the Netherlands, Sweden, and the UK	10.5

(continued)

Table 4 (continued)

Ranking	Reference	Contribution	CPY
10	Kagaari et al. (2010)	Performance management practices, information and communication technology (ICT) adoption and managed performance	3.64
11	Padovani et al. (2014)	Implementing change in a hospital management accounting system	3
11	Munteanu and Newcomer (2020)	Leading and learning through dynamic performance management in government	3
12	Clarke (2017)	Digital government units: origins, orthodoxy and critical considerations for public management theory and practice	2.7
13	Janjua et al. (2019)	Effective performance management of local governments in Khyber Pakhtunkhwa, Pakistan	2.5
14	Mahama et al. (2020)	New development: enabling enterprise risk management maturity in public sector organisations	2
15	Nielsen et al. (2016)	The power reinforcement framework revisited: mobile technology and management control in home care	1.6
16	Ertl et al. (2020)	Ensuring the success of management accounting change in IT departments of public organisations	1
16	Alkaabi et al. (2019)	Assets digitalization: exploration of prospects with better control implementation	1
17	Cosimato et al. (2015)	How to innovate management accounting for public sector: an Italian case study	0.67
18	Schmid (2017)	Big data public controlling fundamental changes in public management	0.5
19	Silva et al. (2013)	A collaborative model of information technology strategic plan for the government sector	0.25
20	Bray et al. (2020)	Performance management and evaluation meets culture and politics: Australia's experience	0
20	Cristofaro et al. (2020)	Measuring healthcare performance in digitalization era: The Pharmacy Unit of Academic Hospital	0
20	Magnusson et al. (2021)	Closeness and distance: configurational practices for digital ambidexterity in the public sector	0

(continued)

Table 4 (continued)

Ranking	Reference	Contribution	CPY
20	Zvereva et al. (2020)	Improving client-oriented approach in the provision of public services in the context of digitalization	0
20	Kurchenkov et al. (2020)	Features of the development of organizational structures of large Russian state-owned companies (based on the example of SC «Roskosmos», SC «Rostekhnologii», SC «Rosatom»)	0

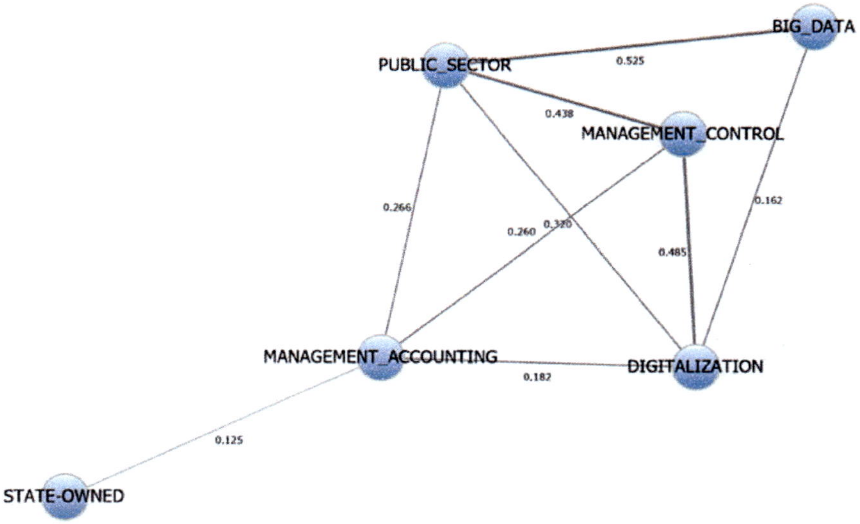

Fig. 2 Frequent pattern extraction (Keyword association: Association >0.4, strong association; 0.4> Association >0.2, moderate association; 0.2> Association, weak association)

focus on the combined use of these keywords. Figure 2 indicates the coefficients showing the influence and correlation among the keywords.

Figure 2 illustrates that public sector and big data, public sector and management control, and management control and digitalization show strong associations, confirming that these keywords are the most used and frequently matched. On the contrary, state-owned and management accounting, and management accounting and digitalization have weak associations. The relation between state-owned and digitalization or big data is almost non-existent because of the absence of these keywords in the contributions. This means that within the selected contributions, the public sector keyword is often used together with big data, suggesting that sometimes, big data is used synonymously as digitalization.

Table 5 Word frequency in contributions

Keywords	Frequency	Percentage (%)
PUBLIC_SECTOR	342	37.46
BIG_DATA	252	27.60
MANAGEMENT_ACCOUNTING	137	15.01
DIGITALISATION	121	13.25
MANAGEMENT_CONTROL	43	4.71
STATE-OWNED	18	1.97

A word frequency analysis was also executed to uncover the word count and the related percentage of occurrence in the selected contributions. More specifically, this analysis enhances the understanding of how many times a specific word appears within the contributions (Provalis Research, 2010). Detailed results of the word frequency are displayed in Table 5, which indicates the topics researchers are interested in, the areas less explored, and the emerging gaps that require attention.

The table above confirms that the main topics, on which researchers have focused so far, are public sector and big data, while management accounting and control, together with digitalization, are less investigated. This result already gives an idea of the topics that need further investigation.

4 Findings

Regarding the specific contents of the 27 contributions, Table 6 shows the results obtained from the coding of the contributions into the following six categories: (A) public sector entity, (B) country of research, (C) management control system, (D) digital tool, (E) research methods, and (F) theory or models.

4.1 *Public Sector Entity*

Concerning the types of public sector entity referred to in each contribution, nine different subcategories were used to classify the 27 contributions: central government (A1), state or regional government (A2), local government (A3), state-owned enterprises (A4), healthcare (A5), education (A6), public utilities (A7), a general subcategory, 'others,' used for contributions not referring to a specific public sector entity (A8), and mixed (A9) for contributions focusing on more than one type of public sector entity (mainly local government, healthcare, and education institutions).

Figure 3 shows that most of the contributions generically address the public sector (26%), are mixed (26%), and focus on state-owned enterprises (18%). Other contributions focus on state or regional governments (15%) and healthcare organizations

Table 6 Coding results

A	Public sector entity	No	%	B	Country of research	No	%
A1	Central government	1	4	B1	Africa	1	4
A2	State/Regional government	4	15	B2	Asia	5	19
A3	Local government	0	0	B3	Europe/UK	9	33
A4	State-owned enterprises (SOE)	5	18	B4	North America	0	0
A5	Healthcare organizations	2	7	B5	South America	1	4
A6	Education institutions	1	4	B6	Oceania	2	7
A7	Public utilities	0	0	B7	Not specified	7	26
A8	Others	7	26	B8	Mixed	2	7
A9	Mixed	7	26		*Total*	*27*	*100*
	Total	*27*	*100*				
C	**Management Control System**	**No**	**%**	**D**	**Digital tool**	**No**	**%**
C1	Strategic planning	4	15	D1	Information Technology (IT)	9	33
C2	Operating system	2	7	D2	E-government	1	4
C3	Business performances	7	26	D3	Mobile technologies and apps	1	4
C4	General management accounting system	14	52	D4	Open Data (OD)	3	11
				D5	Big Data	5	19
	Total	*27*	*100*	D6	Business analytics	2	7
				D7	Multiple tools	6	22
					Total	*27*	*100*
E	**Research methods**	**No**	**%**	**F**	**Theories or models**	**No**	**%**
E1	Case, field study, or interviews	12	44	F1	No model proposed	11	41
E2	Content analysis or historical analysis	1	4	F2	Application of previous models	11	41
E3	Survey, questionnaire, or other empirical work	2	7	F3	Proposition of a new model	5	18
E4	Commentary, normative work, or policy	1	4		*Total*	*27*	*100*
E5	Literature review	10	37				
E6	Mixed	1	4				
	Total	*27*	*100*				

(7%). Finally, a few contributions focus on central governments (4%) and education institutions (4%), while no contributions specifically concentrate on local governments (0%) and public utilities (0%). Local government and public utilities have received less attention because these two types of public sector organizations are included in the mixed category.

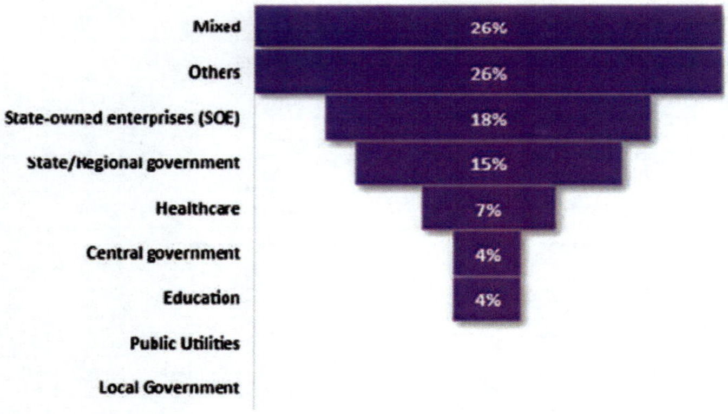

Fig. 3 Contribution distribution by public sector entity (%)

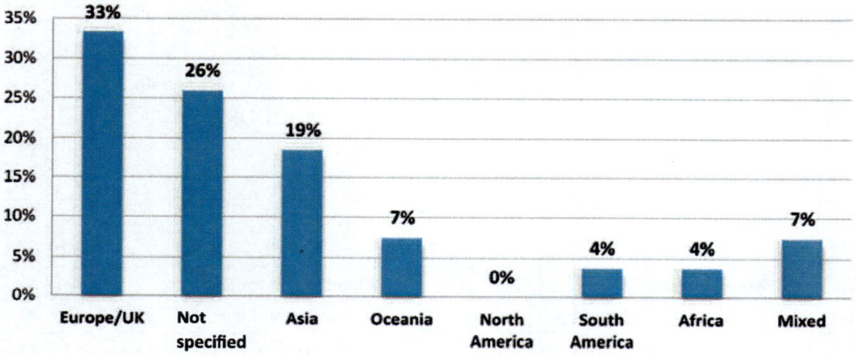

Fig. 4 Contribution distribution by country (%)

4.2 *Country of Research*

'Country of research' refers to the countries on which the contributions focus. Figure 4 presents the contribution distribution by country, showing that public sector research in Europe appears to be well-covered, with nine publications (33%). The contributions that focus on European countries are Italy (3), Germany (2), Sweden (2), France (1), United Kingdom (1), Denmark (1), and Netherlands (1). Some contributions investigate entities worldwide, not focusing on a single country. Such contributions are included in the category 'not specified,' which accounts for 26% of the publications. Another subcategory, 'mixed', includes contributions with more than one country or area (e.g. North and South America together). Figure 4 also shows that some geographical areas such as North America (0%), South America (4%), and Africa (4%) have received less attention.

4.3 Management Control System

The 27 contributions were classified into four types depending on the MCS referred to, namely, strategic planning, operating systems, business performances, and general management accounting systems. Figure 5 illustrates the category 'Management Control Systems' by percentage.

The previous figure four shows that the 27 contributions are quite balanced among the categories identified, with the exception of short-term systems, which are the least widespread. Half of the contributions in the 'general management accounting system' category focused on the public sector in general. Contributions on 'business performances' mainly covered the healthcare system (21%). In this respect, Padovani et al. (2014) highlighted that digitalization to promote organization and process changes have generated significant opportunities to improve overall performance (in terms of key performance indicators). Cristofaro et al. (2020) focused on IT support in public health organizations to improve performance. Maciejewski (2017) argued that big data enables better measurement of employee performance, with positive impacts on public performance. Kagaari et al. (2010) confirmed the positive relationship between performance improvement and information and communication technologies. Another study was carried out to fill the gaps among transparency, decision-making, performance, evidence-based policies and the evaluation of outcomes (Bray et al., 2020). Munteanu and Newcomer (2020) explained the performance measurement capabilities that managers should track to achieve their corporate objectives. Finally, two contributions about business performance focused on improving management performance in government. Chatfield and Reddick (2018) focused on the way to improve governance performance by shedding light on new public administration practices. Janjua et al. (2019) aimed to ensure successful accountability of public performances. Other contributions in business performance

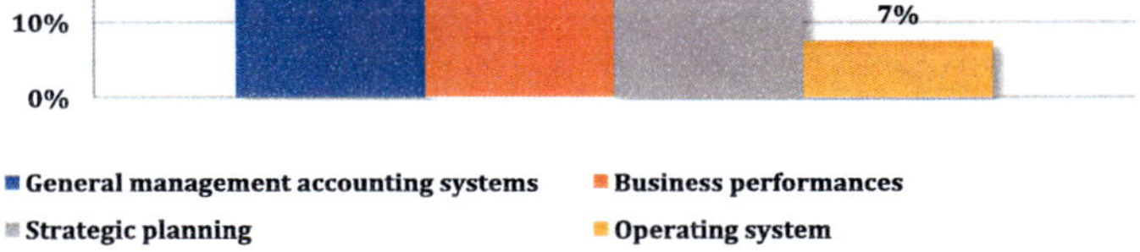

Fig. 5 Contribution distribution by type of management control system (%)

are classified into the subcategories state-owned enterprises, central government, education, and public sector in general, each at 16%. The contributions dealing with 'strategic planning' mainly concerned central governments (71% of all papers on strategic planning).

4.4 Digital Tools

Examining the digital tools treated in the contributions, Fig. 6 shows that the greatest focus is on information technologies (9), followed by multiple tools (this subcategory is used for contributions that refer to more than one digital tool; 6), Big Data (5), Open Data (3), Business analytics (2), E-government (1), and Mobile technologies & Apps (1).

The majority of the contributions focused on information technologies. Taipaleenmäki and Ikäheimo (2013) presented a new framework in which IT acts as a facilitator, promoter, motivator, or even enabler of MCS.

Other contributions emphasized IT's role of supporting performance monitoring in public healthcare to improve the quality of service (Cristofaro et al., 2020). Padovani et al. (2014), focusing on a hospital, analyzed how the implementation of low-cost IT can increase the efficiency and effectiveness of outcomes via improvements of its MCS. Meanwhile, Kagaari et al. (2010) demonstrated that it is fundamental to combine IT with MCS to achieve successful performance management.

The contributions categorized as 'multiple tools' focus on more than one digital tool and mainly includes contributions on e-government, mobile technology, and IT.

Referring to big data, Maciejewski (2017) identified the benefits, disadvantages, and challenges related to their use. Another paper argues about the use of new technologies and big data, opening up opportunities for strengthened evidence-based policy (Bray et al., 2020). Munteanu and Newcomer (2020) emphasized the need for tools and methods for big data analysis such as statistical modelling, data mining models, or machine learning.

Furthermore, Mahama et al. (2020) examined business analytics tools, highlighting their essential enabling role for an effective management accounting, and another work about e-government covered open innovation as an emerging concept that enhances solution-seeking for major policy and management issues (Chatfield & Reddick, 2018).

Nielsen et al. (2016) investigated mobile applications, indicating that the adoption of mobile technology into staff work routines is mainly valuable for administrative management. In this case, technologies can facilitate analytical decision-making for local and provincial supervisors and ensure effective accountability of government officials' performance.

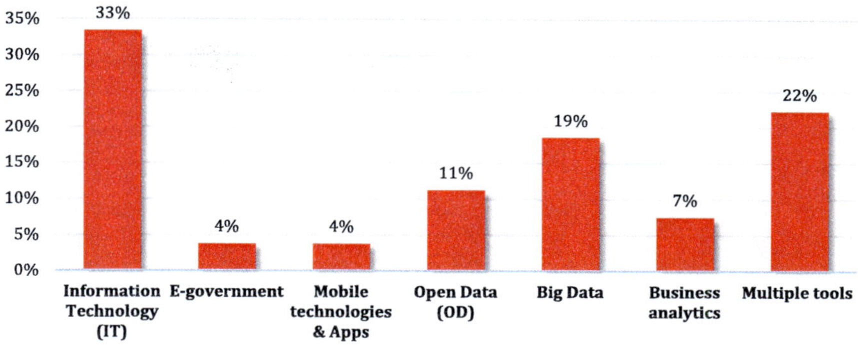

Fig. 6 Contribution distribution by digital tools (%)

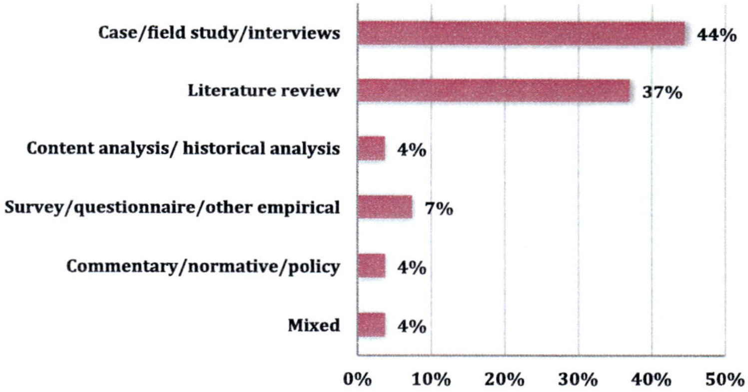

Fig. 7 Contribution distribution by research method (%)

4.5 Research Methods

The research methods adopted in the 27 studies were investigated. As shown in Fig. 7, the lowest-ranking subcategories are 'mixed (contributions that applied more than one research method)', 'commentary, normative work, or policy', and 'content analysis or historical analysis', each with 1 contribution (4% each), followed by 'survey, questionnaire, or other empirical work' (2 contributions, 7%). Scholars tend to use case and field studies, interviews (12 contributions, 44%), and the literature review (10 contributions, 37%).

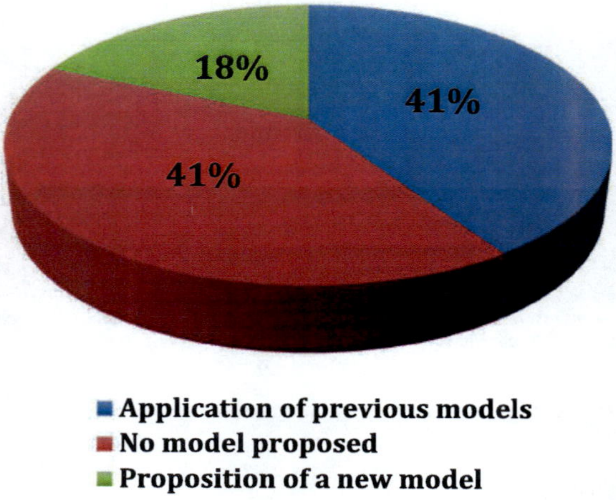

Fig. 8 Contribution distribution by framework or model used (nr.)

4.6 Theories and Models

The category 'theories and models' was adopted to classify whether contributions refer to any theory or model, apply an existing theoretical framework (a set of concepts logically connected and derived from one or more theories) used in the literature, or propose new theoretical frameworks. In the first case, the contribution is grounded in literature but does not recall any theory or model. In the second case (reference to previous models), the contributions refer to the theories or models existing in the literature. In the latter case (proposition of a new model), the studies explicitly develop a new theoretical framework or model related to digitalization. Figure 8 reveals that nearly half of the contributions (i.e. 11 contributions, 41%) ground their arguments in a model already developed in past literature, while 41% of the contributions (11 contributions) do not refer to any model.

Among the five contributions (18%) that propose a new model, some interesting issues emerged. Safarov (2019) presented the first attempt to describe open government data's institutional dimensions. The development of open data policy leads to the delivery of high performance and processing capabilities. The authors identified five different areas: organizational arrangements, public support and awareness, policy and strategy, and legislative foundations and relevant skills.

In the area of open data tools such as Safarov (2019), the article by Munteanu and Newcomer (2020) presented a framework based on open systems performance management and a model of leadership to orchestrate such systems. With this framework, managers can better monitor and measure performance and make strategic decisions to fulfil organizational goals.

The third article with a conceptual model is that of Silva et al. (2013), which is based on the IT strategic plan (ITSP) to identify organization's resources and IT in order to guide the technological and information infrastructure towards strategic goals. The authors filled the gap between IT governance and IT strategic planning with a model that enhances support for decision-making processes.

Ertl et al. (2020) applied a conceptual framework to a concrete case study of a public organization based on four organizational characteristics that influence IT accounting change. The structure enables in-depth insights into IT management accounting departments to discover the results that lead to an effective organizational transformation. This structure can be a powerful tool for effectively shaping the organizational transformation of management accounting, also through the identification of a hybrid department to enhance the dialogue between MCS and IT systems.

Finally, one article presented a mathematical model: Glotko et al. (2020) identified different scenarios to predict government regulation effects on companies and the ability to achieve the desired objectives. Specifically, the researchers proposed to use a framework consisting of four key elements: causes, aims, roles, and principles of government regulation, but it was not possible to identify a new theoretical framework.

5 Discussion

This chapter investigated the research question 'what main evidence does the current literature provide regarding the effects of digitalization on MCS in the public sector?'. The results highlight some relevant issues about the inclusion of digital tools in the MCS of public sector organizations, that is, the design of digital MCS and the influence of digitalization on management control processes.

Specifically, referring to MCS design, it emerged that further investigations are needed especially regarding digital tools. Furthermore, MCS should be better integrated with digital tools to improve their role in interpreting big data and supporting decisional processes, as argued by Nielsen et al. (2016) and Janjua et al. (2019). In addition, digital tools can simplify and optimize MCS in public sector organizations (Zvereva et al., 2020). Schmid (2017) claimed that MCS must take advantage of new technological tools especially since digitalization of MCS in the public sector is still at an embryonic phase, compared with the private sector. Mahama et al. (2020) concluded that business intelligence and analytics, together with MCS, enables effective management activities in public sector organizations, claiming that they can become pioneers through business intelligence and organizational analytics research.

Referring to the design of MCS, it emerged that digitalization allows improvement of the organizational structure and cross-border collaborations (Gao & Yu, 2020; Kurchenkov et al., 2020). Munteanu and Newcomer (2020) claimed that digitalization requires specific skills, especially statistics and database competencies, and an adaptable digital workforce.

In addition, regarding the influence of digitalization, Zvereva et al. (2020), Alcaide Muñoz et al. (2017), and Janjua et al. (2019) stated that the use of digital tools can improve public service accountability and effectiveness, a key aspect measured by

MCS, while other authors highlighted the key role of digital tools for the alignment between goals and actions (Munteanu & Newcomer, 2020; Silva et al., 2013), which is also relevant when implementing MCS.

It has also been observed that digitalization improves the procedures implemented in the public sector (Cristofaro et al., 2020; Kurchenkov et al., 2020), enhancing transparency, innovation, and the quality of public services (Alcaide Muñoz et al., 2017; Cosimato et al., 2015; Gao & Yu, 2020; Janjua et al., 2019; Nielsen et al., 2016; Safarov, 2019; Zvereva et al., 2020), as well as knowledge transfer (Brivot & Gendron, 2011; Wirtz et al., 2019). Furthermore, the efficiency can improve, thanks to the elimination of duplicate business departments and activities, automation and optimization of document and information flow (Gao & Yu, 2020; Kurchenkov et al., 2020), and avoidance of wasted time for both organizations and citizens (Alcaide Muñoz et al., 2017; Bray et al., 2020; Zvereva et al., 2020).

Glotko et al. (2020) reported a positive influence from the use of digital tools on labor productivity (measured by MCS), whereas the use of big data can support employee performance measurement and internal control improvement (Maciejewski, 2017). Finally, some advantages mainly associated with the distribution of organizational power and authority, one of the main issues to solve in MCS, have been observed from the use of mobile technology (Nielsen et al., 2016).

Furthermore, some new gaps, worthy of exploration, emerged. First, such topics remain underexplored in the public sector, requiring more quantitative studies based on surveys, to better generalize the evidence.

The literature review also revealed a lack of innovative technical solutions that can support MCS towards a better focus on government and citizen's needs (Zvereva et al., 2020). Furthermore, a criticism was raised by Cristofaro et al. (2020), highlighting a lack of conceptual models. Cristofaro et al. (2020) concluded that the details on key performance measurement technologies are currently not well understood.

In conclusion, digitalization and big data still have an unexpressed potential in terms of government decision-making processes (Bray et al., 2020) to underline new evidence or satisfy certain needs.

Finally, in the examined literature, mainly positive aspects of digitalization are considered, while difficulties, points of resistance, and the required investment to transition to digital MCS are still underexplored.

6 Conclusions and Implications

This chapter analyzed the state of the art of the literature on digitalization and management control in the public sector. It also identified gaps in the current literature on big data and MCS in public sector organizations through a systematic literature review.

According to the literature review, digitalization promotes organizational structure, cross-border collaborations, internal control, transparency, innovation, and the quality of public services. Furthermore, some researchers discovered that digitalization can simplify and optimize the implementation of management control and performance measurement systems, as well as optimize the time of both enterprises and citizens (Gärtner & Hiebl, 2017; Davenport, 2014; Manyika et al., 2011; McAfee & Brynjolfsson, 2012; McConnell, 2015; Wang et al., 2016).

Another finding is that digitalization can enhance efficiency and the alignment between goals and actions (Leonardi & Treem, 2020). We found that advantages generated by mobile technology are mainly associated with the distribution of organizational power and authority. However, on the downside, the literature review made it clear that digitalization requires specific skills (DeMauro et al., 2016; Wamba et al., 2015), especially statistics and database competencies, which makes it appropriate for the digital workforce. Regarding digital solutions and tools, they can be used to measure employee performance. Some researchers indicated a positive correlation between the use of digital tools and labor productivity (Merchant & Van der Stede, 2007).

There is an evident need to increase the knowledge about technology adoption and true integration with management control and performance measurement systems. This research also identified the absence of innovative technical solutions that facilitate interaction between the government and citizens (Bertot et al., 2010). Big data, generating value through high volume, velocity, and variety (DeMauro et al., 2016; Wamba et al., 2015), can be considered a key digital tool for supporting and improving government decision-making processes (Arnaboldi et al., 2017; Fredriksson et al., 2017). Furthermore, big data can provide valuable support to public managers in making more logical and informed decisions (Manyika et al., 2011). Unfortunately, digitalization is not yet successfully implemented in the public sector (Mullich, 2013).

In summary, this research provides an analysis of the state of the art of the literature on digitalization and MCS in the public sector context, increasing the knowledge for both managers and academics. This literature review provides practical contributions, because it enables public managers and practitioners to gain a better understanding of the status of, main features, benefits, and directions of digitalization and MCS. Furthermore, this review contributes to systematizing the existing literature and identifying gaps and future research avenues, providing several stimuli for researchers.

However, the present literature review has some limitations. First, it is based on a selection of papers published only in international academic journals, not taking into consideration studies elaborated by practitioners. Second, the parameters and keywords used when searching for the literature have an impact on the final sample and the results of the analysis. Third, the coding of the contributions was not always easy. For example, the categorization of the digital tools discussed in the contributions required a subjective classification, because such a classification is still lacking in the management control literature.

7 Future Research Agenda

This literature review has produced new insights into the digitalization in public organizations, especially focusing on MCS tools, design and processes. However, more research can be conducted in this field, for the systematization of this topic. Specifically, future studies could identify a classification of digital tools to generate homogeneity and comparability of the studies. Furthermore, it is necessary to investigate the usefulness of digital tools for measuring public sector organizations' performances and the link with the rewarded system, to enhance MCS capabilities and identify the needs of citizens. It is also important to dig deeper into the role of key digital competences in the public sector in improving management control. Additionally, further studies are needed to investigate in depth how digitalization influences the timing and structures of management control tools, as well as the negative effects of digitalization. Finally, future research can theorize the changes that public sector organizations implement when their MCS become increasingly digitalized. In this review, only loose theoretical frameworks were identified, while it would be interesting to observe this topic under the lens of theories such as the institutional theory or the actor–network theory.

References

The contributions marked with * are included in the systematic literature review.

*Alcaide Muñoz, L., Rodríguez Bolívar, M. P., & López Hernández, A. M. (2017). Transparency in governments: A meta-analytic review of incentives for digital versus hard-copy public financial disclosures. *The American Review of Public Administration, 47*(5), 550–573.

*Alkaabi, A. K. A. S., Karim, A. M., Hossain, M. I., & Nasiruzzaman, M. (2019). Assets digitalisation: Exploration of prospects with better control implementation. *International Journal of Academic Research in Business and Social Sciences, 9*(5), 619–629.

Anessi-Pessina, E., Barbera, C., Sicilia, M., & Steccolini, I. (2016). Public sector budgeting: A European review of accounting and public management journals. *Accounting, Auditing and Accountability Journal, 29*(3), 491–519.

Arnaboldi, M., Busco, C., & Cuganesan, S. (2017). Accounting, accountability, social media and big data: Revolution or hype? *Accounting, Auditing and Accountability Journal, 30*(4), 762–776.

Bertot, J. C., Jaeger, P. T., & Grimes, J. M. (2010). Using ICTs to create a culture of transparency: E-government and social media as openness and anti-corruption tools for societies. *Government Information Quarterly, 27*(3), 264–271.

Bhimani, A., & Willcocks, L. (2014). Digitisation, 'Big Data' and the transformation of accounting information. *Accounting and Business Research, 44*(4), 469–490.

Bonsón, E., Royo, S., & Ratkai, M. (2015). Citizens' engagement on local governments' Facebook sites. An empirical analysis: The impact of different media and content types in Western Europe. *Government Information Quarterly, 32*(1), 52–62.

*Bray, J. R., Gray, M. C., & Stanton, D. I. (2020). Performance management and evaluation meets culture and politics: Australia's experience. *Asia Pacific Journal of Public Administration, 42*(4), 290–302.

*Brivot, M., & Gendron, Y. (2011). Beyond panopticism: On the ramifications of surveillance in a contemporary professional setting. *Accounting, Organizations and Society, 36*(3), 135–155.

Caves, R. W. (Ed.). (2005). Encyclopedia of the city. *Taylor & Francis*. Available at: https://books.google.it/books?hl=en&lr=&id=xrD1iuM_2LgC&oi=fnd&pg=PP2&dq=Caves,+R.+W.+(Ed).+(2005).+Encyclopedia+of+the+City.+Taylor+%26+Francis.+&ots=2azGY3HIso&sig=QDuLKdBtl19_zzZlh9aUIIWjnEw&redir_esc=y#v=onepage&q=Caves%2C%20R.%20W.%20(Ed).%20(2005).%20Encyclopedia%20of%20the%20City.%20Taylor%20%26%20Francis.&f=false

*Chatfield, A. T., & Reddick, C. G. (2018). The role of policy entrepreneurs in open government data policy innovation diffusion: An analysis of Australian Federal and State Governments. *Government Information Quarterly, 35*(1), 123–134.

Chen, P. C. L., & Zhang, C. Y. (2014). Data-intensive applications, challenges, techniques and technologies: A survey on Big Data. *Information Sciences, 275*, 314–347.

CIMA (Chartered Institute of Management Accountants). (2008). Managerial paper 2: Management accounting—Decision making. Prepared by BPP Learning Media. London. Available at: https://www.cimaglobal.com

*Clarke, A. (2017). Digital government units: Origins, orthodoxy and critical considerations for public management theory and practice. *Social Science Research Network Electronic Journal.* Available at: https://doi.org/10.2139/ssrn.3001188.

*Clarke, A. (2020). Digital government units: What are they, and what do they mean for digital era public management renewal? *International Public Management Journal, 23*(3), 358–379.

Côrte-Real, N., Oliveira, T., & Ruivo, P. (2017). Assessing business value of Big Data Analytics in European firms. *Journal of Business Research, 70*, 379–390.

*Cosimato, S., Torre, C., & Troisi, O. (2015). How to innovate management accounting for public sector: An Italian case study. *Journal of US–China Public Administration, 12*(9), 695–705.

*Cristofaro, C. L., Ventura, M., Gentile, T. A. R., Reina, R., & De Francesco, A. (2020). Measuring healthcare performance in digitalisation era: The Pharmacy Unit of Academic Hospital. *Impresa Progetto—Electronic Journal of Management, 2*, 1–20. https://doi.org/10.15167/1824-3576/IPEJM2020.2.1289

Davenport, T. H. (2014). How strategists use "big data" to support internal business decisions, discovery and production. *Strategy and Leadership, 42*(4), 45–50.

De Mauro, A., Greco, M., & Grimaldi, M. (2016). A formal definition of Big Data based on its essential features. *Library Review, 65*(3), 122–135.

Dumay, J., Bernardi, C., Guthrie, J., & Demartini, P. (2016). Integrated reporting: A structured literature review. *Accounting Forum, 40*(3), 166–185.

Ertl, C., Herzfeldt, A., Floerecke, S., & Krcmar, H. (2020). Ensuring the success of management accounting change in IT Departments of Public Organisations. *International Journal of Service Science, Management, Engineering, and Technology, 11*(1), 142–156.

European Commission. (2010). Digitizing public services in Europe: Putting ambition into action. Prepared by Capgemini, IDC, Rand Europe, Sogeti and DTi for the European Commission, Directorate General for Information Society and Media. Available at: https://www.capgemini.com/se-en/wp-content/uploads/sites/29/2017/07/Digitizing_Public_Services_in_Europe__Putting_Ambition_into_Action.pdf

Fredriksson, C., Mubarak, F., Tuohimaa, M., & Zhan, M. (2017). Big data in the public sector: A systematic literature review. *Scandinavian Journal of Public Administration, 21*(3), 39–62.

Gandomi, A., & Haider, M. (2015). Beyond the hype: Big data concepts, methods, and analytics. *International Journal of Information Management, 35*(2), 137–144.

*Gao, X., & Yu, J. (2020). Public governance mechanism in the prevention and control of the COVID-19: Information, decision-making and execution. *Journal of Chinese Governance, 5*(2), 178–197.

Gärtner, B., & Hiebl, M. R. W. (2017). Issues with big data. In Quinn, M., & Strauß, E. (Eds.). *The Routledge companion to accounting information systems* (1st ed., pp. 161–172). Routledge..

*Glotko, A. V., Polyakova, A. G., Kuznetsova, M. Y., Kovalenko, K. E., Shichiyakh, R. A., & Melnik, M. V. (2020). Main trends of government regulation of sectoral digitalisation. *Entrepreneurship and Sustainability Issues, 7*(3), 2181–2195.

Heikkila, T., & Isett, K. R. (2007). Citizen involvement and performance management in special-purpose governments. *Public Administration Review, 67*(2), 238–248.

Isaacs, A. (1996). Oxford dictionary of physics. Available at: https://ui.adsabs.harvard.edu/abs/1996odph.book.....I/abstract

*Janjua, A., Attique, F., Raza, A., & Akbar, W. (2019). Effective performance management of local governments in Khyber Pakhtunkhwa, Pakistan. *International Journal of Productivity and Performance Management, 68*(1), 26-45.

Jarvenpaa, S. L., & Lang, K. R. (2005). Managing the paradoxes of mobile *technology. Information Systems Management, 22*(4), 7–23.

Jin, X., Wah, B. W., Cheng, X., & Wang, Y. (2015). Significance and challenges of big data research. *Big Data Research, 2*(2), 59–64.

*Kagaari, J. R. K., Munene, J. C., & Ntayi, J. M. (2010). Performance management practices, information and communication technology (ICT) adoption and managed performance. *Quality Assurance in Education, 18*(2), 106–125.

Kim, G. H., Trimi, S., & Chung, J. H. (2014). Big-data applications in the government sector. *Communications of the ACM, 57*(3), 78–85.

*Kurchenkov, V. V., Makarenko, O. S., Kurchenkova, M. V., & Brauweiler, H.-C. (2020). Features of the development of organisational structures of large Russian state-owned companies (based on the example of SC 'Roskosmos', SC 'Rostekhnologii', SC 'Rosatom'). In H.-C. Brauweiler, V. V. Kurchenkov, S. Abilov & B. Zirkler (Eds.), *Digitalisation and industry 4.0: Economic and societal development* (pp. 357–371). Springer Fachmedien Wiesbaden. https://doi.org/10.1007/978-3-658-27110-7_25.

Lankshear, C., & Knobel, M. (Eds.). (2008). *Digital literacies: Concepts, policies and practices 30.* Peter Lang. Available at: https://books.google.se/books?id=doVQq67wWSwC&printsec=frontcover&source=gbs_ge_summary_r&cad=0#v=onepage&q&f=false

Leonardi, P. M., & Treem, J. W. (2020). Behavioral visibility: A new paradigm for organisation studies in the age of digitization, digitalisation, and datafication. *Organization Studies, 41*(12), 1601–1625.

*Maciejewski, M. (2017). To do more, better, faster and more cheaply: Using big data in public administration. *International Review of Administrative Sciences, 83*(1_suppl), 120–135.

*Magnusson, J., Khisro, J., Björses, M., & Ivarsson, A. (2021). Closeness and distance: Configurational practices for digital ambidexterity in the public sector. *Transforming Government: People, Process and Policy, 15*(4), 420–441. https://doi.org/10.1108/TG-02-2020-0030

*Mahama, H., Elbashir, M., Sutton, S., & Arnold, V. (2020). New development: Enabling enterprise risk management maturity in public sector organisations. *Public Money and Management, 0*(0), 1–5. https://doi.org/10.1080/09540962.2020.1769314

Manes-Rossi, F., Nicolò, G., & Argento, D. (2020). Non-financial reporting formats in public sector organisations: A structured literature review. *Journal of Public Budgeting, Accounting and Financial Management, 32*(4), 639–669.

Manyika, J., Chui, M., Brown, B., Bughin, J., Dobbs, R., Roxburgh, C., & Hung Byers, A. (2011). Big data: The next frontier for innovation, competition, and productivity. *McKinsey Global Institute.* Available at: https://catalog.lib.kyushu-u.ac.jp/opac_detail_md/?lang=0&amode=MD824&bibid=3144682.

Mauro, S. G., Cinquini, L., & Grossi, G. (2017). Insights into performance-based budgeting in the public sector: A literature review and a research agenda. *Public Management Review, 19*(7), 911–931.

McAfee, A., Brynjolfsson, E., Davenport, T. H., Patil, D. J., & Barton, D. (2012). Big data: The management revolution. *Harvard Business Review, 90*(10), 60–6, 68, 128.

McConnell, A. (2015). What is policy failure? A primer to help navigate the maze. *Public Policy and Administration, 30*(3–4), 221–242.

Merchant, K. A., & Van der Stede, W. A. (2007). *Management control systems: Performance measurement, evaluation and incentives* (4th ed.). Pearson.

Milakovich, M. E. (2012). Anticipatory government: Integrating big data for smaller government. *Internet, politics, policy 2012: Big data, big challenges* Conference Proceedings. Available at: http://blogs.oii.ox.ac.uk/ipp-conference/sites/ipp/files/documents/Anticipatory%20Government%20Oxford.pdf

Mullich, J. (2013). Closing the big data gap in public sector. SURVEY REPORT. Real-time enterprise. Bloomberg Businessweek. Available at: https://www.sap.com/bin/sapcom/fr_be/downloadasset.2013-09-sep-23-16.closingthe-big-data-gapin-public-sector-pdf.html

*Munteanu, I., & Newcomer, K. (2020). Leading and learning through dynamic performance management in government. *Public Administration Review, 80*(2), 316–325.

*Nielsen, J. A., Andersen, K. N., & Danziger, J. N. (2016). The power reinforcement framework revisited: Mobile technology and management control in home care. *Information, Communication and Society, 19*(2), 160–177.

*Padovani, E., Orelli, R. L., & Young, D. W. (2014). Implementing change in a hospital management accounting system. *Public Management Review, 16*(8), 1184–1204.

Petticrew, M., & Roberts, H. (2006). Systematic reviews in the social sciences: A practical guide. *John Wiley & Sons.*

Podsakoff, P. M., MacKenzie, S. B., Lee, J. Y., & Podsakoff, N. P. (2003). Common method biases in behavioral research: A critical review of the literature and recommended remedies. *Journal of Applied Psychology, 88*(5), 879–903.

Provalis Research. (2010). WordStat 6, Content Analysis Module for QDA Miner & SimStat. User's Guide. Available at: https://www.provalisresearch.com/Documents/WordStat6.pdf

Quattrone, P. (2016). Management accounting goes digital: Will the move make it wiser? *Management Accounting Research, 31*, 118–122.

*Safarov, I. (2019). Institutional dimensions of open government data implementation: Evidence from the Netherlands, Sweden, and the UK. *Public Performance and Management Review, 42*(2), 305–328.

*Schmid, A. (2017). Big Data-public controlling fundamental changes in public management. *Public Policy and Administration, 16*(2), 325–334.

Shah, T., Bhatt, C. M., & Ganatra, A. P. (2014). Business analytics–applications and practices for continuous iterative exploration. *CSI Communications,* July, 10–13.

Shaw, J. (2014). Why "Big Data" is a big deal. *Harvard Magazine, 3*, 30–35.

*Silva, W. N., Vaz, M. A., & Souza, J. M. (2013). A collaborative model of information technology strategic plan for the government sector. *International Journal of Distributed Systems and Technologies, 4*(4), 29–38.

*Taipaleenmäki, J., & Ikäheimo, S. (2013). On the convergence of management accounting and financial accounting—The role of information technology in accounting change. *International Journal of Accounting Information Systems, 14*(4), 321–348.

Tammisto, Y., & Lindman, J. (2012, June). Definition of open data services in software business. In Cusumano, M. A., Iyer, B., & Venkatraman, N. (Eds.). *Software Business. Third International Conference, ICSOB 2012, Cambridge, MA, USA, June 18–20, 2012. Proceedings* (pp. 297–303). Springer.

Tranfield, D., Denyer, D., & Smart, P. (2003). Towards a methodology for developing evidence-informed management knowledge by means of systematic review. *British Journal of Management, 14*(3), 207–222.

Von Lucke, J. (2016). Smart government–the potential of intelligent networking in government and public administration. *In 2016 conference for e-democracy and open government (CeDEM)* (pp. 137–144). IEEE.

Wamba, S. F., Akter, S., Edwards, A., Chopin, G., & Gnanzou, D. (2015). How "big data" can make big impact: Findings from a systematic review and a longitudinal case study. *International Journal of Production Economics, 165*, 234–246.

Wang, G., Gunasekaran, A., Ngai, E. W. T., & Papadopoulos, T. (2016). Big data analytics in logistics and supply chain management: Certain investigations for research and applications. *International Journal of Production Economics, 176*, 98–110.

Wirtz, B. W., Weyerer, J. C., & Schichtel, F. T. (2019). An integrative public IoT framework for smart government. *Government Information Quarterly, 36*(2), 333–345.
*Zvereva, A., Ilyashenko, S., & Golubtsova, E. (2020). Improving client-oriented approach in the provision of public services in the context of digitalization. In *Proceedings of the "New Silk Road: Business Cooperation and Prospective of Economic Development" (NSRBCPED 2019),* Atlantis Press. *Advances in Economics, Business and Management Research, 131*, 566–569. https://doi.org/10.2991/aebmr.k.200324.105.

Laura Broccardo, Ph.D., is an Associate Professor in the Department of Management, University of Turin, Italy. Her research interests are in accounting and management control.

Elisa Truant, Ph.D., is an Associate Professor in the Department of Management, University of Turin, Italy. Her research interests are in the area of accounting and management control.

Daniela Argento, Ph.D., is an Associate Professor of Management Control and Accounting in the Department of Business at Kristianstad University, Sweden. She holds a PhD in Public Management and Regulated Sectors from the University of Siena, Italy and her research interests and publications are focused on governance, control and performance of public and hybrid organizations, smart cities, sustainable strategies implementation, as well as accounting change and corporate disclosure practices. Recent projects include Management Control and Control Systems, Strategy and Management Control, Accounting Theory, and Scientific Method.

Chapter 14
Applying Text Mining to Understand Customer Perception of Mobile Banking App

Mouri Dey, Md. Zahedul Islam, and Tarek Rana

Abstract In this big data age, it is imperative to replace the traditional data analysis techniques with big data analytics that can deal with both structured and unstructured datasets from various sources. This study's goal is to provide a method for analyzing unstructured data such as online customer reviews of mobile bank app to better understand customer perceptions. For analyzing customer online reviews, this study makes use of a text mining technique. Pre-processing of the extracted review data, analysis of the sentiment of each review, and an understanding of customer perception and evaluation are all part of the research process. This has come up with some important findings—when looking at it from the perspective of the customer, it was possible to determine which aspects of the app-based banking service are most important to them. As a result, service interruptions can be detected and avoided earlier, resulting in higher customer satisfaction levels. IBBL's bank management should focus more on expanding mobile banking's network reach from a practical standpoint. In order to prevent service failures, they can set up a systematic complaint management system that will allow them to identify and address customer complaints early. In this paper, we use sentiment analysis, one of the text mining applications, to measure service quality using customer reviews of a mobile bank.

Keywords Customer review · Text mining · Topic modeling · Customer perception · Mobile banking app · Performance measures

M. Dey · Md. Z. Islam
University of Chittagong, Chittagong, Bangladesh
e-mail: mouridey@cu.ac.bd

Md. Z. Islam
e-mail: zahedul.islam@cu.ac.bd

T. Rana (✉)
RMIT University, Melbourne, Australia
e-mail: tarek.rana@rmit.edu.au

T. Rana et al. (eds.), *Handbook of Big Data and Analytics in Accounting and Auditing*,
https://doi.org/10.1007/978-981-19-4460-4_14

1 Introduction

In commercial banks, digital servitization is a common practice that leverages the increasing use of smart devices and the internet to provide innovative and digitalized services to their customers, which results in fostering customer loyalty (KM, 2020; Payne et al., 2021; Van der Marel, 2020). With the rise of modern information and communication technologies (ICTs) and the resulting shift in people's lifestyles, banks now have an obligation to provide customers with newer and innovative products and services (Al-Dmour et al., 2020; Rahman & Abedin, 2021; Shankar et al., 2021). Mobile banking app is such type of convenient and smart digital solution for consumers. Therefore, people worldwide are increasingly using mobile banking apps to conduct financial transactions and other financial services, which is a significant trend (Khatun et al., 2021; Leem & Eum, 2021). M-banking is already being used by more than one billion people worldwide, and this number is expected to reach two billion users in just two years, based on Juniper Research's projections. As banking services become increasingly digital, banks are striving to find ways to work with their customers to create value together (Payne et al., 2021). While digital servitization has the potential to benefit both customers and the bank, research into how customers perceive app-based digital banking services is still scarce (Payne et al., 2021; Shaikh, Glavee-Geo, & Karjaluoto, 2021; Rasool et al., 2020). Thus, the aim of this study is to examine the customer perception and sentiments towards mobile app adoption for Islami Bank Bangladesh Ltd. which are critical for profitable service relationships.

Many advantages accrue to both consumers and banks when using a banking app. Services such as account opening, fund transfer, bill payment and account management are available to customers who don't need to visit a branch physically (Malaquias & Silva, 2020; Sharma & Al-Muharrami, 2018). In addition, banks can frequently interact one-on-one with customers to maintain their relationship with them. By adopting the mobile app, customers gain the ability to express their opinions, feedback, and feelings via reviews on a variety of social media platforms, providing banks with a new opportunity to maintain spontaneous attachment with their customers and ensure a sustainable competitive advantage.

Knowledge transforms and creates a new dimension for careful decision-making in various aspects of the organizations when there is an abundance of valuable unstructured data (Eberendu, 2016; Ho et al., 2020). Each second, customer reviews (both positive and negative) and interactions with businesses generate a massive amount of data that reflects the customer perception and intention to the adoption of a product or service. This data is displayed in a variety of forms, including texts, images, symbols and videos. Among all, voluminous textual data is posted frequently which can be extracted conveniently to display deeper insights and sentiments of people. Contrary to this, text data is frequently disorganized and difficult to decipher because of this. That's why business decision makers face significant challenges in dealing with such a large volume of data and extracting valuable insights, as traditional data analytics are unable to match requirements efficiently (Mannering et al., 2020). As a result, it is imperative to develop a mechanism for analyzing online customer feedback to understand customers' perception in order to resolve complaints and improve product or service attributes in future.

Various new techniques have been developed to handle the influx of data from a variety of sources. Sentiment analysis and topic modeling are drawing attention as a research method to understand consumers' in-depth thoughts in banking industry because online reviews and comments from customers have a significant impact on their purchasing decisions (Botchway et al., 2019; Permana et al., 2020). Sentiment analysis, a subset of text mining, applies natural language processing to determine whether the text data contains positive and negative views of individuals which is becoming an increasingly critical manifestation of customer satisfaction and service quality management research (Ali et al., 2020; Koren; Verkijika & Neneh, 2021; Zhao et al., 2019). Sentiment analysis and topic modeling are being applied in a wide range of fields to help with the limitations of existing sociological methods, such as quantitative and objective data that can help with qualitative opinions, extracting valuable information from main keywords, and the relationship between keywords (Jiin & Khamidi; Saputro et al., 2021). Furthermore, it detects the text's underlying emotions and establishes the coherence of the text's implicit topics. Consequently, this study proposes the use of sentiment analysis based on customer reviews to determine the polarity of customers' opinions.

Five sections make up this paper's structure. Section 2 provides an overview of the study's theoretical framework and literature review. Text mining, sentiment analysis, and understanding customer satisfaction using text mining are among the topics discussed. Section 3 goes into detail about the research methodology used to gather and analyze the data for this study, and Sect. 4 discusses the findings. Section 5 concludes with the conclusions and limitations of the study.

2 Literature Review

By facilitating accessibility, account management, transaction, customer service, and security, the use of mobile banking apps in banking operations and transactions adds value to financial services. People who use a mobile app encounter some issues and constraints, which they share or post in the form of a customer review on social media. Customer-generated data, such as online reviews, comments, and responses, has become increasingly important in maintaining customer relationships and idealizing customers' perceptions of a product or service (Xu, 2019). The rapid expansion of this user-generated information in the form of opinions and criticism has been made possible by digital customer-to-customer and customer-to-business interactions on various social media platforms (Xu, 2020). Studying product reviews is a good way to learn about what customers want and how to better serve them in a particular service (Frederick & Bhat, 2021). However, obtaining this important data, including a clear, complete image and quick processing, has always been difficult.

2.1 App-Based Banking Service

A great invention for conducting banking transactions with the help of wireless internet and today most popularly used banking application is named m-banking (mobile banking) (Mulia et al., 2020; Shahid et al., 2022). Among all the invention of applications, mobile banking app is the most effective one as it offers many advantages including security, convenience, ease-of-use, privacy, customization, control, interactivity and availability. Apps are specialized software that can be designed and used to complete specific tasks on a variety of platforms, including smartphones, tablets, and wearable devices. Moreover, it focuses on environmental preservation through energy and resource saving, speed and harmonizes vast customer community in home and abroad (Zahid et al., 2021). So, m-banking can be termed as "pocket bank" as it offers its services without any time and place restrictions (Zhang et al., 2018). Very recently, at the pick time of the COVID-19 pandemic, most of the customers have their banking transaction through mobile banking apps (including mobile financial services) and it creates a new banking experience opening up new opportunity in future (Mustafa, 2021). Besides that, with the rise of smartphones and the government's push for cashless transactions, the adoption of mobile and online banking is increasing at an unprecedented rate.

The majority of apps are available for download on their respective websites from app stores such as the Apple App Store, Google Play, and Amazon App Store (Farooqi et al., 2020; Venkatakrishnan et al., 2020). Large banks in Bangladesh perceive app-based internet banking as a way to focus on providing the best service in terms of security and advanced technology adoption, which has made banking services easily accessible, fast, and comfortable. Many Bangladeshi banks have developed their own internet banking apps to provide all of these services to their customers, recognizing the importance of service quality and customer experience. Customers' interest in mobile-based digital banking is growing, especially among the younger generation, which is more open to using new technologies like apps (M. Ahmed et al., 2020; Khan et al., 2021).

The first private sector Islamic bank in Bangladesh, Islami Bank Bangladesh Limited (IBBL), began its operations on March 13, 1983. The first Islami Bank in Bangladesh, with the largest customer network and more than 63% foreign shareholding, launched their internet banking service, IBBL iBanking, on June 21, 2007, with the strategic goal of ensuring customer satisfaction. According to its users' information IBBL iBanking turned into one of the biggest internet banking service provider of Bangladesh (Akter, 2020). Later it launched mobile app "ismart" for operating banking services in July 2020 (Fig. 1).

With a devotion to serve its customers in the age of digital banking, IBBL offers various services including fund transfer, check book requisition, mobile recharge, bill payment, account information etc. In this study, we have found that IBBL customer relationship department responds immediately (within a few hours/ a day) and shows interest on their customer comments and views. This app has been installed more than 5,00,000 times and rated 4.3. Moreover, users of mobile banking apps can rate

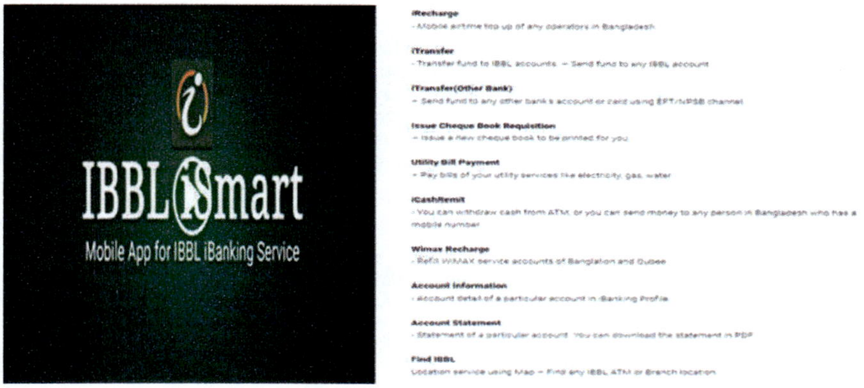

Fig. 1 ismart at a glance (*Source* https://play.google.com/store/apps/details?id=com.ionicframework.icellular894076&hl=en&gl=US)

and review apps in app stores which is a new platform for banks to receive timely feedback from the customers. Besides that, new or potential app users may get useful ideas and information for the review section of the app store.

2.2 Customer Perception of Mobile Banking App

Customer perception refers to how customers perceive a product or a brand. Among many internal and external sources, in recent times online review is an important source to extract and shape customer perception (Auliya et al., 2017). It's an opinion or reaction formed when people notice advertisements, promotions, customer reviews, social media feedback and responses from the company through every direct and indirect interaction. Products/services displaying good rating and reviews create positive impression about the service in the mind of the customers that affect purchase decision of the potential customers (Dwidienawati et al., 2020).

In cross-country perspective, various dimensions have been identified that influence customer perception for mobile banking. Perceived usefulness, relative advantage, quality of system, personal innovativeness, loyalty, usability and self-efficiency are positively perceived by the customers while adopting mobile banking (Esmaeili et al., 2021; Khoa, 2020; Kumar & Shenbagaraman, 2017; Payne et al., 2018). Another study in Bangladesh showed that the most influencing factor is Social influence in adopting mBanking. Besides, Task-technology fit, Technology characteristics, Performance expectancy, Facilitating conditions, Task characteristics, and User adoption have great influence on users' perception and attitude towards mobile banking services (Z. Ahmed et al., 2017). In Malaysia, privacy has been identified as one of the most important influencer to customer perception of mobile banking users

(Tham et al., 2017). In another multi-country study, benefits, trust, loyalty and positive word-of-mouth are positively related with customer satisfaction (Arcand et al., 2017; Sampaio et al., 2017). Mobile self-efficacy, social influence and customer support also influence customer perception (Singh & Srivastava, 2020). In order to customize services by incorporating prerequisites and encouraging the use of mobile banking apps, it's important to examine customers' mindsets and perceptions.

2.3 Text Mining and Sentiment Analysis as Techniques for Extracting Reviews

Text mining is a data analysis technique most widely used technique to elicit strategic information from textual sources like full-text documents, emails, and HTML files. It focuses on extracting business insights by discovering the hidden patterns, user sentiment, themes and topics from textual elements such as posts, comments, reviews, tweets, and blog posts from various social online platforms (Kim et al., 2019). It helps get a sense of peoples' feeling about a brand or a new product quickly and accurately (Mhamdi et al., 2018; Wang et al., 2018). Sentiment analysis, a text mining tool, widely being used to extract either positive or negative reviews or comments of a product or service which is useful to identify the polarity and intensity of sentiments (Chintalapudi et al., 2021; Moutidis & Williams, 2020; Nawab et al., 2020; Neuraz et al., 2020). Sentiment analysis is the use of natural language processing that can be applied to scan online information in order to identify important issues, major problems, and new events. Some of the most commonly used sentiment analysis algorithms include SVM (Support Vector Machine), Naive Bayes, Maximum Entropy, and Matrix Factorization (Mehta et al., 2021).

Questionnaire based survey has been applied for long to measure service quality. However, one disadvantage of this approach is that conducting a survey, collecting required responses, analyzing and interpreting the results to assess service quality takes a significant amount of time and money (Mikalef et al., 2018). Large and diverse data sets from various sources are also increasing enormously, effectively replacing traditional data analytics and transforming the dimension of managerial decision-making in this regard (Wolfert et al., 2017). Businesses can leverage big data analytics to scan and extract useful information from online customer reviews and make data-driven decisions that result in improved business outcomes including improved marketing effectiveness, new revenue opportunities, customer personalization, and operational efficiency. In this connection, machine learning and natural language processing offer some advanced tools that have made it possible to mine voluminous online reviews or texts to supplement or replace traditional methods of service quality measurement and enhancement (Das & Islam, 2021; Muktafin, 2021). Although sentiment analysis has been used to measure service quality in a variety of fields, very few studies has been done on the customer perception of mobile banks using this method. As a result, this study suggests employing sentiment analysis to extract online reviews of Islami Bank's bank app in order to understand and evaluate app users' perceptions, which would help bank management comprehend and focus on customer complaints and concerns in order to improve and diversify services in future.

3 Research Framework

The growth of app based digital banking service has been drawing much attention from customers specially the young generation who are accommodative with adopting digital applications. In this age of increasing smart phone users, mobile app based services are have made banking services easily accessible, fast and comfortable. Keeping this in mind, Islami Bank Bangladesh Ltd (IBBL) has introduced '*ismart*', a mobile app to conduct banking services 24 hours (Fig. 2).

Customer perception is a concept that explains why people act in certain ways and holds certain beliefs about various aspects of life. Self-perception, price perception, and perception of a benefit to one's quality of life are the three categories (Saleem et al., 2015).

Customer perception is heavily influenced by the positive and negative experiences that customers have when interacting with a brand. When a customer posts a review or an opinion about a product, he or she is actually revealing the truths or perceptions about the product. When businesses understand what benefits their customers want, they can focus their efforts on communicating those benefits and, hopefully, creating favorable benefit perceptions in their target market (Veríssimo, 2016). This study's research framework proposed natural language processing as a method for extracting and analyzing app users' reviews in terms of underlying topics so as to comprehend how customers feel about the app and what more they are expecting from this service.

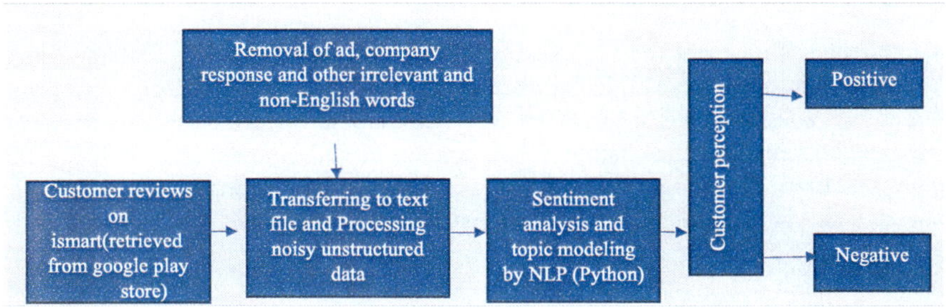

Fig. 2 Research framework

4 Research Methodology

4.1 Research Design

Sentiment analysis has been applied to gauge how customers feel about a bank's mobile app. As a classifier for sentiment analysis, this study utilized Naive Bayes and unsupervised learning approaches (Leem & Eum, 2021). Identifying the sentiment of a mobile bank app review allows us to better understand customer satisfaction, as well as determine the correctness of the sentiment identifier and assess the overall perception of the customers (Leem & Eum, 2021). The sentiment polarity and accuracy of the sentiment analysis are obtained by running natural language technique on users' review data which are noisy and unstructured.

4.2 Research Methods

This section describes how to measure customer perception with the help of user reviews left for Islami Bank Limited Mobile Bank app named ismart. The research procedure includes: (1) extracting users' reviews for Islami bank mobile app from google play store, (2) pre-processing the extracted review data, (3) analyzing the sentiment of each review, (4) understanding perception of consumers by analyzing keyword frequency and network for each polarity, and (5) identifying the key issues that the customers perceive about ismart. Specialized techniques for Machine Learning and Nvivo 12 have been applied for text mining and sentiment analysis respectively.

4.3 Data Collection

We collected data from the Google Play Store for app reviews for Islami Bank. WebHarvy has been operated to extract text data from online customer reviews from September, 2020 to September, 2021. Over 10,000 reviews have been extracted. The extracted contents include customers' comments, company's response, name of the reviewers, likes, symbols and date. After removing symbols, emoticons, non-English language and advertising reviews, 7700 reviews were analyzed.

4.4 Data Pre-processing

Filtering was done at this level to remove words like advertisements, spam, or simple duplicate messages from the raw data that had just been collected. To improve the

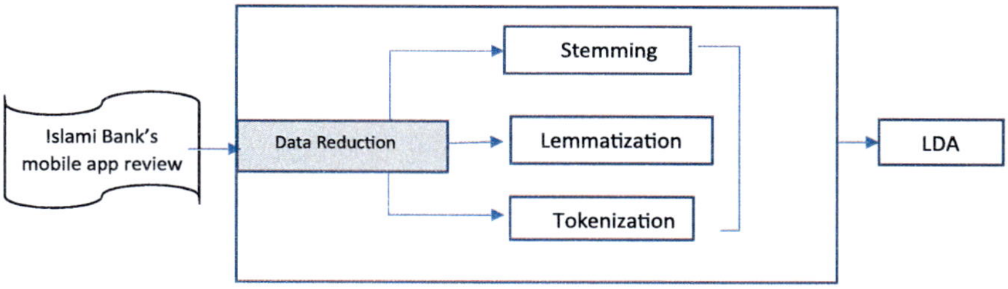

Fig. 3 Data pre-processing

accuracy of the sentiment analysis, we had to convert unstructured data into structured data and remove unnecessary data variables in the pre-processing phase. So, three steps were used to pre-process the data, as shown in Fig. 3. The first step in the data pre-processing process was to tokenize the documents that were extracted from Islami Bank's mobile app review. This process broke down the documents into their parts and turned the sentences into meaningful tokens. The second step was to remove the words that were not important to the study. The third step put the pieces of speech together. This study grouped the words into nouns, adjectives, and adverbs that show how mobile banking services look.

5 Results and Findings

5.1 Term Frequency

Among the 53,909 words to be analyzed from Islami Bank's app reviews from google play store, 7700 words with a word length of two or more letters and TF-IDF (Term Frequency—Inverse Document Frequency) of 0.5 or more were extracted and summarized as listed in Table 1.

The most common word was "good," with 1061 mentions, and other words such as "coverage," "app," "bank" and "nice" were also common. These are all positively mentioned. However, there were also negative words such as "inconvenience," mentioned 114 times. Figure 2 visualizes the word cloud of top 50 most frequent words mentioned in the customer review.

5.2 Sentiment Analysis

The sentiment analysis of 7700 reviews of Islami Bank showed that 61.38% (4727 reviews) of users had a positive sentiment while 6.03% (465 reviews) of users expressed a negative sentiment for this app. This means that while using the mobile

Table 1 Word frequency

Word	Count	Word	Count
Good	1061	thanks	76
Coverage	318	Islami bank	74
apps	300	bill	69
bank	263	problem	68
nice	250	Bangladesh	67
ibbl	173	money	66
account	149	need	64
banking	146	love	61
like	139	better	59
excellent	138	really	57
please	124	update	55
inconvenience	114	email	54
service	105	number	54
time	101	bkash	51
useful	101	branch	51
awesome	90	payment	49
best	90	application	48
great	89	using	48
system	87	smart	46
easy	86	ismart	45
login	85	card	44
transfer	84	ibanking	44
helpful	82	many	44
option	82	just	43
password	79		

bank app, most users are satisfied with the ismart app service and provide a positive response in the form of a positive review. However, the fact that user reviews with negative polarity account for 6.03% of all reviews may lead to negative word of mouth effects. To determine how well the sentiment polarity was classified in the above sentiment analysis, we calculated the accuracy, precision, recall and F-score using the formula in Table 2. Accuracy and recall were high at 84.11 and 94.35%, respectively, while precision was 84.39%. If F-score is more than 70%, it is acceptable (Kwabla et al., 2021).

After conducting sentiment analysis, topic modeling was performed on customer reviews. It was performed to understand the perception of users of mobile app to avail banking service. In this study, we used topic modeling and extracted topic by applying the most widely used LDA (Latent Dirichlet Allocation) algorithm (Amado et al., 2018; Ning et al., 2021).

5.3 Confusion Matrix

A Confusion matrix is an N x N matrix used for evaluating the performance of a classification model, where N is the number of target classes. The matrix compares the actual target values with those predicted by the machine learning model. Confusion matrix gives a holistic view of the performance of machine learning model (Normah, 2019). In this study a confusion matrix is run with the Scikit-learn (sklearn) library in Python.

This matrix produces four outcomes:

True positive (TP): correct positive prediction
False positive (FP): incorrect positive prediction
True negative (TN): correct negative prediction
False negative (FN): incorrect negative prediction

The following matrix can be used to evaluate the performance of a model through the calculation of performance measures like accuracy, precision, recall, and F1-score.

Predicted polarity		Actual polarity	
		Positive	Negative
	Positive	903(TP)	54(FN)
	Negative	167(FP)	267(TN)

Note(s): TP: True Positive, FP: False Positive, FN: False Negative, TN: True Negative

Accuracy: 84.11%; *Precision*: 84.39%; *Recall:* 94.35%; *F score*: 0.8909

Perplexity: − 7.122926519569981 *Coherence*: 0.39307031157060907

5.3.1 Accuracy

Accuracy (ACC) is calculated as the number of all correct predictions divided by the total number of the dataset. The best accuracy is 1.0, whereas the worst is 0.0.

Accuracy = TP + TN/TP + TN + FN + FP

5.3.2 Precision

Precision (PREC) is calculated as the number of correct positive predictions divided by the total number of positive predictions. It is also called positive predictive value (PPV). The best precision is 1.0, whereas the worst is 0.0.

Precision = TP/(TP + FP)

5.3.3 Recall/Sensitivity

Sensitivity (SN) is calculated as the number of correct positive predictions divided by the total number of positives. It is also called recall (REC) or true positive rate (TPR). The best sensitivity is 1.0, whereas the worst is 0.0. Recall = TP/(TP + FN).

5.3.4 F1 Score

The F-score, also called the F1-score, is a measure of a model's accuracy on a dataset. The F-score is commonly used for evaluating the retrieved information search engines when processed in natural languages. The formula for the standard F1-score is the harmonic mean of the precision and recall. A perfect model has an F-score of 1.

$$F_1 = \frac{2}{\frac{1}{\text{recall}} \times \frac{1}{\text{precision}}} = 2 \times \frac{\text{precision} \times \text{recall}}{\text{precision} + \text{recall}} = \frac{\text{tp}}{\text{tp} + \frac{1}{2}(\text{fp} + \text{fn})}$$

5.4 Word Cloud

Word cloud on top 50 frequently mentioned words in the customer reviews. In a word cloud, each word's size indicates its frequency or importance in a given text or subject.

Figure 4a presents top 50 positive reviews. Here the word with biggest size is "coverage". Next comes "account" and "excellent". In Fig. 4b, top 50 negative reviews have been presented. Word with biggest size is "password", then comes "account".

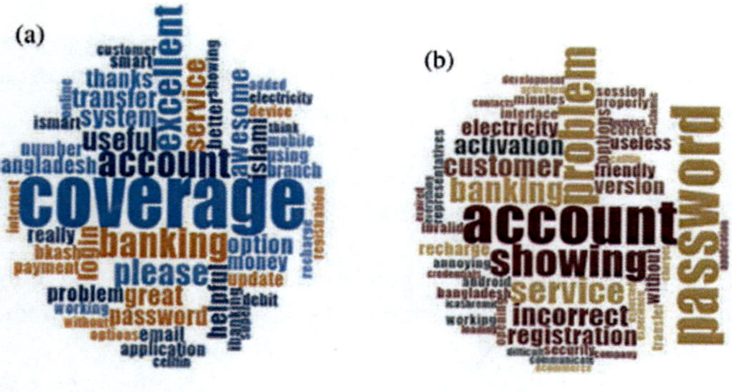

Fig. 4 (**a**) Word cloud (positive reviews), (**b**) Word cloud (negative reviews)

5.5 *Topic Modeling*

Topic modeling is a type of statistical modeling for discovering the abstract "topics" that occur in a collection of documents. Latent Dirichlet Allocation (LDA) is an example of topic model and is used to classify text in a document to a particular topic. It builds a topic per document model and words per topic model, modeled as Dirichlet distributions. The latent Dirichlet allocation (LDA) allows modeling different topics, previously defined according to the distribution of the different terms across reviews (Jeong et al., 2019; Permana et al., 2020). It allows determining the probability of the chosen review belonging to each topic, grouping reviews according to their proximity regarding each considered term. It also helps in identifying which topics are capturing more attention and in finding gaps for future research.

5.5.1 Topic, Sentiment and Frequency

See Table 2.

5.5.2 Topic Visualization

pyLDAVis is the most commonly used and a nice way to visualize the information contained in a topic model. The blue bar width represents the broad frequency of each term, and the width of the red bar represents the specific frequency of the topic for each term (Fig. 5).

When a user moves their mouse over each image (in the tools), a slider appears that allows them to adjust how terms are ranked in the image. Users can quickly determine if a term is highly relevant to the selected topic because of its lift (a high ratio of red to blue) or its probability (a lower ratio of red to blue) (absolute width of red).

5.5.3 Customer Complaints

Upon generating the inherent topics in the corpus, we attempted to identify the relevant concerns that surround the individual topic (Table 3).

Topic modeling revealed four complaint areas namely activation (31%), lack of support service (27%), connectivity (25%) and inconvenience (25%) were summarized and categorized (17%). Following is a list of the four customer complaints and their key words that were retrieved.

Table 2 Review topic, sentiment and frequency

Topic	Representative reviews	Sentiment	Frequency
Performance	Superb apps. I'm just enjoying this app. I feel comfortable when I use this apps for mobile recharge, money transfer to others bank and etc. this apps are very helpful to me but this apps have one bad side that's when I type my email and password and others information then apps is didn't show the letters if IBBl solve it then it'll be well for us… However, thanks a lot IBBl. we're gratitude to IBBL for such a apps ☺😊😍	**Positive**	**1061**
Email	Utter Rubbish, emailed them so many times for years about my issue logging in, no one gets back. when i try login, it says it'll send me an activation email but i never gets the email no matter how many times i try no matter whatever device i try from either android or iOS. simply rubbish…	**Negative**	**33**
Fund Transfer	This is such a wonderful and very helpful app I have ever seen. Islami bank is one of the best banks of our country and also i banking services. As a well-wisher i have a request to ibbl i banking service that fund transfer to mobile banking like bkash, nagad, rocket should be added in the feature of i banking service in the future…	**Mixed**	**66**

(continued)

Table 2 (continued)

Topic	Representative reviews	Sentiment	Frequency
Managing Bank Account	I think It must Add DPS system. Open a DPS in Apps its very helpful for NRB and General People. Such as this system will make more Customers for Your Bank. And Also Add bkash System also. But over all its good apps from IBBL Bank. Thank. Please add all government payment system. Like NID card renew fee Payment. Icashremit service make easy. Make it like DOHA BANK D cardless withdraw. Step-1 Just enter beneficiary number, amount, Tpin and get reference number. send reference to beneficiary. Step-2 Beneficiary just enter his number, enter amount, enter reference number and get OTP from his mobile number, enter OTP. That's it. There no need to register beneficiary. Q. how many beneficiary i can add in ibbl ismart app? Variant types of applications form should be attached to website including (ibanking mobile number change form, dormant account activation form) so that we can perform our ibanking activities without going to branch in person, hoping for the best, Thank You. How can i get the mobile number changing form without signing in? Nice App. very helpful. But the option "download statement" doesn't work properly	**Mixed**	**97**

(continued)

Table 2 (continued)

Topic	Representative reviews	Sentiment	Frequency
Password	Ridiculous Apps. This is worth less app. No update it long time. Forgot password still not working. Shame this digitalization Please inform me the information that, Now I am in Abroad, my mobile not working to get OTP, How I will get OTP by Email If you could add OTP verification via email, we could have used from abroad. I find this app good; however, because OTP verification cannot be done via email, I'm using other bank because they offer OTP verification over email OTP code sending options is so bad, OTP is not working properly, if you informed call center agent, they said we are noted and our team will communicate with you but they will never communicate with you, months to months pass but you can find any solution from Islamic Bank Bangladesh limited Apps is good but f..king OTP system not working. I called many times to head office duty officer (16,259) but nobody solved the problem. First time they say debit not activated then I went to bank for debit activation. Bank officer activated my debit but still same problem. Again, I called 2–3 times to head officers by 16,259 still can't solve the problem. They again say your problem we are noted down. Ohh one more issue email….. I emailed to them with attachment but nobody replies	**Negative**	**29**

(continued)

Table 2 (continued)

Topic	Representative reviews	Sentiment	Frequency
Utility Bill	Everything is perfect but one thing. That is palli biddut prepaid and postpaid. We need it as soon as possible Nice app. Suggestions: 1. Fund transfer to MFS like mcash, bkash, rocket, nagad etc. should be added. 2. Electricity bill payment to Palli Bidyut Prepaid Meter should be added. 3. Add money to other bank accounts or cards should be added. 4. e-commerce to popular sites like daraz, e-valley, bagdoom, ajker deal etc. should be available. 5. Online purchase tickets of bus/railway/airways/launch should be added. 6. Existing services of ibblportal should be available	**Negative**	**54**
Inconvenience	App is good but user not showing all account at a time. Example: account, DPS, credit card. It's helpful very much for user. I can't access to my account even after input my password user I'd. Every time it shows me that service unavailable. Second time I want to log in through another device. Then it showed me that device info, user name, password all are incorrect. Now tell me what to do. It is really disappointing	**Negative**	**258**
Service	Very fantastic and user friendly app The App is very handy This is such a wonderful and very helpful app i have ever seen Easy to use Comfortable and safe superb apps. I'm just enjoying this app!	**Positive**	**147**
Interaction	Smart app Quick service Time saving Customer care dept interacts with the customer one to one regularly	**Positive**	**561**

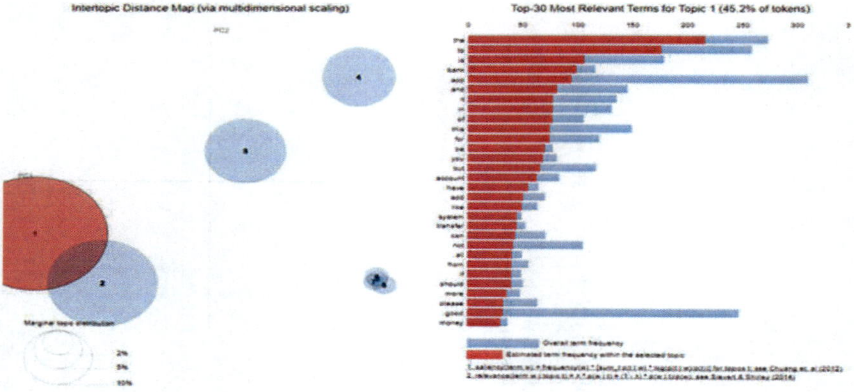

Fig. 5 Topic visualization

Table 3 Topics of customer complaints

Complaints	Words	Percentage
Activation problems	Registration, technology, capacity, maintenance, OTP	31
Unavailability	Utility, Electricity bill, bkash, inconvenience, remote	27
Connectivity	Network, slow, speed, email	25
Inconvenience	Uncomfortable, reinstall, interface, transaction	17

5.6 *Evaluation of Topic Modeling*

The topics generated from the corpus can be evaluated by measuring two popular scores. One is perplexity and another is coherence of topics.

5.6.1 Perplexity

In information theory, perplexity is a measurement of how well a probability distribution or probability model predicts a sample. It may be used to compare probability models. A low perplexity indicates the probability distribution is good at predicting the sample. In this study, the perplexity score is -7.122926519569981. The perplexity, used by convention in language modeling, is monotonically decreasing in the likelihood of the test data, and is algebraically equivalent to the inverse of the geometric mean per-word likelihood. A lower perplexity score indicates better generalization of performance.

5.6.2 Coherence

Topic Coherence measures score a single topic by measuring the degree of semantic similarity between high scoring words in the topic. These measurements help distinguish between topics that are semantically interpretable topics and topics that are artifacts of statistical inference. The coherence score is for assessing the quality of the learned topics. Coherence Score: 0.39307031157060907.

6 Findings and Discussion

This study proposed a method to measure the customer perception, service quality and to find out customer satisfaction with regards to mobile banking apps of Islami Bank Bangladesh Ltd through text mining approach. Over 10,000 reviews related to the Bank were extracted from the Google Play Store, and we have analyzed 7700 comments after removing reviews having advertisement and duplicity. The sentiment analysis interprets that a significant portion (61.38%) of customers shows a positive sentiment while negative sentiment carries a lower weight (6.03%)for Islami Bank app. A significant portion of user community share their positive reviews by mentioning nice, thanks, convenience, good and easy. Some comments contain the word inconvenience, problem when they are facing problems related to utility bills and password issues.

To determine the sentiment polarity was classified in the above sentiment analysis, we calculated the accuracy, precision, recall and F-score. Where accuracy and recall were high at 84.11 and 94.35%, respectively, while precision was 84.39%. If F-score is more than 70%, it is acceptable. Based on this we calculate confusion matrix which produces four outcomes. The result shows highest 903 reviews was true positive (TP) which indicates absolute satisfaction about the mobile app while 267 reviews was true negative (TN) shows absolute dissatisfaction. The remaining reviews are not easily determine with false positive (FP) of 167 and false negative (FN) of 54.After conducting sentiment analysis, topic modeling was performed on customer reviews. It was performed to understand the perception of users of mobile app to avail banking service.

Topic modelling identified 9 major topics covering the captured reviews namely performance, email, fund transfer, account management, password, utility, account, service and delivery of service. Customers are highly satisfied with the performance of the app as the word convenience, availability of services, coverage, connectivity, and activation. Convenience indicates ease of use at the time of completing monetary transactions or other financial assistance by using a mobile banking apps. Mobile banking app use is associated with low apparent risk, high compatibility, high perceived ease of use, and high perceived usefulness accordingly low compatibility, low useful and ease of use and high apparent risk indicating less use of the apps (Veríssimo, 2016). Easy connectivity of the apps including exchange comfort, and ownership/post-ownership comfort anticipate m-banking adoption expectation, with the central driver being the belonging/post-ownership comfort (Shankar & Rishi, 2021).Perceived Transaction Convenience (PTC) having a significant positive relationship with Effort Expectancy (EE) and Performance Expectancy (PE) accordingly identify the behavioral intention of the customers of the respective mobile banking apps (Teo et al., 2015). Banks ought to publicize and advance portable banking through handsets and live show counters at chosen branches monitored by a committed staff to embrace different special exercises for upgrade in computerized proficiency and monetary consideration with other government plans also draw in its clients to introduce banking Apps like BHIM, PhonePe, Payment Banks, and so on to office easy counts on their own palms (Tamilselvi & Balaji, 2019).

On the other way, protection and security, client service, intuitiveness, productivity, and content were the key aspects for ensuring key success of the m-banking apps (Shankar et al., 2020). Services also includes trust which ensures security/privacy and responsibility/fulfillment through enjoyment and sociality (Arcand et al., 2017b). All the services will assist saves money with understanding buyers' assumptions, and give bearings to giving quality m-banking services (Shankar et al., 2020).

Organizations are making better than ever ways for connecting with and including their consumers, and one huge instrument presently involved by organizations for these designs is the application. Companies are creating new and improved ways for engaging and involving their consumers, and one significant tool now used by companies for these purposes is the app. Customers who have cost-and hazard related reservations in regards to application use, promotional activities should impart data which will help them in effectively exploring the applications, assist with establishing more consumer-friendly environments, and provide them with promising circumstances for more savvy choices (Alavi & Ahuja, 2016). Accordingly bank performance does improve on the balance sheet and in customer conversion/retention when the bank has leading-edge mobile banking features along with disciplined cost reduction in front-line tellers and reduction in brick-and-mortar investments. At last, the review shows the fundamental administration suggestions and identifies specific procedures to build up this new business with regards to new innovative advances at the mobile banking application (Muñoz-Leiva et al., 2017).

At last, the review shows the fundamental administration suggestions and identifies specific procedures to build up this new business with regards to new innovative advances at the mobile banking application.ismart users are seemed to be comfortable using it, and they appreciate how well-designed and intuitive it is. Most of the positive reviews focused on how many people were covered by this app-based service's network. As a result of topic modeling, we also gathered negative sentiments, which were depicted in the reviews of customers.

7 Limitations and Future Research

The service quality of the mobile banking app is not the main focus in this study, though the customer perception is trying to identify through subjective judgement. Perception has been gauged only from their online reviews ignoring other social platforms. However, the results of previous studies and the discernment of experts in the relevant field may help alleviate some of this limitation of unstructured data. Future research can be drawn more meaningful results by classifying keywords in terms of service quality and integrating text mining and quantitative study. Secondly, it is considered an influential study to identify the possibility of failure by the intensity of customer complaints and generate a strategy for quick detection and response of failure. Future customer behavioural research should be able to expand by comparing variables of customer complaint and behaviour analysis via customer review analysis.

8 Conclusion

M-banking is an emerging digital banking service that offers potential benefits to the customers that would make banking experience effective and smart. The current study identified by inner sentiments of customers of Islami Bank from voluminous online reviews by applying sentiment analysis and topic modeling. In banking sector, sentiment analysis and topic modeling can effectively be applied to understand peoples' perception about an offer and identify the scope of improvement to ensure customer satisfaction and sustainable competitive advantage.

References

Ahmed, M., Imtiaz, M., & Kauser, A. A. (2020). A comparative study of mobile banking in specific parts of Bangladesh. *International Journal of Science and Business, IJSAB International, 4*(6), 129–139.

Ahmed, Z., Kader, A., Rashid, M., Ur, H., & Nurunnabi, M. (2017). User perception of mobile banking adoption: An integrated TTF-UTAUT model.

Akter, M. (2020). Capital structure of Islami Bank Bangladesh Limited.

Al-Dmour, R., Dawood, E. A. H., Al-Dmour, H., Masa'deh, R., & e. (2020). The effect of customer lifestyle patterns on the use of mobile banking applications in Jordan. *International Journal of Electronic Marketing and Retailing, 11*(3), 239–258.

Alavi, S., & Ahuja, V. (2016). An empirical segmentation of users of mobile banking apps. *Journal of Internet Commerce, 15*(4), 390–407.

Ali, Q., Salman, A., Yaacob, H., Zaini, Z., & Abdullah, R. (2020). Does big data analytics enhance sustainability and financial performance? The case of ASEAN banks. *The Journal of Asian Finance, Economics, and Business, 7*(7), 1–13.

Amado, A., Cortez, P., Rita, P., & Moro, S. (2018). Research trends on Big Data in Marketing: A text mining and topic modeling based literature analysis. *European Research on Management and Business Economics, 24*(1), 1–7.

Arcand, M., PromTep, S., Brun, I., & Rajaobelina, L. (2017). Mobile banking service quality and customer relationships. *International Journal of Bank Marketing.*

Auliya, Z. F., Umam, M. R. K., & Prastiwi, S. K. (2017). Online Costumer Reviews (OTRs) dan Rating: Kekuatan Baru pada Pemasaran Online di Indonesia. *Ebbank, 8*(1), 89–98.

Botchway, R. K., Jibril, A. B., Kwarteng, M. A., Chovancova, M., & Oplatková, Z. K. (2019). *A review of social media posts from UniCredit bank in Europe: A sentiment analysis approach.* Paper presented at the Proceedings of the 3rd international conference on business and information Management.

Chintalapudi, N., Battineni, G., Di Canio, M., Sagaro, G. G., & Amenta, F. (2021). Text mining with sentiment analysis on seafarers' medical documents. *International Journal of Information Management Data Insights, 1*(1), 100005.

Das, R. K., & Islam, M. S. U. (2021). Application of artificial intelligence and machine learning in libraries: A systematic review. *arXiv preprint* arXiv:2112.04573.

Dwidienawati, D., Tjahjana, D., Abdinagoro, S. B., & Gandasari, D. (2020). Customer review or influencer endorsement: Which one influences purchase intention more? *Heliyon, 6*(11), e05543.

Eberendu, A. C. (2016). Unstructured sata: An overview of the data of Big Data. *International Journal of Computer Trends and Technology, 38*(1), 46–50.

Esmaeili, A., Haghgoo, I., Davidavičienė, V., & Meidutė-Kavaliauskienė, I. (2021). Customer loyalty in mobile banking: Evaluation of perceived risk, relative advantages, and usability factors. *Engineering Economics, 32*(1), 70–81.

Farooqi, S., Feal, Á., Lauinger, T., McCoy, D., Shafiq, Z., & Vallina-Rodriguez, N. (2020). *Understanding incentivized mobile app installs on google play store.* Paper presented at the Proceedings of the ACM internet measurement conference.

Frederick, D. P., & Bhat, G. (2021). Review on customer perception towards online food delivery services.

Ho, R. C., Withanage, M. S., & Khong, K. W. (2020). Sentiment drivers of hotel customers: A hybrid approach using unstructured data from online reviews. *Asia-Pacific Journal of Business Administration.*

Jeong, B., Yoon, J., & Lee, J.-M. (2019). Social media mining for product planning: A product opportunity mining approach based on topic modeling and sentiment analysis. *International Journal of Information Management, 48*, 280–290.

Jiin, B., & KHAMIDI, M. F. A study on the perception of walkability in tourist attraction places in Qatar using text mining techniques.

Khan, M. R., Rana, S., & Hosen, M. I. (2021). Impact of trustworthiness on the usage of m-banking apps: A study on Bangladeshi consumers. *Business Perspectives and Research*, 22785337211001969.

Khatun, M. N., Mitra, S., & Sarker, M. N. I. (2021). Mobile banking during COVID-19 pandemic in Bangladesh: A novel mechanism to change and accelerate people's financial access. *Green Finance, 3*(3), 253–267.

Khoa, B. T. (2020). The impact of the personal data disclosure's tradeoff on the trust and attitude loyalty in mobile banking services. *Journal of Promotion Management, 27*(4), 585–608.

Kim, D., Lee, J., So, C. H., Jeon, H., Jeong, M., Choi, Y., . . . Kang, J. (2019). A neural named entity recognition and multi-type normalization tool for biomedical text mining. *IEEE Access, 7*, 73729–73740.

KM, K. (2020). Digitalization of banks: An evidence from India. *IJRAR-International Journal of Research and Analytical Reviews (IJRAR), 7*(1), 571–579–571–579.

Koren, I. K. Improving Nordic Choice Hotels Environmental Sustainability Performance: Understanding Customer Perception and Behaviour.

Kumar, G., & Shenbagaraman, V. (2017). The customers' perception of mobile banking adoption in Chennai City. An empirical assessment of an extended technology acceptance model. *International Journal of Business Information Systems, 26*(1), 46–65.

Kwabla, W., Coulibaly, F., Zhenis, Y., & Chen, B. (2021). Wineinformatics: Can wine reviews in Bordeaux reveal wine aging capability? *Fermentation, 7*(4), 236.

Leem, B.-H., & Eum, S.-W. (2021). Using text mining to measure mobile banking service quality. *Industrial Management & Data Systems.*

Malaquias, R. F., & Silva, A. F. (2020). Understanding the use of mobile banking in rural areas of Brazil. *Technology in Society, 62*, 101260.

Mannering, F., Bhat, C. R., Shankar, V., & Abdel-Aty, M. (2020). Big data, traditional data and the tradeoffs between prediction and causality in highway-safety analysis. *Analytic Methods in Accident Research, 25*, 100113.

Mehta, P., Pandya, S., & Kotecha, K. (2021). Harvesting social media sentiment analysis to enhance stock market prediction using deep learning. *PeerJ Computer Science, 7*, e476.

Mhamdi, C., Al-Emran, M., & Salloum, S. A. (2018). Text mining and analytics: A case study from news channels posts on Facebook *Intelligent Natural Language Processing: Trends and Applications* (pp. 399–415): Springer.

Mikalef, P., Pappas, I. O., Krogstie, J., & Giannakos, M. (2018). Big data analytics capabilities: A systematic literature review and research agenda. *Information Systems and e-Business Management, 16*(3), 547–578.

Moutidis, I., & Williams, H. T. (2020). Good and bad events: Combining network-based event detection with sentiment analysis. *Social Network Analysis and Mining, 10*(1), 1–12.

Muktafin, E. H. (2021). Sentiments analysis of customer satisfaction in public services using K-nearest neighbors algorithm and natural language processing approach. *Telkomnika, 19*(1), 146–154.

Mulia, D., Usman, H., & Parwanto, N. B. (2020). The role of customer intimacy in increasing Islamic bank customer loyalty in using e-banking and m-banking. *Journal of Islamic Marketing.*

Muñoz-Leiva, F., Climent-Climent, S., & Liébana-Cabanillas, F. (2017). Determinants of intention to use the mobile banking apps: An extension of the classic TAM model. *Spanish Journal of Marketing—ESIC, 21*(1), 25–38. https://doi.org/10.1016/j.sjme.2016.12.001

Mustafa, M. (2021). The technology of mobile banking and its impact on the financial growth during the Covid-19 pandemic in the gulf region. *Turkish Journal of Computer and Mathematics Education (TURCOMAT), 12*(9), 389–398.

Nawab, K., Ramsey, G., & Schreiber, R. (2020). Natural language processing to extract meaningful information from patient experience feedback. *Applied Clinical Informatics, 11*(02), 242–252.

Neuraz, A., Lerner, I., Digan, W., Paris, N., Tsopra, R., Rogier, A., . . . Garcelon, N. (2020). Natural language processing for rapid response to emergent diseases: Case study of calcium channel blockers and hypertension in the covid-19 pandemic. *Journal of Medical Internet Research, 22*(8), e20773.

Ning, X., Yim, D., & Khuntia, J. (2021). Online Sustainability reporting and firm performance: Lessons learned from text mining. *Sustainability, 13*(3), 1069.

Normah, N. (2019). Naïve Bayes algorithm for sentiment analysis windows phone store application reviews. *Sinkron: jurnal dan penelitian teknik informatika, 3*(2), 13–19.

Payne, E. H. M., Peltier, J., & Barger, V. A. (2021). Enhancing the value co-creation process: artificial intelligence and mobile banking service platforms. *Journal of Research in Interactive Marketing.*

Payne, E. M., Peltier, J. W., & Barger, V. A. (2018). Mobile banking and AI-enabled mobile banking: The differential effects of technological and non-technological factors on digital natives' perceptions and behavior. *Journal of Research in Interactive Marketing.*

Permana, M. E., Ramadhan, H., Budi, I., Santoso, A. B., & Putra, P. K. (2020). *Sentiment analysis and topic detection of mobile banking application review.* Paper presented at the 2020 Fifth International Conference on Informatics and Computing (ICIC).

Rahman, A., & Abedin, M. J. (2021). The Fourth Industrial Revolution and private commercial banks: The good, bad and ugly. *International Journal of Organizational Analysis.*

Rasool, A., Shah, F. A., & Islam, J. U. (2020). Customer engagement in the digital age: A review and research agenda. *Current Opinion in Psychology, 36*, 96–100.

Saleem, A., Ghafar, A., Ibrahim, M., Yousuf, M., & Ahmed, N. (2015). Product perceived quality and purchase intention with consumer satisfaction. *Global journal of management and business research.*

Sampaio, C. H., Ladeira, W. J., & Santini, F. D. O. (2017). Apps for mobile banking and customer satisfaction: a cross-cultural study. *International Journal of Bank Marketing.*

Saputro, B., Hidayanto, A. N., Abidin, Z., & Paoprasert, N. (2021). Measuring service quality in the telecommunications industry from customer reviews using sentiment analysis: A case study in PT XL Axiata. *International Journal of Innovation and Learning, 30*(2), 188–200.

Shahid, S., Islam, J. U., Malik, S., & Hasan, U. (2022). Examining consumer experience in using m-banking apps: A study of its antecedents and outcomes. *Journal of Retailing and Consumer Services, 65*, 102870.

Shaikh, A. A., Glavee-Geo, R., & Karjaluoto, H. (2021). How relevant are risk perceptions, effort, and performance expectancy in mobile banking adoption? *Research Anthology on Securing Mobile Technologies and Applications* (pp. 692–716). IGI Global.

Shankar, A., Tiwari, A. K., & Gupta, M. (2021). Sustainable mobile banking application: a text mining approach to explore critical success factors. *Journal of Enterprise Information Management.*

Sharma, S. K., & Al-Muharrami, S. (2018). Mobile banking adoption: Key challenges and opportunities and implications for a developing country *Emerging Markets from a Multidisciplinary Perspective* (pp. 75–86): Springer.

Singh, S., & Srivastava, R. (2020). Understanding the intention to use mobile banking by existing online banking customers: An empirical study. *Journal of Financial Services Marketing, 25*(3), 86–96.

Tamilselvi, R., & Balaji, P. (2019). The key determinants of behavioural intention towards mobile banking adoption. *International Journal of Innovative Technology and Exploring Engineering, 8*(10), 1124–1130.

Tham, J., Ab Yazid, M. S., Khatibi, A. A., & Azam, S. F. (2017). Internet and data security–understanding customer perception on trusting virtual banking security in Malaysia. *European Journal of Social Sciences Studies.*

Van der Marel, E. (2020). *Shifting into digital services: Does a crisis matter and for who?* European Centre for International Political Economy.

Venkatakrishnan, S., Kaushik, A., & Verma, J. K. (2020). Sentiment analysis on google play store data using deep learning *Applications of Machine Learning* (pp. 15–30): Springer.

Veríssimo, J. M. C. (2016). Enablers and restrictors of mobile banking app use: A fuzzy set qualitative comparative analysis (fsQCA). *Journal of Business Research, 69*(11), 5456–5460.

Verkijika, S. F., & Neneh, B. N. (2021). Standing up for or against: A text-mining study on the recommendation of mobile payment apps. *Journal of Retailing and Consumer Services, 63*, 102743.

Wang, W. M., Li, Z., Tian, Z., Wang, J., & Cheng, M. N. (2018). Extracting and summarizing affective features and responses from online product descriptions and reviews: A Kansei text mining approach. *Engineering Applications of Artificial Intelligence, 73*, 149–162.

Wolfert, S., Ge, L., Verdouw, C., & Bogaardt, M.-J. (2017). Big data in smart farming–a review. *Agricultural Systems, 153*, 69–80.

Xu, X. (2019). Examining the relevance of online customer textual reviews on hotels' product and service attributes. *Journal of Hospitality & Tourism Research, 43*(1), 141–163.

Xu, X. (2020). Examining an asymmetric effect between online customer reviews emphasis and overall satisfaction determinants. *Journal of Business Research, 106*, 196–210.

Zahid, M., Rahman, H. U., Ullah, Z., & Muhammad, A. (2021). Sustainability and branchless banking: The development and validation of a distinct measurement scale. *Technology in Society, 67*, 101764.

Zhang, T., Lu, C., & Kizildag, M. (2018). Banking "on-the-go": Examining consumers' adoption of mobile banking services. *International Journal of Quality and Service Sciences.*

Zhao, Y., Xu, X., & Wang, M. (2019). Predicting overall customer satisfaction: Big data evidence from hotel online textual reviews. *International Journal of Hospitality Management, 76*, 111–121.

Mouri Dey is currently working as an Associate Professor of Department of Accounting, University of Chittagong, Bangladesh. Her research interests focus on corporate environmental reporting, sustainability reporting, leadership and corporate strategy, corporate governance and data analytics.

Md. Zahedul Islam received an MBA degree in Accounting from the University of Chittagong, Bangladesh. He currently works as an Assistant Professor in the Department of Accounting, University of Chittagong. His current research interests include environmental accounting, environmental sustainability, corporate governance, and capital markets & financial institutions.

Tarek Rana, PhD, MBA, CA, ACMA, is an Associate Professor of Accounting and Data Analytics at RMIT University, Melbourne, Australia. He has considerable professional and industry experience in the areas of business services, taxation, auditing, and financial planning as well as consulting services including performance measurement and risk management. He has undertaken practice focused research projects to deliver long-term social and organizational impact. His current research focuses on the intersection of accounting and data analytics including the implications of emerging technologies on management control systems, performance measurement, risk management, and sustainability.

Part III
Digitalization and Accounting Education

Chapter 15
Integrating Blockchain Technology into Accounting Curricula: A Template for Accounting Educators

Manpreet Singh, Mahesh Joshi, and Sharad Sharma

Abstract This paper provides a guidance note to accounting educators seeking to incorporate applications of blockchain technology (BT) into accounting curricula. This paper is based on review of recent blockchain related publications in the accounting domain. It explains the areas of blockchain relevant to the accounting profession and provides a list of potential topics for inclusion in the accounting curriculum. Potential academic and industry resources that can be used to develop BT materials for integration into the accounting curriculum are also outlined. Being motivated by the need for the accounting profession to update their blockchain-related awareness and skills to meet the expectations of the accounting industry, this paper will help accounting educators as a guidance note in curriculum design and developing their course materials. This paper represents a reference for accounting educators tasked with incorporating emerging technologies into the accounting curricula to prepare work-ready graduates for the rapidly changing accounting profession.

Keywords Blockchain Technology · Accounting curricula · Education · Distributed ledgers · Triple entry system

1 Introduction

Blockchain technology (BT), a highly effective and decentralized form of distributed ledger technology (DLT) (Drescher, 2017), is one of the most important technological developments in recent years (Berryhill et al., 2018; Peters & Panayi, 2016; Subramanian et al., 2018) and has been described as the most transformative innovation in the internet world (Tapscott & Tapscott, 2016). A distributed ledger is spread across

M. Singh · M. Joshi (✉) · S. Sharma
RMIT University, Melbourne, Australia
e-mail: mahesh.joshi@rmit.edu.au

M. Singh
e-mail: s3367226@student.rmit.edu.au

S. Sharma
e-mail: sharad.sharma@rmit.edu.au

T. Rana et al. (eds.), *Handbook of Big Data and Analytics in Accounting and Auditing*,
https://doi.org/10.1007/978-981-19-4460-4_15

geographic locations and institutions for access by multiple users, rather than being centralized and used by a single user (Aggarwal, 2017; Berryhill et al., 2018; Dai & Vasarhelyi, 2017; Ram et al., 2016). Because users can access updated information in the distributed ledger at any point in time, information processing is more time efficient (Peters & Panayi, 2016; Tan & Low, 2019), and thus BT has attracted the attention of corporations, accounting bodies, regulators and various other stakeholders (Byström, 2016; Subramanian et al., 2018).

Given BT's potential to drive simplicity (Midwinter & Sheppard, 2000) and efficiency (Berryhill et al., 2018; Peters & Panayi, 2016; Subramanian et al., 2018), recent years have witnessed increasing use of BT in not only the financial sector but also other sectors, such as manufacturing and healthcare (Attaran & Gunasekaran, 2019; Inside-Higher-Ed, 2018; Ølnes, Ubacht, & Janssen, 2017; Tan & Low, 2017; Yermack, 2017). Supermarkets are using this technology in supply chain processes to track food items, and in the healthcare sector, the application of BT empowers patients through improved transparency and privacy and the ability to obtain their medical records at reduced cost (Attaran & Gunasekaran, 2019; Ølnes et al., 2017; Schmitz & Leoni, 2019; Tan & Low, 2017; Yermack, 2017). Stock exchanges are exploring the ability of BT to enable more accurate and transparent record-keeping of trading of listed equities and their ownership at reduced cost (Yermack, 2017). Institutional participants that have sought to adopt BT include central banks (e.g. Bank of England, European Central Bank, Federal Reserve and Bank of Japan), large commercial banks (e.g. Morgan Stanley, Santanders, Goldman Sachs, Deutsche Bank, Royal Bank of Scotland), global regulators (IMF, BIS and SWIFT), big accounting firms (Deloitte, Ernst & Young (EY), PricewaterhouseCoopers (PwC), KPMG, and international corporations and policy think-tanks (e.g. Capgemini, Accenture, JWT, McKinsey, NBER, World Economic Forum) (Tapscott & Tapscott, 2016).

BT is transforming business, and the positive adaptive responses of businesses are not limited to distribution, health or even government (Smith & Castonguay, 2020). However, in a discussion of the use of BT to improve real-time transactional efficiencies and liquidity for stock exchanges, Yermack (2017) highlighted the disruptive capabilities of BT; that is, improving efficiency may upset the power equation among different stakeholders. Similar apprehensions are apparent in the accounting and auditing profession, where BT seems to threaten the status quo of practices and traditions (Marrone & Hazelton, 2019; Schmitz & Leoni, 2019; Tapscott & Tapscott, 2016; Vigna & Casey, 2019). To address these concerns, researchers across the globe have begun exploring the potential implications of BT for the accounting profession and practice (Schmitz & Leoni, 2019), including for accountants, auditors, regulators and standard setters (Deloitte, 2016; EY, 2017; PwC, 2016; Schmitz & Leoni, 2019). Schmitz and Leoni (2019) noted that the general apprehension of the profession towards BT reflects expectations of redundancy and change and suggested that those in the profession update their skillset in addition to absorbing the inevitable changes that BT will bring. As businesses increasingly use BT, updated skills are essential to fulfil historical expectations of accounting professionals as transaction and information enablers (AICPA, 2017; KPMG, 2018; Schmitz & Leoni, 2019; Vaidyanathan, 2017). Training to address the technical skill gaps of professionals in other fields, e.g. developers, consultants and architects, is already occurring (Chen et al., 2018a; Guang Chen et al., 2018).

Historically, academia has continually updated accounting curricula to broaden skillsets and meet the accounting knowledge requirements of business stakeholders in response to constant changes in business discipline, accounting standards and technological innovations (Chung & Kim, 2016; Owen, 2013; Schmitz & Leoni, 2019; Schwab, 2017). These responses to successive technological and business transactional innovations contributed to the evolution of the accounting profession to its present state. Blockchain is yet another transformative technology that may require updating of skills across many professions and domains (Hoy, 2017). In a questionnaire-based study aimed at gauging the auditing profession's readiness to embrace "disruptive" technologies in the context of BT, Ferri et al. (2020) concluded that performance expectancy and social influence define the intentions of the profession to implement BT. An attempt by De Villiers (2020) to examine the response to transformative technology stopped at identifying principles to guide educators in preparing students for automation and artificial intelligence. Academia has been successful in conveying the rationale for the incorporation of BT in the processing and presentation of accounting information (Bonsón & Bednárová, 2019; De Villiers, 2020) but has not suggested a template and curriculum for producing BT-enabled accounting professionals. This hesitation may reflect a desire for obvious buy-in and demand from the accounting profession and the industry for such inclusion. Given these academic efforts and the increasing integration of BT in other business transactions, we argue that the time has come for educators to include BT in accounting curricula. The theoretical perspective of diffusion of innovation confirms that a range of influences from the external and internal environments determine innovation adoption. This paper seeks to not only reveal these influences but also to meet the education and training needs of industry by helping accounting educators design a strategy to integrate BT in their curricula.

Considering the growing literature on the impact of BT on the accounting, auditing and financial sectors and the emphasis on training future accounting professionals in these related fields (Kuppusamy, 2019), this paper attempts to address the issue of integrating BT into accounting curricula to develop blockchain-related skills among accounting students. In the first phase of this paper, the basic blockchain process, blockchain terminology and the relationship of BT with accounting and auditing are explained based on an extensive review of the literature on BT. The second phase of this paper starts by establishing the relevance of integrating BT in education in general and more specifically in accounting education. This is followed by guidance for accounting educators on curriculum design, including a list of topics to be covered, teaching resources and available reference materials. This effort represents a progression from the rationale for integrating BT in the accounting profession provided by extant research. In so doing, this paper makes several contributions. First, the paper moves to the next stage of efforts to provide a rationale for the inclusion of BT in accounting curricula by providing a template and curricula guidelines. The paper contributes to the development of blockchain accounting materials by accounting educators who are considering adding this topic to their courses. Second, it provides an update on significant developments in the blockchain accounting domain. Third, it provides initial insights on BT and its implications for accounting educators, accounting students and education institutions by providing structured information, concepts and terminologies, potential topics for curriculum development, and relevant information/sources for content development. In the process, the paper makes a significant contribution to the fast-growing BT literature and, more specifically, to the education literature in accounting and other related disciplines. While the effort to integrate BT may be challenging, the growing number of blockchain accounting-related resources available to accounting educators highlighted by this paper can provide reasonable guidance for the successful teaching of BT across the globe.

This paper is structured in the following way.

- Section 2 explains blockchain under the assumption that BT, as a recent phenomenon, requires an introduction. The section provides a detailed BT mechanism relevant to the accounting profession. A glossary of terms for BT is also provided as a starting point that can be further expanded with time and increased usage of BT.
- Section 3 explains the methodology.
- Section 4 focuses on the progress and contributions of BT in the field of accounting. A systematic review of the blockchain literature is conducted to convey the inevitability of integration of BT into accounting curricula. The extant literature providing the rationale for integrating BT into the accounting profession is highlighted. This discussion provides a foundation for Sect. 5 by emphasizing the need for a progression from this rationale to designing a strategy to integrate BT into accounting curricula.
- Section 5 discusses BT and the education sector, including existing and possible uses of BT in the education sector, such as in the administration and delivery of course content. BT is also explained as an educational product, considering the growing demand for training and education in blockchain-related courses across all disciplines.
- Section 6 introduces the suggested curricula and sources of content for academia. This includes guidance materials for accounting educators who are planning to offer blockchain-related basic knowledge to their students in order to enable them to understand the role and impact of blockchain in accounting practice.
- Section 7 concludes the paper.

2 The Blockchain Process

Blockchain is a major technological innovation, a 'trust machine' that is expected to revolutionize society (Tapscott & Tapscott, 2016). It is a decentralized, distributed and public digital ledger (Puthal et al., 2018) that uses a computer network to record transactions. These computers or servers may be based at different locations and accessed/used by many users simultaneously. The transparency and security of transactions are ensured, as altering a single record or transaction requires the alteration of

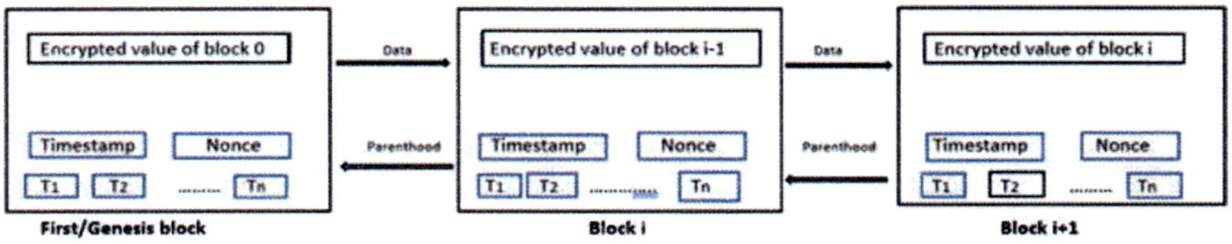

Fig. 1 A sequence of blocks (author design)

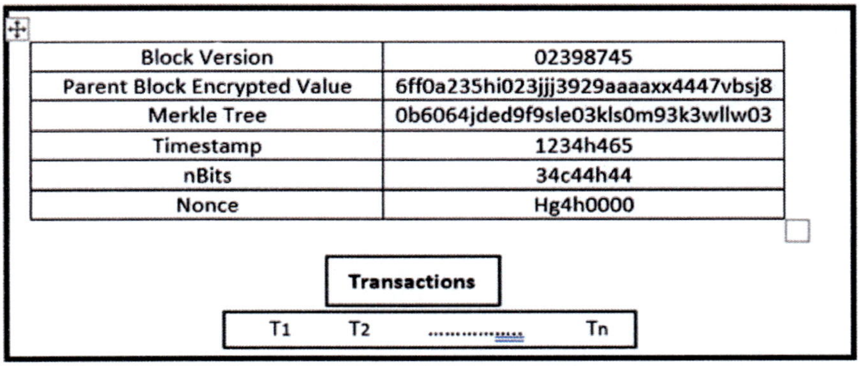

Fig. 2 Block structure (author design)

all subsequent records (Zaghloul et al., 2020). As such, blockchain has the capability of creating trust-based relationships between participants in business transactions even if the participants do not know each other (Drescher, 2017; Tapscott & Tapscott, 2016).

Blockchain is a series of blocks that maintain a full list of transaction records like a traditional public ledger (Yermack, 2015). Each block points to its previous block, or parent block, with a reference that is a hash value[1] of the previous block. The first block of a blockchain is called the genesis block and has no parent block (Xu et al., 2019; Zheng et al., 2018). All blocks are connected by cryptography, and each block contains the address of the preceding block, a timestamp and data.

Each block consists of a block header and block body as shown in Figs. 1 and 2. The block body adopts the following structure:

- Block version: a set of block validation rules
- Parent block hash: the hash value (encrypted data of fixed length) that points to the previous block
- Merkle tree root: the hash value of all transactions in the block
- Timestamp: current time as seconds in universal time since 1/1/1970
- nBits: the programmed form of the target threshold as it appears in the block header.

[1] A hash value is a string value (of specific length) generated by a hashing algorithm.

- Nonce: a random number that is used once in the cryptographic communication. It starts at 0 and increases for every hash.

These blocks of data are stored in nodes[2] (forming a tree-like structure), which can be computers or servers. All nodes are connected to each other, and data exchange between nodes occurs constantly; thus, all nodes stay up to date. There is no central authority that maintains this data or a database. Transactions are secured through cryptography, and thus any alteration of blockchain transactions is impossible (Kokina et al., 2017). Moreover, a transaction cannot be left uncompleted after adding it to the blockchain. This immutability underlies the trustworthiness of blockchain transactions. Traditional or existing systems employ a centralized database that normally stays on the server, and users need to connect to the server to make any modifications of the data. Modifications (alterations or deletions) are possible if the security of the server where the transactions are stored is breached (Li et al., 2020). By contrast, in blockchain, the data are decentralized, that is, not located centrally or at one location, and records are secured with cryptography. Users/participants have unique private keys that are assigned to transactions, and if a record is altered, the whole network will know immediately. In the following section, we cover blockchain fundamentals such as types of blockchain (permissioned and permissionless), distributed ledgers, triple-entry systems and smart contracts to give an overview of how this technology works.

2.1 *Permissioned and Permissionless Blockchain Ledgers*

Blockchain ledgers can be of two types: public or private. In a public network, anyone can access and recommend transactions, whereas in a private network, only authorized participants can participate in or contribute to the network.

A permissionless blockchain is fairly simple, and no authorization is required to be a part of such a blockchain network (Wüst & Gervais, 2018). Because anyone can join, a permissionless blockchain is more decentralized than a permissioned system. In a permissionless blockchain, the public validates the transaction information. No one regulates this process, and the system relies on public agreement on which transactions are considered true. Users who do not trust each other can conduct transactions by using the 'Proof of Work' model in permissionless ledgers. Examples[3] of permissionless blockchains are Ethereum, Bitcoin, Litecoin and Monero.

For permissioned ledgers, there is a limited set of users who have special authorization to read, access and write blockchain data (Vukolić, 2017). Access to view transactions is also restricted depending on the ledger's settings. Permissioned ledgers can enhance accountability because only authorized users can add new transactions. The functionality of permissioned ledgers depends upon protocols that are established

[2] A node is a computer or server that contains a full copy of the transaction history of the blockchain.

prior to programming of the system (Marchionni, 2018). Ripple[3] is an example of a permissioned blockchain.

2.2 Distributed Ledger Technology

DLT is a completely novel way to transfer value between untrusted parties (Elsts A, 2018). DLT is based on a database that is shared and synchronized across different geographical regions called nodes (Maull et al., 2017). No central authority maintains DLT; each node repeats and saves an identical copy of the record and updates itself independently (Ram, 2019). Once the update is completed, then the voting process regarding this latest update starts between the nodes. A majority of the nodes must agree in order to reach a conclusion on whether the update is rejected or accepted. This whole process is called consensus and runs by itself through a program called a consensus algorithm. All nodes are updated on their own after the positive outcome (majority) of the consensus algorithm (Karajovic et al., 2019; Watson & Mishler, 2017).

2.3 Triple-Entry Bookkeeping

Triple-entry bookkeeping is a new type of accounting process that was first proposed in 2005 but has become executable recently with the advent of BT (Dai & Vasarhelyi, 2017). Triple-entry bookkeeping provides enhanced value compared with conventional double-entry bookkeeping (Cai, 2019; Grigg, 2015). For accounting transactions involving strangers, validated transactions are sealed using cryptography into a third entry (AICPA, 2017; Deloitte, 2016; EY, 2017; KPMG, 2018). In simple terms, the triple entry is the product of double entry plus a blockchain ledger using cryptography (Cai, 2019). The blockchain-based ledger provides both parties to a transaction updates on the transaction in real time as well as excellent auditable records (Abreu et al., 2018). Whenever the blockchain ledger is updated with a new transactional record, both parties to the transaction can see and validate the update. Thus, recording transactions on a blockchain ledger provides greater visibility of related transactions and a higher degree of transparency (Ibañez et al., 2020).

2.4 Smart Contracts

Smart contracts are user-defined computer programs that were impossible to execute before the emergence of BT, as programming is done through blockchain (Singh et al.,

[3] Cryptocurrencies include Ripple, Ethereum, Bitcoin, Litecoin, Monero, Dogecoin, Peercoin, etc.

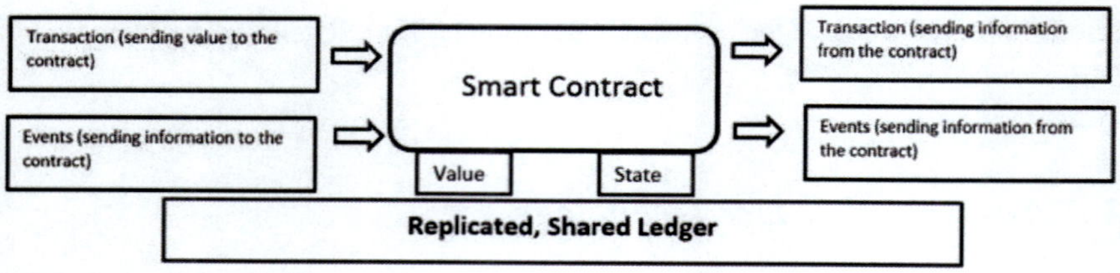

Fig. 3 Smart contract (author design)

2020). Smart contracts provide greater security compared with traditional contract law while reducing transaction costs (Alharby & van Moorsel, 2017; Matthew N. O. Sadiku, 2018). Like a conventional contract, a smart contract describes protocols and fines attached to agreements and automatically imposes these obligations (ICAEW, 2017; Xuan et al., 2020). Smart contracts advance transaction protocols to a new level, as the contracts are self-executed by directly writing the terms agreed on by the parties into lines of software code (ACT-IAC, 2017). Smart contracts deliver a computerized process of obtaining results that is "executed exactly as programmed without any possibility of downtime, censorship, fraud or third-party interference" (Marchionni, 2018). Smart contracts first received notice for their use in crypto exchanges to deal with the high volume of cryptocurrencies (Savelyev, 2017). However, due to their solely electronic nature, software-driven implementation, increased certainty, conditional nature, self-performance and self-sufficiency, smart contracts have since been adopted in a variety of industries, including accounting, automobiles, financial services, healthcare, insurance, real estate and supply chains. Figure 3 presents a simple example of a smart contract that is deployed to a replicated, shared ledger. It can maintain its own state, control its own assets and respond to the arrival of external information or receipt of assets.

2.5 *Basic Blockchain Terms*

Table 1 defines and briefly explains basic terms used in BT. The list is not exhaustive and can be considered a starting point as BT and its applications evolve.

3 Methodology

This paper aims to provide a template to guide accounting educators seeking to incorporate applications of blockchain technology (BT) into accounting curricula. The research was conducted in the following two stages.

Table 1 Blockchain terminology

Authentication	A process to check the user's uniqueness or identity. The request for authentication comes with a set of recognized parameters
Blockchain	A type of distributed ledger that keeps an increasing list of data called blocks. Blockchain is very secure and not easy to modify
Consensus Mechanism	A set of rules that specifies the contributions of various participants of the blockchain to authenticating the transactions without a centralized authority
Crypto Assets	A digital asset intended to work as a medium of exchange using cryptography for various financial transactions and the transfer of assets
Cryptography	A computer term for the conversion of plain text into muddled text and vice versa. Data are stored and transmitted in a specific pattern, and only the people for whom the data were meant can understand or decrypt the pattern. Encryption also helps to protect data from theft and alteration
Cryptographic Signature	The public-key primitives of message authentication with a digital signature; i.e., a technique that binds a person/entity to the ***digital*** data
Distributed Ledger	A database shared and synchronized across different geographical regions called nodes
Initial Coin Offering	The cryptocurrency market equivalent of an IPO for potential investors in the digital currency market as a source of raising funds
Nodes	Keep copies of the data
Public Blockchain	A public network in which anyone can read, submit and validate transactions
Public Key	Non-confidential and available to everyone through the directory. Public key cryptography has the ability to create a digital signature
Private Key	An encrypted key that is known only by the owner or the other party involved in the transaction. It stays in a digital wallet
Privacy	Proper data handling, more specifically, how data are shared with a third party. Another purpose of privacy is to ensure that data are received and read by the intended receiver. Cryptography is used to protect data
Security	Protecting or safeguarding any type of data such as business, personal or transactional data. Security gives an assurance to the receiver that the received message has not been modified. New features such as digital signatures have recently been introduced to securely transmit information

Source AICPA (2017), EY (2017), KPMG (2018)

3.1 Stage 1: Systematic Review

A systematic review was performed to search for relevant studies. A systematic review is applicable because summaries of emerging research implications on a given topic have been shown to be reliable and valid in comparison with controlled trials or case studies (Bonsón & Bednárová, 2019). A systematic review permits the identification, assessment, and understanding of available research and the drawing of logical conclusions based on the findings of the review (Victor, 2008, Dikert et al., 2016). A systematic review follows a staged process: first, the scope of the review is defined by scrutinizing the questions and protocol; then, evidence is selected, and its quality is appraised, followed by data acquisition and synthesis (Popay et al., 2006).

In the present review, published research and sources were identified by using keywords to search publication databases or search engines. The keywords were selected to identify the information content necessary to achieve the purposes of the paper. All results were limited to English only, with no restriction on the year of publication. The Boolean operators were restricted to AND OR. The search strings were as follows:

> ("blockchain" OR "block-chain" OR "distributed ledger") AND "Bitcoin"
> ("blockchain" OR "Accounting" OR "Education") AND ("Accounting and Education" OR "blockchain" OR "Education")

The platforms searched were ScienceDirect, Scopus, and Google Scholar. Sources from large accounting firms and professional accounting bodies were identified by searching their websites and links referenced by published journal articles. Searches were run against the title, keywords or abstract, depending on the search platform, ignoring publication year and quality. The downloaded documents were filtered using the inclusion/exclusion criteria presented below.

Articles were excluded if the abstract, objectives, methodology, results and discussion sections were not relevant to the present theme of the paper. The selection criteria were as follows:

- Only articles published in English were included.
- With respect to document types, only articles in press and review papers were considered; conference papers, book chapters and editorial notes were not considered.
- The article was included if it discussed BT in education as the main theme or examined the use of BT in educational settings.
- Print and online sources on BT from large accounting firms and professional accounting bodies were also included.

All articles were carefully screened based on the above-stipulated inclusion criteria. Finally, 42 articles meeting the inclusion criteria were selected.

3.2 *Stage 2: Developing a Template for Teaching BT*

During this stage, the articles collected in stage 1 were reviewed in order to provide structured information to accounting educators as a source of guidance or template for including BT in their curricula. The template developed in this stage explains the blockchain process to educators, including basic blockchain terminology; suggests ways of integrating BT and other emerging technologies into accounting education; and provides a list of learning and teaching resources for blockchain topics in accounting curricula.

4 Blockchain and Accounting

BT is one of the most welcome technologies of this new era. Digital scientists have categorized BT as a medium- to high-impact technology, and there is consensus that BT has immense potential to benefit accounting and related sectors (Bansal et al., 2018). BT is not the first technological innovation to impact accounting, which has evolved over the years in response to the introduction of computers, ERP and XBRL, among other advances. These innovations were also initially viewed as disruptive by professional accounting bodies but later played a transformative role in bringing the profession to its current stage (Chung & Kim, 2016; Owen, 2013; Schmitz & Leoni, 2019; Schwab, 2017). In the accounting sector, BT may be used by companies to keep or write all of their transactions in a joint location instead of keeping separate records based on transaction receipts, thereby creating an interlocking system of enduring accounting records. Since all entries are distributed and cryptographically sealed, falsifying or destroying them to conceal activity is practically impossible. In practice, this is similar to verification of a transaction by a notary, only in an electronic way (Andersen, 2016).

BT can also be helpful for integrating internal business accounting procedures and safeguarding the integrity of transactions and the visibility of full audit trails of transactions (Dunn, Jenkins, & Sheldon, 2020). According to the core ideas of diffusion of innovation theory (Rogers, 1995), innovations are generally adopted by organizations when they benefit them and rejected when they do not. As BT promises to benefit accounting and auditing firms by allowing for the provision of more transparent and efficient services, its adoption by accounting practitioners and professional accounting bodies confirms the early acceptance of blockchain innovation.

4.1 Benefits of Blockchain for Accountants

Double-entry bookkeeping has been the norm in financial accounting since the Renaissance. This approach significantly reduces conflicts between managers, who can trust the accounts if both sides match (Brandon, 2016) with documentary evidence for audit scrutiny. The advent of computers led to the replacement of physical ledgers at a central location. BT is the next step in the field of accounting: companies can create a joint register in which they record all transactions directly, eliminating the need to keep transactional receipts (Andersen, 2016). Transactions are not stored/recorded in one central location (McKinlay et al., 2016) and are encrypted or sealed with cryptography. Therefore, it is practically impossible to destroy or misrepresent transactions (Andersen, 2016). Blockchain can help reduce the time and cost of auditing if companies standardize their processes, which will allow auditors to authenticate financial data automatically (AICPA, 2017; Shaw, 2018). Auditors can use their newfound spare time to validate other complex transactions and add value to other services.

4.2 Blockchain for Accountants and Auditing Practices

Advocates of BT adoption in accounting believe that fears in the accounting profession of redundancy may not be realized and suggest that accountants and auditors understand and learn this new technology before it becomes a standard requirement (Bonsón & Bednárová, 2019; Schmitz & Leoni, 2019). This game-changing technology (Andersen, 2016) provides many opportunities for accountants to position themselves as forward-thinking (PWC, 2019). Auditors can exploit BT to access real-time data more effectively, increase their efficiency, and enhance sampling and testing in their audit approach, thereby reducing the time and cost of auditing (AICPA, 2017; Fuller & Markelevich, 2020). Auditors can access and validate any record at any time by generating a hash value and comparing the value with the hash value that is timestamped and stored in the blockchain (Shaw, 2018). If the hash values match, then the auditor can trust that the record has not been modified since it was entered into the blockchain. However, clients must give auditors permission to access their financial data at all times for auditing purposes; if not, the promise of BT implementation will not be realized.

Professional and regulatory bodies are still developing their responses to BT (AICPA, 2017; Sinha, 2020). There is a need to change the skill set of professional accountants to focus on digital technology and increased analytical skills, which will require changes in professional training, examination, and employment (Fullana & Ruiz, 2020). Client education should be a priority for professional accounting firms to ensure that clients are satisfied with the new auditing process. Digitization is the way of the future, whether blockchain or another disruptive technology is adopted and impacts the marketplace (AICPA, 2017).

4.3 Blockchain in Accounting Curricula and Challenges to Implementation

DLT has disruptive capabilities to push accountants to change their ways of working, but challenges remain in the implementation of BT in the accounting field (Potekhina & Riumkin, 2017; Shaw, 2018). Current accounting and record-keeping software are not suitable for adopting BT and may not be compatible with blockchain.

Thus, the adoption decision comes with costs for accounting firms in the form of an initial investment in cloud-based accounting software (Appelbaum & Nehmer, 2017) and hiring a blockchain developer to develop a customized user interface according to the firm's needs. These costs may decrease with economies of scale in the development and usage of blockchain accounting software to cater to this emerging marketplace, which will reduce the need for customized blockchain software (Shaw, 2018). Learning the BT software and implementing it in daily operations will also be a challenge for end-users and businesses. BT will be embraced/adopted faster by accounting firms once blockchain software is readily available in the market. Industry-specific blockchain software is not yet available but will be once innovators and investors enter this emerging market to meet growing industry requirements.

5 Blockchain and Education

BT has diverse implications for the education sector. On the one hand, BT can provide use value with the integration of blockchain processes in administrative procedures, which will increase operational efficiency and effectiveness. On the other hand, BT can enhance revenue as an educational product, considering the growing demand for training and education in blockchain-related courses across all disciplines.

5.1 Application and Potential Issues of BT in the Education Sector

The education sector has recently begun using BT to support the administration of academic degree programs and the evaluation of student assessments (Sharples & Domingue, 2016). Administrative uses of BT include developing entire student records, such as students' achievements, academic certificates, and academic outcomes, that can be accessed later for future purposes (Sharples & Domingue, 2016). BT has potential for use by learners and teachers in broader applications such as creating smart contracts for teaching and learning, which could resolve educational issues such as storing student records and evaluating students' work (Chen et al., 2018a; Chen et al., 2018b). Smart contracts can also be used by students to submit assessments using unique IDs; the teacher can review and evaluate the submitted assessments and save the results in blocks (Guang). The University of Nicosia and Sony Global Education (Education, 2018) have used BT to store students' certificates (Sharples & Domingue, 2016) and degree information (Hoy, 2017).

Like accounting, the application of BT in the education sector for administrative purposes faces challenges. It is a complex system, and it is difficult to create smart contracts to evaluate student activities without manual involvement. If such complex systems are built and implemented in the education sector and students' data are added to blockchain ledgers for greater transparency and security (Shetty, Kamhoua, & Njilla, 2019), record modification issues will arise. Other technical issues or barriers that need to be addressed to implement blockchain include a "Proof of Work" consensus mechanism (Vukolić, 2015).

5.2 Teaching of Blockchain

There is an increasing need for a skilled technical workforce in the blockchain domain, including developers, consultants, architects and BT-aware professionals for other allied professions. Technology firms like IBM are developing various BT training initiatives to address this demand for a skilled technical workforce (Turkanović et al., 2018). Educational institutes are also upskilling students and teachers to meet industry requirements; for example, MIT Sloan School of Management has introduced blockchain-specific courses aimed at providing an understanding of BT and its applications in providing solutions to emerging issues. RMIT Australia's Blockchain Innovation hub has introduced short courses addressing skill gaps for developing applications, strategies, and blockchain solutions. Cornell, Duke, Georgetown, and Stanford are running blockchain courses to train students and faculty to bring them up to speed on the newest developments in BT (AICPA, 2017; KPMG, 2018; Schmitz & Leoni, 2019; Vaidyanathan, 2017).

5.3 Including Emerging Technologies in Accounting Education

As technology continues to advance, becomes more cost-efficient, and proliferates throughout nearly every industry, accounting professionals will have to evolve to keep pace with changing requirements (Grech & Camilleri, 2017). Faculty educators and institutes can enable a job-ready workforce by teaching emerging technologies (Turkanović et al., 2018), and accounting is no exception.

Below are some suggestions for introducing these trends in the accounting curriculum or programs:

a. Faculty Volunteers—Faculty members can volunteer to be early adopters and accept the challenge of learning new and emerging trends (Al Harthy et al., 2019). They can subsequently share their acquired knowledge and experiences with other faculty members. Incentives may need to be offered to encourage interest, as many of these courses run on odd schedules (Grech & Camilleri, 2017).
b. Faculty Education—Understanding the function of new and emerging technologies like blockchain and artificial intelligence requires the combined involvement

of students, faculty, and administrators (Grech & Camilleri, 2017). Various institutions and private providers offer online courses on these emerging topics. The Big Four accounting firms have also released resources on emerging trends that can be helpful for learning (Al Harthy et al., 2019; Smith & Castonguay, 2020).

c. Build the Fundamentals First—Students must understand the underlying or basic concepts that drive the technology, and faculty can provide assistance by discussing/teaching these new technologies (Al Harthy et al., 2019) and their implications.
d. Introduce the Profession and Future Growth in Accounting Courses—Faculty need to share recent examples of the use of these technologies in relevant markets (Duan et al., 2017). Graduate courses can be structured based on this knowledge to introduce new trending technologies and case studies based on these tools (Duan et al., 2017). Introducing these courses at the graduate level will position students for upcoming jobs in emerging markets (Smith & Castonguay, 2020).
e. Assign Research Projects and Group Projects on Emerging Technologies—Once students are aware of BT and its implications, their knowledge can be reinforced by open discussions in the classroom, group projects, open-ended questions on exams or writing a research paper (Alammary et al., 2019; Liyuan et al., 2019). An additional benefit of group projects is exposure to interacting with different students, which will prepare them for working with others as professionals in the accounting and finance industry, an extant expectation of the industry (Liyuan et al., 2019). These new trends will not go away anytime soon and have already influenced the accounting and finance profession. Consequently, it is critical to discuss these emerging trends at every opportunity. It is the collective responsibility of educators/institutions to prepare graduates for the workplace of the future (Alammary et al., 2019).

6 Learning and Teaching Resources for Integrating Blockchain Topics into Accounting Curricula

To provide guidance to educational institutions and training providers, Table 2 lists important topics to be taught to future accounting graduates. The table also provides a list of academic and professional resources available for enhancing awareness of BT among accounting educators and students.

Table 2 Topics and resources for teaching blockchain

Topics	Identified resources (books and internet sources)
Basics of Blockchain	• Blockchain Basics: A Non-Technical Introduction in 25 Steps (Drescher, 2017) • Bitcoin Magnet (Aggarwal., 2017) • Blockchain Revolution (Tapscott & Tapscott, 2016) • Bitcoin as a New Asset Class (Ram, 2019)
Triple Entry accounting	• REA, Triple-Entry Accounting and Blockchain: Converging Paths to Shared Ledger Systems (Ibañez, Bayer et al., 2020) • Triple-Entry Accounting with Blockchain: How far have we come? (Cai, 2021)
Real-Time audit	• Blockchain Technology in the Auditing Environment (Abreu, Aparicio et al., 2018) • Auditing Cloud-based Blockchain Accounting Systems (Appelbaum and Nehmer, 2020) • Bitcoin and Blockchain: Audit Implications of the Killer BsBitcoin and Blockchain (Dunn, Jenkins et al., 2020)
Blockchain Security	• Blockchain for Distributed Systems Security (Shetty, Kamhoua et al., 2019) • On Blockchain Security and Relevant Attacks (Moubarak et al., 2018) • A Survey on the Security of Blockchain Systems (Li et al., 2020) • Bitcoin and Blockchain: Security and Privacy (Zaghloul, Li et al., 2020)
Blockchain Architecture	• Architecture for Blockchain Applications (Xu, Weber et al., 2019) • The Blockchain and the New Architecture of Trust (Werbach, 2018) • An Overview of Blockchain Technology: Architecture, Consensus, and Future Trends (Zheng et al., 2017) • Real-time Supply Chain—A blockchain architecture for project deliveries (Helo & Shamsuzzoha, 2020)
Blockchain Standards	• Roadmap for Blockchain Standards—Standards Australia (Meguerditchian, 2017) • Blockchain Standards for Compliance and Trust (Anjum et al., 2017) • Regulating Disruption: Blockchain, GDPR, and Questions of Data Sovereignty (Herian, 2018)

(continued)

Table 2 (continued)

Topics	Identified resources (books and internet sources)
Blockchain Smart contracts	• Smart Contracts: A Primer (Matthew N. O. Sadiku, 2018) • Blockchain Based Smart Contracts (Alharby & van Moorsel, 2017) • An incentive mechanism for data sharing based on blockchain with smart contracts (Xuan et al., 2020) • Blockchain smart contracts formalization: Approaches and challenges to address vulnerabilities (Singh et al., 2020) • Blockchain distributed ledger technology: An introduction and focus on smart contracts (Hamilton, 2020)
Working Papers on Blockchain from Professional Accounting Bodies	• Divided We Fall, Distributed We Stand: The Professional Accountant's Guide to Distributed Ledgers and Blockchain (Vaidyanathan, 2017) • Blockchain Technology and Its Potential Impact on the Audit and Assurance Profession (AICPA, C. C. A., 2017) • Blockchain Technology: A game-changer in accounting? (DELOITTE, 2016) • How blockchain will revolutionize finance and auditing (EY, 2017) • The Blockchain shift will be seismic (KPMG, 2018) • What's Next for Blockchain in 2016? (PWC, 2016)

(continued)

Table 2 (continued)

Topics	Identified resources (books and internet sources)
Research Published in the Accounting Domain	• Accounting and Auditing at the Time of Blockchain Technology: A Research Agenda, (Schmitz & Leoni, 2019) • Accounting for the Bitcoin: Accountability, Neoliberalism and a Correspondence Analysis (Ram et al., 2016) • Bitcoin: Its Economics for Financial Reporting (Tan & Low, 2017) • Bitcoin as a new asset class (Ram, 2019) • Blockchain: Emergent Industry Adoption and Implications for Accounting (Kokina et al., 2017) • Taxation of the Bitcoin: initial insights through a correspondence analysis (Ram, 2018) • The Blockchain and the Future of Everything (Vigna & Casey, 2019) • Towards Blockchain-based Accounting and Assurance (Dai & Vasarhelyi, 2017) • Thinking outside the Block: Projected Phase of Blockchain Integration in the Accounting Industry (Karajovic et al., 2019) • Blockchain and its implications for accounting and auditing (Bonsón & Bednárová, 2019) • Blockchain as a Database Engine in the accounting System (Tan & Low, 2019) • Blockchain and Accounting Governance: Emerging Issues and Considerations for Accounting and Assurance Professional (Smith & Castonguay, 2020) • Should accountants care about blockchain? (Fuller & Markelevich, 2020) • Accounting Information Systems in the Blockchain Era (Fullana & Ruiz, 2020) • The Impact of Artificial Intelligence and Blockchain on the Accounting Profession (Zhang, Xiong et al., 2020) • Opportunities and challenges for accounting professionals (Sinha, 2020) • Blockchain in Accounting Research and Practice: Current Trends and Future Opportunities (Pimentel & Boulianne, 2020) • Ascertaining auditors' intentions to use blockchain technology: evidence from the Big 4 accountancy firms in Italy (Ferri et al., 2020)

7 Conclusion

Interest among businesses, corporations, large accounting and audit firms, professional accounting bodies, banks and financial institutions in fast-emerging BT is growing, which requires that educational institutions and training providers begin developing BT-related training resources and training programs for professionals in various industries. Blockchain developers and industry experts are working constantly to develop ongoing solutions to enhance blockchain's capacity to help various industries process information more smoothly and quickly. Similarly, accounting information system developers are creating solutions for diverse BT applications in information processing for financial reporting, real-time audits, and governance of financial information for financial decision-making. The academic world of accounting is expected to contribute to developing future-ready accounting professionals who can meet the needs of a fast-changing business environment. Such expectations are the result of industry influence and academic efforts to provide a rationale for including BT in accounting curricula as part of the diffusion of innovation. Academic institutions and professional accounting bodies have taken the initiative to provide training to future accountants. The present analysis confirms the theoretical perspective of diffusion of innovation by confirming that accounting educational institutions and training providers have been influenced both externally, i.e., by businesses, accounting practitioners and professional accounting bodies, and internally, i.e., by academia, in the adoption of BT in accounting curricula.

Although the popularity of BT in accounting practice is growing, accounting academics have been relatively cautious in exploring the blockchain sphere and integrating aspects of BT into their curricula. A comprehensive literature search and review indicates that only a few academics have entered the academic domain of blockchain thus far (e.g., Rückeshäuser, 2017; Kokina et al., 2017; Dai & Vasarhelyi, 2017), despite the need to teach this fast-emerging technology to accounting students. By systematizing extant academic and professional discussions of blockchain, this paper explains the basics of BT to academics and justifies the inclusion of blockchain accounting in accounting curricula. Recent updates in blockchain accounting knowledge are collated from publications in accounting journals and guidance materials published by professional accounting bodies and large accounting firms on their websites. The structured information provided here can give accounting educators, accounting students and education institutions useful initial insights on BT and its implications and contribute to the development of blockchain accounting materials by accounting educators who are considering adding this topic to their courses. In addition, a template is provided to guide educators in integrating BT knowledge relevant to financial accounting, management accounting and auditing into accounting curricula. A sequential learning format is recommended that begins with the basics of blockchain and then introduces triple-entry accounting, real-time audits, blockchain security, blockchain architecture, blockchain standards and smart contracts. To facilitate this integration, examples of instructional and research-based resources are provided as a reference point.

By providing structured guidance to accounting educators about integrating BT into accounting curricula, this paper makes a significant contribution to the delivery of accounting education. This paper also makes a practical contribution, as the integration of new technologies into accounting curricula will prepare graduates for employment in the accounting industry and fulfil industry expectations that graduates will have information technology skills relevant to the accounting profession. We argue that this paper represents only the beginning of raising awareness among accounting academics of the need to start incorporating BT into curricula as part of an ongoing effort to understand developments in the field and update instructional materials accordingly. Given the nature and impact of fast-emerging technologies on the accounting profession and practice, accounting educators will continue to need to update their curricula to ensure that students are exposed to and understand BT and other emerging technologies and produce work-ready graduates.

References

Abreu, P. W., Aparicio, M., & Costa, C. J. (2018). *Blockchain technology in the auditing environment.* Paper presented at the 2018 13th Iberian Conference on Information Systems and Technologies (CISTI).

ACT-IAC. (2017). Enabling Blockchain Innovation in the U.S. Federal Government: A Blockchain Primer.

Aggarwal, S. (2017). *Bitcoin magnet* (Vol. 1). Notion Press.

AICPA, C. C. A. (2017). Blockchain Technology and its potential impact on the audit and assurance profession. Retrieved from https://www.aicpa.org/content/dam/aicpa/interestareas/frc/assuranceadvisoryservices/downloadabledocuments/blockchain-technology-and-its-potential-impact-on-the-audit-and-assurance-profession.pdf

Al Harthy, K., Al Shuhaimi, F., & Al Ismaily, K. K. J. (2019). *The upcoming Blockchain adoption in Higher-education: requirements and process.* Paper presented at the 2019 4th MEC International Conference on Big Data and Smart City (ICBDSC).

Alammary, A., Alhazmi, S., Almasri, M., & Gillani, S. (2019). Blockchain-based applications in education: A systematic review. *Applied Sciences, 9*(12), 2400.

Alharby, M., & van Moorsel, A. (2017). Blockchain-based smart contracts: A systematic mapping study. *arXiv preprint* arXiv:1710.06372.

Andersen, N. (2016). *Blockchain Technology: A game-changer in accounting?* Retrieved from

Anjum, A., et al. (2017). Blockchain standards for compliance and trust. *IEEE Cloud Computing 4*(4), 84–90.

Appelbaum, D., & Nehmer, R. (2017). Designing and Auditing Accounting Systems Based on Blockchain and Distributed Ledger Principles. *Feliciano School of Business.*

Appelbaum, D. & Nehmer, R. A. (2020). Auditing cloud-based blockchain accounting systems. *Journal of Information Systems, 34*(2), 5–21.

Attaran, M., & Gunasekaran, A. (2019). Blockchain-enabled technology: the emerging technology set to reshape and decentralise many industries. *International Journal of Applied Decision Sciences, 12*(4).

Bansal, S. K., Batra, R., & Jain, C. N. (2018). Blockchain the future of accounting. *The Management Accountant Journal, 53*(6), 60–65.

Berryhill, J., Bourgery, T., & Hanson, A. (2018). Blockchian Technology and its use in the public sector. *OECD Working Papers on Public Governance, 28.*

Bonsón, E., & Bednárová, M. (2019). Blockchain and its implications for accounting and auditing. *Meditari Accountancy Research, 27*(5), 725–740.

Brandon, D. (2016). The blockchain: The future of business information systems. *International Journal of the Academic Business World, 10*(2), 33–40.

Byström, H. (2016). *Blockchains, real-time accounting and the future of credit risk modeling*. Lund University.

Cai, C. W. (2019). Triple-entry accounting with blockchain: How far have we come? *Accounting & Finance.*

Cai, C. W. J. A., & Finance. (2021). Triple-entry accounting with blockchain: How far have we come? *Accounting & Finance, 61*(1), 71–93.

Chen, G., Xu, B., Lu, M., & Chen, N.-S. (2018a). Exploring blockchain technology and its potential applications for education. *Smart Learning Environments, 10.* https://doi.org/10.1186/s40561-017-0050-x

Chen, G., Xu, B., Lu, M., & Chen, N.-S. (2018b). Exploring blockchain technology and its potential applications for education. *Smart Learning Environments, 5*(1), 1.

Chung, M., & Kim, J. (2016). The internet information and technology research directions based on the fourth industrial revolution. *KSII Transactions on Internet & Information Systems, 10*(3).

Dai, J., & Vasarhelyi, M. A. (2017). Toward blockchain-based accounting and assurance. *Journal of Information Systems, 31*(3), 5–21.

De Villiers, R. (2020). Seven principles to ensure future-ready accounting graduates—A model for future research and practice. *Meditari Accountancy Research*, Vol. ahead-of-print No. ahead-of-print. https://doi.org/10.1108/MEDAR-04-2020-0867

Deloitte. (2016). Blockchain Technology: A Game-changer in accounting? Retrieved from https://www2.deloitte.com/content/dam/Deloitte/de/Documents/Innovation/Blockchain_A%20game-changer%20in%20accounting.pdf

Dikert, K., et al. (2016). Challenges and success factors for large-scale agile transformations: A systematic literature review. *Journal of Systems and Software, 119*, 87–108.

Don Tapscott, A. T. (2016). *Blockchain revolution* (1st ed.). Penguin Books Ltd.

Drescher, D. (2017). *Blockchain basics: A non-technical introduction in 25 steps* (1st ed.). Apress.

Duan, B., Zhong, Y., & Liu, D. (2017). *Education application of blockchain technology: Learning outcome and meta-diploma.* Paper presented at the 2017 IEEE 23rd International Conference on Parallel and Distributed Systems (ICPADS).

Dunn, R. T., Jenkins, J. G., & Sheldon, M. D. (2020). Bitcoin and blockchain: Audit implications of the Killer BsBitcoin and Blockchain. *The accounting review.*

Education, S. G. (2018). Sony global education develops technology using Blockchain for open sharing of academic proficiency and progress records, 22 February 2016.

Elsts A, M. E. a. O. G. (2018). Distributed Ledger Technology and the Internet of Things: A Feasibility Study. *BlockSys 2018.*

EY. (2017). How blockchain will revolutionize finance and auditing. Retrieved from https://www.ey.com/en_gl/digital/blockchain-why-finance-and-auditing-will-never-be-the-same

Ferri, L., Spanò, R., Ginesti, G., & Theodosopoulos, G. J. M. A. R. (2020). Ascertaining auditors' intentions to use blockchain technology: evidence from the Big 4 accountancy firms in Italy.

Fullana, O., & Ruiz, J. (2020). Accounting Information Systems in the Blockchain Era. *Available at SSRN 3517142.*

Fuller, S. H., & Markelevich, A. (2020). Should accountants care about blockchain? *Journal of Corporate Accounting & Finance, 31*(2), 34–46.

Grech, A., & Camilleri, A. F. (2017). *Blockchain in education.* Publications Office of the European Union.

Grigg, I. (2015). *Triple entry accounting*. Systemics Inc. (2005).

Guang Chen, Bing Xu, M. L., & Chen, N.-S. (2018c). Exploring blockchain technology and its potential applications for education. *Smart Learning Environments, 10.* https://doi.org/10.1186/s40561-017-0050-x

Hamilton, M. (2020). Blockchain distributed ledger technology: An introduction and focus on smart contracts. *Journal of Corporate Accounting & Finance, 31*(2), 7–12.

Helo, P. & Shamsuzzoha, A. (2020). Real-time supply chain—A blockchain architecture for project deliveries. *Robotics and Computer-Integrated Manufacturing, 63*, 101909.

Herian, R. (2018). Regulating disruption: Blockchain, Gdpr, and questions of data sovereignty. *Journal of Internet Law, 22*(2), 1–16.

Hoy, M. B. (2017). An introduction to the blockchain and its implications for libraries and medicine. *Medical Reference Services Quarterly, 36*(3), 273–279.

Ibañez, J. I., Bayer, C. N., Tasca, P., & Xu, J. (2020). REA, triple-entry accounting and blockchain: Converging paths to shared ledger systems. *Available at SSRN*.

ICAEW. (2017). Blockchain and future of Accountancy. *ICAEW IT FACULTY*.

Inside-Higher-Ed. (2018). Blockchain Gains Currency in Higher Ed. Retrieved from https://www.insidehighered.com/news/2018/08/13/rising-profile-blockchain-academe

Karajovic, M., Kim, H. M., & Laskowski, M. (2019). Thinking outside the block: Projected phases of blockchain integration in the accounting industry. *Australian Accounting Review, 29*(2), 319–330.

Kokina, J., Mancha, R., & Pachamanova, D. (2017). Blockchain: Emergent industry adoption and implications for accounting. *Journal of Emerging Technologies in Accounting, 14*(2), 91–100.

KPMG. (2018). The Blockchain shift will be seismic. Retrieved from https://home.kpmg/ca/en/home/insights/2018/02/the-blockchain-shift-will-be-seismic.html

Kuppusamy, P. (2019). Blockchain Architecture to Higher Education Systems. *International Journal of Latest Technology in Engineering, Management & Applied Science, VIII*(II), 124–138.

Li, X., Jiang, P., Chen, T., Luo, X., & Wen, Q. (2020). A survey on the security of blockchain systems. *Future Generation Computer Systems, 107*, 841–853.

Liyuan, L., Meng, H., Yiyun, Z., & Reza, P. (2019). *E^ 2 C-Chain: A two-stage incentive education employment and skill certification blockchain.* Paper presented at the 2019 IEEE International Conference on Blockchain (Blockchain).

Marrone, M., & Hazelton, J. (2019). The disruptive and transformative potential of new technologies for accounting, accountants and accountability: A review of current literature and call for further research. *Meditari Accountancy Research, 27*(5), 677–694. https://doi.org/10.1108/MEDAR-06-2019-0508

Marchionni, P. (2018). Next Generation Government Service Bus-The Blockchain Landscape. *Available at SSRN 3141749*.

Matthew N. O. Sadiku, K. G. E., Sarhan M. Musa. (2018). Smart Contracts: A Primer. *Journal of Scientific and Engineering Research.*

Maull, R., Godsiff, P., Mulligan, C., Brown, A., & Kewell, B. (2017). Distributed ledger technology: Applications and implications. *Strategic Change, 26*(5), 481–489.

McKinlay, J., Pithouse, D., McGonagle, J., & Sanders, J. (2016). *Blockchain: Background, challenges and legal issues.* DLA Piper Publications.

Meguerditchian, V. (2017). *Roadmap for blockchain standards report–March 2017*. Standards Australia.

Midwinter, T., & Sheppard, P. (2000). eCollaboration—'The Drive for Simplicity.' *BT Technology Journal, 18*(2), 107–115.

Moubarak, J., et al. (2018). On blockchain security and relevant attacks. *2018 IEEE Middle East and North Africa Communications Conference (MENACOMM)*, IEEE.

Ølnes, S., Ubacht, J., & Janssen, M. (2017). *Blockchain in government: Benefits and implications of distributed ledger technology for information sharing*. Elsevier.

Owen, G. (2013). Integrated reporting: A review of developments and their implications for the accounting curriculum. *Accounting Education, 22*(4), 340–356.

Peters, G. W., & Panayi, E. (2016). Understanding modern banking ledgers through blockchain technologies: Future of transaction processing and smart contracts on the internet of money. In *Banking Beyond Banks and Money* (pp. 239–278): Springer.

Pimentel, E., & Boulianne, E. J. A. P. (2020). Blockchain in accounting research and practice: Current trends and future opportunities. *19*(4), 325–361.

Popay, J., et al. (2006). Guidance on the conduct of narrative synthesis in systematic reviews. *A product from the ESRC methods programme Version 1*, b92.

Potekhina, A., & Riumkin, I. (2017). Blockchain—A new accounting paradigm: Implications for credit risk management.

Puthal, D., Malik, N., Mohanty, S. P., Kougianos, E., & Yang, C. (2018). The blockchain as a decentralized security framework [future directions]. *IEEE Consumer Electronics Magazine, 7*(2), 18–21.

PWC. (2016). What's Next for Blockchain in 2016? Retrieved from https://www.pwc.com/us/en/financial-services/publications/viewpoints/assets/pwc-qa-whats-next-for-blockchain.pdf

PWC. (2019). Blockchain, a catalyst for new approaches in insurance. Retrieved from https://www.pwc.com/gx/en/insurance/assets/blockchain-a-catalyst.pdf

Ram, A., Maroun, W., & Garnett, R. (2016). Accounting for the Bitcoin: Accountability, neoliberalism and a correspondence analysis. *Meditari Accountancy Research, 24*(1), 2–35.

Ram, A. J. (2018). *Taxation of the bitcoin: Initial insights through a correspondence analysis.* Meditari Accountancy Research.

Ram, A. J. (2019). Bitcoin as a new asset class. *Meditari Accountancy Research, 27*(1), 147–168.

Rogers, E. M. (1995). Diffusion of Innovations: Modifications of a model for telecommunications. *Die diffusion von innovationen in der telekommunikation*, Springer, 25–38.

Savelyev, A. (2017). Cryptocurrencies in the system of objects of civil rights. Law. 8, 136–153. *Савельев АИ Криптовалюты в системе объектов гражданских прав//Закон*(8), 136–153.

Schmitz, J., & Leoni, G. (2019). Accounting and auditing at the time of blockchain technology: A research agenda. *Australian Accounting Review.*

Schwab, K. (2017). *The fourth industrial revolution.* Currency.

Sharples, M., & Domingue, J. (2016). *The blockchain and kudos: A distributed system for educational record, reputation and reward.* Paper presented at the European Conference on Technology Enhanced Learning.

Shaw, J. (2018). The blockchain transformation of accounting and auditing. *Oregon Society of CPAs.*

Shetty, S., Kamhoua, C. A., & Njilla, L. (2019). *Blockchain for Distributed Systems Security*: Wiley-IEEE Computer Society Press.

Singh, A., Parizi, R. M., Zhang, Q., Choo, K.-K.R., & Dehghantanha, A. (2020). Blockchain smart contracts formalization: Approaches and challenges to address vulnerabilities. *Computers & Security, 88*, 101654.

Sinha, S. (2020). Blockchain—Opportunities and challenges for accounting professionals. *Journal of Corporate Accounting & Finance, 31*(2), 65–67.

Smith, S. S., & Castonguay, J. J. (2020). Blockchain and accounting governance: Emerging issues and considerations for accounting and assurance professionals. *Journal of Emerging Technologies in Accounting, 17*(1), 119–131.

Subramanian, H., Cousins, K., Dutta, K., Sheth, A., Pineda, J., & Salcedo, E. (2018). Blockchain and Information Systems.

Tan, B. S., & Low, K. Y. (2017). Bitcoin–its economics for financial reporting. *Australian Accounting Review, 27*(2), 220–227.

Tan, B. S., & Low, K. Y. (2019). Blockchain as the database engine in the accounting system. *Australian Accounting Review, 29*(2), 312–318.

Tapscott, D., & Tapscott, A. (2016). *Blockchain revolution: how the technology behind bitcoin is changing money, business, and the world.* Penguin.

Turkanović, M., Hölbl, M., Košič, K., Heričko, M., & Kamišalić, A. (2018). EduCTX: A blockchain-based higher education credit platform. *IEEE Access, 6*, 5112–5127.

Vaidyanathan, N. (2017). Divided we fall, distributed we stand. The Professional Accountant's Guide to Distributed Ledgers and Blockchain. Association of Chartered Certified Accountants.

Vigna, P., & Casey, M. J. (2019). *The truth machine: The blockchain and the future of everything.* Picador.

Victor, L. (2008). Systematic reviewing. *Social Research Update, 54*(1), 1–4.

Vukolić, M. (2015). *The quest for scalable blockchain fabric: Proof-of-work vs. BFT replication.* Paper presented at the International workshop on open problems in network security.

Vukolić, M. (2017). *Rethinking permissioned blockchains.* Paper presented at the Proceedings of the ACM Workshop on Blockchain, Cryptocurrencies and Contracts.

Watson, L. A., & Mishler, C. (2017). Get Ready for Blockchain. *Strategic Finance.*

Werbach, K. (2018). *The Blockchain and the New Architecture of Trust*, MIT Press.

Wüst, K., & Gervais, A. (2018). *Do you need a Blockchain?* Paper presented at the 2018 Crypto Valley Conference on Blockchain Technology (CVCBT).

Xu, X., Weber, I., & Staples, M. (2019). *Architecture for blockchain applications.* Springer.

Xuan, S., Zheng, L., Chung, I., Wang, W., Man, D., Du, X., . . . Guizani, M. (2020). An incentive mechanism for data sharing based on blockchain with smart contracts. *Computers and Electrical Engineering, 83*, 106587.

Yermack, D. (2015). Is Bitcoin a real currency? An economic appraisal. In *Handbook of digital currency* (pp. 31–43). Elsevier.

Yermack, D. (2017). Corporate governance and blockchains. *Review of Finance, 21*(1), 7–31.

Zaghloul, E., Li, T., Mutka, M. W., & Ren, J. (2020). Bitcoin and blockchain: Security and privacy. *IEEE Internet of Things Journal.*

Zheng, Z., et al. (2017). An overview of blockchain technology: Architecture, consensus, and future trends. In *2017 IEEE International Congress on Big Data (BigData Congress)*, IEEE.

Zheng, Z., Xie, S., Dai, H.-N., Chen, X., & Wang, H. (2018). Blockchain challenges and opportunities: A survey. *International Journal of Web and Grid Services, 14*(4), 352–375.

Manpreet Singh Ph.D., has earned a doctorate from the School of Accounting, Information Systems and Supply Chain at the RMIT University, Melbourne, Australia. The research interests are the links between accounting and information systems.

Mahesh Joshi Ph.D., is a Senior Lecturer in Accounting and Financial Planning at RMIT University, Melbourne, Australia. His research interests are corporate social reporting, corporate governance, integrated reporting, intellectual capital, accounting history, accounting education, and emerging technologies in accounting.

Sharad Sharma Ph.D., is a Lecturer in Wealth Management and Taxation in the School of Accounting, Information Systems and Supply Chain at the RMIT University, Melbourne, Australia. He has extensive experience in the banking industry in India. His research expertise is in the areas of behavioral finance, capital markets, IFRS and various aspects of financial reporting and performance. He has published several papers in scholarly academic journals.

Chapter 16
Digitized Simulation and Gamified Pedagogy in a First Year Accounting Core Subject

Viktor Arity, Gillian Vesty, and Belinda Moloney

Abstract The idea of technologically enhanced pedagogy, such as digitized simulation and gamified authentic assessments, in higher education is relatively new but offers the potential to revolutionize classroom delivery. This paper is designed to provide insights into curriculum designs and student responses to the use of innovative assessment in accounting education. This research examines how digitized simulation and serious games can enhance student engagement and help to address cognitive load challenges experienced by students. This paper also provides a case of detailed, practical insights for academics interested in digitizing and gamifying pedagogy for learning, while citing the benefits of serious game use in verifying assessment authenticity.

Keywords Cognitive load · Authentic assessment · Serious games · Discovery-based learning

1 Introduction

In this paper, we contribute to the emerging body of research that examines the ways in which learning design and the use of games and digital innovations can contribute to accounting education. Taking a student-centered learning approach, we examined our course design and its use of technology to enhance student engagement and change the future of accounting education. Students are increasingly required to be equipped with essential work-ready skills in accounting software and digital tools that support data analytics and visualizations for strategic decision making

V. Arity (✉) · G. Vesty
RMIT University, Melbourne, VIC, Australia
e-mail: viktor.arity@rmit.edu.au

G. Vesty
e-mail: gillian.vesty@rmit.edu.au

B. Moloney
Deakin University, Geelong, VIC, Australia
e-mail: belinda.moloney@torrens.edu.au

T. Rana et al. (eds.), *Handbook of Big Data and Analytics in Accounting and Auditing*,
https://doi.org/10.1007/978-981-19-4460-4_16

(ACCA, 2012). Curriculum reviews were prompted by the Australian government policy updates in their aims to foster an increased dialogue between the emerging digital technology industry and education (Commonwealth of Australia, 2016). This research explores the outcomes of embracing technology in accounting curriculum design, through experimenting with self-designed simulations and serious games as well as other readily available software and mobile applications.

Digital simulation and serious games have equally immersive and engaging attributes, often employing specific design features for use in authentic assessments (Egenfeldt-Nielsen et al., 2011). These digital innovations are defined as "…a mental contest, played with a computer in accordance with specific rules that uses entertainment to further government or corporate training, education, health, public policy, and strategic learning objectives" (Zyda, 2005, p. 26), which offer students with a rich opportunity for active exploration of serious intellectual and social problems with minimal risk (Abt, 1987). Games and simulations have proven beneficial in domains including business, health, engineering and science (Routledge, 2016; Sawyer & Rejeski, 2002; Susi et al., 2007) and these mechanisms are increasingly adopted for their use within virtual environment-based staff training (BankersLab, 2013; Routledge, 2016). While simulations and serious games offer the opportunity for innovative and disruptive educational approaches, their pedagogical success depends on ensuring that learning outcomes and design mechanisms are thoroughly considered. Important features include the ability to capture student input data, (Buchinger & Hounsell, 2018) for immediate feedback and the evaluation of cognitively challenging pain points within the learning journey. Instructors can integrate data to map the strengths and the weaknesses of the student responses and adjust the education sessions accordingly. Subsequently, both student and instructors can play an important role in the adaptation and future designs of serious games. Furthermore, simulation and serious games provide a safe way to experiment with learning.

Adopting learning and game mechanics philosophies, students are motivated through the embedded design within serious games features, enabling them to progress through a series of stages and practice their skills through repetition and scaffolded tasks of varying difficulty (Arnab et al., 2016; Routledge, 2016; Subhash & Cudney, 2018). The careful digital design of authentic assessment can bring to life somewhat inaccessible concepts and dry topics within the traditional curriculum. While challenging topics will always remain difficult for students, educational design features must include breaking down large learning components and adopt enhanced guidance with maps, visual aids, instructions and connecting storyboards (Sweller, 1988). These tactics have been demonstrated to be effective in developing digital accounting educational offerings (Arity & Vesty, 2020) and improving student learning experiences with each teaching iteration. Rather than focus on a single serious game or digital simulation, we contribute to this emerging field of research by examining our strategically-designed undergraduate accounting curriculum and reporting on the resulting authentic assessment exemplars. Our examination is conducted through the lens of student engagement, along with the capacity of our revised assessments to mitigate cognitive load challenges.

The research questions addressed within this study include:

RQ1: *How can educators design a digitized course to better support the cognitive burden students face when engaging with challenging concepts?*

RQ2: *How effective are the digitized simulation and serious games design features in addressing the cognitive load burden of students undertaking their first-year accounting core course?*

This research adopted autoethnographic methods to capture a reflective teaching case, alongside the implementation of a survey instrument (questionnaire) and student Course Evaluation Survey (CES) qualitative data to evaluate the efficacy of the curriculum on student's cognitive load burden and engagement respectively. Within this research, lessons learned were documented within the context of delivering a first-year accounting subject as a core component of their business degree, taught within a large Australian university. The research focused on experiential learning, as well as the capacity of the technology and curriculum design features to alleviate the cognitive burden faced by many students who undertake this study while having no prior experience with accounting. While curriculum changes may address calls from the Australian accounting professional bodies for prioritizing technology in accounting education, we were keen to evaluate the pedagogical authenticity of the course, for improved student experiences and learning outcomes.

In the sections that follow, a background overview of extant literature outlines the use of technology in discovery-based learning and the adoption of simulations and serious games in business and accounting education. This is followed by discussion of the theoretical framework, which introduces a combination of digital design features, serious game design principles and cognitive load theory, in order to establish an understanding of accounting education within a systems context. This framework has informed the data collection and analysis process. The research setting comprises a first-year accounting core course, where we describe the development of the curriculum to incorporate simulations and serious games, including a comprehensive, digitized business plan simulation that integrates innovative teaching moments and autoethnographic narratives throughout the 12-week semester. The student's learning journey is mapped according to the Beetham and Sharpe's (2019, p. 265) digital capability checklist. To evaluate the impact on student engagement and cognitive burden, data was collected via a student survey and analyzed along with secondary qualitative survey responses. Following the findings section, we conclude the paper with a discussion of implications and areas for future research.

2 Literature Review

2.1 Curriculum Design and Technology Enhancement: Discovery Learning Versus Direct Instruction

When examining how learning design paired with games and digital innovations can contribute to accounting education, it is important that two types of learning approaches taken by academics are acknowledged. The first, instruction-based learning, is teacher-driven while the second, discovery-based learning is student-centered. The former relies on traditional techniques requiring basic technology, while the latter tends to adopt high-end technology in its approach.

Discovery-based learning, or inquiry-based learning, is a constructivist approach to learning requiring that students to adopt a proactive learning attitude whereby they explore, discover, and invent knowledge (Bok, 2006). A student-centered learning process requires students to identify patterns (Destrebecqz, 2004; Jiménez et al., 1996), elicit explanations (Chi et al., 1994; Rittle-Johnson, 2006), implement manuals (Lazonder & van der Meij, 1993), and perform simulations (Stark et al., 1998) to synthesize, assimilate, and create the target knowledge. Thus, it can be inferred that the degree of autonomy is evidenced by an absence of teacher presence, where minimal assistance is offered to students during the learning process, a key feature of discovery-based learning (Alfieri et al., 2011).

Discovery-based learning is used in different training and learning disciplines. In science subjects that require the development of metacognitive skills, conceptual and procedural knowledge, discovery-based learning is an indispensable learning approach for improving student performance (Nunaki et al., 2019). This learning approach contributes to assessment tasks that require descriptive writing built around text, images and places (Ariyana et al., 2020).

Importantly, discovery-based learning is recognized for building on prior knowledge and supporting the retention of permanent crucial skills (Ramdhani et al., 2017). Other advantages associated with the technique include improved student engagement and motivation in the learning process (Duffy, 2009). There is evidence of enhanced experiment and creativity, particularly as the curriculum can be more readily tailored for individual students for personalized learning experiences (Lee, 2014). This is because discovery-based learning requires the students to individually interact with the environment and make sense of the surroundings (Alfieri et al., 2011).

It is essential that learning designers build content on a pre-existing framework of knowledge, as a necessary pre-condition to ensure that knowledge can be developed by the students drawing from their extant framework (Bruner, 1986). There must also be teacher presence for timely feedback and responding to learner queries. Essentially, the quality of the curriculum is only as good as the instructors' preparedness to anticipate student questions and respond meaningfully. The potential drawback faced within curriculum design potentially reducing the effectiveness of the learning process, occurs when the student-centered learning approach places a demonstrable strain on the working memory of the students during the problem-solving search process (Sweller, 1988). This increases the difficulty of the learning process and hence diverts attention to the cognitive burden faced by students.

While discovery-based learning provides a significant degree of autonomy to the students, instruction-based learning provides little autonomy for students. The format of the teaching delivered in most institutions includes demonstration, guided practice, and independent practice. Students practice under teacher supervision until they achieve mastery (Clark & Mayer, 2016; Mayer, 2011, 2020a). When learning by example, students are taught to employ certain methods and follow instructions to demonstrate their understanding (Mayer, 2020b). This approach fosters teacher presence in the classroom, with teachers as the 'focal point' of this learning method, whereby they provide explicit instructions, examples or demonstration videos to students.

Instruction-based learning can increase the efficiency of learning through reduction in the number of trials, as compared with the trial-and-error approach adopted in discovery-based learning (Ruge et al., 2018). Research demonstrates that repeated instructions avoid the generation of erroneous memory traces established in the discovery-based learning trial-and-error approach. Instruction-based learning ensures that only the correct instructions are retained (Ruge et al., 2018). Furthermore, instruction-based learning places less strain on the working memory of students as it places more emphasis on procedural working memory or on episodic memory traces. This results in faster response times than discovery-based learning, which relies on hypothesis testing that subsequently consumes more time and is more cognitively demanding on the student's declarative working memory (Ruge et al., 2018). In addition, the highly controlled teacher-centered environment has been found to better support students with learning disabilities where it is recognized that only basic academic strategies can be mastered (Gersten et al., 1986).

Nevertheless, while instruction-based learning can increase learning efficiency, this teaching method has been argued to be problematic as students often adopt a passive learning attitude, resulting in minimal information processing and proactive analysis performed by students. They are consequently treated as 'empty vessels', passively receiving knowledge through lectures and direct instructions. Employing this method, any knowledge gained tends to be more short-term by comparison to the discovery-based learning which has longer lasting advantages due to its richer encoding context, yielding better retention and long-term memory retrieval (Ruge et al., 2018).

With no consensus as to which educational design is better, it is argued that the two approaches can potentially be used in tandem with the selected approach depending on the specific learning outcomes required (Oliver & Trigwell, 2005). Together, a blended approach can offer moments where there is a shift from student presence to one of teacher presence, which provides cognitive relief for students, along with opportunities to discuss and reflect the links to learning outcomes (Rodgers & Raider-Roth, 2006). Ultimately, there exists immense potential in adopting technology-based design tactics to help overcome any cognitive challenges that may arise with discovery-based learning and student learning disabilities.

2.2 Introducing Digital Simulation and Serious Games

Digital simulation and serious games arguably provide a social component to learning, which is important for collaborative engagement, alongside specified design features that support educational pedagogy associated with 'learning by doing' (Buchinger & Hounsell, 2018; Carvalho et al., 2015). Learning-by-doing, or discovery-based learning, is arguably suitable for accounting education (Hughes & Berry, 2000). Carefully constructed (accounting and business) scenarios can be presented to students for formation of individually hypothesized and modelled 'what-ifs' that can be tested, experimented with, and challenged (Arnab et al., 2016).

While simulations may mean different things across different settings and disciplines, in general, they aim to simulate reality, or operational representation through imitation (Bell & Loon, 2015; Guetzkow, 1963; Lean et al., 2006), performance (Gee, 2003; Squire, 2006) or problem solving (Squire, 2006). Technology-based simulation within education aims to guide learning through a medium that facilitates interaction with the social and material worlds (Sauer et al., 2000; Squire, 2006), while attempting to reflect or transform student learning (Gredler, 2004). The concepts comprising technology-based simulation and gamification are defined and presented in Table 1.

Simulations are considered evolving case studies with visual, employing video-based content to develop higher order, critical thinking skills and dispositions of participants (Bell & Loon, 2015; Springer & Borthick, 2004). Incorporating participant role playing, simulations help with analyzing problems in a structured fashion (Riley et al., 2013) while reinforcing learning through feedback (Bell & Loon, 2015). While real world environments are mimicked to enhance student engagement (Teach & Schwartz, 2004), benefits include providing learning within a 'safe' setting, rather than practice (Petroski, 2012; Weaver & Erby, 2012) with inherent risk of failing a subject. For example, bankrupting a business or killing a patient is much preferred in simulated workplace scenarios than real life (Gredler, 2004). Attributes such as 'experiential', 'problem-based' and 'the ability to provide immediate feedback' are key to immersive student-centered learning (Blasko et al., 2014; Petroski, 2012) with a superior learning experience. This is largely due to the extrinsic motivation generated by gamification, rewards and change of pace in the classroom (Blasko et al., 2014; Carenys et al., 2016; Clark et al., 2016; Huang et al., 2012). Equally important is the non-linearity of digitized simulation and serious games which contributes to their reusability and authenticity (Routledge, 2016). Randomizing learning design features could result in students playing a simulation multiple times, and enabling learning or improvements with each game. Communication dramatically aids the pedagogical developments in digitized games (Maclean et al., 2016), specifically directed at enhancing individual expertise and learning through group participation.

Lewin et al. (2018) contend that the optimal digital pedagogy is scalable and sustainable with learning designs centered around a community of ideas and features that can be 'shared and re-used' (p. 1132). Innovation and creativity in design is the result of disagreement, debates and not necessarily shared values and coordinated agreement (Stark, 2009). Hence the importance of engaging all stakeholders, including students in digital simulation and serious games design experimentation. In this way, technology in the classroom supports more effective reciprocal dialogue and two-way exchanges of information between teachers and students (Forman & Ansell, 2002). Simulated practice contributes to build the overall confidence of students:

Table 1 Technology based simulation and gamification

Gamification	Focused on applying game mechanics to non-game activities with the intention of making these activities more engaging. Typical game mechanics include levels, badges and achievements to build interest and maintain engagement
Serious Games	Embodying traditional game design methodologies, combined with instructional design approaches to address behavior change in specific subjects. It is not necessary to use game technologies to create a Serious Game. Serious Games are often used to bring content to life through the use of stories, progression and challenges designed to gradually increase a user's awareness of a concept and guide them toward best-practice behavior
Simulations	Providing a realistic representation of a working model of a system or process. Simulations are reliant on behavioral rules and are more true-to-life than Serious Games, perhaps aligned with live case studies
Virtual Worlds	These have the appearance of a game but do not leverage any of the game design mechanics around motivation and engagement that one would associate with a game. They are social places where people can gather in a visual, virtual space
Commercial Off-the-Shelf games for Entertainment	These are games which are produced by the commercial entertainment games industry designed primarily as a leisure activity. These games are typically published by large publishers and have budgets of tens if not hundreds of millions of dollars. These are the games you see on the Xbox and PlayStation
Mobile Games	Typically falling into the casual games genre, mobile games are usually quick to pick up and play and simple to understand. Most consist of simple matching games or traditional card games. Some more complex games are coming onto the market but due to limitations of hardware and software the opportunity for complex games is still nascent
Augmented Reality	Applications that use cameras to superimpose a computer-generated image on a user's view of the real world
Virtual Reality	Computer-generated simulation of a 3D image or environment that can be interacted with in a seemingly real or physical way by a person using special electronic equipment

(continued)

Table 1 (continued)

MMORPGs	Massively Multiplayer Online Role Play Games are game worlds that can support large numbers of players simultaneously

Source Routledge (2016, pp. 24–25)

> Games do something no other form of industry, interaction or media do; they allow you to be bad at them... and they punish you for it by stalling your progress.... One of the features making them perfect for learning and development is this "punishment," the requirement for the learner or player to prove they understand the rules and concepts to progress. (Routledge, 2016, p. 2)

In summary, the attributes that contribute to understanding the success of digital simulation and serious game designs include: (1) the degree to which the game is perceived to challenge individuals; (2) the nature of the individual or group competition; (3) the provision of a meaningful set of rules that engage with the curricula and determine 'fair play'; (4) the provision of goal-oriented tasks to meet competency levels; (5) the decision to situate the game in fantasy and use storytelling for contextual relevance; (6) the flow experience, so that the participant engages more deeply with the game; (8) the level of autonomy or control to give to players of the game; (9) decisions over multimedia embodied in the game and use of visual realism; (10) the extent of feedback to players, and, (11) the ability to which players perceive they have generated real-world skills through playing the game (Carenys et al., 2017, p. 69; Clark et al., 2016; Petroski, 2012). Blasko et al. (2014) further consider cognitive factors, such as learning styles, spatial skills and working memory in design features. Thus, the data generated by observing student progress and gameplay decisions provides the basis for identifying cognitive load challenges and establishes the need for potential design adaptations. In learning algebra, Hedgedus et al. (2015) asserted that dynamic interactive software and wireless networks, in curriculum design, significantly effect student engagement with both procedural and conceptual problems. Further, Xu et al. (2019) linked student engagement to technology-focused learning spaces (e.g. multi-screen space, information sharing, technology-enabled learning support system along with flexible physical spaces and mobile desks) suggesting that flexibility in time and space is important for achieving learning outcomes. Educational factors that influence the choice of technology used in curriculum design include academic expertise, pedagogical experience and the level of student readiness for engaging with alternative forms of teaching (Druzhinina et al., 2018). It is also important that digital technologies should bring both technological and social contexts into account to 'prepare learners for a world pervaded by information, networks, algorithms and data' (Beetham & Sharpe, 2019, p. 1).

While innovations and advancements in educational delivery using virtual reality, artificial intelligence, simulations and serious games are all applicable to accounting and business education, the use of these techniques are not generally assumed in pedagogical designs and tend to be lagging other practitioner fields, such as clinical, science, space and military education (Fletcher, 2009; Watty et al., 2016; Moro, et al., 2022). Understanding accounting as both a social and technical practice is essential for progressing accounting education design (Carnegie et al., 2020). It is also crucial that curriculum designs meet accrediting body requirements including the expectation for students to have enhanced digital capabilities whereby technology is ubiquitous within higher education and the workplace. Some competitive business simulations are directed towards developing algorithmic thinking and understanding of the 'whole' business problem (Marriott, 2004). For example, in business education, simulation participants might be encouraged to consider their hypotheses based on newly presented corporate issues in the field and prescribe corrections (Brooks et al., 2017). The more well-known computer-based simulations include CAPSTONE™, an enterprise-based simulation used in final year undergraduate programs (Teach & Schwartz, 2004) and Harvard Simulations (Working Capital and Balanced Scorecard), Singapore Management University financial accounting game ACE (Seow & Wong, 2013), Kilgors' Balanced Scorecard (Brooks et al., 2017) and Kilgors' Strategic Investment (Brooks et al., 2020). However, only a small number of technology-based games and simulations are used in accounting learning and teaching and fewer exist that would be categorized as 'serious games'. To date, accounting educators and researchers have not fully engaged with the community of practice that views advanced computer technology and gamified simulations as essential part of educational delivery (Clark et al., 2016; Driskell et al., 2017).

Given the recent adjustments towards online teaching as a result of the COVID-19 pandemic, the virtual learning platform is increasingly important, and arguably so is the move away from learning outcomes based on lower order cognition and rote learning that once dominated accounting education. Furthermore, digital simulation and serious games provide greater transparency of student interaction, thus alleviating some of the issues of plagiarism and contract cheating that are persistent and challenging for assessment developers (Bradley, 2015). Further research in the role of design features is essential to best understand the higher order cognitive, intra- and extra-personal skills that are acquired through gamification and simulation (Clark et al., 2016, p. 115). This includes research into student engagement with gamification and simulation, and the teaching support requirements of educators expected to adopt innovative digital designs into their classroom (Blasko et al., 2014). While Huang (2015) argued that success of embracing technology in the classroom is characterized by the teachers' ability to infuse the technologies, equally important is the way in which the adopted technology is influenced by the teaching philosophy. This involves discerning which moments require technology for enhanced teacher presence, versus those that engage student-centred learning.

This literature provides the basis for important curriculum design inclusions, to ensure learners have the opportunity to build their digital capabilities whilst also engaging with challenging accounting concepts and testing their application in an environment where they can safely fail and subsequently engrain new learnings. The effectiveness of the design on addressing the cognitive burden of students is important to ensure active and engaged student participation. This experience provides students with an accessible introduction to the daily tasks of accountants, their decision-making process and prepares students for their ‘real–world’ Work Integrated Learning experience later in their studies.

3 Research Methodology

A mixed-methods approach was adopted to address the research questions, comprising both qualitative and quantitative data. Student survey responses confirmed the suitability of our approach, and collected data was supplemented by autoethnographic accounts of the curriculum design and teaching experiences.

Cognitive load theory underpins our research approach with the pioneer of this theory claiming that educational content should be divided into discrete components (schema) or levels of mastery to reduce **intrinsic** load. Pedagogy should include detailed maps, guides, instructions with timely feedback to students to reduce **extraneous** load. The remaining **germane** load is what students must manage themselves. However, if the intrinsic and extraneous loads are addressed in course design, challenging concepts or topics should overall, be more understandable (Sweller, 1988; Sweller et al., 1998).

A validated cognitive load survey questionnaire designed by Leppink et al. (2013) was adapted and used to evaluate the effectiveness of the digitized simulated assessment task on intrinsic, extraneous and germane cognitive loads. The digitized assessment task flowed throughout the semester and linked to the course content. In Semester 2, 2020, the questionnaire was posted on the course learning management system for all students who had completed the 12-week accounting core course. In total, 139 survey responses were received from a total of 945 students, representing a 14.7% response rate. We removed 5 survey results as they were not usable due to incomplete responses. Final useable survey responses totaled 134.

To understand the overall course satisfaction with the curriculum re-design, student’s qualitative comments were also gathered from the generic student Course Experience Survey (CES) promoted by the university. The CES was distributed to 945 students studying the accounting core course in Semester 2, 2020. In total, 213 responses were received.

To supplement these findings, we also provide a personal narrative of the process and experiences we observed in our curriculum re-design. Autoethnography includes the researcher’s “own intellectual and emotional experiences and insights to generate textured, entangled portrayals of teaching in higher education” (Pillay et al., 2016, p. 1), providing the opportunity to document our personal teaching experiences and supplement these with rich quantitative and qualitative data, collected from student surveys to validate the lived account. Starr (2010a, 2010b) cited the use of autoethnography as an effective methodology for researching education as it constructs new meaning and understanding of the discipline through the lens of personal experience within a constructivist context.

4 New Curriculum Design Features: Process and Experiences

The broad research question asks: How can educators design a digitized course to better support the cognitive burden students face when engaging with challenging concepts? We now explain the steps we have taken to embed a new, digitally-enhanced curriculum in our course. This is guided by the notion of enhancing the experiences of students, while addressing cognitive challenges with design choices.

The course is the first-year accounting core course with around 1,000 students each semester. Only 10% of these students are enrolled in an accounting major, with the remaining students undertaking varying other business degrees. There are also a smaller number of students from other disciplines such as engineering, who study accounting as an elective. Hence, the number of students who may have studied accounting previously is relatively small and it is otherwise assumed students have no prior knowledge. Previously students have claimed this course is both challenging as well as dry and boring. Before we inherited the course, the overall course satisfaction score was low (67%), hence a significant challenge for two of the authors. One supported initial re-design, before jointly commencing the coordination role of this core course in Semester 1, 2019. All 3 authors have previously collaborated in digital innovations in the classroom, experimenting with different models, which is why we decided to introduce these models and our co-designed digital content to improve the outcomes of the accounting core. Our aim was to make accounting fun and replace didactic teaching with interactive sessions to enhance the learning experience (Damron & Mott, 2005).

Previously the course was textbook-driven with a 2-h paper-based exam with a selection of topic questions. In transforming the class, there was a change to case-based illustrations, along with a case-based exam. We decided to move from static to dynamic cases embedded within digital innovations. The curriculum design, including case-based teaching and experimentation with innovative digital technologies were all part of our move to replace exams with authentic assessment. We decided that taking a stepped staged approach and creating multiple low-stake opportunities would also help to check students' progress and learning and provide regular formative feedback (Lambert et al., 2011; Schut et al., 2020). Huxham (2007) argues that combining personalized feedback with model answers is an effective way to help students learn.

Beetham and Sharpe's (2019) digital capabilities checklist (Table 2) was employed to ensure the overall curriculum content supported the move to enhance the digital capabilities of students. Beetham and Sharpe argue that certain design features are required for students to achieve mastery with authors arguing learners should have the opportunity to encounter, practice and receive feedback on their digital capabilities. These include using specialist digital tools, such as those used by accounting practitioners in the workplace. Among the features we considered applicable to accounting practice, were that students should be able to create digital artefacts, find, collate, evaluate and manage data to solve problems and answer questions. Strategic skills

Table 2 Digital Checklist Applied to Curriculum Design

Digitally capable learners should be able to…
Use specialist digital tools of their subject area
Find, collate, evaluate and manage digital information
Manage, analyze and use digital data
Consume and produce ideas in digital media (e.g. spatial, textual, visual, auditory, interactive…)
Create digital artefacts (e.g. web pages, 3D print pieces, code, digital video, infographics …)
Use digital tools to solve problems and/or answer questions
Take part in digital research or professional practice
Collaborate with others using a variety of digital tools and spaces
Participate in digital networks (closed and open)
Develop digital learning skills and habits (e.g. participating, note-making, referencing, quizzing, revising …)
Develop and manage their digital identity and learning outcomes
Consider issues of digital safety, privacy, health and wellbeing, ethics and legality

Adapted from Beetham and Sharpe (2019)

are enhanced through collaboration in digital networks, consuming and producing ideas in digital media, while attention is given to the accounting ethics and legalities of a digitally enhanced world.

The study mapped the digital simulations and serious games content according to the checklist and used other digitized features to form part of the newly designed 12-week curriculum. The significant changes include:

1. *Developing a major assessment piece that invites students to slowly produce a digital artefact as they progress through the course. It is based on their own idea that is designed to solve challenging business problems. It must demonstrate both economic as well as social and environmental sustainability. They demonstrate this by engaging with United Nations Sustainable Development Goals (SDGs).*

Our co-created digital offering, named WritePal, is a dynamic digital simulation tool that is sustainable, scalable and offers a unique staged design, to reduce the cognitive load of students. WritePal can easily be modified with questions and activities that align with specific aspects of the course content, and is accessible on Mobile Phone, Tablet or PC. As outlined in Appendix A, we have designed WritePal so students can create their own simulated business environment, an artefact built on the student's own business ideas. It has 25 staged-release questions, each mapped against the entire course curriculum, but all readily changeable. This staged approach, helps to reduce student stress and alleviates the pressure of last minute, rushed preparation. In addition, the students feel a greater sense of belonging through connecting directly to their teacher through a coded interface. With every stage manageable, we have also found that the tool overcomes issues of poor-quality, even plagiarized submissions. As students can only see a few questions at a time, and cannot predict what future questions might be due to random algorithms, contract cheating is virtually eliminated (Bretag et al., 2019). If students attempt to plagiarize, this will become obvious in the final submission, as they are required to submit through Turnitin originality-checking software and then provide an explanation of how they arrived at their final score. Students were made aware that they cannot change previous inputs without a tutor's feedback and authorization. One of the main design features is that academic staff have regular opportunities for student engagement and feedback, as well as staged marking. We provided video instructions as well as in-simulation guidance, which could be adapted in real-time if multiple queries occurred in class. This reduces staff pressures from receiving repeat email queries, and large block marking burdens, as feedback is provided progressively.

The assessment encourages students to be adaptive and draw on their critical thinking skills. Student input can require text, pictures/diagrams/photos and numerical, which is randomized and coded for self-marking. The communication provided through the interface creates a highly effective learning environment and high levels of student engagement are evidenced with their regular interaction with the tool and their novel business case ideas. The system data demonstrates that students remain actively engaged with the game before and after the due date (see Appendix A). Feedback ensures that students know why their response was correct or incorrect, alongside potential improvements.

The system is flexible and can continually be adapted to include new queries, topics and assessment formats. Students are invited to treat this digital output as an important artefact to include in industry engagement and workplace interviews.

2. *Introducing simulations and serious games to replace static case-based topics.*

We adopted a series of simulations and serious games including Lucro Island and Kilgors Budgeting (Brooks et al., 2020), both of which enrich the student's understanding of important management accounting budgeting nuances. Within Lucro Island, students are introduced to the concept of annual budgeting, which places their learning in a real-life context. Gamified simulations require students to act as consultants and compete to manage their own hotel budgets effectively. A hotel naming activity provided an ice-breaker for students, often prompting humorous ideas. Learning is made fun and competitive through our serious games algorithms, which provide students with immediate feedback on their performance, advice and strategies for improvement. The algorithmic feedback provides immediate visual results on their performance whilst in class. If a student's strategy for 'expenditure on maintenance' is not adequate, their hotel becomes visibly shabbier with graffiti appearing on the facade. If they do not spend enough on their staff or toiletries, customer satisfaction is reduced and bad reviews appear. Students receive feedback in the form of customer complaints, while better performing competitor hotels attract higher occupancy rates. In addition, a detailed feedback report including business financials, customer satisfaction, and industry performance is generated for students to download in the subsequent round of the game. The inbuilt anonymity in the game reporting ensures students do not get embarrassed if they are not on top of the leaderboard.

With Kilgors simulation, students were required to evaluate the different proposals being submitted to the Kilgors' Capital Investment Committee. Students were provided with unique, real-time feedback, depending on their input responses. Every outcome is unique and reliant on the choices of other players, also minimizing plagiarism. Students were required to sit on a virtual committee, recommend a strategic investment, then create a business plan to pitch a performance enhancing idea. Together, these features encouraged real-world, active learning. Without this immediate formative feedback, students might not link their strategies to the success of the business. Students could repeat each activity and make an alternative choice, in order to see what changes occur dependent upon each selection. Active tasks and continual communication within class helped to prepare students for future roles in the workplace, enhancing their decision-making capacity. Serious games created a competitive marketplace within the classroom and every time students engaged, the outcomes also changed, depending on the gameplay, providing learning touchpoints. fun and variety.

With both digital games, students "participate in digital networks", are required to "find, collate, evaluate and manage digital information" and "use digital tools to solve problems and/or answer questions" (Beetham & Sharpe, 2019, p. 265) through the use of spreadsheets, codes and algorithms embedded within the game simulations (Appendix B evidence).

3. *Introduced new topics—Debits/Credits; Capital Budgeting; Data Visualizations; Ethics.*

We extended our financial accounting content with debits and credits, consolidating learning through the Count Fefe App (Financial Education for Future Entrepreneurs [FEFE], http://fefeproject.eu/) with evidence of achievement of Level 2, assessed in class. This was designed to effectively prepare accounting students for their second-year undergraduate curriculum, where a lack of prior debit and credit knowledge often impeded their progress and cognition of Xero and MYOB.

We also introduced capital budgeting within the Kilgors game simulation. While often perceived as too complex for an introductory course, we established this topic as critically important for non-accounting business students who might require knowledge of these techniques in their future workplace (e.g. marketing pitches, management decision making; requests for capital expenditure). The simulation guided student, while the spreadsheets used in class were self-calculating (embedded with formulas), providing students with powerful visual cues to better understand the concept of discounted cash flows.

Thereafter, accounting ethics was introduced into the course, with a focus on technology, big data and algorithm biases that accountants should understand and manage. Implementation of the Bogart Accounting Ethics serious game (cpdaccouting.com) has proven successful, a new serious game that immerses students in a company where there are ethical issues at stake when decision-making.

In the final classes, we introduced students to Tableau analytics software and developed a big data spreadsheet that enabled data visualization of profitable products, whereby students conducted an analysis and presented meaningful graphs. This activity was designed to be low stake, consolidating prior learning and engaging them in an experimental activity that students deemed both enjoyable and creative. Visual step-by-step guides helped novices navigate the system. We asked students to share their visualizations with each other for feedback and discussion (see Appendix C for examples).

This innovative curriculum development exposed students to important topics in a staged, enjoyable and accessible way. Using technology to chunk knowledge into discrete parts for students (Miller, 1956), each activity provided a small, meaningful hurdle, which supported cognitive learning and maintained student engagement, and feedback demonstrated the value and relevance of the learning designs. This discovery is explored further in the following section, through our qualitative and quantitative data, comprising student CES responses and cognitive load survey findings.

5 Survey Findings: CES Data and Cognitive Load Survey

Guided by Beetham and Sharpe (2019) in the development of our digitally-enhanced curriculum, we also incorporated our observed evidence of student engagement with the content into the design, and consequently improved perceived quality of assessments. The survey results demonstrate the improvements made via iterations of design features, which increased engagement with the content.

In addressing the first research question "To what extent do digitized simulation and serious games design features ensure learners build digital capabilities in their first-year accounting core course?" we contend that the following design features have contributed towards enhancing the digital capabilities of our students, along with improved learning outcomes:

- Clear instructions and guidance embedded within the digital tools
- Smaller assessable components (rather than large stake tests/exams)
- Opportunities for low stake contributions and confidence building
- Realistic scenarios with player-led choices that encourage experimentation and failure
- Ability to form student focus group discussions to share experiences and learning outcomes

We noted improved student participation through body language evidence in class, including verbal excitement and physical expressions of elation when accomplishing tasks. This was captured on video or observed when supporting others in the classroom (both online and in face-to-face situations). We also noted that when discussing the content with students, many student queries or comments in the chatbox were quickly responded to by other students, demonstrating they were listening, actively participating, and confident to support others at various stages of understanding. When observing breakout groups (including virtually through LMS tool Collaborate Ultra) the group discussion was dynamic and student-driven. The role of the lecturer in many situations was observing and supporting.

While other accounting courses report dropping attendance rates through the semester, due to withdrawals around census date, or in the later weeks when students lose the passion to continue their studies, we have been able to maintain student numbers and active participation all through the semester, even during the Covid-19 pandemic. This suggests our simulations and serious games are motivating and our staged assessment approach helps students manage their workload better. After implementing these changes to our course, our attendance rate, on average, increased from less than 70% to more than 90% over the semester on average (see Appendix D). Administrative support staff also commented that our course had a very low attrition rate compared to other similar courses. Assessments were mostly completed in full and on time, with higher quality than previous assignments, based on our experience in teaching the course over 10 semesters. After one semester of WritePal implementation the number of extension requests have also diminished from 2.6 to 0.9% with a sizeable 67% decrease in the failure rate, down from 16.1 to 5.3% due to this continued engagement.

In the game's system dashboard, we could also observe whether students improved their performance, due to their responses to the interactive serious game feedback. The chat function ensured students were active participants, which helped us identify if they were making the important theory-into-practice connections. Our approach to digital serious games and simulation encourages peer-to-peer learning, as students played the game individually but later formed groups to submit a report outlining their winning strategies. The effectiveness of this approach was noted in the quality outputs (improved performance) and positive student survey comments. One student commented, "*I enjoy[ed] the group activities because they allow me to gain different perspectives from people in my class and further gain knowledge", and another mentioned, "[t]he entire experience of the hotel [serious game] was fantastic and really underlines the philosophy of learning from experience*" (Participant 1 CES Survey Response).

The diversity in our motivational approaches is appreciated by students, as evidenced by these views: "The group work encourages everyone to participate in completing the assessments. [This] helps us with our teamwork and talking skills" and "All activities we did were engaging, entertaining, and interactive which made me want to participate" and "Teaching quality is fantastic and the best I have experienced over the course of my four-year degree" (Participant 2 CES Survey Response).

Overall, our emphasis on continuous support and inspirational guidance resulted in a 16.6% increase in OSI score of this course from 76.7 to 92.6% in 2021 (see Appendix D).

The survey results (Table 3) helped us address our second research question: *How effective are the digitized simulation and serious games design features in addressing the cognitive load burden of students undertaking their first-year accounting core course?*

Table 3 Student cognitive load survey result summary

	Disagree (%)	Neutral (%)	Agree (%)
Testing Intrinsic Load			
The topics in WritePal seemed more complex than what was covered in class	51.49	14.18	34.33
The business plan development in WritePal covered areas that I perceive as very complex	50.75	11.19	38.06
The activity in WritePal covered concepts and definitions that I perceive as very complex	50.75	9.70	39.55
Testing Extraneous Load			
The instructions and/or explanations in WritePal were very clear	21.64	15.67	62.69
The instructions and/or explanations in WritePal were effective in helping me learn	18.66	15.67	65.67
The instructions and/or explanations in WritePal were clearly written	17.16	15.68	67.16
Testing Germane Load			
WritePal enhanced my understanding of the topic(s) covered	28.36	13.43	58.21
WritePal enhanced my technical skills in developing a business plan	23.88	17.91	58.21
WritePal enhanced my understanding of the business planning activity	18.66	19.40	61.94
WritePal enhanced my understanding of accounting concepts and definitions	19.40	17.17	63.43

To interpret the survey results, we grouped participant responses into Agree (Likert scale 5–7), Neutral (Likert Scale 4) and Disagree (Likert Scale 1–3). The questionnaire (adapted from Leppink et al., 2013) evaluates the effectiveness of the digitized simulated assessment task on student's intrinsic, extraneous and germane cognitive loads.

The first set of three questions in the survey test whether a student's intrinsic load is reduced. Based on the results, around 51% participants indicated a reduction on intrinsic load. The decrease is likely to be caused by breaking the complex schema into smaller topics. While 34–39% of students selected "Agree" category (Likert Scale 5–7), indicating that they did not find the system reducing their intrinsic load, we believe this reverse coding impacted their responses. Due to the way these questions were developed, they required greater interpretation and thought, rather than adopting the personal preference that considers "agree" as always positive. Given the WritePal system only revealed questions when the set time had been reached, some students might have perceived an increase in their intrinsic load as they were unable to predict or see the ensuing questions of the report. Nevertheless, the unsolicited qualitative responses we received from the CES Survey data, which indicated that the intrinsic load was manageable compared to the traditional way of structuring the assignment:

> The use of the WritePal system really puts everything into perspective by breaking it all up into smaller pieces to be completed at separate dates throughout the semester, which is important due to many of us students feeling overwhelmed due to lockdown and other assignments. (CES Survey Data, 2020)

The second set of three questions in Table 3 explore the impact of WritePal on a student's extraneous load. According to the cognitive load theory, the extraneous load can be reduced by providing clear instructions and directed guidance. As previously mentioned, clear and extensive instructions were provided for each question in the form of text and video recordings, including real-time adjustments if more than one student queried the instructions. Together the majority of participants believe their extraneous load is reduced with 62.97, 65.67 and 67.16% participants agreeing that the instructions in WritePal system were clear, effective and clearly written. An unsolicited student comment confirmed this view:

> the business plan made me feel like I could actually properly read the content, absorb the information and then properly apply it. (CES Survey Data)

The germane load is covered by the final set of four questions in the survey. According to cognitive load theory, when learners experience a reduction on intrinsic load and extraneous load, they should experience an increase on germane load and as a result, learn the complex schema easier. The survey results (Table 3) support this claim with approximately 60% participants agreeing that the WritePal system enhanced their understanding of the course topics covered, the underlying concepts, business plan and technical skills required to navigate the simulated business plan.

The following unsolicited qualitative comments received in the CES survey data reflect an overall more manageable study experience. Students suggest they feel less pressured when completing the final report indicating a reduced intrinsic load and extraneous load providing more resources to utilize and increase their germane load capacity.

> The assignments are structured well, with the activities each week corresponding to a small chunk of the overall mark. The staged final report helps immensely as students aren't left to complete a huge full report in the last couple of weeks of the semester.
>
> This course didn't give me stress as much as other courses. I like the way how the teaching team set out the assignment
>
> I guess that alleviates the pressure on more major assessments whereby I could work on my overall semester marks week-by-week
>
> The way the assignments were set out was the most manageable and helpful during these times. The WritePal program was extremely useful and provided us with the best layout in order to succeed
>
> The use of the WritePal system really puts everything into perspective by breaking it all up into smaller pieces to be completed at separate dates throughout the semester, which is important due to many of us students feeling overwhelmed due to lockdowns and other assignments
>
> The distribution of workload is amazing, especially the final exam equivalent [WritePal].

From the word frequency analysis, outlined in Fig. 1, we observe that the most frequent key words: "[less] stress", "apply theory", "enjoy" and "love" indicate that the curriculum design, including the WritePal system has been effective.

Fig. 1 CES survey data word frequency analysis

6 Improving Assessment Authenticity and Further Research

One of the main findings from this research concluded that students participating in the gamified assessment established consistent behaviors of working on their assessments regularly in the classroom and avoided attempts to plagiarize their submissions. Within the assessments there were detailed navigation points, explanations and students always had the opportunity to debrief with peers and their tutors about the unique nature of their simulation and serious games experiences. It did not matter that responses, numbers, costings and decision impacts were different from their peers, as immersive experiences are unique to each student player, and depended on the pathway of choices selected. When presented with a situation where it would take them significantly more effort to take a shortcut (via plagiarizing another student's work) than to improve their knowledge and skills in order to succeed in the game, students opted to participate and have fun in their immersive learning experiences.

This reduction in plagiarism was also highlighted in studies by Malisius (2019) whereby students avoided self-plagiarism of their previously submitted work and instead considered using generating alternative ideas to avoid academic integrity issues within the simulations and serious game play. By creating a unique playing experience, the serious game also provided students with a strong disincentive to plagiarize, given that their spreadsheets and answers would likely be incorrect, as well as reduce their position on the leader board within the competition. Aligning with our experience of students playing serious games, some studies have indicated the benefits of having teaching and support staff "looking over the shoulders" (Egenfeldt-Nielsen et al., 2011, p. 129) of students throughout the game play, which also provides the opportunity of observing gameplay which enables the autoethnographic perspective of the teaching team. Kumar and Bhakar, (2020) cited the significant role of technology in facilitating a student's likelihood to cheat as well as the role of deterrent applications such as Turnitin, as assistants to educate what constitutes high levels of academic integrity.

7 Conclusion, Limitations and Future Research

This paper has provided a deep-dive into the application of using technology to enhance discovery-based learning as an ideal pedagogy for adoption within accounting education. The paper comprises both student responses and an autoethnographic reflection observing the introduction of serious games in the classroom and their impact on students. This research redefines the extant methods of teaching accounting to incorporate gamification and simulation in pedagogical designs. Through the application of serious games, we have observed significant contributions to increase student engagement, reduce cognitive load, and increase overall student satisfaction.

Given our findings that serious games and simulations can effectively reduce the extraneous and intrinsic cognitive load, we also claim that they contribute positively to a student's germane load enabling them to navigate the more complex topics, including debits, credits, and capital budgeting through the simulated activity. Students do not see this activity as burdensome because of the design features within the context of the simulation. Other potential benefits include reducing student attrition, whereby students may previously give up the course, potentially even the degree, based on their perceptions that 'accounting is difficult' and inaccessible from their first encounter. This is particularly so for English as a Second Language (ESL) students whose cognitive load is extended further with language issues. Based on emails correspondence and course enrolment records, this accounting unit is popular with non-business discipline students whereby students report word-of-mouth referrals from peers. This further expands a student's discipline-related or technical knowledge to include a basic understanding of accounting, while promoting increased financial and digital literacy.

However, not all feedback from students was positive. For example, some students found the online delivery more challenging, due to technology issues. The group formation through the learning management system (LMS) was sometimes noted by students to be tedious and time consuming. A very small number of students found the student-centred simulations and serious games harder to follow and preferred a more didactic approach. There were a couple of comments on the interactive 2-h tutorial versus the one-hour asynchronous lecture, which we intend to address in future curriculum updates. These updates will include making the lecture more interactive and offering further reinforcement activities. We also recommend further research to examine the reasons for the negative responses in the cognitive load survey, which indicate that some students (mean 28.8) do not find WritePal reduces their cognitive load.

This study has a few limitations: (1) The intrinsic load questions only asked whether the WritePal design reduces student's cognitive load, not the topic itself. Further experimental research, with control groups, will help to validate inherent assumptions in this study. (2) the first three questions in the validated survey instrument were worded in a way that required a "Disagree" rather than an "Agree" response which might have impacted results. (3) Largely positive feedback for the WritePal was received. Further research with qualitative questions to supplement the quantitative date might draw out any negative impacts and/or further feedback on how the system could be improved. (4) Further research could be expanded to explore the cognitive load challenges associated with using serious games to teach complex topics.

For the accounting education discipline, there is more research that can be conducted in this area. For example, we recommend studying other factors to demonstrate learning is occurring, such as body language responses, eye movement tracking, granular usage details and other biometric indicators. Future research initiatives will expand upon existing knowledge in this area including longitudinal data collection to provide comparison of mark improvement over time. Research that analyses student feedback in more detail, along with exploration of the mechanisms that improve student–teacher interactions would also be useful. Finally, exploration of student perceptions regarding both technology and learning barriers when engaging in serious games is important. From a teacher perspective, we propose that this paper can support educators explore the application of digital offerings in their own classes. Our experiences may also encourage accounting educators to engage in developing their own digitized simulations and serious games, thus contributing to overall enhanced pedagogy across the discipline.

Appendix A: Digital Business Simulation (WritePal)

About WritePal

WritePal enables the student to engage with the development of their own Business Plan by following the guidelines provided by the teacher. The questions can change every semester. At the time of this study, the students were asked to come up with a unique business idea as per detailed questions in each of the following stages:

Stage 1: Name of business and description of business idea, the value chain activities for the business and industry to which it belongs.

Stage 2: Financial analysis of the business idea (details of the costs associated with the idea; and Cost Volume Profit (CVP) analysis).

Stage 3: Measuring the performance of the idea (financial and non-financial) inspired by the United Nations (2018) Sustainable Development Goals (SDGs).

To simulate a business pitch and allow for reflexivity in design, the teacher conducts a review and provides feedback to the students at each stage, suggesting areas that need to be considered or improved.

WritePal Back-End Data

The graph demonstrates students remain active weeks before the due date and log on at different times during the day. Most students are submitting on time with minimal number of extension requests.

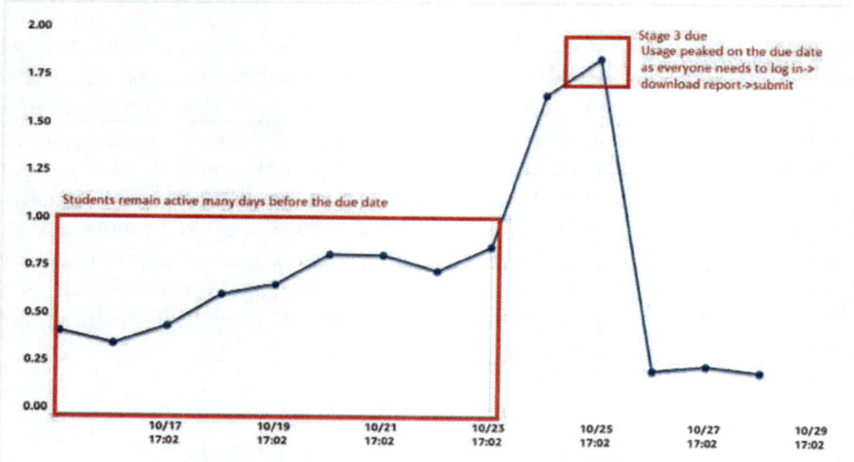

WritePal—Stagged Revealing Question Example

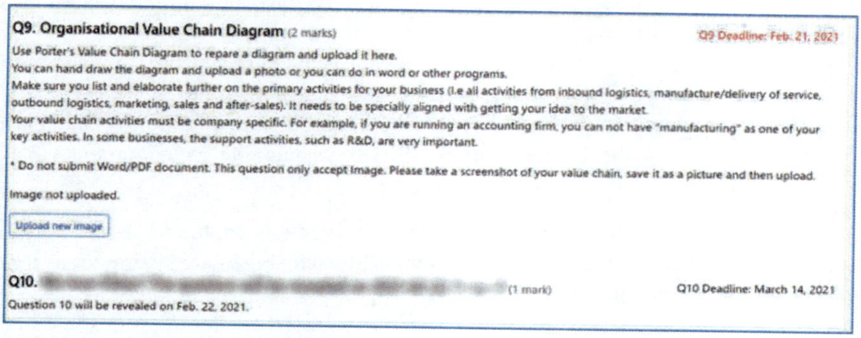

Q9. Organisational Value Chain Diagram (2 marks) Q9 Deadline: Feb. 21, 2021

Use Porter's Value Chain Diagram to repare a diagram and upload it here.
You can hand draw the diagram and upload a photo or you can do in word or other programs.
Make sure you list and elaborate further on the primary activities for your business (I.e all activities from inbound logistics, manufacture/delivery of service, outbound logistics, marketing, sales and after-sales). It needs to be specially aligned with getting your idea to the market.
Your value chain activities must be company specific. For example, if you are running an accounting firm, you can not have "manufacturing" as one of your key activities. In some businesses, the support activities, such as R&D, are very important.

* Do not submit Word/PDF document. This question only accept Image. Please take a screenshot of your value chain, save it as a picture and then upload.

Image not uploaded.

Upload new image

Q10. (1 mark) Q10 Deadline: March 14, 2021

Question 10 will be revealed on Feb. 22, 2021.

WritePal—Teacher's Easy Grading View with Marking Instructions/Rubric

WritePal—Teacher's Class List with Unfinished Work Highlighted

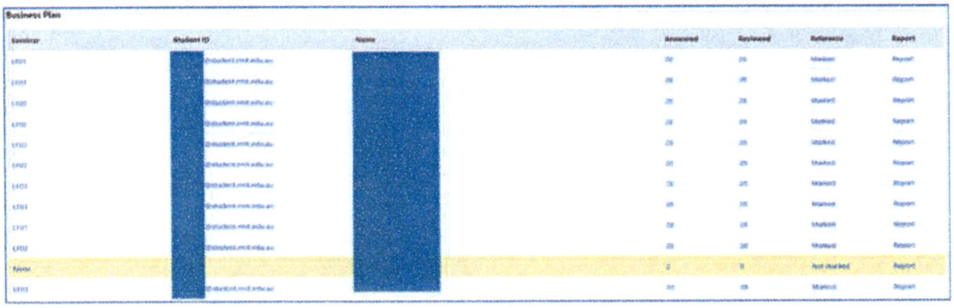

Appendix B: Serious Game (Lucro Island)

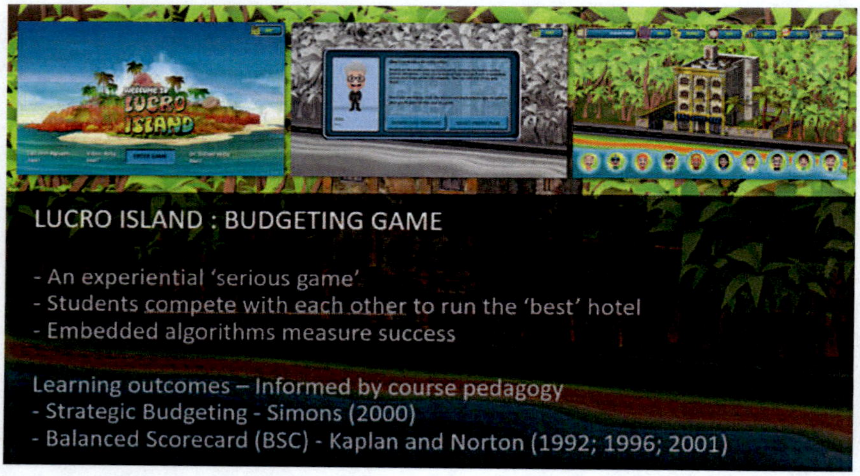

Kilgors Hotels
(fill cells that are shaded green)

3-Star

Hotel Configuration	Single	Double	Family	total
area per room (square metres)	16	20	30	
number of beds per room	1	2	3	
Number of rooms of the first floor - 240 square metre	0	0	8	
Number of rooms on the second floor - 240 square metre	0	12	0	
Nimber of rooms on the third floor - 240 square metre	15	0	0	
number of rooms	15	12	8	35
refurbishment costs (capex) ($/room refurbished)	40,000	62,000	85,000	
planned occupancy rate (%) (open 365 days)	*80%*	*80%*	*80%*	*80%*
average selling price ($/room/night)	160.00	200.00	300.00	

Retail Choices on ground floor	1 or 0	Rent ($ per year)
Café	1	72,000
Restaurant	0	50,000
Laundromat	1	25,000
Travel Agent (Local tours)	1	40,000
Fun Games Parlour	0	60,000
Boutique	0	20,000
Select three retail choices	3	137,000
Pool	1	

Profit Plan	3-Star				
Income Statement					
Accommodation Revenue ($)	**700,800**	**700,800**	**700,800**		**2,102,400**
Food and Beverage (% of accommodation revenue)	*10%*	*10%*	*10%*		
Food and beverage revenue ($)	70,080	70,080	70,080		210,240
Rental Income	45,667	45,667	45,667		137,000
Total sales revenue ($)	816,547	816,547	816,547		2,449,640
Cost of Sales					
Staff Costs (% of accommodation revenue)	*18%*	*18%*	*18%*		
Staff costs ($)	126,144	126,144	126,144		378,432
Purchases (% of accommodation revenue)	*11%*	*11%*	*11%*		
Purchases (toiletries, sheets, towels etc., $)	77,088	77,088	77,088		231,264
Total Cost of Sales ($)	203,232	203,232	203,232		609,696
Gross Profit ($)	613,315	613,315	613,315		1,839,944
Gross Margin (%)	*75%*	*75%*	*75%*		*75%*
Other operating expenses					
Administration Costs ($)	66,667	66,667	66,667		200,000
Marketing Costs ($)	32,662	32,662	32,662	4%	97,986
Utilities - base component	*7,200*	*7,200*	*7,200*		
utilities - activity component	3%	3%	3%		
Utilities cost	28,224	28,224	28,224		84,672
Maintenance (%)	*8%*	*8%*	*8%*		
Maintenance - base component	*7,200*	*7,200*	*7,200*		
Maintenance cost	63,264	63,264	63,264		189,792
Depreciation (straight line depreciation)	76,115	100,384	90,917		267,417
Property taxes	6,667	6,667	6,667		20,000
Insurance	20,000	20,000	20,000		60,000
Interest on loan	75,338	103,320	93,380		272,038
Total Operating Expenses	368,936	421,187	401,781		1,191,904
Operating expenses as % of sales revenue	*45%*	*52%*	*49%*		*49%*
Net Profit ($)	**244,379**	**192,127**	**211,534**		**648,040**

Appendix C: Digital Simulation (CountFefe App)

Appendix D: High Attendance Rates Over the Semesters and Student CES Survey Results

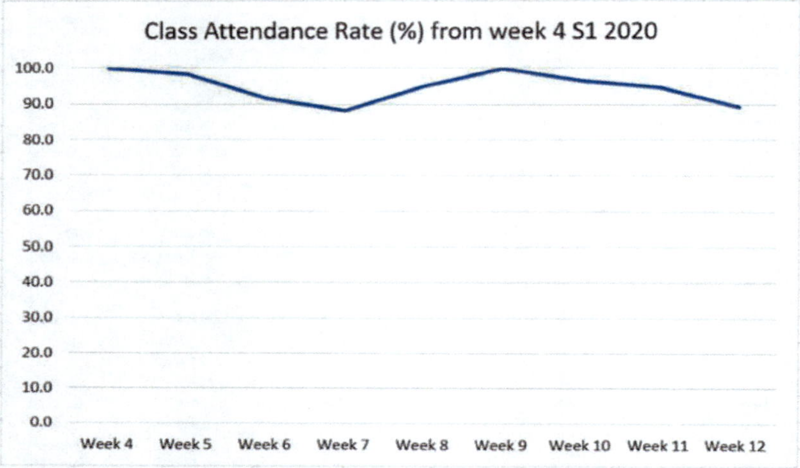

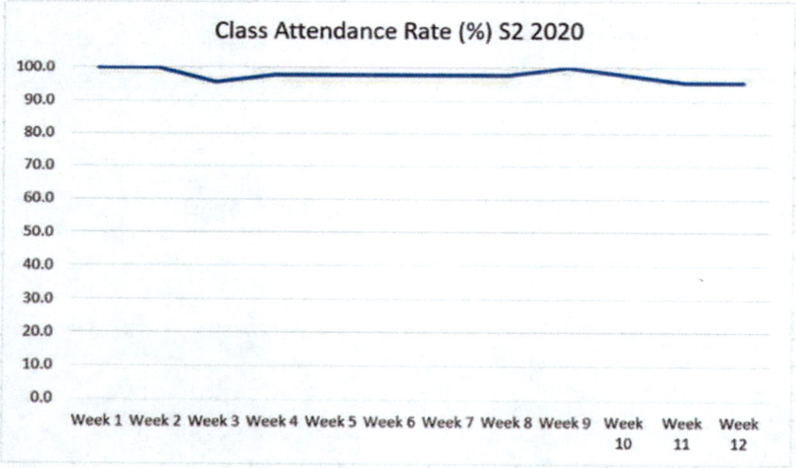

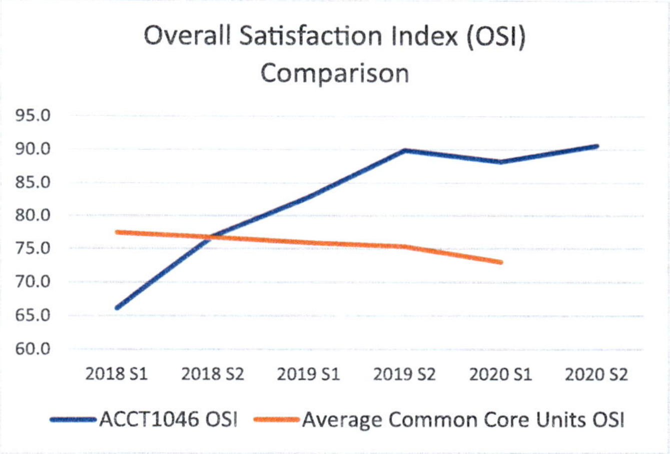

Appendix E: Digital Checklist Applied to Our Curriculum Design

	Digitally capable learners in Accounting are able to…	Mapping capabilities to the curriculum
1	Use specialist digital tools of their subject area	Students use Microsoft Office (including Excel, Teams); Tableau visualization tools) in Lucro Island, Kilgors, WritePal
2	Find, collate, evaluate and manage digital information	WritePal; Lucro/Kilgors by completing spreadsheets and making decisions on the information. Tableau case requires students to create visualizations to address/communicate questions of the data
3	Manage, analyze and use digital data	Use of spreadsheets that comprise numeric, non-numeric such as geographic, date, product descriptive
4	Consume and produce ideas in digital media (e.g. spatial, textual, visual, auditory, interactive…)	Data visualizations with the tableau case; competitive management of hotel budgets on Lucro Island where winners/losers are based on competitor student decisions
5	Create digital artefacts (e.g. web pages, 3D print pieces, code, digital video, infographics …)	WritePal Business Plan is an output of engagement with the digital platform; completed infographics in Tableau

(continued)

(continued)

	Digitally capable learners in Accounting are able to…	Mapping capabilities to the curriculum
6	Use digital tools to solve problems and/or answer questions	Kilgors strategic investment and capital budgeting activities and recommendation of investment alternative; Similarly, Tableau and Kilgors are used to solve problems and answer questions
7	Take part in digital research or professional practice	Students take part in Lucro Island, Kilgors and Bogart ethics game as practicing accountants to engage with the platform and provide solutions. WritePal requires research-related inputs
8	Collaborate with others using a variety of digital tools and spaces	Kilgors, Lucro, Bogart and WritePal have collaborative group activities. Students compete with each other in Lucro. Bogart and Kilgors collaboration is with fictitious characters in simulations
9	Participate in digital networks (closed and open)	Lucro and WritePal are closed networks for interaction between students and with the teacher. Have both student and teacher interface. The LMS and Collaborate Ultra/Teams are used as digital networks to engage students in online activities
10	Develop digital learning skills and habits (e.g. participating, note-making, referencing, quizzing, revising …)	Each of the simulations require students to participate, make notes on their decision choices throughout the simulation. The group discussion and revising of pedagogy is used in the quizzes/group assessment. WritePal and the embedded Micro Credential on Academic Integrity ensures students are equipped with knowledge of referencing, among other features
11	Develop and manage their digital identity and learning outcomes	The student-centred focus of the course design ensures students are in charge of their learning outcomes and outputs. They create a digital identity in the simulations
12	Consider issues of digital safety, privacy, health and wellbeing, ethics and legality	Bogart serious game is designed to immerse students in ethical dilemmas. The WritePal curriculum also embeds a digital Micro Credential on Academic Integrity to equip students with understanding of digital safety, privacy, ethics and legality—in particular, on issues of plagiarism and contract cheating. Student health and wellbeing is directly addressed in the curriculum design and acknowledged by students in CES feedback. WritePal requires students consider health and wellbeing as part of evaluating the SDGs

Adapted from Beetham and Sharpe (2019)

References

Abt, C. C. (1987). *Serious games*. University Press of America.

ACCA. (2012). *Closing the value gap: Understanding the accountancy profession in the 21st century*. White Paper, published August 2012. Association of Chartered Certified Accountants, UK. https://www.accaglobal.com/content/dam/acca/global/PDF-technical/other-PDFs/tech-tp-ctvg.pdf

Alfieri, L., Brooks, P. J., Aldrich, N. J., & Tenebaum, H. R. (2011). Does discovery-based instruction enhance learning? *Journal of Educational Psychology, 103*(1), 1–18.

Arity, V., & Vesty, G. (2020). *Designing authentic assessments: Engaging business students in flow experience with digital technologies*. In T. McLaughlin, et al. (Eds.), *Tertiary education in a time of change: Disruptions challenges and strategies*. Springer Nature.

Ariyana, A., Enawar, E., Ramdhani, I. S., & Sulaeman, A. (2020). The application of discovery learning models in learning to write descriptive texts. *Journal of English Education and Teaching, 4*(3), 401–412.

Arnab, S., Lameras, P., Dunwell, I., Stewart, C., Clarke, S., & Petridis, P. (2016). Essential features of serious games design in higher education: Linking learning attributes to game mechanics. *British Journal of Educational Technology, 48*(4), 972–994.

Bankers Lab. (2013). *A smart guide to serious gaming*. Retrieved 1 February 21, from http://bankerslab.com/blogposts/a-smart-guide-to-serious-gaming-part-1/

Beetham, H., & Sharpe, R. (Eds.). (2019). *Rethinking pedagogy for a digital age: Principles and practices of design*. ProQuest Central. https://repository.jisc.ac.uk/6694/1/DigicapCurriculumDevChecklist.pdf

Bell, R., & Loon, M. (2015). The impact of critical thinking disposition on learning using business simulations. *International Journal of Management Education, 13*(2), 119–127.

Blasko, D. G., Lum, H. C., White, M. M., & Drabik, H. B. (2014). Individual differences in the enjoyment and effectiveness of serious games. In *Psychology, Pedagogy, and Assessment in Serious Games* (pp. 153–174). IGI Global.

Bok, D. (2006). *Our underachieving colleges: A candid look at how much students learn and why they should be learning more*. Princeton University Press.

Bradley, E. G. (2015). Using computer simulations and games to prevent student plagiarism. *Journal of Educational Technology Systems., 2*, 240–252. https://doi.org/10.1177/0047239515617653

Bretag, T., Harper, R., Burton, M., Ellis, C., Newton, P., Rozenberg, P., Saddiqui, S., & van Haeringen, K. (2019). Contract cheating: A survey of Australian university students. *Studies in Higher Education, 44*(11), 1837–1856.

Brooks, A., Vesty, G., & Shackell, M. (2017). *Kilgors wine division: A balanced scorecard simulation*. Presented at MAS/IMA Case Conference in Naperville, Illinois on October 21, 2017.

Brooks, A., Vesty, G., & Taouk, M. (2020). Testing a strategic investment evaluation tool at Kilgors.

Bruner, J. (1986). *Actual minds, possible worlds*. Harvard University Press.

Buchinger, D., & da Silva Hounsell, M. (2018). Guidelines for designing and using collaborative-competitive serious games. *Computers & Education, 118*, 133–149.

Carenys, J., Moya, S., & Perramon, J. (2016). Is it worth it to consider videogames in accounting education? A comparison of a simulation and a videogame in attributes, motivation and learning outcomes. *Spanish Accounting Review, 20*(2), 118–130.

Carenys, J., Moya, S., & Perramon, J. (2017, October). Accounting digital games' effectiveness: A structural equation modeling approach. In *European Conference on Games Based Learning* (pp. 63–70). Academic Conferences International Limited.

Carnegie, G., Parker, L., & Tsahuridu, E. (2020). *It's 2020: What is accounting today? Australian Accounting Review*, pp. 1–9.

Carvalho, M. B., Bellotti, F., Berta, R., De Gloria, A., Sedano, C. I., Hauge, J. B., Hu. J., & Rauterberg, M. (2015). An activity theory-based model for serious games analysis and conceptual design. *Computers & Education, 87*, 166–181.

CES Survey Data. (2020). *Course experience survey 2020*. RMIT University.

Chi, M. T., De Leeuw, N., Chiu, M. H., & LaVancher, C. (1994). Eliciting self-explanations improves understanding. *Cognitive Science, 18*(3), 439–477.

Clark, D. B., Tanner-Smith, E. E., & Killingsworth, S. S. (2016). Digital games, design, and learning. *Review of Educational Research, 86*(1), 79–122.

Clark, R. C., & Mayer, R. E. (2016). *e-learning and the science of instruction* (4th ed.). Wiley.

Commonwealth of Australia. (2016, April 29). The senate environment and communications references committee, "*Game On: More than playing around. The future of Australia's video game development industry*", Australian Senate Standing Committees on Environment and Communications. ISBN 978-1-76010-413-9

Damron, D., & Mott, J. (2005). Creating an interactive classroom: Enhancing student engagement and learning in political science courses. *Journal of Political Science Education, 1*(3), 367–383.

Destrebecqz, A. (2004). The effect of explicit knowledge on sequence learning: A graded account. *Psychologica Belgica, 44*(4), 217–247.

Driskell, T., Driskell, J. E., & Salas, E. (2017). Lexicon as a predictor of team dynamics. In *Team dynamics over time* (pp. 231–257). Emerald Publishing.

Druzhinina, M., Belkova, N., Donchenko, E., Liu, F., & Morozova, O. (2018). Curriculum design in professional education: Theory and practice. *SHS Web of Conferences,* 50.https://doi.org/10.1051/shsconf/20185001046

Duffy, T. M. (2009). Building line of communication and a research agenda. In S. Tobias & T. M. Duffy (Eds.), *Constructivist theory applied to instruction: Success or failure?* (pp. 351–367). Taylor & Francis.

Egenfeldt-Nielsen, S., Meyer, B., & Birgitte Holm Soerensen, B. H. (2011). *Serious games in education: A global perspective.* Aarhus University Press.

Fletcher, J. D. (2009). Education and training technology in the military. *Science, 323*(5910), 72–75.

Forman, E. A., & Ansell, E. (2002). Orchestrating the multiple voices and inscriptions of a mathematics classroom. *Journal of the Learning Sciences, 11*(2–3), 251–274.

Gee, J. P. (2003). *What video games have to teach us about learning and literacy.* Palgrave Macmillan.

Gersten, R., Woodward, J., & Darch, C. (1986). Direct instruction: A research-based approach to curriculum design and teaching. *Exceptional Children, 53*(1), 17–31.

Gredler, M. E. (2004). Games and simulations and their relationships to learning. *Handbook of Research on Educational Communications and Technology, 2,* 571–581.

Guetzkow, H. S. (1963). *Simulation in international relations: Developments of research and teaching* (No. 327 S5).

Hedgedus, S. J., Dalton, S., & Tapper, J. R. (2015). *The impact of technology-enhanced curriculum on learning advanced algebra in US high school classrooms.*

Huang, E. Y., Lin, S. W., & Huang, T. K. (2012). What type of learning style leads to online participation in the mixed-mode e-learning environment? A study of software usage instruction. *Computers & Education, 58*(1), 338–349.

Huang, T. (2015). The technology transfer of the ICT curriculum in Taiwan. *Asia Pacific Journal of Education, 35*(4), 407–422.

Hughes, M., & Berry, A. (2000). Learning by doing: A case study of qualitative accounting research. *Accounting Education, 9*(2), 157–174. https://doi.org/10.1080/09639280010011145

Huxham, M. (2007). Fast and effective feedback: Are model answers the answer? *Assessment & Evaluation in Higher Education., 32*(6), 601–611.

Jiménez, L., Mendez, C., & Cleeremans, A. (1996). Comparing direct and indirect measures of sequence learning. *Journal of Experimental Psychology: Learning, Memory, and Cognition, 22*(4), 948–969.

Kilgors Simulation. (2018). https://kilgors.com/

Kumar, N., & Bhakar, R. K. (2020). Technology vs plagiarism: Friend and enemy. *International Journal of Information Dissemination and Technology, 10*(3), 148–154.

Schuwirth, L. W. T., & Van der Vleuten, C. P. M. (2011). Programmatic assessment: From assessment of learning to assessment for learning. *Medical Teacher, 33*(6), 478–485. https://doi.org/10.3109/0142159X.2011.565828

Lazonder, A. W., & van der Meij, H. (1993). The minimal manual: Is less really more? *International Journal of Man-Machine Studies, 39*(5), 729–752.

Lean, J., Moizer, J., Towler, M., & Abbey, C. (2006). Simulations and games: Use and barriers in higher education. *Active Learning in Higher Education, 7*(3), 227–242.

Lee, D. (2014). How to personalize learning in K-12 schools: Five essential design features. *Educational Technology, 54*(3), 12–17.

Leppink, J., Paas, F., Vleuten, C. P. M. V., Gog, T. V., & Merrienboer, J. J. G. (2013). Development of an instrument for measuring different types of cognitive load. *Behavior Research Methods, 45*(4), 1058–1072.

Lewin, C., Cranmer, S., & McNicol, S. (2018). Developing digital pedagogy through learning design: An activity theory perspective. *British Journal of Educational Technology, 49*, 1131–1144. https://doi.org/10.1111/bjet.12705

Maclean, E. L. (2016, June). Evolution of uniquely human cognition. *Proceedings of the National Academy of Sciences, 113*(23), 6348–6354. https://doi.org/10.1073/pnas.1521270113

Malisius, E. (2019). Academic rigour and video technology: A case study on digital storytelling in graduate-level assignments. In A. Altmann, B. Ebersberger, C. Mössenlechner, & D. Wieser (2019). *The disruptive power of online education: Challenges, opportunities, responses* (Ch 9). Emerald Publishing Limited.

Marriott, N. (2004). Using computerized business simulations and spreadsheet models in accounting education: A case study. *Accounting Education, 13*(sup1), 55–70.

Mayer, R. E. (2011). *Applying the science of learning*. Pearson Merrill Prentice Hall.

Mayer, R. E. (2020a). *Multimedia learning* (3rd ed.). Cambridge University Press.

Mayer, R. E. (2020b). Advances in designing instruction based on examples, *Applied Cognitive Psychology*, Vol.

Miller, D. F., & Logsdon, J. D. (1956). What Is the role of the principal in curriculum work? Initiating the program: How do you organize for action? *The Bulletin of the National Association of Secondary School Principals, 40*(219), 390–394.

Moro, C., Phelps, C., & Birt, J. (2022). Improving serious games by crowdsourcing feedback from the STEAM online gaming community. *The Internet and Higher Education, 55*, 100874.

Nunaki, J. H., Damopolii, I., Kandowangko, N. Y., & Nusantari, E. (2019) The effectiveness of inquiry-based learning to train the students' metacognitive skills based on gender differences, *International Journal of Instruction, 12*(2), 505–516.

Oliver, M., & Trigwell, K. (2005). Can 'blended learning' be redeemed? *E-Learning and Digital Media, 2*(1), 17–26.

Petroski, A. (2012). Games vs. simulations: When simulations may be a better approach. *T+D, 66*(2), 27–29.

Pillay, D., Naicker, I., & Pithouse-Morgan, K. (Eds.). *Academic autoethnographies: Inside teaching in higher education.* Springer.

Ramdhani, M. R., Usodo, B., & Subanti, S. (2017). Discovery learning with scientific approach to geometry. *Journal of Physics: Conference Series, 895*(1), 1–6.

Riley, R. A., Jr., Cadotte, E. R., Bonney, L., & MacGuire, C. (2013). Using a business simulation to enhance accounting education. *Issues in Accounting Education, 28*(4), 801–822.

Rittle-Johnson, B. (2006). Promoting transfer: Effects of self-explanation and direct instruction. *Child Development, 77*(1), 1–15.

Rodgers, C. R., & Raider-Roth, M. B. (2006). Presence in teaching. *Teachers and Teaching: Theory and Practice, 12*(3), 265–287.

Routledge, H. (2016). *Why games are good for business: How to leverage the power of serious games, gamification and simulations.* Palgrave Macmillan UK

Ruge, H., Karcz, T., Mark, T., Martin, V., Zwosta, K., & Wolfensteller, U. (2018). On the efficiency of instruction-based rule encoding. *Acta Psychologica, 184*, 4–19.

Sauer, J., Wastell, D. G., & Hockey, G. R. J. (2000). A conceptual framework for designing microworlds for complex work domains: A case study of the Cabin Air Management System. *Computers in Human Behavior, 16*(1), 45–58.
Sawyer, B., & Rejeski, D. (2002). *Serious games: Improving public policy through game-based learning and simulation.* s.l.: Woodrow Wilson International Center for Scholars.
Schut, S., Heeneman, S., Bierer, B., Driessen, E., van Tartwijk, J., & van Der Vleuten, C. (2020). Between trust and control: Teachers' assessment conceptualisations within programmatic assessment. *Medical Education, 54*(6), 528–537.
Seow, P. S., & Wong, S. P. (2013). *Accounting challenge: Enhancing learning through a mobile game. Accounting Educators Professional Periodical*, pp. 19–21.
Springer, C. W., & Borthick, A. F. (2004). Business simulation to stage critical thinking in introductory accounting: Rationale, design, and implementation. *Issues in Accounting Education, 19*(3), 277–303.
Squire, K. (2006). From content to context: Videogames as designed experience. *Educational Researcher, 35*(8), 19–29.
Stark, R., Gruber, H., Renkl, A., & Mandl, H. (1998). Instructional effects in complex learning: Do objective and subjective learning outcomes converge? *Learning and Instruction, 8*(2), 117–129.
Stark, D. (2009). *The sense of dissonance: Accounts of worth in economic life.* Princeton.
Starr, L. J. (2010a). The use of autoethnography in educational research: Locating who we are in what we do. *Canadian Journal for New Scholars in Education/Revue Canadienne des jeunes chercheures et chercheurs en éducation, 3*(1).
Starr, L. J. (2010b). The use of autoethnography in educational research: Locating who we are in what we do. *Canadian Journal for New Scholars in Education, 3*(1), 1–9.
Subhash, S., & Cudney, E. A. (2018). Gamified learning in higher education: A systematic review of the literature. *Computers in Human Behavior, 87*, 192–206.
Susi, T., Johannesson, M., & Backlund, P. (2007). Serious games: An overview.
Sweller, J. (1988). Cognitive load during problem solving: Effects on learning. *Cognitive Science, 12*(2), 257–285.
Sweller, J., Merrienboer, J. J. G., & Paas, F. G. W. C. (1998). Cognitive architecture and instructional design. *Educational Psychology Review, 10*(3), 251–296.
Teach, R. D., & Schwartz, R. G. (2004). Are business games really delivering what students are led to believe? *Development in Business Simulation and Experiential Learning, 31*, 264–272.
United Nation (UN). (2018). *Sustainable development goals*, United Nations Department of Public Information. https://sustainabledevelopment.un.org/?menu=1300
Watty, K., McKay, J., & Ngo, L. (2016). Innovators or inhibitors? Accounting faculty resistance to new educational technologies in higher education. *Journal of Accounting Education, 36*, 1–15.
Weaver, M., & Erby, L. (2012). Standardized patients: A promising tool for health education and health promotion. *Health Promotion Practice, 13*(2), 169–174.
Xu, Y., Chiu, C. K., & Ye, X. (2019). Understanding the use of technology-enhanced learning spaces in Hong Kong: An exploratory study. *Asia Pacific Journal of Education, 39*(3), 290–309.
Zyda, M. (2005). From visual simulation to virtual reality to games. *Computer, 38*(90), 25–32.

Viktor Arity is an Associate Lecturer in Financial Planning and Taxation in the School of Accounting, Information Systems and Supply Chain at the RMIT University, Melbourne, Australia. He is an active advocate for pedagogical use of digital educational games in tertiary education. His research interests include designing and implementing digital educational games for business education. He is one of the board members of Games for Change Asia Pacific.

Gillian Vesty, Ph.D. is an Associate Professor of Accounting and Deputy Dean of Learning and Teaching in the School of Accounting, Information Systems and Supply Chain at the RMIT University, Melbourne, Australia. She has developed accounting games and simulation tools.

Recent projects include management accounting in public healthcare, serious games, and digital simulation in accounting education, social and environmental health and wellbeing.

Belinda Moloney, Ph.D. is an Associate Professor at the Torrens University, Australia. She is an experienced leader, tertiary educator, IT professional, researcher, change manager and developer, leveraging expertise from education, IT, telecommunications, government and community sectors to bring about positive change and workforce transitions for Deakin University students. She is currently working within the Graduate Employment Division to build career education into scaffolded curriculum touchpoints within undergraduate and postgraduate STEM degrees.

Chapter 17
Roleplay and Interpersonal Skills Self-Efficacy in a Financial Analytics Course

Ling Mei Cong

Abstract This chapter explores how to integrate the in-demand soft skills with the hard skills of financial analytics in an experiential roleplay. Specifically, it examines the impact of the experiential roleplay on MBA students' self-perceived interpersonal skills. Designed using the experiential learning principles for students to practice and reflect, the roleplay is found to improve students' self-perceived interpersonal skills in all 28 survey items except intercultural sensitivity. OLS regressions using the pre-roleplay data show students with longer work experience rated themselves higher for interpersonal skills. However, after the roleplay, difference-in-difference analysis indicates the outcome of the interpersonal skills is not affected by the length of work experience. It implies that students with less work experience did not have a lower level of self-perceived interpersonal skills than peers due to the intervention. This chapter contributes to the literature on self-efficacy theory by providing empirical evidence that roleplays can supplement real-world experience in interpersonal skills development. It offers important insight for educators that work-integrated authentic learning can improve students' self-efficacy and job readiness.

Keywords Roleplay · Experiential Learning · Self-Efficacy · Interpersonal Skills · Financial Analytics

1 Introduction

Financial analytics has become an important area for MBA students to master in recent years. With the explosion of big data, it is increasingly popular for businesses to use data analytics to aid business decisions. The accounting curriculum in MBA has transformed to include more content about data analysis (e.g. scenario analysis) to predict and evaluate financial performance (Fitzgerald, 2021). Huerta and Jensen (2017) note graduates with data analytics skills are in high demand by Big-4 accounting firms. An Ernst and Young's 2015 report indicated "Analytics is

L. M. Cong (✉)
RMIT University, Melbourne, VIC, Australia
e-mail: lingmei.cong@rmit.edu.au

T. Rana et al. (eds.), *Handbook of Big Data and Analytics in Accounting and Auditing*,
https://doi.org/10.1007/978-981-19-4460-4_17

at the heart of every business decision" (p. 11). This prompted the university in this research to introduce the Financial Analytics course in the MBA curriculum.

In the meantime, the GMAC recruiter report (2021) shows that an MBA graduate's three main employment areas are finance/accounting, consulting, and technology. Whilst the employers require the hard skills of analytics, there is increasing attention that employability skills such as interpersonal skills are essential for performance success and career progression (Daff et al., 2012; GMAC, 2021). Kavanagh and Drennan (2008) point out transferable skills, including interpersonal skills are in high demand by the industry for accounting graduates. Meanwhile, there were criticisms in the past that MBA programs had not effectively incorporated soft skills and ethical behavior development into the curriculum, making graduates disconnected to a corporate world (Mitchell et al., 2010; Stewart et al., 2016). McKinsey (2021) notes skill-building efforts after the pandemic would be more focused on 'softer' and advanced cognitive skills.

This study examines the inclusion of an experiential roleplay into the MBA Financial Analytics course to integrate soft skills development with hard skills training. Prior literature has started to explore the soft skills development in the accounting curriculum (e.g. Cegala & Lenzmeier Broz, 2002; Daff, 2013; Gittings et al., 2020; Holsbrink-Engels, 2000; Lane & Rollnick, 2007), though there was very little on MBA accounting courses. This research fills the void of learning design for integration of soft and hard skills to develop versatile graduates who are work ready.

The MBA program that the experiential learning is implemented does not require compulsory prior work experience. It typically has both students who graduated from the undergraduate degree directly and those who are already working in the industry and study part-time. There are both international and domestic students in the program. Three research questions are explored in this study:

- Does the roleplay improve the self-perceived interpersonal skills of MBA students?
- Do students with longer prior work experience rate their self-perceived interpersonal skills higher?
- Does the length of work experience affect the outcome of the interpersonal skills after the roleplay?

2 Literature Review

2.1 *Self-Efficacy Theory*

The self-efficacy theory explains that people tend to undertake tasks or situations that they believe they can handle and avoid the ones that they perceive to be beyond their capabilities (Bandura, 1986, 1991). Personal experience is the most important influence on an individual's self-efficacy. It is more important than observation of others' actions or receiving verbal encouragement. Based on this line of theory, opportunities to practice new skillsets will improve individuals' self-efficacy (Bandura, 1977, 1986, 1991, 2012). This consequently leads to confidence and success in accomplishing tasks that enhance future performance and increase their willingness to try on challenges.

The self-efficacy theory, stemming from the social learning theory, posits an individual's belief systems, environment, and behavioral outcomes greatly affect motivation, wellbeing, and personal accomplishment (Bandura, 1986, 2012). Therefore, a person must believe in his capabilities to succeed in a targeted task (An & Meaney, 2015; Bandura, 1986, 2012; Ramirez et al., 2012; Vodde, 2012). High self-efficacy is associated with resilience to adversity and stress, educational achievement, and employee performance (Ramirez et al., 2012). Success in previous performance, or mastery experiences, can build a person's efficacy. By applying this theory to education, it highlights the importance of practical opportunities for students' self-perception and educational outcomes.

2.2 *Experiential Learning Model*

The experiential learning theory, raised by Kolb's (1984, 2015), argues that learning is a holistic and transformational process. According to Kolb (2015), experience is the foundation of learning and all learning stems from life experiences, including life setting and life path. Specifically, learning takes place by encountering new experiences or re-interpreting prior experience, critically reflecting on the experience and associated emotions, drawing conclusions and implementing new ideas based on experience (Kolb, 2015).

The experiential learning model proposed the four-stage experiential learning cycle: concrete experience, reflective observation, abstract conceptualization, and active experimentation (Kolb, 1984, 2015). During the cycle, students develop skills via learning by doing (Kolb, 1984, 2015). The first two stages form the 'grasping' dimension of learning and the last two stages stand for the 'transforming' stage of learning. Butler et al. (2019) applied the cycle to accounting education as 'Do, Reflect, Think and Apply'.

McCarthy and McCarthy (2006) state that experiential learning provides a direct, personal encounter compared to case studies. Mintzberg (2004) calls for MBA students to conduct fieldwork to obtain essential skills via more personal experience before their graduation. Richardson et al. (2017) note experiential learning provides the actual practice opportunity and is more effective in developing soft skills than learning theories from books.

Building on Bandura (1986, 2012)'s self-efficacy theory and Kolb (1984, 2015)'s experiential learning model, this research explores how the roleplay, which provides learners with authentic opportunities to practice interpersonal skills in a real-world environment, affects students' self-efficacy.

2.3 Experiential Learning and Interpersonal Skill Development

Interpersonal skills, interchangeably called soft skills, are essential to managerial work (Dierdorff et al., 2009). Evans et al. (2009) state employers require accounting graduates to have a high level of interpersonal skills. Communication misunderstandings may result in loss of clients or dissatisfaction (Daff, 2012; Ogilvie, 2006). In contrast, well-developed interpersonal skills build trust with clients and lead to positive outcomes (Daff et al, 2012; McNeilly & Barr, 2006).

Prior studies (Cegala & Lenzmeier Broz, 2002; Daff, 2013; Gittings et al., 2020; Holsbrink-Engels, 2000; Lane & Rollnick, 2007) show role-plays create a safe and controlled environment for students to practice interpersonal communication and receive feedback. Learning by experiencing is an effective method for the development of soft skills, and it involves direct interactions between participants, and between participants and mentors (Richardson et al., 2017). Roleplay can create the kind of interactions desired by using simulations mocking real-world events. It promotes students' active engagement with real-life social environments and facilitates their learning (Finn et al., 2018; Ginting et al., 2020).

Awaysheh and Bonfiglio (2017) posit that experiential learning in MBA can be embedded in a more technical course to enable students to draw from a broad range of topics and their personal experiences. The financial analytics course provides a good opportunity to integrate the interpersonal skills development given GMAC's recruiter surveys show the employers value both technical skills and interpersonal skills for recruitment and employees' performance.

3 The Roleplay Design

The experiential roleplay module was developed in the Financial Analytics course in the host university in 2018. The assessment aimed to integrate the development of interpersonal skills into the MBA curriculum to prepare students to be job ready. Given that the self-efficacy theory predicts students who have been explicitly trained via experiential learning can be more confident and resilient to actual challenges, the authentic pedagogy strives to develop MBA students that meet the "future of work" requirements. The data collection period is from Semester 1 2018 to Semester 2 2019, with an average cohort of around 65 students.

The assessment asks students to undertake a simulation in a mock business enterprise, with actual industry representatives, including CFOs, business consultants, or senior bank managers, acting as 'Senior Executives' in the roleplay. Students form groups of three and interview a 'client' of the mock enterprise and give financial advice. The interview lasts one hour with three steps: (1) meet with the 'Senior Executive' to discuss the interview plan; (2) interview the 'client' with 'Senior Executive' observing; and (3) self-reflection and feedback. Each step is assigned 10 min,

30 min, and 20 min respectively. The teamwork setting enables the development of collaborative problem-solving skills. Students get instant feedback from the role players of 'Senior Executives' in the last step. The feedback is based on marking rubrics and the work experience of 'Senior Executives' and cover both the team and individual performance.

3.1 Before the Roleplay

To prepare for the roleplay, the learning design intends to enable students to engage with the mocked scenario and scaffold the required skills before the assessment. This allows students to comprehend the importance of interpersonal skills and theories about how to acquire the skillset. A dedicated experiential learning module was embedded into Canvas providing comprehensive materials and step-by-step guidelines. The learning materials include exemplar videos that show how consulting companies like McKinsey and Bain & Co conduct the consultation and recruit new graduates using case interviews. It also included a purposeful demonstration video that shows a conversation between an assumed financial consultant and a client with key aspects of interpersonal skills illustrated. The concrete examples provided students with the chance to observe the real-world exemplars and link the concepts to their applications.

Students were given the mock enterprise scenario, assessment instructions and marking rubrics for the assessment. The scenarios were modified from an actual company's events and financial reports. For example, in one semester it used a dairy company that was impacted by a failed marketing strategy to enter a foreign market and the Chief Operating Officer was sent by the company to seek financial advice to improve performance. The accounting challenges in the scenario were built around common financial issues, such as declined cash flow or profit, overstock of inventory, or slow accounts receivable. Detailed instructions on interview skills were given to students before engagement with the roleplay (Bedwell et al., 2014; Trull, 1964). A briefing session is conducted each semester and students were encouraged to have rehearsals before the interview day.

3.2 During the Roleplay

For the actual roleplay, students were self-selected in groups of three to interview a client. The 'business executive' meets with the students first to understand their plan for the interview. For example, they ask students what questions they prepared to ask the client and whether they had any queries. This simulates in the real world that a supervisor gives a task to a junior financial consultant and asks if they have any questions.

The next step is the key part of the roleplay experience. It is mainly divided into 5 stages for students to practice their interpersonal skills based on the scenario and give the client financial advice: (1) Greeting and opening–establishing a relationship; (2) Receiving preliminary information—summarize & check accuracy; (3) Engaging with the client—gathering more detailed information and active dialogue to explain accounting principles and financial ratios in plain language; (4) Evaluating information received and communicating your preliminary advice—ensure client's understanding of advice and (5) Closing the interview. During this phase, the business executive sat quietly in a corner of the room to observe the performance of the students. They also used the marking rubrics to grade the students' performance at the individual and group levels. The role-player for the client was instructed to have reactions based on the students' questions and responses. For instance, they could pretend to be impatient and have a busy schedule. This tests students' ability to show empathy and use strategies to build rapport and trust. They could also pretend to not understand the financial jargon and need more clarification. Also, as COOs, they could simulate rejecting students' recommendations because not all the financial measures will benefit their interests. The role-players for clients all had industry experience, hence it was relatively easy for their actions to mimic the real-world situations. This created an excellent social and natural environment for experiential learning.

3.3 After the Roleplay

The last step of the interview is self-reflection and feedback. The Business Executive would first ask students to critically reflect on their performance. Given students were relatively clear about the expectations and marking rubrics, they usually would honestly self-evaluate their strengths and weaknesses during the roleplay. They also commented on their peer's performance and their collaboration during the self-reflection. Often students also said they realized what they understood didn't mean they could perform like it. This forms an important part of the learning experience given the experiential learning model emphasizes that conscious reflection enables a deeper conceptualization and interpretation of the required skillsets. It helps them to internalize the learning based on the fresh experience and adjust their actions in the future workplace.

The business executive then commented on the students' performance based on their observation and linked to students' self-reflection. Their feedback was both based on the rubrics and their life experience to give constructive advice for further improvement. The instant feedback enabled students to understand where their interpersonal skills levels were and how they could leverage their strengths and enhance the weaker areas. The role-players of the client were also encouraged to give their opinion on the live interactions with the students. For example, they might comment on whether they felt it was a warm and inviting conversation, or whether there was a specific moment that they felt awkward. The authentic and honest opinion gives a rare chance for training before students step into the workplace. A debriefing session was also organized by the lecturer to ask students to discuss their reflections on the roleplay experience in class. This fosters critical reflection and enables a potential long-term deep understanding of the interpersonal skills and techniques for client interviewing.

4 Research Method

This research uses a questionnaire to evaluate if the roleplay improves students' self-perception of interpersonal skills and the other two research questions. The questionnaire was distributed both before and after the simulation to all participating students using two anonymous online surveys. The first survey was circulated to students one week before the roleplay and the second survey was distributed after the written task associated with the roleplay was completed. Students were advised that participation was entirely voluntary and anonymous, and their participation or not would not affect their grades.

The interpersonal skills items in the questionnaire adopt Klein et al.'s (2006) taxonomy of 12 IPS covering two key dimensions: communication and relationship building. The instrument includes 28 IPS questions that are measured on a 5-point scale (1 = I am poor at this, 2 = I am only fair at this, 3 = I'm ok at this, 4 = I'm good at this, 5 = I'm extremely good at this). The survey also asked demographic questions such as their nationality, age bracket and the number of years of experience. For the post-roleplay survey, an open-ended question was added. Other than that, the pre- and post-roleplay survey questions were the same to enable comparison.

To test the first research question, t-tests were conducted for the pre- and post-self evaluation scores for each survey item. To answer the second research question, it used the pre-roleplay survey only and OLS regressions were conducted for the overall IPS score and the subtotals for communication and relationship building skills. For the third research question, OLS regressions were performed to assess if students' interpersonal skill outcomes were affected by the length of work experience.

The survey was distributed to students enrolled into the Financial Analytics course from January 2018 to December 2019. Altogether 4 cohorts of students participated in the simulation and a total of 214 students were invited to fill in the questionnaires. A total of 75 responses were received for the pre-roleplay survey and a total of 66 students participated in the post-roleplay survey. This results in a response rate of 35% and 31% for the pre- and post-roleplay surveys respectively.

5 Results

The survey results show students' profile is consistent with the overall MBA program student profile at the host University. Demographic questions were captured and coded in the following variables (Table 1).

Responses from the pre-roleplay survey show the majority of students were below 30 years old, with 36.49% between 20 and 24 years old and another 36.49% between 25–29 years old. Meanwhile, 21.62% were between 30 and 34, 4.05% were between 35–39 with the rest (1.35%) between 55 and 59. The male (51%) and female students (49%) were roughly equal. The majority (77% of the total) were international students and 82% of the students surveyed studied full-time. The work experience of participating students ranged from 0 to 20 years, and the average length of work experience was 4.87 years. The majority had less than 4 years of work experience (44%) or no work experience at all (20%). Another 20% had 5–9 years of experience and 16% of the respondents had more than 10 years of work experience. This data highlights the potentially high value of the roleplay in providing relatively inexperienced students with exposure to mocked real-world experiences and helping them prepare to be job ready.

5.1 Roleplay and Self-Perceived IPS Improvement

Table 2 shows results from the comparison of the 12 IPS before and after the roleplay, including detailed mean value contrasts for the 28 questionnaire items. To test the first research question, t-tests were used to assess if the differences in the mean IPS scores for pre- and post-roleplay periods were statistically significant.

As illustrated in Table 2, overall, the average total IPS score from the pre-roleplay survey was 100.54, in contrast to 113.53 from the post-roleplay survey, and the difference was highly significant at the 1% significance level. For each of the 12 IPS, the average post-roleplay survey score was significantly higher than the pre-roleplay result, except for intercultural sensitivity. Specifically, for communication

Table 1 Demographic characteristics coding

Variable	Coding
Age	1 (20–24); 2 (25–29); 3 (30–34); 4 (35–39); 5 (40-44); 6 (45-49); 7 (50-54); 8 (55-59)
Gender	0 (female); 1 (male)
International	0 (international student); 1(domestic student)
Full-time	0 (full-time study); 1 (part-time study)
Work status	1 (full-time); 2 (part-time); 3 (casual); 4 (unemployed)
Work experience	Number of years of work experience

skills, the total sub-scores were 31.59 and 37.10 for pre- and post-roleplay periods respectively and the difference was highly significant at the 1% significance level. The following communication skills: active listening, oral communication, and assertive communication were found to have significantly increased, at the 1% significance level, whilst written and non-verbal communication skills were significant at the 5% significance level.

Table 2 Pre-roleplay and post-roleplay IPS mean scores and t-tests

No	Question	Pre-roleplay mean	Post-roleplay mean	Difference	*t*-tests
Communication skills					
Active Listening (AL)					
1	Paying close attention to what is being said	3.62	4.24	0.62	0.000***
2	Asking the other party to explain exactly what he or she means	3.48	4.15	0.67	0.000***
3	Requesting that ambiguous ideas or statements are repeated	3.23	3.94	0.71	0.000***
AL	**Subtotal**	**10.33**	**12.33**	**2.00**	**0.000*** **
Oral Communication (OC)					
4	Sending verbal messages constructively	**3.46**	**4.06**	**0.60**	**0.000*** **
Written communication (WC)					
5	Writing clearly and appropriately	3.52	4.00	0.48	0.008***
6	Communicating intended meaning	3.57	4.23	0.66	0.000***
WC	**Subtotal**	**7.09**	**8.23**	**1.14**	**0.050** **
Assertive communication (AC)					
7	Directly expressing feelings, preferences, needs, and opinions in a way that is neither threatening nor punishing to another person	3.66	4.09	0.44	0.008***
8	Proposing ideas	3.62	4.27	0.65	0.000***
AC	**Subtotal**	**7.28**	**8.36**	**1.08**	**0.000*** **

(continued)

Table 2 (continued)

No	Question	Pre-roleplay mean	Post-roleplay mean	Difference	*t*-tests
Non-verbal communication (NVC)					
9	Reinforcing or replacing spoken communication through the use of body language, gestures, voice, or artefacts	**3.43**	**4.12**	**0.69**	**0.000*** **
1–9	**Subtotal**	**31.59**	**37.10**	**5.51**	**0.017** **
Relationship-building skills					
Cooperation and coordination (CC)					
10	Understanding and working with others in groups or teams	3.87	4.18	0.31	0.039**
11	Offering help to those who need it	3.79	4.24	0.45	0.002***
12	Pacing activities to fit the needs of the team	3.46	4.00	0.54	0.001***
CC	**Subtotal**	**11.12**	**12.42**	**1.30**	**0.001*** **
Trust					
13	Willingness to be vulnerable to the actions of another party based on the expectation that certain actions important to the me will be performed	**3.23**	**3.91**	**0.68**	**0.001*** **
Intercultural Sensitivity (IS)					
14	Appreciating individual differences among people	3.79	4.18	0.39	0.020**
15	Interacting with culturally diverse others	4.07	4.18	0.11	0.485
IS	**Subtotal**	**7.86**	**8.36**	**0.50**	**0.103**

(continued)

Table 2 (continued)

No	Question	Pre-roleplay mean	Post-roleplay mean	Difference	*t*-tests
Service Orientation (SO)					
16	Predispositions and an inclination to provide service, to be courteous and helpful in dealing with customers, clients, and associates	3.85	4.22	0.37	0.032**
17	Exceeding customer's expectations	3.67	3.97	0.30	0.089*
18	Ability to maintain positive client relationship	3.84	4.24	0.40	0.014**
19	Representing the organization to customers and the public	3.67	4.09	0.42	0.009***
SO	**Subtotal**	**15.03**	**16.52**	**1.49**	**0.020****
Self-presentation (SP)					
20	Influencing the reactions and images people have of me and my ideas	3.39	3.82	0.43	0.017**
21	Positively influencing work associates	3.59	3.94	0.35	0.026**
SP	**Subtotal**	**6.98**	**7.76**	**0.78**	**0.013****
Social influence (SI)					
22	Guiding people toward the adoption of specific behaviors, beliefs, or attitudes	3.41	3.94	0.53	0.002***
23	Influencing the distribution of advantages and disadvantages within an organization through one's actions	3.28	3.88	0.60	0.000***
SI	**Subtotal**	**6.69**	**7.82**	**1.13**	**0.000*****

(continued)

Table 2 (continued)

No	Question	Pre-roleplay mean	Post-roleplay mean	Difference	*t*-tests
Conflict resolution and negotiation (CRN)					
24	Advocating one's position with an open mind	3.59	3.94	0.35	0.060*
25	Not taking personally other members' disagreements	3.57	3.73	0.15	0.429
26	Putting oneself in the other's shoes	3.69	3.97	0.28	0.141
27	Following rational argument and avoiding premature evaluation	3.56	3.94	0.38	0.031**
28	Trying to synthesize the best ideas from all viewpoints and perspectives	3.64	4.06	0.42	0.008***
CRN	**Subtotal**	**18.05**	**19.64**	**1.59**	**0.000****
10–28	**Subtotal**	**68.95**	**76.43**	**7.48**	**0.002*****
IPS	**Total**	**100.54**	**113.53**	**12.99**	**0.000*****

Meanwhile, for relationship-building skills, the post roleplay score was 76.43, which was significantly higher than the pre-roleplay survey score of 68.95 at the 1% significance level. Of all Relationship-Building skills, cooperation and coordination, trust, social influence, and conflict resolution and negotiation were found to have significantly increased at the 1% significance level. Meanwhile, service orientation and self-presentation improved at the 5% significance level. Again, intercultural sensitivity was the only Relationship-Building skill that was not perceived to have enhanced significantly in the survey. It seems the roleplay was successful in providing students with stepstones to advance their interpersonal skills which will benefit their future career path.

Results also show the average post-roleplay scores in each of the 12 IPS increased compared with the pre-roleplay survey. For the 5 communication skills, the average increase in the mean score was 0.61 out of 5. For the 7 relationship-building skills, the average increase in the mean score was 0.39 out of 5, which was lower than the growth in communication skills. It shows the experiential simulation, which is an interview roleplay via teamwork, may be more effective in improving communication skills compared with relationship-building skills. The highest increase in the mean score was for Item 3 active listening. This suggests the roleplay initiative greatly lifted students' confidence and self-perception of their competency in active listening, an attribute that is highly valued in the workplace. This makes sense given the roleplay is designed as an experiential activity that requires students to empathize with the client's feelings and build trust with the clients.

Moreover, for the additional question on students' self-perception of whether they believed they improved their interpersonal skills through the roleplay experience, 78.13% of students answered a 'yes', supporting the conclusion that the experiential roleplay was largely successful in achieving its intended outcomes. Qualitative feedback showed students greatly appreciated the live and instant feedback from industry executives, which they would not get from a traditional assessment such as a case study.

5.2 Work Experience and Self-Perceived IPS Before the Roleplay

Table 3 shows results from the regression to test the second research question. The OLS regression uses the pre-roleplay data to test the relationship between self-perceived IPS score and the length of work experience. The regression controls for age, gender, domestic vs international student, study mode and work status. Since domestic vs international student has a high correlation (Cr = 0.81) with the study mode, the study mode is removed from the equation to avoid any multicollinearity issue. Results show the model overall was highly significant at the 1% confidence level (F = 3.823). The coefficient for Work Experience was highly significant at the 5% level and was positively related to the overall self-perceived IPS score. This means students who had longer prior work experience rated themselves higher for the IPS score. It is consistent with the self-efficacy theory that personal experience affects students' self-perception of their skills and people are more confident with tasks they have performed from previous life experiences. All other control variables were not significant.

Table 3 Work experience and self-perceived IPS scores OLS regression

	Coefficients	*t* Stat	*P*-value
Intercept	89.644	10.621	0.000***
Age	−0.091	−0.043	0.966
Gender	−3.917	−0.939	0.352
International	7.147	1.217	0.229
Work status	1.686	0.837	0.406
Work Experience	1.570	2.341	0.023**
F-statistic			3.823***
R^2			0.257
N			75

Table 4 Work experience and self-perceived communication skills OLS regression

	Coefficients	*t* Stat	*P*-value
Intercept	27.865	9.443	0.000***
Age	−0.126	−0.168	0.867
Gender	−2.116	−1.450	0.153
International	3.639	1.773	0.082
Work status	0.859	1.219	0.228
Work Experience	0.455	1.942	0.057*
F-statistic			3.404***
R^2			0.236
N			75

Table 5 Work experience and self-perceived relationship-building skills OLS regression

	Coefficients	*t* Stat	*P*-value
Intercept	61.779	10.551	0.000***
Age	0.034	0.023	0.982
Gender	−1.801	−0.622	0.536
International	3.508	0.861	0.393
Work status	0.828	0.592	0.556
Work Experience	1.115	2.396	0.020**
F-statistic			3.741***
R^2			0.254
N			75

Tables 4 and 5 further demonstrate the relationship between work experience and the two dimensions of the IPS score: communication skills and relationship-building skills. In both models, the coefficients on work experience were positive and significant at 10% and 5% respectively. Again, this means students with more work experience rated themselves higher for both dimensions compared with students with less experience.

5.3 *Work Experience and Self-Perceived*

5.3.1 IPS After the Roleplay

To test the third research question, the difference-in-difference regression was conducted. A dummy variable "WE < 4 Yrs" was created and it was coded zero (0) for students with work experience less than 4 years and one (1) otherwise. 'Pre_Post' was coded one (1) for the post-roleplay survey for zero (0) for pre-roleplay survey. An interaction terms of "WE x Pre_Post" was used to capture the difference-in-difference

Table 6 IPS skills outcome and work experience length

	Coefficients	*t* Stat	*P*-value
Intercept	93.864	13.173	0.000
Age	2.160	1.991	0.050
Gender	−1.784	−0.566	0.573
International	7.377	1.701	0.093
Work status	1.920	1.184	0.240
WE < 4 Yrs	−11.115	−2.679	0.009***
WE x Pre_Post	2.738	0.440	0.661
Pre_Post	8.800	1.992	0.050**
F-statistic			6.976***
R2			0.362
N			141

and whether work experience length affected the post-roleplay IPS outcome. Results are reported in the below Table 6.

Results show that the model was overall highly significant at the 1% significance level (F = 6.976). The coefficient on the "WE < 4 Yrs" was highly significant (at 1% significance level). This means, before the roleplay, students with work experience higher than 4 years had a higher level of self-perceived interpersonal skills. This is consistent with the findings from research question 2. Meanwhile, the coefficient on the 'Pre_Post' was also significant at the 5% level. This indicates, for the treatment group of students with less than 4 years of experience, the improvement in interpersonal skills was significant after the roleplay. The interaction term is, however, not significant. This shows the outcome of the interpersonal skills after the roleplay is not affected by the length of work experience. It implies that students with less work experience did not have a lower level of self-perceived interpersonal skills than peers due to the intervention.

This finding has significant implications for educators and institutions. Whilst prior work experience affects students' self-perceived level of IPS, the roleplay simulation can be used to improve students' IPS skills and their self-efficacy. This means by providing simulated real-life experience, institutions can create a safe and controlled environment for students to experience and practice interactions with clients to develop their interpersonal skills. The improved self-efficacy as indicated by the study will make students more confident to handle workplace tasks and challenges more proficiently (Bandura, 1986, 2012). Simulations such as roleplays can be a supplement for real experience to give precious opportunities to practice soft skills before they step into the society. This is particularly important for students with less work experience. The concrete experience and instant feedback from industry partitioners facilitates learning by doing. The roleplay learning design gives students expectations, demonstrations, theories to enable abstract conceptualization. By going through the experiential learning cycle, students engage with the roleplay to advance their cognitive and behavioral outcomes. This will modify their action choices in new situations. Therefore, grasping and transformative experience helps internalize the skills development and apply them to the actual workplace with confidence in the future.

The above results are also consistent with industry practitioners' anecdotal observations of students' performance. The learning design used industry practitioners as supervisors for the roleplay assessment. They gave students marks and written feedback based on rubrics. Their feedback indicates they perceived students in the roleplay overall demonstrated a reasonable level of interpersonal skills benchmarking against employees in their organizations. They indicated graduates who performed well in the roleplay experience would be competitive in the job interviews and more ready for real-world tasks. This means the simulations can speed up the learning cycle for new hires and get them into the action mode of a mature employee quicker.

6 Conclusion

This chapter examines the impact of a roleplay on MBA students' interpersonal skills in a Financial Analytics course. This industry-engaged roleplay aimed to ensure students possess interpersonal skills in addition to hard (e.g. analytical) skills and thus become job ready. Using a 28-item questionnaire, this study tests three research questions based on the self-efficacy theory. It provides important empirical evidence on how experiential learning can impact students' self-perception of their interpersonal skills.

Results indicate simulated roleplay experience can enhance students' self-perceived interpersonal skills. The intervention outcome is not affected by the work experience, which means although before the roleplay, students with longer work experience rated themselves higher in IPS scores, the difference is negligible after the roleplay. Findings from this result have significant implications for work-integrated learning in higher education. It highlights the importance of practical and reflective experience on the development of students' employability skills. Although students with longer prior experience had a higher level of self-efficacy before the roleplay, students with less prior experience caught up on interpersonal skills through the roleplay mastery experience. This means the opportunities for encountering and practicing a new experience can make up for life experience, even if it is simulated. Educators and institutions should recognize the benefits of such opportunities and invest in practice-based or work-integrated learning opportunities to nurture workplace capabilities.

This research has its limitations and future research could further extend the evidence for the self-efficacy theory. It did not use the traditional questionnaire comprising eight qualitative questions to directly measure self-efficacy. To enable an empirical analysis of the level of interpersonal skills, the survey was based on Klein et al. (2006) quantitative tool for interpersonal skills measurement. Due to limitations of the host institution, we could not collect data from prior MBA students who did not have the roleplay experience as a control group. Despite the limitations, this chapter offers important empirical evidence on the impact of experiential learning on students' self-perceived interpersonal skills. It provides significant contributions to the line of literature on experiential learning and self-efficacy. It also supplies a learning design exemplar for integrating soft skills with hard skills in a Financial Analytics course.

References

An, J., & Meaney, K. S. (2015). Inclusion practices in elementary physical education: A social-cognitive perspective. *International Journal of Disability, Development and Education, 62*(2), 143–157.

Awaysheh, A., & Bonfiglio, D. (2017). Leveraging experiential learning to incorporate social entrepreneurship in MBA programs: A case study. *The International Journal of Management Education, 15*(2), 332–349.

Bandura, A. (1977). Self-efficacy: Toward a unifying theory of behavioral change. *Psychological Review, 84*(2), 191.

Bandura, A. (1986). The explanatory and predictive scope of self-efficacy theory. *Journal of Social and Clinical Psychology, 4*(3), 359–373.

Bandura, A. (1991). Social cognitive theory of self-regulation. *Organizational Behavior and Human Decision Processes, 50*(2), 248–287.

Bandura, A. (2012). On the functional properties of perceived self-efficacy revisited. *Journal of Management, 38*(1), 9–44.

Bedwell, W. L., Fiore, S. M., & Salas, E. (2014). Developing the future workforce: An approach for integrating interpersonal skills into the MBA classroom. *Academy of Management Learning & Education, 13*(2), 171–186. https://doi.org/10.5465/amle.2011.0138

Butler, M. G., Church, K. S., & Spencer, A. W. (2019). Do, reflect, think, apply: Experiential education in accounting. *Journal of Accounting Education, 48*, 12–21. https://doi.org/10.1016/j.jaccedu.2019.05.001

Cegala, D. J., & Lenzmeier Broz, S. (2002). Physician communication skills training: A review of theoretical backgrounds, objectives and skills. *Medical Education, 36*(11), 1004–1016.

Daff, L. (2012). Lessons from successes in medical communication training and their applications to accounting education. *Accounting Education, 21*(4), 385–405.

Daff, L. (2013). Accounting students' reflections on a course to enhance their interpersonal skills. *Accounting Education, 22*(6), 563–581.

Daff, L., De Lange, P., & Jackling, B. (2012). A comparison of generic skills and emotional intelligence in accounting education. *Issues in Accounting Education, 27*(3), 627–645.

Dierdorff, E. C., Rubin, R. S., & Morgeson, F. P. (2009). The milieu of managerial work: An integrative framework linking work context to role requirements. *Journal of Applied Psychology, 94*(4), 972.

Ernst & Young's. (2015). *Becoming an analytics driven organization to create value.* https://assets.ey.com/content/dam/ey-sites/ey-com/en_gl/topics/digital/ey-global-becoming-an-analytics-driven-organization.pdf

Evans, E., Tindale, J., Cable, D., & Hamil Mead, S. (2009). Collaborative teaching in a linguistically and culturally diverse higher education setting: A case study of a postgraduate accounting program. *Higher Education Research & Development, 28*(6), 597–613.

Finn, K. E., Yan, Z., & McInnis, K. J. (2018). Promoting physical activity and science learning in an outdoor education program. *Journal of Physical Education, Recreation & Dance, 89*(1), 35–39.

Fitzgerald, S. (2021). MBA in business analytics: Big data is a big deal. https://fortune.com/education/business/articles/2021/05/04/mba-in-business-analytics-big-data-is-a-big-deal/

Ginting, H., Mahiranissa, A., Bekti, R., & Febriansyah, H. (2020). The effect of outing Team Building training on soft skills among MBA students. *The International Journal of Management Education, 18*(3), 100423.
Gittings, L., Taplin, R., & Kerr, R. (2020). Experiential learning activities in university accounting education: A systematic literature review. *Journal of Accounting Education, 52*, 1–13.
Graduate Management Admissions Council (GMAC). (2021). *Demand of graduate management talent: 2021 Hiring projections and salary trends access the report, blog, and infographic Corporate Recruiters Survey 2021.* https://www.gmac.com/-/media/files/gmac/research/employment-outlook/2021_crs-demand-of-gm-talent.pdf
Holsbrink-Engels, G. A. (2000). Designing role-plays for interpersonal skills training. *Performance Improvement, 39*(9), 32–39.
Huerta, E., & Jensen, S. (2017). An accounting information systems perspective on data analytics and Big Data. *Journal of Information Systems, 31*(3), 101–114.
Kavanagh, M. H., & Drennan, L. (2008). What skills and attributes does an accounting graduate need? Evidence from student perceptions and employer expectations. *Accounting and Finance, 48*, 279–300.
Klein, C., DeRouin, R. E., & Salas, E. (2006). Uncovering workplace interpersonal skills: A review, framework, and research agenda. In G. P. Hodgkinson & J. K. Ford (Eds.), *International Review of Industrial and Organizational Psychology*, vol. 21, 80–126. Wiley and Sons, Ltd.
Kolb, D. (2015). *Experiential learning: Experience as the source of learning and development*. Pearson Education.
Kolb, D. A. (1984). *Experiential learning: Experience as the source of learning and development* (D. A. Kolb, Ed.). Prentice-Hall.
Lane, C., & Rollnick, S. (2007). The use of simulated patients and role-play in communication skills training: A review of the literature to August 2005. *Patient Education and Counseling, 67*(1–2), 13–20.
McCarthy, P. R., & McCarthy, H. M. (2006). When case studies are not enough: Integrating experiential learning into business curricula. *Journal of Education for Business, 81*(4), 201–204.
Mckinsey. (2021). *Building workforce skills at scale to thrive during and after the COVID-19 crisis*. https://www.mckinsey.com/business-functions/people-and-organizational-performance/our-insights/building-workforce-skills-at-scale-to-thrive-during-and-after-the-covid-19-crisis
McNeilly, K. M., & Barr, T. F. (2006). I love my accountants–they're wonderful: Understanding customer delight in the professional services arena. *Journal of Services Marketing., 20*(3), 152–159.
Mintzberg, H. (2004). Managers not MBAs: A hard look at the soft practice of managing and management development. *Management Today, 20*(7), 10–13.
Mitchell, G. W., Skinner, L. B., & White, B. J. (2010). Essential soft skills for success in the twenty-first century workforce as perceived by business educators. *Delta Pi Epsilon Journal, 52*(1), 43–53.
Ogilvie, R. (2006). Conversation comes easy. *Charter, 77*(6), 33–35.
Ramirez, E., Kulinna, P. H., & Cothran, D. (2012). Constructs of physical activity behaviour in children: The usefulness of social cognitive theory. *Psychology of Sport and Exercise, 13*(3), 303–310.
Richardson, J. C., Maeda, Y., Lv, J., & Caskurlu, S. (2017). Social presence in relation to students' satisfaction and learning in the online environment: A meta-analysis. *Computers in Human Behavior, 71*, 402–417.
Stewart, C., Wall, A., & Marciniec, S. (2016). Mixed signals: Do college graduates have the soft skills that employers want? *Competition Forum,* 14(2), 276. American Society for Competitiveness.
Trull, S. G. (1964). Strategies of effective interviewing. *Harvard Business Review, 42*(1), 89–94.
Vodde, R. F. (2012). Changing paradigms in police training: Transitioning from a traditional to an andragogical model. In *Police organization and training* (27–44). Springer.

Ling Mei Cong, PhD is an Associate Professor of Accounting and Deputy Dean of Learning and Teaching in the Graduate School of Business and Law at the RMIT University, Melbourne, Australia. She coordinates and teaches accounting courses in the EMBA and MBA programs. Her research interests are mainly in corporate governance, financial reporting quality, sustainability reporting, and capital markets. She is an executive leader in Higher Education. Specialized in using technology to enhance student experience.

Chapter 18
Data Analytics in an Undergraduate Accountancy Programme: The Spaced Retrieval Method

SzeKee Koh, Hwee Hoon Lee, and Arif Perdana

Abstract The accountancy profession is now challenged by the pace of technological advancement and the ubiquitous digitalization leading to data explosion and advanced analytics. Digital technology is also replacing mundane tasks and manual work which accountants undertook in the past. Besides data analytics skills, accountants now need to possess critical thinking skills, knowledge of data science tools and communication skills. Consequently, equipping accounting professionals with data analytics skills is critical. Professional accounting bodies address this need by emphasizing continuing professional education and developing guidelines for data analytics. At the same time, higher education institutions are taking the initiative to integrate data analytics into their accounting curricula. However, given the numerous professional accreditation requirements that higher education institutions must fulfill, a big challenge remains for any institution to insert rigorous data analytics training into their existing curriculum. This chapter describes the development of a data analytics roadmap for undergraduate accountancy education—from reviewing our academic and industry data analytics curricula and evaluating existing modules that could be integrated with relevant data analytics topics, to seeking feedback from industry partners regarding the curriculum model we had developed. In delivering our curricula across the levels of study, a spaced retrieval teaching technique was opted to ensure that students could progressively develop data analytics competencies.

Keywords Accounting Education · Data Analytics Competencies · Undergraduate Curriculum · Spaced Retrieval

S. Koh (✉) · H. H. Lee · A. Perdana
Singapore Institute of Technology, Singapore, Singapore
e-mail: SzeKee.Koh@Singaporetech.edu.sg

H. H. Lee
e-mail: hweehoon.lee@singaporetech.edu.sg

A. Perdana
e-mail: arif.perdana@monash.edu

T. Rana et al. (eds.), *Handbook of Big Data and Analytics in Accounting and Auditing*,
https://doi.org/10.1007/978-981-19-4460-4_18

1 Introduction

The accountancy profession is now challenged by the pace of technological advancement and the ubiquitous digitalization leading to data explosion and advanced analytics. While the future of the accountancy profession looks promising with the advancement of technology, of concern is the possibility of accountants becoming redundant (Richins et al., 2017), as mundane tasks and manual work undertaken by accountants could be replaced by machines. History, though, has shown that the role of humans in many professions are not likely to be replaced by machines. Although the capacities of robots and automation have been enhanced, human workers remain indispensable to perform useful tasks in an economy (Mokyr et al., 2015). The use of digital technologies in the accounting profession, therefore, might not replace accountants. Rather, it promises new career opportunities for accountants who are able to harness the new technology to deliver higher value services to their clients.

Digitalization of businesses and advanced technological tools bring about more data today than ever before (Smolan & Erwitt, 2012). Zwitter (2014) suggests that up to year 2003, approximately 5 billion gigabytes of data were generated from the beginning of recorded history, compared to the same amount generated every 10 seconds in year 2015. These big data can be translated into huge amounts of valuable information vital for businesses to succeed in the new digitalized world. Therefore, accountants must equip themselves with skills in processing and analyzing data. In fact, Association of Chartered Certified Accountants (ACCA) named data analytics as one of the drivers of change for the transformation of future accounting and auditing practice and competencies (ACCA, 2016). Furthermore, with the help of advanced technologies, organizations can identify new sources of data that may exist internally and externally, which can potentially be exploited. Accountants can leverage data analytics and cultivate future opportunities to accelerate organization growth, competitive advantage and value creation (EY, 2015). Consequently, data analytics is an essential skill future accountants must possess.

Institutes of higher education and universities play an important role in providing fundamental professional training to future accountants. With the increasing need for future accountants to have the fundamental data analytics skillsets, accountancy programmes in the higher education sector must develop relevant curricula to meet the accounting industry's digital needs (Paul & MacDonald, 2020). Implementation of data analytics in accounting curricula, however, requires thoughtful consideration. Implementation issues are reflected in the following questions: *What are the types of data analytics skillsets that accountancy students need be equipped with? What are the courses relevant for teaching data analytics? Would it be necessary to have separate courses for data analytics or to have data analytics topics embedded into existing courses? What technologies should be used to run the data analytics courses? Is data analytics solely about the use of sophisticated technologies for analysis?*

Furthermore, to maintain accreditation credentials with local and/or international accounting professional bodies, many universities' accounting programmes are packed with a long list of pre-requisite technical courses (such as accounting systems and processes, audit and assurance, business law, economics, ethics, finance and finance management, management accounting, quantitative methods, information technology and taxation). This leaves very little curriculum space for universities to plan a comprehensive data analytics knowledge matrix without extending the programme duration. Hence, university administrators will need to design an appropriate curriculum to meet all stakeholders' expectations.

While prior studies have shed some light on the integration of data analytics in the higher education curricula (see, for example, Gupta et al., 2015; Mitri & Palosay, 2015; Wilder & Ozgur, 2015), their focus was on the business school curricula, with little discussion relevant to accountancy programmes. An exception is Dzuranin et al. (2018), who proposed data analytics implementation approaches in the accounting curriculum. This chapter describes our experience in developing an integrated approach to improve data analytics competencies for students in an accountancy undergraduate programme at a public autonomous university in Singapore. Autonomous universities (AUs) in Singapore receive funding from the government and are given the flexibility to strategize, innovate, and differentiate themselves in their pursuit of excellence in education, research and service (Singapore Ministry of Education, n.d.).

In our review of the curriculum, a data analytics roadmap was first identified, and a knowledge matrix set as the learning outcomes. In other words, upon completion of the programme, students should have the competencies to analyze the relationships and patterns from data and to perform a decision optimization. The knowledge matrix was split into four stages: collecting, storing, processing, reporting, analyzing, forecasting, pre-emption analyzing of data and reporting the findings and solutions through visualization techniques. We then explored the spaced retrieval method to break the knowledge matrix into bite-size components and to be integrated into various modules spread out across the entire programme. The spaced retrieval teaching approach promotes repeated recalling of information across multiple study and recall sessions. Students attained data analytics competency through learning the knowledge from basic/foundation level through to the intermediate level, and finally, the applied/advanced level. Each level was reinforced and interlinked with common learning points so that students could see how topics were connected across modules and knowledge levels.

Since its inception, the programme has graduated four cohorts of students. On average, in excess of 90% of graduates obtained full time employment within 6 months of their graduation, with more than 80% of the employed graduates working in the four major accounting entities in Singapore in the assurance, taxation, data analytics and corporate advisory divisions. The average starting salaries were also among the highest relative to those earned by accountancy graduates from the other local universities. In response to our new curriculum model, our graduates commented that the spaced retrieval teaching technique had helped them attain the data analytics competencies needed for their careers in accountancy.

The remainder of this chapter is organized as follows: background discussion on the perceived importance for accountants to possess data analytics skillset for the new digital economy as well the various curriculum designs to embed the learning of data analytics for university students, followed by discussion of the spaced retrieval teaching technique to reinforce learning outcomes and of our integrated teaching approach to embed the teaching of data analytics to our students, and finally, the concluding section of the chapter.

2 Background

2.1 Data Analytics for Accountants

With the emergence of big data, data analytics has been attracting interest from both professionals and academics. While the core idea of data analytics to generate insights from data and information has long been acknowledged, ubiquitous digitization, high performing computing and sophisticated analytical software have added new value to the field of data analytics. The explosion of data sources and the speed of technology have further created a wider spectrum of business opportunities for companies who are now able to utilize analytic techniques to develop data-driven innovations. As a professional dealing with data and business, accountants should be at the forefront of data analytics initiatives. Furthermore, the use of data analytics in accounting is unavoidable since it affects the way accountants process information and arrive at decision making (Amani & Fadlalla, 2017; Li et al., 2018). For example, financial statements in several countries around the world are now delivered through the eXtensible Business Reporting Language (XBRL) and other semantic web solutions, making them more interactive to users. Data collection can be further expanded through customers' or users' digital trail on the web or application interface (Bhimani & Wilcocks, 2014). Therefore, data analytics can assist accountants to further analyze the narrative across multiple channels of financial activities disclosure to identify investor sentiment and future stock performance (Amani & Fadlalla, 2017).

Data analytics can also bring about operational changes to how accountants discharge their de facto fiduciary duties. For example, for auditors, data analytics allows continuous auditing (CA) (Alles et al., 2008) and big data audit analytics (Setty & Bakhshi, 2013). CA processes are made possible due to the automated acquisition of accounting data and transactions. Given the massive amount of data from enterprise applications that can be readily accessed by auditors, analyses can now be performed on the entire data population instead of sample data (Li et al., 2018). Data analytics also permits auditors to undertake audit analytics, draw conclusions from a large amount of data, and identify meaningful patterns and associations within the data (Setty & Bakhshi, 2013). In addition, data analytics can facilitate more accurate business forecasting (Rikhardsson & Yigitbasioglu, 2018). The use of data visualization for analytical purposes also helps auditors to identify existing or potentially fraudulent future activities (Dilla & Raschke, 2015).

In short, the current landscape of data analytics requires accountants to keep abreast of their skillsets. Accountants are required not only to excel in their domain knowledge but also to apply this knowledge to help build the data model, process the data, as well as ascertain the meaning of the data to provide informed data-driven insights.

2.2 *Data Analytics in Accounting Education*

Responding to the surge in demand for data analytics skills, institutes of higher learning and universities around the world are compelled to embed more data analytics content into their modules (Dzuranin et al., 2018). Academic accreditation bodies, professional bodies, and industry are now placing demands on institutions of higher learning and universities to produce graduates equipped with data analytics skills.

The Association to Advance Collegiate Schools of Business (AACSB) International Accounting Accreditation Standard A7: Information Technology Skills and Knowledge for Accounting Graduates states that:

> Consistent with a mission, expected outcomes, and supporting strategies, accounting degree programmes include learning experiences that develop skills and knowledge related to the integration of information technology in accounting and business. Included in these learning experiences are the development of skills and knowledge related to data creation, data sharing, data analytics, data mining, data reporting, and storage within and across organizations (Information Technology Skills and Knowledge for Accounting Graduates) (AACSB International, 2014: 3)

AACSB encourages institutions of higher learning and universities to embed information technology related topics, including data analytics, throughout the curriculum, use relevant technology, and expose students to real-world practices reflecting the complexities of business.

Association of Chartered Certified Accountants (ACCA) suggests that the utilization of smart software and systems in the accounting field will be more pervasive than ever before. Manual bookkeeping and tedious, mundane accounting tasks would no longer be burdensome. Reflecting on this, ACCA proposes digital skill as a relevant skill. Future accountants must be aware of existing accounting and auditing applications, emerging digital technologies, as well as the way these technologies can be applied to solve complex business issues (ACCA, 2016).

From the industry's perspective, the World Economic Forum (WEF) projected that big data analytics and machine learning are among the top five technologies that companies are likely to adopt (Centre for the New Economy & Society, 2018). This trend will certainly transform the employment landscape. Future accountants, for example, will work on predictive modelling rather than focus on historical reporting. Hence, there will be an expectation that accountants are trained to be detail-oriented, fluent in documentation, familiar with multiple business contexts, capable of exercising judgment and interpretation, able to use relevant technology for their work, and able to advise companies and businesses (Haverson, 2014).

To meet professional accreditation requirements and industry's needs, institutes of higher learning and universities have been working to integrate data analytics competencies into their curricula. The implementation of data analytics, however, creates challenges because the field of data analytics is linked to multiple disciplines, such as information systems and technology, communication, and domain-specific knowledge (i.e., finance and accounting). Dzuranin et al. (2018) proposed three strategies to embed data analytics into the accounting curriculum: (a) a focused approach, (b) an integrated approach, and (c) a hybrid approach. The first approach requires separating data analytics modules from the existing accounting modules; the second approach attaches relevant data analytics topics into the existing accounting modules; and the third approach is a combination of the first two approaches.

Besides excelling in the core technical skills of data analytics, accountants will need to master *complimentary* skills. Dzuranin et al. (2018) highlight that to do well in data analytics tasks, one would also need to have three other skills: (a) critical thinking, (b) data comprehension and analysis, and (c) communication skills. Critical thinking skills include formulating relevant questions, identifying problems, being able to identify the required data to address the problems, and conducting data exploration. To be able to think critically, accounting students must understand their domain knowledge well. Understanding the data necessitates comprehending the type of data, relational and non-relational database, data retrieval, data cleansing and data loading. Students must be able to use technology to perform analytical work (i.e., descriptive, diagnostic, predictive, and prescriptive). In a similar vein, understanding data and performing analysis refer to tool skills. To handle massive amounts of data and the complexity of business, students have to be armed with tools to solve problems. Finally, accounting students must also be able to effectively communicate analytical results, both written and oral, to different audiences. Thus, all three skills of critical thinking, data comprehension and analysis, and communication skills are needed for accounting graduates to develop data analytic competencies to provide professional services to their clientele.

2.3 *Spaced Retrieval Teaching Technique*

While it is easy for any Accountancy School to realize the importance of integrating data analytics skills in their programme curriculum, with the various accreditation requirements (for example, AACSB, Professional Accounting bodies), the challenge lies in finding learning opportunities amidst the limited curriculum spaces. To integrate comprehensive data analytics in learning, the traditional teaching approach of including all there is to know about data analytics into one module, in hope that students will learn the required competencies, may not work. Instead, alternative teaching methods need to be considered.

Learning is understood to have taken place when people encode or study new material and are able to form meaningful connections and create enriched knowledge structures (Blunt & Karpicke, 2014). Often, the ultimate test of whether a student has mastered the knowledge is through a summative assessment of a subject matter at the end of the teaching term. Performance in the summative assessment is then the yardstick to quantify the level of mastery and competency that the student has gained. Such a learning design may not yield the best results in student learning, as students are unable to enjoy long-term retention of the knowledge learnt. In other words, especially in an examination-orientated environment, students learn merely to pass summative assessments.

Retrieval-based learning, on the other hand, promotes repeated recalling of information across multiple study and recall sessions. Information acquired through repeated retrieval practice is more resistant to interference, shows a lower forgetting rate and remains accessible in situations where a person must multitask when attentional processes are heavily loaded (Karpicke, 2012; Racsmány et al., 2018). Repeated retrieval-based learning is found to produce superior long-term retention relative to imagery-based and verbal elaborative study. The benefits of retrieval practice stem from processes involved in recollecting the context of a prior learning episode (Karpicke & Smith, 2012; Karpicke et al., 2014).

Retrieval learning, therefore, is the practice of actively recalling information and knowledge learnt. It strengthens the learning process by drawing out learned concepts and forces students to augment the memories of what they have studied, giving the memories more permanence in their long-term memories (Karpicke & Blunt, 2011; Karpicke & Roediger, 2007, 2008; Pyc & Rawson, 2009, 2010; Roediger & Karpicke, 2006). To illustrate, Petrovic-Dzerdz's (2019) study analyzed the application of learning gamification principles in online, open-book, multiple-choice tests to motivate students to engage in repeated retrieval-based learning activities. She found a strong positive correlation between the number of successful retrieval attempts in these tests—that covered content from the course textbook—and long-term knowledge retention demonstrated in a live, final, closed-book, cumulative examination.

3 The Case Study

3.1 The Institute of Higher Learning

The institute of higher learning in this case study is a publicly funded autonomous university (AU) in Singapore. The university launched its undergraduate accountancy degree in 2014. Unlike other Singapore AUs which emphasize academic learning, this university offers a unique learning experience for its students by integrating learning from school, industry and the community. It offers applied degree programmes targeted at growth sectors of the economy with a unique pedagogy that integrates work and study. The university's curricula have strong linkages with industry's needs. This linkage is reflected in the compulsory practical job internship (lasting up to 12 months) with relevant industries. The accountancy programme, in this case, requires all its students to undergo a prolonged internship (minimum of 8 months) with one of the public practicing accounting entities in Singapore. The students may work in the audit and assurance (including audit analytics) division, taxation division, internal audit division, or corporate advisory division.

The accounting programme is a three-year direct honors bachelor's degree programme. In their final term of academic studies, students can elect to study a specialization area (from Financial Accounting, Management Accounting, Auditing, Taxation and Finance). The specialized areas allow students to gain in-depth professional knowledge in the chosen discipline. To date, the university has conferred the accountancy degree to more than 500 graduates, and the degree has received recognition and accreditation from the local and overseas professional bodies.

3.2 Curriculum Design—Integrating Data Analytics

If there is one thing academics and practitioners agree on, it is that data analytics is one of the most essential skills in the future. Debate, however, continues about the best way to implement data analytics in higher education. For instance, at the business school, the scope of data analytics is different from that at the school of computer science. Business school graduates typically will work in management positions instead of computer related jobs. They will need hybrid skills, meaning that they must have sufficient knowledge of their domain to be able to identify and frame business problems and exploit opportunities and, at the same time, be able to use multiple data analytics related technologies to leverage their ability in solving business problems and complexity (Wilder & Ozgure, 2015). In the graduate business school, the focus is on students' ability to use data analytics technology instead of their ability to develop data analytics technology.

Specific to the accounting discipline, data analytics is a task-oriented focus (Schneider et al., 2015). Schneider et al. (2015) suggest that infer, predict, and assure tasks are generally used for data analytics related issues. The tasks are applied to accounting information systems, auditing, financial accounting, management accounting and taxation. Infer tasks include identifying audit issues, detecting inefficiency in business operation, and detecting potential fraud. Predict tasks comprise several tasks such as predicting future financial accounting figures, identifying potential future fraud, and advising tax planning. Assure tasks focus on evaluating financial performance, identifying performance gap, and evaluating risk assessment indicators (Schneider et al., 2015).

The emergence of data analytics allows accountancy programmes in higher education institutions the opportunity to provide a talent pipeline to contribute to business value creation (Lawson et al., 2014, 2015). This opportunity is timely for accountancy programmes to equip their graduates to meet the high demand for data analytics

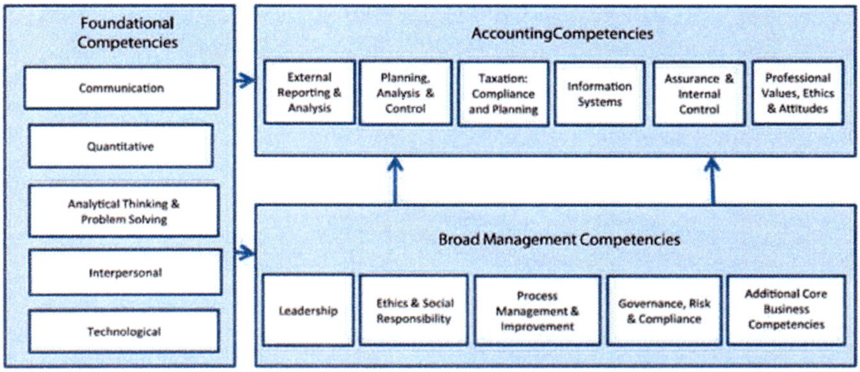

Fig. 1 Framework for accounting competency integration (Lawson et al., 2014, 2015)

competencies. Furthermore, to ensure students keep abreast of changing, complex business issues across multiple organizational contexts, accounting curricula need to be tightly connected with industry and meet professional requirements. In support of this close alignment, the Pathways Commission proposed a competency framework for accountancy students (Behn et al., 2012). The competencies are divided into three categories: foundational, accounting and broad management. Figure 1 shows the competency framework.

The skills required in data analytics, such as critical thinking, tools and communication, align with the above competency framework. The foundational competencies provide the basis for students to understand what and why data analytics should be applied. The accounting competencies help students to experience how data analytics can be applied in reporting, planning, taxation, information systems, assurance and internal control and professional ethics. Last but not least, broad management competencies help students understand where the data analytics can be improved or where it can help improve broad organizational processes, such as in process management. Within broad management competencies, improvement competencies help students effectively utilize data management, while Governance, Risk and Compliance competencies equip students with the ability to assess risk through analytics.

In line with the above competency framework, our curriculum was designed using a 3D formula with real-world interaction: (1) Democratization of technology, (2) Domain Knowledge, and (3) Dynamic learning. Figure 2 illustrates the curriculum design.

This design of the accounting curriculum seeks to build a strong foundation of domain knowledge a professional accountant must possess, that is, in the areas of foundational business knowledge (such as economics, marketing and management, financial literacy and the legal framework of business), and professional accountancy competencies (such as financial accounting, management accounting, assurance, taxation and finance). The notion of democratization of technology emphasizes

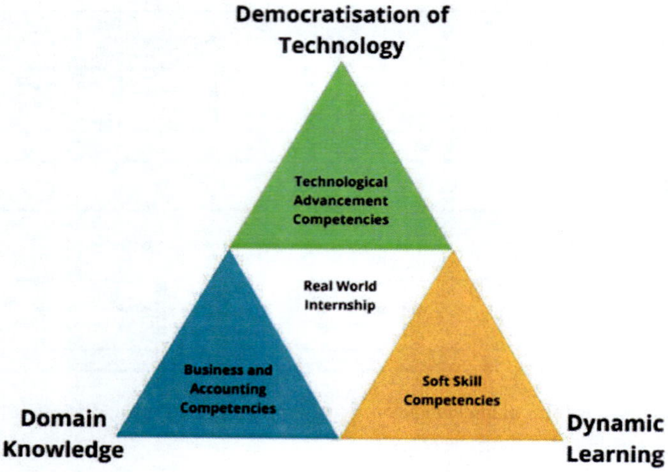

Fig. 2 Curriculum design

students' readiness for digital transformation. Students are taught skills to perform data science related tasks that will enhance their value propositions. The data analytics competency roadmap is integrated into the curriculum to allow conceptualization of the applications of data analytics to accounting subjects. The last "D" relates to dynamic learning. Other than core competencies in technical and technology subjects, "soft skill" and critical thinking competencies are equally important attributes in job applicants (Hodge & Lear, 2011; Robles, 2012). Outcomes on dynamic learning were, therefore, included in the curricula.

Finally, a unique characteristic of the programme is the integrating of real work experience and study, allowing students to practice what they have learnt in classes in a real workplace setting. Prior to launching the programme, industry practitioners' feedback on the programme's curricula was collected to ensure that the learning outcomes met the employers' expectations of required skills.

3.3 *Essential Data Analytics Skills*

In designing the roadmap detailing the essential skills of a professional accountant to perform data analytics related tasks, the skillset competencies required by data analysts, engineers or scientists were scanned. Holtz (2014) provides a summary on the 8 data science skills required by data analysts, learning engineers, data engineers and data scientists: (1) programming, (2) data visualization and communication, (3) data intuition, (4) statistics, (5) data wrangling, (6) machine learning, (7) software engineering, and (8) multivariable calculus and linear algebra. While the above attributes (with skills 1 to 6 identified by senior industry professionals and accountants in business as the most relevant) form the ultimate data skills checklist for the data scientist, professional accountants do not need to have the same level of competencies as the data science experts. However, accountants do need to possess some of the data skills to perform their role. At a minimum, accountants should be able to understand the structure of data sciences and be able to communicate confidentially with the data science experts at work. Consequently, three main essential data analytics skills were selected for inclusion in the programme's digital transformation learning matrix: (1) technological advancement and tools skills, (2) critical thinking skills, and (3) communication skills.

3.3.1 Technological Advancement and Tools Skills

Technology is constantly being developed and quickly advancing at an unprecedented rate, from data storage to data processing, and from data analytics to artificial intelligence. Paperwork is now largely being replaced by digital documentation. The way organizations collect data is changing as well. Information can now be automatically collected via barcodes, sensors, and mobile platforms. Unfortunately, gaps remain between constant change in technology, individual capability and individual progress. Technology is progressing at a faster rate than individuals' capability and business growth (Deloitte University Press, 2016).

According to KPMG (2017), digitalization is the catalyst for significant business process changes. Digitalization in accounting involves paperless accounting, systems' interfaces, process automation, system uniformity, integrated consolidation systems, big data analysis, visualization, and cloud computing (KPMG, 2017). Similarly, ACCA (2017) suggested that digital or technology awareness was becoming more essential to future accountants and auditors than ever before. Accountants and auditors must be aware of and familiarize themselves with the existing or emerging digital solutions and technologies and their capabilities to help accounting practices, solve problems, and run business processes efficiently. Apart from having an awareness of digital solutions and technologies, accountants and auditors must understand the risks and challenges associated with the use of digital solutions and technologies so as to optimize the use of the technologies and at the same time, be able to mitigate potential risks arising from the use of these technologies (ACCA, 2017).

To ensure that our students would have the technological advancement and tools skills, emphasis was placed on their ability to identify the types of data needed to resolve a business problem data, to make use of those data and perform deep analytics using advanced technology tools so that they are able to make optimal decisions. Figure 3 presents the roadmap and knowledge matrix developed for our programme.

The knowledge matrix includes knowing how to collect, store and process raw data into useful information, how to utilize data to perform predictive analyses to aid forecasting and pre-emptive business measures and how to convert all the useful deep analyses information into a "story" and propose solutions. Included in this category

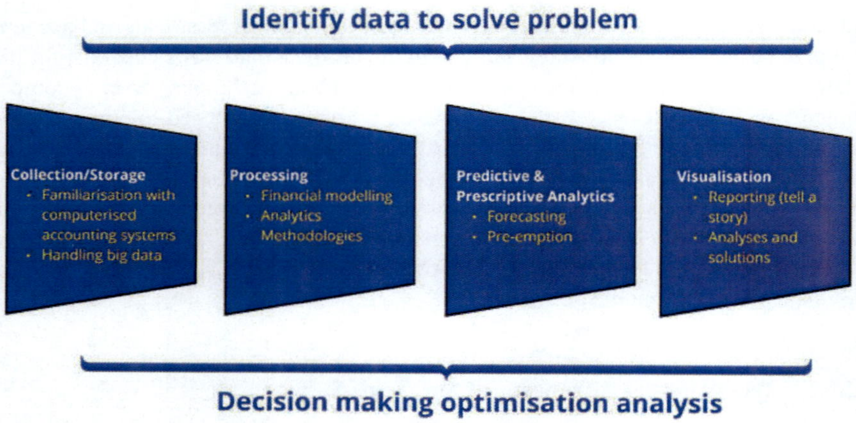

Fig. 3 The data analytics roadmap and knowledge matrix

of technological advancement and tools skills are data science skills (see Table 1) embedded in our curricula.

While the above skillsets formed a data analytics checklist for the programme, the intended outcome was not to produce a data scientist; rather, they were meant to equip our students to work with data scientists. For example, past studies have suggested that equipping students with programming skills is associated with cognitive benefits including reasoning, creative thinking, and mathematical skills (Meyer, 2015; Scherer et al., 2019; Tuomi et al., 2017). As such, basic programming skills, such as programming with Python or Java, may indeed be beneficial to future accountants (PricewaterhouseCoopers, 2015). While programming skills can add value, the accounting curriculum itself does not need to require students to be an expert in coding with programming languages. Encouraging students to understand how a programming language works and doing so in a non-formal setting would be sufficient. Therefore, accountancy students are not required to code extensively. However, they must at least understand how to execute the code and the overall structure of the coding. In fact, with packages publicly available for data analytics purposes, such as R and Python, accounting students would just need to understand how the packages can help them solve data analytics problems and be able to run the packages and modify them, if necessary. RStudio IDE (Integrated Development Environment) is a platform with nearly 18,000 packages for diverse analyses ranging from statistical analysis to machine learning, while Python has 200,000 packages. In short, the above skillsets aimed to produce professional accountants capable of harnessing big data to advance professionally in this era of digital transformation. If external expert assistance is needed (such as extensive coding), accountants should be able to seamlessly communicate their needs to the coding experts.

Table 1 Technological advancement and tools skills—data science skills

Data science skills	Our knowledge matrix and specific competencies
Programming	Students are taught the essentials of database concepts. They are also taught some programming and database querying languages to aid their data mining and analysis competencies
Data intuition	Students are taught to identify comprehensive business scenarios to become a data-driven problem solver. From understanding the big picture of the dataset to presenting the underlying story of the analysis results, students are taught how to communicate with data science experts using the language of the field
Statistics and predictive analysis	Students are expected to undergo business quantitative analyses training, including cleansing of data and management of data, and running of predictive modelling using commercially available statistics software
Data wrangling	Students are taught to deal with imperfections in data and to validate data for usage in analysis. For example, they identify multiple types of fields, such as DATE, INTEGER, or TEXT. Each data type has its own characteristics which can influence the result of the analysis
Machine learning	Fundamental learning on machine learning methods is provided. For example, SAP analytics is used to teach common algorithms in the business sector, and Azure ML is taught to expose students to machine learning. This helps the students to understand the predictive analytics algorithm, robotic process automation as well as the way artificial intelligence can be used, so as to enhance the students' ability to provide a higher level of work for their stakeholders
Software engineering	Students are not expected to design or develop information systems. Instead, students are taught to customize the syntaxes or commands inside existing software. Students are also exposed to developing automation apps/bots for the most common accounting functions

3.3.2 Critical Thinking Skills

Critical thinking is recognized as another essential skill for future accountants and auditors (ACCA, 2016). Critical thinking reflects the ability to reason logically, think reflectively and judge skillfully (Butler et al., 2017). Critical thinking also includes the ability to evaluate whether the presented information is reliable, identify connections and patterns, and determine actions to be taken (Gut, 2011; Spector, 2019). The application of critical thinking may be broad or domain specific. Broadly, general critical thinking skills, such as problem solving, analytic thinking, decision making, reasoning, argumentation, interpretation, synthesis, evaluation, collaboration, communication, and self-directed learning, can be applied in multiple disciplines (Moallem et al., 2019). When applied to a specific domain, critical thinking skills need to be paired with domain skills. For example, in the accounting arena, critical thinking may involve the ability to (1) link accounting theory and practice, (2) evaluate accounting principles and practices used in corporate reporting, (3) understand analytical methods to solve existing or potential problems, (4) make inferences and arrive at a conclusion following the analysis, and (5) evaluate evidence both for and against particular assertions while maintaining a constructive attitude (ACCA, 2016).

Various pedagogical approaches can be found in the literature on developing critical thinking. For example, students can be asked to reflect on particular problems via problem based learning, group discussions and sharing sessions (Huang, Hung & Cheng, 2012; Kim et al., 2013; Moallem et al., 2019; Yang & Wu, 2012). Critical thinking skills can serve as an indicator of students' comprehension of problems. Spector (2019) notes that critical thinking reflects students' engagement in analysis, synthesis, problem-solving, evaluation and reflection. When working with data, accountants and auditors require critical thinking ability, using logical reasoning to identify the strengths and weaknesses of multiple options for problem solving and arrive at relevant conclusions.

For this reason, the critical thinking skills category was embedded in our curricula. In particular, students were taught to formulate relevant questions and identify the problems and required data needed for analyses to address the problems. Compulsory design thinking training was introduced to our students, where they were given real life business problems and taught to provide solutions through the 5-stage process of empathize, define, ideate, prototype and test. Using both technological advancement and tools skills and critical analysis competencies, the students would critically identify comprehensive business problems to provide data-driven innovative solutions.

3.3.3 Communication Skills

The ability to communicate is another important skill in accounting education (Dzuranin et al., 2018; Lawson et al., 2014, 2015). As mentioned, equipping students with data analytics skills also means developing their ability to "effectively communicate processes and outcomes of data analytics" (Dzuranin et al., 2018: 33). Where data are to be reported, whether written or oral, the focus would be on both content and delivery. In most instances, results are presented to influence decision-making or action.

Key communication skills for students in a data analytics module could include knowledge of different types of writing and presentations expected in the accounting community, knowledge of document design and use of visuals, effective use of language, and knowledge of ethical communication. To guide their search for answers to problems, accounting and auditing students need to know how to ask the right questions (Dzuranin et al., 2018). This entails the use of questioning strategies when probing, such as asking 'who', 'what', where', 'when', 'why', 'how' and 'what else' questions, asking for contrary evidence, and clarifying understanding. At the same time, to function effectively as interviewers, students need to be active listeners, as relating with the other party on an interpersonal level helps to build rapport and trust.

Results from data analysis might be presented in a written report or an oral presentation. Students might be required to produce different types of reports, namely, reports for clients such as audit reports, and reports for management, such as cost-and-profit analysis and sales analysis. Students should know organization patterns and language functions, such as defining, describing, comparing, inferring, and recommending. Students' reports should also display aspects of effective writing, such as accuracy, clarity, coherence, conciseness, and fluency. Finally, students need to be conscious of formatting requirements in the design of documents, to add clarity to their data presentation. Once the data is clean and prepared, students can perform exploratory data analysis for accounting data. Students may be required to present their findings in an oral presentation. Raw data alone is not useful to the audience; the presenter needs to ask relevant questions about the data to turn it into meaningful information that leads to decisions and actions. A great way to do this is to tell a data-driven story (Lawson et al., 2014, 2015).

Presenting data visually, whether in a written or oral report, is yet another communication skill that students should possess. Besides using data (or statistical evidence) in visuals, the presenter may utilize other forms of evidence, namely, narrative (or anecdotal) evidence, casual (explanatory) evidence and expert (confirmation) evidence (Hornikx, 2018). Use of narratives relates closely to telling a story. In the presentation of data, narrative evidence could lend credibility to the analysis (Han & Fink, 2012). In fact, messages conveyed through both narrative evidence and statistical evidence have been found to be more persuasive than messages using only either form of evidence (Allen et al., 2000).

The final point on communication skills for accounting students concerns ethics. As potential accounting professionals, students need to realize they have a responsibility to present data ethically. Ethical communicators are honest, giving credit to others whose work they have referenced, and they respect confidentiality of sensitive information. Most importantly, ethical communicators do not distort the interpretation of findings or mislead the audience with flawed conclusions.

This category of communication skills, therefore, occupied a place in the accounting curricula. Equipped with communication skills and the ability to convert data information into a story, our students were taught extensively data visualization and communication (Table 2).

Table 2 Technological advancement and tools skills—data science skills

Data Science skills	Our knowledge matrix and specific competencies
Data visualization and storytelling	Extensive training on data visualization and communication of reports is provided. Students are equipped with skills to describe findings using visual aids that appeal to their audiences, and to convert technical information into a non-technical story that can be understood by all audiences

After mastering the essential technical skills of collecting, storing, processing and analyzing voluminous big data, students were introduced to the "telling a story using visual aids" skillset. Extensive training on data visualization and the art of communication was also introduced in class. Students were taught to use commercially available visualization software (e.g., Tableau) to "tell the story". The use of commercially available visualization packages (such as Tableau or Power BI) prepares the students to be industry ready, such that they would not need training during employment on the use of the same packages.

3.4 Data Analytics Implementation Approach

Following the design of the data analytics integration roadmap and the essential knowledge matrix and skillsets, the integrated approach was identified as the most suitable for our accounting programme. Two approaches were, in fact, considered. Firstly, dedicated modules for data analytics could be developed separately from our professional accountancy core modules. These could include specific modules such as programming for analytics (i.e., *Programming for Business Analytics, Introduction to Programming*, and *Python Programming* etc.). This approach allows the data analytics related modules to be distinguished from the existing core modules.

Most of the other Singapore AUs have chosen this path in their introduction of data analytics in their accounting curricula. However, given the stringent accreditation requirements set by the accounting professional bodies, very little curriculum space within our programme was available to include many specific and dedicated modules for data analytics. As a result, if this approach was adopted, only a small number of specific and isolated modules could be offered to our students, with little possibility of covering the knowledge matrix that they could possibly master. In addition, in response to the frequent comment that students easily forgot what they had learnt in specific and isolated modules, our aim was to help students retain what they had learnt.

Instead of using the first approach, the programme opted to integrate data analytics skills in the professional accountancy core modules (i.e., *Financial Accounting Analytics and Automation, Digital Accounting and Visualization, Forensic Auditing and Analytics.*) This approach allowed us to customize and conceptualize the data analytic applications in specific accounting domains, such that students could learn to value data analytic applications in various accounting professional contexts. Furthermore, the approach allowed us to implement the spaced retrieval learning technique, where relevant data analytics topics were broken into bite-size bits and embedded in various professional accountancy core modules (to form the conceptualization of the topics within the accounting domain areas). Figure 4 presents the breakdown of data analytics topics for bite-size teaching.

The data analytics knowledge matrix was first categorized into three levels: (1) Basic/Foundation, (2) Intermediate, and (3) Applied/Advanced. This approach aligns with the proposed data analytics integration technique suggested by Qasim et al.

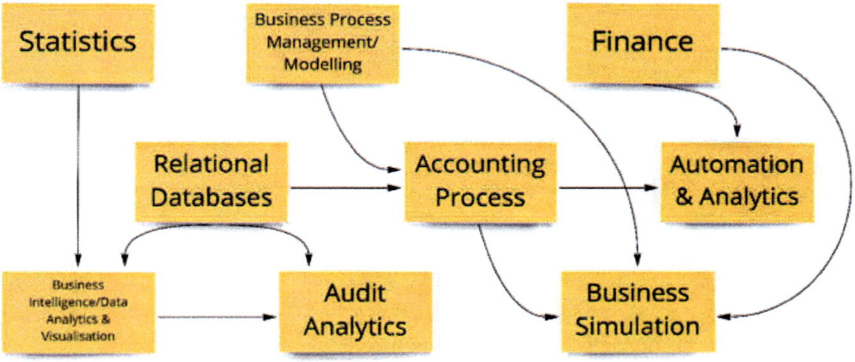

Fig. 4 Bite-size teaching of data analytics

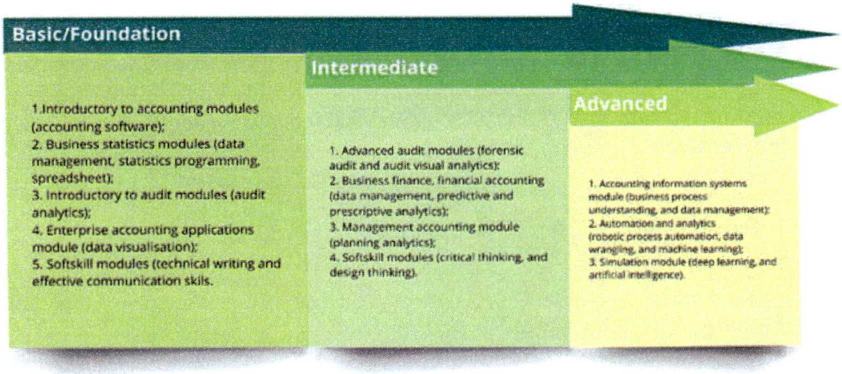

Fig. 5 Spaced retrieval-based learning

(2020). Data analytics should be taught progressively from introductory to intermediate, and then to advanced levels. The breaking down of the learning matrix into bite sizes and into different levels of difficulty creates a lego-building learning approach aimed at helping students to achieve mastery of data analytics skillsets. As the imparting of these skillsets is also distributed throughout the degree programme across various modules with linked data analytics learning points, students were repeatedly recalling information across multiple modules. Figure 5 illustrates how the learning of data analytic topics was spaced out.

At the end of each module, students were expected to complete and pass the respective summative assessments. As all the modules have linked data analytics learning points, students could learn and connect the various learning points of data analytics. Furthermore, in their final term of study, students were required to complete an accounting analytics capstone module with a dissertation based on a real-life business problem. Students had to provide sound solutions based on the entire spectrum of analytics skills they had learnt. As argued by retrieval-based learning advocates, this method strengthens the students' learning process by drawing out learned concepts and forcing them to augment the memories of what they had studied, thereby giving the recall more permanence in their long-term memories.

3.5 *Students' and Industry Reactions*

Our study was approved by our university's Institutional Review Board. We surveyed one cohort of our students to gather their feedback on the data analytics training they had completed (Table 3). A total of 144 final year students took part in the survey. These students had completed 8 months of internship. On a 5-point Likert scale, a positive average of 4.33 was recorded, signifying students' approval of the training received.

More than 500 students have completed and graduated from this accountancy programme. The programme has also received positive verbal feedback from employers on the data analytics skillset displayed by our graduates. Furthermore, the first three graduate employment surveys commissioned by the Singapore Ministry

Table 3 Survey results on students' feedback on the data analytics training

Measurement	Mean (n = 144)	SD (n = 144)	Minimum	Maximum
During my internship engagement I am able to perform tasks that require data analytics skills	4.22	0.64	2	5
The data analytics training was effective in terms of illustrating important and applied concepts on data analytics	4.34	0.57	3	5
The data analytics training was effective in terms of equipping me with the competencies to perform analytics tasks using relevant applications (i.e., Spreadsheets, Data Analytics and Visualizations)	4.27	0.56	3	5
The data analytics training I have gone through is aligned with the company's data analytics related tasks during my internship engagement	4.25	0.69	2	5
I believe that having strong competencies in data analytics will add value for my future career	4.54	0.51	3	5

of Education revealed that more than 90% of our graduates were employed within six months of completing their studies. The surveys also revealed that our graduates were earning about 3% more on the median gross monthly salary compared to what graduates from the other AUs (same degree duration of 3 years as ours) were earning.

Although no statistical link has been drawn between the implementation of data analytics topics in our curricula and the employment success of our graduates, what is evident is that job recruiters value the quality of accountancy graduates produced by this university.

4 Conclusion

Professional accountants are the traditional custodians of business strategies, transactions and processes, and most prominently, financial records and finances. Although the accountancy profession has always been working with data and employing analytical tools to solve business issues, the current business, data and technological landscape has evolved far more rapidly than expected. In the age of digital disruption, corporate leadership is ever more reliant on accounting professionals to strategize and provide advice on cognitive and data driven businesses.

Given their expertise knowledge, accounting professionals will play a key role helping businesses to transform and flourish in the new digital world. Therefore, to be that useful linkage, accountants must have data analytics competency. They must embrace digital transformation and be savvy about using data analytics tools. The current shortage of data analytics talent provides accounting students with the opportunity to occupy the data analytics space. Even though data analytics is increasingly gaining traction in business and industry, the supply of data analytics talent remains inadequate (Pompa & Burke, 2017). Similarly, recruiting and retaining data analytics experts continues to be difficult (Ransbotham et al., 2015). IBM predicted the number of data analytics job listings in the US to grow 15% from 2,350,000 in 2015 to approximately 2,720,000 in 2020 (Columbus, 2017). The shortage of data analytics talent also exists in Asia Pacific countries (Pompa & Burke, 2017). Hence, given that universities are the training ground for the accounting profession, universities' degree programmes should embed a data analytics competencies roadmap.

In conclusion, in implementing a data analytics training into our accountancy degree programme, a bite-size and spaced retrieval-based learning approach was adopted, with no compromise to the required technical knowledge to include in our curriculum so as to satisfy accreditation requirements from accounting professional bodies. In view of further industry and service revolutions to our profession, accounting curricula must be constantly revised to meet industry needs.

Acknowledgements We thank the participants at 2019 CTLA: 12th Annual American Accounting Association (AAA) Conference on Teaching and Learning in Accounting, 5th Asian Conference on Education & International Development (ACEID 2019) and The National Association of CPAs in

Education 6th mid-Year Accounting Teachers' International Conference for their helpful comments. We would also like to thank the anonymous reviewers for their suggestions provided.

References

AACSB International Accounting Accreditation. (2014). *AACSB International Accounting Accreditation Standard A7: Information technology skills and knowledge for accounting graduates: An interpretation.* AACSB international Committee on Accreditation Policy.

Allen, M., Bruflat, R., Fucilla, R., Kramer, M., McKellips, S., Ryan, D., & Spiegelhoff, M. (2000). Testing the persuasiveness of evidence: Combining narrative and statistical forms. *Communication Research Reports, 17*(4), 331–336.

Alles, M., Kogan, A., & Vasarhelyi, M. (2008). Putting continuous auditing theory into practice: Lessons from two pilot implementations. *Journal of Information Systems, 22*(2), 195–214.

Amani, F., & Fadlalla, A. (2017). Data mining applications in accounting: A review of the literature and organizing framework. *International Journal of Accounting Information Systems, 24*, 32–58.

Association of Chartered Certified Accountants (ACCA). (2016). *Professional accountants—The future: Drivers of change and future skills.* https://www.accaglobal.com/content/dam/members-beta/docs/ea-patf-drivers-of-change-and-future-skills.pdf. Accessed on 1 January 2019.

Association of Chartered Certified Accountants (ACCA). (2017). *The digital accountant: Digital skills in a transformed world.* ACCA.

Behn, K., Ezzell, W., Murphy, L., Rayburn, J., Stith, M., & Strawser, J. (2012). The pathways commission on accounting higher education: Charting a national strategy for the next generation of accountants. *Issues in Accounting Education, 27*(3), 595–600.

Bhimani, A., & Willcocks, L. (2014). Digitisation, 'Big Data' and the transformation of accounting information. *Accounting and Business Research, 44*(4), 469–490.

Blunt, J., & Karpicke, J. (2014). Learning with retrieval-based concept mapping. *Journal of Educational Psychology, 106*(3), 849–858.

Butler, H., Pentoney, C., & Bong, M. (2017). Predicting real-world outcomes: Critical thinking ability is a better predictor of life decisions than intelligence. *Thinking Skills and Creativity, 25*, 38–46.

Centre for the New Economy and Society. (2018). *Insight report: The future of jobs report 2018.* World Economic Forum. www.weforum.org/docs/WEF_Future_of_Jobs_2018.pdf. Access on 1 January 2019.

Columbus, L. (2017). IBM predicts demand for data scientists will soar 28% by 2020. *Forbes.* https://www.forbes.com/sites/louiscolumbus/2017/05/13/ibm-predicts-demand-for-data-scientists-will-soar-28-by-2020/#499d0f837e3b. Accessed on 1 January 2019.

Deloitte University Press. (2016). *Global human capital trends—The new organization: Different by design.* Deloitte Development LLC, US.

Dilla, W., & Raschke, R. (2015). Data visualization for fraud detection: Practice implications and a call for future research. *International Journal of Accounting Information Systems, 16*, 1–22.

Dzuranin, A., Jones, J., & Olvera, R. (2018). Infusing data analytics into the accounting curriculum: A framework and insights from faculty. *Journal of Accounting Education, 43*, 24–39.

Ernst and Young (EY). (2015). *Becoming an analytics-driven organization to create a value—A report in collaboration with Nimbus Ninety.* EYGM Limited. https://www.ey.com/Publication/vwLUAssets/EY-becoming-an-analytics%E2%80%93driven-organisation-to-create-value/$FILE/EY-becoming-an-analytics%E2%80%93driven-organisation-to-create-value.pdf. Accessed on 1 January 2019.

Gupta, B., Goul, M., & Dinter, B. (2015). Business intelligence and big data in higher education: Status of a multi- year model curriculum development effort for business school undergraduates,

MS graduates, and MBAs. *Communications of the Association for Information Systems, 36*, Article 23.

Gut, D. (2011). Integrating 21st century skills into the curriculum. In G. Wan & D. M. Gut (Eds.), *Bringing schools into the 21st Century* (pp. 137–157). Springer.

Han, B., & Fink, E. (2012). How do statistical and narrative evidence affect persuasion? The role of evidentiary features. *Argumentation and Advocacy, 49*(1), 39–58.

Haverson, A. (2014). *Why predictive analytics should be "a CPA thing."* AICPA.

Hodge, K., & Lear, J. (2011). Employment skills for 21st century workplace: The gap between faculty and student perceptions. *Journal of Career and Technical Education, 26*(2), 28–41.

Holtz, D. (2014). *What is data science? 8 skills that will get you hired in data.* Udacity School of Data Science. https://blog.udacity.com/2014/11/data-science-job-skills.html. Accessed 6 January 2020.

Hornikx, J. (2018). Combining anecdotal and statistical evidence in real-life discourse: Comprehension and persuasiveness. *Discourse Processes, 55*(3), 324–336.

Huang, K., Hung, K., & Cheng, C. (2012). Enhancing interactivity in geography class: Fostering critical thinking skills through technology. *Problems of Education in the 21st Century, 50*, 32–45.

Karpicke, J. (2012). Retrieval-based learning: Active retrieval promotes meaningful learning. *Current Directions in Psychological Science, 21*, 157–163.

Karpicke, J., & Blunt, J. (2011). Retrieval practice produces more learning than elaborative studying with concept mapping. *Science, 331*, 772–775.

Karpicke, J., & Roediger, H. (2007). Repeated retrieval during learning is the key to long-term retention. *Journal of Memory and Language, 57*, 151–162.

Karpicke, J., & Roediger, H. (2008). The critical importance of retrieval for learning. *Science, 319*, 966–968.

Karpicke, J., & Smith, M. (2012). Separate mnemonic effects of retrieval practice and elaborative encoding. *Journal of Memory and Language, 67*, 17–29.

Karpicke, J., Lehman, M., Aue, W. (2014). Retrieval-based learning: An episodic context account. In B. Ross B (Ed.), *The psychology of learning and motivation.* Elsevier.

Kim, K., Sharma, P., Land, S., & Furlong, K. (2013). Effects of active learning on enhancing student critical thinking in an undergraduate General Science course. *Innovative Higher Education, 38*(3), 223–235.

KPMG. (2017). *Digitalization in accounting—Study of the status quo in German Companies.* KPMG AG.

Lawson, R., Blocher, E., Brewer, P., Cokins, G., Sorensen, J., Stout, D., Sundem, G., Wolcott, S., & Wouters, M. (2014). Focusing accounting curricula on students' long-run careers: Recommendations for an integrated competency-based framework for accounting education. *Issues in Accounting Education, 29*(2), 295–317.

Lawson, R., Blocher, E., Brewer, P., Morris, J., Stocks, K., Sorensen, J., Stout, D., & Wouters, M. (2015). Thoughts on competency integration in accounting education. *Issues in Accounting Education, 30*(3), 149–171.

Li, H., Dai, J., Gershberg, T., & Vasarhelyi, M. (2018). Understanding usage and value of audit analytics for internal auditors: An organizational approach. *International Journal of Accounting Information System, 28*, 59–76.

Meyer, C. (2015). *Should accounting students learn to code?* https://www.aicpa.org/interestareas/accountingeducation/newsandpublications/should-accounting-students-code.html. Accessed 1 January 2019.

Mitri, M., & Palocsay, S. (2015). Toward a model undergraduate curriculum for the emerging business intelligence and analytics discipline. *Communications of the Association for Information Systems, 37*, Paper 31.

Moallem, M., Hung, W., & Dabbagh, N. (2019). *The Wiley handbook of problem-based learning.* Wiley.

Mokyr, J., Vickers, C., & Ziebarth, N. (2015). The history of technological anxiety and the future of economic growth: Is this time different? *Journal of Economic Perspectives, 29*(3), 31–50.

Paul, J., & MacDonald, L. (2020). Analytics curriculum for undergraduate and graduate students. *Journal of Innovative Education, 18*(1), 22–58.

Petrovic-Dzerdz, M. (2019). Gamifying online tests to promote retrieval-based learning. *International Review of Research in Open and Distributed Learning, 20*(2), 24–43.

Pompa, C., & Burke, T. (2017). *Data science and analytics skills shortage: Equipping the APEC workforce with the competencies demanded by employers.* APEC Human Resource Development Working Group. https://www.apec.org/-/media/APEC/Publications/2017/11/Data-Science-and-Analytics-Skills-Shortage/217_HRD_Data-Science-and-Analytics-Skills-Shortage.pdf. Accessed on 1 January 2019.

PricewaterhouseCoopers. (2015). *Data driven: What students need to succeed in a rapidly changing business world.* PricewaterhouseCoopers LLP.

Pyc, M., & Rawson, K. (2009). Testing the retrieval effort hypothesis: Does greater difficulty correctly recalling information lead to higher levels of memory? *Journal of Memory and Language, 60*, 437–447.

Pyc, M., & Rawson, K. (2010). Why testing improves memory: Mediator effectiveness hypothesis. *Science, 330*, 335.

Qasim, A., Issa, H., El Refae, G., & Sanella, A. (2020). A model to integrate data analytics in the Undergraduate Accounting Curriculum. *Journal of Emerging Technologies in Accounting, 17*(2), 31–44.

Racsmány, M., Szollosi, A., & Bencze, D. (2018). Retrieval practice makes procedure from remembering: An automatization account of the testing effect. *Journal of Experimental Psychology: Learning, Memory, and Cognition, 44*(1), 157–166.

Ransbotham, S., Kiron, D., & Prentice, P. (2015). Minding the analytics gap. *MIT Sloan Management Review.* https://sloanreview.mit.edu/article/minding-the-analytics-gap/#:~:text=Minding%20the%20Analytics%20Gap%20With%20more%20access%20to,ability%20to%20apply%20them%20effectively%20to%20business%20issues. Accessed on 1 January 2019.

Richins, G., Stapleton, A., Stratopoulos, T., & Wong, C. (2017). Big data analytics: Opportunity or threat for the accounting profession? *Journal of Information Systems, 31*(3), 63–79.

Rikhardsson, P., & Yigitbasioglu, O. (2018). Business intelligence and analytics in management accounting research: Status and future focus. *International Journal of Accounting Information Systems, 29*, 37–58.

Robles, M. (2012). Executive perceptions of the top 10 soft skills needed in today's workplace. *Business and Professional Communication Quarterly, 75*(4), 453–465.

Roediger, H., & Karpicke, J. (2006). Test-enhanced learning: Taking memory tests improves long-term retention. *Psychological Science, 17*, 249–255.

Scherer, R., Siddiq, F., & Sánchez Viveros, B. (2019). The cognitive benefits of learning computer programming: A meta-analysis of transfer effects. *Journal of Educational Psychology, 111*(5), 764–792.

Schneider, G., Dai, J., Janvrin, D., Ajayi, K., & Raschke, R. (2015). Infer, predict, and assure: Accounting opportunities in data analytics. *Accounting Horizons, 29*(3), 719–742.

Setty, K., & Bakhshi, R. (2013). What is big data and what does it have to do with IT audit? *ISACA Journal, 3*, 1–3.

Singapore Ministry of Education. (n.d.). *Post secondary.* https://www.moe.gov.sg/education/post-secondary. Accessed 1 June 2020.

Smolan, R., & Erwitt, J. (2012). *The human face of big data.* Against All Odds Productions.

Spector, J. (2019). Complexity, inquiry critical thinking, and technology: A holistic and developmental approach. In T. D. Parsons, L. Lin, & D. Cockerham (Eds.), *Mind, brain and technology learning in the age of emerging technologies* (pp. 17–26). Springer.

Tuomi, P., Multisilta, J., Saarikoski, P., & Suominen, J. (2017). Coding skills as a success factor for a society. *Education and Information Technologies, 23*(1), 419–434.

Wilder, C., & Ozgur, C. (2015). Business analytics curriculum for undergraduate majors. *INFORMS Transactions on Education, 15*(2), 180–187.

Yang, Y., & Wu, W. (2012). Digital storytelling for enhancing student academic achievement, critical thinking, learning motivation: A year-long experimental study. *Computers and Education, 59*(2), 339–352.

Zwitter, A. (2014, July). Big data ethics. *Big Data and Society, 1*, 1–6.

SzeKee Koh, Ph.D. is an Associate Professor and currently serves as the Director of Programmes for the Business, Communication and Design (BCD) Cluster at the Singapore Institute of Technology (SIT), overseeing the strategic positioning of all the programmes within the BCD Cluster. His research interests include the areas of capital structure, corporate bankruptcy, corporate social responsibility, socially responsible investments, corporate life cycle and accounting education. He had completed applied research with industry partners including RSM Singapore and Institute of Singapore Chartered Accountants with the findings published in the ISCA's journal as well as in the newspapers including the *Business Times* and the *Straits Times*.

Hwee Hoon Lee, Ph.D. is an Assistant Professor at the Centre for Communication Skills at the Singapore Institute of Technology (SIT). Her research interests include teaching and learning issues in higher education, language teaching and testing, workplace communication, technical communication, and verbal and non-verbal communication.

Arif Perdana, Ph.D. is an Associate Professor at Monash University, Indonesia. Prior to working in academia, he worked in the IT service and finance industry. His research interests are in Data Science and Analytics, Digital Technology Strategy, and Management Information Systems. He has done industrial research and consultancy with institutions in Australia, Singapore and Indonesia. He has also secured several academic and industrial research grants from Australian, Indonesian, and Singaporean institutions in the areas of data analytics, fintech, digital health, and blockchain.

Chapter 19
Learning Analytics in Informal, Participatory Collaborative Learning

Michelle L. F. Cheong, Aditya V. Singh, Jean Y.-C. Chen, and Bing Tian Dai

Abstract Learning Analytics was recognized to be "the third wave of large-scale developments in instructional technology". Learning Management Systems (LMSs) have been widely adopted as the learning analytics tools because the captured data represents how the learners' interact with the system during formal learning. However, most LMSs' analytics models do not capture learning activities outside the systems. We built an integrated Telegram mobile application and a web-based portal discussion forum, to enable informal, participatory and collaborative learning beyond the classroom. We analyzed student-initiated question-and-answer discussion posts where our machine learning algorithm will predict the quality of the posts, and the system will prompt the students to improve their posts. With six in-built engagement features, our system generated higher number of high-quality posts, resulting in better learning outcomes among the students. Based on three implementation runs in an undergraduate course, our results show that there were positive correlations between post quality and student assessment outcomes. Students who used the system could achieve higher knowledge gain, and in-class intervention by the course instructor to review the weekly discussion posts will further improve knowledge gain. Mandatory participation benefitted the academically stronger students, while academically weaker students will need positive intervention actions when mandatory use of the system is enforced. We envisage that our system can be a successful alternative for workplace learning and ultimately contribute to organization knowledge creation. Using the system, working professionals can post questions and answers shared among peers within their own organizations and learn through such informal discussions, which can be blended seamlessly in their day-to-day workflow. While our

M. L. F. Cheong (✉) · A. V. Singh · J. Y.-C. Chen · B. T. Dai
Singapore Management University, Singapore, Singapore
e-mail: michcheong@smu.edu.sg

A. V. Singh
e-mail: adityavs.2017@mitb.smu.edu.sg

J. Y.-C. Chen
e-mail: jeanchen@smu.edu.sg

B. T. Dai
e-mail: btdai@smu.edu.sg

T. Rana et al. (eds.), *Handbook of Big Data and Analytics in Accounting and Auditing*,
https://doi.org/10.1007/978-981-19-4460-4_19

system has not been implemented in workplace learning, we attempt to draw inference from our implementation results, to understand the parallels in the business organization context.

Keywords Q&A Forum · Text mining · Natural language processing · Machine learning · Impact assessment · Informal learning · Participatory collaborative learning · Workplace learning

1 Introduction

Learning Analytics (LA) was defined as "the measurement, collection, analysis and reporting of data about learners and their contexts, for purposes of understanding and optimizing learning and the environments in which it occurs" during the First International Conference on Learning Analytics and Knowledge (LAK11) in 2011. In the same year, Brown (2011) touted LA to be "the third wave of large-scale developments in instructional technology", after the first wave where learning management system (LMS) was used in education in the 1990s, and the addition of social networking and cloud-based applications into LMS during the second wave.

Past works in LA focused on assessing students' learning behavior (Blikstein, 2011), predicting student performance (Pardos et al., 2013; Romero-Zaldivar et al., 2012), increasing reflection and awareness (Ali et al., 2012), prediction of drop-out, student satisfaction and retention (Dekker et al., 2009; Guo, 2010), and improving feedback and assessment services (Barla et al., 2010; Worsley & Blikstein, 2013).

Literature reviews on LA have been done by Papamitsiou and Economides (2014) and Viberg et al. (2018). Papamitsiou and Economides (2014) focused on LA and Educational Data Mining (EDM), and their impact on adaptive learning supported by empirical evidence from 40 case studies conducted between 2008 and 2013. They highlighted four major directions of LA/EDM empirical research including pedagogy-oriented issues, contextualization of learning, networked learning, and educational resources handling. They also suggested incorporating other emerging technologies with LA/EDM such as game-based learning, mobile learning, sensorimotor learning, intelligent tutoring systems, and fully automated educational recommender systems. Viberg et al. (2018) analyzed 252 papers on LA in higher education published between 2012 and 2018 to discover evidence on four propositions (1) LA supports learning and teaching, (2) LA improvements in students' learning outcomes, (3) LA is deployed widely, and (4) LA is used ethically. Their analysis revealed that LA is still an evolving field and evidence related to each proposition is estimated to be about 35% for Proposition (1), 9% for Proposition (2), 6% for Proposition (3), and 18% for Proposition (4). There is thus insufficient evidence to suggest that the potential for LA has been transferred into higher education practice. In addition, the focus in LA research has shifted from prediction (e.g. drop-outs and grades) towards deeper understanding of students' learning experiences. We attempt to understand students' learning experiences and measure learning better in our research work using the CAT-IT system which we have developed and implemented.

To perform LA, LMSs have been widely adopted as the LA tools because the structured data captured represents how the learners interact with the system during formal learning. However, most LMS analytics models do not capture learning activities by the learners outside the LMS (Long and Siemens, 2011). Learners continue to learn informally beyond the formal settings due to the distributed and network nature of interactions among them. Such informal learning can occur on other platforms such as blogs, chats, YouTube videos, and using mobile devices. Informal learning has been explored in past research, where learners learn from their peers within their network, and even beyond their network, and positive learning outcomes have been reported (Falchikov, 2001; Kim, 2015; McMaster et al., 2006).

With technology enhanced learning, learning can be omni-directional among instructors and peers, and effective learning can go beyond the normal classroom. Several papers have highlighted the need for analytics in education to be "transformative, altering existing teaching, learning, and assess processes, academic work, and administration" (Long and Siemens, 2011), and to "increase the scope of data capture so that the complexity of the learning process can be more accurately reflected in analysis" (Siemens, 2013). Our research work thus aims to achieve several of the highlighted areas including using a purposefully built system which integrates mobile applications (Telegram) and web-based portal to increase and to enable active participatory and collaborative learning beyond the classroom, and to improve the data capture outside formal learning. Our work is also to respond to the call by Viberg et al., (2018) to transfer more LA practices into higher education towards deeper understanding of students' learning experiences, by using text mining and Natural Language Processing (NLP) to analyze students' informal post contributions to achieve such deep understanding.

One key twenty first century skill that students need to have is "the ability to ask and answer important questions, to critically review what others say about a subject, to pose and solve problems, to communicate and work with others in learning, and to create new knowledge and innovations" (Trilling & Fadel, 2009). One way to develop such skill is through participatory learning that involves "cooperative learning tasks which are dialogic in nature and involve student-to-student interaction, rather than just teacher-student interaction" (Cahill et al., 2014). Past research works have reported that students' participations in online forums have positive impact on their learning and were positively correlated to their performance in the course (Cheng et al., 2011; Romero et al., 2013; Yoo & Kim, 2012). In addition, if the posts are visible to many students to read and re-read, there are benefits in the quality of the posts contributed by the students (Wise et al., 2014).

There are many discussion forums available both publicly and within LMS that aim to achieve this objective. These platforms while popular, suffer from several ineffectiveness including,

- Students' tendency to post condensed versions of their own ideas rather than responding to the ideas of others (Hara et al., 2000; Larson & Keiper, 2002)

- Discussions are often shallow (Gunawardena et al., 1997)
- Students' tendency to attend to unread posts and most recent posts, rather than posts with important content, and difficulty in promoting interactive dialogues (Gao et al., 2013)
- Little support for convergent processes and lack of timely feedback (Gao et al., 2013)

To overcome the ineffectiveness of existing discussion forums, the new platform should have three new features suggested by Gao et al. (2013). Firstly, to foster an online community, provide timely feedback, encourage information sharing and support collaborative problem solving, some incentive mechanisms can be designed into the environment. Secondly, the lack of convergence requires a system that can go beyond knowledge sharing to include active processing and synthesizing of the information provided by the community. Thirdly, the use of multi-functional environments that can integrate new media technology to facilitate learning at different phases, such as asynchronous and synchronous discussions.

Our work is different from previous works in two main areas. Firstly, we used our in-house developed system (CAT-IT), different from traditional LMS, which we have incorporated the three suggested features to facilitate active and meaningful online discussions for students at our university, assisting them to acquire the important twenty first century skill in asking and answering questions, and to facilitate collaborative learning. Secondly, due to the high effectiveness of our system, we were able to collect a large number of high quality and truthful posts for data analysis to assess the impact of our system on collaborative learning, and to answer the following research questions:

- RQ1: Do students who posted higher quality posts (not quantity) perform better in the course? And if so, do students need to be sufficiently motivated extrinsically to contribute high quality posts?
- RQ2: Is there a difference in knowledge gain for students who used the system based on mandatory participation versus voluntarily participation, and comparing with students who have no access to the system?
- RQ3: Will in-class intervention to review the weekly post improve students' knowledge gain?
- RQ4: Is mandatory participation effective for different students with different academic strengths?

The purpose of analytics is to produce actionable intelligence, and in the field of LA, the equivalent would be to take actions to improve learning for the learners so as to achieve better learning outcomes. Campbell and Oblinger's (2007) five-step model of learning analytics include 'Capture', 'Report', 'Predict', 'Act', and 'Refine'. The 'Act' step includes making appropriate interventions, and the 'Refine' step includes refining the future practices to achieve better learning outcomes. Similarly, the LA Cycle as proposed by Clow (2012) depicts the cycle with four linked steps: (1) learners, (2) generate data, (3) data that is used to produce metrics, analytics or visualization, and (4) feedback to learners through one or more interventions. Several other literatures also echoed such importance (Brown, 2011; Elias, 2011; Long and Siemens, 2011). With the answers we can conclude for the four research questions listed, we will discuss the actions to be taken to improve the learning for our students.

Apart from education, can our system be implemented at actual business workplace, in the form of workplace learning? Workplace learning is defined as "formal and informal knowledge or learning experiences that people receive whilst they are acting in working environments and/or ecosystems using systems or information sources managed by their employer or self-managed" by the LACE LAW Manifesto (Cardinali et al., 2015). At this LACE meeting held in April 2015, a list of experts from the EU discussed and recommended future policies that should be adopted on LA for the training of workforce. It was mentioned that "the growth of digitalized tools for training at the workplace in the last years has led to the necessity of Learning Analytics tools that are able to track the experience of users and to evaluate the performance and quality of the materials provided". This will imply the need to develop new pedagogical and IT tools that will aim to reduce the gaps in the twenty first century skills, which is also an objective our system aims to achieve.

"Professional development and workplace learning opportunities are beginning to offer targeted just-in-time resources and educational experiences to support workers' development of skills and knowledge required for a rapidly progressing technological society." (Dawson et al., 2015). Increasingly, we are seeing organizations subscribing to commercial learning platforms such as LinkedIn Learning where working professionals can learn from video courses taught by industry experts in various topics including software, business and creative skills. Such online learning platforms including Coursera, Khan Academy, Udacity, Udemy, are all based on learning from external experts by watching video course deliveries and attempting tutorial questions. We hope that our CAT-IT system can be one such tool to capture learning within the organization, where the experts are professionals themselves who work in the organization, sharing their knowledge with their colleagues. We will attempt to draw inference from our implementation results, to understand the parallels in the business organization context.

The focus of this chapter is on LA based on the analysis of the posts data from three implementation runs in an undergraduate course in Spreadsheets Modeling and Decision Making at our university. We will discuss our research method and data collection in Sect. 2; explain our Q&A forum system highlighting the thoughtfulness score prediction, post quality improvement, and the effectiveness of the six in-built incentive and engagement mechanisms in Sect. 3. We will then discuss the implementation runs and the results obtained which attempt to answer the four research questions in Sect. 4. Based on the results obtained, we will close the loop by proposing actions which can be taken to improve the system's functionality, implementation settings, and ultimately students' learning in Sect. 5. In Sect. 6, we will discuss how we envisage that our system can be a successful alternative for workplace learning and ultimately contribute to organization knowledge creation. We end this chapter with our conclusions in Sect. 7.

2 Research Method and Data Collection

We have implemented the Q&A forum over three runs for an undergraduate course in Spreadsheets Modeling and Decision Making, each run over a 15-week duration. We have selected this course because the course instructors involved are part of the research team who designed and developed the system, and the implementation of such a system requires subject matter expertise of the course materials. Six hundred students from the six schools (Law, Accountancy, Business, Economics, Social Sciences and Information Systems) at our university were involved, and these students can be in their first to fourth year in their respective undergraduate course, but mostly in their sophomore year. 90% of our students are local students, with 10% international students. For the three runs, we have 128 students (3 sections) in Run 1, 147 students (4 sections) in Run 2, and 325 students (8 sections) in Run 3.

We imposed different settings for the three runs to achieve different insights and to provide answers to our research questions.

- To answer RQ1, we use Run 1 (3 sections with 128 students) where students have their thoughtfulness scores earned form 5% weightage (Sections G15 and G16) or 10% weightage (Section G1) of their overall course grade, to serve as extrinsic motivation factor to participate. We want to assess how the students' course performance correlate with their post quality, and how much extrinsic motivation will be ideal.
- To answer RQ2, we use Run 2 (4 sections with 147 students), where two sections had 5% weightage (Sections G10 and G12), one section had 10% weightage (Section G1), and one section had 0% weightage (Section G13) which represented voluntary participation. We had three additional sections of students with no access to the Q&A forum to act as the control group, to compare knowledge gain via mandatory versus voluntary participation, and compared to without the use of the forum.
- To answer RQ3, we use Run 3 (8 sections with 325 students), where all eight sections had 5% weightage, with three of the sections (Sections G2, G9 and G10) subjected to intervention actions during the immediate next in-class session, to compare knowledge gain with and without intervention actions. The intervention actions include going through the posts generated the week before to clarify doubts and correct any misconceptions.
- To answer RQ4, we use Run 2 and Run 3 to understand how the normalized knowledge gain distributes among the students with different academic strengths. In addition, we compare the normalized knowledge gain among students from different degree programs, based on Run 3 data, to apply the conclusions from RQ4 to different students in different degree programs.

Note that the section IDs are not running numbers because some sections did not participate in our implementation runs. For students who participated in the three implementation runs, either with the use of the forum or without the forum as control group, they understood that their participation was for research purpose and did not feedback any inequity in learning experience or assessment. In the case where students were subjected to 5% or 10% weightage of the final grade, they did not provide any negative feedback due to mandatory participation, as students in other sections who did not participate in the implementation runs, had other equivalent participation assessment component in place.

The method to collect data on the students' posts was aligned with the requirements set by the Institutional Research Board (IRB) to ensure the protection of the rights, safety, and welfare of human research participants. Several mechanisms were put in place,

- When the student signs up for an account to use the Q&A system, a Consent Form for Research Participation will be shown to explain the research purpose and its terms and conditions, and to seek the student's consent to allow his/her forum participation data to be collected and analyzed.
- Participation in the Q&A Forum could be compulsory in some cases, as the marks attained will form part of the overall grade of the course, which can be considered as the extrinsic motivation factor for participation. In cases where participation is not compulsory, where marks attained do not form part of the overall grade, students will still be graded for the participation in the course using other means. For such students where participation is not compulsory, we rely on our system's in-built engagement features (explained in Sect. 3.2) to motivate participation. However, consent to data collection is optional, thus the student can participate but reject data collection. Student will then receive a copy of the consent form via email.
- Student will set an Avatar name or nickname during account setup to protect his/her real identity to participate in the Q&A forum.
- The faculty members teaching the course do not have direct access to the user account details which are directly linked to the post data collected. This means that faculty members do not know which Avatar name corresponds to which student, thus will not know which post was contributed by which student.
- To link the data collected with actual course performance, only the Research Engineer managing the system will perform the linkage, with students' identity information removed. This means that faculty members only know the aggregated data with the related statistical information.

3 Integrated Telegram and Web-Based Forum System

We have developed our system (CAT-IT) as shown in Fig. 1. The student can interact with the system via the Telegram Application (on their mobile phones) or the Web-based forum (on their computers). The Telegram Application can be programmed to prompt and guide students using customized buttons, to post questions and answer questions. In addition, we also programmed a chat-bot (which we have called it our 'CAT bot') to post questions periodically (about one question every one to two days) from the question bank, to keep the discussion lively. The Web-based Forum has full

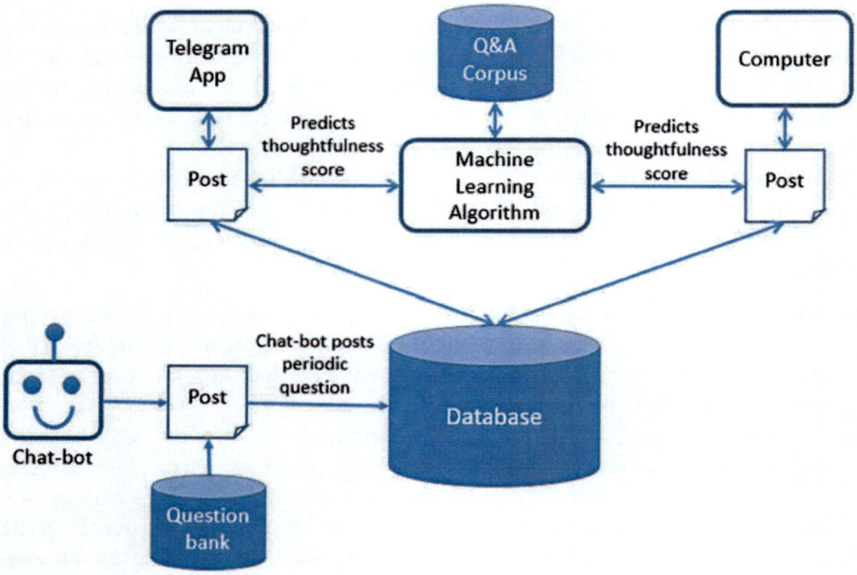

Fig. 1 Schematic of CAT-IT system

functionality which can allow the students to post questions and answers, view and search for posts, and to view their own statistics. The statistical information includes their thoughtfulness scores earned, in-game coins earned, and leader board ranking to date.

Within our system, we encompassed the three new features suggested by Gao et al., (2013). For the first feature, we have designed six in-built incentive and engagement mechanisms in our Q&A system. For the second feature, our system is capable of automatic thoughtfulness score (quality measure) assessment of question and answer posts, using text mining and Natural Language Processing (NLP) methodologies, and prompts the students to improve on their posts, thereby invoking deeper thinking and learning, beyond just knowledge sharing. For the third feature, our system is an integrated Telegram and web-based forum which are synchronized real-time, so that student learning and sharing can occur anytime and anywhere, and with many students concurrently. The success of our system implementation depends on active student participation and high quality post contributions, which will be discussed in the following two sub-Sects. 3.1 and 3.2.

3.1 Thoughtfulness Score Prediction and Post Quality Improvement

High quality posts will benefit both the asker and the answerer, as well as all students who viewed and learned from the posts, as supported by Wise et al., (2014). Sonntag (2004) proposed to measure text quality in four dimensions including contextual, intrinsic, representation, and accessibility. For online posts, we focused on assessing the contextual dimension in terms of relevancy and representation for ease of understanding and interpretability. As such, we used thoughtfulness score to measure if a statement contains insightful reasoning and relevance to the issues discussed, as suggested by Gottipati and Jiang (2012).

To build the initial corpus to train the machine prediction, the research team collected and shortlisted an initial data set of 2377 posts with 340 questions, from the public forum on Excel (www.excelforum.com) over a four-month period (from June to September 2017). The two course instructors, who were part of the research team, are subject matter experts who labelled the posts on a scale of 0 to 5, where 0 means that the post is not thoughtful, to 5 which means that the post is thoughtful with clear explanation, examples, references and suggested Excel formulas and interpretations.

We have selected the random forest algorithm, after testing several machine learning algorithms, to predict the thoughtfulness score of the questions and answers posted. The text features used for machine prediction include structural, syntactic, discourse and other features. Structural features include average number of characters per word, average number of words per sentence, number of words, average parse tree height, and average number of subordinate clauses per sentence. Syntactic features include average number of noun phrases per sentence, average number of verb phrases per sentence and average number of pronounce phrases per sentence. Discourse relations include expansion relation, comparison relation, and contingency relation. Other features include the number of reference links and number of Excel formulas provided in the post content, and the question type. Students who participated in the discussion forum do not know the text features used to predict the thoughtfulness score, so they will not be able to game the system.

For example, the first question post below scores 1.85 for thoughtfulness, while the second question post scores 2.7, based on the text features. The total thoughtfulness score attained by each student over the entire course duration will be converted to 5% or 10% of the final grade (for those who were subjected to mandatory participation), by pro-rating their individual score against the highest scoring student.

Question Post 1:

For Assignment 2 Q3 on the Club 2010 age verification, let's say if A is born on 23 February 1997, and today's date is 24 February 2018, I tried a few methods but the calculated age was 21 instead of 20. Is it possible to calculate age according to birth date instead of just year? I have tried a few methods including INT, DATEDIF and YEARFRAC but it gives the same answer.

Question Post 2:

Hi, I know this has been asked a few times, but sometimes I STILL cannot get the optimal answer!! I know that solver tries to find a solution closest to the initial conditions, but most of the time, the global optimal answer is not close to the initial conditions and I get another answer instead. I can only get the global optimal answer when I manually type in a value close to the global optimal answer, but I don't always know the global optimal answer beforehand. I have tried using Evolutionary but it requires for both variables to have an upper and lower bound (I've set it such that variables are "=" or have both "<=" and ">=", but it still gives me the same message so help). But then again, Evolutionary may take too long so how should I use GRG Nonlinear to get the global optimal answer? I've selected GRG Nonlinear Multistart already (which also takes very long btw), so what else can I do to ensure I get the global optimal solution? During tests and exams, is it okay if I don't get the global optimal answer even though my model and constraints and everything else is the same?

Details of the entire data analytics process including data preparation, text pre-processing, feature selection, models and comparison are described in our earlier paper Cheong et al. (2018). As new posts were collected using our own system, they were labelled again by the same instructors and added to the corpus to re-train the machine. This will ensure that the algorithm prediction of the thoughtfulness score is maintained consistently according to the scoring method.

After the thoughtfulness score is predicted and shown to the student, the system then prompts the students to improve their posts, which will result in higher quality posts. Past research has shown that by providing immediate feedback and giving the participant an opportunity to revise answers to open-ended questions resulted in higher scores for the participants in an experiment carried out by Attali and Powers (2010).

In our implementations over three runs, the number of students, number of active students (those who posted questions and/or answers), number of posts created, and number of posts with second attempt, are given in Table 1.

Analysis of the posts with second attempt show that a high percentage of the second attempts improved in post quality, as shown in Table 2. We tested the null hypothesis (H0) that the chance of improving a post on second attempt was not significantly different from random chance, using the binomial test. We rejected H0 for all three runs where their p-values are much smaller than 0.05, representing that they are all significant. Thus, we can conclude that when prompted to improve their posts, some students will choose to do so, and among those who did, a large percentage managed to improve their posts, leading to higher quality posts, fulfilling

Table 1 Information about the three implementation runs

	Run 1	Run 2	Run 3
Number of students	128	147	325
Number of active students	101	115	244
Number of posts created by active students (excluding questions posted by chat-bot)	1025	1128	2486
Number of posts with second attempt	73	55	101

Table 2 Percentage of second attempts with improved thoughtfulness score

	Run 1		Run 2		Run 3	
	Improved	Reduced	Improved	Reduced	Improved	Reduced
Question	8 (57.1%)	6 (42.9%)	27 (71.1%)	11 (28.9%)	48 (78.7%)	13 (21.3%)
Answer	48 (81.4%)	11 (18.6%)	12 (70.6%)	5 (29.4%)	32 (80.0%)	8 (20.0%)
Total	56 (76.7%)	17 (23.3%)	39 (70.9%)	16 (29.1%)	80 (79.2%)	21 (20.8%)
p-value	5.27×10^{-6}		0.0025		2.73×10^{-9}	

the objective of our system. It is worthwhile to note that currently our system is unable to provide suggestions on how to improve the posts, which will form part of our future research work.

3.2 Incentive and Engagement Mechanisms

To achieve high participation rates in our system, apart from imposing 5% or 10% weightage as part of their final grade, we have designed six incentive and engagement mechanisms to ensure students remain engaged in using the Q&A forum. These mechanisms include:

- Avatar identity: To overcome the fear of being ridiculed when posting seemingly silly questions or the fear of providing the wrong answers, our students participate in the Q&A forum using their individual avatar identity to provide them a safe environment to post freely. This is also part of the IRB requirement for collecting data on human subjects.
- Real-time ranking: The avatars are ranked based on their cumulative thoughtfulness score earned to incite students' desire to stay at the top of the leader board.
- In-game coins: Together with the thoughtfulness scores earned, students will earn in-game coins which can be used as bounty to buy quick response for the best answer provided within a user-set time limit.
- Auto-routing of unanswered questions: To improve participation especially for the quiet students in class, posted questions which are unanswered after the time limit will be automatically routed to the top five and bottom five students according to their rankings. The top five students are chosen as they have shown to be highly participative and are knowledgeable to ensure higher quality posts, while the bottom five students are chosen to encourage them to participate so that they will not be left out of the system.
- Emotional cues: There are two buttons which the students can use to express their responses to posts. The "Need Improvement" button is to encourage other users to improve the current post, while the "Up-Vote" button is to identify good posts to draw attention to students to re-read such good posts.

- Chat-bot: The chat-bot will ask questions periodically (on average one question every one to two days) from a question bank to drive student participation, as students found it easier to respond to questions asked, than to ask a question. Note that the chat-bot does not answer any questions. From the data collected from Run 2 and Run 3, the chat-bot posted 140 questions in Run 2 (compared to 299 questions and 829 answers by students), and 280 questions in Run 3 (compared to 504 questions and 1982 answers by students). These chat-bot questions attracted 127 and 264 answers in Run 2 and Run 3 respectively, which is about one student answer to one chat-bot question.

With these mechanisms, we achieved high participation rates (number of active students / number of students) of 78.9% in Run 1, 83.7% in Run 2, and 75.1% in Run 3. Such high participation rates resulted in a large number of meaningful posts contributed by the students, with 1025 in Run 1, 1128 in Run 2, and 2486 in Run 3. This translates to about 10 meaningful post per active student. Such high participation rates and high average number of posts per active student were unseen in past literature that we are aware of as reported in Cheong et al. (2019).

4 Implementation Results

In Sect. 3, we have discussed our system and its effectiveness in generating high quality posts with high student participation rates. We will now discuss the implementation results to answer research questions RQ1 to RQ4, in the next three sub-Sects. 4.1, 4.2 and 4.3. Sub-Sect. 4.1 will answer RQ1, RQ2 and RQ3, while sub-Sect. 4.2 will answer RQ4. Sub-Sect. 4.3 will further extend the results for RQ4 to cater to different students in different degree programmes.

4.1 Assessment Results and Normalized Knowledge Gain

The main purpose of designing, developing and implementing our Q&A forum is to enhance out-of-class collaborative learning, to allow students to learn to ask good questions, provide good answers, and to learn from posts contributed by other students.

In Run 1, we correlated the average thoughtfulness scores of the students in each section with their respective scores attained in quizzes and final exam (Table 3). The average thoughtfulness scores for the two sections with 5% weightage (G15 and 16) are higher than that of the section with 10% weightage. All results displayed positive correlations between the average thoughtfulness scores with scores attained in quizzes and final exam, and most of the p-values are < 0.05, except for G16 quizzes (p-value $= 0.0541$) and for G1 final exam (p-value $= 0.1274$). While the correlation values are between 0.2333 to 0.4734, such modest values are expected when one

Table 3 Correlation between average thoughtfulness scores and assessments for Run 1

			Quizzes		Final Exam	
Section	# of Posts	Average Thoughtfulness	Correlation	p-value	Correlation	p-value
G1 (10%)	603	2.22	0.3169	0.0361	0.2333	0.1274
G15 (5%)	174	2.28	0.4734	0.0018	0.4112	0.0076
G16 (5%)	248	2.38	0.2993	0.0541	0.3684	0.0164

considers that there are many other factors which will affect students' performance, as supported by Cheng et al. (2011).

Thus, we can conclude for RQ1 that students with higher thoughtfulness scores (contributed higher quality posts) tend to perform better in assessments with appropriate extrinsic motivation, and 5% weightage is more ideal than 10%.

In Run 2 and Run 3, we conducted pre-test and post-test (both using multiple-choice questions) with the students, to assess their normalized knowledge gain with and without using the Q&A forum (in Run 2), and with and without in-class interventions while using the Q&A forum (in Run 3). Pre-test and post-test have been used to measure improvement in learning before and after the students have completed the course. Delucchi (2014) used pre-test and post-test to measure student learning in social statistics course and using paired sample t-test, he revealed statistically significant gains in knowledge for each course section, and all sections combined. Using the post-test results, he recommended pedagogy improvements such as revising the post-test content which students performed poorly or increase emphasis and class time on these hard topics. Pre-test results can be used to identify student's prior knowledge enabling faculty to spend lesser time on those areas. Kinoshita et al. (2017) explored using normalized gain scores to assess the positive influence of active learning in a lecture hall as compared to traditional lecturing in introductory environmental engineering course. Using independent samples t-test, they showed statistically significant differences between the two instructional methods, which concludes that learning gains were on average 16.7% higher for active learning versus traditional lecture-only learning.

Our pre-test contained 28 MCQ questions on using Excel spreadsheet functions to perform calculations, data filtering, data lookup, and questions on concepts relating to distribution functions for data simulations, consistent with the topics covered in the course. The post-test also contained the same 28 MCQ questions, however for questions that involved calculations, the input values were changed which will result in different answer options. For both runs, the students were given the pre-test at the start of the course to assess their initial knowledge before going through the course, while the post-test was given at the end of the course before the final exam. We advised students to leave the answer empty if they did not know the answer to any question, to prevent the situation where students managed to obtain the correct answer due to random selection. Pre-test and post-test scores did not count towards the final grade, and only students who completed both tests were included in the data set for analysis.

Table 4 Normalized knowledge gain in Run 2

Group	# of Students*	Average A	Average B	Normalized knowledge gain	% Increase
No system (G8, G9 & G11)	100	0.309	0.564	0.370	–
0% (G13)	37	0.354	0.598	0.378	+2.2
5% (G10 & G12)	61	0.328	0.597	0.401	+8.4
10% (G1)	34	0.266	0.558	0.397	+7.3

* includes only students who took both pre-test and post-test

We computed the normalized knowledge gain using the formula, Normalized knowledge gain = (B–A)/(1–A) where A = normalized pre-test score and B = normalized post-test score, as given in Hovland et al. (1949), which is the same as that used by Kinoshita et al. (2017).

For Run 2, apart from the four sections of students (Sections G1, G10, G12 and G13) who had access to the Q&A forum, three additional sections (Sections G8, G9 and G11) of students who did not have access were also given the same pre-test and post-test, so that we can perform added-value comparison.

From Table 4, we can see that students who had access to the Q&A forum had higher normalized knowledge gains as compared to students who did not. For Section G13 (0% voluntary participation), the normalized knowledge gain was slightly higher (+2.2%) than students with no access to the system. For mandatory use of the system (5% and 10% weightage) for online discussion, the students achieved higher knowledge gain (+8.4% and + 7.3%). While we were unable to prove statistical significance to answer RQ2 confidently, our result suggests that there could potentially be a positive difference in knowledge gain for students who used the system based on mandatory participation versus voluntarily participation, and in general, gained more knowledge than students who have no access to the system.

In Run 3, we implemented the system for eight sections of students, all with the same mandatory 5% weightage. Three out of the eight sections (Sections G2, G9 and G10) had in-class interventions to review the weekly posts during the immediate next class to clarify doubts and clear misconceptions raised in the posts, while the remaining five sections did not. We observe from Table 5 that sections with in-class intervention attained a higher normalized knowledge gain (+11.2%) than sections without in-class intervention. We performed a one-tailed test using Welch's t-test ($t = -1.63$, Df = 214), and obtained a p-value of 0.05 which is very close to the critical value of 5%. Thus, we can conclude for RQ3 that in-class intervention to review posts to clarify doubts and clear misconceptions was effective in improving knowledge gain.

Table 5 Normalized knowledge gain in Run 3

Group	# of Students*	Average A	Average B	Normalized knowledge gain
No intervention (G11, G12, G13, G14 & G15)	172	0.267	0.534	0.365
With intervention (G2, G9, G10)	100	0.288	0.577	0.406 (+11.2%)

* includes only students who took both pre-test and post-test

Table 6 Top vs bottom 10% knowledge gainers in Run 2

Group	# Students*	Top 10% gainers		Bottom 10% gainers	
		#	% of group	#	% of group
No system (G8, G9 & G11)	100	7	7.0	10	10.0
0% (G13)	37	3	8.1	1	2.7
5% (G10 & G12)	61	10	16.4	7	11.5
10% (G1)	34	4	11.8	6	17.6
TOTAL	232	24	–	24	–

* includes only students who took both pre-test and post-test

4.2 *Academic Strengths Comparison*

In this section, we focus on answering RQ4 to understand how the normalized knowledge gain distributes among the students with different academic strengths, using the results from Run 2 and Run 3. We filtered out the top 10% knowledge gainers (based on 90th percentile knowledge gain value) and bottom 10% knowledge gainers (based on 10th percentile knowledge gain value), for each implementation groups.

In Run 2, we observe from Table 6 that among the top 10% knowledge gainers, 5% and 10% weightage groups have more than 10% (16.4% and 11.8% respectively) of their respective groups being among the top 10% knowledge gainers. While those with no system and 0% weightage have less than 10% (7.0% and 8.1% respectively) of their respective groups being among the top 10% knowledge gainers. Such an initial observation aligns with our earlier observation that mandatory use of the system for online discussion will benefit the students more in learning and gaining knowledge, resulting in a higher percentage of students among the top 10% knowledge gainers.

For the bottom 10% gainers, the results show that mandatory participation with 5% and 10% weightage groups still have more than 10% (11.5% and 17.6% respectively) of their respective groups being in the bottom 10% knowledge gainers. This is a shocking discovery. It shows that the system did not seem to benefit these students when mandatory participation was enforced. A detailed analysis of the students in terms of their pre-test and post-test scores is necessary, to better understand how they responded to mandatory participation.

Table 7 Pre-test score, post-test score, normalized knowledge gain for top and bottom 10% with mandatory use of system (5% and 10%) in Run 2

Group	# of Students	Average A	Average B	Normalized knowledge gain
Top 10% knowledge gainers	14	0.332	0.829	0.740
Bottom 10% knowledge gainers	13	0.311	0.334	0.030

With the 14 students identified in the top 10% knowledge gainers, and another 13 students identified in the bottom 10% knowledge gainers, who were subjected to mandatory use of the system (5% and 10%), we computed their normalized pre-test and post-test scores, and normalized knowledge gain, as given in Table 7. We observe that the top 10% gainers have a higher average pre-test score (0.332) than the bottom 10% gainers (0.311). This shows that these top 10% gainers had better knowledge already at the start of the class as compared to the bottom 10% gainers. With the mandatory participation in using the systems, the top 10% gainers attained very significant average knowledge gain of 0.740. On the other hand, the bottom 10% gainers attained only very little average knowledge gain of 0.030. We performed a Welch's t-test ($t = 30.99$, $\mathrm{Df} = 19$), and obtained a p-value of 0.00 representing statistical significance. This suggested that mandatory participation suits the academically stronger students, while weaker students will not gain much knowledge under mandatory usage of the system. One plausible reason is that under mandatory participation, our system measures the quality of posts using thoughtfulness score and uses it as part of the student's overall grade. For the academically weaker students, contributing high quality posts spells intrinsic challenge for them, even when forced to do so.

Next, we focused only on the bottom 10% knowledge gainers, and determine if mandatory participation (5% and 10%) versus voluntary participation (0%) and no access to system, would result in any difference in their knowledge gain. Our Welch's t-test ($t = 0.798$, $\mathrm{Df} = 21$) obtained p-values of 0.21 (one-tailed test) and 0.43 (two-tailed test), suggesting no statistical difference in their knowledge gain. This means that for the weaker students, their knowledge gain will not be positively affected by mandatory participation in the forum. This brought us to explore whether mandatory participation with intervention actions would be able to assist the weaker students better in knowledge gain.

We performed similar top 10% versus bottom 10% knowledge gain analysis for the students in Run 3, where all students were subjected to mandatory participation (5%), and three sections of students had intervention actions, while five sections of students did not. There were 27 students in the top 10% and 29 students in the bottom 10%, based on 90th percentile and 10th percentile knowledge gain values respectively. From Table 8, we can see that the top 10% gainers have almost the same percentage

(9.9% and 10%) of students regardless of whether there were intervention actions or not. For the bottom 10% gainers, a higher percentage (12.8%) of students were in the no intervention group, while only 7% of the students were in the intervention group.

With the 27 students identified in the top 10% knowledge gainers, and the other 29 students identified in the bottom 10% knowledge gainers, we computed their normalized pre-test and post-test scores, and normalized knowledge gain, as given in Table 9. For the top 10% gainers, our Welch's t-test ($t = 0.113$, $Df = 20$) obtained p-values of 0.46 (one-tailed test) and 0.91 (two-tailed test), suggesting no statistical difference in their knowledge gain, with or without intervention actions. However, for the bottom 10% gainers, our Welch's t-test ($t = 2.339$, $Df = 9$), obtained p-values of 0.023 (one-tailed test) and 0.047 (two-tailed test), suggesting that there is statistical difference in their knowledge gain, when intervention actions were added.

Table 8 Top vs bottom 10% knowledge gainers in Run 3

Group	# Students*	Top 10% gainers		Bottom 10% gainers	
		#	% of group	#	% of group
No intervention (G11, G12, G13, G14 & G15)	172	17	9.9	22	12.8
With intervention (G2, G9 & G10)	100	10	10.0	7	7.0
TOTAL	272	27	–	29	–

* includes only students who took both pre-test and post-test

Table 9 Normalized knowledge gain for top and bottom 10%, with and without intervention actions in run 3

Group	# of Students	Average A	Average B	Normalized knowledge gain
Top 10% knowledge gainers (No intervention)	17	0.268	0.806	0.735
Top 10% knowledge gainers (With intervention)	10	0.367	0.830	0.733
Bottom 10% knowledge gainers (No intervention)	22	0.298	0.335	0.051
Bottom 10% knowledge gainers (With intervention)	7	0.270	0.344	0.099

Table 10 Normalized knowledge gain by degree programs

Degree Program	# Students*	Average A	Average B	Normalized knowledge gain	Admission grade profile◇
Law	1	0.222	0.815	0.762	AAA/A
Accountancy	42	0.306	0.610	0.438	AAB/B
Business	104	0.280	0.557	0.385	ABB/C
Economic	40	0.270	0.544	0.376	BBC/B
Information Systems	50	0.293	0.541	0.350	BBC/B
Social Sciences	35	0.202	0.470	0.336	BBC/B

* includes only students who took both pre-test and post-test
◇based on Cambridge GCE A level results (10th percentile)

Thus, we can conclude for RQ4 that mandatory use of the system for online discussion will benefit the academically stronger students, while academically weaker students can benefit from mandatory use the system only when in-class intervention was provided to help them further.

4.3 Degree Programs Comparison

In this section, we perform the comparison of normalized knowledge gain among students from different degree programs so as to apply the conclusions for RQ4 for different students. We used the results from Run 3, since all the sections were subjected to the same mandatory 5% weightage. From Table 10, we can see that apart from the single Law student, Accountancy students attained the most knowledge gain, followed by Business students, Economics students, Information Systems students, and lastly Social Sciences students. This result is consistent with the admission grade profile of the students in each program, where Accountancy students have a better grade profile, followed by Business students, and then the students from the remaining three programs. Our t-test showed that the difference in normalized knowledge gain between Accountancy and Information Systems ($t = 2.452$, p-value $= 0.016$), and between Accountancy and Social Sciences ($t = 2.534$, p-value $=$ 0.013) were significant.

With the top 10% and bottom 10% knowledge gainers results based on degree programs in Table 11, we can see that students from Information Systems and Social Sciences programs have the least percentage of students in the top 10% group, and were among the highest percentage of students in the bottom 10% group. Again, this is consistent with the grade profiles of the students. Based on our conclusion for RQ4, we can suggest that students from Information Systems and Social Sciences need positive intervention actions when mandatory use of the system is enforced.

Table 11 Top vs bottom 10% knowledge gainers by degree programs

Degree	# Students*	Top 10% Gainers		Bottom 10% Gainers	
Programs		#	% of group	#	% of group
Law	1	1	100	0	0
Accountancy	42	5	11.9	2	4.8
Business	104	8	7.4	7	6.7
Economic	40	9	22.5	7	17.5
Information Systems	50	2	4.0	7	14.0
Social Sciences	35	2	5.7	6	17.1
TOTAL	272	24	–	24	–

* includes only students who took both pre-test and post-test

5 Closing the Loop

We aim to close the loop after we have understood how the students learn while using the system. The results from our three implementation runs, using different settings, allow us to explore which setting will work best for different types of students, and also what improvements can be added to the system.

Firstly, analysis of the posts data established that students who achieved higher average thoughtfulness scores performed better in the course assessments. This implies that students who posted higher quality posts performed better. Our system currently only prompts the students to improve their posts by displaying the predicted thoughtfulness scores, which resulted in some students re-posted better posts trying to get higher scores, while some chose not to re-post. We want to improve the system to provide automated guidance or suggestions to the students on how and in what areas to make improvements to their posts. The guidance or suggestions could be in terms of providing further explanation, giving examples, and/or providing comparisons. In this way, we can expect even higher quality posts which will benefit all the students who learn from the posts.

Secondly, students who used the system seemed to achieve higher knowledge gain as compared to those who did not, and weaker students who used the system coupled with in-class intervention actions will achieve positive knowledge gain. This insight tells us that the system is effective in helping students gain more knowledge, and in-class intervention will add value. The suggested future action would be to have course instructors review the posts on a weekly basis during in-class lessons or participate in the Q&A forum themselves, so that students can get clarifications on the questions and answers posted, and not be left with the ambiguity of not knowing if their contributed answers are correct or not. It also presents a good opportunity to identify and re-visit difficult topics which have the most questions asked. This is supported by Cheng et al. (2011) who suggested that the "implementation of an online discussion forum is beneficial even if a teacher only invests minimal time on the forum." There have been forms of intervention actions implemented in past case experiments to assist learners who are potentially at risk (Rienties et al., 2017). In one case, emails were sent to learners-at-risk to encourage them to reflect upon their study progress as a form of progress check, and to provide information on how to move forward. In the second case, a sophisticated system with machine learning method was used to predict learners who are likely not to submit the next assessment, and the system will recommend the best study materials for successful completion of the assessment.

Thirdly, we found that different types of participation work best for different types of students. Without in-class intervention, mandatory participation benefitted the academically stronger students, while the academically weaker students need positive intervention actions when mandatory use of the system is enforced. This can impact how the Q&A forum should be implemented based on the composition of students from different degree programmes in the section, to decide how much and the types of intervention actions should be included.

6 Implications for Workplace Learning

We hope that our CAT-IT system can be a successful alternative for working professionals to acquire knowledge which are specific to their business domain areas in an informal setting. Using the system, working professionals can post questions and answers shared among peers within their own organizations and learn through such informal discussions, which can be blended seamlessly in their day-to-day workflow. The LACE LAW Manifesto highlighted an important point on "blending analytics and learning innovation to conceive and implement new working environments capable to constantly analyze, diagnose, and support the performance of users, and offer them context-aware and intelligent learning experiences directly at the workplace, in their day-to-day workflow, is going to be crucial for the workforce of the future." (Cardinali et al., 2015).

While our system has not been implemented in real business organization learning, we attempt to draw inference from our implementation results. Firstly, analysis of the posts data established that students who achieved higher average thoughtfulness scores performed better in the course assessments. Drawing the parallel to business organization context, we envisage that employees who share more thoughtful questions and answers will achieve better work outcomes. Secondly, our system is effective in helping students gain more knowledge, and in-class intervention will add value. Translating that to business organization context, due to the use of the system, employees in the organizations will gain more knowledge and some form of positive intervention from experts (who could be senior mentors with deep knowledge of the business) will enhance knowledge gain further. Thirdly, we found that different types of participation work best for different types of students. To ensure the effectiveness of such a system in a business organization implementation, different settings may be needed to suit different types of roles and personas within the organizations. Our proposed extension in implementing our system in informal workplace learning is

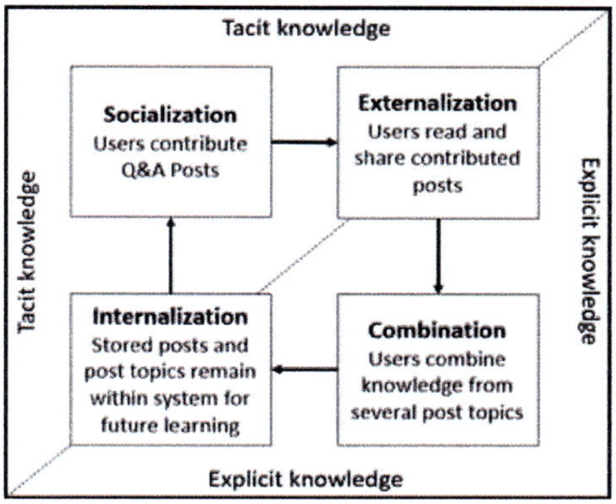

Fig. 2 Map of CAT-IT implementation into organization knowledge creation process

aligned with Sambrook's (2005) definition of learning in work which is "associated with the more informal processes that are embedded in activities, such as observing, asking questions, problem solving, doing projects, mentoring and coaching others, and participating in ad hoc discussions."

Successful individual learning can support organization learning, where the aim is to transform individual knowledge into organizational knowledge. Organization knowledge creation theory views organization learning as a dynamic process involving tacit and explicit knowledge processes. The creation of organizational knowledge is a spiral process repeated in four phases: socialization, externalization, combination and internalization (Nonaka & Konno, 1998). In the socialization phase, there is tacit knowledge sharing among individuals. The tacit knowledge is then translated into explicit forms that can be understood by others in the externalization phase. When the explicit knowledge held by different individuals is combined, sorted, or categorized, such enhanced explicit knowledge will be disseminated to members of the organization in the combination phase. The final internationalization phase requires the conversion of the enhanced explicit knowledge into organization's tacit knowledge. We hope that the implementation of our system in organization learning will be able to contribute to the organization knowledge creation process. In Fig. 2, we attempt to map our system implementation into the four phases corresponding to that of the organization knowledge creation process.

7 Conclusions

Learning Analytics has been both a research and practice application area in education. Many learning technologies, such as LMS have incorporated LA to allow educators to collect and analyze data on students' learning, so as to enhance learning and achieve better learning outcomes. Our intelligent integrated Telegram and web-based forum enables informal, participatory learning outside the classroom and was shown to increase knowledge gain, and different implementation settings were found to suit different student profiles and backgrounds. We proposed that our system can be a successful alternative for workplace learning and ultimately contribute to organization knowledge creation, and we attempt to draw inference from our implementation results, to understand the parallels in the business organization context.

References

Ali, L., Hatala, M., Gašević, D., & Jovanović, J. (2012). A qualitative evaluation of evolution of a learning analytics tool. *Computers & Education, 58*(1), 470–489.

Attali, Y., & Powers, D. (2010). Immediate feedback and opportunity to revise answers to open-ended questions. *Educational and Psychological Measurement, 70*(1), 22–35.

Barla, M., Bieliková, M., Ezzeddinne, A. B., Kramár, T., Šimko, M., & Vozár, O. (2010). On the impact of adaptive test question selection for learning efficiency. *Computers & Education, 55*(2), 846–857.

Blikstein, P. (2011). Using learning analytics to assess students' behavior in open-ended programming tasks. In P. Long, G. Siemens, G. Conole, & D. Gasevic (Eds.), In *Proceedings of the 1st International Conference on Learning Analytics and Knowledge (LAK 11)* (pp. 110–116). New York, NY: ACM.

Brown, M. (2011). Learning analytics: The coming third wave. *Educause Learning Initiative Brief, 1*(4),1–4.

Cahill, H., Coffey, J., Lester, L., Midford, R., Ramsden, R., & Venning, L. (2014). Influences on teachers' use of participatory learning strategies in health education classes. *Health Education Journal, 73*(6), 702–713.

Campbell, J. P., & Oblinger, D. G. (2007, October). Academic analytics. EDUCAUSE Quarterly.

Cardinali, F., van der Schaaf, M. F., Scheffel, M., Paini, M., Vanarwegen, M., Glaser, J., Kismihok, G., Chazerand, P., & Flocken, S. (2015). The LACE learning analytics in the workplace (LAW) Manifesto. https://dspace.library.uu.nl/handle/1874/326614

Cheng, C. K., Pare, D. E., Collimore, L.-M., & Joordens, S. (2011). Assessing the effectiveness of a voluntary online discussion forum on improving students' course performance. *Computers & Education, 56*, 253–261.

Cheong, M. L. F., Chen, J. Y.-C, & Dai, B.T. (2018, December 4–7). Integrated Telegram and web-based forum with automatic assessment of questions and answers for collaborative learning. *Proceedings of IEEE International Conference on Teaching, Assessment and Learning for Engineering TALE 2018*. Wollongong, Australia. https://doi.org/10.1109/TALE.2018.8615137

Cheong, M. L. F., Chen, J. Y.-C, & Dai, B. T. (2019). An intelligent platform with automatic assessment and engagement features for active online discussions. Presented at 32nd International Conference on Industrial, Engineering and Other Applications of Applied Intelligent Systems, IEA/AIE 2019 (pp. 730–743). Advances and Trends in Artificial Intelligence, LNAI 11606.

Clow, D. (2012). The learning analytics cycle: Closing the loop effectively. In *Proceedings of the 2nd International Conference on Learning Analytics & Knowledge (LAK 12)* (pp. 134–138). Vancouver, BC, Canada.

Dawson, S., Mirriahi, N., & Gasevic, D. (2015). Importance of theory in learning analytics in formal and workplace settings. *Journal of Learning Analytics, 2*(2), 1–4. https://doi.org/10.18608/jla.2015.22.1

Dekker, G. W., Pechenizkiy, M., & Vleeshouwers, J. M. (2009). Predicting students drop out: A case study. In T. Barnes, M. Desmarais, C. Romero, & S. Ventura (Eds.), *Proceedings of the 2nd International Conference on Educational Data Mining* (pp. 41–50).

Delucchi, M. (2014). Measuring student learning in social statistics: A pretest-posttest study of knowledge gain. *Teaching Sociology, 42*(3), 231–239. https://doi.org/10.1177/0092055X14527909

Elias, T. (2011). Learning analytics: Definitions, processes and potential.

Falchikov, N. (2001). *Learning together – Peer tutoring in higher education.* RoutledgeFalmer.

Gao, F., Zhang, T., & Franklin, T. (2013). Designing asynchronous online discussion environments: Recent progress and possible future directions. *British Journal of Educational Technology, 44*(3), 469–483.

Gottipati, S., & Jiang, J. (2012). Finding thoughtful comments from social media. *Proceedings of COLING 2012: Technical Papers* (pp. 995–1010).

Gunawardena, C. N., Lowe, C. A., & Anderson, T. (1997). Analysis of a global on-line debate and the development of an interaction analysis model for examining social construction of knowledge in computer conferencing. *Journal of Educational Computing Research, 17*(4), 397–431.

Guo, W. W. (2010). Incorporating statistical and neural network approaches for student course satisfaction analysis and prediction. *Expert Systems with Applications, 37*(4), 3358–3365.

Hara, N. M., Bonk, C. J. M., & Angeli, C. M. (2000). Content analysis of online discussion in an applied educational psychology course. *Instructional Science, 28*, 115–152.

Hovland, C. I., Lumsdaine, A. A., & Sheffield, F. D. (1949). A baseline for measurement of percentage change. In C. I. Hovland, A. A. Lumsdaine, F. D. Sheffield (Eds.), *Experiments on mass communication* (pp. 284–292). Wiley.

Kim, C. L. (2015). Preliminary empirical model of crucial determinants of best practice for peer tutoring on academic achievement. *Journal of Educational Psychology, 107*(2), 558–579.

Kinoshita, T. J., Knight, D. B., & Gibbes, B. (2017). The positive influence of active learning in a lecture hall: An analysis of normalised gain scores in introductory environmental engineering. *Innovations in Education and Teaching International, 54*(3), 275–284. https://doi.org/10.1080/14703297.2015.1114957

Larson, B. E., & Keiper, T. A. (2002). Classroom discussion and threaded electronic discussion: Learning in two arenas. *Contemporary Issues in Technology and Teacher Education, 2*(1), 45–62.

Long, P., & Siemens, G. (2011). Penetrating the fog. Analytics in learning and education. EDUCASE *Review, 46*(5), 31–40.

McMaster, K. L., Fuchs, D., & Fuchs, L. S. (2006). Research on peer assisted learning strategies: The promise and limitations of peer mediated instruction. *Reading & Writing Quarterly: Overcoming Learning Difficulties, 22*, 5–25.

Nonaka, I., & Konno, N. (1998). The concept of "Ba": Building a foundation for knowledge creation. *California Management Review, 40*, 40–54.

Papamitsiou, Z., & Economides, A. A. (2014). Learning analytics and educational data mining in practice: A systematic literature review of empirical evidence. *Educational Technology & Society, 17*(4), 49–64.

Pardos, Z. A., Baker, R. S. J. d., San Pedro, M. O. C. Z., Gowda, S. M., & Gowda, S. M. (2013). Affective states and state tests: Investigating how affect throughout the school year predicts end of year learning outcomes. In D. Suthers, K. Verbert, E. Duval, & X. Ochoa (Eds.), *Proceedings of the 3rd International Conference on Learning Analytics and Knowledge* (pp. 117–124). New York, NY: ACM.

Rienties, B., Cross, S., & Zdrahal, Z. (2017). Implementing a learning analytics intervention and evaluation framework: What works? In B. K. Daniel (Ed.), *Big data and learning analytics in higher education* (pp. 147–166), Springer International Publishing. https://doi.org/10.1007/978-3-319-06520-5_10

Romero, C., Lopez, M.-I., Luna, J.-M., & Ventura, S. (2013). Predicting students' final performance from participation in on-line discussion forums. *Computers & Education, 68*, 458–472.

Romero-Zaldivar, V.-A., Pardo, A., Burgos, D., & Kloos, C. D. (2012). Monitoring student progress using virtual appliances: A case study. *Computers & Education, 58*(4), 1058–1067.

Sambrook, S. (2005). Factors influencing the context and process of work-related learning: Synthesizing findings from two research projects. *Human Resource Development International, 8*, 101–119.

Seimens, G. (2013). Learning analytics: The emergence of a discipline. *American Behavioral Scientist, 57*(10), 1380–1400.

Sonntag, D. (2004). Assessing the quality of natural language text data. GI Jahrestagung.

Trilling, B., & Fadel, C. (2009). *21st century skills: Learning for life in our times.* John Wiley & Sons.

Viberg, O., Hatakka, M., Bälter, O., & Mavroudi, A. (2018). The current landscape of learning analytics in higher education. *Computers in Human Behavior, 89*, 98–110.

Wise, A. F., Hausknecht, S. N., & Zhao, Y. (2014). Attending to others' posts in asynchronous discussions: Learners' online listening and its relationship to speaking". *International Journal of Computer-Supported Collaborative Learning, 9*, 185–209.

Worsley, M., & Blikstein, P. (2013). Towards the development of multimodal action based assessment. In D. Suthers, K. Verbert, E. Duval, & X. Ochoa (Eds.), *Proceedings of the 3rd International Conference on Learning Analytics and Knowledge* (pp. 94–101). New York, NY: ACM.

Yoo, J., & Kim J. (2012). Predicting learner's project performance with dialogue features in online Q&A discussions. In S. A. Cerri, W. J. Clancey, G. Papadourakis, K. Panourgia (Eds.), *Intelligent tutoring systems.* ITS. Springer. https://doi.org/10.1007/978-3-642-30950-2_74

Michelle L. F. Cheong, Ph.D., is a Professor of Information Systems (Education), Associate Dean, SCIS Post-Graduate Professional Education, and Doctor of Engineering in the School of Computing and Information Systems at the Singapore Management University, Singapore. She is an experienced academic with a demonstrated history of working in the higher education industry. She is skilled in Data Science and provides professional training and consulting for mid- to senior-level professionals in various industries.

Jean Y.-C. Chen, Ph.D., is a Systems & Learning Instructor in the MITB (Artificial Intelligence) Programme at the Singapore Management University, Singapore. Her research interest includes computer aided instruction, data mining, learning (artificial intelligence), natural language processing, and text analysis.

Bing Tian Dai, Ph.D., is an Assistant Professor of information Systems (Education) and Director of MITB (Artificial Intelligence) Programme, School of Computing and Information Systems, Singapore Management University, Singapore. His research interest are data management and analytics, data mining on social network with interactions, and topic and sentiment analysis.

Chapter 20
A Research on Digitalization and Performance in Higher Education Between Hybridity and Algorithms

Lino Cinquini and Sara Giovanna Mauro

Abstract The phenomenon of digitalization has spread in the field of education and research, as demonstrated by the digitalization of teaching and training methods, the use of digital technologies for conducting research and the spread of the concept of the 'digital university'. One of the main expectations is that digitalization can improve the performance of universities, supporting the delivery of more efficient and effective services. Nevertheless, the relationship between digitalization and performance measurement and management has so far been under-investigated. This chapter studies how this relationship has been addressed in the academic debate by conducting a review of the literature on the topic. The analysis of the literature allows the identification of key themes, both previously studied and future research areas. The findings show that, in most cases, attention has been paid to the effect of the use of digital tools on (student) performance by investigating the adoption of digital teaching/learning tools and resources. Next, attention has been directed to the use of digital tools to measure the performance of universities. However, digitalization does not concern only tools, but it implies changes in the language used in universities, calling for further research on the costs and benefits of digitalization, going beyond the technicalities of digital tools to investigate performance and changes in academia as a result of the digitalization of the language.

Keywords Digital · Performance measurement · Literature review · University · Hybridity · Algorithm

L. Cinquini
Institute of Management, Sant'Anna School of Advanced Studies of Pisa, Pisa, Italy
e-mail: l.cinquini@santannapisa.it

S. G. Mauro (✉)
University of Modena and Reggio Emilia, Modena, Italy
e-mail: saragiovanna.mauro@unimore.it

T. Rana et al. (eds.), *Handbook of Big Data and Analytics in Accounting and Auditing*,
https://doi.org/10.1007/978-981-19-4460-4_20

1 Introduction

At a time when digital tools have a primary role to play in society and in the governance of public administrations (Andrews, 2019; Dunleavy et al., 2005), digital technologies are considered a possible tool for a more efficient, effective and transparent delivery of public services, including educational services. The phenomenon of digitalization has spread in the field of education and research, as made clear by the digitalization of teaching and training methods, the use of digital technologies for conducting research and, more generally, the spread of the concept of the 'digital university' (Hazemi et al., 2012; Johnston et al., 2019), which summarizes the key changes occurring in the higher education field.

Digitalization is based on the use of digital technologies that are expected to overcome physical barriers and distances and generate a significant amount of data allowing multiple analyses. One of the main expectations is that the data can be also used in decision-making processes to improve the effectiveness of services and stakeholder relations through the provision of smart services and the creation of public value (Agostino & Arnaboldi, 2017; Andrews, 2019).

Despite the expected potential benefits of digitalization, this process creates many challenges that are complex to manage (Andrews, 2019; Gamage, 2016; Nørreklit et al., 2019; van der Voort et al., 2019). Not only may the results not live up to expectations, thereby generating inefficiencies and complexity as demonstrated by the development of new forms of 'robotic bureaucracy' (Bozeman & Youtie, 2020), but the widespread adoption of a digital language may generate the deeper transformation of universities, further changing their identity (Nørreklit et al., 2019).

The changes linked to technological innovation have occurred within a scenario of reforms that have been affecting universities for several decades, together with a growing internationalization and competition in the sector and the influence of a widespread managerial logic (Dal Molin et al., 2017; Dobija et al., 2019; Ferlie et al., 2008; Hemsley- Brown & Oplatka, 2006; Humphrey & Gendron, 2015; King, 2000; Parker, 2002; Pianezzi et al., 2020; Rebora & Turri, 2013; Tieghi et al., 2018). According to this logic, a crucial role has started to be played by the measurement and management of performance to strengthen economy, efficiency and effectiveness in the delivery of public services where the citizens or—in the case of higher education—the students are considered as 'clients'. The centrality of performance evaluation in university governance is also evident in the adoption of performance-based budgeting and funding tools for resource management (Ezza et al., 2019). The adoption of these managerial practices and tools in the field of higher education has enlivened a debate on their critical impacts on universities and academics' role, identity and final performance (e.g., Francesconi et al., 2020; Grossi et al., 2020; Humphrey & Gendron, 2015; Parker, 2011; Rebora & Turri, 2011). In this context of reforms, the growing adoption of digital tools and technologies has further contributed to shaping the performance of universities, influencing how the various teaching, research and third mission activities carried out by universities are realized and then evaluated (e.g., Giovanelli et al., 2017; Nørreklit et al., 2019). The impact is even more evident in times of crisis such as the COVID-19 pandemic.

Despite the relevant and growing debate on digitalization (Gil-García et al., 2018), and even though performance measurement in the public sector and state universities is not a new aspect of the literature, the relationship between digitalization and performance measurement and management of public organizations is still under-explored (Agostino & Arnaboldi, 2017; Agostino et al., 2021; Lavertu, 2016; Nørreklit et al., 2019). However, as the debate described above suggests, it is important to go deeper into the topic, to understand its crucial aspects, identify the perspectives through which the topic has mainly been studied until now and set a future research agenda. For this reason, this research aims to identify and analyze the most significant contributions published in international scientific journals through a systematic review of the literature. We have searched for international contributions about digitalization and performance in universities through an examination on portals such as Scopus and EBSCO. The identified papers have been analyzed through both a descriptive and a thematic analysis. The focus of the analysis has been on understanding how digitalization and performance have been jointly interpreted and studied within the field of higher education.

For the purposes of this research, a broad interpretation of the concept of performance has been adopted to find out how the contributions on the theme have defined the term 'performance' itself. The multidimensional concept of performance has been used with different meanings and for different purposes over time, in line with the different paradigms adopted by public administrations (e.g., Public Administration, New Public Management, New Public Governance) (Pollitt, 1986; van Dooren et al., 2015). This term can be used to indicate the ability of an organization to achieve its objectives, which translates into an analysis of efficiency, effectiveness and cost-effectiveness and increasingly also an analysis of quality, user satisfaction and ability to ensure fair services. The concept of performance has become increasingly multidimensional to take into consideration the multiple missions ascribed to universities, ranging from teaching to research and the third mission and the different levels, ranging from the individual level to the department and university levels, at which performance can be measured.

The chapter is structured as follows: the next section provides a reflection on the key transformations undertaken by universities over the last several years to provide the background of the research. The third section illustrates the research methodology and the fourth section describes the framework of analysis. The fifth and sixth sections present the results of the analysis and the last section draws conclusions and implications of the research.

2 Universities Between Hybridity and Algorithms

The motivation of this research is rooted in the recent literature addressing the main features of the university change process. Universities have certainly undertaken a significant process of change over the last several decades and two main macro-trends are identified and discussed here: the hybridization of the higher education system and the digitalization process.

The first macro-trend of reforms is visible in the hybridity of the higher education field. Hybridity can be interpreted as the interface between public, private and civil society through different ownership modes, competing types of institutional logic, diverse funding bases and/or various forms of controls (Johanson & Vakkuri, 2017). The higher education field can be considered a relevant example of hybridity from multiple perspectives, as listed below and then discussed:

- The *hybridity of values and types of logic* since universities are now led by different (and contrasting) types of logic and values, such as managerial logic and academic logic;
- The *hybridity of funding arrangements*, as the resources allocated to universities can come from multiple sources, both public and private;
- The *hybridity of controls*, as financial, societal, professional and bureaucratic controls co-exist.

Starting with the first perspective, the 'massification' of the higher education sector and the growing competition, even beyond national boundaries, have been corroborated by the widespread development of a managerial logic (Ferlie et al., 2008; Hemsley-Brown & Oplatka, 2006; King, 2000; Parker, 2002; Pianezzi et al., 2020). In the spirit of New Public Management (NPM) and the adoption of market-based reforms, the higher education field has seen a growing competition for students and research funding (Ferlie et al., 2008). The competition has stimulated the creation of an evaluative culture and required the development of performance measurement and management systems coherent with the process of the marketization of higher education (Espeland & Sauder, 2007). Consequently, the adoption of the business language has contributed to reshaping the identity and role of universities (Parker, 2011), influencing and hybridizing their logic and values. In an attempt to become a 'profitable organization', academics are pushed towards the attainment of new objectives and the achievement of new performance targets. University and journal rankings have been used to define what is *good* and have influenced academics' decisions about where to publish and how much effort to devote to their different duties (Agyemang & Broadbent, 2015).

In this hybrid corporatized university (Parker, 2011), academic logic and managerial (business) logic can then co-exist (Grossi et al., 2020; Guarini et al., 2020), reinforcing the hybridity of public value creation and the ambiguity of the university's performance measurement systems (Pekkola et al., 2020; Vakkuri & Johanson, 2020). Distinct from the academics, there are manager-academics, who are academics who hold a management position, which can create daily tension in the work management (Ferlie et al., 2008; Pekkola et al., 2020). On the one hand, the managerial (business) logic is visible in the tendency towards measuring performance, allocating funds based on results and managing universities as corporate organizations aimed at attaining a good position in the rankings; on the other hand, the professional (academic) logic is visible in the freedom of research and teaching, in the pursuit of scholarly knowledge and reputation and managing the university as a professional organization: both these types of logic co-exist and call for careful management (Lepori & Montauti, 2020) to cope with the tendency to replace academic values with managerial (business) values. In fact, the risk that has been observed and discussed by scholars is that the managerial logic is becoming predominant, transforming and challenging the academic (professional) logic. Academic creativity and freedom are challenged by the search for external legitimacy and resources (ter Bogt & Scapens, 2012). Neo-liberal values and principles have reformed the identity of academics (van Helden & Argento, 2020), who have been transformed into academic performers driven by conformity (Gendron, 2008). The 'neoliberal metrical governmentality' has constrained freedom, quality and societal benefit, assigning more relevance to quantity and managerial control (van Houtum & van Uden, 2020). This critical debate poses important questions about the extent to which it is still possible to detect an academic (professional) logic, or whether this logic has been hybridized by the managerial logic.

The diffusion of the managerial logic is visible predominantly in the growing relevance of performance measurement and management systems. In the higher education field, the impact on the object of performance measurement systems is significant, since these systems are not able to consider the complexity of reality (Kure et al., 2021). What should be measured? And how? The complexity is exacerbated by the multiple goals and functions universities must fulfil: they are required to carry out teaching activities to train future generations; at the same time, they are expected to conduct innovative research to contribute to the development of organizations and society and to interact with society, communicating and sharing the results of the research activities. Consequently, the use of the performance systems may vary, ranging from a symbolic, external legitimacy-driven use to a 'rational' use, which influences decision-making (Dobija et al., 2019).

Concerning the second perspective, the hybridity is partly enhanced by the multiple funding arrangements used by universities to obtain the resources to be competitive. In addition to the different legal status of private and public universities, the diversification of funding sources is a consequence of the decrease in government funding and the necessity of finding new sources by increasing collaboration with businesses (Boitier & Rivière, 2013). The integration of private and public sources reinforces the hybridity of the entrepreneurial corporatized university, in parallel with the development of performance-based funding (King, 2000), which links the allocation of funds to the results measured and strengthens the managerial logic.

Consequently, universities' and academics' activities have been subject to multiple new forms of control. There is a stress on financial control, efficiency and value for money (Ferlie et al., 2008). In parallel, societal control is pushed by stakeholder engagement and the growing demands for relevant outcomes to be obtained by universities, as shown by the call for a sustainable university. Finally, professional and bureaucratic controls are carried out on the academic work. The pervasive development of an audit culture has resulted in a shift towards bureaucratic control and a lower level of trust (Craig et al., 2014). The co-existence of multiple controls can be considered a further sign of hybridity in the higher education field, since it fosters hybridity, and is simultaneously influenced by the hybridization process of logic, values and funding mechanisms.

To sum up, as is also pointed out by recent reviews of the literature on the topic, hybridity of knowledge-intensive public organizations, including universities, exists and is increasingly recognized (Argento et al., 2020; Grossi et al., 2019). It can be detected mainly with reference to the existence of multiple goals, competing types of institutional logic, diverse funding mechanisms and various forms of controls and accounting tools in the higher education field.

The second macro-trend of reforms occurring in the higher education field is visible in the digitalization process and the development of algorithm-based governance systems. The growing attention paid to performance measurement and management has resulted in the definition of performance metrics suitable for translating and communicating the performance of a university in numbers and rankings. This dominant calculative technology is facilitated by the spread of algorithms, increasingly employed to measure performance with important changes in university governance. Recently, the academic debate has recognized and investigated the development of 'algorithmic regulation' and 'algorithmic governance', which refer to systems that use algorithms to drive decision-making (Katzenbach & Ulbricht, 2019; Lodge & Mennicken, 2019). A shift from governing by numbers to governing by data is recognized as well as the consequent challenges, which recall and resemble performance measurement challenges (Lodge & Mennicken, 2019). Indeed, algorithms bring multiple challenges due to the difficulty in assessing quality and outcomes and in driving decision-making based on the results of algorithmic computations. Algorithms can lack transparency (Katzenbach & Ulbricht, 2019) and increase ambiguity. Further, they can introduce new layers of difficulty. For instance, their increasing use can automate certain activities, in areas such as university research grants and contract administration, including the automatic sending of emails for reporting and compliance purposes, and lead to new forms of 'robotic bureaucracy' (Bozeman & Youtie, 2020).

The two macro-trends of hybridization and digitalization have been discussed here as separate, but in practice they are inter-linked. On the one hand, the increased use of the digital technology and algorithms can be considered a further driver of the hybridity of universities and of their performance measurement and management systems. The reasons are multiple. The adoption of digital tools and languages further transforms the activities carried out (e.g., teaching, research, communication) and their measurement (Nørreklit et al., 2019), introducing a new language different from the academic and managerial ones and a new type of control. The digital language transforms the space where academics work and strongly influences the communication mechanisms whereby actors establish their relationships, both internal and external to the universities. This occurs in parallel with a non-digital space and way of communicating in the higher education field, which still exist. Further, the availability of digital tools and data paves the way to new types of control over the activities carried out by academics, widening the spectrum of tasks under control. Finally, the digitalization process can also contribute to reinforcing the quantitative measurement of performance by supporting the production and communication of numbers and data, spreading the use of 'rankings' and 'ratings' and exacerbating the tensions between managerial logic and academic logic. On the other hand, the ongoing hybridization of universities fosters the development and adoption of digital technologies to obtain the necessary data to cope with the multiple information needs and accountability requirements of the field and to increase service efficiency and effectiveness.

Considering this background of literature, the current research is exploratory in nature. It has been designed to investigate the focus of the studies carried out on the topic of digitalization and performance in the higher education field, in order to assess the extent to which the orientation of the research questions is intertwined with the path of change described above. Specifically, we aimed to investigate (a) the purpose of digitalization these research studies consider: for example, if the contributions are focused on the use of digital tools to measure the performance of universities or on the measurement of the performance of universities that have implemented digital modes of teaching or that have adopted e-governance models; (b) if the focus of performance is mainly conceptualized taking into account an external or an internal perspective. Further, the methodological approach of the research and the context analyzed are interesting aspects to be detected. In sum, the current research aims at analyzing a scientific debate still in evolution, being exploratory in nature, and at identifying emerging issues and possible areas for future research through a systematic review of previous studies.

3 Research Method

This research is based on a systematic analysis of the international literature published in academic journals across disciplines, designed to be both methodologically rigorous and theoretically interesting. Paper search and analysis were conducted through a well-documented process (Tranfield et al., 2003) consisting of the following phases.

The first phase consisted of the definition of the search protocol. The keywords to guide the paper search and the databases used to search for papers were first defined. The keywords were formulated to reflect the two key dimensions of this analysis: field of reference and theme. Regarding the field of reference, namely the higher education field, the most commonly-used terms were identified to represent the university world (higher education; universit*). To delimit the theme of the analysis, a combination of keywords was used to capture both the dimension of digitalization (digital*; big data) and the dimension of performance (performance).

Multiple searches were conducted on two distinct databases: EBSCOHost (Business Source Complete) and Scopus. While EBSCO is a predominantly economic, business and social science database, Scopus is a bibliographic database of abstracts and citations from scientific literature that indexes journal titles in the scientific, medical, technical and humanistic fields. For this reason, searches on the Scopus database were delimited, giving priority to the business, management and accounting areas. In addition, three additional research strings guided the selection of the studies:

- *First parameter* (language): to avoid translation problems, only papers written in English were selected.
- *Second parameter* (time period): the research did not impose time constraints as it was aimed at identifying the origin of the academic debate on the topic under analysis.
- *Third parameter* (source): the analysis was limited to articles published in academic journals. Analysis of literature is usually characterized by an evaluation of the quality of documents, often replaced, as in this case, by the evaluation of journals (Tranfield et al., 2003). Journals were classified according to the information reported on the SCImago portal.

Table 1 summarizes the key elements of the search protocol.

Once keywords, databases and search protocol were defined, the second phase consisted of the creation of the dataset. In this phase, the database searches were carried out (step A) and the records obtained were analyzed on the basis of title and abstract to select only papers in line with the research theme (step B). The papers resulting from each database were integrated and duplicates were deleted (step C). Finally, the papers were subject to further careful reading by the two researchers, who separately evaluated each paper to ensure its relevance to the research topic.

Table 1 The search protocol

SCOPUS	
Boolean/phrase	("higher education" or "universit*") AND ("digital*" or "big data") AND ("performance") in TITLE—ABSTRACT—KEYWORDS
Language	English
Document type	Paper
Source	Journal
Research field	Business, management and accounting
EBSCO	
Search 1	
Boolean/phrase	("higher education" or "universit*") AND ("digital*") AND ("performance") in ABSTRACT
Language	English
Source	Journal
Search 2	
Boolean/phrase	("higher education" or "universit*") AND ("big data") AND ("performance") in ABSTRACT
Language	English
Source	Journal

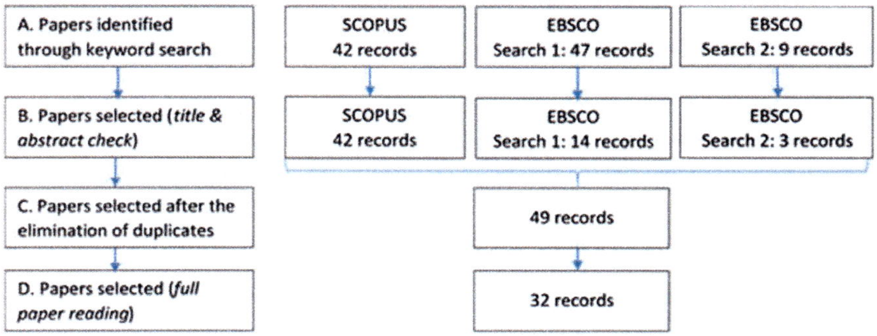

Fig. 1 The search process

Discordant cases were discussed and the final dataset was defined (step D). Figure 1 illustrates the various steps and the results of each step.

The final dataset is composed of 32 papers, which were the subject of the analysis described in the next section.

4 The Framework of Analysis

The analysis of the selected papers was carried out in two phases. In a first descriptive phase, the dataset was analyzed in order to identify and categorize the distinctive elements of the papers considering the following elements:

- *Year of publication*
- *Disciplinary area*: the journals in which the papers of the dataset were published were classified with respect to their main disciplinary area as indicated on the SCImago portal.
- *Methodology*: papers were classified into 'empirical' or 'conceptual' research (Anessi-Pessina et al. 2017; Flick, 2009), where empirical papers are qualitative, quantitative or mixed approach research based on the collection and analysis of empirical material, while conceptual papers include literature reviews, normative documents discussing best practices or developing conceptual models on the topic of interest.
- *Research context*: the geographical continent in which the research was conducted was considered in order to define the research context.

These four elements represent key factors in defining the characteristics of a set of academic studies allowing the analysis of: (1) the time span in which the different contributions on the topic were published and the academic interest developed, (2) the disciplinary approach to the topic, (3) the methodology adopted to investigate the topic and (4) the context in which the research was conducted.

In the second phase, a thematic analysis was carried out in order to deepen the analysis of the papers and identify the main issues addressed thus far. The analysis started from the study of the research questions and the objectives of each paper to find out the key themes, namely the purpose of the digitalization analyzed by the studies of the dataset. The coding scheme was developed in an interactive way. The papers were read individually by the researchers, to suggest a possible classification. In this regard, reflecting on the focus of each paper of the dataset, some 'labels' were formulated and proposed to classify and codify the various themes. In total, ten labels were initially coined by the two researchers (e.g., e-governance; digital governance; digital learning; digital academic scholarship). The classification proposal was discussed in order to converge on a common coding scheme. In some cases, it appeared that different terms were proposed by researchers to identify similar themes (e.g., e-governance and digital governance). Hence, they were made homogeneous (e.g., digitalization of governance and services). In other cases, the researchers further analyzed the papers to find the most appropriate labels (e.g., digital academic scholarship) comparing the classifications. In the end, a list of four labels was set to identify the purpose of the digitalization: digitalization of learning/teaching; digitalization of performance system; digitalization of academic work; digitalization of governance and services. The agreed labels were jointly assigned to the papers. After the analysis of the purpose of digitalization, notes were taken on the conceptualization and focus of performance in each paper to find out whether the interest was, for instance, in student performance, departmental performance, the performance of digital tools and so on.

The results of the descriptive and thematic analysis are discussed in the next sections.

5 Description of the Dataset

The analysis of the year of publication clearly shows a growing trend that has seen a significant increase in contributions on the subject over the last three years (Fig. 2). The apparently smaller number of papers published in the year 2020 can probably be explained by the fact that the search was conducted in the first half of 2020. The topic remains highly topical and evolving.

The analysis of the journals in which the papers under analysis were published highlights the interdisciplinary/multidisciplinary nature of the debate on the subject. The analysis was conducted considering the primary area of reference of the journals on the SCImago portal. The results highlight the predominance of articles published in 'business, management, & accounting' and 'social science' journals. Numerous other studies have been published in journals belonging to different disciplinary areas, which include 'engineering', 'decision sciences' and 'computer sciences' and finally 'economics, econometrics, & finance' (Table 2). Hence, the topic under analysis appears to have been investigated across multiple disciplines. The journals in which the papers of the dataset were published often belong to different disciplines,

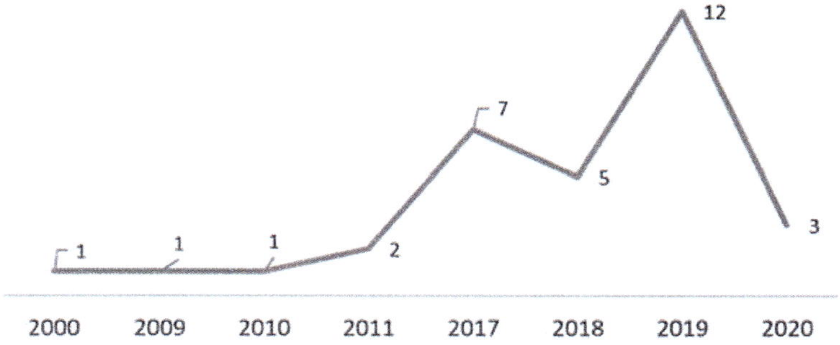

Fig. 2 The distribution of the papers over time

suggesting an openness to multidisciplinary and interdisciplinary studies. The variety of journals and disciplinary areas can first be explained considering the multidisciplinary nature of the theme itself, ranging from the analysis of computer systems and tools supporting the digitalization of processes and activities (e.g., as shown by the fields of computer sciences, engineering, etc.) to an in-depth examination of the implications that these systems and tools have on governance systems and university planning and control processes (e.g., business, management and accounting; social sciences). However, the analysis of the papers has shown that the interdisciplinary nature of the journals is not always reflected in the studies. Indeed, a real integration of different disciplines in addressing the linkage between digitalization and performance is not visible.

The analysis of the methodological approach of the papers under analysis then highlighted the predominance of empirical papers (n. 22) compared to conceptual papers (n. 10). Among the empirical papers, it is interesting to highlight the presence of research conducted through quasi-experimental designs (n. 5), aimed mainly at verifying the impact of digital teaching tools on students' learning. In a few cases (n. 2), there are also mixed approach papers, carried out through questionnaires and interviews. Among the remaining empirical papers, quantitative research is the main component (n. 9).

Finally, the analysis of research contexts (Table 3) shows a significant interest in the topic in Asia in recent years (publications are concentrated between 2017 and 2020). In particular, the attention seems to be greater in developing contexts, such as Malaysia and Indonesia. Next, America and Europe represent equally investigated contexts and in particular the first paper of the dataset published in 2000 deepened the case of a university library in California.

Table 2 The disciplinary approach

Disciplinary area	No. of papers
Business, Management, and Accounting; Social Science	8
Business, Management, and Accounting	5
Business, Management, and Accounting; Engineering	4
Business, Management, and Accounting; Computer Science; Decision Science	2
Business, Management, and Accounting; Decision Science	2
Business, Management, and Accounting; Economics, Econometrics, and Finance	2
Engineering; Social Sciences	2
Social Sciences	2
Business, Management, and Accounting; Energy; Engineering; Environmental Science	1
Business, Management, and Accounting; Psychology	1
Economics, Econometrics, and Finance	1
Engineering	1
Arts & Humanities; Business, Management, and Accounting; Economics, Econometrics, and Finance; Social Sciences	1

Table 3 The distribution of the papers over space

Research context	No. of papers
Asia	9
America	6
Europe	6
Africa	2
Oceania (Australia)	2
N/A	7

6 A Thematic Analysis

The thematic analysis led to the identification of four main thematic areas, each of which corresponds to a specific purpose of the digitalization process shown in the corresponding label. In this perspective, we identified four main themes emerging from the analysis of the research focus, namely:

- the digitalization of learning/teaching resources and tools ('Digitalization of learning/teaching')
- the digitalization of performance measurement systems ('Digitalization of performance system')
- the digitalization of the work carried out by the academics with reference to the multiple activities usually performed, from teaching to research and third mission

Table 4 The purpose of digitalization

Research themes	No. of papers
Digitalization of learning/teaching	15
Digitalization of performance system	8
Digitalization of academic work	5*
Digitalization of governance and services	5*

* One study has been included in both the categories

and consequently the perceptions of the academics of their role in this digital context ('Digitalization of academic work')

- the digitalization of governance and university structures and services ('Digitalization of governance and services').

This analysis made it possible to recognize the different interpretations of the phenomenon of digitalization in the context of universities with reference to the papers analyzed (Table 4, Appendix).

The results of this analysis highlighted the significant predominance of the 'Digitalization of learning/teaching' dimension. Specifically, 47% of the papers in the dataset analyzed the digitalization of teaching methods and resources used by students to carry out their university studies.

There is also a growing interest in the 'Digitalization of performance system' dimension, since these studies have been published mostly in the last few years, even though the papers on this topic are published in interdisciplinary journals with a limited contribution from management and accounting journals.

Residual attention seems to be devoted to the theme of 'Digitalization of governance and services' and 'Digitalization of academic work', with one study dealing with both perspectives. In this regard, it is interesting to note that the studies that have adopted the 'Digitalization of academic work' perspective are also the most recent (all published in 2019) with a more critical approach to the topic, which has initiated a discussion on the transformation of academics in the digital age.

The analysis focusing on the interpretation of digitalization and the investigation of its purpose was integrated with the analysis focusing on performance in this debate, distinguishing whether the performance is conceptualized considering mainly an external or an internal perspective. In the first case, it implies that performance is built mostly around the need to satisfy expectations and the needs of external stakeholders, while in the second case, an internal approach reveals more attention being paid to how performance is conceptualized and managed to consider internal concerns.

6.1 Digitalization of Learning/Teaching

The analysis of the papers shows that the predominant interpretation of digitalization with respect to learning and teaching methods is complemented by the analysis of student performance. Research has mainly investigated the impact of digital modes of teaching on students' learning outcomes and demonstrated how their use allows for a general improvement in learning (e.g., Hamzah et al., 2019). In some cases, the perception of performance has been analyzed, as in the case of Foster and Stagl's work (2018), which examined student satisfaction with the use of an alternative teaching mode, defined as an 'inverted classroom model', according to which the key contents of a course are delivered through video lectures and online tools, while classroom lessons are dedicated to moments of interaction and discussion. The research on online teaching and learning modes also sees a growing interest in studying the impact of online social networks on student performance (e.g., Gonzalez et al., 2019). In most cases, therefore, the focus has been on the effects generated on students and performance has been measured in terms of students' satisfaction or achievements (external perspective). Accordingly, it can be stated that an external market approach is prevalent whereby universities are considered providers of services to students, who measure the performance of university courses based on the extent to which courses meet their expectations (Vakkuri & Johanson, 2020). In a more limited number of cases, research has focused on requirements necessary for the effectiveness of digital teaching (e-learning) and for a transition to digital resources (e.g., Farhan et al., 2019; Tay & Low, 2017). In these latter cases, which represent a residual component, a broader perspective is adopted, recognizing both the different variables which influence the performance of digital processes and the different actors involved.

6.2 Digitalization of Performance System

The papers included in the category 'Digitalization of performance system' are studies that investigate tools or models facilitating performance assessment and improvement. The majority of these studies analyze the use of digital tools, algorithms and analytics to measure performance. The focus is on the digitalization of the tools used to measure performance and this perspective is then analyzed in combination with the focus on performance, namely with the level at which performance is measured. In this latter regard, attention has mainly been paid to the potential of digital technologies and digital datasets to support the measurement of student performance by assessing student assignments or their achievement of learning outcomes. This approach confirms the predominant tendency towards the adoption of a market-driven orientation focusing on the student perspective (external perspective). In a few other cases, digital frameworks are proposed to measure performance from a more comprehensive perspective, for instance, in terms of resource utilization (utilization rate of university human resources, utilization rate of school buildings), which can ultimately influence the number of graduates (Huan & Bo, 2018), or combining people, process, technology, change management and communication and governance elements (Al Rashdi & Nair, 2017). Finally, Attaran et al. (2018) have explored how analytics can be used in higher education institutions in order to improve performance, for instance, by identifying at-risk students and helping them, or finding potential donors. From this perspective, the role of technology is investigated as a driver of performance rather than as a tool to measure results.

6.3 Digitalization of Academic Work

The category 'Digitalization of academic work' includes studies discussing the figure of the academic in the new digital context, addressing the issue of performance measurement and critically discussing its multiple dimensions and implications. This perspective allows a discussion of the consequences that a digital transformation can have on interpreting and perceiving one's work. In this regard, the research of Nørreklit et al. (2019) explores the consequences that a digital language, introduced into universities through performance measures based on digital tools, can have on the work of the academic, through a significant change in the academic 'cognitive habitus', that is the social space in which academics traditionally confront and carry out their activities. The tension between the core values of accounting research (as the search for novel, rigorous, significant and authentic research) and the metrics used to measure the quality of academic research is recognized and discussed in light of the digitalization of tools and processes (Guthrie et al., 2019; Nørreklit et al., 2019). The growing reliance on rankings and their integration with citations, big data and digital metrics (e.g., n. of paper downloads) have reinforced the development of an evaluative culture and can contribute to penalizing academic freedom in favor of a culture of excellence (Guthrie et al., 2019). The availability of research in online repositories, indexing systems and the consequent online visibility of academics are all factors used by researchers themselves to assess the scientific publication performance based on 'empirical evidence' (Sasvári & Nemeslaki, 2019). This latter study reveals how the publication strategy can be dictated by the leading rankings and how, when national and international rankings and indexing systems are not aligned, performance assessment can diverge and the same university, department or scholar can be assessed positively or negatively based on the language and perspective adopted. This leads to reflection on the significant implications that digitalization is having on the academic sector and on the future of the 'public intellectual' (Murphy & Costa, 2019), who is increasingly becoming a digital academic entrepreneur (Rippa & Secundo, 2019). Interestingly, the discussion of the concept of 'Digital academic entrepreneurship' identifies the following key reflection points: Why are digital technologies adopted for academic entrepreneurship? What are the forms of digital academic entrepreneurship (e.g., start-ups supported by digital technologies)? Who are the stakeholders involved? How do the digital technologies support academic entrepreneurship (e.g., free online courses, experimental labs, social media)? (Rippa & Secundo, 2019). Digitalization is claimed to be able to support the creation of a more open community, the achievement of greater knowledge sharing and facilitation of innovation by exploiting the potential of new digital technologies to increase the number of potential users of digital products and services. At the same time, digitalization poses new challenges and may not live up to its expectations. A contradiction emerges observing, on the one hand, the expected benefits of a web-based academic scholarship and, on the other hand, the apparent decline of the public intellectual (Murphy & Costa, 2019).

According to this category of studies, the need emerges for 'looking at the web beyond its functional use as a tool and interpreting it simultaneously as a field of practice and a space of empowerment' which leads 'to new understandings of digital practices' (Murphy & Costa, 2019: 208). Digital technologies create a new space in which to act and communicate and impose a new language, which can create a new culture that excludes scholarly insights (Nørreklit et al., 2019). Therefore, it becomes of pivotal importance to pay further attention to the understanding of digital technologies in order to be aware of their potential implications and manage their use and integration in the governance systems of universities.

6.4 Digitalization of Governance and Services

The 'Digitalization of governance and services' category includes studies that have analyzed the digitalization of governance structures and services, such as the digitalization of the library, the wireless campus and the digitalization of communication with the consequent expected improvement of performance (e.g., Miller et al., 2018; Rankin, 2000). For instance, the study by Rankin (2000) focuses on the 'disrupted' changes in the university library determined by the development of digital technologies. The implications of these changes are broadly discussed, including the impact on infrastructure, staff competences, development of consortia and design of research and teaching programmes.

Another study deals with the relevance of training to improve digital competences and consequently to improve the 'customer' perceptions, by stressing the role of digital tools to implement training courses (Miller et al., 2018). In particular, the study addresses the potential positive impact on staff motivation obtained by the employment of digital tools, such as digital rankings, whereby the staff can monitor the advancement of their competences (Miller et al., 2018). In these studies, performance is loosely conceptualized since there is a broad claim of the benefits of digitalization, which can range from improved communication and speedy information to easier access to resources by students and staff and improved transparency. However, these benefits are not critically discussed or empirically analyzed, with the exception of one research study, which combines the analysis of governance and the role of academics (Nørreklit et al., 2019). This latter study by Nørreklit et al. has critically analyzed the application of governance models driven by digital technologies to the measurement of performance, pointing out the controversial effects on the academic role, as discussed in the previous section.

6.5 *A Summary of the Results of the Thematic Analysis*

The following matrix summarizes the results of the thematic analysis, highlighting the internal, external or mixed focus of performance enhanced by the digitalization of processes and activities within the different purposes of digitalization as identified in this thematic analysis (Fig. 3).

7 Discussion and Conclusions

The current review analyses the academic literature on digitalization and performance in universities in order to identify the perspectives through which the topic has mainly been studied in order to understand the key aspects of the debate and to identify possible areas for future development. The search conducted has identified 32 papers, published in academic journals across different disciplines. A steady increase in publications over the last four years highlights the growing interest in the topic.

FOCUS OF PERFORMANCE	PURPOSE OF DIGITALIZATION: LEARNING/ TEACHING	PERFORMANCE SYSTEM	ACADEMIC WORK	GOVERNANCE & SERVICES
EXTERNAL	Performance as meeting the students' expectations through the digitalization of tools and resources	Performance as students' achievements measured through digital tools		
INTERNAL		Performance as resource utilization measured through digital tools	New conceptualization of performance as impacted by digital technologies IT-based performance measurement models transforming the academic language	IT-based performance measurement models transforming the academic language
MIXED	Performance as novel digital teaching made possible through the consideration of different interests and needs	Performance as result of a mix of factors, internal and external to the university, identified/ managed through digital tools		E-governance and digitalization of services as a tool to improve performance

Fig. 3 Thematic analysis

The studies, mainly of an empirical nature, have spanned several continents, with a particular focus on developing contexts.

The thematic analysis of the papers included in the dataset has highlighted the prevailing interpretation of digitalization as an opportunity to innovate and expand teaching and learning methods. This translates into a specific focus on student performance and satisfaction. The majority of the studies in the dataset reveal a concern for external accountability, towards students or towards institutions in the sector in order to ensure their satisfaction, rather than towards internal actors.

In turn, the impact of digitalization on the various activities of academics (research and third mission), and even more on their perception of the role to be played in new contexts, is not sufficiently recognized or analyzed (Nørreklit et al., 2019).

Further, according to the papers analyzed, significant attention has been paid to digitalization as a *tool* whereby it is possible to deliver new services (e.g., digital courses) with effects on performance or whereby it is possible to measure performance. In this latter regard, according to the dataset, more attention has thus far been paid to the study of digital tools through which performance can be measured rather than to the object of their measurement and how this information is then discussed and used (even digitally). Most of these studies seem to adhere to a market approach, within which universities are service providers, where digitalization supports the meeting of the needs and expectations of constituencies and performance is pursued by legitimization through satisfaction (Vakkuri & Johanson, 2020).

However, digitalization does not concern only instruments, but it transforms the way of acting, interacting and achieving results, often replacing dialogue with unidirectional communication of data. It introduces a new language that significantly changes what the academic has to do, how it has to be done and how it will be evaluated (e.g., everyone's 'performance' becomes visible to all in an immediate but partial way). A digital language changes communication and relationships between actors, namely between academics and students, as well as among academics, between academics and the non-scientific community and between academics, managers and administrators. The new digital language therefore also influences the way of understanding and measuring performance and making decisions. According to the dataset analyzed, these impacts of digitalization have received only limited attention. If, on the one hand, digitalization opens the way to new opportunities and possibilities for actors (e.g., distance learning, greater sharing of events and scientific results), on the other hand, it creates new challenges that need to be critically and carefully analyzed. The benefits of digitalization can be overcome by its costs. In fact, the hybridity of knowledge-intensive public organizations such as universities—if considering the existence of multiple goals, competing types of institutional logic among academics and managers, diverse funding mechanisms and various forms of controls and accounting tools—renders the relationship between digitalization and performance a very sensitive topic. As Vakkuri and Johanson (2020) have observed, there are ambiguities associated with measuring performance in hybrid organizations that need to be carefully considered to mitigate new variations of performance measurement ambiguities, disappointments and problems.

The review shows that the debate on digitalization *and* performance in the higher education field is still under-developed and fragmented. Several issues are addressed in the papers of the dataset, ranging from the digitalization of teaching to the digitalization of governance structures and performance systems. However, there is a limited conceptualization and analysis of the multiple links existing between these issues and between them and performance. The studies are published in journals belonging to different disciplinary fields and this may suggest that several streams of literature exist to address specific issues, with a limited use of interdisciplinary approaches to the topic. The conceptualization and discussion of performance considering the development of digitalization thus call for further analysis. While the debate on the implications of performance measurement and management is quite developed, and recognizes the critical effects deriving from an excessive focus on measures, indicators and rankings (e.g., Dobija et al., 2019; Humphrey & Gendron, 2015; Pianezzi et al., 2020), the role of digitalization in this debate is not explicitly recognized and discussed.

In only a few cases, digitalization is explicitly explored as a tool for obtaining information and consequently supporting and revising decision-making. In this regard, our review points out the limited attention paid to analyzing whether digitalization can contribute to increasing the relevance of performance measurement and changing the role played by academics. Further, according to our dataset, accounting journals have dedicated limited attention to this topic, which confirms that the implications of digitalization on accounting systems and accountability mechanisms are explored in only a limited way (Agostino et al., 2021). From one perspective, it emerges that digitalization is changing the higher education field from multiple perspectives, contributing to making it more complex, variegated and hybrid. Indeed, the studies in the dataset have pointed out the changes that have occurred in activities, structures and services. However, we found a restrained analysis of the underlying and more profound changes in behaviors and values from digitalization.

7.1 Research Agenda

In this context and on the basis of the analysis of the papers, several aspects call for further research, as listed below and then discussed:

- Digitalization of the language and not only of the tools: what are the implications?
- Effects on performance: of what? For whom?
- Accounting implications of digitalization
- Digitalization and the multiple missions of university: an integrated perspective
- Digitalization not as a panacea: costs and benefits

First, the strand of study focusing on metrics and digital tools to support performance measurement requires going beyond the analysis of the technicalities of these tools and instead deepening the object of the measurement, the identification of appropriate measures and how performance information is communicated and used through the digital tools. Does the interpretation of the concept of performance change as a result of the digitalization of the language used in universities? Does the availability of multiple and real-time data change the decision-making process? These research questions put further emphasis on the role of the academic in this new context characterized by the spread of digitalization. Moreover, the studies focusing on the 'Digitalization of performance system' are published in interdisciplinary journals but with a limited contribution from management and accounting journals, whose contribution could be stronger to shed light on the implications of digitalization on accounting systems and accountability mechanisms. The availability of new and multiple data does not leave the decision-making processes within universities unchanged.

In addition, studies focusing on the performance analysis of universities that have started digital activities should not be limited to the consideration of the phenomenon of digitalization as applied to teaching and learning; they need to investigate the other activities and dimensions of university governance. A more integrated approach is suggested. This also implies that more attention can be paid to the performance of other activities affected by digitalization (apart from teaching).

Finally, and most importantly, digitalization does not concern only tools, but it creates a new space and language, which can significantly influence the governance of universities and the work of academics. Therefore, it becomes pivotal to further investigate the costs and benefits of digitalization improving the understanding of this complex phenomenon and considering the perspective of the different actors involved, both external and internal.

7.2 Limitations

The work has some limitations. The research, although conducted through a transparent, replicable process based on objective parameters, is affected by the subjectivity with which researchers have defined these parameters. In this regard, research has focused on academic papers, and excludes, for instance, papers presented at conferences or working papers. Although they may be interesting works, these contributions have been excluded in accordance with the parameters usually used for a systemic review and aimed at assessing the quality of the contributions according to standardized and generally agreed standards. Furthermore, the dataset that is analyzed may be considered to be affected by the limited number of studies. Nevertheless, this represents an important result of the research since it points out the still limited extent of the investigation of the topic.

Acknowledgements The current research has been carried out as a part of the international research project funded by EURAM—European Academy of Management (2020). A previous version of this research has been published in the proceedings of the Italian Conference SIDREA 2020.

Appendix

See Table 5.

Table 5 The purpose of digitalization (article title/year)

Digitalization of learning/teaching	
Project, technology and active (PROTECTIVE) learning model to develop digital literacy skills in the twenty-first century	2020
Augmented reality as a digital teaching environment to develop spatial thinking	2017
Design, implementation, and evaluation of an inverted (flipped) classroom model economics for sustainable education course	2018
Digital game-based learning as an innovation to enhance student's achievement for Arabic language classroom	2019
Digitalization of learning resources in a HEI—a lean management perspective	2017
Do Badges Affect Intrinsic Motivation in Introductory Programming Students?	2020
Influence of home media technologies on academic performance of undergraduates	2011
Key factors for defining the conceptual framework for quality assurance in e-learning	2019
Leading entrepreneurial e-learning development in legal education: A longitudinal case study of "universities as learning organizations"	2017
Project, technology and active (PROTECTIVE) learning model to develop digital literacy skills in the twenty-first century	2020
Student attitudes and behaviors towards digital textbooks	2011
Students' perceptions on the use of mobile learning to improve writing proficiency in the mute	2019
The impact of digital citizenship instruction through flipped classroom model on various variables	2018
The Impact of Providing Unlimited Access to Programmable Boards in Digital Design Education	2009
University students and online social networks: Effects and typology	2019

(continued)

Table 5 (continued)

WhatsApp and academic performance among undergraduate students in Ghana: Evidence from the University of Cape Coast	2019
Digitalization of performance system	
A business intelligence framework for Sultan Qaboos University: A case study in the Middle East	2017
A classification algorithm analysis of students' ict competency level using data mining technique	2020
Application of the big data grey relational decision-making algorithm to the evaluation of resource utilization in higher education	2018
Evaluating what students know: Using the rosE portfolio system for institutional and program outcomes assessment tutorial	2010
Identifying patterns of students' academic performance from tracer evaluation using descriptive data mining	2019
Impacting Big Data analytics in higher education through Six Sigma techniques	2017
Opportunities and challenges for big data analytics in US higher education: A conceptual model for implementation	2018
Towards next generation rubrics: An automated assignment feedback system	2017
Digitalization of governance and services	
A decade of restructuring at Meriam Library, California State University, Chico	2000
E-governance in education sector	2019
To Infinity and Beyond—Gamifying IT Service-Desk Training: A Case Study	2018
Moving towards digital governance of university scholars: instigating a post-truth university culture	2019
The antecedent of continuance usage intention of electronic government service by integrating UTAUT and perspectives of expectation-confirmation models in the conflict environment	2017
Digitalization of academic work	
Digital academic entrepreneurship: The potential of digital technologies on academic entrepreneurship	2019
Digital scholarship, higher education and the future of the public intellectual	2019
Moving towards digital governance of university scholars: instigating a post-truth university culture	2019
The cruelty of data about scientific publication performance: An assessment of the visibility of Hungarian social science by analyzing Hungary's main repository	2019
What counts for quality in interdisciplinary accounting research in the next decade: A critical review and reflection	2019

References

(An additional reference list, see below)

Agostino, D., & Arnaboldi, M. (2017). Social media data used in the measurement of public services effectiveness: Empirical evidence from Twitter in higher education institutions. *Public Policy and Administration, 32*(4), 296–322.

Agostino, D., Saliterer, I., & Steccolini, I. (2021). Digitalization, accounting and accountability: A literature review and reflections on future research in public services. Financial Accountability & Management.

Agyemang, G., & Broadbent, J. (2015). Management control systems and research management in universities. *Accounting, Auditing & Accountability Journal, 28*(7), 1018–1046.

Andrews, L. (2019). Public administration, public leadership and the construction of public value in the age of the algorithm and 'big data.' *Public Administration, 97*(2), 296–310.

Anessi-Pessina, E., Barbera, C., Sicilia, M., & Steccolini, I. (2016). Public sector budgeting: A European review of accounting and public management journals. *Accounting, Auditing & Accountability Journal, 29*(3), 491–519.

Argento, D., Dobija, D., & Grossi, G. (2020). The disillusion of calculative practices in academia. *Qualitative Research in Accounting & Management, 17*(1), 1–17.

Boitier, M., & Rivière, A. (2013). Freedom and responsibility for French universities: From global steering to local management. *Accounting, Auditing & Accountability Journal, 26*(4), 616–649.

Bozeman, B., & Youtie, J. (2020). Robotic Bureaucracy: Administrative Burden and Red Tape in University Research. *Public Administration Review, 80*(1), 157–162.

Craig, R., Amernic, J., & Tourish, D. (2014). Perverse audit culture and accountability of the modern public university. *Financial Accountability & Management, 30*(1), 1–24.

Dal Molin, M., Turri, M., & Agasisti, T. (2017). New Public Management Reforms in the Italian Universities: Managerial Tools, Accountability Mechanisms or Simply Compliance? *International Journal of Public Administration, 40*(3), 256–269.

Dobija, D., Górska, A. M., Grossi, G., & Strzelczyk, W. (2019). Rational and symbolic uses of performance measurement: Experiences from Polish universities. Accounting, Auditing & Accountability Journal.

Dunleavy, P., Margetts, H., Bastow, S., & Tinkler, J. (2005). New Public Management is dead: Long live digital-era governance. *Journal of Public Administration Research and Theory, 16*, 467–494.

Espeland, W. N., & Sauder, M. (2007). Rankings and reactivity: How public measures recreate social worlds. *American Journal of Sociology, 113*(1), 1–40.

Ezza, A., Fadda, N., Pischedda, G., & Marinò, L. (2019). Il "grande gap": Gli effetti del performance budgeting sulle politiche di reclutamento delle Università italiane. *Management Control, 2*, 99–121.

Ferlie, E., Musselin, C., & Andresani, G. (2008). The steering of higher education systems: A public management perspective. *Higher Education, 56*(3), 325.

Flick, U. (2009). *An Introduction to Qualitative Research.* Sage Publications.

Francesconi, A., Guarini, E., & Magli, F. (2020). Distorsioni nel sistema di accountability delle Università: Analisi di un caso. *Management Control, 1*, 59–86.

Gamage, P. (2016). New development: Leveraging big data' analytics in the public sector. *Public Money & Management, 36*(5), 385–390.

Gendron, Y. (2008). Constituting the academic performer: The spectre of superficiality and stagnation in academia. *European Accounting Review, 17*(1), 97–127.

Gil-García, J. R., Dawes, S., & Pardo, T. A. (2018). Digital government and public management research: Finding the crossroads. *Public Management Review, 20*(5), 633–646.

Giovanelli, L., Rotondo, F., & Marino, L. (2017). A performance management system to improve student success in Italian public universities: Conditions and critical factors of an IT system. In

N. G. Castellano, R. Lamboglia, & D. Mancini (Eds.), *Reshaping accounting and management control systems* (pp. 203–219). Springer.
Grossi, G., Kallio, K. M., Sargiacomo, M., & Skoog, M. (2019). Accounting, performance management systems and accountability changes in knowledge-intensive public organizations. *Accounting, Auditing & Accountability Journal, 33*(1), 256–280.
Grossi, G., Dobija, D., & Strzelczyk, W. (2020). The impact of competing institutional pressures and logics on the use of performance measurement in hybrid universities. *Public Performance & Management Review, 43*(4), 818–844.
Guarini, E., Magli, F., & Francesconi, A. (2020). Academic logics in changing performance measurement systems. *Qualitative Research in Accounting & Management, 17*(1), 109–142.
Hazemi, R., Hailes, S., & Wilbur, S. (2012). The digital university: Reinventing the academy. Springer Science & Business Media.
Hemsley-Brown, J., & Oplatka, I. (2006). Universities in a competitive global marketplace: A systematic review of the literature on higher education marketing. *International Journal of Public Sector Management, 19*(4), 316–338.
Humphrey, C., & Gendron, Y. (2015). What is going on? The sustainability of accounting academia. *Critical Perspectives on Accounting, 26*(C), 47–66.
Johanson, J. E., & Vakkuri, J. (2017). Governing hybrid organisations: Exploring diversity of institutional life. Routledge.
Johnston, B., MacNeill, S., & Smyth, K. (2019). *Conceptualising the digital university: The intersection of policy, pedagogy and practice*. Springer.
Katzenbach, C., & Ulbricht, L. (2019). Algorithmic governance. Internet. *Policy Review, 8*(4), 1–18.
King, A. (2000). The changing face of accountability: Monitoring and assessing institutional performance in higher education. *The Journal of Higher Education, 71*(4), 411–431.
Kure, N., Nørreklit, H., & Røge, K. M. (2021). Objective and results-based management of universities: Constructing reality or illusions? *Financial Accountability & Management, 37*(2), 204–230.
Lavertu, S. (2016). We all need help: "Big data" and the mismeasure of public administration. *Public Administration Review, 76*(6), 864–872.
Lepori, B., & Montauti, M. (2020). Bringing the organization back in: Flexing structural responses to competing logics in budgeting. *Accounting, Organizations and Society, 80*, 101075.
Lodge, M., & Mennicken, A. (2019). Reflecting on Public Service Regulation by Algorithm. *Yeung K* (pp. 178–200). Algorithmic Regulation, Oxford University Press.
Nørreklit, L., Jack, L., & Nørreklit, H. (2019). Moving towards digital governance of university scholars: Instigating a post-truth university culture. *Journal of Management and Governance, 23*(4), 869–899.
Parker, L. D. (2002). It's been a pleasure doing business with you: A strategic analysis and critique of university change management. *Critical Perspectives on Accounting, 13*(5–6), 603–619.
Parker, L. (2011). University corporatisation: Driving redefinition. *Critical Perspectives on Accounting, 22*(4), 434–450.
Pekkola, E., Pinheiro, R., Geschwind, L., Siekkinen, T., Carvalho, T., & Pulkkinen, K. (2020). Nested hybridity and value definition in public higher education: A conceptual view. In J. Vakkuri & J. Johanson (Eds.), *Hybrid Governance* (pp. 59–80). Organisations and Society.
Pianezzi, D., Nørreklit, H., & Cinquini, L. (2020). Academia After Virtue? An Inquiry into the Moral Character (s) of Academics. *Journal of Business Ethics, 167*, 571–588.
Pollitt, C. (1986). Beyond the managerial model: The case for broadening performance assessment in government and the public services. *Financial Accountability & Management, 2*(3), 155–170.
Rebora, G., & Turri, M. (2011). Critical factors in the use of evaluation in Italian universities. *Higher Education, 61*(5), 531–544.
Rebora, G., & Turri, M. (2013). The UK and Italian research assessment exercises face to face. *Research Policy, 42*(9), 1657–1666.

Ter Bogt, H. J., & Scapens, R. W. (2012). Performance Management in Universities: Effects of the Transition to More Quantitative Measurement Systems. *European Accounting Review, 21*(3), 451–497.

Tieghi, M., Orelli, R. L., & Padovani, E. (2018). Accounting reform in Italian universities. Internal response to accounting change. *Management Control, 1*, 117–138.

Tranfield, D., Denyer, D., & Smart, P. (2003). Towards a methodology for developing evidence-informed management knowledge by means of systematic review. *British Journal of Management, 14*(3), 207–222.

Vakkuri, J., & Johanson, J. E. (2020). Failed promises–performance measurement ambiguities in hybrid universities. *Qualitative Research in Accounting & Management, 17*(1), 33–50.

van Dooren, W., Bouckaert, G., & Halligan, J. (2015). *Performance management in the public sector*. Routledge.

van Helden, J., & Argento, D. (2020). New development: Our hate–love relationship with publication metrics. *Public Money & Management, 40*(2), 174–177.

van Houtum, H., & van Uden, A. (2020). The autoimmunity of the modern university: How its managerialism is self-harming what it claims to protect. Organization.

van der Voort, H. G., Klievink, A. J., Arnaboldi, M., & Meijer, A. J. (2019). Rationality and politics of algorithms. Will the promise of big data survive the dynamics of public decision making? *Government Information Quarterly, 36*(1), 27–38.

The papers of the dataset (cited in the text)*

Afful, B., & Akrong, R. (2019). WhatsApp and academic performance among undergraduate students in Ghana: Evidence from the University of Cape Coast. *Journal of Education for Business, 95*(5), 288–296.

Al Rashdi, S. S., & Nair, S. S. K. (2017). A business intelligence framework for Sultan Qaboos University: A cas e study in the Middle East. *Journal of Intelligence Studies in Business, 7*(3), 35–49.*

Apolinar-Gotardo, M. (2020). A classification algorithm analysis of students' ict competency level using data mining technique. *International Journal of Scientific and Technology Research, 9*(3), 3256–3258.

Attaran, M., Stark, J., & Stotler, D. (2018). Opportunities and challenges for big data analytics in US higher education: A conceptual model for implementation. *Industry and Higher Education, 32*(3), 169–182.*

Carbonell Carrera, C., & Bermejo Asensio, L. A. (2017). Augmented reality as a digital teaching environment to develop spatial thinking. *Cartography and Geographic Information Science, 44*(3), 259–270.

Faaeq, M. K., Abdullah, S. S., Faieq, A. K., Al-Salami, Q. H., Alsamarraie, R., Mohammed, A. O., & Rasheed, M. M. (2017). The antecedent of continuance usage intention of electronic government service by integrating UTAUT and perspectives of expectation-confirmation models in the conflict environment. *International Journal of Economic Research, 14*(19), 311–323.

Facey-Shaw, L., Specht, M., van Rosmalen, P., & Bartley-Bryan, J. (2020). Do Badges Affect Intrinsic Motivation in Introductory Programming Students? *Simulation and Gaming, 51*(1), 33–54.

Farhan, M. K., Talib, H. A., & Mohammed, M. S. (2019). Key factors for defining the conceptual framework for quality assurance in e-learning. *Journal of Information Technology Management, 11*(3), 16–28.*

Foster, G., & Stagl, S. (2018). Design, implementation, and evaluation of an inverted (flipped) classroom model economics for sustainable education course. *Journal of Cleaner Production, 183*, 1323–1336.

Gonzalez, R., Gasco, J., & Llopis, J. (2019). University students and online social networks: Effects and typology. *Journal of Business Research, 101*, 707–714.*
Guthrie, J., Parker, L. D., Dumay, J., & Milne, M. J. (2019). What counts for quality in interdisciplinary accounting research in the next decade: A critical review and reflection. *Accounting, Auditing and Accountability Journal, 32*(1), 2–25.*
Hamzah, M., Ghani, M. T. A., Daud, W. A. A. W., & Ramli, S. (2019). Digital game-based learning as an innovation to enhance student's achievement for arabic language classroom. *International Journal of Recent Technology and Engineering, 8*(3), 2108–2112.*
Hava, K., & Gelibolu, M. F. (2018). The impact of digital citizenship instruction through flipped classroom model on various variables. *Contemporary Educational Technology, 9*(4), 390–404.
Huan, J., & Bo, R. (2018). Application of the big data grey relational decision-making algorithm to the evaluation of resource utilization in higher education. *International Journal of Enterprise Information Systems, 14*(2), 43–55.*
John, D. S., & Md Yunus, M. (2019). Students' perceptions on the use of mobile learning to improve writing proficiency in the MUET. *Pertanika Journal of Social Science and Humanities, 27*(2), 1481–1492.
Krishnaprabu, S. (2019). E-governance in education sector. *International Journal of Recent Technology and Engineering, 8*(1). ISSN: 2277–3878.
Laux, C., Li, N., Seliger, C., & Springer, J. (2017). Impacting Big Data analytics in higher education through Six Sigma techniques. *International Journal of Productivity and Performance Management, 66*(5), 662–679.
Miller, C. L., Grooms, J. C., & King, H. (2018). To infinity and beyond—gamifying IT service-desk training: A case study. *Performance Improvement Quarterly, 31*(3), 249–268.*
Murphy, M., & Costa, C. (2019). Digital scholarship, higher education and the future of the public intellectual. *Futures, 111*, 205–212.*
Nathawitharana, N., Huang, Q., Ong, K.-L., Vitartas, P., Jayaratne, M., Alahakoon, D., Midford, S., Michalewicz, A., Mort, G. S., & Ahmed, T. (2017). Towards next generation rubrics: An automated assignment feedback system. *Australasian Journal of Information Systems, 21*, 1–20.
Nørreklit, L., Jack, L., & Nørreklit, H. (2019). Moving towards digital governance of university scholars: Instigating a post-truth university culture. *Journal of Management and Governance, 23*(4), 869–899.
Radu, M. E., Cole, C., Dabacan, M. A., Harris, J., & Sexton, S. (2009). The Impact of Providing Unlimited Access to Programmable Boards in Digital Design Education. *IEEE Transactions on Education, 54*(2), 174–183.
Rankin, J. E. (2000). A decade of restructuring at Meriam Library, California State University, Chico. *The Bottom Line, 13*(1), 26–33.*
Rippa, P., & Secundo, G. (2019). Digital academic entrepreneurship: The potential of digital technologies on academic entrepreneurship. *Technological Forecasting and Social Change, 146*, 900–911.*
Rohman, F., Fauzan, A., & Yohandri, Y. (2020). Project, Technology and Active (PROTECTIVE) learning model to develop digital literacy skills in the 21st century. *International Journal of Scientific & Technology Research, 9*(1), 12–16.
Sasvári, P. L., & Nemeslaki, A. (2019). The cruelty of data about scientific publication performance: An assessment of the visibility of Hungarian social science by analyzing Hungary's main repository. *Corvinus Journal of Sociology and Social Policy, 10*(2), 125–146.*
Siraj, F., & Bakar, N. A. A. (2019). Identifying patterns of students academic performance from tracer evaluation using descriptive data mining. *International Journal of Recent Technology and Engineering, 8*(2S2), 187–191.
Tay, H. L., & Low, S. W. K. (2017). Digitalization of learning resources in a HEI–a lean management perspective. *International Journal of Productivity and Performance Management, 66*(5), 680–694.*

Trevitt, C., Steed, A., Du Moulin, L., & Foley, T. (2017). Leading entrepreneurial e-learning development in legal education: A longitudinal case study of "universities as learning organisations." *The Learning Organization, 24*(5), 298–311.
Ukwueze, F. N. (2011). Influence of Home Media Technologies on Academic Performance of Undergraduates. *Journal of Home Economics Research, 14*, 255–262.
Weisberg, M. (2011). Student attitudes and behaviors towards digital textbooks. *Publishing Research Quarterly, 27*(2), 188–196.
Williams, J. M. (2010). Evaluating what students know: Using the RosE portfolio system for institutional and program outcomes assessment tutorial. *IEEE Transactions on Professional Communication, 53*(1), 46–57.

Lino Cinquini, Ph.D., is Professor of Business Administration and Management Accounting at the Institute of Management, Scuola Superiore Sant'Anna of Pisa, Italy. His main research areas are Management Accounting and Performance measurement in public and private organizations. He is Editor-in-Chief of Journal of Management and Governance.

Sara Giovanna Mauro, Ph.D., is currently Assistant Professor at the Department of Economics "Marco Biagi", University of Modena and Reggio Emilia, Italy. She holds a Ph.D. in Management and her primary research interests are in public sector budgeting, accounting and performance management.

Chapter 21
Online Household Waste Management: Measurement, Reporting and Awareness Education

Elspeth McKay, Tehmina Khan, and David Teh

Abstract Managing household waste has become a real problem in Australia. One solution is to deal with this dilemma with a circular economy model of waste management; encompassing the repair, reuse and recycling of materials to get as much use out of waste material as possible, identified as a priority for the Victorian State Government. Households play a critical role in all stages of waste management, including reducing, reusing and recycling their waste materials. Research shows undertaking such measures has a dramatic and material impact on the generation of such household waste. This chapter describes a project aimed at evaluating an online interactive training-tool designed to increase awareness of effective household waste management (HWM) strategies. The waste management training-tool will be free and made available to Australian households in Victoria through their mobile phones. The Rasch psychometric model will be used to assess the impact of this waste management training-tool, to provide expected percentages of behavioral improvement.

Keywords Household waste management · Training-tool · Rasch psychometric model · Accounting · Data analytics · Australia

1 Background

The reality of not dealing with the issue of solid waste management is undoubtedly capturing global research attention. We have been looking the other way for far too long now while rubbish piles up, causing important global public health and environmental damage. Measurement of this ecological disaster has resulted in the view that

E. McKay · T. Khan (✉) · D. Teh
RMIT University, Melbourne, VIC, Australia
e-mail: tehmina.khan@rmit.edu.au

E. McKay
e-mail: e.mckay@cogniware.com.au

D. Teh
e-mail: david.teh@rmit.edu.au

T. Rana et al. (eds.), *Handbook of Big Data and Analytics in Accounting and Auditing*,
https://doi.org/10.1007/978-981-19-4460-4_21

doing nothing has economic costs to society 5–10 times greater than the financial costs of proper waste management practice (Wilson, 2016). Since the 2018 international embargo on accepting our solid waste, knowing how to deal with Australian waste products is now a critical problem. There are a variety of opinions on how to mitigate this growing dilemma. Some industrial waste experts feel the solution to the rising landfill is to charge more for dumping such waste as landfill, while others promote subsidies to recycling plants. A more pragmatic view is to focus closely at the root of the problem—the generation of household waste (MacKenzie, 2018). To tackle the looming crisis at an Australian governmental level, the State Parliament of Victoria convened a Legislative Council Environment and Planning Committee to urgently inquire into current circumstances in municipal and industrial recycling and waste management (Baker et al., 2019).

The terms of reference included the following requirements: (1) the responsibility of the Victorian Government to establish and maintain a coherent, efficient and environmentally responsible approach to solid waste management across the State, including assistance to local councils; (2) to ascertain whether the newly implemented international embargo towards receiving Australia's waste was anticipated and responded to appropriately; (3) identify short and long-term solutions to the recycling and waste management system crisis; (4) develop strategies to reduce waste generation and better manage all waste such as soft plastics, compostable paper and pulp, and commercial waste; (5) conduct relevant reviews, inquiries and reports into the waste and recycling industry in other Australian jurisdictions and internationally; and (6) any other related matters (Baker et al., 2019) pp: ix–x].

1.1 Measurement and Reporting for Waste Management: Accounting and Data Analytics Potential

Seminal research in the area of environmental management accounting in the context of local government waste management has been undertaken by (Qian et al., 2011). Qian et al. (2011) have highlighted the issue of lack of accounting information as measurement and reporting practice, in the context of waste management. This has resulted in a negative influence on accountability and efficiency of waste and recycling management.

The current environment in Australia, requires a better, more value adding approach to waste management accounting which needs to encompass a comprehensive understanding of full costs (including externalities) of waste management (Qian et al., 2011).

To promote efficient, value adding and quality waste management, extensive monitoring data on waste generation needs to be collected (Niska & Serkkola, 2018). Advanced data analytical approaches such as self-organizing maps and k-means algorithm have been used in Europe to generate detailed household waste information for optimal waste collection and recycling initiatives (Niska & Serkkola, 2018).

Geographic Information Systems (GIS) have allowed the generation of large data sets, consisting of millions of entries of waste fractions, weights and locations to result in waste collection improvements and efficiencies of routes (Shahrokni, Van_der_Heijde, Lazarevic, & Brandt, 2014).

Technologies such as Internet of Things (IoT) are transforming waste management logistics and waste monitoring, thus increasing cost and time reductions (Malapur & Pattanshetti, 2017).

Environmental management accounting implementation for waste management improvement initiatives has been widely applied in Europe and Asia with impressive results (Bartolomeo et al., 2000; Burritt et al., 2019). Use of big data enabling technologies which facilitate Cloud infrastructures (Chen et al., 2013); which include IoT (Dai et al., 2020; Dogan & Gurcan, 2019) and GIS can result in achieving dramatic waste management efficiencies in Australia (Zhou et al., 2016). They have the potential to facilitate better implementation of environmental management accounting for waste management efficiencies. Discussed below is a potential educational project to improve household waste management behaviors (Babaei et al., 2015; Bartelings & Sterner, 1999) in the State of Victoria. Education and awareness related costs have been identified as critical, yet unrecognized behavior improving costs in EMA (Bennett et al., 2002; Qian et al., 2018; Qian et al., 2018).

2 Project Introduction

Household waste management (HWM) behavior is the problem we address in this project. Households all around Australia have been facing the critical question of dealing with waste effectively. Key issues relevant to these households continue to be:

- the contamination of co-mingled recycling (Cleanaway, 2018) which is negatively impacting the ability of waste material to be sold and recycled, and
- forty per cent of waste in municipal landfill bins is organic (Pickin et al., 2018), and that waste is contributing to the production of greenhouses gases, including methane(CSIRO, 2016).

Promotion of the circular economy model of waste management encompasses the repair, reuse and recycling of materials to get as much use out of these waste materials as possible identified as a priority of the Victorian Government (deWit et al., 2019). Households can, therefore, play a critical role in all stages of waste management from a circular economy perspective, including reducing, reusing and recycling. Undertaking such measures can have a dramatic and material impact on a household's generation of waste (ABS, 2007).

2.1 Rationale

Our interactive mobile phone training-tool is the first of its kind, engaging households for Victoria's waste management. It will convey useful waste management information in a simple yet effective manner through a mobile phone for private HWM education. A preliminary search for waste management tools reveals waste management software applications for industrial use only, for example, substances of concern in products (Capterra, 2020; SCIP, 2020). Instead, our mobile phone HWM training-tool will focus on the key factors contributing to the Victorian state government's predicament. The solutions provide simple familial waste management actions that make vast differences, as graphical statistics that are easy to understand and entertaining, giving positive behavioral reinforcements to keep household members engaged.

We will focus on two aspects relating to HWM: education (create an understanding of the problematic issues, and household actions (simple behaviors and their implemented steps) for reduced waste creation that contribute to the circular economy (deWit et al., 2019). This project represents the general community's use of digital technologies to transform their lives through education and training, tapping into the cultural, social and economic benefits for all Victorian citizens.

To this end, this project's initiative uses mobile phone technologies to reach diverse and disadvantaged groups to address a significant community and environmental issue. There is no doubt that waste management is a severe problem for the Australian State of Victoria, reaching a crisis point during the last couple of years since the imposed international embargo on accepting our waste. The average Australian household produces 1.5 tons of waste in a year (Dufton, 2018), and Australians let A.U. $8 billion worth of edible household food go to waste (ABC-News, 2013). This digital HWM training-tool's primary users/beneficiaries are Victorian households, family members, including young children, teens, adults, and elderly citizens. Other benefits include: environment-less waste going to landfills; enhanced recycling facilities; and empowered community involvement with Victorian Local Government jurisdictions. The initial project scope is the Melbourne metropolitan local government areas, within the Australian State of Victoria.

This chapter describes a prescriptive information systems design (ISD) methodology (McKay, 2018) for managing the requirements for an efficient and effective HWM training-tool. A hierarchy task analysis (McKay & Mohamad, 2018) conducted to depict awareness for household waste expressed as the HWM skill development matrix adapted from (McKay & Mohamad, 2018).

Figure 1 shows the result of the task hierarchy analysis, which identified the HWM test instrument specification matrix devised to design household waste management skills and knowledge as test-items. The horizontal axis depicts the training-tool's instructional objectives, the vertical axis used for noting HWM content (or learning/training domain), as shown in more detail in (McKay, 2000). The learning domain shown here is a continuum along the vertical axis, beginning with HWM concepts at one end, developing into more complex conceptual tasks at the other.

Instructional Objectives : HWM Skill Development

		Declarative		Procedural			
		Verbal information skill	Intellectual skill	Intellectual skill	Cognitive Strategy	Cognitive Strategy	
		Concrete concept	Basic rule	Higher-order-rule	Identify sub-tasks	Knowing the 'how'	
		Knows basic terms	Discriminates	Problem solving	Recognizes unstated assumptions	Recall simple prerequisite rules & concepts	
		Knows 'that'	Understands concepts & principles	Applies concepts & principles to new situations		Integrates learning from different areas into a plan for solving a problem	
Task No:	Learning Domain:						Totals:
3	Waste recydining				2 questions		3
2	Reuse	1 question	1 question	2 questions	1 question		2
1	Repair	2 questions	1 question	2 questions			2
	Totals:	3 questions	2 questions	4 questions	3 questions	2 questions	14

Fig. 1 HWM skill development matrix. Measuring HWM awareness outcomes

There were three-categories of digital skill identified along this continuum. The instructional objectives consisted of two-categories of specific HWM knowledge.

Along the horizontal axis, the three skill/knowledge categories of HWM involve two classes of declarative knowledge/skill (McKay, 2000; Theng, 2012): (1) verbal information:*(knowing isolated rules with no real need for understanding* [Theng, 2012]); (2) intellectual capacity: (*knowing how to discriminate between concepts and principles*). Procedural knowledge expressed as two classes: (1) intellectual skill: (*higher-order-rules for HWM problem-solving*); (2) cognitive strategy: (*recognizing sub-tasks*).

3 HCI and Waste Management

Over the last couple of decades, there has been a combined approach to urban management research to focus on the potential of using digital technologies to address the challenge of environmental sustainability.

More recently, the stance taken concentrates on technologies and communications as knowledge networks to address environmental sustainability issues (Ciocoiu, 2011), including waste management. As for information and communications technologies (ICT) impacting on waste management (Berkhout & Hertin, 2004), there are direct effects that are mostly negative; use and disposal of hardware including computers and screens (quite relevant at a household level). Indirect effects are mostly positive as ICT deemed to contribute to increasing efficiency of production processes through 'computer-aided design,' incorporating higher speeds and scales of production.

From a waste management perspective, ICT that includes the Internet of things (IoT) offers potential for increasing efficiencies through implementation of better conventional waste management techniques. Such techniques include: waste monitoring; more efficient dealing with waste volumes; and more accurate waste sorting. Research suggests cities further develop waste management strategy and policy to promote automated resource efficiency with IoT technologies. Having IoT embedded in waste management systems improves resource efficiency, tracking and measurement when acting as an accountability mechanism for waste management governance and cities' reporting of waste management (Teh & Khan, 2020).

Behavioral aspects of ICT potentially have both positive and negative outcomes. A key positive result is a shift to a service economy with associated lower energy and use levels. The negative aspect relates to increases in demand, which negates any positive outcomes from such a change to a service economy (Berkhout & Hertin, 2004). From an HWM perspective, this project's focus is on using a mobile phone training application to positively create HWM awareness.

3.1 Awareness

Although HWM is a national issue in Australia, a localized focus through proper consultation and communications is critical to get a coherent environmental message across to households (Evison & Read, 2001). The general public appears to be much less concerned about household waste disposal than other environmental issues, including traffic congestion, biodiversity loss and chemicals in food (Evison & Read, 2001; Onyx-Environmental-Trust, 1999). Recycling levels in households are generally deemed to be low. Recycling and other types of waste management need to be adequately communicated to the public to positively influence residents' habits, behaviors, and traditions and achieve goals of recycling and recovery (McDonald & Ball, 1998). Awareness and attitudes of people in communities are crucial as their understandings of HWM play a critical role in addressing environmental issues due to waste generation (Momoh & Oladebeye, 2010). Something as rudimentary as the separation of waste into the right bins can be a challenge for some households and requires positive influencing through communications of such personal factors such as attitudes, knowledge and personality variables (Momoh & Oladebeye, 2010). Therefore, this HWM awareness training-tool's main aim is to influence household behaviors towards improvements in personal factors that should positively impact practices towards better waste management at the household level.

4 ISD for Courseware Training

Instructional systems design (ISD) concerns a structured process for designing and developing performance assessment and training solutions (McKay, 2018). Since the advent of Web 2.0, interest in human–computer interaction (HCI) increased (McKay, 2008), affording innovative digital economy transformation reform, shifting the global community from thinking of technology per se towards understanding the changes taking place (Weill & Woerner, 2018). Consequently, corporate CEOs have been busy reinventing their business models to support the next-generation Digi-enterprise (Kerr, 2014). Digitization of the economy extends throughout all sectors (Weill, 2013), where the central theme is to achieve greater customer-centricity. However, the distance education and training sector worked as the earliest next-generation business sector to engage with digital transformation well before Web 2.0 by the universities of Queensland and Western Australia. The information communications technology (ICT) educational/training-tools were slow to adopt customer-centric pedagogy models (T. Evans, 2006). Instead, they were mainly transferring paper-based instructional resources into digital-based files as page-turners devoid of interactive tasks and meaningful feedback.

An evaluation of the primary ISD factors used for designing the HWM training-tool examines the tension between maintaining a well-informed community on awareness measures and effective ISD practice by probing the current training waste management models used by leading Australian industry experts. The study will follow an experimental research design to investigate the effectiveness of using the training-tool for community households to operationalize the interactive effect of instructional format (text-based, text-plus-graphics, text-plus-audio, text-plus-graphics-plus-audio) on training performance outcomes.

4.1 Training-Tool Development

Prescriptive ISD elements that promote successful training outcomes follow the well-known instructional design (ID) principles (M. D. Merrill, 2002a, 2002b) (see Table 1), which involve five principles. (1) a demonstration such as a screen-show or video clips with guided navigation to general information or an organizing structure for a particular instance. Further training enhancement is achievable through peer discussion and demonstration. (2) application, where trainees apply the new knowledge to a newly defined problem using a case study example, complete with suggested solutions and corrective feedback. (3) a task-centered instructional strategy, such as providing more solutions to a given problem graded in a simple-to-complex task progression. (4) the activation principle, where trainees can activate relevant prior knowledge or experience. Best results occur when people are encouraged to share their training activities with others who have previous experiences for further reflection. (5) integration of training newly acquired knowledge on HWM into their everyday world (see Table 2).

Stemming from educational/social science fields, learning by doing with goal-based scenarios (Schank et al., 1993/1994) to depict human behavior have been adopted by many training programs (Biech, 2015; Clark & Mayer, 2013). The quality of Web-based training improved when it offered the possibility of 'doing' over 'telling' (Schank, 2002). Hence, the following six Schank strategies, integrated into the ISD to manage requirements for efficient and effective courseware development, incorporate a goal-based scenario approach (Hsu & Moore, 2011), include:

- learning/training goals to set out the expected procedural or declarative knowledge (Brinck, 2016; McKay & Mohamad, 2018);
- training mission as buy into the training session (Schank et al., 1993/1994);
- cover story acting as a marketing tool (Pallarito, 2012) to catch the trainee's eye;
- scenario operations instructional/training activities the trainees need to perform to fulfil the training mission. They may involve decision points, together with examples and non-examples (Hsu & Moore, 2011) to show the consequences of following or not following the scenario examples described by Merrill (M. D. Merrill, 2002a);
- resources that relate to the information that the trainee requires to complete the training session (Lehman & Conceição, 2010); and
- Feedback: training resources must provide two types of feedback (Heron, 2011).

Table 2 presents the ISD framework used to develop the mobile phone courseware modules on awareness for HWM, which aligns with the Merrill principles of instruction (D. M. Merrill, 2009) and his previous knowledge navigation strategies (M. D. Merrill, 2002a), together with the Schank goal-based strategies (Schank et al., 1993/1994).

Demonstration (D. M. Merrill, 2009): Table 2 shows how the HWM training-tool courseware follows the prescriptive ISD described by McKay (McKay, 2018). The overall training goals demonstrate the circular economy model's main factors (repair, reuse and recycling). While it is equally important to convey the training-tool mission (promote awareness of effective HWM strategies) expressed in simple concepts to initiate user 'buy-in' by explaining 'what's in this for them.' Feedback opportunities afford a formative check-list approach during the training to encourage 'feel good' training experiences.

Application (D. M. Merrill, 2009): the cover story given to set the context for the user. Advantages of understanding the circular economy from a local user's point of view. Here is where the examples and non-examples reside in the training-tool (including the consequences for not following HWM principles

Task-centered scenarios (D. M. Merrill, 2009): the training-tool activities list informational HWM modules. They are presented in no particular order, with a heavy emphasis on experimentation, reaching out to others (Lehman & Conceição, 2010), and feedback opportunities to track skill/knowledge development progress. Chances for trying out newly acquired skills/HWM knowledge provide feedback on progress.

Activation (D. M. Merrill, 2009): reiterative quiz/drag-and-drop modules afford continual HWM skill/knowledge development. A help-desk module links the user to progress and training-tool issues to increase a happy experience with the training-tool (Lehman & Conceição, 2010). The psychometric evaluation of the HWM training-tool, requires the training strategy variables operationalized as text-based, text-plus-graphics, text-plus-audio, and text-plus-graphics-plus-audio) provide the research

Table 1 Combined strategies for courseware ISD practice. ISD framework adapted McKay (2018, p. 9)

Merrill's principles	Schank's strategies	Implications for IS courseware design prescription
	Learning/training goals	• Outline required outcome expectations • Provide mechanisms for participant feedback on training experience
Demonstration	Training mission	• Provide communiqué to promote opportunit for trainee buy-in. Show them what's in it for them
Application	Cover story	• Create motivational tools to engage interest • Provide examples of how the training can be applied in new circumstances
Task-centred	Scenario operations	• Provide corrective feedback • Provide an instances pool of examples and non-examples • Show the consequences of following a non-example
Activation	Resources	• Provide multiple instructional sequences to include: textual, static graphics, multimedia video clips, etc • Embed several case-study examples to highlight training activities in different environments • Provide opportunity to engage with training colleagues to integrate new knowledge and personal experiences
Integration	Feedback	• Provide formative (during the training activities) feedback • Provide an embedded training quiz that allows reiterative participation • Provide summative (testing at the end of the training session) feedback

experimental design requirements for data analysis (McKay, 2000). Key user characteristics such as age range, educational level, occupation, and familial household membership arrangements, provide the pertinent data for conducting a differential item functioning (DIF) analysis drawing on the Rasch measurement theory (Boone et al., 2014). These results provide expected percentages of behavioral improvement to communicate the research results. The starting point is to examine the waste management questionnaire results in terms of the individual participant/person Likert agreement-scores relative to each participant's agreement-score and each questionnaire items behavior relative to each questionnaire item on a standard unidimensional scale. This known as the Person-Item Threshold Distribution where people and Likert agreement levels are displayed together on the same scale.

Integration (D. M. Merrill, 2009): there are formative feedback opportunities sprinkled throughout the training-tool. It is essential to create opportunities for the user to feel they can share their experiences with others (Lehman & Conceição, 2010). Likewise, the summative feedback gives closure to the user and provides qualitative and quantitative data for analysis. It should be noted here that the initial

Table 2 HWM courseware mapped to ISD practice. ISD framework adapted (McKay, 2018, p. 9)

Merrill's principles	Schank's strategies	Implications for IS-design prescription
	Learning/training goals	• Outline required outcome expectations • Provide mechanisms for participant feedback on training experience
Demonstration	Training mission	• Provide communiqué to promote opportunit for trainee buy-in. Show them what's in it for them
Application	Cover story	• Create motivational tools to engage interest • Provide examples of how the training can be applied in new circumstances
Task-centred	Scenario operations	• Provide corrective feedback • Provide an instances pool of examples and non-examples • Show the consequences of following a non-example
Activation	Resources	• Provide multiple instructional sequences to include: textual, static graphics, multimedia video clips, etc • Embed several case-study examples to highlight training activities in different environments • Provide opportunity to engage with training colleagues to integrate new knowledge and personal experiences
Integration	Feedback	• Provide formative (during the training activities) feedback • Provide an embedded training quiz that allows reiterative participation • Provide summative (testing at the end of the training session) feedback

HWM training-tool 'standard university ethics' declaration statements reside where instances of data collection occur.

5 HCI Changing Community Awareness

Total global waste is expected to double from nearly 2 billion tons in 2016 to an estimated 4 billion tons by 2050 as consumer-oriented urban populations grow. As population growth increases consumption and waste, managing this waste is becoming an ever-greater challenge. The waste management crisis intensified when the 2018 international embargo on acceptance of Australian solid waste. Melbourne is Australia's fastest-growing city in the State of Victoria, which has doubled the amount of waste it generates in the past 20 years (Knight, 2019). Similar problems mounted in other Australian states such as New South Wales and Queensland, even though government collects 'huge' levy gains (Hannam, 2019). More sustainable waste management is urgently needed.

Due to the lack of community awareness and environmental awareness among the community and the general public, this results in inappropriate and inefficient disposal of waste and waste management (Kumar et al., 2011). As evidenced above in this paper, the situation is not necessarily better in developed countries. High living standards and per capita income lead to high rates of buying, consuming, and refusing, resulting in more waste (Mmereki et al., 2016). Human activities create waste; however, it is how this waste is handled, stored, collected and disposed of which matters. Research has shown poor waste management has an enormous impact on health, the local and global environment, and the economy. Improper waste management usually results in down-stream costs higher than what it would have cost to manage the waste properly in the first place (Hoornweg & Bhada-Tata, 2012; Zurbrügg, 2003). Also, waste management cannot be entrusted to civic bodies; instead, active involvement of everyday citizens and local communities through awareness generation and a participatory approach should be adopted by governments (Das et al., 2019).

Therefore, it boils down to encouraging the community and general public through education and awareness on waste management. It is about creating or enhancing the general public's understanding of waste management practices and the problematic issues around waste and their household actions; achieving this is changing their mindset and behaviors. The success of this HWM awareness training-tool ultimately lies in the community's response and take-up if we are to contribute to the circular economy. When used regularly, will address the lack of HWM awareness because it appeals to society at large, is interactive, fun and straightforward to use, explained elsewhere as the human-dimension of HCI (McKay, 2008).

HWM training-tool deployment to educate, train, and facilitate household waste contributions implements more effective community-based actions for Victorian waste management. Encouraging such community awareness for HWM also supports the A.U. $129 million spent on the digital economy to take a holistic approach to reduce, reuse and recycle state waste. For example, we are reforming the use of the kerbside recycling local council roll-outs of four color-coded bins to homes across the State. The idea is to encourage better HWM to sort waste, recyclables and organics, into categories such as: food and garden organics; glass and plastics; metal and paper recycling (Andrews, 2020).

5.1 Project Aims

This project aims to initiate a change in the community's awareness, behaviors and actions, through implementing well-informed, motivated and enthusiastic knowledge (Lehman & Conceição, 2010) on better HWM strategies. The training-tool also serves as a tool of hope and perception of positivity at an individual and community level, making a positive difference—contributing to the overall Victorian local government waste and recycling system and strategies. The project stages include:

1. examine current knowledge of waste management practices in general, and in particular, in the State of Victoria;
2. define HWM training through a task analysis;
3. instructional systems design processes;
4. develop system specification;
5. build system;
6. system deployment (testing/feedback);
7. marketing and monitoring activities;
8. analyze psychometric feedback data (Andrich, 2011);
9. report; and
10. project dissemination.

5.2 *Behavioral Change Analysis*

Although attitudes form a prime antecedent to 'pro-environmental HWM behaviors, it is unclear what precisely those attitudes and practices might be (Tucker & Speirs, 2003). One recent research study found that pro-environmental behavior, such as the habit of reusing plastic bags and reducing wastefulness, could promote a higher level of home composting practice (Loan et al., 2019). This project will further analyze what attitudes and behaviors drive change in waste management practices to afford positive behavioral reinforcements and keep household members engaged (Lehman & Conceição, 2010). The resulting psychometric testing will determine people's probability of experiencing similar benefits from using the same digital HWM tool (Andrich, 2011). The success of such a training-tool will ultimately lie in the user's responses. As mentioned before, the training-tool affords household members to create or enhance their understanding of waste management practices, uncover problematic HWM issues, and step up in waste management awareness by changing their behaviors and actions. However, this requires users to reflect on current behaviors and food-related attitudes, beliefs, and lifestyles and changing waste management behaviors – by helping them understand and track their waste management practice across time. The Rasch psychometric model will be used to assess such impact of the waste management training-tool.

Similarly, this will also allow the researchers to understand the complexities of how households deal with waste in the home (Barr et al., 2019). Some significant factors that influenced families to waste management involve: home composting knowledge (Edgerton et al., 2009); attitudes toward home composting (Edgerton et al., 2009; Tucker & Speirs, 2003) the total quantity of food waste generated (Bennagen et al., 2002); and time spent on home composting according to (Bennagen et al., 2002; Edgerton et al., 2009).

Australians let A.U. $8 billion worth of edible food go to waste (Tucker & Speirs, 2003). This analysis can shed light on the understanding of other diverse factors that can influence food-wasting behaviors at the household level to design waste management systems and policies to reduce food waste. This analysis will assess several variables, for example, perceptions of the households' current waste management practices (by considering their waste management practices or food wasting in broader contexts, and comparing to their social circles, such as neighbors, family, and friends, then comparing to their past and future projected behaviors), the perceptions of the municipal waste management system, self-reported waste behaviors, environmental beliefs, and socio-demographic characteristics. Improved household-level waste behaviors allow for the development of targeted place-specific policy interventions and create a sense of capacity to change household behaviors and reduce waste to landfill and solve food wastage issue (Parizeau et al., 2015). It is essential to understand how new behaviors can be stimulated continuously amongst some of the population and how they are maintained throughout time.

It is imperative to understand householders' behaviors in a broader context of other systemic factors that involve: the current waste management practices and systems; local government capacities and priorities; and cultural factors, such as the 'throwaway society' (D. Evans, 2012) or 'out of sight, out of mind' attitude toward waste which is common in Canadian society (deCoverly et al., 2008); as well as other various institutional and cultural factors that can influence individual environmental beliefs and behaviors (Shove, 2010). The next section considers some of these project risks.

5.3 *Main Risks*

The main project risk is the engagement of a suitable application developer for the training-tool, within budget. The developer needs to have the technical skills (and demonstrated experience) of building similar digital tools and the ability to make the training-tool simple and fun to use (Lehman & Conceição, 2010). The project team has access to a range of developers through previous university research projects and will review and select the most appropriate.

A second risk is not having access to relevant data (McKay & Mohamad, 2018), and statistical evidence on household waste specifically focused on Victoria. The logistics of this issue is solved by accessing numerous databases available through the researchers' university library and approaching Municipal Councils directly.

A third risk is poor take-up of the mobile training-tool by households to allow for statistical analysis or positively impact. This risk will be mitigated by approaching several Municipal councils for advertising in their newsletters/website.

5.4 *Project Monitoring*

The Team Leader will have fortnightly meetings to discuss progress and review the critical path and potential issues. The 12-month project Gantt chart with allocated resources will have a critical pathway monitored fortnightly and address any technical, schedule or supply problems (Hass, 2007).

The project focuses on improving waste management training for households, including children, teenagers, adults, and the elderly. Many individuals perceive the waste management problem as an issue that is beyond their control. They feel helpless and confused; they do not know what measures they can implement to make a difference. This project will substantially impact changing behaviors at individual levels for all Victorian families who are willing to access the online tool.

6 Long-Term Sustainability

The main costs are the design, build and testing of the mobile phone HWM training-tool. Once the tool is freely available to Victoria's households, data on use and impact will be automatically collected throughout the online tool's life. The researchers will analyze the data to determine the effects of the training-tool on households, their decision-making, perceptions, and whether the tool has impacted their self-efficacy perception for waste management.

If successful, the tool will be offered for trial with a broader range of local councils and then modified for other Australian jurisdictions and domestic use.

7 Summary

Managing household waste has become a real global problem, with extra burdens on Australian refuse management. The circular economy model of waste management (repair, reuse and recycling of materials) provides an opportunity to adopt solutions that impact the digital economy proving the 'waste not, want not' proverb. To this end, the Victorian State Government in Australia aims to get as much use of waste material as possible. Households play a critical role in all waste management stages, including reducing, reusing and recycling their waste materials. This paper describes a project in progress that aims to evaluate a mobile phone HWM training-tool designed to increase awareness of effective household ways to deal with household waste.

References

ABC-News. (2013). Do Australians waste $8 billion worth of edible food each year? https://www.abc.net.au/news/2013-10-08/food-waste-value-australia/4993930?nw=0

ABS. (2007). *Household waste, Australian bureau of statistics report 4102.0—Australian social trends*. https://www.abs.gov.au/AUSSTATS/abs@.nsf/Latestproducts/E1E64A4DB813BC8BCA25732C00207FF7

Andrews, D. (2020). *Transforming recycling In Victoria*. Transforming recycling in Victoria. Victorian Government (www.vic.gov.au). Government Printer.

Andrich, D. (2011). Rating scales and rasch measurement. *Expert Review Pharmacoeconomics Outcomes Research, 11*(5), 571–585.

Babaei, A. A., Alavi, N., Goudarzi, G., Teymouri, P., Ahmadi, K., & Rafiee, M. (2015). Household recycling knowledge, attitudes and practices towards solid waste management. *Resources, Conservation and Recycling, 102*, 94–100.

Baker, M., Crowe, K., Petrie, A., & Donohue, J. (2019). *Inquiry into recycling and waste management: Final report*. https://www.parliament.vic.gov.au/file_uploads/LCEPC_59-02_Inquiry_into_recycling_and_waste_management__6hNrvBj7.pdf (pp. 94, Session 2018–2019). Victorian Government Printer.

Barr, S., Guilbert, S., Metcalfe, A., Riley, M., Robinson, G., & Tudor, T. (2019). Beyond recycling: An integrated approach for understanding municipal waste management. *Applied Geography, 39*, 67–77.

Bartelings, H., & Sterner, T. (1999). Household waste management in a Swedish municipality: Determinants of waste disposal, recycling and composting. *Environmental and Resource Economics, 13*(4), 473–491.

Bartolomeo, M., Bennett, M., Bouma, J. J., Heydkamp, P., James, P., & Wolters, T. (2000). Environmental management accounting in Europe: Current practice and future potential. *European Accounting Review, 9*(1), 31–52.

Bennagen, M. E., Nepomuceno, G., & Covar, R. (2002). *Solid waste segregation and recycling in Metro Manila: Household attitudes and behavior* Quezon City. https://www.cleanaway.com.au/sustainable-future/contamination-main/

Bennett, M. D., Bouma, J. J., & Wolters, T. J. (2002). *Environmental management accounting: Informational and institutional developments* (Vol. 9). Springer Science & Business Media.

Berkhout, F., & Hertin, J. (2004). De-materialising and Re-materializing: Digital technologies and the environment. *Futures, 36*(8), 903–920.

Biech, E. (2015). *101 Ways to Make learning Active Beyond the Classroom*(pp. 320). http://au.wiley.com/WileyCDA/WileyTitle/productCd-1118971981.html

Boone, W. J., Staver, J. R., & Yale, M. S. (2014). *Rasch analysis in the human sciences*. Springer.

Brinck, I. (2016). Developing an Understanding of Social Norms and Games: Emotional engagement, nonverbal agreement, and conversation. *Theory & Psychology, 24*(6), 737–754.

Burritt, R. L., Herzig, C., Schaltegger, S., & Viere, T. (2019). Diffusion of environmental management accounting for cleaner production: Evidence from some case studies. *Journal of Cleaner Production, 224*, 479–491.

Capterra. (2020). Waste management software. https://www.capterra.com/waste-management-software/

Chen, M., Jin, H., Wen, Y., & Leung, V. C. (2013). Enabling technologies for future data center networking: A primer. *IEEE Network, 27*(4), 8–15.

Ciocoiu, C. (2011). Integrating digital economy and green economy: Opportunities for sustainable development. *Theoretical and Empirical Researches in Urban Management, 6*(1), 33–43.

Clark, R. C., & Mayer, R. E. (2013). *Scenario-based e-learning: Evidence-based guidelines for online workforce learning*. USA.

Cleanaway. (2018). What is recycling contamination. https://www.cleanaway.com.au/sustainable-future/contamination-main/

CSIRO. (2016). Climate change in Australia: Projections for Australia's NRM regions—Greenhouse gases. Planning for climate change in natural resource management. Department of Agriculture, Water and the Environment.

Dai, H. N., Wang, H., Xu, G., Wan, J., & Imran, M. (2020). Big data analytics for manufacturing internet of things: Opportunities, challenges and enabling technologies. *Enterprise Information Systems, 14*(9–10), 1279–1303.

Das, S., Lee, S. H., Kumar, P., Kim, K. H., Lee, S. S., & Bhattacharya, S. S. (2019). Solid waste management: Scope and the challenge of sustainability. *Journal of cleaner production*, 228, 658–678.

deCoverly, E., McDonagh, P., O'Malley, L., & Patterson, M. (2008). Hidden mountain: The social avoidance of waste. *Journal of Macromarketing, 28*(3), 289–303.

deWit, E., Plant, J., & McIntosh, E. (2019). Victoria in the midst of a waste crisis: Broad scale reform recommended. https://www.nortonrosefulbright.com/en/knowledge/publications/efdc1538/victoria-in-the-midst-of-a-waste-crisis-broad-scale-reform-recommended#section2.

Dogan, O., & Gurcan, O. F. (2019). Applications of big data and green IoT-enabling technologies for smart cities. In *Handbook of Research on Big Data and the IoT* (pp. 22–41). IGI Global.

Dufton, E. (2018). 13 Plastic-free household products you should be using. https://www.lifestyle.com.au/shopping/13-plasticfree-household-products-you-should-be-using.aspx

Edgerton, E., McKechnie, J., & Dunleavy, K. (2009). Behavioral determinants of household participation in a home composting scheme. *Environment and Behavior, 41*(2), 151–169.

Evans, D. (2012). Beyond the throwaway society: Ordinary domestic practice and a sociological approach to household food waste. *Sociology, 46*(1), 41–56.

Evans, T. (2006). Distance education in Australia. *European Journal of Engineering Education, 20*(2), 233–234. https://doi.org/10.1080/0304379950200213

Evison, T., & Read, A. (2001). *Local authority recycling and waste—Awareness publicity/promotion, 32*(3–4), 275–291.

Hannam, P. (2019). NSW 'waste crisis' looms even as government collects 'huge' levy gains. https://www.smh.com.au/environment/sustainability/nsw-waste-crisis-landfill-levy-gains-20190104-p50pp3.html.

Hass, K. (2007). The blending of traditional and agile project management. *Project Smart*. http://cs.anu.edu.au/courses/COMP3120/local_docs/readings/the-blending-of-traditional-and-agile-project-management.pdf

Heron, G. (2011). Examining principles of formative and summative feedback. *British Journal of Social Work, 41*(2), 276–295.

Hoornweg, D., & Bhada-Tata, P. (2012). *What a waste: A global review of solid waste management*. Urban Development Series Knowledge Papers No. 15. World Bank. Washington, DC. https://openknowledge.worldbank.org/handle/10986/17388

Hsu, C.-Y., & Moore, D. R. (2011). Formative research on the goal-based scenario model applied to computer delivery and simulation. *The Journal of Applied Instructional Design, 1*(1), 13–24. www.jaidpub.org

Kerr, D. (2014). Digital banking: BBVA's González—The digital banker. https://www.euromoney.com/article/b12kknhm1qdwms/digital-banking-bbvas-gonz225lez-the-digital-banker?copyrightInfo=true.

Knight, B. (2019). Recycling crisis prompts call to switch to six-bins system for Victorian rubbish collection. https://www.abc.net.au/news/2019-10-20/recycling-crisis-victoria-considers-increasing-kerbside-bins/11617258

Kumar, G., Kar, S., & Jain, A. (2011). Health and environmental sanitation in India: Issues for prioritizing control strategies. *Indian Journal of Occupational and Environmental Medicine, 15*(3), 93.

Lehman, R. M., & Conceição, S. C. O. (2010). *Creating a sense of presence in online teaching: How to "be there" for distance learners*. John Wiley.

Loan, L. T., Takahashi, Y., Nomura, H., & Yabe, M. (2019). *Modeling home composting behavior toward sustainable municipal organic waste management at the source in developing countries*. https://kyushu-u.pure.elsevier.com/en/publications/modeling-home-composting-behavior-toward-sustainable-municipal-or

MacKenzie, I. A. (2018). The recycling crisis in Australia: Easy solutions to a hard problem. https://theconversation.com/the-recycling-crisis-in-australia-easy-solutions-to-a-hard-problem-95231

Malapur, B. S., & Pattanshetti, V. R. (2017). *IoT based waste management: An application to smart city. Paper presented at the International Conference on Energy, Communication, Data Analytics and Soft Computing* (ICECDS).

McDonald, S., & Ball, R. (1998). *Public participation in plastics recycling schemes, 22*(3–4), 123–141.

McKay, E. (2000). Measurement of cognitive performance in computer programming concept acquisition: Interactive effects of visual metaphors and the cognitive style construct. *Journal of Applied Measurement, 1*(3), 257–286.

McKay, E. (2008). *The human-dimensions of human-computer interaction: Balancing the HCI equation* (Vol. 3, 1st ed.). IOS Press.

McKay, E. (2018). Prescriptive training courseware: IS-design methodology. *Australasian Journal of Information Systems, 22*. https://doi.org/10.3127/ajis.v22i0.1675

McKay, E., & Mohamad, M. (2018). Big data management skills: Accurate measurement. *Research and Practice in Technology Enhanced Learning, 13*(1), 1–24.

Merrill, D. M. (Ed.). (2009). *First principles of instruction. Instructional design theories and models: Building a common Knowledge base (Vol. III)*. Routledge.

Merrill, M. D. (2002a). First principles of instruction. *ETR&D, 50*(3), 43–59. http://www.indiana.edu/~tedfrick/aect2002a/firstprinciplesbymerrill.pdf

Merrill, M. D. (2002b). Pebble-in-the-pond model for instructional development. *Performance Measurement, 41*(7), 39–44. http://mdavidmerrill.com/Papers/Pebble_in_the_Pond.pdf

Mmereki, D., Baldwin, A., & Li, B. (2016). A comparative analysis of solid waste management in developed, Developing and Lesser Developed Countries. *Environmental Technology Reviews, 5*(1), 120–141.

Momoh, J., & Oladebeye, D. (2010). Assessment of awareness, attitude and willingness of people to participate in household solid waste recycling programme in Ado-Ekiti, Nigeria. *Journal of Applied Sciences in Environmental Sanitation, 5*(1).

Niska, H., & Serkkola, A. (2018). Data analytics approach to create waste generation profiles for waste management and collection. *Waste Management, 77*, 477–485.

Onyx-Environmental-Trust. (1999). *National survey on waste*. Oxford Oxford Brooks University.

Pallarito, K. (2012). Cover story: Head off the competition with marketing strategies that Work. *Hearing Journal, 65*(7), 16,18,20,22. https://doi.org/10.1097/01.HJ0000416271.13977.8d

Parizeau, K., & von-Massow, M., & Martin, R. (2015). Household-level dynamics of food waste production and related beliefs, attitudes, and behaviours in guelph, Ontario. *Waste Management, 35*, 207–217.

Pickin, J., Randell, P., Trinh, J., & Grant, B. (2018). National waste report 2018. In: Department of the Environment and Energy. https://www.environment.gov.au/system/files/resources/7381c1de-31d0-429b-912c-91a6dbc83af7/files/national-waste-report-2018.pdf

Qian, W., Burritt, R., & Monroe, G. (2011). Environmental management accounting in local government: A case of waste management. *Accounting, Auditing & Accountability Journal*, 93–128.

Qian, W., Burritt, R. L., & Monroe, G. S. (2018). Environmental management accounting in local government: Functional and institutional imperatives. *Financial Accountability & Management, 34*(2), 148–165.

Schank, R. C. (2002). *Designing World-Class E-Learning: How IBM, GE, Harvard Business School, & Columbia University are succeeding at e-Learning*. McGraw-Hill.

Schank, R. C., Fano, A., Bell, B., & Jona, M. (1993/1994). The design of goal-based scenarios. *The Journal of the Learning Sciences, 3*(4), 305–345.

SCIP. (2020). New SVHC requirements are coming—Are you ready? https://echa.europa.eu/waste-operators

Shahrokni, H., Van_der_Heijde, B., Lazarevic, D., & Brandt, N. (2014). *Big data GIS analytics towards efficient waste management in Stockholm. Paper presented at the 2014 conference ICT for Sustainability*. Paris.

Shove, E. (2010). Beyond the ABC: Climate change policy and theories of social change. *Environment and Planning A, 42*(6), 1273–1285.

Teh, D., & Khan, T. (2020). As cities grow, the internet of things can help us get on top of the waste crisis. https://theconversation.com/as-cities-grow-the-internet-of-things-can-help-us-get-on-top-of-the-waste-crisis-127917

Theng, L. F. (2012). *Incorporation of Gagn's instructional design in a student-centred multimedia learning environment.* (Master of Science thesis). Multimedia University, Malaysia. (1585768).

Tucker, P., & Speirs, D. (2003). Attitudes and behavioural change in household waste management behaviours. *Journal of Environmental Planning and Management, 46*(2), 289–307.

Weill, P. (2013). Peter weill on digitally driven customer-centricity: An interview with the chairman of MIT-CISR. https://www.bcg.com/publications/2013/digital-transformation-financial-institutions-peter-weill-digitally-driven-customer-centricity.aspx

Weill, P., & Woerner, S. L. (2018). *What's Your Digital Business Model? Six questions to help you build the next-generation enterprise.* Harvard Business Review Press.

Wilson, D. C. (2016). *Responding to the global waste management crisis.* UNEP & ISWA. https://wasteaid.org/responding-global-waste-management-crisis/

Zhou, J., Feng, K., Pei, Z., Meng, F., & Sun, J. (2016). Multivariate analysis combined with GIS to source identification of heavy metals in soils around an abandoned industrial area Eastern China. *Ecotoxicology, 25*(2), 380–388.

Zurbrügg, C. (2003). Urban solid waste management in low-income countries of Asia—How to cope with the garbage crisis. http://www.sandec.ch/Publications/PublicationsHome.htm#SWM

Elspeth McKay, Ph.D., involves developing specialist e-Learning tools that implement digital transformation precision. After 25-years at RMIT University in Melbourne, Australia, she is moving back into her private consultancy, Cogniware. She also holds further qualifications in Instructional Design, Computer Education and Business Information Systems, and is passionate about designing effective eLearning resources for industry training/reskilling programmes and the education sector. She has published extensively in the research fields of HCI and educational technology, with more than 150 peer-reviewed research papers, several educational technology books and has been awarded numerous awards for funded projects.

Tehmina Khan, Ph.D., is a Senior Lecturer in Accounting at RMIT University, Melbourne, Australia. She undertakes research in the area of sustainability (including SDGs, measurement and reporting), accounting and accountability, information systems and internet technologies. Recent projects involve advanced data analytics, artificial intelligence, and machine learning to address sustainability related problems.

David Teh, Ph.D., works in the School of Accounting, Information systems and Supply Chain at the RMIT University, Melbourne, Australia. He focuses on understanding business's challenges and needs, and creating practical solutions, to make visible outcomes and real impact. He has a strong passion for and/or expertise in sustainability, strategy, process improvement, risk management, and technology (data analytics).

Chapter 22
Does Virtual Reality Enhance Taxation (Capital Allowances) Learning? An International Study

Terry Filer and Marc Holmes

Abstract Taxation undergraduate students in Wales, Singapore and China experienced virtual reality (VR) in their learning of taxation, where a real-world capital allowances scenario supported student learning of the topic. Experiential learning can help students improve their understanding of the subject and gain valuable skills for employment or further studies e.g. professional qualifications. Virtual reality is an immersive learning experience that can help students improve their understanding. As a visual learning approach, students are more likely to be able to recall their visual experiences. VR has the benefit of participators experiencing "presence" in their learning, putting themselves in the virtual world making it a memorable and often an enjoyable experience. This study compares student perceptions from students at each of the three universities using a voluntary questionnaire, accessed via a QR reader, before the VR session to capture their knowledge and use of technology plus their thoughts on using VR for learning. A further questionnaire after the VR session captured student's thoughts on their VR learning experience, did they enjoy the experience, did it help their understanding, and would they like to use it more in their studies? A summary of the results demonstrates the majority of students indicated: they were positive about using VR for learning; VR enhanced their learning experience; VR improved tax understanding; They enjoyed using VR; and they would like to see more VR in their studies.

Keywords Virtual reality · Experiential learning · Taxation · Capital allowances · Immersive technology

T. Filer (✉) · M. Holmes
Swansea University, Swansea, Wales, UK
e-mail: T.filer@swansea.ac.uk

M. Holmes
e-mail: marc.holmes@swansea.ac.uk

T. Rana et al. (eds.), *Handbook of Big Data and Analytics in Accounting and Auditing*,
https://doi.org/10.1007/978-981-19-4460-4_22

1 Introduction

Prospective students of accounting are often attracted to study the subject as salary levels are competitive and accounting graduates can gain access to employment opportunities after graduating (Complete University Guide, 2021; UCAS, 2021). Employers often provide study support to graduates in the form of financial support for further education and materials plus paid study time to sit examinations to attract the best candidates as employees and to retain staff by helping them gain a professional accounting qualification (Moy, 2002). Developing accounting talent in house is a considerable investment for many firms but one that can often reap rewards in providing trainees a broader knowledge of the business and industry and to gain deep industry specific knowledge (*Guardian*, 2021).

Many Higher Education Institutions (HEI's) have gained exemptions from professional accounting qualifications allowing bachelors accounting graduates part qualified accountant status thereby minimizing the number of professional accounting examinations they need to sit (Apostolou & Gammie, 2014). Therefore, studying an Accounting related degree helps students to become a professionally qualified accountant in a shorter time period. Added benefits for students in qualifying sooner is the ability to increase their earnings and to be promoted at a faster pace than those students who join the profession directly after school and complete their accountancy studies either by day release or in the evenings at a tertiary college.

Furthermore, qualified accountants enjoy flexibility within the profession to move around various sectors throughout their career leading to a fulfilling working life with plenty of variety (ACCA, 2021).

Academia is one such destination where one often finds accounting instructors holding professional accounting qualifications together with working experience prior to entering the academic community. Many students choose to study at university with the intention of obtaining a good degree outcome that will enable them to gain future employment in the career of their choice. Students often enjoy learning from academic staff that have industry experience as this provides an insight on how that sector operates (Kutluk et al., 2015). Indeed, academics can be inspirational to students who can often decide on a specific career path based on their enjoyment of a subject taught at university or on recommendation from their lecturers (Bradley et al., 2015). Case studies provided by accounting instructors are often based on their industry experience and take a problem based learning approach, which together with the passion for their subject and the real world application of accounting knowledge fuels the student's interest in their chosen field of study and is found to be effective learning approach (Stanley, 2012).

Traditional teaching approaches have previously focused on a "chalk and talk delivery" or are delivered using slides to discuss concepts followed by relevant examples and numerical practice questions. These questions are usually based on explanative text scenarios that require students to use their own imagination and prior experiences to visualize the scenario provided (Kern, 2002).

Instructors at Swansea University aim to bring their subjects alive by introducing real world case studies as part of the students learning to improve student engagement and interest in their accounting studies. However, most case studies are based on explanative text scenarios that require students to use their own imagination, prior experiences, and English proficiency to visualize the scenario provided.

Hence each student's learning experience can be very different and the use of some words that have dual meanings such as plant can lead to confusion, where some students could be thinking of the garden variety compared with the alternative meaning which refers to large manufacturing equipment that is actually intended in the scenario. These issues can be overcome by using photographs or videos to demonstrate the case study being discussed (Carney, 2002), although these mediums are useful they do not provide the same learning experience as visiting a business premises in person. Where students could meet the client, raise queries, note any issues, and view the business premises and equipment first-hand.

From a practical perspective, it is often not possible to take a large class of accounting students to visit a business premises to experience a real-world accounting issue due to logistical challenges, safety, and cost. Hence, the use of a virtual world could be used to overcome the in-person challenges.

Ideally, tax instructors would teach the subject of capital allowances by arranging a visit to a local business as learning by first-hand experience could improve student understanding of the topic (Clayton, 2004) where students could view business assets in situ to consider their value and eligibility. However, where an in-person visit is not practical the use of virtual reality (VR) can allow students to gain real world capital allowances experience by immersing themselves into a VR case study. Indeed, it is often through a client visit when the whole perspective of the business is appreciated (Whitten, 2004).

Through prior professional working experience of submitting a large capital allowances claim for a consortium company, the taxation instructor wished to provide a similar case study experience for undergraduate taxation students when they studied the topic of capital allowances in class. By using a real world case study students would be provided with the opportunity to gain a better appreciation of the more contentious areas that needed to be explored in more detail to draw up an accurate capital allowances claim that meets the relevant criteria for tax authorities. Using textbook case studies tends to provide a scenario that is far more straight forward than that encountered in the real world. VR provides an ideal medium to present a real-world case study where students could virtually visit their client's premises to consider eligible assets to include in their capital allowances claim.

2 Benefits of Virtual Reality

Objective of this study is to explore if VR enhances student learning of the taxation topic capital allowances and to make an international comparison. Where the benefits of an international study will allow tax instructors to deepen their understanding of student learning and explore possibilities for improvement (Blömeke & Paine, 2008).

In the context of this study VR is defined as a 360-degree set of photographs that are viewed as a set of scenarios and accessed using a specialized VR headset.

The benefits of VR learning are providing students with an immersive experience similar to actually being there (Slater & Sanchez-Vives, 2016) without the logistical or risk factors of physically being there (Deb et al., 2017) as the learner could come to harm. In this study access to a similar real world business premises would not be possible for a large student cohort due to logistical issues where there is simply not enough space to accommodate the number of students who wished to view the premises and the danger aspect of accessing a roof top and plant rooms containing sophisticated machinery in a controlled environment. However, VR opens up the possibility of providing real world experiences in a virtual setting that is safe and accessible to all (Squelch, 2001).

For the taxation instructor wishing to providing students with an enjoyable learning experience based on the real world, VR opens up new possibilities to provide students with an experiential learning experience that can improve their understanding of the subject (Kolb, 2014) and gain valuable skills for their employability after graduating or in support of further accounting studies e.g. professional qualifications.

VR as a pedagogic approach has been successfully used in STEM education settings for many years, where student learning in the key areas of knowledge acquisition, understanding, recall and engagement showed improved performance compared to more traditional teaching approaches (Allcoat, 2018). Existing literature in this area is indicative that VR and AR environments improve learning outcomes and are worthwhile in tertiary education settings as they are known to raise the level of student engagement, promote self-learning, enhance spatial ability, help to improve student confidence and enjoyment in their learning (Papanastasiou, 2019). By providing an immersive environment through VR, accounting educators can increase learning opportunities for students where they can gain a holistic experience that could not be provided by visiting in person due to the issues of cost or for impractical reasons due to insufficient space (Schott, 2018). Furthermore, some learning environments could be too dangerous to visit in person e.g. mines, oil rigs, heavy machinery industries and for firefighting training (Engelbrecht, 2019). Through the medium of VR anything is possible where environments can be adapted to achieve learning outcomes. In accounting education, VR has been utilized successfully by the educator for both taxation and auditing subjects through the study of assets, which are easily adapted into a virtual environment and developed into a case study. Students visit the case study to discuss and develop their understanding of the risks and effects on valuation relating to the audit of financial statements or the values used in taxation computations.

However, VR is not the only format that could be used as other effective alternatives including photographs or videos can be beneficial, however neither of these options involve an immersive experience which is the closest to actually being present. Immersive experiences provide a more realistic experience for the students

(Psotka, 1995). Being in the moment or using a visual approach is a very powerful way to learn as it provides a memorable experience that students can recall (Burmark, 2002) when required in the future for either assessment purposes or when students leave University and start working in the accounting profession. Another benefit of immersive technology is that students follow their naturally inquisitive mind to explore the space that they are in either physical or virtual, the same element of surprise and interest take place which can benefit student learning (Siegle, 2019).

Furthermore, the experience can be so powerful that VR users forget where they are and can accidently walk into items around them (Sieberth, 2019).

To overcome the problem of collision accidents while viewing VR, students are encouraged to work in pairs or small groups to share the VR headsets where one student views the case study while another takes notes and ensures the student comes to no harm through their viewing experience. Indeed, when demonstrating VR to accounting colleagues at a conference some have physically tried to walk around the premises assuming they were present in the scenario. This concept of presence is often more enjoyable (Baumgartner et al., 2008; Junghyo Lee, 2019) and memorable for students (Tussyadiah et al., 2018) who can better recall the scenario and their learning of the topic when required to do so.

3 Collaboration Opportunities

Taxation instructors at Swansea university in collaboration with a VR expert from Swansea university's engineering department were able to adapt a text-based case study into a VR case study that could be accessed by all students studying the module. Benefits of collaborative working can achieve shared working goals and greater productivity (Johnson & Johnson, 2009).

Students at Swansea university first experienced VR in 2018 and were very positive about their learning experience. Based on the positive student response received on the initial pilot project, VR is now fully incorporated into teaching and learning the topic of capital allowances where final year taxation students experience their practical seminar using VR every year.

This study seeks to evaluate accounting student's perceptions on the use of VR in their studies of taxation—capital allowances and how this compares with other undergraduate accounting students experience internationally. By extending the study from a single country to an international comparison further evidence of student perceptions on the use of VR for taxation learning can be gained and the effects compared.

An opportunity to involve a Singaporean institution arose by invitation, through the Chartered Institute of Accountants in England and Wales (ICAEW) conference proceedings where the Singaporean university became aware of VR being used to teach undergraduate students in the UK. The Singaporean university wished to share new pedagogical approaches to accounting and taxation learning within their own faculty which resulted in an academic visit being arranged for June 2019. Visiting

Table 1 Cohort numbers

Country of institution	Student cohort size
Wales, UK	182
Singapore	140
China	160

academics have the opportunity to share new learning approaches and best practice with the visiting university (Gao & Liu, 2020) with the aim of improving the quality of teaching and learning at both institutions.

An opportunity to include a Chinese university in the study was possible through a joint program delivery between the Chinese university and Swansea university. One of the modules taught to undergraduate accounting students on the program is the same UK tax module that is delivered to Swansea university students in Wales. The tax instructor is keen to ensure equal opportunities are provided to the Chinese partner students therefore arrangements were made to ensure the Chinese students experienced the same VR exercise in September 2019. Students studying taxation on the joint program are taught in English, so delivery of the 2-h lecture and 1-h VR capital allowances exercise was presented by the same tax instructor.

All students from the three participating institutions were studying a bachelor's degree and had previously studied capital allowances before experiencing the VR case study. Student cohort numbers from each of the institutions featuring in this international study are shown in Table 1.

4 Equipment

Equipment for the case study is an important element of the student experience as some individuals experience motion sickness which can provide a negative experience for that student (Nichols & Patel, 2002). To overcome this problem after the initial pilot using google cardboard headsets plus the student's own smart phone, Swansea University purchased Oculus Go headsets. The benefits of using Oculus Go compared with cardboard headsets are a more immersive experience through the ability to adjust the headset for improved comfort plus a head strap to hold the headset firmly in place allowing the user's hands to be free (see Photo 1). Eye spacing is improved with a different shape of lens viewer making viewing more comfortable for all users irrespective of the width between their eyes. This helps to overcome motion sickness as some individuals, particularly females have a narrower gap between their eyes hence fixed spacing headsets tend to be wider to accommodate as many different eye gaps as possible and will usually be a wider setting. This issue can be resolved to some extent by sharing the headset with other students and limiting the amount of time experiencing VR.

Oculus Go headsets can also accommodate students that wear glasses so that they can remain on while viewing the VR case study or students can choose to remove

Photo 1 Oculus Go VR headsets

them depending on their personal preference. For hygiene reasons wipes are provided so students can clean the lens and fitting area between each student's use. Oculus Go headsets were purchased for around £200 each where Swansea university invested in 15 headsets, a reasonable number for a group of up to 40 students.

Viewing the VR exercise through dedicated use VR headsets allows the instructor to pre-install the software ready for student use before a seminar session, hence, saving time in the learning environment.

Previous use of VR using cardboard headsets were reliant on students downloading the capital allowances app on their own smart phones. Due to the different operating systems android and apple and the variety of smart phones available some students were unable to run the app in VR mode so having pre-installed headsets saved time in resolving students' technical queries. This allowed more time to focus on the learning aspects of capital allowances and required less support from the instructor.

5 Methodology

Using Swansea University campus as the business premises, the taxation instructor compiled a case study that provided virtual visits to a number of locations containing assets that could attract capital allowances. These locations included plantrooms, areas on top of buildings, kitchens and gyms plus offices and classrooms. Each area contained assets that were eligible for capital allowances together with some that were not. Students were required to call on their prior learning of capital allowances via the learning resources available on the virtual learning environment (VLE) and

Photo 2 Opening frame for the capital allowances exercise

through the material delivered in a two-hour lecture prior to the seminar session where VR was presented.

Photo 2 demonstrates the opening frame for the VR capital allowances exercise—Monarch Flight School based at Swansea university bay campus.

5.1 Compiling the Capital Allowances Scenario

Using a 360-degree camera the taxation instructor obtained permission to access areas within the campus that contained relevant assets that could be considered eligible for capital allowances. As some of these areas were only accessible using estate services personnel the building services manager accompanied the instructor throughout the campus tour. Areas such as plantrooms are inherently dangerous places to visit due to the equipment housed there and hazards such as low ceilings and high steps to navigate. Having an experienced estates manager available also provided the opportunity to gain useful information on what the pieces of equipment were together with an indication of their value. Accessing the roof space is a potentially dangerous area with a risk of falling. Having an experienced estates manager present during the visit ensured no damage came to the equipment and the taxation instructor's safety was maintained at all times. Photo 3 demonstrates the roof space housing solar panels that attract 100% capital allowances.

Initially the photographs were captured from several locations across the Bay campus after the photographs were taken the instructor decided on a themed case study around the information that was already provided. Swansea University Engineering Department housed a flight simulator, so the case study was themed on a

Photo 3 Rooftop of the building housing solar panels in room 2

flight training school called the Monarch Flight Training School that had classrooms, a gym, kitchen, outdoor exercise area and equipment housed in plant rooms and on the roof (Photos 4 and 5).

Each photo was provided with a specific room number for ease of reference during the student's learning.

Photo 4 A plant room containing air handling units in room 10

Photo 5 Gym equipment in room 6

Table 2 List of the VR case study rooms students would visit virtually

Room	Description
1	Overview of Bay campus showing location of the case study (Photo 2)
2	Roof of plant room with solar panels (Photo 3)
3	Plant room with air conditioning
4	Kitchen with ovens and other equipment
5	Classroom with flight simulator
6	Gym (Photo 5)
7	Foyer with moveable partitions
8	Foyer 2 with lift
9	Plant room with building management system and air compressors
10	Plant room with air handling units (Photo 4)
11	Plant room with heating pipework
12	Plant room with condenser boilers
13	Plant room with building management system

A list of the various locations/rooms are provided in Table 2.

With the support of VR experienced engineering staff, each scenario was produced using Unity, a specialist software to develop VR projects. The tax instructor's role was to provide relevant comments to each scenario in the photographs where text boxes were created next to the object in the photograph for students to consider. Furthermore, the 360-degree photographs were linked by inserting a green sphere to advance through the rooms and a red sphere to go backwards. Photo 2 demonstrates a green sphere only as this is the first photo in the case study. To negotiate around the case study, students click on a green circle to go forward or a red circle to go backwards in a consecutive order.

The learning behind the case study is that students virtually visit the client's premises with the view of preparing a capital allowances computation from the assets that the business Monarch Flying School owned. Students had the opportunity to learn which assets were eligible for which type of capital allowance available through a two-hour lecture provided before the VR case study was presented. Students should also have been aware that some capital allowances attracted 100% relief whereas others attracted a lower percentage and some assets are not eligible for capital allowances for example the building structure itself.

As stated above each scenario or room contained assets that were eligible for capital allowances at either 100%, 18%, 6% or not eligible. Students needed to identify the asset, its cost and then decide on its eligibility. Once all the assets had been considered the capital allowances computation could be calculated for the business. Through prior study sessions, students were aware of the benefits of capital allowances in reducing taxable trading profits and hence a lower amount of tax payable for that business. Students were fully aware that their main aim in the exercise was to maximize the amount of the capital allowances claim.

Working in pairs or small groups of up to four students each group was provided with an Oculus Go headset that contained the case study saved as an APK app that could be accessed via the device's main menu. The same app was used for all students as this provides a better comparison of results.

Although Chinese tax is different to UK tax the Chinese students are studying UK modules on a joint BA Accounting program. Singaporean students also study capital allowances on their taxation module therefore the VR exercise is deemed appropriate for all three student cohorts.

During each VR session the tax instructor with support from engineering staff set the scene in a seminar group containing around 30 students per group. Having a small group is more manageable should the students experience any technical issues with the headset for example adjustment for comfort or support on how to progress from one room to another and technical capital allowances support, if required. Oculus Go headsets are used with a handheld pointer that the students use for menu control and for moving around the case study by clicking on the green or red circles within the case study app.

Another reason for students to work in small groups is to ensure the safety of the VR user so that they avoid collision accidents with items in the room or with other students. Students were free to decide if they wish to stand or sit during their VR experience depending on their preference. It was quite surprising to see some students able to wear the VR headsets and write notes at the same time, although most students viewed the case study while another student made notes.

From a timing perspective each VR seminar took approximately one hour which also provided time to introduce the activity for the students, view the case study, record their findings, and produce a capital allowances computation. In the final 15 min the instructor held a class discussion on how each group treated the assets while providing the correct solution. This feedback session is an important part of the learning experience (Blair et al., 2013) as it is how students check their understanding on the application of capital allowances in the case study. When compared with a text only based case study the VR exercise provided more of a challenge as it required students to make assumptions on assets eligibility, an element that is not usually present in the text only based questions when students are deciding what is or is not allowable. It is this element where the instructor is bringing their prior professional experience into the classroom using a problem-based learning approach based on their prior working knowledge of the subject. In this case the instructor had previously spent a year preparing and negotiating a multi-million capital allowances claim as part of their accounting role in industry (Breton, 2010).

6 Results

6.1 Results from the VR Pre-session Questionnaire

A pre-session questionnaire built using Survey Monkey was provided to all students at the start of the session before the VR exercise commenced. The same questionnaire was used in Wales, China, and Singapore. Students accessed the pre session questionnaire via a QR code reader using their mobile phones. Questions in the pre session questionnaire requested students to provide demographic information on the students age, gender, degree program plus their general feelings towards exploring new ideas and general technology competency in their own view. Followed by more specific questions on their prior experience of VR plus their perceptions on whether they think VR will help them understand tax better. The number of students who participated in the survey by institution are summarized in Table 3.

Due to a follow up email sent to all Chinese students enrolled on the taxation module more students responded to the post-session questionnaire than the pre-session. Overall, 90 Chinese students participated in the VR seminar session but not all of them completed the questionnaires.

Results of the pre-session questionnaire can be found in Table 4.

The results in Table 4 illustrate that the majority of students from all three institutions are between the ages of 20 and 25 years old with the Singaporean students being slightly older with 78% aged between 22 and 25 years old whereas 70% of both Welsh and Chinese students are between the ages of 20 to 21 years. From the gender perspective we find that there are slightly more females involved in the questionnaire at 57% overall and 41% of males. 2% of students overall preferred not to specify their gender. From an individual institution perspective there are more males participating in Wales and more females participating in China and slightly more females participating in Singapore at 55% compared with 41% of males. 92% of the respondents are studying a bachelor's in accounting with a small percentage of 3% studying finance, 1% studying law and 4% studying another degree (Table 5).

Results from question 4 asked the students how often they explore something that is completely new. This question explores the student's natural curiosity to try out new ideas. From the student responses we find that the majority of students, 48% occasionally explore something new with 30% seldom exploring new ideas, 1% never and 21% regularly. The most explorative students are the Chinese followed by Welsh. Question 5 asked students to describe their general competency in technology. We find the overall result demonstrates 11% of the students considered themselves to be

Table 3 Number of participating students by institution

	Wales, UK	China	Singapore	Total
Pre-session questionnaire	78	56	78	212
Post-session questionnaire	42	80	50	172

Table 4 Demographic results from the pre-session questionnaire

	Wales		China		Singapore		Total	
	No. of students	%	No. of students	%	No. of students	%	No. of students	%
Question 1—How old are you?								
A. 18–19 years	2	3%	12	21%	0	0%	14	7%
B. 20–21 years	57	73%	39	70%	13	17%	109	51%
C. 22–25 years	19	24%	5	9%	61	78%	85	40%
D. 26 years and older	0	0%	0	0%	4	5%	4	2%
	78	100%	56	100%	78	100%	212	100%
Question 2—What is your gender?								
A. Male	41	53%	14	25%	32	41%	87	41%
B. Female	37	47%	40	71%	43	55%	120	57%
C. Other	0	0%	1	2%	0	0%	1	0%
D. Prefer not to say	0	0%	1	2%	3	4%	4	2%
	78	100%	56	100%	78	100%	212	100%
Question 3—What degree program are you studying towards?								
A. BSc/BA Accounting (including Accounting and Finance	75	96%	44	79%	76	97%	195	92%
B. BSc/BA Finance	3	4%	2	4%	1	1%	6	3%
C. BSc/BA Law	0	0%	3	5%		0%	3	1%
D. Other degree	0	0%	7	13%	1	1%	8	4%
	78	100%	56	100%	78	100%	212	100%

experts, 62% considered themselves better than novice but not expert, which is the majority and 24% considered themselves as novices in their technology competency. 3% responded that they were not interested in technology and rarely use it unless essential. From an individual institution perspective, we find that both Welsh and Singaporean students have a response of 68% where students indicated they were better than novice but not expert compared with 45% of the Chinese students. A higher percentage of Chinese students at 18% consider themselves as expert compared with 13% of Welsh students and 5% of Singaporean students.

Table 5 Technology questions from the pre-sessional questionnaire

	Wales		China		Singapore		Total	
	No. of students	%	No. of students	%	No. of students	%	No. of students	%
Question 4—How often do you explore something that is completely new to you?								
A. Regularly	20	26%	15	27%	10	13%	45	21%
B. Occasionally	35	45%	24	43%	42	54%	101	48%
C. Seldom/not often	22	28%	15	27%	26	33%	63	30%
D. Never	1	1%	2	4%	0	0%	3	1%
	78	100%	56	100%	78	100%	212	100%
Question 5—How would you describe your general competency in technology?								
A. Expert	10	13%	10	18%	4	5%	24	11%
B. Better than novice but not expert	53	68%	25	45%	53	68%	131	62%
C. Novice	14	18%	18	32%	19	24%	51	24%
D. Not interested in technology and rarely use it unless essential	1	1%	3	5%	2	3%	6	3%
	78	100%	56	100%	78	100%	212	100%
Question 6—What types of technology do you use?—tick all that apply to you								
A. Computer/laptop	76	97%	40	71%	78	100%	194	92%
B. Cell phone/tablet (mobile devises)	74	95%	44	79%	77	99%	195	92%
C. Social media (Twitter, WhatsApp, Facebook etc.)	66	85%	28	50%	76	97%	170	80%
D. YouTube videos	65	83%	16	29%	78	100%	159	75%
E. Entertainment—Music	68	87%	37	66%	71	91%	176	83%
F. Entertainment—TV and movie streaming	57	73%	27	48%	59	76%	143	67%
G. Google and/or other search engines for shopping, etc.	70	90%	27	48%	73	94%	170	80%
H. On-line gaming applications	41	53%	20	36%	40	51%	101	48%
I. Other	5	6%	10	18%	10	13%	25	12%
Question 7—On average how much time do you spend on technology on a daily basis?								
A. 0 to 1 h	1	1%	6	11%	0	0%	7	3%
B. 2 to 4 h	16	21%	31	55%	16	21%	63	30%
C. 5 to 7 h	38	49%	13	23%	30	38%	81	38%

(continued)

Table 5 (continued)

	Wales		China		Singapore		Total	
	No. of students	%	No. of students	%	No. of students	%	No. of students	%
D. 8 to 10 h	15	19%	3	5%	11	14%	29	14%
E. >10 h	8	10%	3	5%	21	27%	32	15%
	78	100%	56	100%	78	100%	212	100%

Question 6 asked the students to tick all the types of technology they use; the results here demonstrate that 92% of all the students use computers and laptops with 92% overall result for cell phones and 80% tablets. Overall, 80% of the students used social media where both the Singaporean and Welsh students have a higher percentage at 97% and 85% respectively. The low Chinese result of 50% is not surprising due to the Chinese government restrictions on the use of the social media examples provided on the questionnaire. For accessing YouTube videos 100% of the Singaporean students utilize these compared with 83% of Welsh students and just 29% of Chinese students, again Chinese students are restricted on the use of YouTube and a Chinese alternative may be available. Overall, 83% of the students used technology to listen to music with 91% of Singaporean students, 87% of Welsh students and 66% for Chinese students. For TV again both Singaporean and Welsh students have a fairly high percentage at 76% and 73% respectively followed by 48% for Chinese students. Results of student use of internet search engines overall percentage is 80% with the highest percentage again from Singaporean students (94%) followed by Welsh students (90%) and Chinese students (48%). For gaming purposes, the highest percentage here was Welsh students where 53% said they used technology for online gaming followed by Singaporean students at 51% and then Chinese students at 36% for other purposes the overall here is 12%.

Surprisingly overall, the majority of students from all three institutions had not used VR before (35%), led by Singaporean students where 49% had not used VR before and then Chinese students 30% and finally Welsh students at 24%. Of the students that had used VR before 32% of Welsh students had used it in an education setting followed by 21% of Chinese students and just 4% of Singaporean students.

Overall, 32% of students had used VR for entertainment purposes with the highest percentage of 41% coming from Singaporean students followed by Welsh at 29% and then Chinese at 21% a much lower percentage of students had utilized VR for both entertainment and education at 15% overall with the Chinese students' percentage being the highest followed by Welsh and then Singaporean students.

Question 9 asked students their feelings towards using VR in their seminar class. It was surprising to see 38% of students overall indicating they were very positive towards the idea with 31% slightly positive, 26% neutral and 5% slightly negative and none very negative. When we consider the results individually by institution, we find that the largest positive response at 84% is from Chinese students followed by Singaporean students at 64% and Welsh students at 63%. More of the Singaporean students were neutral at 35% compared with 26% Welsh and 14% of Chinese students. A higher number of Welsh students were slightly negative at 12% compared with just 2% of Chinese students and 1 Singaporean student. Overall, the results demonstrate that the students were positive about receiving a VR case study so were open minded to a new learning approach.

Question 10 asked students do you think that VR technology will help you understand tax better?

Results demonstrate the highest number of positive responses came from Chinese students at 75% followed by Welsh students at 55% and Singaporean students at 36%. From these results one can conclude that Singaporean students are more skeptical about the use of VR for learning and would probably reserve their position until they had experienced VR. The highest number of students indicating they were not sure were from Singapore at 55% followed by Welsh students with 36% and then Chinese students at 21%. Those students who indicated that they thought that VR would not help them understand tax better and choose either not really or no definitely not, were approximately the same overall at 9% for Welsh and Singaporean students and just 4% from Chinese students. Conclusions we can reach here is that the Singaporean students were reserving their position until they had actually experienced the case study through VR whereas Welsh and Chinese students were more optimistic that VR could help them understand tax better maybe through previous use of VR or through their trust of the instructor.

6.2 *Results from the VR Post-session Questionnaire*

After the students had experienced VR in their capital allowances taxation learning, towards the end of the session students were provided with a post VR questionnaire, accessed via a QR code and collated in Survey Monkey, which captured their thoughts on their feelings of utilizing VR in the seminar session as demonstrated in Table 6.

Responses to Question 1 from the post session questionnaire demonstrated that overall, 86% of the students were either very positive or slightly positive towards their VR experience. Where 12% were neutral and just 3% were either slightly or very negative. From each institution 90% of Singaporean students were positive compared with 87% of Chinese students and 78% of Welsh students. There were more neutral responses from Welsh students compared with Chinese and Singaporean at 14%, 13% and 8% respectively. Overall, the highest number of students who were negative towards the process were from Wales at 7% followed by Singapore at just 2%, none of the Chinese students were negative towards the experience.

Question 2 asked students if VR enhanced their learning experience in class, here we find that 81% overall said either yes definitely or yes to some extent with 11% who indicated they were unsure and 9% answered no. Question 3 asked students if VR helped them understand tax better, again the most positive students were the Chinese at 76% followed by Singaporean students at 72% and finally Welsh students at 64%. Overall, 18% of all students indicated they were unsure. The highest number

Table 6 Post VR questionnaire questions 1 to 4

	Wales		China		Singapore		Total	
	No. of students	%	No. of students	%	No. of students	%	No. of students	%
Question 1—Now that I've had the opportunity to use VR in my seminar, my feelings towards the process are								
A. Very positive	15	36%	47	59%	28	56%	90	53%
B. Slightly positive	18	43%	22	28%	17	34%	57	33%
C. Neutral	6	14%	10	13%	4	8%	20	12%
D. Slightly negative	2	5%	–	0%	1	2%	3	2%
E. Very negative	1	2%	–	0%	0	0%	1	1%
	42	100%	79	100%	50	100%	171	100%
Question 2—Did you find that VR enhanced your learning experience in class?								
A. Yes (definitely)	11	26%	35	44%	25	50%	71	42%
B. Yes (to some extent)	19	45%	28	35%	19	38%	66	39%
C. Not sure	4	10%	13	16%	2	4%	19	11%
D. Not really	7	17%	2	3%	4	8%	13	8%
E. No (definitely not)	1	2%	1	1%	0	0%	2	1%
	42	100%	79	100%	50	100%	171	100%
Question 3—Do you think that VR technology helped you to understand tax better?								
A. Yes (definitely)	8	19%	32	41%	11	22%	51	30%
B. Yes (to some extent)	19	45%	27	35%	25	50%	71	42%
C. Not sure	4	10%	17	22%	9	18%	30	18%
D. Not really	9	21%	2	3%	4	8%	15	9%
E. No	2	5%	–	0%	1	2%	3	2%
	42	100%	78	100%	50	100%	170	100%
Question 4—Did you enjoy using VR during the lecture?								
A. Yes (definitely)	20	48%	40	51%	28	56%	88	51%
B. Yes (to some extent)	13	31%	23	29%	19	38%	55	32%

(continued)

Table 6 (continued)

	Wales		China		Singapore		Total	
	No. of students	%	No. of students	%	No. of students	%	No. of students	%
C. Not sure	4	10%	13	16%	2	4%	19	11%
D. Not really	4	10%	3	4%	0	0%	7	4%
E. No (definitely not)	1	2%	–	0%	1	2%	2	1%
	42	100%	79	100%	50	100%	171	100%

of negative responses came from Welsh students at 26% followed by Singaporean students at 10% and just 3% from Chinese students.

Question 4 asked students if they enjoyed using VR. We find that 83% overall agreed with 11% unsure and 5% who disagreed. When we break that down to the individual institutions, we find that the greatest enjoyment was experienced by Singaporean students at 94% followed by Chinese students at 80% and finally welsh students at 79%. One can conclude here that the vast majority of students enjoyed using VR as a learning tool in their seminar. Table 7 results below demonstrates the final four post questionnaire questions.

When asked the question would the students like to see more VR technology being used in their lectures and seminar classes overall, we find 77% of the students agreed with 15% who were unsure, 9% disagreed. Individually, the highest positive response of 85% were from Chinese students followed by Singaporean students at 83% and finally Welsh students at 57%. We can conclude from this question that students would like to see more VR technology but there is a small number of students who were not positive about their experience.

Question 6 asked the students how often do they think VR should be used? Overall results demonstrate 27% of students would like to use VR weekly followed by 32% monthly, 24% once a semester and 9% annually. 8% stated never. Students who would like to use VR more frequently was highest for Singaporean students at 64% followed by Chinese students at 62% then welsh students at 48%. One can also conclude here that of the students would like to utilize VR more often the majority at 32% felt that once a month was the most appropriate time period.

Question 7 asked students if they would like to see VR used in other modules. Overall results demonstrate 71% of students said yes (yes definitely or yes maybe), 20% said maybe and just 8% said no.

The final question asked students if they would explore VR technology after the seminar session in their everyday life, in other words how interested in VR they were and would they like to use it for other applications. Results demonstrate overall 75% of the students said yes (definitely or maybe) followed by 20% who said not really and 4% who said no.

Table 7 Post VR questionnaire questions 5 to 8

	Wales		China		Singapore		Total	
	No. of students	%	No. of students	%	No. of students	%	No. of students	%
Question 5—Would you like to see more VR technology used in your tax lectures and seminars?								
A. Yes (definitely)	16	38%	45	57%	22	45%	83	49%
B. Yes (to some extent)	8	19%	22	28%	17	35%	47	28%
C. Not sure	7	17%	10	13%	8	16%	25	15%
D. Not really	10	24%	1	1%	1	2%	12	7%
E. No (definitely not)	1	2%	1	1%	1	2%	3	2%
	42	100%	79	100%	49	100%	170	100%
Question 6—How often do you think VR should be used in lectures and seminars?								
A. Never	3	7%	10	13%	1	2%	14	8%
B. Once a year	4	10%	7	9%	4	8%	15	9%
C. Once a semester	15	36%	13	16%	13	26%	41	24%
D. Once a month	16	38%	19	24%	19	38%	54	32%
E. Once a week	4	10%	30	38%	13	26%	47	27%
	42	100%	79	100%	50	100%	171	100%
Question 7—Would you like to see VR technology used in other modules?								
A. Yes (definitely)	17	40%	34	43%	27	54%	78	45%
B. Yes (maybe)	7	17%	25	31%	13	26%	45	26%
C. Maybe	7	17%	17	21%	10	20%	34	20%
D. Not really	8	19%	3	4%	0	0%	11	6%
E. No (definitely not)	3	7%	1	1%	0	0%	4	2%
	42	100%	80	100%	50	100%	172	100%
Question 8—Would you explore VR technology after the lecture in your everyday life?								
A. Yes (definitely)	12	29%	30	38%	15	30%	57	33%
B. Yes (maybe)	14	33%	35	44%	24	48%	73	42%

(continued)

Table 7 (continued)

	Wales		China		Singapore		Total	
	No. of students	%	No. of students	%	No. of students	%	No. of students	%
C. Not really	14	33%	11	14%	10	20%	35	20%
D. No (definitely not)	2	5%	4	5%	1	2%	7	4%
	42	100%	80	100%	50	100%	172	100%

7 Conclusions

Overall, one can conclude that the majority of students from all three institutions:

- enjoyed using VR
- felt it enhanced their learning
- helped them understand tax better
- would like to see more VR used in their learning on a regular basis
- will explore VR technology further

Students comments from a selection of student's individual handwritten sheets handed in after the VR seminar are listed below:

"New, eye opening. Out of classroom experience without leaving the classroom."

"Using VR to learn was an interesting experience as it was my first time using it for educational purposes."

"I think it's very interesting and fun because we rarely have interactive learning during class. I feel that VR helps us to experience the "real" situation on how we could differentiate what to claim or not to claim for capital allowances. It helps to understand better on this topic, I love it ❤ Thank you for giving us this opportunity to experience this ☺"

"It's so fun! U feel like its real hands on exercise! Experienced on my seat rather than going out of school! Hope to be able to see more VR experiences in the future. Interactive practice is the best ☺. Might not have time to do VR practice in class but definitely do not mind doing it at home."

"More VR please!"

"It is more engaging and interesting to learn using VR as we can see how the items are structured in the rooms instead of only looking at words."

"VR enhances the learning process. It creates engagement between the classmates. It is a creative way of allowing students to apply the theory learnt."

"I think it was great, as it is interactive and users would enjoy the experience of using VR as part of learning."

"It is a good way of capturing student's attention and then interest in learning. As sometimes, some of the topics are mundane. Using VR will stir the interests of students."

"It's pretty fun and engaging. Something different from the pen and paper learning."

> "Using VR is a great way to enhance learning and putting theory into practice without having to physically leave the classroom. It allows us to explore the various venues which might be inaccessible. Rather than studying the theory, I would prefer to learn through VR."
>
> "This is one interesting method for learning it would be great if this is used in most learning in the future. It would be great if we were allowed to select our choice & answer the questions using the VR."
>
> "Good learning platform and get to experience real-life. Able to apply why we learn in tax into real life. A bit dizzy after a while."
>
> "Fun, very different from our usual type of lectures. Engaging. However, it makes for a slightly dizzy experience after using it for a while."
>
> "I think it is quite fun and interacting using VR than the usual classroom style of learning things. Realistic scenarios, suitable for a different learning environment. Do not have to travel to the "real" place/site and you can see it through VR."
>
> "I think it is an interesting way to learn. Being able to see the item in VR is quite visual for us to decide if we can claim capital allowances for it. It would be hard to imagine if it wasn't for the VR. It is quite cool also that we got to go in and see what kind of items an actual company would have."
>
> "Very interesting way of learning, helps with remembering what was taught. The lesson was fun and enjoyable."
>
> "It was interactive and engaging. I have enjoyed it and would like to see it being used for learning more often. It was easy to navigate as well."
>
> "It is very interactive especially that, there is ability to virtually visualize the different assets and etc. in the different rooms. I think that using VR enhances my learning as it is very experiential and "hands on."

As demonstrated above the evidence gained from the international study supports the conclusion that the majority of students from all three institutions enjoyed their VR experience and found it helpful in their capital allowances taxation studies. A small number of students did not enjoy the experience which was mainly due to feelings of motion sickness. These students should be encouraged to keep their VR sessions short, be provided with an alternative headset or encouraged to take on the note taking role within the group.

There are further benefits to students as a result of their real-world VR capital allowances case study which is the opportunity to increase their employability from the workplace skills, they have gained by completing a technical capital allowances computation and soft skills from teamworking. These personal attributes are sought by employers from graduates applying as candidates for a trainee role. Photos 6, 7, and 8 show students from each institution working on their VR capital allowances case study during their seminar session.

8 Limitations of the Study and Areas for Further Exploration and Research

This study focuses on an international comparative study on the use of VR for taxation students on the topic of capital allowances. The study could be further developed

Photo 6 Swansea Taxation Students

Photo 7 Singaporean Taxation Students

by including additional taxation topics for example inheritance or death taxes and other accounting subjects such as management accounting, financial accounting, and auditing. Further research could explore if the benefits of using VR is evident if it is used more extensively than one case study during the duration of the module of study through a cross-sectional study over time or by involving the same students based on a longitudinal study to explore if the findings are consistent over a number

Photo 8 Chinese Taxation Students

of years. Both approaches could provide further evidence on the benefits of VR in accounting education and are recommended to provide further support of the pedagogic approach.

References

ACCA. (2021, April 21). *ACCA Global*. Retrieved from Whatever you're looking for, a career in finance and accountancy can help you get there. Here's why...It's highly flexible: https://yourfuture.accaglobal.com/global/en/your-career/why-accountancy.html

Allcoat, D. (2018). Learning in virtual reality: Effects on performance, emotion and engagement. *Research in Learning Technology, 26*. https://doi.org/10.25304/rlt.v26.2140

Apostolou, B., & Gammie, E., (2014). The role of accreditation in accounting education. In R. M. Wilson, *The Routledge companion to accounting education* (Chapter 29). Routledge.

Baumgartner, T., Speck, D., Wettstein, D., Masnari, O., Beeli, G., & Jäncke, L. (2008). Feeling present in arousing virtual reality worlds: Prefrontal brain regions differentially orchestrate presence experience in adults and children. *Frontiers in Human Neuroscience, 2*, 8. https://doi.org/10.3389/neuro.09.008.2008

Blair, A., Curtis, S., Goodwin, M., & Shields, S. (2013). What feedback do students want? *Politics, 33*(1), 66–79. https://doi.org/10.1111/j.1467-9256.2012.01446.x

Blömeke, S., & Paine, L. (2008). Getting the fish out of the water: Considering benefits and problems of doing research on teacher education at an international level. *Teaching and Teacher Education, 24*(8), 2027–2037. https://doi.org/10.1016/j.tate.2008.05.006

Bradley, S., Kirby, E., & Madriaga, M. (2015). What students value as inspirational and transformative teaching. *Innovations in Education and Teaching International, 52*(3), 231–242. https://doi.org/10.1080/14703297.2014.880363

Breton, G. (2010). Some empirical evidence on the superiority of the problem-based learning (PBL) method. *Accounting Education*, 1–12. https://doi.org/10.1080/096392899331008

Burmark, L. (2002). *Visual literacy: Learn to see, see to learn.* Association for Supervision and Curriculum Development.

Carney, R. L. (2002). Pictorial illustrations still improve students' learning from text. *Educational Psychology Review, 14*, 5–26. https://doi.org/10.1023/A:1013176309260

Clayton, K. S. (2004). Utilizing service-learning in accounting programs. *Issues in Accounting Education, 19*(4), 469–486. https://doi.org/10.2308/iace.2004.19.4.469

Complete University Guide. (2021, April 22). *The Complete University Guide*. Retrieved from The Complete University Guide: https://www.thecompleteuniversityguide.co.uk/student-advice/careers/what-do-graduates-do-and-earn#Whatdograduatesearn. Accessed on 22 April 2021.

Deb, S., Carruth, D. W., Sween, R., Strawderman, L., & Garrison, T. M. (2017). Efficacy of virtual reality in pedestrian safety research. *Applied Ergonomics, 65*, 449–460. https://doi.org/10.1016/j.apergo.2017.03.007

Engelbrecht, H. L. (2019). A SWOT analysis of the field of virtual reality for firefighter training. *Frontiers in Robotics and AI, 6*, 101. https://doi.org/10.3389/frobt.2019.00101

Gao, Y., & Liu, J. (2020). Capitalising on academics' transnational experiences in the domestic research environment. *Journal of Higher Education Policy and Management*. https://doi.org/10.1080/1360080X.2020.1833276

The Guardian. (2021, April 20). *The Guardian.* Retrieved from theguardian.com/careers/in-house-training-accountancy-scheme-route-finance: https://www.theguardian.com/careers/in-house-training-accountancy-scheme-route-finance

Johnson, D. W., & Johnson, R. T. (2009). An educational psychology success story: Social interdependence theory and cooperative learning. *Educational Researcher, 38*(5), 365–379.

Junghyo Lee, J. K. (2019). The adoption of virtual reality devices: The technology acceptance model integrating enjoyment, social interaction, and strength of the social ties. *Telematics and Informatics, 39*, 37–48. https://doi.org/doi.org/10.1016/j.tele.2018.12.006

Kern, B. (2002). Enhancing accounting students' problem-solving skills: The use of a hands-on conceptual model in an active learning environment. *Accounting Education*, 235–256. https://doi.org/10.1080/09639280210141680

Kolb, D. (2014). *Experiential learning: Experience as the source of learning and development*. FT Press.

Kutluk, F. A., Donmez, A., & Gülmez, M. (2015). Opinions of university students about teaching techniques in accounting lessons. *Procedia—Social and Behavioral Sciences, 191*, 1682–1689. https://doi.org/10.1016/j.sbspro.2015.04.155

Moy, J. S. (2002). The career choice of business graduates: SMEs or MNCs? *Career Development International, 7*(6), 339–347. https://doi.org/10.1108/13620430210444367

Nichols, S., & Patel, H. (2002). Health and safety implications of virtual reality: A review of empirical evidence. *Applied Ergonomics, 33*(3), 251–271. https://doi.org/10.1016/S0003-6870(02)00020-0

Papanastasiou, G. D. (2019). Virtual and augmented reality effects on K-12, higher and tertiary education students' twenty-first century skills. *Virtual Reality, 23*, 425–436. https://doi.org/10.1007/s10055-018-0363-2

Psotka, J. (1995). Immersive training systems: Virtual reality and education and training. *Instructional Science, 23*, 405–431.

Schott, C. M. (2018). Virtual reality and situated experiential education: A conceptualization and exploratory trial. *Comput Assist Learn, 34*, 843–852. https://doi.org/10.1111/jcal.12293

Sieberth, T. D. (2019). Applying virtual reality in forensics—A virtual scene walkthrough. *Forensic Science, Medicine and Pathology, 15*, 41–47. https://doi.org/10.1007/s12024-018-0058-8

Siegle, D. (2019). Seeing is believing: Using virtual and augmented reality to enhance student learning. *Gifted Child Today, 42*(1), 46–52. https://doi.org/10.1177/1076217518804854

Slater, M., & Sanchez-Vives, M. V. (2016). Enhancing our lives with immersive virtual reality. *Frontiers in Robotics and AI, 3*, 74. https://doi.org/10.3389/frobt.2016.00074

Squelch, A. (2001). Virtual reality for mine safety training in South Africa. *Journal of the South African Institute of Mining and Metallurgy, 101*(4), 8. https://hdl.handle.net/10520/AJA0038223X_2672

Stanley, T. (2012). Problem-based learning: Does accounting education need it? *Journal of Accounting Education, 30*(3–4), 267–289. https://doi.org/doi.org/10.1016/j.jaccedu.2012.08.005

Tussyadiah, I. P., Wang, D., Jung, T. H., & Tom Dieck, M. C. (2018). Virtual reality, presence, and attitude change: Empirical evidence from tourism. *Tourism Management, 66*, 140–154. https://doi.org/10.1016/j.tourman.2017.12.003

UCAS. (2021, April 28). *Explore subject guides*. Retrieved from UCAS: https://www.ucas.com/explore/subjects/accounting

Whitten, C. S. (2004). Accounting service-learning experiences and the IRS volunteer income tax assistance programme: A teaching note. *Accounting Education, 13*(1), 101–112. https://doi.org/10.1080/0963928042000182475

Terry Filer is an Associate Professor of Accounting and Taxation at Swansea University, UK, and a Fellow of the Chartered Association of Certified Accountants (FCCA) with extensive industry experience. After 20 years in industry and practice, she moved into the education sector initially teaching ACCA professional qualifications at Gower College Swansea, moving to Swansea University in 2010 where she now teaches taxation and accounting. She focuses on pedagogic research to improve learning and assessment in taxation, auditing and accounting subjects. She uses virtual reality to experience case studies through immersive learning. Students find this approach helpful to better understand how the subject relates to the business world and is an enjoyable way to learn.

Marc Holmes, Ph.D. is a Virtual Reality Research Officer at Swansea University, UK. He worked with the Medical Engineering department to create an app in which students can assemble a full-scale skeleton from a floating jumble of bones. Users physically 'pick up' the bones using VR controllers and hang them on a frame. The bones must be assembled in the correct order to stay in place. Once assembled, users can select each one individually to answer a multiple-choice question about its name. A timer is included, so students can try to beat the clock and even compete against their peers.

Chapter 23
How Blockchain Is Transforming Accounting, Auditing and Finance: A Systematic Review

Manpreet Singh, Mahesh Joshi, Sharad Sharma, and Tarek Rana

Abstract Blockchain technology (BT) has been receiving increasing attention from the academics and practitioners, in terms of its emergence, evolution, transformation, potential disruptions, technical aspects, and implications on accounting, auditing and finance practices. Through a review of the 51 papers published from 2015 to 2021 in Scopus indexed academic journals in accounting and auditing. Based on the analysis of the selected papers, this chapter charts the current knowledge on BT, examines key themes identified from the literature, and recommends opportunities for future research. The chapter finds that the innovation and ensuing disruption of BT is still in an emerging phase, particularly the scope and influence in the accounting, auditing, and finance practice and research. The findings of this chapter can be used by the key stakeholders involved in professional practice in the accounting and auditing domain. The chapter offers avenues for future research seeking to develop theory and align theory-practice.

Keywords Blockchain · Emerging technology · Accounting · Auditing · Finance · Literature review

1 Introduction

The disruptive potential of blockchain technology (BT) to alter many business models and activities is widely recognized (Ali et al., 2020; Du et al., 2019; Grant & Hogan, 2015; Millar et al., 2018; Nagy et al., 2016; Schuelke-Leech, 2018). BT applications can improve efficiency, transparency, cost and security across many types of business and social transactions (Clemons et al., 2017; Economist, 2015; Iansiti &

M. Singh · M. Joshi · S. Sharma · T. Rana (✉)
RMIT University, Melbourne, VIC, Australia
e-mail: tarek.rana@rmit.edu.au

M. Joshi
e-mail: mahesh.joshi@rmit.edu.au

S. Sharma
e-mail: sharad.sharma@rmit.edu.au

T. Rana et al. (eds.), *Handbook of Big Data and Analytics in Accounting and Auditing*,
https://doi.org/10.1007/978-981-19-4460-4_23

Lakhani, 2017; Krugman, 2013). In addition, the continuity of long-standing businesses and professions depends on their ability to update/adapt their value adding models through digital transformation which can take the form of digital platforms or software that supports innovation and implementation of BT (CBINSIGHTS, 2021; Erik et al., 2018; Ølnes et al., 2017). BT is not only a supporting technology or tool but is also a transformative force with potential to impacts accounting transactions and financial analysis as well as connecting them with the legal contracts, product validation, and keeping trails for audit and verification (Turker & Bicer, 2020).

Although BT emerged with the technology of cryptocurrency (Nakamoto & Bitcoin, 2008), its scope has since widened beyond digital currency (Abreu et al., 2018; Swan, 2015). Blockchain 1.0 encompassed digital payment systems which is referred to as the digital and/or cryptocurrency phase (Potekhina & Riumkin, 2017) (Brukhanskyi & Spilnyk, 2019). Blockchain 2.0 brought digital finance into being, as its applications include the transfer of assets other than currency, such as stocks, bonds, loans, mortgages, and titles, via smart contracts (Abreu et al., 2018; Christidis & Devetsikiotis, 2016). Blockchain 3.0 represents the application of BT beyond business transactions—in government, health, science, arts & culture, supply chain management, market monitoring, smart energy, and copyright protection—to promote a digital society (Engelhardt, 2017; Hyvärinen et al., 2017; Kim & Laskowski, 2018; O'Dair & Beaven, 2017; Radanović & Likić, 2018; Savelyev, 2018). Blockchain 2.0 has attracted attention in finance, accounting and auditing (Turker & Bicer, 2020), among other business transaction-related fields (Abreu et al., 2018). A passing glance at the literature shows that academia has been striving to explain the benefits and applications of BT to provide buy-in while placating the fears of stakeholders about BT implementation and implications (Al Harthy et al., 2019; Coyne & McMickle, 2017; Duan et al., 2017; Vigna & Casey, 2016).

BT may completely change accounting, auditing, and control activities, and consequently there is huge interest in BT among professionals in these fields. For example, BT is playing a significant role in financial innovation, and its increasing use in payments is driving the fintech revolution (Ali et al., 2014, 2020; Kshetri, 2018). As described by Abreu et al. (2018), BT allows developers to create decentralized applications with unique sets of rules for validating transactions known as smart contracts (Christidis & Devetsikiotis, 2016; Hamilton, 2020), which have wider applications beyond digital currency. Concerns in the accounting and auditing professions have centered on challenges in developing and implementing processes and practices (Krugman, 2013), not only for the development of effective regulations and standards (Kiviat, 2015) but also for advising businesses and other parties on their transactions (Bonsón & Bednárová, 2019). As a new and rapidly pervasive phenomenon, extensive academic studies of BT in multiple directions are justified, but consolidation of the extant literature is urgently needed to avoid further duplication of effort, to understand the implications of BT for the accounting, auditing and finance professions, and to provide direction for future research.

This study conducts a systematic review of the relevant literature to understand and consolidate academic efforts on the applications of BT in the financial, accounting and auditing sectors. This review includes dominant themes in the literature and possible applications and impacts of BT for both business and society. In particular, this chapter seeks to understand the disruptive potential and educational and technical implications of the application of BT in the financial, accounting and auditing sectors. To achieve this objective, three research questions are devised. *RQ1: How has BT disrupted the accounting, auditing and finance professions?* A systematic analysis of the main benefits of BT will provide a clearer picture of the incentives driving stakeholders to adopt and deploy BT, which will help researchers and practitioners understand and build upon the needs that BT is effectively addressing across business and society at large. *RQ2: What are the practical implications of BT for the accounting, auditing and finance professions? RQ3: What is required for BT education and training for the accounting, auditing and finance professions?* This question was designed to understand the barriers and problems that these professions (and others) will face due to the lack of blockchain professionals/practitioners/courses. The search timeline for the systematic review of scholarly research on BT in the business literature included the years 2015–2021. The subject areas were limited to accounting, auditing and finance, and 51 articles were selected for inclusion in content and thematic analyses to identify research patterns.

This study offers several useful contributions for promoting the use of BT in finance, accounting and auditing, as well as other business transactions. First, it is one of the first efforts to consolidate academic research on BT and its implications for the accounting, auditing and finance professions. Second, based on a discussion of the advantages and challenges of BT for the accounting and auditing professions, this study offers propositions on how accounting and audit practices must change to leverage new opportunities in BT advancement with the support of current and future accountants and auditors (Fuller & Markelevich, 2020). Third, it provides insights for regulators, policy makers and other stakeholder groups with significant roles in the BT ecosystem. The unfounded fears and arguments of stakeholders who are habituated to existing arrangements may constrain BT. As these stakeholders are confronted by the technological advancement of BT and are required to act, this study can serve as a useful reference for the development of standards, policies and regulations. Finally, this study aims to support scholars, leaders and decision-makers in thinking about the benefits and risks of BT and associated knowledge gaps to guide future research and applications.

The remainder of the chapter is structured as follows. Next, the methodology used to systematically select the primary studies for analysis is described. Papers in the subject fields of accounting, auditing and finance are then analyzed, including geographical distribution, journals, highly cited papers, and so on. The content of the papers is analyzed based on the main research themes. This is followed by a future agenda, and the chapter ends with conclusions and recommendations.

2 Methodological Approach

Due to the rapid growth of publications in accounting, auditing (Appelbaum & Nehmer, 2020; Kaaniche & Laurent, 2017) and finance, investigating relevant articles for evidence-based practice is not a manageable task for experts (Ali et al., 2020; Dai & Vasarhelyi, 2017). Experts in accounting and finance must exercise caution in decision-making based on studies that may be limited by biases (Abbas et al., 2008). Evidence-based practice requires strong facts based on research (Dai et al., 2019). Systematic reviews are one of the strongest sources of evidence-based financial practice (Evans, 2003). The research implications generated by systematic studies are more reliable and valid than those from controlled trials or case studies (Bonsón & Bednárová, 2019). Through systematic reviews, a researcher can identify, assess, and understand available research and reach logical conclusions based on the findings (Dikert et al., 2016; Victor, 2008). Systematic reviews are an effective way of addressing fragmentation as a means of evaluating and interpreting a particular research topic or phenomenon of interest (Kitchenham & Charters, 2007). Thus, a key objective of our systematic reviews is to clearly provide evidence that can be used to improve the consistency and validity of research findings (Coren & Fisher, 2006; Kitchenham & Charters, 2007).

A staged process is followed when conducting a systematic review: first, the scope of the review is defined, and the questions and protocol are developed; next, the evidence is selected; and, finally, the quality of the evidence is appraised, and the data are acquired and synthesized (Popay et al., 2006).

Guidelines are essential in performing a systematic literature review (Kitchenham & Charters, 2007). The present systematic review follows the guidelines and procedures described by Kitchenham and Charters (2007), Tranfield et al. (2003), and Ali et al. (2018). The planning, execution, and reporting phases of the review were conducted iteratively to ensure a thorough evaluation of the literature. IEEE Xplore Digital Library, ScienceDirect, ACM, and Google Scholar were searched using the following search strings:

("blockchain" OR "block-chain" OR "distributed ledger") AND "Bitcoin"

("blockchain" OR "Accounting" OR "Auditing" OR "Finance" OR "Assurance") AND ("Accounting and Auditing" OR "Accounting and Finance" OR "Auditing and Finance")

The searches were run against titles, keywords, and/or abstracts, depending on the options available in the search platform. The searches were conducted on different dates in September 2021, but all studies published up to this date were processed.

2.1 Inclusion and Exclusion Criteria

The following inclusion criteria were applied to select eligible studies:

- Papers written in English.

- Papers centered solely on BT in the accounting, auditing and finance fields.
- Papers published between January 2015 and October 2021.
- Peer-reviewed papers published in a conference proceeding or journal.

The exclusion criteria were as follows:

- Papers focused exclusively on business intelligence, cloud computing, and computer technology.
- Papers reporting general results on BT irrelevant to the fields of interest.
- Gray literature such as blogs, law notes, magazine articles, articles without references, duplicate articles, posters, and government documents.
- Papers not available in English.
- Papers without full-text availability.

2.2 Selection Results

The process of identifying and including papers in the systematic review is illustrated in Fig. 1. Our initial search of the four databases in September–October 2021 yielded 701 articles. Eliminating duplicate papers, papers without full-text availability, and papers that were not focused on BT left 481 papers. In the next round of assessment, papers that were too technical were excluded, and the remaining articles were assessed based on their abstracts and read in full to confirm that they fulfilled the study parameters. Ultimately, 51 papers were selected for inclusion.

3 Results of the Review

The 51 articles selected for inclusion were analyzed in terms of journals, research topics, citations, and so on to depict the research status of blockchain in the fields of accounting, auditing and finance more comprehensively. Several review papers have played an important role in the study of blockchain (Xu et al., 2019. For instance, Li and Wang (2017) investigate the influence of blockchain on supply chain practices and policies. Zhao et al. (2016) suggest that blockchain will be widely adopted in finance and lead to many business innovations and research opportunities. Figure 2 categorizes the sample according to the area of publication; 43% of the studies are in the field of accounting, followed by 21% in the financial sector and 14% in blockchain as a disruptive technology.

3.1 Geographical Distribution

The 51 papers were drawn from 13 countries and regions; the specific data are shown in Fig. 3. The United States and Australia were the top two countries by number of papers published on blockchain, and the United States produced more than one third

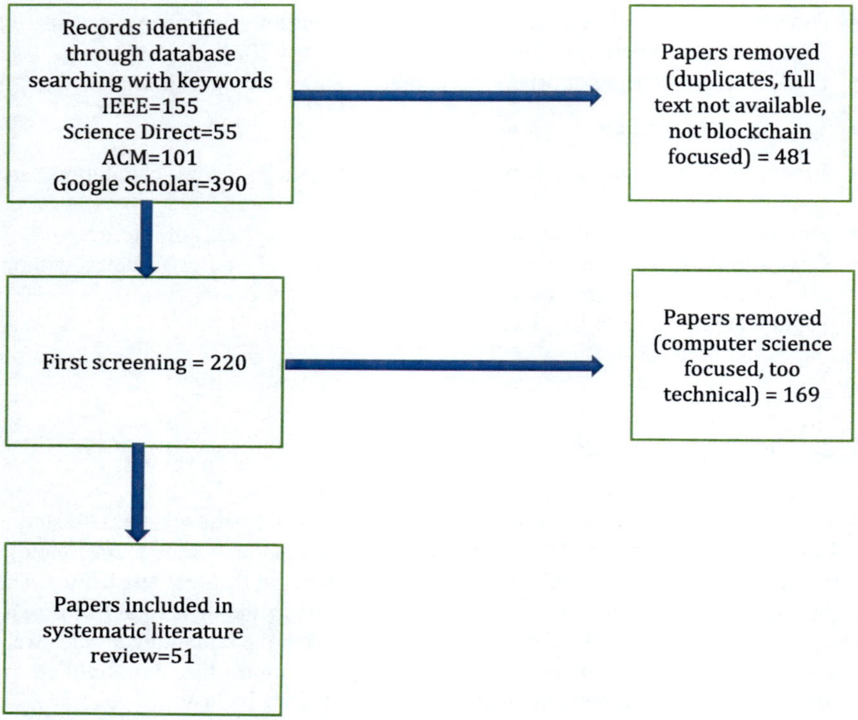

Fig. 1 The process of selecting papers for the review

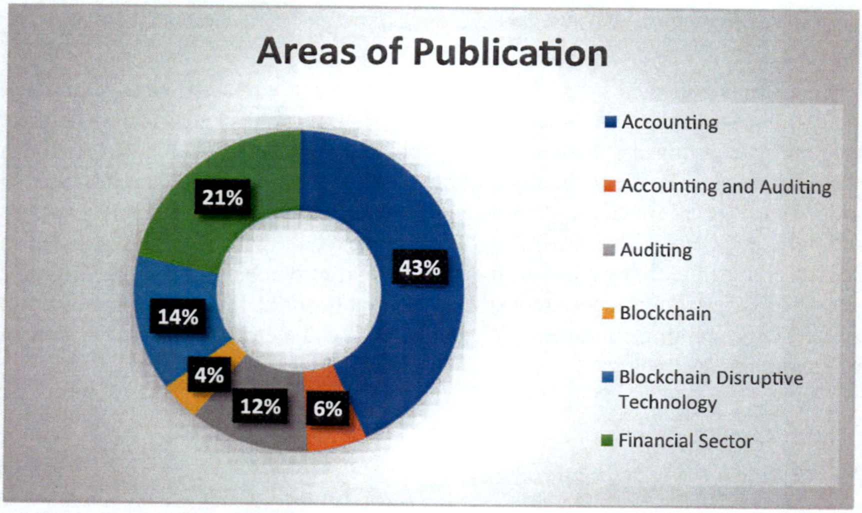

Fig. 2 Distribution by areas of publication

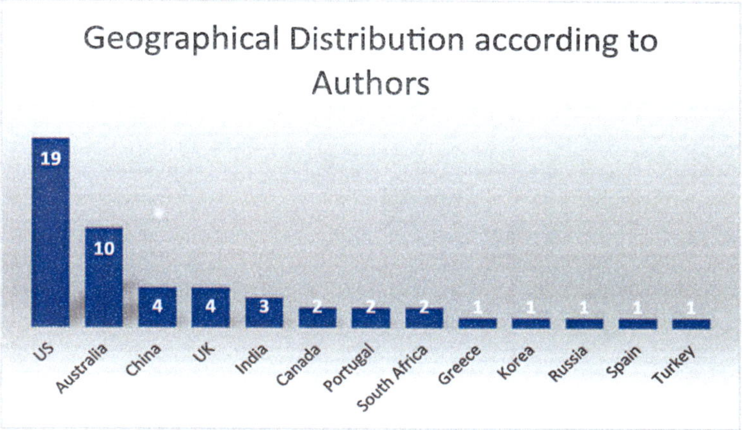

Fig. 3 Geographical distribution of selected papers

of the total articles. At the time of data collection, China and UK had contributed 4 papers each, ranking third and fourth. This distribution shows that blockchain is still an emerging research area that awaits entry by a broader field of countries and scholars.

3.2 Distribution by Journals

The 51 included papers were published in 29 journals. The top 8 publication companies are shown in Fig. 4. First was Elsevier, followed by Emerald and Wiley. Most of the papers in Elsevier and Emerald journals were published in 2018, with a few in 2015 and 2016. Papers in Wiley journals were generally published in 2015, 2016 and 2019. The distribution by year of publication is shown in Fig. 5 and highlights the recent growth in this field.

3.3 Most Influential Articles

The 51 papers were cited a total of 2261 times. The most influential articles, with more than 100 citations each, are listed in Fig. 6. The most popular article in our data set is Casino et al. (2019), which has 370 citations in Google Scholar. This suggests that this article, which proposes that the real applications of blockchain have not yet been realized, has strongly influenced blockchain research. The other highly cited articles describe how blockchain affects and functions in various areas, such as accounting and finance. Since blockchain is an emerging technology (Smith &

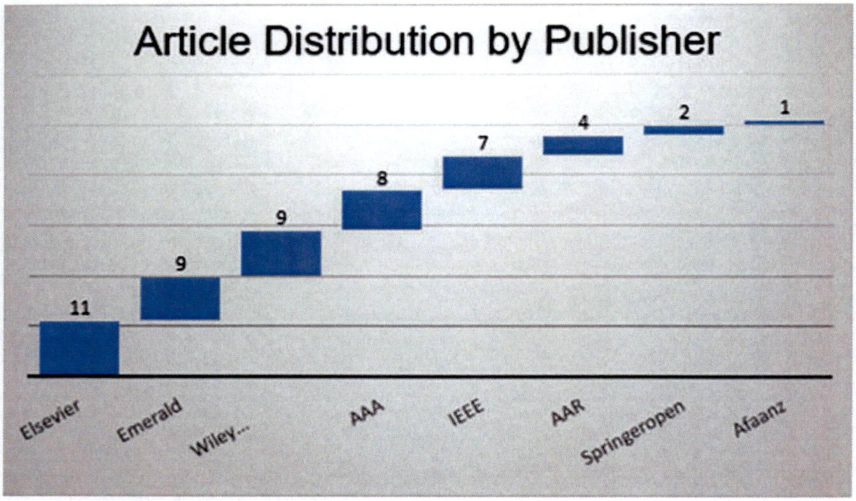

Fig. 4 Distribution by journals

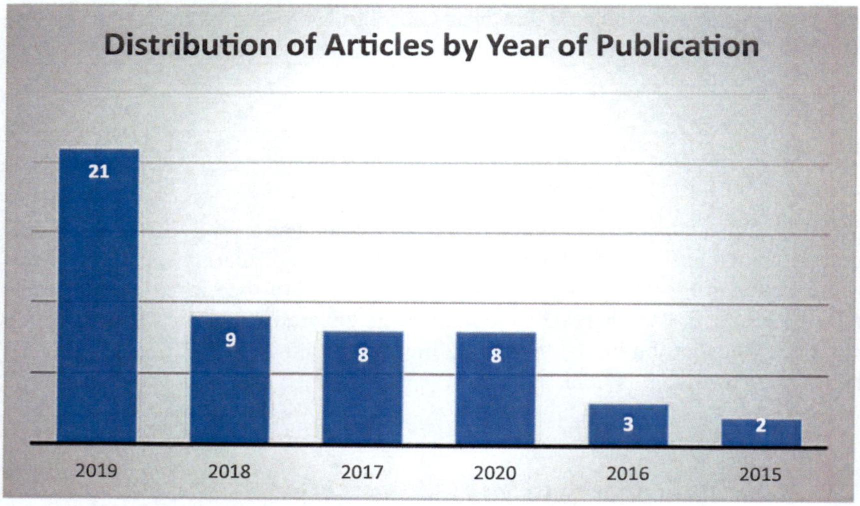

Fig. 5 Distribution by year of publication

Castonguay, 2020), it is particularly necessary to explore how blockchain can be incorporated into various industries and fields.

Papers	Citations
A systematic review of blockchain-based applications	370
Toward blockchain-based accounting and assurance	265
Blockchain and its impact on financial services	261
Defining and identifying disruptive innovations	184
Can blockchain serve an accounting purpose	154
Blockchain technology in finance	138

Fig. 6 Top five papers by citations

4 Thematic Analysis from the Review

Identifying research themes is crucial to understanding a research field and exploring future research directions. Here, keywords were used to explore research themes, as keywords are representative and concise descriptions of article content. First, the most used keywords were identified: "blockchain," "accounting," "auditing," and "finance". Although the potential for blockchain applications goes far beyond digital currencies, bitcoin (Raiborn & Sivitanides, 2015) and other cryptocurrencies are widely discussed in the set of articles as an important blockchain application scenario in the accounting and finance industry. In addition, many researchers regard the combination of blockchain with finance as an important financial technology (Coyne & McMickle, 2017; Moll & Yigitbasioglu, 2019).

Next, keyword clustering analysis was performed to identify the research themes. Four clusters were identified and labeled cluster #1, "Blockchain's implications for accounting, auditing and finance"; cluster #2, "Blockchain as a disruption in accounting, auditing and finance"; cluster #3, "Blockchain education and training"; and cluster #4, "Technical aspects of blockchain in accounting and auditing".

Several researchers have studied blockchain as a disruption, its technical aspects, implications for different areas and the role of the education system (Casino et al., 2019). Every new technology goes through a phase of "digital disruption" in which no one knows how professionals and industries will react to the new technology (Marrone & Hazelton, 2019). Blockchain is in the initial phase of digital disruption (Brennan et al., 2019). Blockchain is gaining momentum as industries begin investing in and implementing BT as early adopters (Dai et al., 2019). In the healthcare sector, blockchain can play an important role in centralizing electronic health records (Halamka et al., 2017), research data, eliminating prescription drug fraud, and reducing administrative overhead (Engelhardt, 2017). In the music industry, blockchain could improve the accuracy and availability of copyright data and significantly improve the transparency of the value chain (O'Dair & Beaven, 2017).Applications of BT to streamline transactions and settlement processes could effectively reduce the costs associated with manual operations (Sheetal Sinha &

Bathla, 2019). The fintech revolution brought by blockchain has received extensive attention (Yang & Li, 2018; Zhang et al., 2020). Researchers agree that this emerging technology may transform traditional trading methods and practices in the financial industry (Ashta & Biot-Paquerot, 2018; Chen, 2004; Kim & Sarin, 2018). Gomber et al. (2018) discuss transformations in four areas of financial services: operations management, payments, lending, and deposit services. Casino et al. (2019) and Dierksmeier and Seele (2018) address the impact of BT on the nature of financial transactions from a business ethics perspective Iansiti and Lakhani (2017), Schmitz and Leoni (2019) and Vincent et al. (2020) analyze the inherent features of blockchain and point out that much work remains before blockchain can be applied extensively. The characteristics of BT RE discussed from multiple perspectives. For example, Xu (2016) explores the types of fraud and malicious activities that BT can prevent and identifies attacks to which blockchain remains vulnerable. Meanwhile, Aune et al. (2017) propose a cryptographic approach to solving information leakage problems in blockchain. A handful of researchers discuss the supporting role played by blockchain in the sharing economy. Pazaitis et al. (2017) describe a conceptual economic model of blockchain-based decentralized cooperation that might better support the dynamics of social sharing. Sun et al. (2016) discuss the contribution of emerging blockchain technologies to the three major factors of the sharing economy (i.e., human, technology, and organization). They also analyze how blockchain-based sharing services contribute to smart cities.

5 Discussion

The themes were intended to provide a comprehensive overview of blockchain research in various sectors such as accounting, auditing, and finance. The papers were also coded for important topics, and a single paper could have multiple topics. For example, one study focused on blockchain in the context of accounting, and another explored blockchain in accounting and auditing as well as accounting and finance (Kaaniche & Laurent, 2017), so we coded for each of these categories separately (Angeles, 2019; de Ridder et al., 2017). The greatest share of papers in the data set focus on blockchain in accounting (43%), followed by finance (22%), and auditing (12%); the remaining papers are related to blockchain as a disruptive technology or combinations of accounting and auditing.

5.1 *Real-Time, Recordkeeping, Transparency, Fraud Detection*

The papers focusing on accounting (43%) reveal that implementing BT is not a linear, rational, or deterministic process (Cai, 2018; Moll & Yigitbasioglu, 2019). There are many uncertainties, so experiments are needed to fully understand the technology and its limitations. Furthermore, new technological applications often result in changes in human behavior (Brennan et al., 2019; DeSanctis & Poole, 1994).

Early adopters of BT claimed that this new technology would enable real-time accounting rather than updating of books and records on a monthly or quarterly basis (Byström, 2019). A ledger that cannot be altered or destroyed would improve the trustworthiness of financial statements (Byström, 2019). Dai and Vasarhelyi (2017) conclude that BT can facilitate a real-time, verifiable, and transparent accounting ecosystem. Wang and Kogan (2017) recommend blockchain as an accounting system due to its power in real-time accounting and auditing, as well as fraud detection. Rückeshäuser (2017) criticizes the application of blockchain in accounting and questions the immutability of blockchain based on decentralization and technological rigor. She challenges the notion that blockchain will prevent fraud by senior management. Other authors warn that the integrity of blockchain is only as good as the data that are recorded (Prewett et al., 2020). For BT to work well, large data volumes are needed, which could reduce transaction costs but might increase the time required to process transactions (Davidson et al., 2016).

5.2 Technological Aspects

The potential benefits of BT make it attractive to most organizations. BT implementations are largely technology driven, and often various combinations of technologies are needed to make the BT architecture fit organizational applications (van Engelenburg et al., 2017). BT is distributed in nature, so organizations must undergo major structural transformations to work with customized BT applications and reap the potential benefits (Frizzo-Barker et al., 2020). Whereas the control of traditional information systems (Rossi et al., 2019) is relatively straightforward, the distributed nature of BT requires changes in responsibilities and new governance approaches. Implementing BT without extensive changes might limit its benefits (Millar et al., 2018). Currently, most BT projects are technology driven to explore the potential benefits, but as BT matures, societal challenges must become central (Millar et al., 2018). Lazanis (2015) predicts that blockchain will completely transform the accounting profession. Bumgarner and Vasarhelyi (2018) anticipate that auditing will increasingly rely on external sources of information, such as blockchain, and auditors' roles will be greatly reduced or even eliminated (Turker & Bicer, 2020). Appelbaum and Nehmer (2017) consider opportunities for auditors to modernize their audit procedures by taking advantage of the capabilities of BT. If companies keep all their transactions and balances on blockchain, it will not be necessary for auditors to provide opinions on financial statements, as the potential for tampering and mistrust will be eliminated (Byström, 2019). Internal auditors of companies using blockchain could conduct continuous internal audits, with audit trails and account analysis at the push of a button. Rooney et al. (2017) list the challenges of blockchain for internal auditors: they will have to access information in new formats (Cruz et al.,

2018); maximize the value of real-time continuous information; and work collaboratively with internal auditors from other organizations. Blockchain will improve the effectiveness of organizations' risk management, control, and governance processes (Rooney et al., 2017; Yoo, 2017).

At the technical level, numerous challenges in BT remain to be resolved. Yli-Huumo et al. (2016) explore the technical limitations of blockchain in-depth in their systematic review guided by Swan's (2015) framework. They enumerate challenges such as throughput, latency, size, bandwidth, security, wasted resources, usability, versioning, hard forks, scalability, reliability, volatility, negative environmental impact, and lack of universal standards and multiple chains (Dai et al., 2019; Kruglova & Dolbezhkin, 2018). Scalability is proving to be an issue as blockchain's popularity grows (Chang et al., 2020), since its initial design was not intended for wide-scale use and adoption. Blockchain scaling has been an active area of technical research for several years, and a variety of solutions are currently being tested (Kasireddy, 2017; Treleaven et al., 2017). Risks to reliability refer to the fact that BT can maintain information integrity but cannot guarantee the reliability of information added in the first place (Lindman et al., 2017; Soma Sinha, 2020). This could have serious negative impacts on smart contracts such as land registries (Cruz et al., 2018; Hamilton, 2020; Lemieux, 2016). As blockchain remains in the early phases of maturation, volatility remains a concern, especially for cryptocurrencies (Yuan et al., 2020). All these challenges can influence spikes and crashes in the cryptocurrency market as investors continue to grapple with the actual versus perceived value of this new asset class (Soma Sinha, 2020).

5.3 Financial Aspects

Papers focusing on finance (22%) often discuss the current and speculative opportunities and challenges of incorporating blockchain into various institutional processes (Lindman et al., 2017). Although one of blockchain's core characteristics is its ability to side-step traditional intermediaries, many banks and financial institutions are striving to adopt the benefits of distributed ledger technology (Ying et al., 2018) while mitigating third-party risk (Canaday, 2017; Sheetal Sinha & Bathla, 2019). Overall, the literature reveals that major institutions have a positive outlook toward improving efficiencies and lowering costs through BT (Liu et al., 2019; Yoo, 2017). Conceptual framework studies examine blockchain's potential to bring transparency, efficiency and cost savings to the financial sector (Glaser, 2017; Ko et al., 2018; Orel et al., 2004). Some articles also highlight the fact that BT may require changes to regulations at almost every level of society: individual corporations (Yermack, 2017), national governments (De Meijer, 2016), and the financial industry as a whole (Primm, 2016).

Several studies explore blockchain's financial benefits. Fanning and Centers (2016), Yoo (2017) and Zalan (2018) highlight the financial and economic opportunities associated with blockchain for international business and entrepreneurship with a focus on the accelerated internationalization of firms that are 'born global' on blockchain. The interconnected concepts of security, privacy, and data ownership are cited as benefits of blockchain. Blockchain's decentralized structure (Nærland et al., 2017) facilitates these features of the technology (Liu et al., 2019). Blockchain also has the potential to increase business efficiency and lower transaction costs (Kokina et al., 2017). For instance, *regtech*, or regulation technology, is designed to improve the effectiveness of financial services regulation (Birch et al., 2016) and (Yu et al., 2018). One of the most compelling and progressive benefits of blockchain is lower transaction costs for remittances, which are a lifeline for millions of people around the world, especially in rural areas and across the global south (Larios-Hernández, 2017). Blockchains like Ripple reduce the costs of remittances for both banks and end users. Since blockchain is designed to eliminate fraud and bypass software malfunctions, value transactions in these distributed networks (Paech, 2017) can be processed almost immediately, even before they are confirmed on the blockchain (Greenspan, 2016; Larios-Hernández, 2017). Cong et al. (2018) assess the paradigm shift blockchain represents for accounting and auditing organizations, which have built their empires on the centralized concept of keeping data within four walls (Shaw, 2018; Wang & Kogan, 2018).

The benefits of BT are often framed in technological, structural, or financial terms (Ram et al., 2016; Schmitz & Leoni, 2019). In 2009, Santoshi Nakamoto highlighted the fact that blockchain overrides the root problem of trust concerning conventional currencies and the global economy (Dowd & Hutchinson, 2015). This trust-free concept now extends beyond digital currencies to include smart contracts (Cruz et al., 2018; Hamilton, 2020) that automate various management functions using code (Brühl, 2017; Buterin, 2014; Gainsbury & Blaszczynski, 2017). Blockchain can facilitate governance functions such as voting and forming coalitions (Zhao et al., 2016), thereby allowing small investors, entrepreneurs, and creatives to be involved in corporate governance and protect their rights and interests. Blockchain could be used to promote transparency and greater equity in the music industry by addressing issues of ownership and payments and creating a single universal database of copyrights (O'Dair & Beaven, 2017; Tan & Low, 2019).

5.4 Disruption

There is a debate about the exact meaning of "disruptive technology" and how to predict which technologies will be particularly disruptive (Klenner et al., 2013). Questions remain about what causes technology to be disruptive and the nature of the disruption. Thinking about the actual process of creating technologies may be helpful for providing insights into the disruption process. Bringing new technologies and services to market is an essential driver of economic prosperity and domestic job growth. Moreover, there is almost unquestioning faith that new technologies will solve many of the problems and inefficiencies that exist within society. However, technological development and innovation are inherently tied to the economic system and, by extension, to the changes, inequalities, and interactions within that system. The discovery, evolution, and emergence of new technologies are influenced by the innovation ecosystem, which is, in turn, influenced by changing technologies and institutions.

Disruptive technologies are closely tied to innovation. Firms that can create and exploit emerging technologies and capture or create markets can add significant value to their bottom line (Christensen, 2013; Nagji & Tuff, 2012). Therefore, there is a great desire to understand and explain disruptive technologies. Technological innovation is the core of an innovation economy. New products, services, and knowledge create value, solve problems, and increase quality of life. However, new technologies are quickly replaced in the race for innovation. Bower and Christensen assert that disruptive technologies are those that cause an upheaval in the existing market structure and dominant firms (Christensen & Bower, 1996). These technologies initially operate at the margins but eventually displace conventional technologies. Frequently, the disruptive technology is cheaper, simpler, more convenient, and more reliable than the dominant technology and includes features that current customers do not care about (Christensen, 1997). Therefore, luxury and niche products, services, and technologies are not necessarily disruptive, even if they are innovative or revolutionary.

However, disruptions can occur in other ways. Disruptive technologies can be classified as disruptive when they overthrow existing (or widely accepted) scientific paradigms, ideas, or methods (Kuhn, 1970). This is a disruption in knowledge. New services or new processes can cause disruptions. Disruptions can also occur when relationships or social interactions are transformed. The disruption of emerging technologies may come not so much from the disruption of the marketplace or existing technological paradigms but from the disruption of the existing model of capitalism, organizational structures, or social interactions.

By Christensen's definition, disruptive technologies are essentially commercial disruptions that occur in an existing marketplace when a new product or service (a technology) is introduced. In refining and expounding his explanations of disruptive technologies and disruptive innovations, Christensen notes that three theories are at the heart of disruptive innovations (Christensen et al., 2004). The first is the Disruptive Innovation Theory, which posits that new organizations use simple, convenient low-cost innovations to create growth and triumph over powerful incumbents (p. xv). The second theory is the Resources, Processes, and Values (RPV) Theory, which explains that these three components collectively establish a firm's strengths and weaknesses. Finally, the Value Chain Evolution Theory states that a firm needs to directly control its value chain and solve the problems that would otherwise prevent that firm from capturing value from its activities. More recent scholarship seeks to expand Christensen's definition of disruptive innovations. Govindarajan and Kopalle (2006) broaden Christensen's definition to include both high-end and low-end disruptions. Yu and Hang (2011) distinguish between disruptive innovation and destructive innovation. They note that disruptive innovation does not always come from new entrants into the market or from start-ups. Christensen, however, continues to adhere closely to his original conceptualization (Christensen et al., 2008; Christensen &

Euchner, 2011; Gobble, 2015). As a result, it is difficult to reach consensus on a definition of disruptive technology.

The framework of two orders of technological disruption builds on Christensen's theories of disruptive technologies. A first-order disruption is a localized change within a market or industry. This type of disruption accepts Christensen's conceptualization of disruptive technology but is not limited by it. A first-order disruptive technology can come from a start-up, a new entrant to a market, or an existing firm. It is the disruption to an existing market that establishes a technology as a first-order disruptive technology, not where the disruption comes from. This first-order level is the type of disruption that is the focus of much of the business literature on innovation and disruption. Second-order disruptions are technological disruptions that ripple through society, creating large-scale change. That is, these technologies disrupt social interactions and relationships, organizational structures, institutions, public policies, and (sometimes) the physical environment (i.e., micro-level disruptions).

Technological innovations are often classified into two types: (1) revolutionary, discontinuous, breakthrough, radical, emergent or step-function technologies and (2) evolutionary, continuous, incremental or 'nuts and bolts' technologies (Florida & Kenney, 1990; Morone, 1993; Utterback, 1994). First-order and second-order disruptions should not be confused with revolutionary versus incremental technologies. Both first-order and second-order disruptions are revolutionary forms of technological innovation. The difference between them is the magnitude of the disruption.

Often, an emerging technology can improve or displace others (Christensen, 2013; Kokina et al., 2017). One of the major questions across the article data setis how blockchain may disrupt existing technologies (Frizzo-Barker et al., 2020). If BT effectively diffuses into corporate culture as the new system of recordkeeping, accountants may see a diminishment or evolution of their role (Fuller & Markelevich, 2020). Brandon (2016) explores future blockchain-based accounting practices for businesses, including the growth of accounting systems from single-entry ledgers to triple entries (debit, credit, and cryptographic signature of transaction). This is another area that requires more research as it unfolds.

5.5 *Education*

Education is facing major challenges that go beyond the mere optimization of teaching-learning processes (Bartolomé & Steffens, 2011) in response to the changes in knowledge produced by technologies that alter not only customs but also ways of thinking, evoking a Frankenstein's syndrome state (Postman, 2011). Can BT provide a solution to some of these problems?

It would be a mistake to assume that this technology will be applied immediately or in the coming years. Instead, this is an exploratory period, and these technologies may never develop further or in this direction. The fervor with which some sectors of the education system are pursuing BT has raised concerns about both the origins of this enthusiasm and the consequences that a literal application of current technology could have. Speaking of the consequences of implementation is as speculative as much of the literature that is promoting it. Nonetheless, it is essential to ask questions about the ideologies and agendas of the institutions, enterprises, initiatives, or projects that are intended to be based on education using BT.

Watters (2016) cites three key elements of the imagined future in the discourse on BT in education that deserve special attention:

- The anti-institutional disposition of BT.
- Its dependence on decentralization (technologically and metaphorically), which may dismantle rather than democratize the public sector.
- The invocation of trust (and mistrust) as the key social behavior mediated by technology.

Bellver (2017) summarizes criticisms of BT use in education in the following points:

- Usually related to certification.
- Those offering criticisms have an interest as state, international, or global shared repositories but are limited to an institution that does not offer advantages concerning the current electronic certificates.
- It is a technology in an experimental stage. The only consolidated implementation is the Bitcoin system.
- It is a technology with an overly complex implementation based on the social implementation of terribly problematic matters (such as the use of public-key cryptography) at considerable cost both economically and in terms of energy.
- It ensures the validity of transactions, but the problem of the detailed certification and reputation of the custom learning remains unresolved.
- If the transaction record is public and unchangeable, the user loses the right to privacy and the definition of their curriculum vitae. They cannot choose parties they would prefer to show it to or hide it from.
- Exaggerating the potential of BT to transform education implies reducing, once again, education to evaluation and evaluation to the certification of competencies.
- The underlying ideology of BT is libertarian liberalism or libertarianism. Transferring this ideology to education would support a global certification utopia in which everyone participates in the same plan as current educational institutions.

Some articles consider BT in the early development stage in education. Its evolution in the coming years will show whether we are moving toward more economical and easy-to-use systems. Others refer to the use of BT to solve the first problem: academic certification. Others raise some complex challenges, such as respect for an individual's privacy regarding elements of their curriculum vitae or the need to validate the accreditation that picks up the chain. Finally, some articles refer to the ideology that allegedly underlies this technology.

In the growing literature on BT, the main emphasis is on training future accounting professionals in these new emerging technologies (Kuppusamy, 2019). Academia is continually updating the accounting curriculum to broaden students' skillsets and meet the accounting knowledge requirements of business stakeholders in response to constant changes in accounting standards and technological innovations (Chung & Kim, 2016; Owen, 2013; Schmitz & Leoni, 2019; Schwab, 2017). These responses to successive technological and business transactional innovations have contributed to the evolution of the accounting profession to its present state. Blockchain is yet another transformative technology that may require updating of skills across many professions and domains (Hoy, 2017).

6 Future Research Agenda

The economic benefits of blockchain have been studied extensively. For an individual business, it is important to understand the effects of blockchain applications on the business's organizational structure, mode of operation, and management model. For the market as a whole, it is important to determine whether blockchain can resolve the market failures brought by information asymmetry and increase market efficiency and social welfare. However, understanding the mechanisms through which blockchain influences corporate and market efficiency will require further academic inquiry. Privacy protection and security issues require more attention from BT researchers. Although all blockchain transactions are anonymous and encrypted, there is still a risk of data hacking (Lindman et al., 2017). In the security sector, there is a view that absolute security can never be guaranteed wherever physical contact exists. Consequently, the question of how to share transaction data while also protecting personal data privacy is particularly vital in both academic and social practice.

Initial coin offerings (ICOs) and cryptocurrency markets have grown rapidly. Their growth raises many interesting questions, such as how to manage digital currencies. The majority of previous research has focused on the determinants of the success of ICOs, and future research should begin discussing how to regulate cryptocurrency and the ICO market. The success of BT in digital currency applications before 2015 caught the attention of many traditional financial institutions. Blockchain continues to reinvent itself and is now more than capable of meeting the needs of the finance industry. Large-scale applications of blockchain are possible in many areas of finance, such as banking, capital markets, internet finance, and related fields. The deep integration of BT and fintech will continue to be a promising research direction.

In short, the first important research direction is understanding the mechanisms through which blockchain influences corporate and market efficiency. The second potential research direction is privacy protection and security issues. The third relates to the management of digital currencies and regulation of the cryptocurrency market. The fourth potential research direction is how to deeply integrate BT and fintech. The final topic is cross-chain technology—if each industry has its blockchain system, then researchers and developers must discover new ways to exchange data. This is the key to achieving the Internet of Things (Christidis & Devetsikiotis, 2016). Businesses that require accounting settlement and crowdfunding, data storage and sharing, supply chain management, and smart trading can benefit considerably from applying BT.

The sharing economy is often defined as the sharing of goods and services among individuals on a peer-to-peer basis. In the future, sharing among enterprises may become an important part of the new sharing economy. Consequently, building blockchain interconnections may become a distinct trend. These interconnections will facilitate linkages between processes of identity authentication, supply chain management, and payments in commercial operations. They will also allow instantaneous information exchange and data coordination among enterprises and industries.

The traditional accounting business and educational environments are changing in response to a constantly digitalizing world but not quickly enough to meet the requirements of a blockchain accounting system. Major overhauls of the educational system and business structure may be needed. This study facilitates the identification of research areas and implications and provides a useful baseline for practitioners, professionals, and academics, who can monitor the state of the art in the disruption of accounting, auditing and finance by BT by highlighting how blockchain is changing traditions and what actions are required.

7 Conclusion

This chapter presents a comprehensive overview of blockchain and its potential to enhance accounting, auditing and finance activities. This topic is still immature. Blockchain is one of the most revolutionary technologies available today, but unlocking its true potential requires more than technical improvements. Whereas scalability, latency, privacy, security and authentication are widely recognized as significant obstacles to further maturation of blockchain, organizational and human issues remain in the shadows but are critical to implementing a blockchain solution at the organizational level.

Despite the widespread deployment of blockchain applications, many issues have yet to be addressed. Addressing these issues will increase not only the scalability and efficiency but also the durability of blockchain. The features offered by BT are not unique when considered individually, and most of the mechanisms they are based on are well known. However, the combination of these features makes BT ideal for many applications and justifies the intense interest in BT among several professions/industries. As BT matures, applications are expected to penetrate more industries/domains than those covered here.

As theoretical applications transition to proof-of-concept successes, BT will become an integral part of the information technology ecosystem. BT will undoubtedly have a tremendous impact on the financial sector, and one of the most challenging areas will be financial accounting. Blockchain has the potential to greatly increase accounting information and reduce errors in disclosures and earnings management. Moreover, the role of financial, taxation, and management information systems accountants will change. They will no longer be expected to record transactions and make financial statements; instead, they will validate both the source documents and reasonability of smart contracts used in accounting blockchain. This potential impact is generally recognized and intensely studied by accounting and auditing professional bodies. However, for most accountants, blockchain remains an "exotic" technology that is mostly related to cryptocurrencies. This limited understanding not only undermines their ability to take full advantage of blockchain accounting but also misses a unique opportunity to participate in the process of designing blockchain solutions for their clients.

References

Abbas, Z., Raza, S., & Ejaz, K. (2008). Systematic reviews and their role in evidence—Informed health care. *JPMA: The Journal of the Pakistan Medical Association, 58*(10), 561.

Abreu, P. W., Aparicio, M., & Costa, C. J. (2018). *Blockchain technology in the auditing environment.* Paper presented at the 2018 13th Iberian Conference on Information Systems and Technologies (CISTI).

Al Harthy, K., Al Shuhaimi, F., & Al Ismaily, K. K. J. (2019). *The upcoming blockchain adoption in higher-education: Requirements and process.* Paper presented at the 2019 4th MEC International Conference on Big Data and Smart City (ICBDSC).

Ali, O., Ally, M., & Dwivedi, Y. (2020). The state of play of blockchain technology in the financial services sector: A systematic literature review. *International Journal of Information Management, 54*, 102199.

Ali, O., Shrestha, A., Soar, J., & Wamba, S. F. (2018). Cloud computing-enabled healthcare opportunities, issues, and applications: A systematic review. *International Journal of Information Management, 43*, 146–158.

Ali, R., Barrdear, J., Clews, R., & Southgate, J. (2014). Innovations in payment technologies and the emergence of digital currencies. *Bank of England Quarterly Bulletin, Q3*, 262–275.

Angeles, R. (2019). Blockchain-based healthcare: Three successful proof-of-concept pilots worth considering. *Journal of International Technology and Information Management, 27*(3), 47–83.

Appelbaum, D., & Nehmer, R. (2017). *Designing and auditing accounting systems based on blockchain and distributed ledger principles.* Feliciano School of Business.

Appelbaum, D., & Nehmer, R. A. (2020). Auditing cloud-based blockchain accounting systems. *Journal of Information Systems, 34*(2), 5–21.

Ashta, A., & Biot-Paquerot, G. (2018). FinTech evolution: Strategic value management issues in a fast changing industry. *Strategic Change, 27*(4), 301–311.

Aune, R. T., Krellenstein, A., O'Hara, M., & Slama, O. (2017). Footprints on a blockchain: Trading and information leakage in distributed ledgers. *The Journal of Trading, 12*(3), 5–13.

Bartolomé, A., & Steffens, K. (2011). Technologies for self-regulated learning. In *Self-regulated learning in technology enhanced learning environments* (pp. 21–31). Brill.

Bellver, C. (2017). Blockchain en educació? Per a qué? [Fichero de video]. *Seminario del Centro de Educación y Nuevas Tecnologías (CENT).* Universidad Jaume I de Castellón. Recuperado de http://cent.uji.es/pub/seminari-blockchain

Birch, D., Brown, R. G., & Parulava, S. (2016). Towards ambient accountability in financial services: Shared ledgers, translucent transactions and the technological legacy of the great financial crisis. *Journal of Payments Strategy & Systems, 10*(2), 118–131.

Bonsón, E., & Bednárová, M. (2019). Blockchain and its implications for accounting and auditing. *Meditari Accountancy Research, 27*(5), 725–740.

Brandon, D. (2016). The blockchain: The future of business information systems. *International Journal of the Academic Business World, 10*(2), 33–40.

Brennan, N. M., Subramaniam, N., & van Staden, C. J. (2019). *Corporate governance implications of disruptive technology: An overview*. Elsevier.

Brühl, V. (2017). Virtual currencies, distributed ledgers and the future of financial services. *Intereconomics, 52*(6), 370–378.

Brukhanskyi, R., & Spilnyk, I. (2019). *Cryptographic objects in the accounting system.* Paper presented at the 2019 9th International Conference on Advanced Computer Information Technologies (ACIT).

Bumgarner, N., & Vasarhelyi, M. A. (2018). Continuous auditing—A new view1. In *Continuous auditing*. Emerald Publishing Limited.

Buterin, V. (2014). DAOc, DACs, DAs and more: An incomplete terminology guide. Available online: https://blog.ethereum.org/2014/05/06/daos-dacs-das-and-more-anincomplete-terminology-guide/. Accessed 20 October 2021.

Byström, H. (2019). Blockchains, real-time accounting, and the future of credit risk modeling. *Ledger Journal, 4*(4), 40–47.

Cai, C. W. (2018). Disruption of financial intermediation by FinTech: A review on crowdfunding and blockchain. *Accounting & Finance, 58*(4), 965–992.

Canaday, T. (2017). Evolving a payments business to meet the demands of a distributed economy. *Journal of Payments Strategy & Systems, 11*(1), 15–22.

Casino, F., Dasaklis, T. K., & Patsakis, C. (2019). A systematic literature review of blockchain-based applications: Current status, classification and open issues. *Telematics and Informatics, 36*, 55–81.

CBINSIGHTS. (2021). *Banking is only the beginning: 58 big industries blockchain could transform.* CBINSIGHTS. https://www.cbinsights.com/research/industries-disrupted-blockchain/

Chang, V., Baudier, P., Zhang, H., Xu, Q., Zhang, J., & Arami, M. (2020). How blockchain can impact financial services—The overview, challenges and recommendations from expert interviewees. *Technological Forecasting and Social Change, 158*, 120166.

Chen, C. (2004). Searching for intellectual turning points: Progressive knowledge domain visualization. *Proceedings of the National Academy of Sciences, 101*(suppl 1), 5303–5310.

Christensen, C., & Euchner, J. (2011). Managing disruption: An interview with Clayton Christensen. *Research-Technology Management, 54*(1), 11–17.

Christensen, C. M. (1997). *The innovator's dilemma: How new technologies cause great firms to fail*. Harvard Business School Press.

Christensen, C. M. (2013). *The innovator's dilemma: When new technologies cause great firms to fail.* Harvard Business Review Press.

Christensen, C. M., & Bower, J. L. (1996). Customer power, strategic investment, and the failure of leading firms. *Strategic Management Journal, 17*, 197–218.

Christensen, C. M., Anthony, S. D., & Roth, E. A. (2004). *Seeing what's next: Using the theories of innovation to predict industry change.* Harvard Business Press.

Christensen, C. M., Kaufman, S. P., & Shih, W. C. (2008). Innovation killers. *Harvard Business Review, 86*, 98–105.

Christidis, K., & Devetsikiotis, M. (2016). Blockchains and smart contracts for the internet of things. *IEEE Access, 4*, 2292–2303.

Chung, M., & Kim, J. (2016). The internet information and technology research directions based on the fourth industrial revolution. *KSII Transactions on Internet & Information Systems, 10*(3), 1311–1320.

Clemons, E. K., Dewan, R. M., Kauffman, R. J., & Weber, T. A. (2017). Understanding the information-based transformation of strategy and society. *Journal of Management Information Systems, 34*(2), 425–456.

Cong, Y., Du, H., & Vasarhelyi, M. A. (2018). *Technological disruption in accounting and auditing.* American Accounting Association.

Coren, E., & Fisher, M. (2006). *The conduct of systematic research reviews for SCIE knowledge reviews*. SCIE.

Coyne, J. G., & McMickle, P. L. (2017). Can blockchains serve an accounting purpose? *Journal of Emerging Technologies in Accounting, 14*(2), 101–111.

Cruz, J. P., Kaji, Y., & Yanai, N. (2018). RBAC-SC: Role-based access control using smart contract. *IEEE Access, 6*, 12240–12251.

Dai, J., He, N., & Yu, H. (2019). Utilizing blockchain and smart contracts to enable audit 4.0: From the perspective of accountability audit of air pollution control in China. *Journal of Emerging Technologies in Accounting, 16*(2), 23–41.

Dai, J., & Vasarhelyi, M. A. (2017). Toward blockchain-based accounting and assurance. *Journal of Information Systems, 31*(3), 5–21.

Davidson, S., De Filippi, P., & Potts, J. (2016). *Economics of blockchain*. Available at SSRN 2744751.

De Meijer, C. R. (2016). The UK and blockchain technology: A balanced approach. *Journal of Payments Strategy & Systems, 9*(4), 220–229.

de Ridder, C. A., Tunstall, M. K., & Prescott, N. (2017). Recognition of smart contracts in the United States. *Intellectual Property & Technology Law Journal, 29*(11), 17–19.

DeSanctis, G., & Poole, M. S. (1994). Capturing the complexity in advanced technology use: Adaptive structuration theory. *Organization Science, 5*(2), 121–147.

Dierksmeier, C., & Seele, P. (2018). Cryptocurrencies and business ethics. *Journal of Business Ethics, 152*(1), 1–14.

Dikert, K., Paasivaara, M., & Lassenius, C. (2016). Challenges and success factors for large-scale agile transformations: A systematic literature review. *Journal of Systems and Software, 119*, 87–108.

Dowd, K., & Hutchinson, M. (2015). Bitcoin will bite the dust. *Cato Journal, 35*(2), 357–382.

Du, W. D., Pan, S. L., Leidner, D. E., & Ying, W. (2019). Affordances, experimentation and actualization of FinTech: A blockchain implementation study. *The Journal of Strategic Information Systems, 28*(1), 50–65.

Duan, B., Zhong, Y., & Liu, D. (2017). *Education application of blockchain technology: Learning outcome and meta-diploma*. Paper presented at the 2017 IEEE 23rd International Conference on Parallel and Distributed Systems (ICPADS).

Engelhardt, M. A. (2017). Hitching healthcare to the chain: An introduction to blockchain technology in the healthcare sector. *Technology Innovation Management Review, 7*(10), 22–34.

Erik, P. M., Vermeulen, M. F., & Kaal, W. (2018). Why blockchain will disrupt corporate organizations—What can be learned from the "digital transformation." *The Journal of the British Blockchain Association, 1*(2), 6352.

Evans, D. (2003). Hierarchy of evidence: A framework for ranking evidence evaluating healthcare interventions. *Journal of Clinical Nursing, 12*(1), 77–84.

Fanning, K., & Centers, D. P. (2016). Blockchain and its coming impact on financial services. *Journal of Corporate Accounting & Finance, 27*(5), 53–57.

Florida, R., & Kenney, M. (1990). High-technology restructuring in the USA and Japan. *Environment and Planning A, 22*(2), 233–252.

Frizzo-Barker, J., Chow-White, P. A., Adams, P. R., Mentanko, J., Ha, D., & Green, S. (2020). Blockchain as a disruptive technology for business: A systematic review. *International Journal of Information Management, 51*, 102029.

Fuller, S. H., & Markelevich, A. (2020). Should accountants care about blockchain? *Journal of Corporate Accounting & Finance, 31*(2), 34–46.

Gainsbury, S. M., & Blaszczynski, A. (2017). How blockchain and cryptocurrency technology could revolutionize online gambling. *Gaming Law Review, 21*(7), 482–492.

Glaser, F. (2017). *Pervasive decentralisation of digital infrastructures: A framework for blockchain enabled system and use case analysis*. Paper presented at the Proceedings of the 50th Hawaii international conference on system sciences.

Gobble, M. M. (2015). The case against disruptive innovation. *Research-Technology Management, 58*(1), 59–63.

Gomber, P., Kauffman, R. J., Parker, C., & Weber, B. W. (2018). On the fintech revolution: Interpreting the forces of innovation, disruption, and transformation in financial services. *Journal of Management Information Systems, 35*(1), 220–265.

Govindarajan, V., & Kopalle, P. K. (2006). Disruptiveness of innovations: Measurement and an assessment of reliability and validity. *Strategic Management Journal, 27*(2), 189–199.

Grant, G., & Hogan, R. (2015). Bitcoin: Risks and controls. *Journal of Corporate Accounting & Finance, 26*(5), 29–35.

Greenspan, G. (2016). *Four genuine blockchain use cases.* MultiChain [blog], 10.

Halamka, J. D., Lippman, A., & Ekblaw, A. (2017). The potential for blockchain to transform electronic health records. *Harvard Business Review, 3*(3), 2–5.

Hamilton, M. (2020). Blockchain distributed ledger technology: An introduction and focus on smart contracts. *Journal of Corporate Accounting & Finance, 31*(2), 7–12.

Hoy, M. B. (2017). An introduction to the blockchain and its implications for libraries and medicine. *Medical Reference Services Quarterly, 36*(3), 273–279.

Hyvärinen, H., Risius, M., & Friis, G. (2017). A blockchain-based approach towards overcoming financial fraud in public sector services. *Business & Information Systems Engineering, 59*(6), 441–456.

Iansiti, M., & Lakhani, K. R. (2017). The truth about blockchain. *Harvard Business Review.* hbr.org/2017/01/the-truth-about-blockchain. Accessed February, 2, 2019.

Kaaniche, N., & Laurent, M. (2017). *A blockchain-based data usage auditing architecture with enhanced privacy and availability.* Paper presented at the 2017 IEEE 16th International Symposium on Network Computing and Applications (NCA).

Kasireddy, P. (2017, August 23). *Blockchains don't scale. Not today, at least. But there's hope.* Medium: Hackernoon. https://hackernoon.com/blockchainsdont-scale-not-today-at-least-but-there-s-hope-2cb43946551a

Kim, H. M., & Laskowski, M. (2018). Toward an ontology-driven blockchain design for supply-chain provenance. *Intelligent Systems in Accounting, Finance and Management, 25*(1), 18–27.

Kim, S., & Sarin, A. (2018). Distributed ledger and blockchain technology: Framework and use cases. *Journal of Investment Management.* https://doi.org/10.2139/ssrn.3373347

Kitchenham, B., & Charters, S. (2007). *Guidelines for performing systematic literature reviews in software engineering.* Technical Report EBSE 2007–001, Keele University and Durham University.

Kiviat, T. I. (2015). Beyond bitcoin: Issues in regulating blockchain tranactions. *Duke Law Journal, 65,* 569.

Klenner, P., Hüsig, S., & Dowling, M. (2013). Ex-ante evaluation of disruptive susceptibility in established value networks—When are markets ready for disruptive innovations? *Research Policy, 42*(4), 914–927.

Ko, T., Lee, J., & Ryu, D. (2018). Blockchain technology and manufacturing industry: Real-time transparency and cost savings. *Sustainability, 10*(11), 4274.

Kokina, J., Mancha, R., & Pachamanova, D. (2017). Blockchain: Emergent industry adoption and implications for accounting. *Journal of Emerging Technologies in Accounting, 14*(2), 91–100.

Kruglova, I. A., & Dolbezhkin, V. A. (2018). *Objective barriers to the implementation of blockchain technology in the financial sector.* Paper presented at the 2018 International Conference on Artificial Intelligence Applications and Innovations (IC-AIAI).

Krugman, P. (2013, December 28). Bitcoin is evil. *The New York Times.*

Kshetri, N. (2018). 1 blockchain's roles in meeting key supply chain management objectives. *International Journal of Information Management, 39,* 80–89.

Kuhn, T. S. (1970). *The structure of scientific revolutions* (Vol. 111). University of Chicago Press.

Kuppusamy, P. (2019). Blockchain architecture to higher education systems. *International Journal of Latest Technology in Engineering, Management & Applied Science, VIII*(II), 124–138.

Larios-Hernández, G. J. (2017). Blockchain entrepreneurship opportunity in the practices of the unbanked. *Business Horizons, 60*(6), 865–874.

Lazanis, R. (2015). *How technology behind Bitcoin could transform accounting as we know it*. Retrieved August, 23, 2017.

Lemieux, V. L. (2016). Trusting records: Is Blockchain technology the answer? *Records Management Journal, 26*(2), 110–139.

Li, X., & Wang, C. A. (2017). The technology and economic determinants of cryptocurrency exchange rates: The case of Bitcoin. *Decision Support Systems, 95*, 49–60.

Lindman, J., Tuunainen, V. K., & Rossi, M. (2017). *Opportunities and risks of blockchain technologies—A research agenda*. Academic Press.

Liu, M., Wu, K., & Xu, J. J. (2019). How will blockchain technology impact auditing and accounting: Permissionless versus permissioned blockchain. *Current Issues in Auditing, 13*(2), A19–A29.

Marrone, M., & Hazelton, J. (2019). The disruptive and transformative potential of new technologies for accounting, accountants and accountability. *Meditari Accountancy Research, 27*(5), 677–694.

Millar, C., Lockett, M., & Ladd, T. (2018). Disruption: Technology, innovation and society. *Technological Forecasting and Social Change, 129*, 254–260.

Moll, J., & Yigitbasioglu, O. (2019). The role of internet-related technologies in shaping the work of accountants: New directions for accounting research. *The British Accounting Review, 51*(6), 100833.

Morone, J. G. (1993). Technology and competitive advantage—The role of general management. *Research-Technology Management, 36*(2), 16–25.

Nærland, K., Müller-Bloch, C., Beck, R., & Palmund, S. (2017). *Blockchain to rule the Waves-Nascent design principles for reducing risk and uncertainty in decentralized environments*. Paper presented at the ICIS.

Nagji, B., & Tuff, G. (2012). A simple tool you need to manage innovation. *Harvard Business Review, 5*, 2–12.

Nagy, D., Schuessler, J., & Dubinsky, A. (2016). Defining and identifying disruptive innovations. *Industrial Marketing Management, 57*, 119–126.

Nakamoto, S., & Bitcoin, A. (2008). *A peer-to-peer electronic cash system*. Bitcoin. https://bitcoin.org/bitcoin. pdf

O'Dair, M., & Beaven, Z. (2017). The networked record industry: How blockchain technology could transform the record industry. *Strategic Change, 26*(5), 471–480.

Ølnes, S., Ubacht, J., & Janssen, M. (2017). *Blockchain in government: Benefits and implications of distributed ledger technology for information sharing*. Elsevier.

Orel, N. A., Ford, R. A., & Brock, C. (2004). Women's financial planning for retirement: The impact of disruptive life events. *Journal of Women & Aging, 16*(3–4), 39–53.

Owen, G. (2013). Integrated reporting: A review of developments and their implications for the accounting curriculum. *Accounting Education, 22*(4), 340–356.

Paech, P. (2017). The governance of blockchain financial networks. *The Modern Law Review, 80*(6), 1073–1110.

Pazaitis, A., De Filippi, P., & Kostakis, V. (2017). Blockchain and value systems in the sharing economy: The illustrative case of backfeed. *Technological Forecasting and Social Change, 125*, 105–115.

Popay, J., Roberts, H., Sowden, A., Petticrew, M., Arai, L., Rodgers, M., Britten, N., Roen, K., & Duffy, S. (2006). *Guidance on the conduct of narrative synthesis in systematic reviews*. A Product from the ESRC Methods Programme Version, *1*, b92.

Postman, N. (2011). *Technopoly: The surrender of culture to technology*. Vintage.

Potekhina, A., & Riumkin, I. (2017). *Blockchain—A new accounting paradigm: Implications for credit risk management* (Dissertation). Retrieved from http://urn.kb.se/resolve?urn=urn:nbn:se:umu:diva-136867

Prewett, K. W., Prescott, G. L., & Phillips, K. (2020). Blockchain adoption is inevitable—Barriers and risks remain. *Journal of Corporate Accounting & Finance, 31*(2), 21–28.

Primm, H. (2016). Regulating the blockchain revolution: A financial industry transformation. *Review of Banking & Financial Law, 36*(1), 75–91.

Radanović, I., & Likić, R. (2018). Opportunities for use of blockchain technology in medicine. *Applied Health Economics and Health Policy, 16*(5), 583–590.

Raiborn, C., & Sivitanides, M. (2015). Accounting issues related to Bitcoins. *Journal of Corporate Accounting & Finance, 26*(2), 25–34.

Ram, A., Maroun, W., & Garnett, R. (2016). Accounting for the Bitcoin: Accountability, neoliberalism and a correspondence analysis. *Meditari Accountancy Research, 24*(1), 2–35.

Rooney, H., Aiken, B., & Rooney, M. (2017). Q & A. Is internal audit ready for blockchain? *Technology Innovation Management Review, 7*(10), 41–44.

Rossi, M., Mueller-Bloch, C., Thatcher, J. B., & Beck, R. (2019). Blockchain research in information systems: Current trends and an inclusive future research agenda. *Journal of the Association for Information Systems, 20*(9), 14.

Rückeshäuser, N. (2017). *Distributed ledgers for the prevention of accounting fraud: Blockchains between expectations and reality.* Albert-Ludwigs-Universität Freiburg.

Savelyev, A. (2018). Copyright in the blockchain era: Promises and challenges. *Computer Law & Security Review, 34*(3), 550–561.

Schmitz, J., & Leoni, G. (2019). Accounting and auditing at the time of blockchain technology: A research agenda. *Australian Accounting Review, 29*(2), 331–342.

Schuelke-Leech, B.-A. (2018). A model for understanding the orders of magnitude of disruptive technologies. *Technological Forecasting and Social Change, 129*, 261–274.

Schwab, K. (2017). *The fourth industrial revolution.* Currency Books.

Shaw, J. (2018). *The blockchain transformation of acoounting and auditing.* Oregon Society of CPAs. Retrieved from https://www.orcpa.org/writable/files/Publications/Magazine-Articles-PDF/blockchain_story_excerpt.pdf

Sinha, S. (2020). Blockchain—Opportunities and challenges for accounting professionals. *Journal of Corporate Accounting & Finance, 31*(2), 65–67.

Sinha, S., & Bathla, R. (2019). *Implementation of blockchain in financial sector to improve scalability.* Paper presented at the 2019 4th International Conference on Information Systems and Computer Networks (ISCON).

Smith, S. S., & Castonguay, J. J. (2020). Blockchain and accounting governance: Emerging issues and considerations for accounting and assurance professionals. *Journal of Emerging Technologies in Accounting, 17*(1), 119–131.

Sun, J., Yan, J., & Zhang, K. Z. (2016). Blockchain-based sharing services: What blockchain technology can contribute to smart cities. *Financial Innovation, 2*(1), 1–9.

Swan, M. (2015). *Blockchain: Blueprint for a new economy.* O'Reilly Media, Inc.

Tan, B. S., & Low, K. Y. (2019). Blockchain as the database engine in the accounting system. *Australian Accounting Review, 29*(2), 312–318.

The Economist. (2015). The promise of the blockchain: The trust machine. *The Economist, 31*, 27.

Tranfield, D., Denyer, D., & Smart, P. (2003). Towards a methodology for developing evidence-informed management knowledge by means of systematic review. *British Journal of Management, 14*(3), 207–222.

Treleaven, P., Brown, R. G., & Yang, D. (2017). Blockchain technology in finance. *Computer, 50*(9), 14–17.

Turker, I., & Bicer, A. A. (2020). How to use blockchain effectively in auditing and assurance services. In *Digital business strategies in blockchain ecosystems* (pp. 457–471). Springer.

Utterback, J. M. (1994). Radical innovation and corporate regeneration. *Research Technology Management, 37*(4), 10.

van Engelenburg, S., Janssen, M., Klievink, B., & Tan, Y.-H. (2017). *Comparing a shipping information pipeline with a thick flow and a thin flow.* Paper presented at the International Conference on Electronic Government.

Victor, L. (2008). Systematic reviewing. *Social Research Update, 54*(1), 1–4.

Vigna, P., & Casey, M. J. (2016). *The age of cryptocurrency: How bitcoin and the blockchain are challenging the global economic order.* Macmillan.

Vincent, N. E., Skjellum, A., & Medury, S. (2020). Blockchain architecture: A design that helps CPA firms leverage the technology. *International Journal of Accounting Information Systems, 38*, 100466.

Wang, Y., & Kogan, A. (2017). *Designing privacy-preserving blockchain based accounting information systems.* Retrieved from https://doi.org/10.2139/ssrn.2978281

Wang, Y., & Kogan, A. (2018). Designing confidentiality-preserving Blockchain-based transaction processing systems. *International Journal of Accounting Information Systems, 30*, 1–18.

Watter A. (2016). *The blockchain for education: An introducation.* Retrieved from http://hackeducation.com/2016/04/07/blockchain-education-guide

Xu, J. J. (2016). Are blockchains immune to all malicious attacks? *Financial Innovation, 2*(1), 1–9.

Xu, M., Chen, X., & Kou, G. (2019). A systematic review of blockchain. *Financial Innovation, 5*(1), 27.

Yang, D., & Li, M. (2018). Evolutionary approaches and the construction of technology-driven regulations. *Emerging Markets Finance and Trade, 54*(14), 3256–3271.

Yermack, D. (2017). Corporate governance and blockchains. *Review of Finance, 21*(1), 7–31.

Ying, W., Jia, S., & Du, W. (2018). Digital enablement of blockchain: Evidence from HNA group. *International Journal of Information Management, 39*, 1–4.

Yli-Huumo, J., Ko, D., Choi, S., Park, S., & Smolander, K. (2016). Where is current research on blockchain technology?—A systematic review. *PLoS ONE, 11*(10), e0163477.

Yoo, S. (2017). Blockchain based financial case analysis and its implications. *Asia Pacific Journal of Innovation and Entrepreneurship, 11*(3), 312–321.

Yu, D., & Hang, C. C. (2011). Creating technology candidates for disruptive innovation: Generally applicable R&D strategies. *Technovation, 31*(8), 401–410.

Yu, T., Lin, Z., & Tang, Q. (2018). Blockchain: The introduction and its application in financial accounting. *Journal of Corporate Accounting & Finance, 29*(4), 37–47.

Yuan, H., Chen, X., Wang, J., Yuan, J., Yan, H., & Susilo, W. (2020). Blockchain-based public auditing and secure deduplication with fair arbitration. *Information Sciences, 541*, 409–425.

Zalan, T. (2018). Born global on blockchain. *Review of International Business and Strategy, 28*(1), 19–34.

Zhang, Y., Xiong, F., Xie, Y., Fan, X., & Gu, H. (2020). The impact of artificial intelligence and blockchain on the accounting profession. *IEEE Access, 8*, 110461–110477.

Zhao, J. L., Fan, S., & Yan, J. (2016). *Overview of business innovations and research opportunities in blockchain and introduction to the special issue.* SpringerOpen.

Manpreet Singh has earned a doctorate from the School of Accounting, Information Systems and Supply Chain at the RMIT University, Melbourne, Australia. The research interests are the links between accounting and information systems.

Mahesh Joshi is a Senior Lecturer in Accounting and Financial Planning at RMIT University, Melbourne, Australia. His research interests are corporate social reporting, corporate governance, integrated reporting, intellectual capital, accounting history, accounting education, and emerging technologies in accounting.

Sharad Sharma is a Lecturer in Wealth Management and Taxation in the School of Accounting, Information Systems and Supply Chain at the RMIT University, Melbourne, Australia. He has extensive experience in the banking industry in India. His research expertise is in the areas of behavioral finance, capital markets, IFRS and various aspects of financial reporting and performance. He has published several papers in scholarly academic journals.

Tarek Rana is an Associate Professor of Accounting and Data Analytics in the School of Accounting Information Systems and Supply Chain, at RMIT University, Melbourne, Australia. He earned a PhD in Accounting at the University of New South Wales (UNSW) Australia and an MBA from the University of Saskatchewan, Canada. He has considerable professional and industry experience in the areas of business services, taxation, auditing, and financial planning as well as consulting services including performance measurement and risk management. His current research focuses on the intersection of accounting and data analytics including the implications of new technologies on management control systems, performance measurement, risk management, and sustainability where he draws on textual analytics, machine learning and artificial intelligence theories and practices. His research papers appeared in international and interdisciplinary scholarly journals such as *The British Accounting Review, Accounting Auditing and Accountability Journal, Financial Accountability & Management, Intelligent Systems in Accounting, Finance & Management, Qualitative Research in Accounting and Management, Meditary Accountancy Research, Business Strategy and the Environment, Public Money & Management, Journal of Accounting & Organisational Change, Journal of Cleaner Production, and Journal of Intellectual Capital.*

Index

A
Absolute sustainability, 6, 107, 108, 111, 114, 117, 120–122, 124–127
Accounting, 2–12, 18, 21–25, 37, 42–44, 46, 47, 50–59, 68, 71, 99, 110, 123, 133–137, 139, 140, 142, 143, 145, 147, 148, 150, 151, 153–156, 158, 159, 165–174, 178, 179, 184, 192, 196, 197, 209–215, 217, 221, 228, 229, 231, 240, 243, 245, 248, 258–260, 264, 271, 274, 301, 338–340, 343, 344, 346–351, 355, 356, 362, 363, 368–371, 374, 376, 377, 380, 381, 395, 396, 398–400, 416–420, 422–430, 432, 433, 468, 470, 472, 473, 475, 477, 480–482, 484, 510–513, 519, 530, 536–539, 541, 543–545, 547, 549–553
Accounting curricula, 8, 339, 340, 344, 347, 348, 351, 355, 356, 416, 423, 429, 430, 433
Accounting education, 8, 9, 217–219, 221, 223, 224, 226, 339, 347, 356, 361, 363, 366, 369, 380, 381, 397, 428, 512, 531
Accounting for sustainability, 245
Accounting informatization, 165, 173
Accounting technology, 3, 43, 52, 57
Algorithm, 8, 9, 11, 19, 34, 73–82, 97, 181, 244, 249, 314, 318, 341, 343, 368, 373, 374, 427, 447, 448, 465, 468, 476, 484, 493
Analytical procedures, 19, 20, 25, 45, 55
Analytics, 2, 3, 5–8, 10, 11, 18, 20, 23, 37, 95, 127, 173, 174, 210, 211, 242, 257, 281, 286, 298, 301, 375, 416, 418, 420, 423, 425, 427, 430, 432, 433, 441, 442, 458, 476
Artificial intelligence (AI), 2–6, 8–12, 42, 51, 53–56, 58, 67, 83, 89, 93–101, 106, 114, 115, 117, 118, 120–122, 126, 127, 134, 153, 178, 237, 241, 243, 244, 246, 248, 249, 258, 261, 263, 265, 268–270, 273, 274, 339, 350, 368, 425, 427
Audit analytics, 18, 20, 418, 422
Audit efficiency, 2, 18
Auditing, 2–6, 8–12, 18–22, 24, 37, 42–47, 50–58, 99, 174, 178–180, 184, 197, 261, 338, 339, 347, 348, 355, 416, 418, 419, 422, 428, 512, 530, 536–539, 543–545, 547, 552, 553
Australia, 6, 56, 59, 178, 181, 183, 185, 186, 189, 190, 214, 222, 245, 290, 292, 350, 362, 474, 492, 493, 496, 497, 500, 504, 539
Authentic assessment, 362, 371

B
Big data analytics (BDA), 42, 51, 53, 55, 134, 237, 241–244, 246, 314, 419, 484
Big data (BD), 3, 5, 10, 11, 18, 20, 26, 37, 42–45, 47–50, 54–56, 58, 106, 114, 115, 117, 118, 121, 122, 126, 127, 159, 165, 170, 173, 174, 178, 196, 209–213, 231, 242–244, 281–284, 286, 288–294, 297, 298, 301–303, 375, 395, 416, 418, 425, 426, 430, 469, 470, 477, 484, 493
Blockchain, 2, 6, 10, 46, 47, 178–185, 192, 194–197, 200–202, 250, 339–343,

T. Rana et al. (eds.), *Handbook of Big Data and Analytics in Accounting and Auditing*,
https://doi.org/10.1007/978-981-19-4460-4

345–350, 355, 536–539, 541–547, 549, 551–553
Blockchain technology (BT), 6, 47, 178–180, 182–185, 193–197, 200, 201, 337–340, 343, 344, 346–352, 355, 356, 535–537, 539, 543–547, 549–552
Bookkeeping, 4, 10, 133–160, 166, 168, 169, 171, 184, 343, 347, 419
Budgeting, 8, 12, 24, 143, 211–213, 231, 286, 288, 373, 374, 380, 388, 464

C

Capital allowances, 10, 511, 513–516, 518, 519, 524, 528, 529
Cloud accounting, 164–174
Cloud computing, 18, 46, 164, 166, 167, 242, 425, 539
Cognitive load, 8, 362, 363, 368, 370, 372, 375–378, 380, 381
Committee of Sponsoring Organizations of the Treadway Commission (COSO), 256–261, 273
Controversies, 48, 69–76, 78–83, 111, 114, 117–119, 121
Corporate social performance (CSP), 4, 5, 11, 66–69, 82, 83, 93, 94
Corporations, 18, 24, 90–92, 97, 134, 135, 142, 201, 338, 355, 546
Customer perception, 310, 313–316, 327, 329
Customer review, 310, 311, 313, 314, 316–318, 320, 327, 329

D

Data analytics, 8, 9, 12, 18, 23, 25, 43–45, 52, 54, 55, 58, 159, 210, 211, 216, 240, 243, 310, 314, 361, 395, 416–420, 422–426, 428, 430–433, 448
Data analytics competencies, 417, 420, 423, 433
Data sources, 7, 43, 44, 114, 196, 209–218, 221–223, 226–233, 243, 282, 418
Data visualization, 17–28, 30, 32–37, 212, 257, 375, 387, 418, 424, 429
Digital, 6, 8, 12, 56, 57, 134, 136, 141, 142, 157, 171, 178–184, 197, 201, 202, 240–242, 280, 281, 283, 286, 288–292, 294, 298, 301–304, 310–312, 315, 329, 340, 345, 347, 348, 361–363, 365, 366, 368, 369, 371–376, 380, 381, 387, 388, 416–419, 424–426, 433, 464, 468–470, 472, 473, 475–480, 482–484, 494, 495, 497, 502, 503, 536, 543, 547, 551
Digital economy, 56, 164, 183, 417, 496, 501, 504
Digitalization, 8, 134–137, 141, 156–159, 197, 202, 257, 280–284, 287, 289–294, 297, 300–304, 324, 416, 425, 464–466, 468, 469, 472–484
Discovery-based learning, 363–366, 380
Distributed ledgers, 179, 181, 185, 337, 338, 342, 345, 538, 546
Document review, 173

E

Earth system, 106, 107, 122
Education, 8, 9, 54, 58, 82, 113, 183, 214, 217–219, 222–224, 227, 231, 284, 285, 294, 295, 298, 339, 340, 346, 348, 349, 355, 361, 362, 366, 368–370, 397, 410, 416, 417, 422, 440, 441, 443, 459, 464–469, 477, 481, 483, 484, 494, 497, 501, 510, 512, 523, 543, 549, 550
Emerging technology(ies), 3, 10, 12, 18, 42–45, 47, 51–59, 165, 173, 178, 237, 240, 241, 246, 347, 350, 355, 356, 440, 541, 544, 548–550
Enterprise Risk Management (ERM), 256–261, 271, 273, 274
Entrepreneurship, 148, 156, 159, 285, 288, 477, 484, 546
Environment, Social, Governance (ESG), 4–7, 10, 11, 66–73, 75, 77, 80–83, 89–100, 105, 106, 109–127, 256–261, 264–274
ESG ratings, 3, 5, 11, 12, 66–71, 75, 76, 80, 82, 91–98, 113, 124, 126, 268
Experiential learning, 363, 396–400, 409–411, 512

F

Finance, 4, 5, 11, 12, 25, 68, 81, 92, 95, 96, 111, 113, 121, 152, 155, 164, 210, 214, 217, 221, 226, 228, 229, 231, 240, 256, 266, 269, 351, 396, 417, 420, 422, 423, 433, 472, 520, 536–539, 541, 543, 544, 546, 551, 552

Financial analytics, 395, 396, 398, 401, 410, 411
Financial materiality, 4, 11, 67, 109, 110, 113, 115, 121, 122
Forecasts, 21, 24, 165, 212, 215, 229
Fraud detection, 22, 55, 545

H
Household waste management (HWM), 493–498, 500–502, 504
Hybridity, 8, 465–468, 480

I
Immersive technology, 513
Impact assessment, 56
Informal learning, 441
Integrated control, 7, 256, 271
Integrated reporting, 274
Internet of Things (IoT), 165, 173, 183, 237, 241–248, 250, 289, 291, 493, 495, 496
Interpersonal skills, 396–401, 406, 407, 409–411

L
Literature review, 43, 281, 282, 284, 286, 288, 299, 302–304, 311, 440, 471, 538

M
Machine learning (ML), 4–7, 9–12, 67, 71–76, 80–83, 93–97, 99, 100, 115, 126, 137, 138, 142, 145–147, 153, 244, 249, 298, 314, 319, 419, 424, 426, 427, 447, 458
Management accounting, 7, 144, 165, 172, 210–212, 231, 282, 283, 286, 288–295, 297, 298, 301, 355, 373, 417, 422, 423, 492, 493, 530
Management control, 7, 12, 134, 143, 213, 258, 271, 280, 282–284, 290, 293, 294, 301–304
Measurement Error, 94
Mobile banking app, 310–312, 314, 327–329

N
Natural language processing (NLP), 42, 115–117, 121, 126, 127, 311, 314, 315, 441, 446

P
Participatory Collaborative Learning, 9
Performance measurement, 22, 260, 297, 302, 303, 465–468, 474, 477, 480–482
Public sector, 280–284, 290, 292–298, 301–304, 465, 550

Q
Q&A forum, 443–445, 449–452, 457, 458

R
Rasch psychometric model, 502
RegTech, 178, 195
Regulation, 4, 6, 45, 47, 57, 58, 89–91, 135, 136, 138–142, 147, 155–159, 168, 179, 180, 184, 200, 202, 263, 264, 274, 288, 289, 291, 301, 468, 536, 537, 546, 547, 551
Reporting standards, 266, 268
Roleplay, 396–402, 406, 407, 409, 410

S
Sales predictions, 211, 213–218, 221, 226–228, 230, 231, 233
Self-efficacy, 314, 396–398, 407, 409–411, 504
Serious games, 8, 362, 363, 365–369, 372–376, 379–381
Small business, 4, 134, 135, 144, 145, 148, 149, 152, 154, 157, 159, 171, 186, 191, 195
Smart agriculture, 245, 250
Smart waste management, 245–247
Smart Water Utilities Management, 246, 247
Socially responsible investment (SRI), 5, 11, 66, 68, 81, 82, 93, 98–100, 109, 114, 121, 258
Social media, 7, 18, 114, 115, 117, 118, 178, 209–211, 214–217, 220, 222, 225–231, 233, 242, 243, 310, 311, 313, 478, 522, 523
Spaced retrieval, 417, 418, 430, 433
Sustainability, 4–6, 69, 70, 81, 82, 91–93, 95, 98, 106, 107, 110–115, 117, 118, 120–127, 236, 237, 240, 241, 243–245, 247, 249, 256, 257, 259, 261–273, 495
Sustainability reporting, 4, 5, 256, 274

Sustainable Development Goals (SDGs), 121, 122, 126, 237–250, 262, 266, 381, 388

T

Taxation, 10, 178, 192, 197, 200, 417, 422, 423, 511–516, 519, 520, 524, 529
Tax compliance, 6, 178, 200, 201
Tax losses, 6, 178, 185, 186, 189–196, 199–201
Text mining, 311, 314, 316, 327, 329, 441, 446
Topic modeling, 311, 318, 321, 327–329
Training-tool, 494, 496–504
Triple-entry systems, 342

U

Undergraduate curriculum, 374
University, 9, 50, 54, 169, 214, 349, 363, 370, 396, 398, 402, 416–422, 432, 433, 442–444, 464–469, 473, 475–483, 497, 503, 510, 511, 513–516

V

Vietnam, 42, 43, 46, 47, 51–59
Virtual reality (VR), 9, 10, 368, 511–516, 518–520, 523–531

W

Workplace learning, 443, 458, 460